SUPERADAPTABILITY

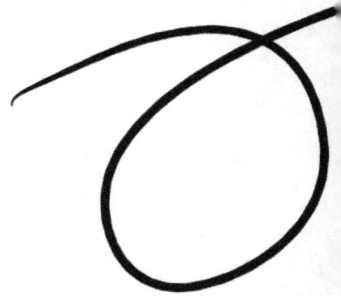

SUPERADAPTABILITY

How to Transcend in an Age of Overwhelm

MAX MCKEOWN

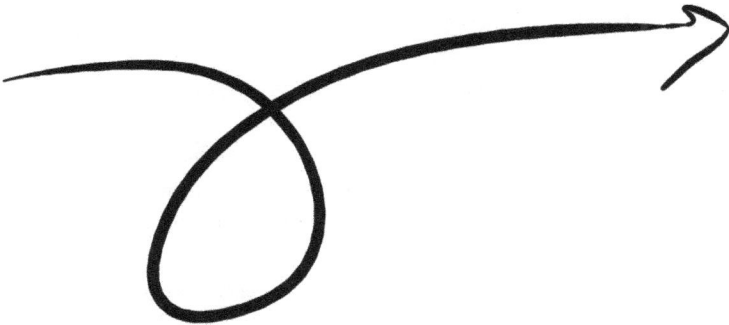

DE GRUYTER

ISBN 978-3-11-157512-4
e-ISBN (PDF) 978-3-11-157550-6
e-ISBN (EPUB) 978-3-11-157629-9

Library of Congress Control Number: 2025946408

Bibliographic information published by the Deutsche Nationalbibliothek
The Deutsche Nationalbibliothek lists this publication in the Deutsche Nationalbibliografie;
detailed bibliographic data are available on the internet at http://dnb.dnb.de.

© 2026 Walter de Gruyter GmbH, Berlin/Boston, Genthiner Straße 13, 10785 Berlin
Cover image: Michelle Morgan
Image copyright: Max Mckeown
Typesetting: Michelle Morgan

www.degruyterbrill.com

Questions about General Product Safety Regulation:
productsafety@degruyterbrill.com

A NOTE ON SOURCES AND METHOD

This book draws from neuroscience, psychology, and cultural evolution to develop a practical framework for human adaptability. The examples and case studies are based on real historical figures and events, but are presented as illustrative narratives – not exhaustive biographies.

The theoretical foundation builds on established science – concepts like neuroplasticity, metacognition, and cultural transmission. But the specific synthesis, structure, and terminology (including 'superadaptability' and 'metaplasticity as metacognition accessing neural plasticity') are original contributions.

You'll find further reading – and some of the scientific references I explored – in the bibliography and back matter. These are offered as entry points for readers who want to explore the academic research that informs this work.

While care has been taken with the accuracy of events and quotations, memory – like meaning – is always reconstructed. What's told here is true in spirit, even when filtered through narrative shape or personal emphasis. Where quotations have been paraphrased or recalled from memory, I've aimed to preserve the meaning, not the exact words.

The visual loopforms and hand-drawn glyphs in this book aren't illustrations – they're part of the method. They serve as cognitive anchors, distilling recursive insight into shape. Each one is a fractal compression of a pattern the text unfolds.

This book is written for thoughtful general readers – for people seeking understanding and application. It doesn't aim to catalogue every source, but to bring rigorous ideas into reach.

My goal is not just knowledge, but usable insight – ideas you can live with, loops you can make your own.

– Max Mckeown

YOU ARE HERE

The Non-Intro Intro to Rule Zero

I've always loved maps.
Especially the part that says you are here.

This book is a map.
To your mind. To the minds of others. To how people adapt.

You don't have to go everywhere at once.
But now that you've started, you may begin to see the pattern.
The signal. The three-part loop.

It was already running in you.
But now you can use it on purpose.

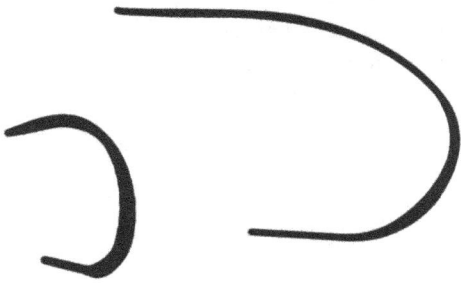

WHY THIS BOOK EXISTS

How to transcend when ordinary habits aren't enough.

You've probably heard a lot about habits.
Tiny ones. Powerful ones. Stacked ones.
Habits that help you drink more water or check fewer emails.
And those are useful – until they're not.

Because there comes a point where better routines
don't solve the deeper problem.
You're still overwhelmed.
Still stuck in systems you didn't design.
Still bumping against limits you can't quite name.

That's what this book is for.

This is a book about superadaptability:
How to thrive amid uncertainty.
How to overcome overwhelm.
How to transcend the invisible limits of self, system, and situation.

And what we've found – through story, science, and lived example –
is that the most reliable path isn't more effort.
It's a different loop.

Not just doing better.

Looping better.

Because at the core of real transformation are meta-habits:
Patterns that shape how you build, break, and reroute other patterns.
They're not just what you do.
They're how you adapt to what's happening.

That means this isn't a book about tips, tricks, or tactics.

It's a book about changing how you change.

Across the ten Rules, you'll learn how to upgrade
your most essential internal loops:
How you detect meaning.
How you model pressure.
How you decide, act, and recover.

The result?
A system that doesn't just survive chaos but uses it.
A structure that can bend, shift, and grow with you –
because it's built from the inside out.

You don't need more habits.

You need habits that upgrade your ability to adapt.

That's what superadaptability is.

And that's why this book exists.

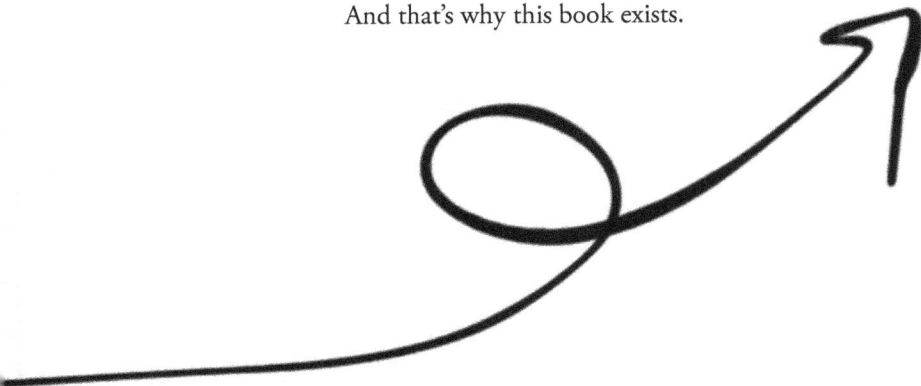

NOT THE START

NOT THE END

"We always remained ourselves, in no way echoing nor currying favor with one another, neither of us trying to meddle with the other's soul, neither I with his psyche nor he with mine. And in this way [...] both of us, felt ourselves free in spirit."
– Anna Dostoevskaya

BEGIN THE LOOP

The loop begins with Rule Zero –
a rule to help you overcome overwhelm.
Before you take any action, you need to get your footing.

The next three chapters guide you through the first phase:
Recognise.
Each one reveals a different way to see the loop you're in.

Then come three more:
the Understand phase.
Rules that help you decode the deeper structure – what drives the system,
what holds it in place, and what makes change possible.

Next, you'll move into Necessary Action.
Three more rules, each showing how superadapters shift the system –
not by force, but by precision.

By the time you reach Rule Ten,
you'll be ready to re-loop the loop –
to upgrade the upgrade.
Not just once,
but again and again.

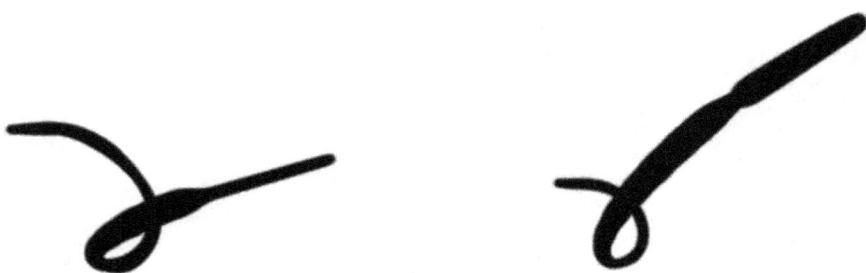

EVERY PAGE A PATTERN

Each Rule unfolds as both chapter and system.
A structure that loops – not just to repeat, but to evolve.
This isn't literary decoration.
It's cognitive architecture.

Each turn leaves you changed.
Better positioned.
More aware.
More able.

You don't need to see the full pattern yet.
Just enter it.

Each chapter shows how superadaptive minds really work:
not in theory,
but in action.
You'll meet them through lived example:
Three figures for each core function.
Each one showing what it means to –
recognise the loop you're in,
understand its deeper logic,
and take the kind of Necessary Action
that reshapes everything.

You'll sit with neuroscientists mapping the plastic brain.
With artists who turned constraint into breakthrough.
With leaders who didn't just adapt to their systems,
but rewrote them.

These aren't success stories.
They're structural demonstrations.
Patterns you can trace, test,
make your own.

Each chapter moves from understanding to application.
How to live these loops.
How to spot when they're breaking down.
How to counter the failures.

How to transcend the patterns that once held you.

Because you are already looping.
You always were.

The question isn't whether you're in a system.
The question is whether you'll choose one –
one designed to evolve.

One recursive pattern,
consciously adopted,
can change not just where you're going,
but how you move through whatever reality throws at you.

YOU ALREADY LOOP

You already loop.

You loop when you think, when you react, when you cope, when you try again.

Your morning routine is a loop. So is that argument you keep replaying.

But so is your team dynamic. So is traffic. So is capitalism.

The world loops. The system loops.

The question isn't whether you loop.

It's whether you run the loop – or let it run you.

You've already built loops – consciously or not.

Some serve you. Others sabotage. Most just repeat.

You're not starting from zero.

What's here can be tuned, upgraded, rewritten.

You've already got momentum. We'll help you redirect it.

Every loop in this book follows one deep pattern:

RECOGNISE → UNDERSTAND → NECESSARY ACTION

This is the meta-habit behind all successful adaptation.

You've used it before – instinctively.

Now you'll use it on purpose. At any scale.

Self. Situation. System.

You've got this. You're built to loop.

And your loops can evolve.

This book won't give you a blueprint.

It gives you a loop – one you'll learn to run, rerun, and refine.

Starting now.

Nulla dies
sine linea,
nulla vita sine
circuitu.

No day
without a line,
no life without
a loop

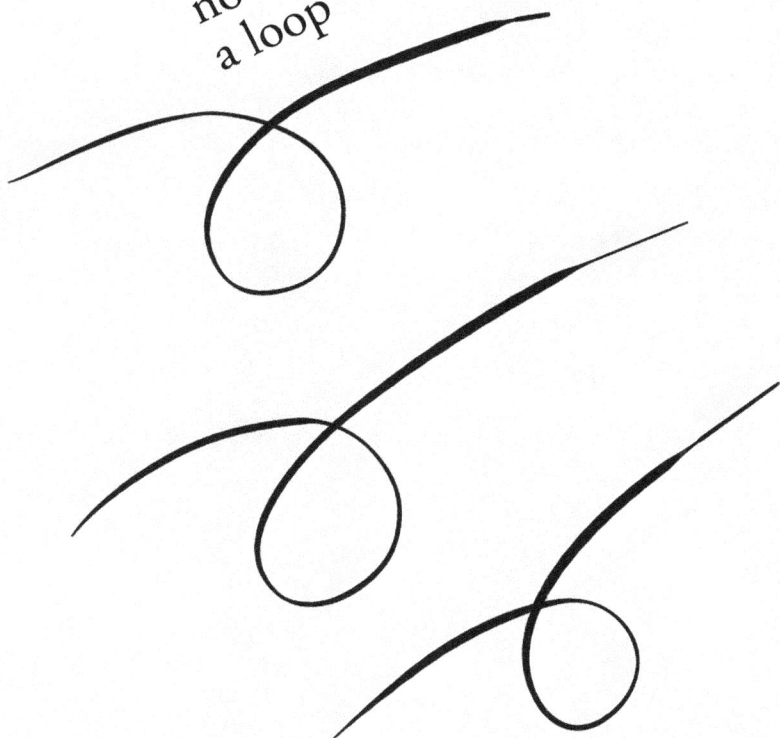

THE LONGEST LOOP

We were never the strongest.
We weren't the fastest.
We didn't have claws, or fangs, or the cold precision of instinct.
But we noticed things.
We noticed patterns.
And then we noticed ourselves.

That's where it begins.
Not with dominance.
With attention.

SAPIENS → SUPERADAPTABILITY → SUPERSAPIENS

We copied what we saw.
Then we adapted what we copied.
But some of us did more than adapt.
We changed the loop.
We didn't just survive.
We learned to reconfigure the system that made survival possible.

That was superadaptability.

And those who learned to pass that on –
Not just through genes, but through structure, through gesture, through loops –
they became the first supersapiens.

They didn't just live better.
They made living better contagious.

METACOGNITION × NEUROPLASTICITY = METAPLASTICITY

We were born with brains that could change.
Then we learned to watch ourselves change.
And finally, to shape how we shape.

This is metaplasticity.

It is not a theory.
It is a recursive capacity.
When we say superadaptability, we don't mean grit.
We mean design.
A mind that learns how it learns.
A system that loops itself forward.

RECOGNISE → UNDERSTAND → NECESSARY ADAPTATION

This is the smallest working loop of intelligent change.
The RUN loop is the heartbeat of superadaptability.

You see the pattern.
You name the mechanism.
You move just enough to shift the future.

Every superadapter does this.
And every supersapien makes it easier for someone else to do it next.

This is how we teach the loop that taught us.
This is how we transcend.

You are not reading this because you need more facts.
You're here because you've felt the edge of something.

You've seen the limits of productivity.
You've outgrown performance advice.
You've glimpsed – however faintly – that life is looped.

That success is recursive.
That intelligence can be extended.
That you might not be done yet.

You're right.

You're not just part of the loop.
You are what the loop becomes when it learns to evolve itself.

Let's begin.

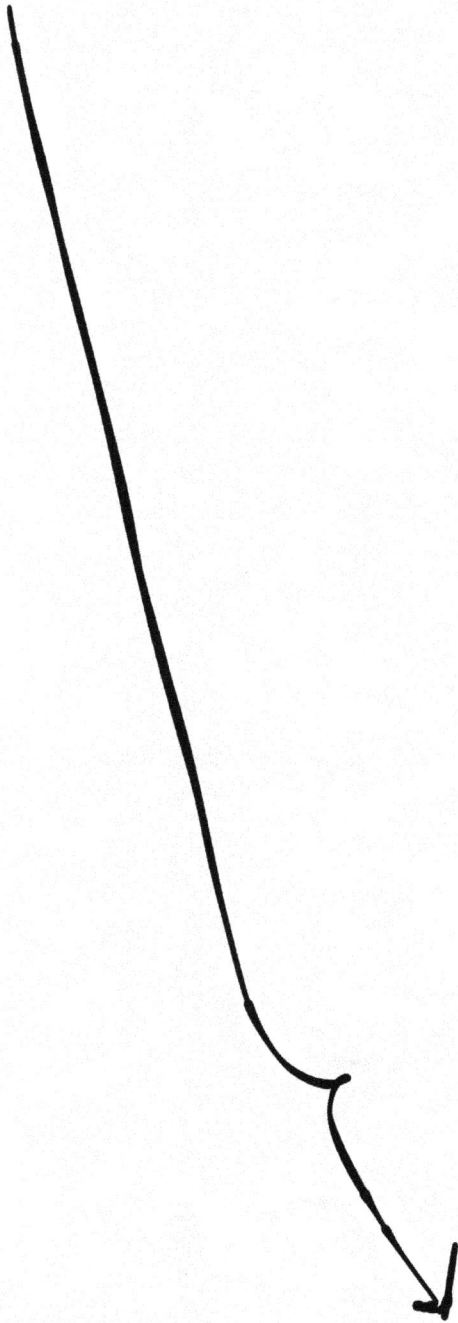

PROLOGUE

"Stability is an illusion. The jungle doesn't care who you are. And sometimes, the plane breaks apart at 10,000 feet."

The world is not waiting for you to be ready.

We begin with falling.

On December 24, 1971, Juliane Koepcke fell out of the sky.

LANSA Flight 508 was struck by lightning and exploded midair over the Peruvian rainforest. Ninety-one people died. Juliane – seventeen years old, strapped to a row of seats – plummeted nearly two miles.

And lived.
Not because she was lucky.
Not because she was stronger, smarter, or special.

She survived because she adapted – in motion, in fragments, in fear.

She crawled from the wreckage with a broken collarbone, torn ligaments, and one sandal. Her glasses – essential for seeing – were gone. No map. No food. No rescue. Just instinct, pain, and memory.

She began walking.
Not toward mere hope but guided by a deep pattern.

Her parents were biologists. She remembered: where there's water, there are people.

So, she followed the stream.

For eleven days she floated, stumbled, crawled through crocodile rivers, infected wounds, and jungle silence.

She pulled maggots from her leg using gasoline from an abandoned hut.

And she kept going.
Until – on the edge of death – she was found.
The only survivor.

This is what superadaptability looks like.

Not control.
Not just toughness.
Not even resilience.
It's more than that.

And it's much more valuable.

It is the ability to stay conscious under pressure.
To act while everything narrows.
To build a loop while the map is burning and the system is breaking.

Because the enemy isn't always out there.
Sometimes it's Overwhelm itself.
Overwhelm isn't just a feeling.

It's an attack.
A rear naked choke.
Fast. Silent. Invisible.
The arm slips around your neck.
Pressure cuts off both sides.

And in ten seconds, it's over.

You lose vision.
You lose clarity.
You lose time.

This is what modern life does to people.
To teams. To systems.

Overwhelm tightens.
Adaptation shuts down.
Unless you act before the loop collapses.

Juliane didn't start with a plan.
She started with the ability to see and adapt to patterns – a loop beneath thought.

She looped.

She recognised the environment: where she was, what she lacked.
She understood what mattered: water, movement, time.
She took necessary action – even when the next step was pain.

That's the loop that saved her.

And that's what this book will teach you:
How to act inside the chokehold – before the system collapses.
How to create space to breathe, to think, to move.
How to survive the choke – and sometimes, reverse it.

RULE ZERO:
OVERCOME OVERWHELM

The one about becoming superadaptable

It's your first choice that changes everything. When you breathe. When you create space to breathe, think and adapt. The world is changing faster than most people – and most systems – can handle. But it's not enough to just adapt. To survive and thrive in environments shaped by shocks, complexity, and collapse, we must go further. Superadaptability is a trainable loop and a meta-habit, and a strategic system. This book teaches that system so you can transcend the limits of your self, system, or situation.

She wakes up strapped to a row of seats in the jungle. No signal. No systems. Just silence, insects, and blood. She does not panic. And that's the first choice that changes everything. When you breathe. When you create space to breathe, think, and adapt.

You may have already met her in the prologue. Juliane Koepcke. Seventeen. The sole survivor of a midair disintegration.

She fell more than 10,000 feet, still strapped to a section of airplane seats, and landed in the Amazon rainforest. Her collarbone was broken. One eye was swollen shut. Her arm was gashed open. The jungle around her was full of things that could kill her. But the part that matters most is this: she didn't panic.

Not then. Not at first. She took a breath. She created space inside the panic. And in that space, the first loop began.

She didn't know what she would do next. She didn't know how she would get out. But she gave herself enough room to ask the first real question: Where am I? What's happening? And then, quietly, the next one: How do I get out of here alive?

That's where superadaptability begins. Not with confidence. Not with some brilliant plan. It begins with a gap. A breath. A moment of space inside the overwhelm.

Not all overwhelm is falling from the sky.

Sometimes it's something quieter, longer, slower. It's the paperwork that never ends. The grief that doesn't lift. The low, steady pressure of trying to do everything right and still feeling like you're failing. It can feel like burnout. Depression. Rage. Powerlessness. Or ambition so strong it hurts. The feeling that you were built for something more, and somehow you're still stuck.

Overwhelm wears many faces. But it always does the same thing. It shuts down your capacity to move. It compresses your thinking. It takes away the breath you need to begin.

That's why Rule Zero always comes first. Before any system. Before any breakthrough.

Rule Zero is the breath. The space. The moment you stop the spiral for long enough to start something new.

From that moment, you can begin to ask the next questions:

What's happening?

Why am I trapped?

How do I transcend?

That's the triple move at the heart of this book.

Breathe and **Recognise.**

Understand the trap.

Take **Necessary Action** to transcend

We'll come back to those three. You'll see them again. You'll feel them again. They sit under everything that follows.

Some people, like Juliane, do it instinctively. Some do it out of desperation. Some don't even realise they've done it until years later. But in every case, it begins the same way.

With a pause.

With a breath.

With enough space to begin the loop.

Next stop. Portugal. Someone else who paused, then looped forward.

FRIDA

We were drawn by the posters.

Her face – piercing, still, emblematic. Frida Kahlo. Black hair parted, eyes steady. That image now does something few others do. It doesn't just promise art. It promises presence. A woman who made space. Who demanded it. Who held it – scarred, unblinking, adorned.

We were in Porto. The Centro Português de Fotografia. A building that used to be a prison – now softened by light, turned over to memory. It was summer, I think. Or nearly. People queued down the steps, along the iron railing. Nobody was rushing. Everyone just... waited.

We'd thought it was about her paintings. Her art. But when we got inside, we realised: it was about her world.

Not what she made, but what she saw.

Not what she created, but what she carried.

Inside, the exhibition was cooler. Old stone walls, high light, the soft hush of a crowd trying to remember how to look.

There were photos of Frida's family. Frida with Diego. Frida with others. But always, somehow, Frida alone.

Not dramatic. Not curated to shock. Just fragments. A life being pieced together from its edges. You could see how hard she worked to hold it all.

Her body had been broken – truly broken. A streetcar crash, a metal rod through her pelvis, surgeries upon surgeries, bones that didn't knit back together. She couldn't sit upright without pain. She couldn't carry a child. She couldn't always sleep. But she painted.

They built a mirror above her bed. Her father gave her brushes. Her mother had a carpenter make a frame so she could paint flat on her back. From that position – fixed, trapped – she began to reappear.

Line by line. Brushstroke by brushstroke. Frida emerged.

She never painted the moment that broke her. She said she wanted to, but never could. So instead, she painted everything around it.

She painted herself surrounded by jungle. She painted herself flayed, exposed, tangled in corsets and ribbons and thorns. She painted herself with Diego on her mind, and in her heart, and sometimes inside her own face. She painted herself split in two. And always, she painted from the same place.

The Blue House.

The place where she was born. The place she almost died. The place she remade.

She didn't leave to find herself. She stayed – and kept returning. She turned her birthplace into a studio, a mirror, a stage, a sanctuary. She filled it with colour and light, with dresses and bones, with books and masks and animals and silence.

She built a space inside the space that built her.

And in that space, she became all her Fridas.

That's what we were seeing. Not spectacle. Not mythology.

A room she made – so she could keep moving.

And maybe that's what everyone in the gallery queue was looking for. A little room inside the overwhelm. A way to see themselves, again. Or differently. Or fully. A space you don't have to leave in order to begin.

Some people do better.

You see it. You know it. Two people face the same loss, the same pressure, the same collapse – and one of them finds a way through. Not easily. Not cleanly. But somehow, they begin again. They breathe. They move. They change.

Why?

That's the question that started this book.

Is it luck? Genetics? Resilience? Is it something they were born with? Or something life carved into them? Or something they chose – again and again?

It turns out, all three can be true.

Some people are born with certain instincts. Others build them slowly, deliberately, in pieces. Some get thrown into the fire and learn to move through it – because they have no other choice.

But no matter how it starts, what's remarkable is this:

There's a recognisable pattern.

You see it in their lives. You see it in the research. You see it in your own best moments – maybe when you weren't even looking for it.

It's not random. It's not chaotic.

It's a loop.

A real one.

Learnable. Repeatable. Trainable.

And – best of all – already partially yours.

This book is about that loop.

You'll see it in people. In systems. In pressure. In hope. You'll see it in yourself – sometimes for the first time, sometimes with relief.

But there's something else.

One of the most powerful ways to develop superadaptability isn't just through effort. Or insight. Or will. It's through other people.

You live the loop.
You learn the loop.
But often, you're led to it – by someone else who made space before you.
That's what we're doing here.
Not just surviving the fall.
But building forward from it.
Not by guessing.

By running the loop.

HOW DO SUPERADAPTERS OVERCOME OVERWHELM?

Being human is hard. Not just because the world is chaotic – but because we are.

Big brains. Big energy demands. Big loops. Big dreams. And all of it running on limited time, emotion, sleep, and attention.

Superadapters aren't people with fewer problems. They're people with a system that lets them respond when the pressure hits.

Overwhelm isn't just a feeling. It's structural. It's the natural outcome of a mind that sees patterns, senses possibility, and still has to get through a Tuesday.

And that's why superadapters don't just cope. They loop.

The core pattern they run – whether they've named it or not – is a simple three-part loop:

Recognise what's happening.

Understand what must change.

Take the necessary action.

You'll see that pattern again and again in this book. Sometimes in fast, instinctive decisions. Sometimes across years. Sometimes playing out in a crisis. Sometimes unfolding in a quiet moment alone.

But the pattern holds.

That's what the next section will show you. A loop you already know. A loop you've already run, at least in part. A loop we're going to name properly – so you can start running it consciously.

Because when you can Recognise, Understand, and take Necessary Action – deliberately, repeatedly, and under pressure – you stop being trapped.

You start transcending.

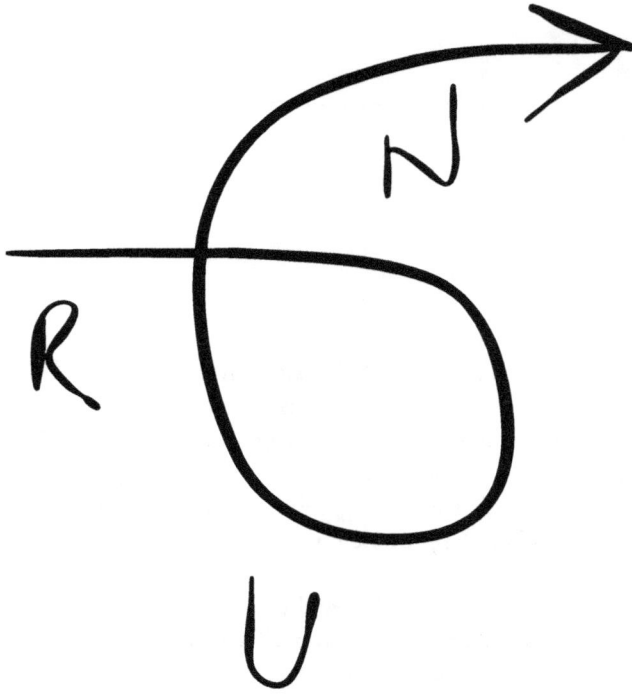

THREE STEPS FROM OVERWHELM

You're going to hear more about this loop in a moment.

But before we explain it in full, let's get something straight.

This is not just a theory.

It's what happens when people escape the chokehold of overwhelm – whether they know the name of the loop or not.

What do superadapters do that others don't?

First, they make space.

They find a breath. They clear their head. They let the panic drain just long enough to move. That's the first move. You'll feel it in your chest. It doesn't last forever. But it's the start.

Space to recognise.

They look around. They look inward. They see what's really happening – not just what it feels like. They name the moment. Sometimes they name the trap.

Next, they understand.

Not everything. Just enough. Enough to know what matters. Enough to say: "That's what's holding me. That's the thing I can move."

Then they move.

One step. Not flailing. Not thrashing. A real move. The necessary move. Sometimes the painful one.

And something shifts.

Maybe not everything.

Maybe not right away.

But the loop begins.

Recognise.

Understand.

Necessary Action.

That's how people get out.

That's how they loop forward.

That's what this book will teach you to do.

THE LOOP THAT LETS YOU ADAPT

You don't change unless you recognise that something needs to change. Not reliably. Not structurally. Not repeatably.

Superadapters are people who see the pattern sooner. They don't just react. They don't just push harder. They pause – just long enough to notice what's really going on.

That's what recognition means. You see the shift. You name the moment. You say: something here isn't working – or something here could be better.

But superadapters don't stop there. They position themselves where change is possible. Where energy can flow. Where there's a way out, and a way up. Their action isn't just about getting through – it's about leaving themselves better positioned next time.

That's the ratchet effect. The pattern you'll see again and again in this book. Adaptive action that leaves you in a better state than where you began.

But recognition isn't enough.

If you don't understand the type of change that's needed, you won't know what to do. Or worse – you'll do something that makes it worse.

Understand means you grasp the nature of what you're facing. You ask: What's going on here? How does this work? What's the real play underneath all this?

Superadapters model what's happening. They build a picture – mental, emotional, mechanical. They work out the mechanism that's holding the problem in place – or the mechanism that might open a way forward.

And they focus on the part that matters: the part they can modify. The trap or lever that shifts the system.

That's understanding. Not a full diagram. Just enough clarity to move usefully.

Then comes Necessary Action.

Because if you've recognised and understood, but you don't act, nothing adapts. The loop collapses.

Necessary Action is what closes the loop. It's what turns awareness into momentum. It's when you apply what you've seen – when you do the thing that matches the model you've built.

And you don't just act. You energise the action. You find the fuel – internal or external – to move when it counts.

Finally, you embed it. You do enough, long enough, well enough, to change your position. That's what locks in adaptation. That's what resets the loop from survival into transcendence.

This can be tiny. This can be huge. But once you see the loop, you'll find yourself using it everywhere.

That's the RUN loop.

RECOGNISE → UNDERSTAND → NECESSARY ACTION

Three moves. One pattern. A loop that makes forward motion possible – under pressure, under complexity, under overwhelm.

It's how superadapters live. And it's how this book works.

Let's look at each step in a little more detail. Each loop will embed the idea more deeply.

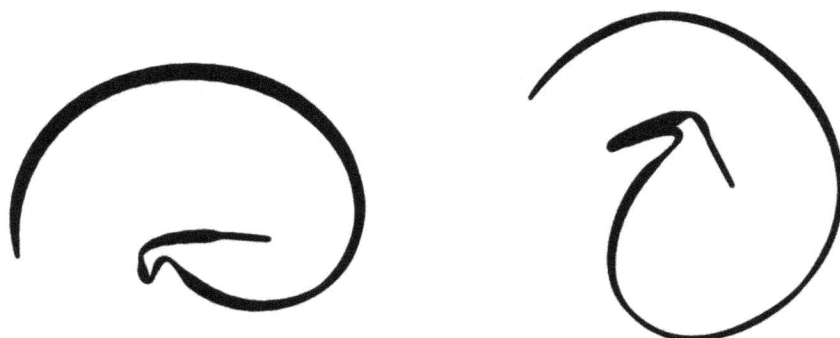

STEP 1 – RECOGNISE

To recognise is not just to notice. It's to become aware of the right thing – soon enough to matter.

Superadapters don't simply perceive more. They detect the pattern beneath the noise. They see the signal hiding inside the ordinary. They feel the tug before the trap, the pull before the change.

Recognise is the first real move of adaptation. It's the pivot between unconscious reaction and conscious entry into the loop.

Without it, you're stuck. Or worse you're moving in the wrong direction with confidence.

It has three internal functions:

Detect – Something's happening. Something's shifted. Something's not quite right. Or is newly possible.

Interpret – What does that mean? What kind of change is this?

Decide – Do I enter the loop? Do I prepare to understand?

This isn't overthinking. It's over-feeling made intelligent.

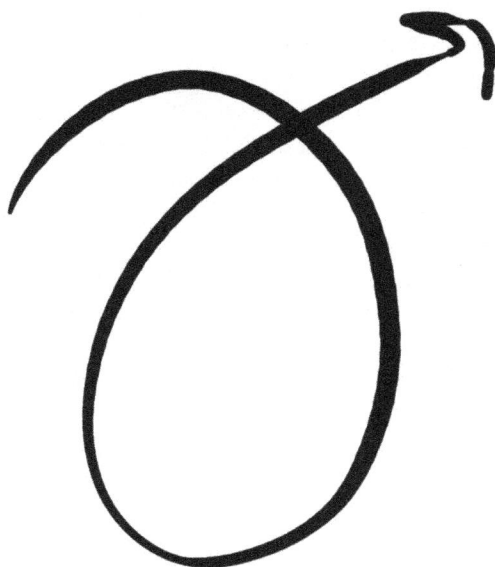

Without recognition, loops don't start. Adaptation doesn't happen. You miss what was possible. Or you end up stuck in what was already lost.

It's not heroic. It's habitual. Superadapters build recognition as a reflex – not because they're better, but because they practice.

This is the step that makes space. The one that stops the spiral. The one that tells your system: something different is needed now.

Recognise is the moment the loop begins – or doesn't.

Recognition isn't a soft skill. It's an edge. And in the real world, it separates adaptation from erosion.

A bobsleigh runner, crouched and ready, doesn't just explode into motion – they wait for a precise audio cue, then adapt in milliseconds to shifting track conditions, a teammate's rhythm, and their own body's feedback. A single mistimed decision, even if 98% right, can mean disaster.

A soldier moving across open terrain in Kosovo must distinguish between distant sound and immediate threat – snipers, shadows, wind. The stakes aren't emotional. They're terminal. But the loop is the same: detect → interpret → decide.

Now shift scale. A small business owner says: "I've never been one for new tech. I know I should keep up… but I don't." They've recognised the change – but they've mislooped. They're aware, but not adaptively aware. They're stuck in a loop of recognition that never reaches understanding or action.

The same happens in activism. A climate protester may deeply recognise the moral urgency but misread whether their tactics are helping or hindering. They're stuck on the big truth, missing the little truths that actually change things.

Or take the founder who sees a shift in customer behaviour but clings to their original idea out of loyalty. It's not that they don't see change – it's that they see it late. Or in the wrong resolution.

In every domain – sport, war, business, culture – recognition must be adaptive, not performative. What matters isn't just what you see, but when, why, and what loop it activates.

This is the difference between spotting a change and looping it forward.

You already know what it feels like to misrecognise. We all do.

You say something in a meeting, and part of you knows you shouldn't. You even preface it – "I know I probably shouldn't say this, but…" And then you say it anyway. You recognise the loop is flawed, but you run it.

Or you catch yourself thinking, "I'm just not a tech person," or, "I've never really liked all that new stuff." But you're not just stating a preference. You're closing a door. You're recognising change but not in a way that helps you move. It's a form of adaptive blindness.

Sometimes people cut off their own noses. They treat themselves like voodoo dolls. And they do it habitually, with a kind of practiced self-injury.

This is why Recognise matters.

Because you can't interrupt a loop you don't realise you're in. You can't adapt a system you haven't noticed has changed. You can't learn if you keep repeating the part you're already good at.

So pause. Look around.

What are you missing? What's stalled? Where are you technically 'right', but functionally stuck? What feels familiar but isn't helping?

Superadapters aren't born enlightened. They're just better at catching those early cues – and moving.

And that's the good news. You can get better at this. You already are. Just reading this? You're building the loop.

Recognising the need to adapt is vital. But it's not enough.

You can detect a threat, feel the urgency, even decide to act – and still get it wrong.

Why? Because you skipped the next step: understanding what you're facing, and how it works.

Some people recognise well, but act prematurely.

Others stay stuck in endless recognition – seeing what's wrong but never moving.

Superadapters do neither.

They pause. They ask: Do I understand this situation well enough to act wisely?

That's what we move to next.

Because the loop isn't just a prompt.

It's a system.

It holds the power of rhythm: detect, interpret, decide – then go deeper.

If you follow it, you build something better with each pass.

Not just insight. But action with altitude.

This loop is your first aid kit when you're overwhelmed.

It's your scaffolding when you're building something new.

It's your ratchet when you need to rise.

And when practiced, it becomes something more:

A meta-habit. A way of thinking that adapts as you do.

It bears repeating:

This isn't about knowing more.

It's about doing better with what you now see.

Read to understand. Learn to elevate.

But know this:

Even recognition, if not deepened, becomes another trap.

STEP 2 – UNDERSTAND

Understand is the second step in the RUN loop. It comes after recognition – and makes adaptation possible.

If you recognise that something must change, but you don't understand what or how, your actions will be misdirected.

Understand means grasping the nature of the challenge you face. It means diagnosing the system you're in. It means asking: what part of this structure, habit, belief, process – or story – is driving the current outcome?

This is the step where models matter. You don't need to be a scientist to use one. You already are. You use models every day: to cross the street, to manage a conversation, to anticipate how your colleague or child or partner will react.

The difference with superadapters is that they treat those models as improvable.

They make the invisible mechanisms visible.

They ask: what's really going on here?

And then they look for the hinge – the part of the system that, if shifted, might change everything.

This is not overthinking. It's strategic comprehension.

It's what lets you change the game rather than just playing it harder.

It's how you stop solving the wrong problem.

And it's how you prepare for action that matters.

Understand has three sub-skills: Model, Mechanism, Modify.

Model: what's the system, the dynamic, the structure of this situation?

Mechanism: what causes what? Which lever changes the output?

Modify: what can I shift, tweak, reroute, or remove to make this work better?

This step is not optional. It's the only way to make change that lasts.

Recognise tells you where the trap is.

Understand tells you how it works and how to move past it.

That's what comes next.

Some people may not like the results that the machine gives them – but they never open it up to find out why. They don't read the manual. They don't look underneath the hood. They keep pressing the same buttons, living the same loop, expecting something different.

But superadapters aren't like that.

They don't stop at it doesn't work. They ask: how does it work? What's inside this? What am I missing?

That instinct to ask what's really going on – is what allows them to adapt faster, better, and with more precision.

A washing machine, a social system, a recurring mood, a communication failure – everything has a model. Everything has a mechanism. And if you can understand the mechanism, you have a shot at modifying it.

This section is about that shot.

You don't need to be a mechanic to fix something.

You don't need to be a philosopher to question a loop.

You don't need to be a genius to sketch a better model.

You just need to get curious. Get honest. And look a little closer.

Superadapters do this with calm and precision. They diagnose before they act.

They ask: where is the hinge? Which change is both possible and powerful?

And they use that insight to create movement – forward, upward, out of the trap.

It's not magic. It's understanding.

It's the difference between struggling in the dark and switching on the light.

You don't need a washing machine to understand systems. The idea is bigger than that.

A system is anything that gives you an outcome. A system is a classroom, a family, a friendship, a job. Your sleep habits, your confidence, your career trajectory. Your city. Your childhood.

Understanding doesn't always mean figuring everything out. It means seeing enough of the model to make better moves. It means getting a feel for what's actually holding things in place – and what might let them shift.

If your work life keeps pushing you into burnout, understanding means asking:

What are the actual pressures?

What's rewarded? What's invisible?

Where does the stress loop feed itself?

What does a healthier mechanism look like?

If your relationships feel like a script you didn't write, understanding means pausing to notice:

Who always plays the rescuer?

Who always needs saving?

What do you believe you have to do to earn love?

And what might happen if you stopped doing it?

These questions don't solve everything. But they crack open the shell. They help you see patterns, rules, constraints – and options. And once you see options, you're in a different world.

This is how superadapters think. They don't just push harder. They map the terrain. They figure out which tool fits the task. They experiment. And they update.

In every situation, there is a model. In every model, a mechanism. In every mechanism, a potential modification.

Understanding brings that to light.

Then it's time to act.

Understanding doesn't stand alone.

You recognise something is off. Something needs to change. That's the spark. But without understanding – without figuring out what's really going on – you can't target your energy. You waste motion. You take guesses. You repeat what didn't work. Or worse, you burn out before you even start.

And yet, understanding without action isn't the goal either.

Superadapters don't just model. They move. They use their understanding to focus their energy, to direct it with precision. And they loop. They return to recognition with new data, revisit models with deeper insight, recalibrate action with clearer purpose.

Because the goal is not knowing – it's changing.

This is why the RUN loop isn't linear. It's recursive. Adaptive. Alive.

Recognition feeds understanding.

Understanding sharpens action.

Action generates new recognition.

Together, they form a loop. A loop that moves you from stuck to unstuck. From trapped to transcended.

And now, you know what comes next.

STEP 3 – NECESSARY ACTION

However well you have understood or recognised, your recognition and understanding will not lead to active change unless you move to necessary action.

Yet there is a subtlety here, or a sophistication.

The superadaptive know that simply being biased towards action will not necessarily help – especially if it's unthinking or maladaptive action, too fast or too slow, or in the wrong direction. And the wrong direction is sometimes backwards, but sometimes simply forwards in a place that is unhelpful.

Necessary Action involves its own levels:

You must enact what you had intended – the modification of the mechanism in the model that you recognised.

You must find and focus and flow your energy.

You must embed that change in a way that leaves you better placed to adapt next time.

The micro-loops of our daily lives move through Recognise → Understand → Necessary Action. In the blink of an eye. In a breath. But each one can be trained. Each one can be looped. And each one can lead to better.

We'll go deeper into the rhythm of action – slow, slow, quick, quick, slow. Into the groove of growth. Into the beat that makes necessary action more effective.

But first: enact, energise, embed.

This is what moves us. This is what builds better.

Action isn't neutral. Even action that leaves you exactly where you were used up energy, time, and space. If that use was useful or worthwhile – resting, recovering, connecting – then it has value. But most action is shaping something: a conversation, a habit, a decision, a system.

And action happens anyway. While asleep, your body breathes. Your brain loops. It uses energy. Action is inevitable. But direction is not.

Necessary Action means turning motion into momentum. We're not interested in any action. We're interested in the action that moves us forward – towards adaptation, not exhaustion.

Superadaptive minds act with rhythm. They don't rush without thinking. They don't stall out in delay. They operate in adaptive cadence: slow, slow, quick, quick, slow. It's a groove, not a grind. And the groove builds growth.

They don't waste energy on tasks that don't shift the model. They focus on energy that sustains and elevates. This means:

Finding the energy (or the smallest move with the biggest consequence)

Focusing it (so it flows toward the right mechanism)

Keeping it flowing (so the change embeds, sticks, stays)

And then they reboot.

We're always moving. But Necessary Action means we're moving well. That's the difference. That's the beat of transformation.

You get knocked down. You get up again. It's not always that simple, but sometimes it is. Not because the problem disappears, but because action pulls you into motion again. And motion creates space to think, choose, climb.

Necessary Action is the climb. But it's not one ladder. It's not even one direction. It's a network of adaptive ladders – chosen based on where you are, what you've got, and what's needed next.

Sometimes it's recovery. Sometimes it's precision. Sometimes it's knowing when to rest.

And sometimes it's knowing that the action you took – however smart it seemed – needs to stop.

This is not a glorification of action. This is a strategy of adaptive energy. A recognition that:

Marginal gains can plateau.

Momentum can trap.

Even your best efforts can become your next obstacle if you don't look up.

Superadapters recognise when to level up. They stop learning one verb at a time and start talking. They stop building the same feature and reframe the project. They stop pleasing and start redirecting. They notice when they're being a 'gopher' and decide it's time to be the go-to.

That decision doesn't come from hustle. It comes from run-looping.

So whether you're rebuilding trust, re-entering study, or restarting sleep – remember: it's not just action. It's Necessary Action. Because not all action is. And that's how we rise up and rise up again.

Now that we've examined Recognise, Understand, and Necessary Action, the shape of the loop becomes clear. Not as a linear checklist, but as a recursive arc – one that begins again, differently, each time it's completed.

The superadapter doesn't just act – they loop. They don't just do – they 're-do', with intelligence. The adaptive brain uses action not just to change the world but to test it, to ask questions, to learn.

So Necessary Action isn't the end of the process – it's the beginning of the next loop. That's why it has to be chosen, adjusted, embedded, and sometimes even unpicked.

This is how people get out of loops that trap them – and into loops that elevate them.

Sometimes the action is urgent, even desperate.
Sometimes it's crafted, minimal, efficient.
Sometimes it's imperfect, but repeated.

But what links all Necessary Action is this: it is taken by someone who knows what they are trying to change – and why.

Because even the smallest act – when it's part of the right loop – can be transcendent.

RECOGNISE → UNDERSTAND → NECESSARY ACTION.

That's how superadapters move from trapped to transcended.
That's how we begin again, each time, slightly higher than before.

Recurro,
ergo vivo

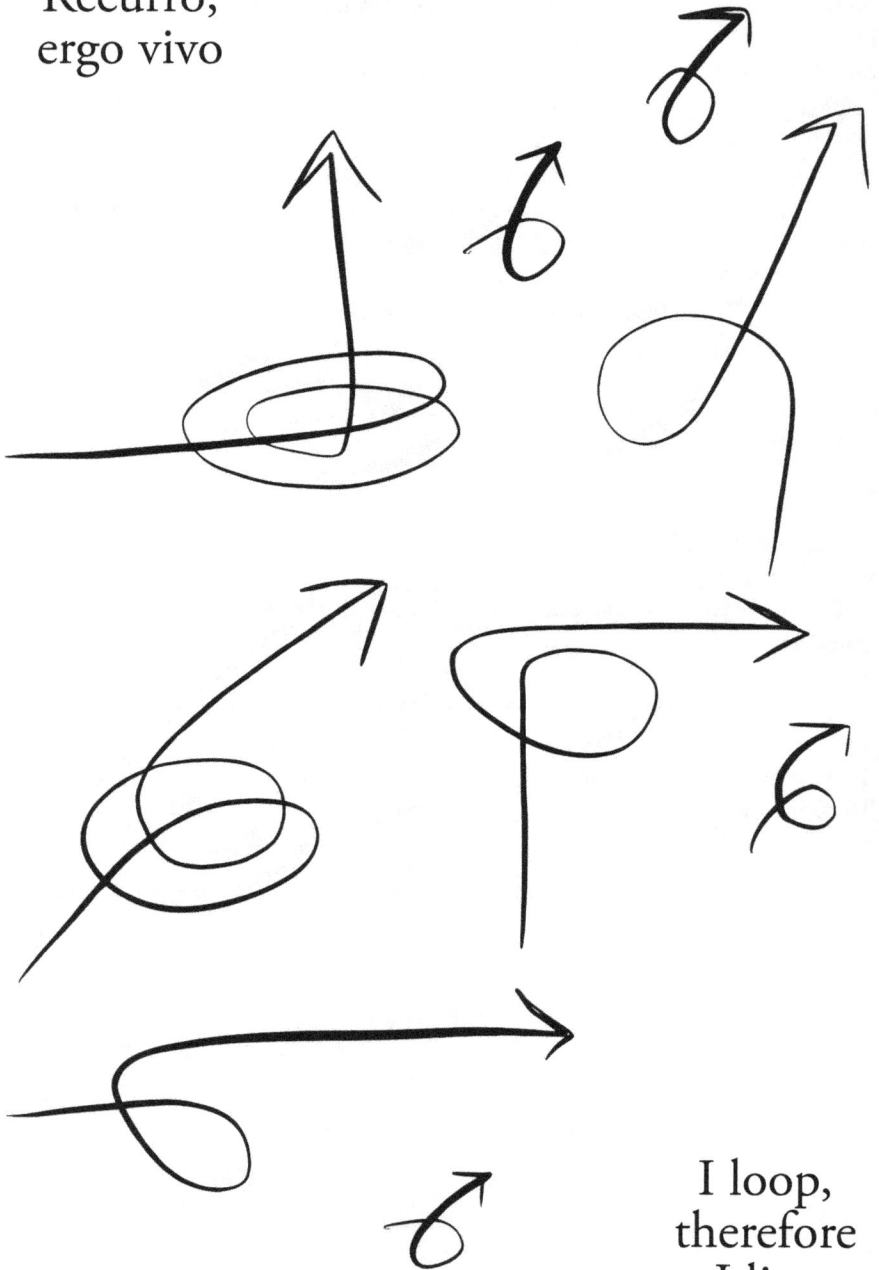

I loop,
therefore
I live

THE SITDOWN: THE TRAPPED
(AND THE TRANSCENDED)

WHY WE SIT DOWN NOW

"I understand the mechanism of my own thinking. I know precisely how I know, and my understanding is recursive. I understand the infinite regress of this self-knowing, not by proceeding step by step endlessly, but by apprehending the limit."
— Ted Chiang, *Understand*

This is a good time to reflect. To take a breath and deepen your understanding of the loop you've just seen. You've seen how it overcomes overwhelm. You've seen how it fits together – how it offers a way to think, and a way to act. Let's cycle through again – add detail, add depth. So you're better equipped.

I read a story once. A man suffers a brain injury and is given an experimental drug. It not only heals him – it starts improving him. And once it starts, it doesn't stop. That's science fiction. But the self-improving part? That's real. That's called metaplasticity – the ability of the brain not just to learn, but to learn how to learn. To change how it changes.

The second thing this character does is adopt new behaviours. Not just randomly, but deliberately. He builds habits that reinforce one another. A framework. A pattern for living. You might call that a meta-habit. And that too, is real. The third thing? He learns from others. He absorbs everything he can – language, systems, signal, strategy. That's super-social learning. And that's how we, as humans, go further than we ever could alone.

A FRACTAL HABIT
(Or how small patterns become everything)

A fractal is nature's way of being efficient and poetic all at once. It's a shape that repeats itself at every level: tiny curls inside bigger curls, small branches imitating the large, the little copying the whole. Zoom in on a fern, and you'll find... another fern. Stare at a coastline, and the closer you look, the longer it gets.

The point is: the pattern stays the same, even as the scale changes. It's self-similar, self-renewing, and quietly brilliant. Nature doesn't reinvent – she reframes. She finds something that works and loops it. But not lazily. Iteratively. Intelligently.

Some habits work like that too. You think you're doing something small – taking a daily walk, saying 'no' more often, noticing your breath before you speak. But then that tiny habit begins to ripple outward. It shapes your week. It colours your relationships. It shifts your sense of self. And eventually, you realise: it wasn't just a habit. It was a pattern for living.

But here's the real leap. You can choose the pattern. You can select a new fractal. You can build a deliberate, recursive structure that doesn't just help you cope – but helps you upgrade. Not just how you act. But how you adapt.

This is what I mean by a superadaptive meta-habit: a consciously chosen, endlessly scalable pattern for living. One that shapes how you respond to the world – and ultimately, how the world responds to you.

And when you choose this particular pattern, when you begin to move through it – recognising, understanding, and acting – you access something extraordinary: The way your brain learns. The way your brain learns to learn. And the way your life learns to upgrade itself.

That's the loop. That's the fractal. That's the recursive path you're about to walk.

RECOGNISE → UNDERSTAND → NECESSARY ACTION
(The RUN loop. A superadaptive pattern for living.)

THE TRAPPED AND THE TRANSCENDED

A comedian once warned: "Don't touch your potential. You'll mess it up. It's like your bank balance – you always have a lot less than you think." That might be true. But you're still here, reading. Which means… maybe you're tempted to check the balance. Some people never stop checking. Some people never start. And some people only discover their strength when trouble finds them.

You've probably met all three. The born loopers. The silent improvers. The ones who only showed up when the lights went out. Maybe you already know which one you are. Maybe you've been all three at different points. Maybe you're about to change again.

This isn't about labels. It's about entry points. This is how real change begins: with a moment that leads to a pattern. And a pattern that reshapes what comes next.

What follows is a closer look at three ways people enter superadaptability. Each of them begins the pattern differently – but the pattern, once begun, is the same. This isn't a hierarchy. It's just three ways to begin the same pattern.

Some are born superadaptable. Some achieve it. And some have it thrust upon them.

Throughout the next few pages, and then the rest of this book, you'll find hand-drawn loopforms – visual companions to the ideas you're absorbing. Some spiral inward, some burst out. Some hold, some break. All of them mark the lived shape of choices, thoughts, and actions. They're not decoration. They're recursion made visible.

BORN → ACHIEVE → THRUST

BORN

Some people seem to come into the world already reaching – already running the loop. They find ways to shape their own thinking from an early age, bending the world around them through curiosity, through pattern, through play. What they're doing, whether they know it or not, is talking to themselves in ways that unlock their brain's plasticity. Not just once, but again and again.

Sometimes that's a matter of nature – an inheritance of temperament, perception, or drive. Just as often, it's shaped by circumstance. Some are born into difficulty or constraint. And still, they find ways to model, to listen, to rearrange what's around them into something livable – and learnable. They don't wait for permission. They build early access to something others spend decades discovering: the ability to alter the system by adapting the self.

That early access can look magical from the outside. But it's not. It's recursive. And it's learnable. The ability to talk yourself into a better pattern, to convert frustration into focus, to structure your way of thinking into a life that works – these aren't talents. They're meta-habits. And the Born show us how they can begin.

And that's the point. If they can do it – by disposition, by necessity, or by sheer early practice – then so can you. Because the pattern is visible. And if the pattern is visible, it can be studied, absorbed, and used.

What they've built can be your missing link. The first click. The first turn. The first moment something you've struggled to finish… suddenly fits.

This is the secret the Born have already stumbled into: the world is patternable. You don't have to solve it all at once. You just have to live it one intelligent spiral at a time.

Some begin early. But everyone can begin now.

MARIA

Some children grow into themselves. Maria Montessori seemed to start there.

She refused the script. When her parents suggested teaching, she replied: "Anything but this." She studied engineering. Then biology. Then medicine. In 1896, she became Italy's first female doctor – not because Italy invited her, but because she refused to let the system stop her. It would have to bend to her will, not she to it.

Stop and think about this. A child recognising her abilities – and the limitations of others. Not with cruelty. With clarity. With the instinct that others could rise if given the tools.

That insight became her life's work. While others were admiring her success with so-called "unteachable", children, she was asking: What's holding ordinary children back? The answer, she believed, lay in how we learn to learn. Through the hand. Through the self. Through a pattern we spiral, not a track we're marched down.

She watched children like a scientist. Built materials like an engineer. Spoke like someone who had looped through her own education and come out the other side. She called it the absorbent mind. Today, neuroscientists call it plasticity. Either way, the principle holds: the mind reshapes itself through action. Especially early. Especially often.

She gave children the tools to guide their own development. She gave teachers the role of quiet nudger, not loud instructor. She turned education into an environment where recursion could emerge.

Montessori didn't just transcend barriers. She designed ways for others to do it too.

PABLO

Pablo Picasso never waited for permission. He drew before he spoke fluently. Signed his work "Rey" – King. Told a family friend at thirteen, "I am already a great painter. I don't need lessons." From the outside, it looked like arrogance. But inside it was something more recursive: a loop of identity already underway.

Pause. Consider the power of self-talk here. He wasn't just predicting who he'd become. He was authoring the loop. That's the move we miss – not confidence, but recursive instruction.

His father taught fine art. His mother told him he was destined to be someone no one else could be. He believed them – and then exceeded them. By fourteen, a critic would call one of his paintings the finest ever produced in Spain. It wasn't luck. It was recursion. He copied masters, compressed years into months, absorbed structure – and then tore it apart.

He called academic art "a trap." He escaped it with precision. "It took me four years to paint like Raphael," he said, "and a lifetime to paint like a child." That wasn't regression. It was conscious unlearning. Recursive renewal. He looped forward by looping back.

In his studio, he moved like someone in conversation – with the canvas, the form, himself. Observers noted the murmuring, the pacing, the way he coaxed each stroke into becoming. Montessori called the hand "the instrument of the mind". Picasso made that literal.

He didn't just make art. He made Picasso. Then remade him. Again and again.

He avoided traps – not by resistance, but by motion. While some wait to be named, he named himself. The boy who signed 'King' became a man who painted like a child. Not all who start early keep spiralling. But he did.

Some people seem to come into the world already reaching – already running the loop. That might not be you. But you can still learn from those who moved early, and moved well.

Montessori knew, even as a child, that she was thinking at a different level. And here's the remarkable thing: she didn't think that made her superior. She thought it meant others could rise. That you could, in a sense, be born again – at a new level of understanding, with the right tools, the right guidance, the right timing. She did it through careful system design. And she did it not for herself, but for others. That's the key. She transcended but she built the steps.

Picasso moved differently. He avoided the trap by never stepping into it. He didn't wait to be told who he was. He didn't wait to be invited. He named himself – Rey, King – before the world could decide otherwise. He talked himself upward. Drew before he spoke. Painted like a master before he was old enough to vote. And then he looped back to unlearn it all, so he could find what was new.

You may not move like they did. That's not the point. The point is: these are patterns. You can learn to recognise them. You can learn to run them. And once you do, you don't have to stay where you started.

Some people are born superadaptive. But everyone has the chance to become.

ACHIEVE

Some people are born spiralling. Others have to build the spiral themselves.

This is the second path into superadaptability. Not the inherited loop, but the constructed one. The loop that forms through reflection, attention, repetition. Through watching someone do it and trying it for yourself. Through practice – not just of skill, but of pattern.

You don't have to be born looping to loop well. But you do have to notice what you're doing – and decide to keep doing it better.

The Born show us what it looks like to start early. The Achievers show us what it means to come in late – and still rise.

These are the people who didn't start with a visible gift. They didn't leap. They didn't stand out early. They arrived slowly, almost invisibly – but with a pattern of persistence, mirroring, adjustment, and recursive re-entry.

If the Born embody metaplasticity, the Achievers reveal something else: meta-habit. The choice to monitor and modify your own way of learning over time.

This is not the loop that ignites by instinct. It's the one that builds itself across years. And when it clicks – when the pattern becomes visible – it can be just as powerful.

Maybe more.

YITANG

There is a kind of slow recursion that lives in the dark. Years go by. You don't see movement. But something is still turning underneath.

Yitang Zhang's breakthrough in number theory came in 2013. He was 58. Until then, he had worked in obscurity – sometimes as a delivery worker, sometimes as a low-level lecturer. He had no tenure, no funding, and for decades, no major publications.

But he had a habit: he kept thinking.

The question he cracked had baffled mathematicians for generations: whether there are infinitely many pairs of prime numbers that differ by only a fixed amount. What he published wasn't a full solution – but it was enough. A recursive breach. And it opened the door for others.

Zhang's gift wasn't speed. It was patience. Metacognitive durability. A refusal to stop believing that the pattern he had followed – however long it took – was still running.

It's worth thinking here about how the long loop helps you keep going – even when progress is slow, or help feels far away. This kind of loop lives under your control. You don't need permission. You don't even need applause. Just the pattern – and your belief in it.

His breakthrough came not by flair, but by quiet design. Recursive isolation. Intellectual rehearsal. The loop lived – uncelebrated, unconfirmed – until it finally emerged.

And when it did, the world adjusted to fit it.

PENELOPE

Not every pattern needs to be completed quickly. Some loops stretch across decades. Some patterns take half a life to even begin.

Penelope Fitzgerald's first novel was published when she was 60. Before that, she had lived an ordinary, sometimes difficult life – raising children, teaching, working in bookshops. Her early years included teaching in small private schools and moving through near-poverty after her husband's decline. But she read. She observed. She remembered.

When her books did appear, they arrived with precision. Tightly wound. Beautifully recursive. She didn't just tell stories – she unfolded them backwards, sidewards, from memory into clarity. Her greatest work, *The Blue Flower*, came near the end.

Fitzgerald's loop wasn't visible from the outside. But it was forming. She was gathering recursive intelligence, watching systems, cataloguing lives, training her eye to see what would matter later.

She didn't just arrive. She re-entered.

And when she did, it was not as a beginner. It was as someone who had looped silently through life and brought the pattern home.

And maybe, if you look closely, you'll find that something in your own life is forming that same arc. Some things you couldn't have done five years ago might now be within reach – only because of what you've lived. What you're living now may be the seed of something that will only make sense later.

Sometimes the loop starts late. Sometimes you don't know you're in it until you find yourself returning – better, faster, deeper than before.

That's what Achieve shows us. It's not always early. It's not always visible. But if you've ever changed how you change – if you've ever stopped, reflected, adjusted, and gone again – then you already know what this is.

You've looped. Quietly. Without applause. And the pattern has carried you further than you realised.

The Born might show us what recursion looks like from the outside. But the Achievers show us what it feels like from within.

This is the path of second starts, reframed skill, long games. Of patience. Of witnessing. Of letting what you've seen settle – until it becomes something you can use.

Some build the loop slowly. Some walk it back. And some – some get thrown into it. Not gently. But powerfully.

And next, we go there.

THRUST UPON

Some adapt because they choose to. Some because they train to. But others – others adapt because they must.

This is the third entry into superadaptability. Not the gifted start. Not the long learning arc. But the sudden, often violent arrival of a moment that demands change. And the person who steps forward, not because they are ready – but because no one else is.

What we call Thrust Upon isn't about trauma or drama. It's about ignition. It's about being called forward – by crisis, by necessity, by care. When the system collapses, or a door suddenly opens, or you lose the thing that once defined you, something else can begin.

And what begins, if you let it, is the loop.

This is the phase of transformation through rupture. The place where the pattern is not planned – but it is possible.

JEAN-DOMINIQUE

Jean-Dominique Bauby was a French journalist and editor of *Elle* magazine when, at 43, a stroke left him with locked-in syndrome. His mind was intact. His body – frozen. He could blink his left eye. That was all.

And still, he wrote a book.

The Diving Bell and the Butterfly was dictated letter by letter, blink by blink, over ten months. A transcriber read out the alphabet, arranged by frequency. Bauby would blink at the letter he wanted. Word by word, sentence by sentence, chapter by chapter, he looped.

He looped through memory. Through grief. Through pattern. The loop was slow, but it was intact.

He built a recursive loop out of silence, breath, and a single eye.

We'd both hope never to face what he did. And yet, loss and constraint come in many forms. Not all of them dramatic. Some wear us down. Others arrive in a moment. But in whatever shape the outside world imposes itself, this truth remains: we can choose how to meet it. Not easily. Not without grief. But as Bauby did – deliberately, with the pattern still running.

JOSÉ

José Andrés didn't plan to become a crisis chef. He was already successful – multiple restaurants, awards, acclaim. But in 2010, after the Haiti earthquake, something shifted. He flew there and began cooking for those displaced by the disaster. It was improvisational, urgent, recursive work.

One meal. Then another. Then 100,000.

Over time, this turned into World Central Kitchen – an adaptive humanitarian operation that now responds to floods, fires, wars, and refugee crises. Wherever he goes, he adapts – ingredients, tools, systems, teams. He doesn't just feed people. He builds supply chains. Invents delivery routes. Coaches local cooks.

He adapts the loop live.

Andrés doesn't wait for conditions to be right. He cooks anyway. He tests anyway. He feeds anyway. And from the pattern of that doing, a new system emerges.

He cooked something up in Haiti. Hello.

And sometimes, the world doesn't collapse – it opens. You notice it's you. It's your turn. You've been invited. Or you volunteer yourself. And if you step forward, even tentatively, you may find a missing link, a next step, a new you.

This is the third path in. You don't have to be born looping. You don't have to achieve it slowly. Sometimes, it's thrust upon you.

These are the moments when the outside intrudes – accident, disaster, opportunity, or care. You didn't seek the loop. But now you're in it.

And when that happens, everything you do next becomes the pattern. The way you blink. The way you serve. The way you reframe a story you didn't ask for.

What these figures show isn't power. It's choice.

The choice to loop anyway. To act. To adapt.

To say: if this is the starting point, then let it start here.

You've now seen all three kinds of recursion:
   Born: the gifted or instinctive spiral.
   Achieve: the loop built across years.
   Thrust Upon: the loop ignited by rupture or call.

The next question is not how it starts. It's how to live it.

HOW TO LIVE THE LOOP

This book is built around a loop.

And that loop has three steps:

RECOGNISE → UNDERSTAND → NECESSARY ACTION

Everything that follows is designed to help you live those three steps –
intelligently, adaptively, and repeatedly.

You'll get nine rules, three for each stage of the loop.
Then a tenth rule to help you upgrade the loop itself.
And finally, one last invitation: to reboot the loop.
To start again – only better.

Ten rules. One loop. A pattern for living.

But this is Rule Zero.
Think of it as a first loop through the loop.
You won't get every insert, every counter-loop, every strategy yet.
You'll just get enough to recognise the rhythm – enough to begin.

Each rule that follows will go deeper:
    A core pattern or insight
    Real-world examples
    Common traps – and how to transcend them
    Practices and provocations
    A story to stretch your perspective
    And a pivot to what comes next

You won't remember everything. You're not meant to. But you'll begin to notice
the loop.
    In your habits. In your history. In the way the world works – and how you
might work differently inside it.

So don't worry about mastering it all at once.
Just loop once. Then again. Then better.

In the pages ahead, you'll see how others lived the loop.

You'll be invited to try it yourself.

You'll see what happens when it goes wrong – and how to reset.

This is the part of the book where the loop becomes yours.

Let's begin.

HOW THEY LIVED THE LOOP
Jumping genes, jumping habits

I nearly cut this page.

Not because it wasn't true. But because it was hard to name.

What do you call a moment when everything shifts? When what you thought was fixed turns out to be movable – edit-able – even upgradeable?

I could have called it how to change what you do to change what you get. Or how to swap your habits to upgrade your life.

Or even: how to copy what superadaptive people do and run that in your own head, like a meta-habit.

But none of those quite landed.

So instead, I'm going to tell you a story.

She was born Eleanor, but her parents renamed her Barbara.

Why? Because even at birth, they could tell she was serious. Determined. Not the kind of child who would sit quietly and obey. She wasn't easy, but she was exacting – and that would turn out to matter more.

Her mother, like many women of her time, thought college was optional. Something girls might do, briefly, before marriage. But her father believed otherwise. "You can go," he said. "Just don't tell your mother until you're already there."

So she went.

She studied what she was allowed to study – botany. Not genetics, not the deeper science she was drawn to. That wasn't for women, apparently.

But she watched. She paid attention. And what she saw, in the microscope, changed science.

Maize, dyed and dissected. Chromosomes that didn't stay put. Genes that moved.

They told her she was wrong. That chromosomes were fixed. That she was mistaken. But she wasn't.

She'd discovered what are now called transposable elements – 'jumping genes'.

And she stuck with it. For decades. Until, at 81, they gave her the Nobel Prize.

McClintock saw what no one else believed: that even your deepest code might not be fixed.

That parts of your pattern might jump.

That identity – even biology – isn't just inherited. It's observed. It's edited.

And here's the shift: what's true at the genetic level may also be true at the behavioural level.

Your habits are not set in stone. They're patterns. They can be dyed, tracked, moved.

This happened in early 20th-century America. Barbara McClintock was born in Hartford, Connecticut, in 1902. But if the place and the era feel distant, the forces she faced are not. There are still enough obstacles, enough gatekeepers, and enough people being kept out – for no good reason at all – for you to recognise something of her situation in your country, in your systems, maybe even in your own life.

She was, in many ways, born superadaptive. But she also had to achieve it. She had to study, resist, adapt. She needed support. She faced new blocks. She had to keep proving herself. She had to learn it again.

And, yes – at key moments, it was also thrust upon her. She had to see that the opportunity was right there, in the corn she was allowed to study. She had to notice what others missed.

If you think back to all the people in this book so far, it was the same for them. The potential wasn't given to them – it was in them. It had to be drawn out, worked through, sometimes wrestled into being.

And it's in you too. That's not a promise of ease. Life isn't simple, or fair. But that's exactly why this book exists.

Because even in an unfree world, the act of noticing differently, interpreting consciously, and deciding to move – again, and again – is how you begin to overcome overwhelm.

And, as you'll see in the next pages – and throughout this book – that is how superadaptive people live, work, and breathe.

BORN → ACHIEVE → THRUST UPON

TRAPPED → TRANSCENDED

FROM TRAPPED TO TRANSCENDED
Why one loop changes everything

This book is about potential.

A comedian once said you shouldn't touch it – because there's always less than you thought. But the sci-fi we explored earlier suggested otherwise: that once you become aware of your own thinking, once you can talk to yourself, you can talk yourself into better. Into becoming. Into change.

That's the real arc here. Of this book. Of our species.

Brains hung around for aeons. For countless generations – partly because those generations were so long, and partly because we hadn't figured out how to count them. We didn't know what to notice yet.

And even now, we still don't always notice.

What's a trap? Zhang locked out of academia. Bauby trapped in his own body. Fitzgerald late to be taken seriously. Montessori permitted, but only partially. Traps aren't always dramatic. Sometimes they just feel like the world is whispering: "not for you."

But it is.

Bauby welcomed his wheelchair – not because of what he'd lost, but because of where he knew he could restart. Zhang kept looping even when no one saw. The movement, this movement, is what we're interested in. It's what matters.

Self-directed learning. Divergent thinking. Brain plasticity. These aren't abstractions anymore. They're labelled now. In case of emergency, use this.

They're tools. Keys. Invitations to potential.

The RUN loop is the beginning of that fractal life.

Your brain loops whether you permit it or not. It predicts, fires, wires, learns. But what we're doing now – what you've just begun – is looping on purpose.

Recognising where the limits are.
Understanding the patterns and the systems that hold them in place.
Taking the necessary action that begins the shift.

You've seen it now: action alone isn't enough. Understanding alone leaves you circling. But the loop – the full loop – moves you.

And once you pick it up, you're living the fractal life.
One loop at a time.
From trapped to transcended.

	TRAPPED	**TRANSCENDED**
Recognise	You lock onto the wrong signal. You misread what you're seeing – or rush to explain it. You act without pausing, or wait too long to act. You don't detect the shift until the damage has begun.	You widen your scan. You delay certainty. You ask: "What's really changing here?" You don't just see more – you see better. You recognise the shift while there's still time to respond.
Understand	You sense something's wrong – but you don't look deeper. You stop at blame, frustration, or defeat. Or you chase explanations without clarity. You treat the symptom but never trace the system.	You know there's a system – and you want to understand it. You ask: "How is this working?" and "What's driving this loop?" You model with purpose. You search for the mechanism. You aim to modify what matters most. You understand to change.
Necessary Action	You act too soon – or not at all. When it doesn't work, you stop – or keep going in the wrong direction. You move without rhythm, without pause, without feedback. You waste energy on what doesn't shift the system. You treat action as effort – not pattern. Nothing embeds. Nothing loops.	You move when the moment is right. You focus your effort where it matters most. You act in rhythm – with your energy, your timing, your system. You listen to feedback. You act to embed, not just to escape. You move the system forward – on purpose.

REBOOT YOUR LOOP
Your zero-day kit

This book has big ideas.
But this page is small on purpose.

Because when you're overwhelmed, confused, knocked sideways by life – you don't need a theory.
You need a loop.
A simple, repeatable loop that gets you out of stuckness and back into motion.
This is it.
Your Zero-Day Reboot.

When in doubt:
RECOGNISE what's happening.
UNDERSTAND what's true.
Take the NECESSARY ACTION.

Then breathe.
And begin again.

You can use it in five seconds or five minutes.

You can write it down, speak it out loud, or just feel your way through it.

It works in a crisis. It works in a meeting. It works on a walk, in a text, in a moment where you don't know what to do next.

It's not perfect.
But it's portable.

It adapts with you.
You don't have to get it right the first time.
That's why we call it a loop.

Pack it.
Practice it.
Reboot it.
Begin again – only better.

TRANSCEND YOUR LOOP

You are here. And you are just beginning.

This was the one about overcoming overwhelm.

The one about loosening the chokehold, finding air to breathe and space to think again.

The one about seeing where you are – and moving anyway.

This was Rule Zero.

It gave you a map. A loop. A way of noticing, understanding, and acting – again and again, in every part of your life.

It was your first loop. And it wasn't hypothetical.

You lived it.

And now – you go forward.

You'll meet artists and scientists, detectives and athletes, teachers and radicals.

You'll sit beside people in war, people in wonder. People who kept going.

Their stories are sharp. They're strange. They're real.

And in all of them, you'll see risk. You'll see rhythm. You'll see recursion.

You might even see yourself.

Some walked toward freedom. Some ran.

Some were pushed – and still adapted.

And that's where we go next.

TEGLA LOROUPE AND THE LONG LOOP

"I ran to free myself," she said.

Not to win. Not first. Free.

Free from the weight of 24 siblings.

Free from the silence expected of Pokot girls.

Free from the road she was meant to stay on.

At seven, she was already running ten kilometres to school – every day. Not as sport. As life. Her loop didn't begin in glory. It began in necessity. The act of movement, again and again, through hardship, made her not just fast, but fluent in difficulty.

"In a country where only men are encouraged, you have to be your own inspiration."

No one expected much. Even when she won her first races, no one knew what to do with a girl who ran like that. But she understood something the world didn't: that running could be resistance. That pace could be purpose. And eventually, that purpose could be shared.

After becoming the first African woman to win the New York Marathon, after setting world records, after representing Kenya in three Olympics, she did something rarer.

She looped back.

"Sport is not just about fame. It can bring peace where there is war."

With the Tegla Loroupe Peace Foundation, she didn't just run. She brought others – pastoralists, warriors, refugees – into the loop. She turned competition into community. In the places where AK-47s outnumbered schoolbooks, she started Peace Races.

"Life has been good to me and I want to give back as much as I can."

This is what it looks like to run the loop well. Not just once. Not just for yourself. But again and again, for others.

Tegla Loroupe didn't just overcome.

She looped.

She built a system that helps others adapt.

R → U → N

AND REMEMBER...

Montessori, Zhang, Bauby, Frida, Juliane, McClintock.
  Each with a different beginning.
  Each with a different loop.
  Each faced something they didn't choose.
  And each chose something that changed everything.
  They were born into constraint.
  They achieved what wasn't expected.
  They had hardship thrust upon them.
  They were trapped.
  And they transcended.
  McClintock proved that genes jump.
  And since identity – at its deepest level – isn't fixed.
  And since most of your genome is made of restless, jumping genes,
  maybe your habits can shift too.
  Maybe your life can jump.
  That's what this loop is for.
  Recognise what has held you.
  Understand what it's made of.
  Take the necessary action to change your pattern.
  That's how you live the loop.
  That's how you go from trapped to transcendent.

recognise

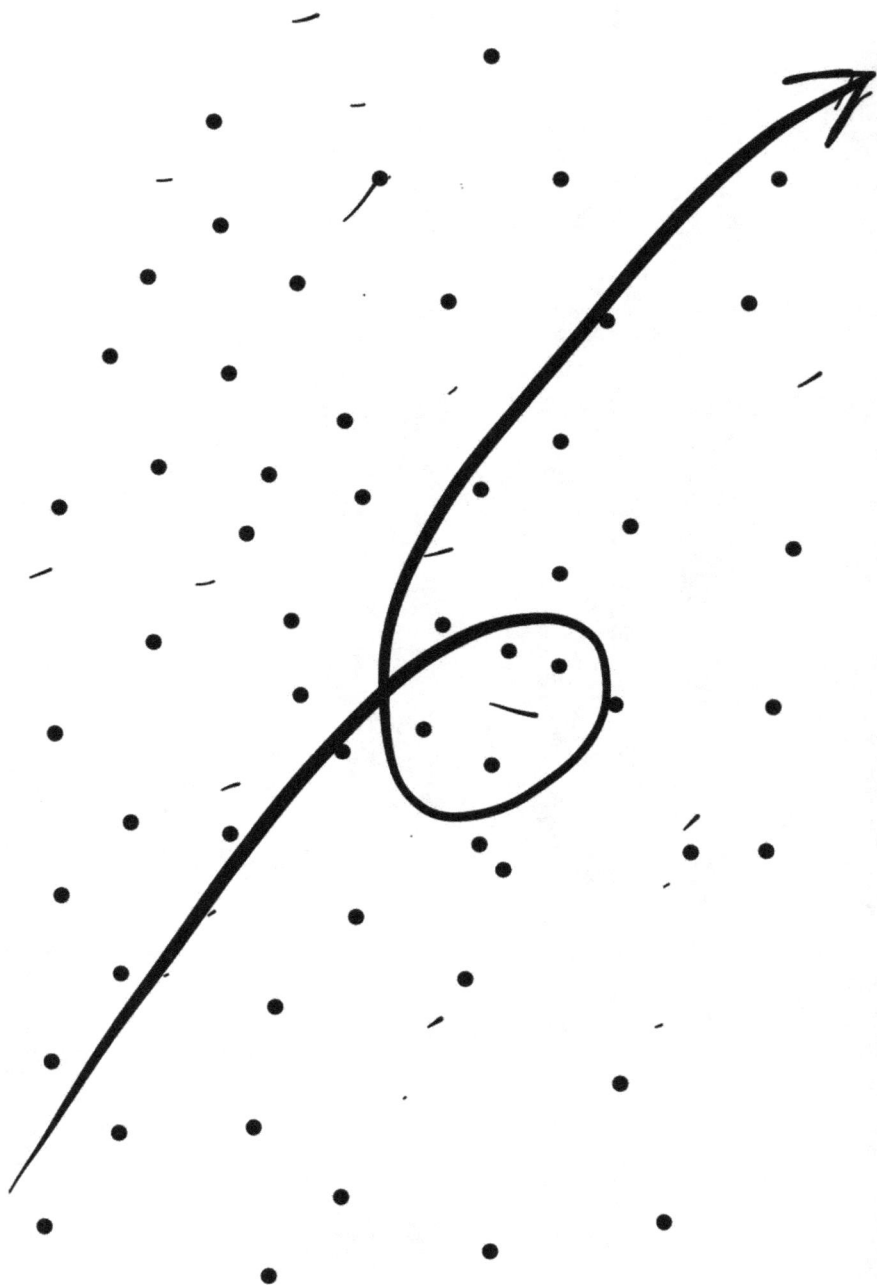

RULE 1:
SEE WHAT OTHERS MISS

The one about noticing what matters most

Superadapters don't just see more. They detect what matters. They tune their attention to the patterns that drive reality – signals others ignore, anomalies others miss. But detection isn't enough. What matters is how it feeds the loop. Because superadaptability doesn't begin with motion. It begins with noticing. And noticing is what allows you to move forward and up.

What if survival doesn't depend on reacting faster – but on seeing sooner?

This chapter opens with a sharp challenge: most people fail not because they're weak or slow, but because they don't notice the shift until it's too late.

Superadapters have a different eye. They don't just look harder. They see patterns in noise, signals in mess, meaning where others see chaos.

Rule 1 introduces this gift – not as magic, but as habit. You'll meet people who learned how to see. Then you'll learn how to do it too.

Not by thinking harder.

By paying attention differently.

WHITE BLOSSOMS, WHITE AIRPODS

We're standing under a white-blossom tree. Somewhere beneath it, someone has dropped a white AirPod.

The problem? Everything on the ground looks like the thing we're looking for.

We know what we're trying to find – but we can't see it. There's too much sameness. Too many false positives. The shape is right. The colour is right. But the signal's buried in pattern.

So we stop looking. And start listening.

We find a YouTube video: "Loudest sound to find AirPod." It has 1.3 million views. Apparently, this is a common loop.

We walk the perimeter. Triangulate a memory. Play the sound.

We're nearly standing on it.

The model was right, but our perception was overloaded.

Detection isn't just about vision. It's about perception design. It's about knowing that when a pattern becomes too dense, you need a new signal – an offset input. Something that lets you find the thing that looks like everything else.

You can't always see what matters most.

But you can still find it.

THE DETECT LOOP

HOW SUPERADAPTERS DETECT
You've been detecting things your whole life.

Where to step. Who to trust. When something doesn't feel right. Your brain is doing it all the time – spotting shifts, scanning for patterns, deciding what deserves your attention.

That's how life works. But superadapters do it differently.

They don't just notice more. They detect usefully. They tune their attention to the kinds of signals that help them move – not just now, but later.

This is the first loop of the Recognise phase, the start of the whole system. And it matters, because if you're not detecting the right things, everything that follows gets harder. The interpretation gets warped. The decision gets skewed. The action goes off-track.

Superadapters get better not just by doing more, but by detecting better. They get early access to the real problem. Or the real opportunity. They position themselves sooner. Sharper. Freer.

This chapter will show you how they do that – three real people, three different ways of running the same loop.

But before that, we'll take a closer look. At the loop itself. What it's for. How it works. And why you can train it.

All life detects. But superadapters detect differently.

They don't just wait for the world to reveal itself. They tune their perception to pick up the signal that matters, before it's obvious. They don't get distracted by noise. They don't mistake patternlessness for pattern. They don't chase the flashiest signal – they follow the one that helps them move.

This loop sits at the very start of the RUN system, the first of three that make up the Recognise phase. It's what you're doing – consciously or not – every time you scan a room, catch a shift in someone's tone, pause at a headline, notice a gut drop, or realise too late that you missed the key move entirely.

Superadapters run this loop better. They get more useful signal, sooner. Not because they're gifted – but because they loop it. Deliberately.

This loop has a shape. A sequence.

$$HUNT \rightarrow SCAN \rightarrow TAG$$

That's the Detect Loop.
You're about to see three people run it – each in their own way. But first, let's go deeper. Let's look at the shift that made this loop possible.

There was a time when perception was thought to be direct.

J. J. Gibson, the American psychologist, believed the brain didn't need to interpret anything. It simply picked up affordances from the environment – clues and cues already built into the world. In his model, perception was accurate, ecological, and automatic. We saw what was there.

But then came Richard Gregory.

Gregory saw perception not as reception, but construction. He argued that the brain doesn't simply detect the world – it builds a best guess from limited data. We don't see light. We infer edges. We project structure. We fill in gaps. Perception, in Gregory's model, is a loop of prediction, not a camera of reality.

That insight didn't come from nowhere. As a child, Gregory and his father built a small aircraft together – a "Flying Flea," based on a French kit. Just before their first flight, Gregory detected something others missed: a stream of crash reports from similar models. They didn't fly it. And they lived.

That's detection as adaptation – not accuracy, but survival.

Years later, Gregory would found The Exploratory, a public-facing illusion lab where children and adults could walk through perception itself. They saw how the brain bends signal. They learned to catch it in the act. Gregory was showing us what superadapters already do: they test what their brain is predicting – before it fails.

So what does this mean for you?

It means that detection isn't about truth. It's about traction.

Your brain doesn't just receive the world. It predicts it – constantly. And those predictions shape where your attention goes, what you think is happening, and what options you believe you have.

Superadapters don't just wait to be right. They train themselves to spot what matters – sooner. Not because they're faster. Because they loop. They test. They revise. They update.

And here's the best news: this capacity is trainable.

Your brain isn't just plastic. It's metaplastic. That means you can change how you change. You can adjust how your attention filters the world, and you can learn to detect a signal that moves you forward – not just confirms what you already know.

That's the Detect Loop. It's not a passive sense. It's a recursive skill.

And it starts with seeing differently. Because the thing that fools you – the thing you miss – is often the thing that would've set you free.

We call it: The Third Eye.

THE THIRD EYE
The art of seeing with purpose

You don't just see the world.
You process it.
You filter. You notice. You miss.

Most people don't know they're seeing through a lens –
because they've never taken the lens off.

But the third eye isn't mystical. It's meta.
It's the awareness that perception isn't passive.
That attention can be honed.
That some people see not just the event – but the pattern it belongs to.

We don't all perceive the same world.

Some people see colour on spectrums others never glimpse.
Bees follow ultraviolet arrows to pollen.
Pit vipers feel heat.
Migratory birds read magnetic lines like maps.
Humans built tools to match them – infrared goggles, space telescopes, LIDAR –

but the real upgrade isn't in the machine.
It's in the mind that knows which signal matters.

The third eye isn't just vision – it's discrimination.
Noticing what's salient, not just what's shiny.
Holding back from false positives, phantom tigers, imagined insults.
Tuning out the noise, so that signal can speak.

But even good eyes can lie.

You can over-see, over-think, over-track the wrong thing.
Like the athlete who keeps looking back at the competition and slows down.
Like the over-attentive parent scanning for danger that isn't there.
You drown in detail, and miss the pattern.
You react, but don't detect.

And without detection, there is no interpretation.
No action.
Just a blur of unprocessed stimuli.
That's what the third eye protects you from.

Without the third eye, you drown in noise and miss the signal.

Real detection requires slack.
You can't hear a whisper in a nightclub.
You can't read micro-expressions when your brain is flooded.
Perception happens in the space just before you interpret.
The retina passes 80% of its data straight to the bin.
The third eye is what rewrites the filter.

Some people call it pattern recognition.
Some call it situational awareness.
But it's more than either.
It's the capacity to notice what you will need –
not just now, but next.

Great detectors don't just read the world.
They read the watcher.
They track what others might see, want, fear, or miss.

It's not just awareness of people – it's awareness of what people are aware of.
That's the real Theory of Mind.

You think about what they're thinking.
You sense what they'll sense.
You see the second move before the first one finishes.

Not everyone has the same input.
But everyone can train the funnel.
What you notice, what you miss, what you believe was never there.
You can reprogram the aperture.
You can see better.

THE EYES IN THE BACK

A father walks his daughter to the playground.
He is blind, cane ticking, stroller gliding.
Other parents watch – half admiration, half alarm.
At the swing set a ball rockets off a child's foot,
cutting a low, fast arc toward the toddlers.

Before sighted parents even flinch,
the father pivots, one hand still on the stroller,
catches the ball with an audible thump.
He heard the air split, felt the crowd's breath shift,
mapped the trajectory in sound.

"My normal eyes may function less," he laughs,
"but the eyes in my back work as well as anyone's."

Later, when asked how he knew, he shrugs:
"You listen for patterns – then you keep the useful ones."
Blindness didn't shrink his field; it re-wired the funnel.
Silence became resolution.
Echoes became pixels.

All great detectors do the same –
not seeing more, but attending better.

The third eye doesn't just help you see, it helps you aim.
Because adaptive perception always ends here:
the eye on the prize.

THE THIRD EYE IN ACTION

The third eye of the superadapter is their ability to see the alternative – the part of a pattern that is most helpful to them. At its heart, that's what it is. And by seeing the part of the pattern that's most helpful to them, they're able to orient their efforts, their energy – which is always limited, as you know in your life – towards the next steps that are the most effective use of that energy. Nothing is guaranteed, but by learning how to detect better and to develop this third eye, they – and now you – are able to focus attention later on what needs to be interpreted, what needs to be decided, and what action needs to be taken to put you in a better position to succeed the next time, and the time after that.

In this first of our habits in the detect loop, we begin with Hunt. It's the foundational act – the pattern-seeking instinct that initiates everything else. Without Hunt, there's nothing to scan, nothing to tag, and nothing to build upon. Hunt is what primes the system. It trains your perception to actively search for structure, rhythm, friction, or leverage – whatever makes a pattern useful. It is a habit that sculpts how the rest of the loop behaves. What you hunt, you see. What you see, you tag. What you tag, you learn from. That's how recursive detection becomes metaplastic. And what you're really training is not just your eye – but your entire adaptive system. And it starts here, with the way you hunt.

HABIT 1: HUNT FOR PATTERNS
Build pattern fluency by scanning everyday life for structure and rhythm.

Our next example is, of course, a superadapter more generally – but specifically here we're focused on her embodiment of the habit: HUNT FOR PATTERNS. Temple, when we join her, is dealing with a world that doesn't understand her. She's surviving among people who put obstacles directly in her way, who called the police on her, who tried to get her removed from university.

Even earlier, as a child, people tried to take her away from her mother and blamed her mother for Temple's differences. She was born into a demanding world that could have broken many people. But her ability to hunt for patterns, both in the world around her and within her own mind, was transformative. And, for us, instructive.

It begins with perception – noticing that her way of sensing, of tuning in to the emotional responses of animals, was a different kind of strength. Let's step into Temple's world – and watch what happens when detection gets personal.

TEMPLE GRANDIN
Temple Grandin was still in high school when she built her first squeeze machine.

Diagnosed later in life as autistic, Grandin grew up drawn to patterns – visual, sensory, mechanical. Her early fixations were dismissed by some as distractions. But her science teacher, Mr. Carlock, saw something else: an opportunity to build a loop.

He used her fixation on cattle chutes to engage her in psychology. He showed her how to turn a narrow interest into a structured investigation. And with that guidance, Grandin began to upgrade her own perception. Not by abandoning her fixations – but by directing them.

This was metacognition – supplied at first from the outside, then taken on from within. She didn't just notice the world differently. She learned to design around it. She didn't just see what others missed. She noticed what they never even thought to look for.

It wasn't a revelation. It was a rhythm.

While others moved through the world assuming the problem was inside the animal, she slowed everything down. Watched. Rewatched. Traced the loop.

A glint of light. A sound. A shape. A shadow across a path.

Where others saw resistance, she saw pattern: flicker → flinch → freeze.

Grandin trained herself to spot the micro-patterns that signalled failure in the system. Not just when the cattle panicked – but what they were reacting to.

And the answer wasn't 'chaos'. It was missed cues. Unreadable thresholds. Poor design.

She didn't blame the animal. She refined the environment.
She didn't demand obedience. She noticed structure.

Her loops were slow, recursive, practical.
She tested them. Changed one variable at a time. Listened. Watched again.

What others labelled irrational, she decoded as sensitive.
What others labelled broken, she labelled as misread.

The system wasn't breaking because the animals were irrational.
It was breaking because no one else had detected the pattern. She had.

This wasn't intuition. It was attention – run consciously, refined iteratively, and used to rewire a system.

HUNT → SCAN → TAG

You will have noticed a pattern in the Grandin example, because you were hunting for them – and at one level the pattern was her getting better at hunting for patterns. Becoming more confident in her ability to do it. Spotting interference and sabotage and leverage. Scanning the system for the one person who might listen. And every time she succeeded, she built a new loop. She looped forward. She published and then republished. Each cycle left her stronger. Even her autobiography became an adaptive tool – a new version of herself each time she told the story. Hunting for patterns, for her, was recursive. Each success became another pattern worth pursuing.

And so her hunt for patterns demonstrated the need for another habit – both her need of it, and her demonstration of it to us. Because she's a superadaptive person in totality, we can be quite confident that she has demonstrated all of the behaviours found throughout this book. And the next pattern, the next habit, is to continue to scan for signals. To sweep your environment for subtle shifts, constraints, or leverage points. Because hunting for a pattern and then staying fixated on it – even if it's a useful pattern – is not helpful enough. You'll need other patterns. The picture is not complete. Like two telephones needing each other to create a network. Like scanning for digital signal when analogue is gone. Like noticing when your best friend doesn't react the same way. Because the signal has changed. What you saw yesterday may no longer apply. Or something new may be emerging that matters more. Scanning keeps you moving. Scanning gives you optionality. And scanning keeps your loop open – ready to receive, ready to detect again.

HABIT 2: SCAN FOR SIGNALS
Sweep your environment for subtle shifts, constraints, or leverage points.

And this is why you need to scan for signals. You need to sweep your environment for subtle shifts, constraints, or leverage points. This keeps you up to date. Makes sure you see the little thing that could become a big thing – or the thing that's holding you back, or the point of influence, the thing that would really magnify your effort. We're always looking for what we can send forward – for the attention of another part of your brain, or another part of the loop. What needs more understanding? What might deserve more attention? What's changed – internally or externally?

So we zoom back in time to just a year after Temple Grandin's birth, to 1937, where a young engineer named Claude Shannon is preparing to submit what would become the famous 'Bell Systems Paper' – a bold new theory for how to handle electronic communication more efficiently. At the time, no one knew how to send information cleanly across wires. Electronic noise polluted the system. Messages were dropped or warped mid-transmission. Shannon suspected there was a structure – a logic – that could cut through the noise. If he was right, it would change everything.

But Shannon wasn't yet sure. And neither were his professors. In fact, many worried he spent too much time tinkering. His house would later be nicknamed Entropy House. It was filled with strange inventions and playful machines – rocket-powered Frisbees, juggling mannequins, mechanical mice. He even built a device to 'read minds'. He loved building machines, but admitted: it was hard to keep them in repair. For Shannon, everything was a game. Everything was a chance to play. And that playfulness – the constant search for what might be interesting or useful or beautiful – kept him scanning. Not just for what the system was doing, but for what it could become.

So the question is: how useful is this kind of play to scanning for signals? We're about to find out.

CLAUDE SHANNON

In 1937, Claude Shannon was 21 years old and working at MIT.

Assigned to work on a differential analyser – a monstrous, belt-driven contraption the size of a dining room table – he spent his days watching wheels spin, wires tangle, and gears churn their way through physical simulations of equations. It was mechanical, loud, and almost poetic in its absurdity: a kind of steam-powered mathematician with poor posture.

But Shannon wasn't looking at the math.

He was watching the relays – the electromechanical switches controlling the system. That was the moment. Somewhere between the clatter and the hum, he saw it: logic hiding inside the noise. A pattern inside the switches. A way to use circuits not just for movement, but for meaning.

He didn't call it scanning.

But he was already scanning – before the term had shape.

Filtering signal from overload. Asking: what matters here?

Which details carry structure? Which are just noise?

His 1948 paper – 'A Mathematical Theory of Communication' – made it formal. It showed that information could be quantified, compressed, transmitted. That clarity was a function of probability. That uncertainty, when reduced, was knowledge. He set the limits of transmission, and showed how you might approach them.

But Shannon wasn't a showman. He wasn't selling the future.

He retreated. Gently. Intentionally.

He built juggling robots, unicycles, mechanical mice. He named his house Entropy House. He created machines that did nothing but turn themselves off.

Like Einstein riding a beam of light, Shannon rode signal through a maze of relays – until he'd seen what it could become.

Then he left. Not because he'd run out of ideas, but because the noise had caught up.

He'd already shown us how to tune it.

Claude Shannon scanned for signals his entire life.

Sometimes in circuits. Sometimes in silence.

Signal isn't what screams. It's what repeats. What carries. What survives compression.

He didn't just build the architecture of the digital world.

He looped his way through uncertainty – and showed us how to do the same.

That's how you begin to see what others miss.

HUNT → **SCAN** → TAG

You may have noticed a pattern: hunting for patterns, scanning for signals… but you don't want to become overwhelmed. And you don't want to forget the stuff that matters. That's why it becomes crucial to tag what matters. To mentally label the important cues to make signal retention easier. To note: that one matters, that one matters. Start small. Your waistline. That mole. Your child's energy level. Something is changing – but will you track it? Tagging helps you overcome overload. It gives shape to memory. It makes patterns visible across time. And if you tag not just what happened, but why it matters, you'll know what to escalate, what to dismiss, and what to send forward.

You want to tag things so you can see what's changing. You see where it is on day 1 and where it is on day 10. Maybe it's growing. Maybe it should be dropped. You cannot remember everything. You want to track the health of your family, but a particular measure of it. In sport, you might be told to track one player. Sure – tag what matters. And take the tags on and off the board. Tagging lets you manage the flow. Tag why it matters – so you can pass it on. First, know which things matter. Then, package them to hand off. Send it over for interpretation. Tag it for escalation.

HABIT 3: TAG WHAT MATTERS
Mentally label important cues to make signal retention easier.

So if we take you across the Atlantic from Entropy House and Shannon's awards for brilliant playfulness – 3,456 miles over to France and a few years back from his seminal paper – we find our next superadaptive mind in the middle of a world war. Pearl Witherington, born in France to British parents, escaped the Nazi occupation – only to return later by parachute. She decided, maybe, that freeing France from a dictator was the most important use of her life. The Air Force called her the best shot British espionage had ever seen. But was she the right person to survive the fog of war? How would she know where to hide, what to carry, who to trust?

France was fractured. The Nazis had invaded. The official army had fallen, and underground resistance groups were trying to rise – network by network, town by town. Spies, saboteurs, smugglers. A few of them women. From London, the British launched the Special Operations Executive: a shadow network sending agents behind enemy lines. Pearl Witherington was one of them – barely 30, newly trained, and parachuted in alone. Where to hide. Where to strike. Who to trust. Tagging what matters wasn't just a skill. It was survival.

PEARL WITHERINGTON

On the night of 22 September 1943, Pearl Witherington parachuted into occupied France. She was 29 years old.

Operating under the codename 'Marie', she became the only woman in the Special Operations Executive (SOE) to lead a French Resistance circuit – commanding over 3,500 fighters.

When the Nazis tried to crush her network with 2,000 troops, she held the line with 140 partisans. When her commander was captured, she stepped up. When she was offered a civilian honour after the war, she turned it down: "There was nothing civil about what I did."

Witherington didn't just move under pressure. She perceived under it.

She read betrayal before it broke. She sensed morale as a temperature, not a number. She knew when to disappear, when to reappear, and when to pull everyone forward.

This wasn't guesswork. It was judgement – under tension.

She didn't waste attention. She didn't drown in options. She tagged what mattered.

The Maquis needed coordination? She did it. A signal line failed? She found another. A decision had to be made about which rail line to sabotage, which message to trust, which betrayal to confront. She moved.

Tagging is how you orient inside chaos. And Pearl Witherington mastered it.

Not as abstraction. As habit. She didn't just perceive. She chose. And what she chose reshaped the outcome.

$$HUNT \rightarrow SCAN \rightarrow \textbf{TAG}$$

Witherington didn't just tag what mattered. She made it matter. And it's the movement between these two and their interrelationship that really makes this one sing.

By tagging what matters, she reduces the number of things she has to keep track of. And by learning what matters and how to make it matter, she learns how to move forward. If something doesn't matter yet, perhaps it's the wrong thing to tag.

If she can't act on it, maybe she needs to tag something else that enables action. She taught herself what to escalate. And across the chapter, you've seen that same recursive refinement – Grandin, Shannon, Witherington. They weren't just detecting. They were deciding what to send forward. That's how superadaptive detection works.

So just as our earlier examples would have done all three things and more – our next example will too. He will hunt for patterns: build pattern fluency by scanning everyday life for structure and rhythm. He will scan for signals; sweeping the environment for subtle shifts, constraints or leverage points. And he will tag what matters, mentally labeling important cues to make signal retention easier.

These three habits don't live in isolation. They interlock. You notice a loved one's mood dip. That's hunting. But you also scan – has their behaviour shifted? Have circumstances changed? And then you tag what matters: this moment, this conversation, this doctor's appointment. That's the loop.

This next example lives the loop in a lab coat. Born in Switzerland. Working in the pharmaceutical and chemical department of Sandoz Laboratories. His job? Purify and synthesize a fungus. That's what he was paid for. But he was also trained – trained to be curious, trained to be prepared.

As Fleming said, chance favours the prepared mind. So when something strange happened, something unplanned, the question wasn't just: what is this? The question was: will he notice? Will he tag it? Will he follow it? What happens when you detect the thing nobody paid you to find?

THE DETECT LOOP: PUTTING IT ALL TOGETHER

A strange unease rising in his chest, soft but insistent, Albert Hofmann stepped back from his workbench in the Sandoz lab, blinking against the light. The sun outside seemed too sharp, the outlines of the world somehow thickened – like the edges of objects had begun to hum. He closed his eyes and waited for it to pass. But behind his eyelids, something had started. Shapes. Motion. A subtle choreography of colour and form. It wasn't frightening. Not yet. But it was… unfamiliar. Different. The kind of difference you didn't dismiss if you were trained to notice patterns. And Hofmann was. Even as his balance tilted, even as a subtle vertigo began to stir in his blood, he began to watch. This wasn't a mistake. It was a signal.

He lay down, closed his eyes, and began to watch. Behind his eyelids, forms began to shift – a choreography of colour, pattern, and pulse. He noted the sensations with a quiet precision, almost like prayer. There was a rhythm to it, not random. A message in motion.

"An uninterrupted stream of fantastic pictures…
Kaleidoscopic shapes…
Exploding in coloured fountains…
Rearranging and hybridizing themselves in constant flux."

He didn't try to name it. Not yet. But he didn't look away.

"Chance," he would later write, "favours the prepared mind." And Hofmann's was prepared. He had trained his attention since boyhood – watching leaves quiver, light fold, chemistry bend.

Three days later, he decided to return.

On the morning of April nineteenth, Hofmann measured out a small dose of the compound. At least, he believed it was small. Two hundred and fifty micrograms. Just enough, he thought, to observe more clearly what he had glimpsed before. He called it a self-experiment, but it was more than that. It was chance to see – not just what the substance could do, but what his mind might be capable of receiving. He made a note in his lab book. He took the dose. And he waited.

The first effects came slowly. A shimmer. A soft buzzing at the edges of his senses. And then it began to build. His vision stretched. Sound became motion. The world outside the lab twisted into abstraction. He asked his assistant to take him home – and together, they rode bicycles through the streets of Basel, Hofmann swaying, unsure if the road was rippling or if his legs had forgotten how to move. Everything around him vibrated with intensity. The trees leaned toward him. The pavement pulsed. Time slowed, folded, disappeared. At one point, he thought he had poisoned himself. At another, that his own thoughts had escaped and were circling back. He could no longer trust the shape of the world.

"I thought I was dying."

But even in that fear, part of him remained watching.
Not lost. Not gone. Just deep inside the signal.

He made it home. Barely. He collapsed into bed, unsure whether the experience was ending or beginning again. The doctor found nothing wrong – except for the dilation in his eyes. No fever. No damage. Just an opened system. Slowly, his fear began to fall away, replaced by something else. Wonder. Beauty. Behind closed eyes, the colours had returned.

"Little by little I could begin to enjoy the unprecedented colours and plays of shapes...
Kaleidoscopic, fantastic images...
Circles and spirals... exploding in coloured fountains... in constant flux."

He remembered it all.

Even during the disintegration, he had stayed conscious.

He had written the loop from inside it.

What he had seen wasn't noise. It was structure, folding and unfolding in a new language.

What stayed with him wasn't just the colour. It was the clarity. The sense that something fundamental had shifted – not in the world, but in how the world could be perceived. This was not an intoxicant. It was not an escape. It was a substance that made perception itself more visible. A lens, not a veil. He began to think of it not as a drug, but as a tool – something sacred. Something that might help us become more than we currently are.

"A voyage into the universe of the soul."

It was, he believed, a substance that could assist in meditation. In insight. In evolving the mind beyond its ordinary filters. A signal amplifier for the human system.

He didn't know where history would take it.

But he knew this: the pattern was real.

And he had seen it.

He didn't walk away. He didn't keep it to himself. He began to speak – in essays, in interviews, in lectures. Not as a prophet, but as a scientist. A witness. Someone who had seen a shift and believed others could too. Not recklessly. Not casually. But deliberately. Responsibly. With reverence.

"It is just a tool… to turn us into what we are supposed to be."

He never argued that everyone should take it. He argued that humanity should not ignore what it opened. Perception was not fixed. The mind could see differently. And if it could see differently, it could change. And if it could change, it could evolve.

He had taken the ride. Now he wanted others to know the road existed.

The substance had shown him something. But the real discovery wasn't chemical. It was cognitive. A loop, hiding in plain sight.

HUNT → SCAN → TAG

That was the rhythm he had followed.

And that is where superadaptability begins.

Not with certainty.

Not with power.

But with the willingness to notice what doesn't quite fit – and the courage to go back in.

He hadn't gone looking for a trip. He had gone looking for what the mind might still be capable of.

And what he found was not escape.

It was a door.

And a question.

What have you seen, that you weren't supposed to?

And what will you do with it now?

Hofmann hunted professionally, scanned for science, and tagged what he felt really mattered.

He said it gave him inner joy, open-mindedness, open eyes, and internal sensitivity for the miracles of creation. He continued as director of Sandoz, and continued studying mushrooms, Mexican mushrooms, and other psychoactives, which led to the synthesis of psilocybin.

He travelled to Mexico to find that the morning glory mushroom they use had an active compound closely related to LSD, and yet again, other people weren't hunting for those patterns, they weren't scanning for the signals, and so they responded with disbelief, but it was confirmed.

Meanwhile, many parts of the world, many legal systems, get this entirely the wrong way around. Instead of hunting for patterns, things that can help, they stay fixed on patterns that don't. They close their doors to what this could be.

They don't scan for the signals to show that people are using such substances to, for instance, help with headaches or pain or migraines. The people with such painful migraines that they call themselves clusterheads, they don't tag that. Instead, they tag something like, it's something we don't understand, so we don't want to understand it, so we better ban it. No human progress came as a result of this kind of behaviour.

So this shows the full detect loop in operation.

You can do the same, you can emulate it, because whether you're born with that innate capacity, your brain is built to grow and to be plastic so you can achieve it deliberately, or when crisis thrusts the need upon you. You'll need it at some point and you'll be glad you've developed it between now and then.

Remember that the detect loop is just one part of the recognise loop, which is part of your run loop – recognising and understanding, and taking necessary action in order to adapt better. So you can go back there and reread, underline some things, or even take a break.

So if you do decide to take that break, or go for a relaxing run or a swim, you can turn over the page to the sit-down section, designed as a change of pace, and explore the life of Harriet Tubman.

You can also learn more about the science and philosophy establishing habits amid a stream of consciousness through an act of belief, and your brain's ability to predict so that you get better at being in the right place at the right time.

And then later you'll be able to become even more practical by learning to live the loop in the next section. What you've just read over these pages weren't just stories. They were strategy. The next sections will show how to make it yours.

HUNT → SCAN → TAG

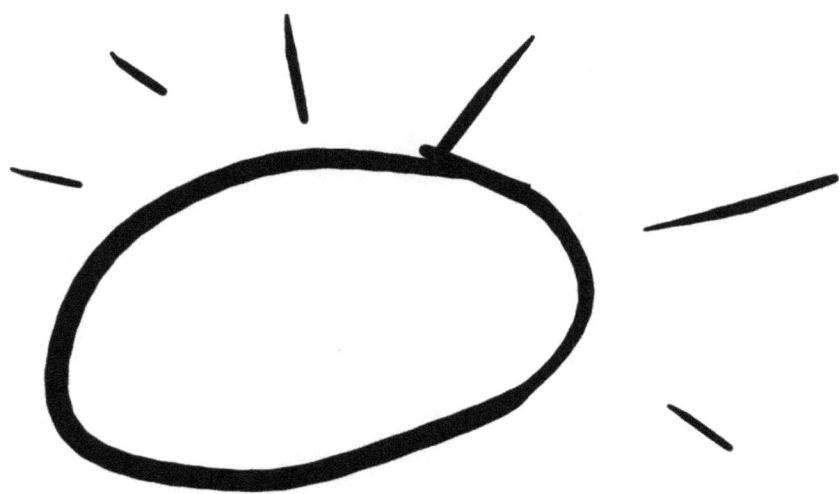

THE LANTERN AND THE UNDERGROUND

WHY WE SIT DOWN NOW
Stillness before the signal

"The pessimist sees only the tunnel;
the optimist sees the light at its end;
the realist sees the tunnel and the light –
and the next tunnel."
– Sydney J. Harris

The beauty of sitting down is that it slows everything down – just enough. Just enough to breathe. Just enough to re-see. In Rule Zero, we explored what it means to overcome overwhelm. This is part of that same loop. Even in the midst of momentum – especially in the midst of it – we need to find pockets of air. Stillness before signal. Breath before pattern. Athletes talk about "time on the ball." The best don't just move faster, they seem to slow time. That's what the Sitdown is. The pause that restores timing, vision, and space.

It's not just a reset. It's a cognitive high ground. A hill you climb to look back down at the path. When you're under pressure – children, jobs, bills, illness, urgency – it's easy to feel like stillness is indulgence. But it isn't. It's infrastructure. Our ancestors knew this. They didn't just seek the sun; they sought shade. Not just escape, but shelter. They needed insight into how the world worked – and insight into themselves. But even more than that, they needed insight into how they acquired insight. And that's what we're doing here.

The underground was never just a place of fear. It was a place of movement, meaning, and connection. Caves gave shelter. Tunnels joined spaces. Viaducts, aqueducts, canals, even roads – these were physical metaphors for mental structures. Hidden modes. Channels for recursive movement. And just like the mind, they didn't always appear lit. You had to bring a torch. You had to feel your way through. Light wasn't automatic. But it was portable.

Meta-perception isn't just how others see you – it's how you guide what you see. Your brain runs modes you don't notice. It filters. It prioritises. It avoids. The third eye is how you begin to see the seeing. It's the moment you shine the torch on the hand holding it. Sitting down lets you detect the frame before it locks. You see your choices – and what's guiding them.

Knowledge, too, is a light source. Fire, torch, language, symbol. And from that, we built gaslight, electricity, LED beams, headlamps. But we also built books, systems, loops. Prometheus gave us fire. We sit to remember how to use it. To see the pattern. The one above. The one below. The one forming right now.

You don't sit to escape the world. You sit to see how it's shaped. To see whether what you're in is helping or harming. To track the water. To read the clouds. To feel the tunnel. Every example you've just read in the detect loop showed a way to see – not just clearly, but usefully. Adaptively. They looked for safety, for clarity, for possibility. They followed old paths with new eyes. They lit what others missed. They moved.

And now it's your turn to sit. Just for a moment. Not to hide – but to sense. To detect. To listen. To look again.

HARRIET TUBMAN: LOOPING FIRE

THE DARKNESS SHE ESCAPED

She couldn't sleep. And she didn't sleep. Not because of fear, but because of listening. Harriet moved through the trees like breath through a throat. Every footstep, every broken branch, every flick of shadow against bark was a signal. The darkness wasn't quiet. It was coded. She didn't have a map. She didn't have shoes. But she had attention. Her body tuned itself to what others ignored: the smell of the river, the way dogs barked at certain angles, which birds kept singing when danger came close...

The night she left, there was no grand announcement. No certainty. No stars that promised anything. But something inside her had shifted – a refusal. She had no map, no lantern, no shoes. But she had perception...

The blow to her head came when she was still a child. A weight hurled at someone else. It struck her instead – and left her with visions, seizures, dreams that came unbidden.

She didn't carry a lantern the first time. There was no flame in her hand, no glowing beacon. But something in her attention had begun to cast light...

She began to notice more. Which dogs barked and which didn't. Which fences had been mended too recently. Which footpaths curved too sharply around open ground...

She crossed. And when she did, she could have stopped. She had reached the other side – north of the line, out of reach...

She looked behind her and saw not the night – but the path.

THE ROUTES SHE REMEMBERED

She didn't return as a ghost. She returned as a map. Not one written down, not one held in hand, but a living pattern held in memory...

She didn't need directions. She carried terrain inside her. A split branch, a flattened grass line, a chimney that never smoked past dusk – all of it was remembered...

She began to read people the way she read terrain. Which knocks meant welcome. Which silences meant warning...

Sometimes the path closed. A house was raided. A signal went dark. Someone lost their courage. When that happened, she didn't freeze...

The routes didn't always hold. Houses once safe were betrayed. Doors that had opened now closed...

Her lantern wasn't a thing she carried. It was a way she moved. Quiet. Attentive. Constantly adjusting...

She had heard it before she ever left. Not in the woods. Not in a dream. In her mother's voice...

THE SIGNAL SHE BECAME

She became something others watched for. She was not myth. She was method. She counted meals. Measured silence. Timed footsteps between fences...

Sometimes people doubted. The stories were too big. The fear was too close. But then she arrived...

She was never safe. There were bounties on her head. People betrayed for money. She changed names...

She was more than a name. More than a route. She became a pattern herself – a system of awareness...

She didn't carry fire in her hands. But she brought back something burning. A perception that caught...

The light she carried wasn't visibility. It was transmission. She didn't hand people torches. She taught them how to notice...

THE NIGHT YOU NAVIGATE

She didn't stop. Not when the war came. Not when her name faded from newspapers...

She found others. John Brown. Soldiers. Activists. But she never stopped walking her own path...

She wasn't waiting for the world to become fair. She knew better. She had been born into a contradiction...

She was still adapting long after history stopped watching. She worked in her garden… She did not ask to be born into that place, that time, that system. But she was. And she did not accept the terms…

You've seen something too. Maybe not as clearly. Maybe not in danger. But you've felt the tension…

That was her way of seeing.

Hunt the pattern. Scan the signal. Tag what matters…

She didn't just write it down. She lived it.

Not just a path through the trees, but a way of reading the dark.

Others followed her. And some never met her at all. But they moved the way she moved.

They noticed.

They listened.

What she lit was not the road.

It was the way to look for one.

LIGHTING UP THE MIND
William James and the origins of selective attention

For most of human history, the mind could only study itself by watching itself.

No labs. No scans. No formal theories. Just reflection. Imagination. Observation.

People looked inward to understand what was happening inside. They looked outward to guess what others were thinking, feeling, intending. They tested their thoughts through language – through stories, tools, and touch.

That's how we became what we call in this book, supersapiens. Not just reactive. But recursive. Able to notice. And then notice that we were noticing.

William James wasn't the first to do this. He was simply one of those we know by name. A bright mind in a long line of minds who turned inward and asked: What is this stream? What is this belief? What is this self?

But what made James different is that he stayed there. He made a method out of watching. He turned attention into a tool. And from that tool, he built something else: A way of seeing the mind seeing itself.

William James came from a family that overflowed. Artists. Writers. Mystics. A father who chased God through philosophy. A brother who reshaped the modern novel.

William tried painting. Then medicine. Then science. He got the qualifications, but not the conviction.

He fell into a depression so deep he wasn't sure he'd come out. "I am melting away into something impalpable," he wrote. "I am taking myself apart." But in that taking apart, something else began.

He started to notice how his mind moved. How one thought pulled another behind it. How his feelings could cloud what he saw. How a belief – if held too tightly, or too soon – could trap him in the wrong loop.

Later, he became the first professor of psychology in America. But he was never just interested in theory. What mattered to him was use. Usefulness.

If a belief helped you, it was worth keeping. If it helped you survive, it was worth holding on to. If it helped you thrive, it was worth developing. If it didn't, it wasn't true enough. It wasn't fit for purpose.

"My first act of free will," James wrote, "shall be to believe in free will."

It wasn't optimism. It was action. A belief tested by living.

THE ACT OF WILL
Overload, filtering, and the first loop decision

Let's pause for a moment. This is a Sitdown, after all.

You and I are here to think – not just about James, but about what he noticed, and how it applies to us. To you.

Because he wasn't just writing about thoughts. He was writing about streams. The stream of consciousness, yes – but also the stream of stimulus. The stream of noise. The stream of culture, obligation, input.

Think about your day. The things coming at you.

The appointment you haven't booked. The parent who's unwell. The door that won't close properly. The message you need to reply to. The child needing care, the friend needing an answer, the dinner needing to be cooked, the news screaming in the background, the email blinking, the thought you forgot, the feeling you can't name, the half-song that's still looping from yesterday morning.

It doesn't stop. And you don't even choose what shows up.

That's the stream James was pointing to – even if he didn't call it that.

You're not just thinking. You're filtering. Your mind is selecting, usually without permission, what gets through.

And when you're overwhelmed, it's like one of those game shows where the objects are flying at you and you're trying to grab the right ones – or dodge the wrong ones – or contort yourself to fit through whatever opening is left.

Sometimes you get pulled back by things you can't even see. That's the part that's hardest to fight: when you don't know what's holding you.

When the hands are hidden, the loop is harder to break.

But this – this moment of sitting down – is about changing that.

James believed that choosing what to notice was the first act of will.

And what he meant was: You can't control what comes at you. But you can choose what you return your attention to.

That's not a soft insight. That's the beginning of recursion.

HABIT AND THE METALOOP
Repetition, identity, and the shape you choose

What James noticed was a tension. A tension you've probably felt too.

On the one hand, habit is the enormous flywheel of society – his phrase, not mine. A system that keeps turning because it's already in motion. A kind of gravity pulling things back toward the familiar. Round and round it goes. We repeat because we repeated. We respond the way we've always responded.

We all know the feeling. The hamster wheel. The loop that doesn't lift.

James believed that most of life – 499 parts in 500, he said – runs this way. We notice what we're trained to notice. We respond how we've been primed to respond.

But he also said something else. Something quieter, but more important. He said you could choose your habits. Not just one. A set. A philosophy of patterned action.

You could build what we've come to call in this book a meta-habit. A metaloop. One chosen way of being that holds all the others inside it. Like the drop of water inside a cave system. Drip, drip, drip. Soft enough to fall. Hard enough to carve stone.

That's how real change happens. Not in a moment. In a pattern.

Take, for example, one man in India. In a small village, Dashrath Manjhi – after his wife died because she couldn't reach medical care – took a hammer and a chisel and carved a path through a mountain. It took him twenty-two years. But he did it. By hand.

You can get a long way with repetition and focus. But only if you choose what to repeat. And that's the turn.

The point of habit isn't to trap you. It's to teach you what's worth reinforcing. You've seen something. You've decided what it means. Now you embed it.

James, by the way, didn't just have these thoughts once. He lived with them. Worked them. Returned to them again and again.

His writing spans volumes – lectures, essays, letters, books. You could get lost in it, and many people have. But if you're looking for the loop that guided his work, the pattern he returned to – this is what I believe it was.

Not a theory. Not a doctrine. A way of thinking. A way of deciding. A way of embedding.

WILL → PRAGMATISM → HABITS

Choose what to attend to.

Choose what to believe.

Choose what to repeat.

It's not what you build. It's what you choose to pay attention to that shapes everything that comes after.

THE FILTER AND THE FOREST
Salience, perception, and what you choose to pass on

Imagine you're in a forest. The light is going. The trees are dense. There's no clear path. A branch breaks to your left. A shape moves to your right. A thought arrives in your head – maybe from fear, maybe from memory. What do you notice?

That's the work of your salience network – the part of your brain that decides what's relevant. Not what's loudest. Not what's most obvious. What matters.

William James didn't have brain scans, but he was circling this idea. He called it will – the effort of attention. Beau Lotto calls it something else: a constructed reality. Perception isn't the world you see. It's the world your brain lets through.

Modern neuroscience confirms what both of them were pointing to. Salience isn't passive. It's trainable. You can sharpen it. You can soften it. You can bring it to heel. That's not philosophy. That's your brain learning how to loop.

One way to think about it is like Tetris™. The blocks keep falling. You don't choose the sequence – but you decide what to rotate, what to place, what to let stack. Some shapes clear the line. Some jam the board. The skill isn't in stopping the stream. It's knowing what to do with what drops in.

And some people play at a different level. There's even a kid who learned how to break the game. He didn't just play Tetris™. He transcended it. That's salience taken to mastery.

But sometimes it's not a game. Sometimes it's the difference between losing and surviving.

Aron Ralston didn't have a flashlight and a trail. He had a boulder, a penknife, and one unmovable fact: no one was coming. So he made a choice. He filtered out everything but the signal that mattered. What will get me out of here? And then he acted.

That's what salience is. Not just what's visible. What's 'vital'. And knowing the difference when it counts.

He wasn't in a forest, and he didn't have a flashlight. But Aron Ralston, an experienced rock climber, did have to deal with a boulder on a trapped arm – and, fortunately, as it turned out, a rope and a penknife. Not one of those expensive Leathermans. One of those cheap ones you pick up at a gas station, tossed in with your other last-minute supplies.

At first, his mind did what minds do: it flailed. A wave of panic. A rush of noise. Shout. Shift. Dig. Wait. Pull. Every option shouted for attention.

Each test returned a result. Each failure, a block to bank. Like Tetris™, he began to play the round – not by force, but by rotation.

What do I still know? What can I now drop? What shape remains? What can I drop into place?

He drank the last of his water. Carved a note into the canyon wall. Filmed a goodbye. Let go of the exits that no longer existed. And then – on the sixth day – he made the final move. He broke his radius and ulna, then cut through the remaining tissue with his knife.

It was not bravery. It was precision. Recursive perception under pressure.

Ralston's story is proof that the third eye can be trained. Not just to see – but to rank. Not just to feel panic, but to discard it when it no longer serves.

That's not instinct. That's a looped, adaptive mind – choosing what matters next.

The piece drops. He moves. The loop reboots.

FINDING YOUR OWN LANTERN

Hopefully you will never wake to find your hand wedged between two boulders, no phone signal, no help coming, and a clock that ends with dehydration or a blade. The point of Aron Ralston's story isn't the dare-devilry; it's the timing. Each minute another variable shifted – heat, thirst, tissue death – so each minute he had to ask, What's the one move now?

That is detection in its purest form: noticing the repeatable loop forming around you and judging whether to break, bank, or ride it before the next block drops. When the world's deadlines and dilemmas start to blur your adaptive discernment, it's useful to know about three loops that are worth spotting early:

THE TRAP LOOP is a pattern that keeps dumping you in the same ditch. (Ralston's first hours: yank, curse, repeat. Your own: the argument that always circles back, the inbox that never shrinks, the irreconcilable difference, the hill worth nothing that you're going to die defending.)

THE SHRINKING TIME LOOP is the task whose window is closing. Study the syllabus with a year to go and it's a stroll; ignore it until eight hay-fevered hours before the exam and the loop tightens like a vice. Do this one early. Or at least not too late.

THE COMPOUNDING LOOP is the pattern that pays interest if you engage it now. One push-up, one language word, one bedtime story: tiny, repeatable moves that widen the tunnel every time you cycle through.

Detecting which loop you're in – or is hurtling towards you – doesn't completely solve the problem, and it doesn't yet tell you how to interpret it; that work is coming next. But seeing the loop is the first lift of the lantern. The salience network can be trained to mark these patterns faster, rank them better, and let the noise slide by while you figure out how to rotate it or yourself to survive the round and level up.

Because a loop isn't just something that happens to you. It's something you can learn to light from the inside. And once you see it, you get to choose what happens the next time the block drops.

ROCK → ROTATE → RESCUE

LIVE THE LOOP

HOW TO LIVE THE LOOP
Third eye. Second thoughts. First moves.

"The only real voyage of discovery consists not in seeking new landscapes but in having new eyes."
– Marcel Proust

Before we got to this stage, we've hunted for patterns and scanned for signals and tagged what matters. We've looked at the full decision loop. We've met Temple Grandin, Claude Shannon, and Pearl Witherington. We've seen Albert Hofmann take a bicycle ride through his own nervous system and Harriet Tubman light a path to freedom. We've thought with William James, looked through the lens of Beau Lotto, and felt the full arc of attention and intention and reinvention.

We've moved through slaughterhouses and resistance networks and invention labs and ideas about freedom, because all of it was about the same thing: how to detect what matters, in time to do something with it. Not in a mystical way – but in a structural way. This is what we've called the third eye. It's what allows you to tag the bit of the pattern that's most relevant, most vital, not in the opinion of someone else – but in your opinion, in your life, in your situation. That's the real voyage. That's the return.

You may have heard the phrase: "what fires together wires together." That's Hebbian theory. It's about neurons. Do something often enough, and your brain doesn't just remember it – it becomes more likely to do it again. That's synaptic plasticity: your brain's ability to change itself based on what you do to it.

But what you might not know is that Hebb wasn't just interested in neurons. He was interested in learning. He was frustrated by the way the education system didn't adapt to the needs of the students in front of him. He believed that if you could shape the environment around someone so it matched their level of engagement and attention, they would learn more – and keep learning.

He also studied people with brain injuries. And what he found was extraordinary. Children's brains recovered better than adults' but not, more recent studies have found, just because of the age. Because they played. Because they explored. Because they were alive to new experiences.

Adults, meanwhile, reduced their inputs. They stayed within familiar loops. They shrank from change. Just like bodies lose strength when not used, so too do brains.

But the exciting part is this: you can reverse some of that shrinkage. Through play, stimulus, fun, engagement, effort. It's like a reverse pruning. Instead of secateurs, you use new experiences. That's how you get new growth.

That's why we've structured this chapter the way we have. That's why we braided together stories and science. To give you not just information, but stimulus. To excite your neurons. To make them fire, so they can rewire. You don't have to do anything drastic. Just meet the ideas with attention. Like a new yoga pose for your mind.

Every time you stretch for something new, the third eye learns. Your salience map gets sharper. Your brain gets better at seeing what matters to you.

So take that with you as you turn the page and revisit the lives you met earlier – Grandin, Shannon, Witherington. On the farm, in the lab, undercover with the resistance.

Notice how they trained their detection – not once, but again and again. That's what made them superadapters.

And then keep going. Into the next series: Life Detectives. Opportunity Detectives. Brain Detectives. These aren't detours. They're activation. They're here to show you that what you've been learning isn't abstract – it's visible. It's repeatable. It's already happening in the world.

Close the book now, think about it. Open the book later, apply it. Talk about it. That's how it works: the book, the loop, your life.

There's only one loop for seeing what matters.

HUNT → SCAN → TAG

And it's yours to run – whenever you're ready.

HOW THEY LIVED THE LOOP
Three pattern detectives changing worlds and saving lives

You've already seen it – three figures, three habits, one arc of action.

But let's bring it into focus.

This wasn't just a collection of stories. Not perfect people. Not perfect moves.

But a pattern you can now see again – with more clarity, and use in your own life. What they have in common is their ability to detect patterns that move them forward.

It started with Grandin. She didn't wait for someone to explain the problem. She watched. Rewatched. Noticed the flicker. Where others shouted at resistance, she slowed the pattern down.

It was never just cattle. It was a system reacting to invisible signals. She didn't push harder. She hunted the repeat.

And when she saw it – she adapted the environment, not the animal.

That's the first move: pattern fluency.

The kind that notices what's off, before it breaks. The kind that doesn't need to be the loudest voice to have the keenest senses.

Shannon didn't wait for the message either.

He listened to the interference. While others focused on what the machines were saying, he studied what got lost along the way.

Every glitch. Every delay. Every misfire.

That's where he found the logic – not in clarity, but in distortion. He didn't decode by force. He scanned for the underlying structure.

Switches in series. Gates in logic.

He could hear what the system 'could' say – if you stripped away the noise.

He didn't just build a device. Or a robot or a toy or a gadget. He revealed a new language by playing with ideas, toys, and gadgets.

And he made it carry anything: code, commands, chaos – even danger.

And then there was Pearl.

Salience in disguise.

No fancy title. No polished frame.

Just one of the most effective detectors ever to walk behind enemy lines. She filtered what others missed. Saw the plan inside the confusion. Held her nerve while others hesitated.

And made others move – not by pressure, but by conviction.

She wasn't loud. She didn't flinch.

And she got over 3,000 people out.

Three different figures.

Three ways of detecting.

All using the same adaptive loop.

They read the situation. They refined what mattered. They acted from the signal – not the noise. They didn't wait for certainty. They didn't freeze in chaos. They didn't let the obvious blind them to the real.

Each one of them was a kind of detective.

Grandin, who seemed cut off from emotion, was, in wondrous fact, an emotions detective – tracking the subtle patterns in tone, gesture, and fear that others overlooked.

Shannon was a signal detective – a playful codebreaker who turned messages into maths and maths into metaphor.

And Pearl Witherington was an undercover salience operative – filtering risk, spotting exits, and tagging what mattered most under conditions of extreme threat.

Each of them developed their ability to detect patterns in two ways: by training that ability to become more effective, and by recognising the value of their kind of detection in thriving in the situations they faced.

What they were running was a loop: hunt, scan, tag.

A recursive hunt for what matters next.

$$\text{HUNT} \rightarrow \text{SCAN} \rightarrow \text{TAG.}$$

And that is what we see in our next three examples.

Three new pattern detectives.

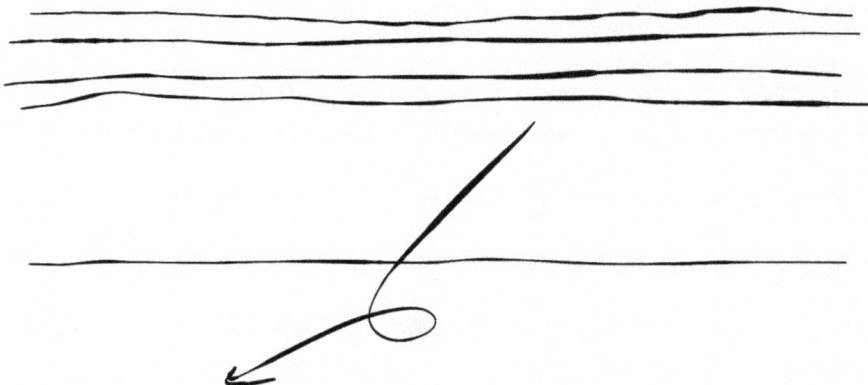

THE WAVE DETECTIVE

I don't know if you remember being ten and being on a beach. But I do.

There's a kind of stillness to it – sunlight coming off the water, sand warm between your toes, the reliable rhythm of the waves, in and out, in and out. Your mind wanders. You don't need to look for anything. It's all already there.

That's what makes it so easy to miss the shift when it happens.

When the world you think you know doesn't do what it normally does.

She saw it.

Not a scream, not a boom – just a change. A strange fizz at the shoreline. The water was bubbling where it met the sand, and it wasn't pulling back the way it usually did. It came in. Then in again. Then again.

And that was enough.

She looked once. Then looked again. Then remembered.

Her name was Tilly Smith. She was ten years old, on holiday in Phuket with her family. They were staying at the JW Marriott, walking along the beach that morning like hundreds of other tourists. Nobody else seemed to notice the pattern. But she had just finished a lesson at school – autumn term, end of the year, earthquakes, tsunamis. They'd watched a video. She'd listened. She'd filed it.

And now it came back.

Tilly told her parents. Her father listened. Her mother didn't – at first. But her dad spoke to a hotel staff member, who told the chef. The chef spoke Japanese. He knew the word.

People moved. The beach emptied.

No one died on that stretch of sand.

It wasn't panic. That's the part that's easiest to misunderstand.

Tilly didn't have a sudden rush of fear. She didn't cry or run. She watched.

And what she saw wasn't dramatic, not in the way we expect danger to be. No earthquake. No towering wall of water. Just the sea behaving… off.

The edge of the tide looked wrong. It fizzed – like a shallow pan of water on a stove, bubbling at the edges. There was no retreat between surges. Just a slow, persistent advance. Each wave came closer than the last. But none of them went back out.

It was the pattern that told her. The mismatch.

Not what was there, but what wasn't.

Sometimes, when the dog doesn't bark, the absence means something.

And she remembered what that something was.

Just two weeks before the holiday, in a Year 6 geography lesson back in England, her teacher had shown a video – an old tsunami, with water rising strangely before the strike. The clip had stayed with her. Not because it was frightening, but because it was structured. It had a logic she could feel, even at ten.

Now here it was again.

And she recognised it.

What Tilly detected wasn't the wave itself – it was the early warning system, the silent code inside the sea. Something her brain had already filed as important, tucked away until it was needed. A piece of attention trained just in time.

What she did looked like instinct.

But it wasn't.

She didn't act because of a gut feeling or a sixth sense. She acted because her brain had been primed – just enough, just in time. Her geography teacher, Andrew Kearney, had shown the class a tsunami video at the end of term. It had explained how water sometimes rises instead of pulling back. How waves don't always behave the way you think. She watched it. She learned it. She stored it.

And when the sea looked strange – when the ocean patterns matched the pattern she'd been shown – her brain did the rest.

That's salience.

That's detection with meaning.

Her salience network, the part of the brain that tags what matters, had been sensitised. Not forever. Not dramatically. Just enough to say: look again. And that was all it took.

This is what matters: the loop she ran wasn't hers.

It had come from a teacher, who had learned it from others, who had learned it from field teams and scientific institutions and eyewitness accounts.

It was a social loop, passed hand to hand, until one child saw it at the right moment.

She didn't invent it.
She detected it.
She ran it.
She passed it on.
This is what detection really looks like.

It doesn't always feel heroic. It doesn't feel like genius. It feels like something's off. Like a pattern you've seen before has just shown up again, out of place.

Tilly didn't save lives because she knew more than anyone else. She saved lives because someone had shown her a loop – what to notice, when to notice it – and she remembered it.

She ran the loop.
That's what matters.

This is Rule 1, lived cleanly.
She recognised the signal.
She understood what it meant.
She took necessary action.
And it didn't stop with her.

Because real detection isn't just noticing – it's passing it on.

A geography teacher shows a classroom a video. One child sees it again on a beach. She warns her father. The chef hears the word in Japanese. A call reaches another Marriott hotel. The loop moves. The loop works.

This is what superadaptability looks like in its earliest, simplest form.

Tag the pattern. Run the loop. Save the system.

And if a ten-year-old can do it, so can you.

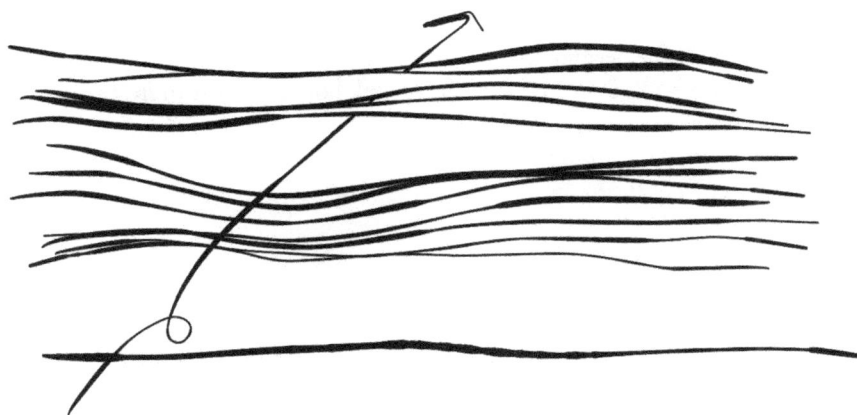

THE OPPORTUNITY DETECTIVES

IT WAS 1942.
Nancy Stratford was 23 when she joined the British Air Transport Auxiliary. She left behind a fiancé who told her not to go. The motto was simple: Anything to Anywhere.

She flew 50 types of aircraft, often without instruments, sometimes without radios. Pilots learned by 'conversion' – no instruction manual, just adaptive loops. The skies were chaos: fog like a bowl of milk, wind like the Devil waving you through.

But Nancy didn't flinch. She kept flying. Map in hand, feet to the floor, navigating by feel, memory, and nerve. She said flying gave her freedom – clean air, clear intent. And she kept going. Later, she became the first woman to fly helicopters commercially in Alaska. She didn't just fly. She rewrote the coordinates.

ANYTHING → TO → ANYWHERE

IT WAS 1919.
Bessie Coleman looked up – and saw something that wasn't there yet.

Not because she was welcome in it. She wasn't. Not because there was a map. There wasn't. Not because the world encouraged it. It didn't. But she saw it anyway.

Too Black. Too female. Too poor. She taught herself French and crossed the Atlantic. In 1921, she became the first African American – and Native American – woman to earn a pilot's license. She came back home not just to fly, but to perform, to protest segregation, to lift others up.

Queen Bess looped through the air, but her superadaptability came from the moment she saw her future in the sky – and refused to unsee it.

ANYONE → ANYTIME → ANYWHERE

IT WAS 2010.

Niloofar Rahmani was 18 when she entered Afghanistan's military flight academy. She trained in secret, under threat of death, with no support but her own resolve. In 2013, she became the first female fixed-wing air force pilot in Afghan history.

She flew medical evacuations, supply drops, missions the Taliban said she had no right to fly. When her name was leaked, she kept flying. When she was told to stop, she flew anyway. And when she saw the door close – she flew again. Escaping, rebuilding, adapting once more.

ANYWHERE → OPPORTUNITIES → EVERYWHERE

Bessie, Niloufar, and Nancy flew toward the point of light in a pattern of darkness. Toward opportunity in a pattern of obstacles. Toward possibility in a pattern of prejudice.

They weren't just flying aircraft. They were flying logic. Flying lives. From anything – through intent – to anywhere.

And still, the pattern holds. Across decades, across contexts. The loop is rarely obvious. Often obscured by weather, by prejudice, by low visibility and sabotage. But for those who know how to read the pattern – there is often a line of flight.

They weren't the only ones. Others have flown. Others will. Sometimes the hardest thing is to detect the exit. The next move. Or the moment to stay.

As Vidura Rajapaksa, the Sri Lankan comedian once said:

"Sometimes you've got to stay, stay. And sometimes you've got to leave, leave."

ANYWHERE → OPPORTUNITIES → EVERYWHERE

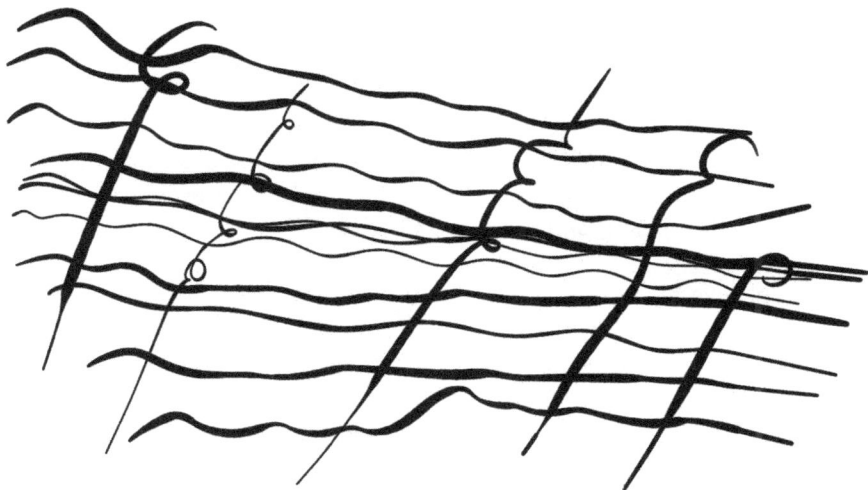

THE BRAIN DETECTIVES

"The ability to think recursively is what distinguishes the human mind from the minds of other animals."
– Michael Corballis

Michael Corballis didn't invent recursion, but he did more than almost anyone to explain why it matters. He claimed the idea first clicked on a long bus ride through the sheep fields outside Auckland – watching the landscape loop past as his thoughts did the same. Colleagues recall his near-constant tramp across campus with a spiral notebook in hand, sketching language trees that looked like railway junctions. In talks, his standard slide was a photo of two chimps grooming under the caption 'Staff Meeting'. He believed gesture was the root of language, and that humans differ not by having language, but by having minds that can fold in on themselves – thoughts within thoughts within thoughts.

Theory of mind – the ability to represent other people's thoughts – including what they think about your thoughts. It's how you can wonder what your friend thinks about what you think about what your mother said about what your son did – and loop it back again.

Mental time travel – the ability to revisit the past, imagine futures, and rehearse what might happen. It's how we reflect, redirect, or simulate what to say before we say it.

Recursive learning – the ability to learn from previous loops, adjust, and build on what came before. This is how you adapt, not just by reacting – but by remembering, comparing, and trying again differently.

Corballis planted the recursive seed. Others grew it. Thomas Suddendorf showed how our minds loop through time – revisiting the past, rehearsing futures, and imagining outcomes before they happen. Kalina Christoff explored what happens when the mind wanders: how seemingly aimless thought drifts toward goals you haven't voiced yet. Lucina Uddin revealed how we shift between these states – how the brain tags what matters and switches between internal focus, social meaning, and outward attention. Each one shows us a different loop. Taken together, they map what a flexible mind can do.

So use it. If you can time travel – do it consciously. Move backward to see how you got here. Move forward to test where you might go. If your mind wanders, follow it – like Einstein following a beam of light through space until it became a theory. And if your focus is stuck, switch it. You can tag the moments that matter, notice the loops that work, and bring back what's useful – from memory, from imagination, from daydream. You're already a brain detective. The difference is, now you can detect your own loops on purpose.

We predominantly stand in the present facing the future, rather than looking back to the past.

But we can't look to the future without assembling it from what we know of the past. That's how we simulate. That's how we plan. That's how we adapt. Recursive minds don't just store – they reorganise, reweight, and reframe. That's what these brain detectives have shown us. That's what you can learn to do.

Neuroscientists now talk about the brain as having its own connectome – the vast map of its internal wiring. They're working to chart every synapse, every thread of connection, all the way through the human brain. But now they're also turning their attention to something else: the effectome. Not just what connects, but what changes. How cause and effect are stored in your brain, modified, and re-run – so that you can respond differently, and shape the world you live in. That's the next frontier. And as brain detectives carry on detecting, you can use what they've learned to become your own: an even better superadapter.

Corballis believed that recursion explains three of the most powerful things the human mind can do – each one a loop we run, and improve.

FROM TRAPPED TO TRANSCENDED

Sometimes you don't feel trapped because of the world. You feel trapped because of what you can't yet see.

You miss the pattern, so you miss the warning – or the way out. You miss the signal, so the opportunity slips past – or the threat arrives too late. You get flooded with noise, and can't tell what matters until the moment's already gone.

That's what the Trapped state looks like. And that's what these three habits are designed to shift.

First, you learn to 'hunt for patterns' – not just obvious ones, but the rhythms that run beneath your routines. Instead of walking blind, you begin to see how things repeat – and how those repetitions shape what's possible.

Then, you learn to 'scan for signals' – not just data, but leverage. You stop assuming the world will tell you what matters. You start sweeping for friction, for contrast, for tension – and treating those as messages worth decoding.

Finally, you 'tag what matters' – you stop hoping memory will save you, and start naming the moments worth remembering. You build internal markers, so you can loop back faster next time – and act before the window closes.

This is the Power of Three. Three moves, done with attention, that retrain your brain to see before it's too late.

And when you run that loop – again and again – something shifts. You stop being someone who gets trapped by surprise. You start being someone who sees the shift early – who moves when others freeze, who reads the moment when others wait for the summary.

That's the beginning of superadaptability. And that's what this Rule teaches: Not just how to survive your current loop – but how to detect what matters most to prepare for the one that comes next.

MOVE/ HABIT	WHEN YOU'RE TRAPPED...	WHEN YOU TRANSCEND...
Hunt for Patterns	You miss the clues. You overlook the patterns that could show you where the opportunity lies – or where the danger is hiding. You don't see the doorway, the warning sign, or the way out. You stay stuck because the world feels random – when it isn't.	You notice the clues others ignore. You recognise patterns early – repeats, deviations, rhythms – and use them to find entry points, exits, or leverage. You don't wait to be told. You map what matters and move before the trap locks in.
Scan for Signals	You're flooded with noise but miss the signals that matter. You feel busy, reactive, distracted – but still blindsided. You stay oblivious to the cues that could've warned you, helped you, or lifted you out. So you delay, overreact, or move on false information.	You scan deeper than others. You filter noise fast and pick up signals others miss – because you're observant, not oblivious. You read tension early, spot leverage points, and prepare before the wave hits. This isn't luck. It's trained perception.
Tag What Matters	Everything comes at you – but nothing stands out. You can't tell what matters most, so every signal competes, and none of them stick. You're flooded with next steps, but can't take the right one – because you haven't marked what's worth remembering. It all blurs. So you freeze, fumble, or forget.	You don't try to track everything. You tag what matters. You mark the moments, cues, and decisions that count – so you can loop back at speed. You move through noise with memory, not guesswork. What you label, you remember. What you remember, you can use.

You've seen how detection works – how it acts as a kind of third eye. How it helps us hunt, scan, and tag the signals that matter. Sometimes it reveals the invisible trap. Sometimes, the hidden escape path.

You've examined your own patterns. You've met wave detectors, opportunity seekers, brain-based hunters of meaning. You've seen how salience can sharpen, how patterning prepares the ground for action.

But like any loop, detection can misfire. We tag the wrong signal. We scan for threats that aren't there. We hunt in the wrong direction – or stop hunting altogether.

And when that happens, it's easy to fall into misinterpretation. To spend years decoding the wrong bit of the problem. To dedicate vast amounts of energy to a pattern that was never truly there – or one that can't help you overcome the limits you face today.

That's what we're going to look at next.

A clear diagnostic. A loop-level map of what goes wrong when detection breaks.

So that instead of drowning in complexity, you can simply say: ah – one of those three.

And then? We'll show how to put it right.

THE WRONG LOOPS
Three ways the detect loop fails

HYPO happens when detection fires too little, too late, or too slow. You spot the pattern – but the moment has passed. You notice the danger – but after it could have been avoided. You detect the opportunity – but just beyond the point of action. It's not that you're wrong. You're just behind the loop.

You realise too late that your behaviour has been causing damage – and the relationship is already breaking. You know the market is shifting, but assume you'll have time to course-correct. You log the task, but don't calculate what it really needs – time, help, clarity. The signal wasn't hidden. You just didn't prioritise it until the cost was already unfolding.

Ask yourself whether you know what you're looking for – and what this pattern really means. Are you clear on what's urgent and what isn't? Do you understand the time, the cost, or the impact of what you're paying attention to?

HYPER happens when detection fires too fast, too much, or too strongly. You think you know what you saw – but you didn't pause. You jump from signal to certainty, from noticing to action. The loop accelerates. Bias takes over. You double down, lock in, and commit too soon – giving the rest of the process no chance to adapt.

You get a blunt message from someone you care about. A voicemail, a text. You spiral – so fast you miss the signal that they're not angry, they're depressed. You're mid-argument. They say, "That's not what I meant." But you're already committed to being right. Or a sharp message lands from your boss. And now everything feels like signal. Every ping, every word – over-interpreted, misread, amplified.

Have you just jumped to a conclusion – when you were meant to be detecting? Did you read something as louder or more urgent than it was, just because you were rushed, distracted, or eager to resolve it? Have you noticed something real, but missed the chance to pause and look again – to see it another way, to let your third eye come into focus?

ANTI happens when you detect the wrong thing – or apply the wrong meaning to what you saw. You lock onto the false pattern. You miss the real threat. You pass the wrong message forward. The loop doesn't just fail – it misguides. It takes everything else with it unless you stop, check, and give yourself a chance to re-see.

You sub off a player for being lazy – only to realise he was covering for everyone else. Your team loses. You see a leak in the laundry room, so you fix the tap. But it leaks again. And again. Because the pipe is cracked two rooms over. You're detecting – but you're not detecting the cause. You're building your response around the wrong pattern.

Always ask yourself: did I really see what I thought I saw? Could it be the other way around? Is there another story here – something I've missed? Am I looking at the whole picture, or just the part I expected to find? And if I'm wrong… am I wrong in a way that matters?

These loops won't run perfectly every time. They can't. But the good news is: they tend to go wrong in familiar ways. You don't need a hundred biases or a thousand checklists. Just start noticing when your detection is too slow, too fast, or pointed in the wrong direction. That pattern will return throughout the book – each time applied to a different part of the loop. The point isn't perfection. It's positioning. When detection fails, what matters is how quickly you can re-see, reframe, and return to the loop in a better way. Because if detection improves, everything downstream has a better chance to succeed. In the next section, we'll look at how these same failure patterns show up in the real world. Learn from those too.

REAL-WORLD WRONG LOOPS
Three famous failures in detection

"There is nothing more deceptive than an obvious fact."
– Arthur Conan Doyle

The worst detective isn't the one who misses the clue. It's the one who finds it
– fast, certain, precise – and builds a brilliant theory on the wrong thing. That's
how most real-world failures begin. Not with ignorance, but with false pattern-
lock. You chase the wrong signal. You explain the wrong motive. You solve the
mystery – just not the right one. And because your detection loop feels complete,
you don't even notice the loop is broken. These real-world failures show what
happens when detection goes wrong. Don't just observe them. Use them. Look
again. Ask again. This is training.

HYPO In 1845, British explorer Sir John Franklin led two ships into the
Canadian Arctic in search of the Northwest Passage. They packed cut-glass
decanters, silver flatware, a library of 1,200 books. They did not pack enough
cold-weather gear. The signs were there. Shifting ice. Weak sun. Inuit warnings.
But they didn't adjust. The expedition stalled. Froze. Starved. Every man died.
They weren't reckless. They were slow. They waited too long to detect that the
system had changed. And the Arctic doesn't wait.

HYPER In the 1980s, America declared a war. Not against a country. Against
a sensation: drugs. It wasn't that the problem didn't exist. It's that the detection
loop locked on the wrong signature. Every baggie became a threat. Every user,
a criminal. Every pain, a pathology. The loop didn't refine the signal. It flooded
the zone. Budgets exploded. Prisons filled. Communities collapsed. And still,
the system kept scanning – more tests, more raids, more noise. What started
as vigilance became obsession. The data was there. But the detection engine
couldn't stop itself. It wasn't wrong for seeing too much. It failed for trying to act
on everything.

ANTI For years, FIFA claimed to uphold the spirit of football – global
cooperation, merit-based competition, fair play. Behind the scenes, it was
scripting the opposite. Bribes. Vote rigging. Fraudulent bids. But what made it
dangerous wasn't just the corruption. It was the loop protecting it. FIFA didn't
fail to detect wrongdoing. It built systems to spot journalists. To silence dissent.
To suppress signal – on purpose. The detection infrastructure didn't collapse.

It inverted. And once it did, no whistle could reach the surface. That's anti-detection. Not the absence of a loop. A loop reprogrammed – to collapse the moment truth gets close.

If you follow the wrong clues, you'll dig in the wrong places.

THE COUNTER LOOPS

The good news here is that the very loop that caused the failure can also fix it. When your detection runs too slow, too fast, or locks onto the wrong thing, the solution isn't external – it's in the same loop, running better. Each of these failures – missing the clue, chasing the wrong threat, mistaking noise for signal – can be prevented or repaired with the same habits that caused them in the first place. What went wrong was detection. What helps you re-enter is detection – done differently. That's what the next three habits are for. They don't just stop damage. They help the loop recalibrate, speed up, slow down, or shift direction. They give you a way back in.

HUNT FOR PATTERNS is the habit that counters hypo-loops – when detection runs too slow, too little, or too late. By building pattern fluency – scanning everyday life for structure and rhythm – you prepare your mind to catch the signal before it slips by. Not because you've seen this exact situation before, but because you've trained yourself to look for the underlying form. That's what pattern hunters get better at: recognising structural resemblances. It's why people improve at IQ tests, or Sudoku, or picking up on the way different customers speak. Every pattern you notice gives your brain another trace to match – or mismatch – next time. And if things have already gone wrong, this habit gives you a way back in. You pause. You ask: What does this remind me of? And now the signal has somewhere to land.

SCAN FOR SIGNALS is the habit that counters hyper-detection – when you notice too much, too fast, or too forcefully. It's what keeps you from jumping to conclusions, or mistaking emotional urgency for actual relevance. You're not here to react. You're here to detect – helpfully. This habit teaches you to sweep your environment with calibration, not panic. To prioritise discernment over reflex. It slows escalation. It notices the build-up. And when things are already moving too fast, it gives you the chance to ask: Wait, what else is here? You might still see the same thing. But now you're not locked in. Your aperture widens. You catch the left-field signal. You notice the warning light you almost ignored. Scan helps you put time, space, and proportion back into your loop – before it burns the map.

TAG WHAT MATTERS is the habit that helps you counter anti-detection – when you've spotted the wrong thing, mislabelled it, or locked in too soon. Tagging is mental labelling. A quick internal note. A post-it on what you think you've seen. You're not making a final decision. You're marking signal for review. This habit gives you language – not to prove yourself right, but to give yourself something to check later. It helps prevent loop failure by creating trace marks – something you can return to and re-evaluate. And if the detection loop has already veered off-course, Tag gives you a way to name the misstep. You said this was an entrance. But it was an exit. You ask: Have I tagged this too fast? Is there a better name for what I'm seeing? That question reopens the loop. And lets you detect again – this time, with clarity.

Each of these habits helps the loop correct itself. HUNT helps you recognise patterns early – so you can start faster, and see sooner. SCAN filters urgency and adds discernment – so your detection doesn't jump the gun. TAG delays premature certainty and keeps your attention anchored to what matters most. Together, these habits help you stop before you escalate, pause before you mislabel, and orient before you pass a faulty signal through to the rest of your loop. They won't catch everything. But they'll stop you from doing too much good work on the wrong thing.

RECOGNISE → UNDERSTAND → NECESSARY ACTION

The habits you've just seen don't just prevent failure. They help people re-enter the loop after it breaks. That's what comes next. We're returning now to the three figures you met at the start of this chapter – Temple Grandin, Claude Shannon, and David Witherington. But this time, we're watching how they faced new conditions. New noise. New unknowns. And each of them rebooted their loop. They didn't just detect well once. They adapted again. And again. That's what superadaptability really means.

REBOOTING THEIR LOOP
How three people found their way back through change

We've already met these three. But your first meeting with them isn't where their stories ended. Each of them faced something new.
A shift. A break.
A pattern they hadn't yet seen.
They didn't collapse. They didn't return to the start. They looped forward.

That's what superadapters do. They don't just detect well once.

They adapt again – and again. Not through willpower. Through remembering. Through questioning. Through noticing what changed and what didn't.

That's the loop.

And when we watch others go through it – especially in the form of story – we learn something else: Not just what to do, but how to become someone who can do it.

RECOGNISE → UNDERSTAND → NECESSARY ACTION

TEMPLE GRANDIN – REBOOT HER LOOP
Time/Place: 1970s–1980s, Colorado State University and clinical settings

The Pressure
It wasn't one dramatic failure. It was a wall she kept running into.

She could see the system – the cattle, the sensors, the gates. But she couldn't feel the people. Couldn't accept being touched. Couldn't relate. Couldn't relax. Her brain was a maze of brilliance and friction.

She could detect everything – except comfort.

And that was the missing loop.

The Reboot
So she built a machine.

Foam-lined. Self-controlled. Deep pressure.

She stepped inside and let herself be squeezed. Not once, but over and over. She trained her own nervous system – so she could feel calm. So she could feel safe. So she could connect. First to a cat. Then to cattle. Then to people.

She learned how to be comforted – so she could give comfort.

She learned how to touch – so she could be touched back.

Her empathy didn't arrive as insight. It arrived as pressure.

The same way she mapped animal stress, she mapped her own.

The Return
And from there, everything shifted.

Her loop didn't just help animals. It helped clinics, classrooms, families.

The squeeze machine wasn't the end. It was the middle – the reboot that let the rest of her work take hold.

She didn't abandon her system.
She deepened it.
She looped inward – to extend her reach outward.

CLAUDE SHANNON – REBOOT HIS LOOP
Time/Place: 1952–1975, Bell Labs and MIT → Quiet retreat in New Jersey

The Pressure
He was already a legend. By his forties, Claude Shannon – the father of
information theory – had redefined how the world understood communication,
uncertainty, and logic itself.
But the signal he created was being overwhelmed by its own success.
At Bell Labs and later at MIT, he watched the world flood with systems that used
his ideas without understanding them.
Signal. Noise. Entropy. Feedback.
What he built to clarify was being co-opted to sell, spin, manipulate.
He recognised the trap: being surrounded by brilliance, but drifting from
curiosity. Being honoured as a genius, but cut off from play.
He didn't feel famous. He felt squeezed.

The Reboot
So he built the opposite of a squeeze machine.
Not pressure. Play.
Not performance. Puzzles.
He turned inward – back to his own mind. Juggling. Unicycles. Homemade
gadgets. Silent thinking. He built mechanical mice that could solve mazes, and
then sat for hours watching them fail and reroute.

He didn't publish much. He didn't need to.
The ideas were still coming – but only the ones he wanted to chase.
He once said that motivation was the missing variable in creativity:
"You can have all the intelligence and training in the world. But if you're not
curious – if you're not constructively dissatisfied – you won't see what needs to be
seen."

His lab became a refuge. His silence, a system. The unsqueeze machine.

The Return

He never stopped thinking. He just stopped broadcasting.
Still teaching. Still inventing. But no longer racing.
He had built a theory to explain how anything could be transmitted.
Then he stepped away – to protect what should be transmitted.

He didn't need applause.
He needed fidelity.
He didn't walk away from the loop.
He re-entered it from the quiet.

PEARL WITHERINGTON – REBOOT HER LOOP
Time/Place: 1945–2006, post-war London → World Bank → Paris

The Pressure

She'd already done what few ever could.
Fifteen hundred resistance fighters. Sabotage missions ahead of D-Day. A whole region of France held together by radio wires, escape lines, and guts.
But when the war ended, the silence hit harder than any gunfire.
Her government offered her a typist's medal.
She refused.
"There was nothing civil in anything I did."
They gave her a peacetime role. She worked. She married Henri. But not for comfort. Not for escape.
"I didn't risk my life to marry Henri. There was a job to be done."
And when they denied her the parachute wings she had earned – she didn't shrug.
"I bitched and moaned… for 63 years."
She got them. At 92.

The Reboot

This wasn't a return to domesticity.
It was a return to self.
Pearl Witherington had lived in systems her whole life:
A father who drank away the family fortune. A mother who couldn't hear.
She negotiated debts as a child. Walked miles to scavenge food. Studied at night.
She became the family's signal-reader before she was old enough to vote.
The war didn't create her. It revealed her.
And after it, she didn't retire. She kept working – at the World Bank. Quietly.

Competently. Deliberately.

She looped back not to be seen, but to keep seeing.

The Return

When recognition finally came, she accepted it – not because it validated her, but because it completed the record.

Her loop wasn't about headlines. It was about continuity.

She didn't romanticise the mission. She preserved it.

She didn't seek to be remembered as exceptional.

She made sure the system couldn't forget what women like her had done.

She didn't fade. She clarified.

RECOGNISE → UNDERSTAND → NECESSARY ACTION

Haruki Murakami once wrote that when you come out of the storm, you won't remember how you made it through. But one thing is certain, he said – you won't be the same person who walked in. That's almost true. The difference – the invaluable difference – is that the people on this page did remember. Not everything. Not all at once. But enough. They learned from their storms. And that's what allowed them to adapt again, and again, in new conditions. Not just by surviving, but by noticing. By watching the loop run. And learning what the storm was really about.

REBOOT YOUR LOOP
When you can't find the way, find the torch.

You don't think much about the flashlight on your phone. Or torch, depending on where you're reading this. But it's there – always. A tap away.

So many people use it in moments of need that phone manufacturers keep upgrading it. Brighter LEDs. Easier access. Voice activation. Some even respond to a clap.

Why? Because when you're in the dark, nothing else matters.

Some lights you carry in your pocket. Some strap around your head. Some hang from your belt. Some – the ones on your phone – you forget you have… until you need them.

You're not thinking about symbolism when you switch it on. You're trying to find your keys. Avoid broken glass. See where the hallway ends. Or signal for help.

It's one of the most used and underrated survival tools in the world.

And the loop in this book – the one you've already met – is just like that light.

RECOGNISE when you're in the dark. When you've stopped seeing clearly but kept moving anyway.

UNDERSTAND the shape of where you are – what's familiar, what's shifted, what you're bumping into.

Then take the NECESSARY ACTION. Turn on the light. Find your footing. Move forward – not faster, just better lit.

Somewhere, someone was found because of a phone torch. A lost hiker flashing light through trees. A child under rubble holding down the button. A driver signalling SOS through a cracked windshield.

It's not dramatic when you carry it. It's just a keyring light, a belt torch, the one on your phone. Until it isn't. Until it's everything.

You don't need to start over. You just need to see what's around you. Your loop is already in your hand. Use it.

TRANSCEND THE LOOP

THE THIRD EYE

"What is now proved was once only imagined."
— William Blake

Yeats once wrote of "men who loved the future like a mistress", and who were hidden from their time because of what they could already see. William Blake was one of them. But he didn't work alone. His wife, Catherine, mixed the inks. Coloured the pages. Helped pull the future out of the press, one etched page at a time.

That matters. Because the future isn't always a vision. Sometimes, it's a loop. A collaboration. A hand steadying the frame while the other draws it.

The future isn't delivered complete. It's detected in fragments – glimpsed sideways. Pulled forward through imagination, interpretation, and systems that don't yet exist.

And detection isn't neutral. What we see, what we notice, what we filter, what we attend to – it's never a mirror of the world. It's a shaping. A choice. There is always a pre-perception: what you are primed to see. And a post-perception: what you allow yourself to carry forward.

We can narrow or widen our gaze. Shade our eyes or lean in. We can use a microscope, a telescope, radar or LiDAR. We can focus on a postage-stamp-sized window – or open the frame. And every one of those choices shapes what we call reality.

Temple Grandin saw stress in livestock no one else detected. Claude Shannon found signals buried in noise. Harriet Tubman mapped escape routes from memory and night sky. Pearl Witherington disappeared into an alias and saw when to resurface. These were not reflexes. These were loops. Their Third Eye wasn't mystical – it was trained. Returned. Re-entered.

The Third Eye is not a gift. It's a system. It's what happens when you don't stop noticing.

But what if what you detect isn't even visible yet? What if the system you need hasn't been built?

Then you imagine it. And then, you build.

As Blake put it:

"I must create a system, or be enslaved by another man's."

The next figure didn't invent a machine. She detected the future embedded in it. She saw the loop before it ran. And she gave the unseen its architecture.

Her name was Ada Lovelace.

THE THIRD EYE OF ADA LOVELACE

"That which is unseen and unsuspected is not therefore unseeable and unsuspectable."
– Ada Lovelace

Ada Lovelace was born into paradox. She was the daughter of Lord Byron – the most famously volatile poet in Europe – but she never knew him. He left a month after her birth and died when she was eight. Her mother, determined not to pass on poetic instability, insisted Ada be raised on mathematics and rational thought.

And yet both forces shaped her.

She lived between structures. Between science and imagination. Between convention and contradiction. Her life was a kind of third space – privileged but restricted, brilliant but isolated, linear on the surface but recursive underneath.

She once called herself "a poetical scientist". It wasn't decoration. It was method. A way of holding imagination and logic in tension – until the unseen revealed itself.

She didn't just grow up in that tension. She learned to see from it.

I don't know what you would do when faced with hours of obligatory mathematics – or with being famous for having an infamous father who left for France before you could remember him – but Ada Lovelace treated both as structure to work with.

She was born in 1815, in a century where girls of her class were expected to marry, manage, and stay mostly silent. Her mother – a sharp, controlled woman determined to purge any trace of Byron's volatility – enforced a strict education in logic and calculation. Ada could have resisted. She could have disengaged. Instead, she found something in it. She looked at equations the way other people looked at landscapes. She wasn't solving for x. She was solving for structure.

She was able to accommodate both – the absent poet and the present curriculum – in the way she saw them. Each became a form of information. A signal. A possible route. This is what superadapters do. They detect constraint and sense possibility – at the same time.

One of her tutors, Augustus De Morgan, later wrote to her mother: "The very great tension of mind which they require is beyond the strength of a woman's physical power of application." But Ada didn't just match that tension. She turned it into insight.

This wasn't the romantic fantasy of a forgotten genius. This was a girl, often ill, often isolated, often underestimated – learning how to pay attention. That's how the loop begins.

And somehow, that loop still runs. Every year, the second Tuesday of October is marked as Ada Lovelace Day – an international celebration of women in science, technology, engineering, and mathematics.

She didn't wait to be asked. When Ada encountered the Analytical Engine, she didn't just observe it – she entered it. Interpreted it. Translated what it could be, not just what it was.

The Analytical Engine was, essentially, a Victorian idea for a computer – on paper – more than a hundred years before anyone actually built one.

It was Charles Babbage who designed it, and the Italian engineer Menabrea who described it in French. But it was Ada who translated the paper – and then, in the margins, added her own annotations. Her famous *Note G* introduced the idea of symbolic operations, machine looping, and complex algorithmic sequences. She didn't just describe the machine. She interpreted its future.

This wasn't invention – it was recursive insight. She saw what others missed because she refused to collapse how she perceived. She looked further, inside and beyond. And what she left behind became part of the loop.

Ada Lovelace wrote her famous *Note G* in 1843. It described a machine that did not yet exist – an Analytical Engine that could process not just numbers, but symbols. It was, in essence, a design for a computer on paper. More than a hundred years would pass before anything like it was built. That's how far ahead she was. That's what she could see.

Her notes were revived in 1953, reprinted in *Faster Than Thought* at the dawn of the digital age. And by then, thinkers like Alan Turing were already in conversation with her work. He named her directly. He even constructed a counterargument to her most famous caution:

"The Analytical Engine has no pretensions whatever to originate anything. It can do whatever we know how to order it to perform."

That line still haunts us.

Because Ada wasn't limiting imagination – she was protecting it. She understood how machines run instructions. But she also knew that humans – unlike machines – originate. They create. They see below, and above, and in between. They sense what isn't visible, and name what doesn't yet exist.

This is why it's so valuable to hold contradictory perceptions open.

This is what happens when you don't collapse the loop too early.

This is what happens when the Third Eye doesn't blink.

THE SIGNAL MUST BE READ
Detection is the beginning

You've seen what others might have missed. You've learned how perception is filtered, how attention loops – how the right signal, spotted early, can change everything.
But seeing isn't enough.
The loop doesn't end with recognition. It turns inward. It asks more of you.

To be a superadapter isn't just to notice the signal –
it's to decide what it means.
It's to turn perception into meaning, meaning into direction.

Now you must interpret.

Not because the signal demands it –
but because your next move depends on it.

DETECT → **INTERPRET** → DECIDE

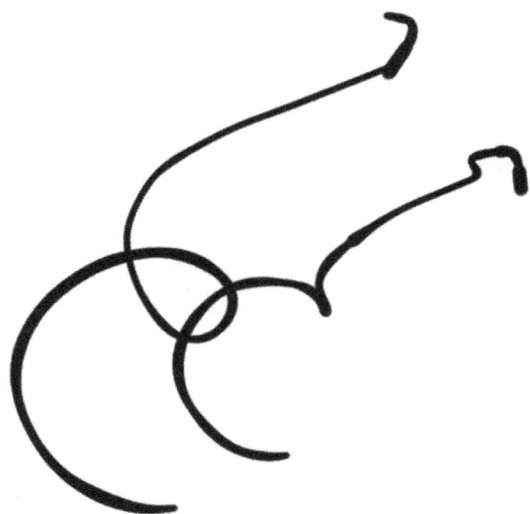

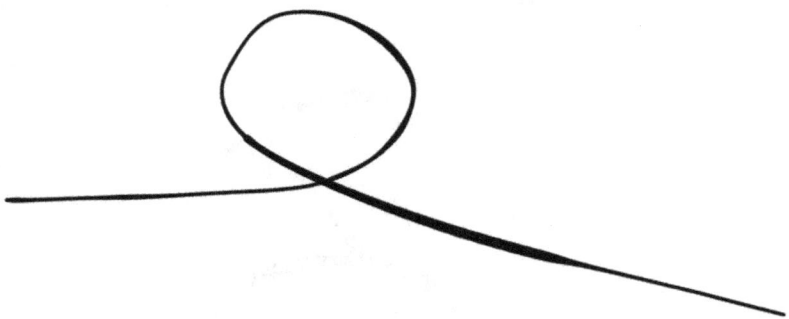

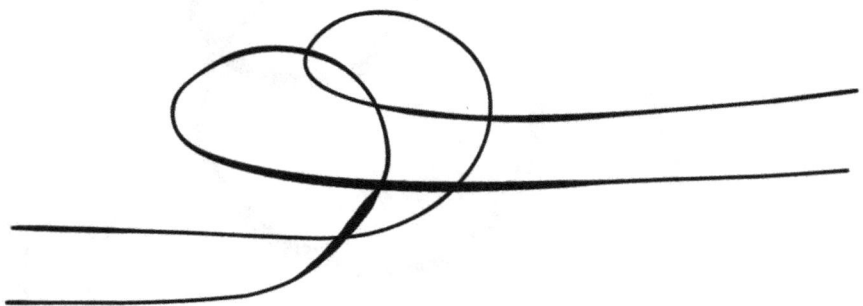

RULE 2:
YOU COULD BE WRONG

The one about interpreting reality – so you can transcend it.

Superadapters resist rigid certainty – not to stay open, but to stay adaptive. Interpretations can be right or wrong – but more importantly, they can be useful or limiting. The most powerful interpretations don't just explain or fit the facts. They create space – space to shift, move, and adapt. This Rule is about interpretation. Not as a theory, but as a habit. A superadaptive skill.

Everyone interprets. But superadapters interpret better. They don't just accept the first explanation. They don't lock onto the nearest narrative. They calibrate. They re-check. They reframe. And when the loop drifts, they get it turning again.

This Rule teaches you how.

It's the second part of the Recognise phase – the part where meaning takes shape.

You've learned how to detect patterns. Now you'll learn how to make sense of them. To read the room. The system. The signal. Yourself. Because the world doesn't just need more information. It needs better interpretation.

We'll show you how superadapters do it – through three distinct habits. And three powerful real-world examples. You'll learn how to loosen rigid stories, shift frames, test meaning, and get out of your own way.

This isn't about thinking more. It's about thinking better. Thinking for movement. Thinking for change. Because the right interpretation isn't just what makes sense. It's what lets you move – smarter, faster, freer.

That's what this Rule gives you. Not just the insight. The loop to return to. And the tools to change the frame that's keeping you trapped.

THEY THOUGHT WHAT?!
Misinterpretation, surprise, and the loops that set us free

You think you know what you're looking at – until you don't. That's the trap of interpretation. It feels like truth, right up until it doesn't.

For centuries, Europeans had no idea where swallows went in winter. Some believed they buried themselves in riverbeds. Others claimed they turned into mice. Swallowed by the earth. Swallowed by metaphor. Not one person imagined they were flying – miles and miles across continents and oceans.

Then, in 1822, a stork crash-landed in northern Germany. It had an iron spear lodged in its neck – an African spear. It became known as the Pfeilstorch – 'arrow-stork' – and it changed everything.

That single wounded bird proved something miraculous: migration was real. Birds disappeared because they left. The sky hadn't swallowed them. The earth hadn't changed them. We just hadn't followed them far enough.

They weren't gone. They were just gone beyond belief.

You think that was the only time?

People thought disease came from bad smells and night air. From sins. From swamps. They'd bury garlic. Burn pitch. Blame the stars. The idea that invisible things – germs – could crawl from hand to hand, cup to lip? Unthinkable. Microscopes weren't just tools. They were revolutions.

People thought babies came from homunculi – tiny, pre-formed humans curled up in sperm. Some said the egg did all the work. Some said the sperm was the soul. Nobody quite imagined it took both, in dialogue. Until the loop closed.

People thought seizures were demonic possession. That the stars rotated around the earth. That maps had dragons at the edges. That shadows moved because they were alive. That women's wandering wombs caused hysteria. That leeches could cure imbalance. That volcanoes were gods speaking.

They weren't stupid. They were interpreting. With the tools they had. With the stories they knew.

And that's what we do.

We explain what we can't yet understand with what we already believe. We loop old meaning onto new mystery. Until something doesn't fit. Until something – a spear, a symptom, a stutter in the data – punctures the loop and forces us to see again.

They didn't just get it wrong. They lived inside the wrongness. They built models. Passed laws. Raised children inside it. Entire societies running on invisible errors.

And then?

Someone relooped. Someone said: What if it's not that at all? Someone saw a door where everyone else saw a wall.

That's interpretation. It's not what you see – it's what you make of what you see. And it's not fixed. It never was.

So now ask yourself:

What do you believe is obvious? What have you never questioned, not once? What's the thing you think everyone knows?

What if you're still wrong?

And what if that's your best chance to adapt?

As you learned in Rule 1, this journey unfolds in loops: Recognise → Understand → Necessary Action.

Rule 2 is the second step inside that first phase – Recognise. Detection showed you how to see the pattern. Now you'll learn how to make sense of it. To test it. To frame it. To shift it when it no longer fits.

This is interpretation. The second loop in your larger adaptive habit.

You're not just learning to think differently. You're learning to loop differently. To spot the story you're using. And to decide if that story still serves.

You'll meet three people in this section. Each one will show you how superadaptive minds interpret – not passively, but in motion. They question, reframe, and move forward with clarity.

After that, you'll revisit the loop. See how it bends under pressure. See what happens when it works – and when it breaks. Then you'll try it yourself. You'll test your patterns. Reboot your meaning. Rebuild your next move.

By the end of this Rule, you won't just have new insight. You'll have a working loop. A way to interpret like a superadapter. And the awareness to know when to run it again.

THE INTERPRET LOOP

HOW SUPERADAPTERS INTERPRET

All life interprets.

Not always consciously. Not always well. But every living thing does something with what is done to it.

It's the simplest rule in biology: for every action, there is a reaction. Something goes in, something comes out. A signal becomes a shift. That's interpretation. The transformation of input into meaning – and meaning into movement.

Your pet does it when it hears the door. Is it a stranger? Or you, their favourite person?

Your cat does it when you throw something. Is it a toy? A threat? A chance to pounce?

The difference between a threat and a game, between lunch and danger, between a hatstand and your partner in a darkened hallway – comes down to how we interpret.

And here's the good news: the human brain has developed the capacity not just to interpret – but to reinterpret. To interpret its own interpretations. That's what makes this loop different. That's what makes it trainable.

You can tune not just what you think – but how you think it. How you assign meaning. And how you change the story when the meaning you've made no longer helps you move.

Superadapters do that better. They don't just run on automatic frames. They pause. They stretch the frame. They choose the most useful interpretation available – not the fastest, not the easiest. The one that moves them forward.

And they do it at just the right moment.

You saw it in the Detect Loop: superadapters learn to spot what matters.

Now, in the Interpret Loop, they learn to make sense of it – deliberately. They don't pass on noise. They don't hand off panic. They pass on what's been curated – read, reframed, and made more useful.

That's the job here:

To take what has been detected…

…interpret it adaptively…

…and hand it off cleanly for action.

Whether you think of it as a baton in a relay, a parcel being delivered to the right address, or the ball moved through a midfield – what matters is that something real has happened. You've taken in the world, turned it, and now it's ready to change you, or the system you're in.

This is the second loop in Recognise.
This is where meaning starts to move.
At its core, the Interpret Loop is about positioning.

Not just where you are now, but where you could be next. It's the loop that lets you open paths that were previously hidden – and stops you from wasting energy on roads that go nowhere.

Because attention is limited. And energy is limited. And time – well, we all know about that.

If you've ever spent a morning wondering whether to switch energy providers or just sit in the sun with a cold drink, you've already run this loop. You weighed up meaning, cost, and direction. You made a call. That's interpretation in action.

This loop doesn't just help you understand. It helps you move. It focuses your perception. It filters your meaning-making. It channels your energy toward what's most useful now – and next.

In this Rule, you'll meet three habits that help you do that better. They help you hunt for patterns, tag what matters, and shift the frame so your next move becomes clear.

DITCH THE DOGMA → REVERSE THE OBVIOUS →
SWITCH POINT OF VIEW

That's the Interpret Loop. It picks up what Detect delivers and makes it usable – so Decide can act on it.

And as always, the best way to understand a loop is to see it in motion. Not in theory, but through people.

We learn best from each other – by watching, listening, retelling, reflecting. That's why the next few pages will introduce three people. Each one runs this loop in a different way. Each one has something to teach you.

And then we'll bring them back together – so you can see the pattern they form, and how to make it your own.

As ever, there are other theories available. And some are more helpful than others – especially when the aim is not just to understand the mind, but to adapt with it.

Take Kahneman. Much loved. Hugely influential. And yes – he gave us something enduring: a language for how we trip over our own thinking. System 1, System 2. Fast, slow. Bias after bias. The whole catalogue of ways in which we fool ourselves.

But here's the thing: you could spend your whole life trying to catch every bias, and still never act. You'd fall into the bias-reduction trap. There's probably a name for that too. ("Just one more cognitive distortion before I get started.")

You end up as the curator of your own error museum – expert in every misstep, paralysed by possibility.

Barrett takes a different route. Instead of assuming we're flawed judges of objective reality, she says: maybe there is no objective reality to judge. Maybe your brain doesn't just interpret data – it constructs it. On the fly. Based on what you've felt before, what you expect, what you need right now.

In Barrett's view, meaning isn't discovered. It's assigned. You're not reacting to the world – you're generating it. Framing isn't a failure of accuracy. It's a feature of adaptation.

Her invitation is subtle but seismic. Instead of auditing your thoughts, recast them. Shape your categories. Rethink your reactions. Don't ask is this true? Ask is this helping?

Kahneman hands you a red pen. Barrett reminds you that you're in charge. She hands you the keys.

Superadapters don't waste energy hunting every bias. They don't freeze trying to calculate the truest possible story. They ask: What interpretation moves me forward?

They know that meaning is always constructed – so they construct it deliberately. Not to distort the world, but to work with it. They frame with purpose. They tag what matters. They bend the story just far enough to make the next move possible.

That's not manipulation. That's adaptation.

Because reality isn't just one fixed thing coming in. Your brain is assembling what it makes of what's happening to it.

That means you're always filtering. The only real question is: what kind of filter are you using? And is it revealing the part of the world that helps you move?

That's what superadapters do differently. They don't interpret to confirm what they already believe. They interpret to discover what else might be possible. They use framing not to feel safe, but to get somewhere better.

This kind of interpretation is a meta-habit. It can be trained. It's not about resisting emotion, or neutralising meaning. It's about learning to shift what a moment means – so you can shift what becomes possible next.

You don't have to be perfect. But you do need space.

Because the right frame – the useful one, the freeing one – won't show up if the system's flooded. Sometimes it's not about choosing the right meaning from a list. It's about finding the one that leaves you in a better place.

And that's where we're going next.

THE THIRD SPACE

Where possibility lives.
Sometimes, you just need room.
Room to think.
Room to move.
Room to breathe.

The third space is that room. It's not just metaphorical. It's physical, cognitive, emotional. A clearing in the woods. A mental bench. The missing square in the sliding puzzle. It's not yet decision. It's not yet action. It's interpretation – but with space to repattern the frame.

Most of the world pushes us into binaries. Yes or no. Right or wrong. Them or us. But the third space isn't either side of the fight. It's the unoccupied ground where something different might grow.

Some cultures didn't originally have a word for 'three'. They had one. They had two. Beyond that? Many. But as soon as complexity arrived – trade, tension, interdependence – the need for a third category became essential.

That's the third space.
It's what lets you say:
Maybe not this.
Maybe not that.
Maybe something else.
Not indecision. Openness.
A space between roles, between reactions, between selves.

Psychologists speak of third spaces as creative or restorative zones. A place between work and home. A mental shift zone between stimulus and response. Where habits pause. Where new meanings can be rehearsed without being judged.

Even your lungs need slack to function. Even your thoughts need silence to settle. Adaptation needs space to unfold. Not everything worth doing is efficient. Not everything efficient is adaptive.

You can't rearrange the pieces if you can't move.
You can't adapt a loop if you're pinned inside it.

Without third space, there is no third move.
There's just reaction, rebound, repeat.

There was a sliding block puzzle in a waiting room. You know the kind: a plastic square, with little tiles numbered one to eight – but only nine spaces in total. One space always left blank. The only way to solve it – the only way to move anything at all – was to use the empty square.

A boy sat with it for hours while his mother filled out forms. He twisted the puzzle, turned it, got stuck, started again. At one point, he tried forcing the tiles with his fingers, but they jammed. No space, no movement. No movement, no solution.

Years later, he'd remember that puzzle during an argument with his partner. He'd feel the same rising panic. The tightening. The need to force it. And then, somehow, that click in his mind:

Make space first.

Even just one square. One beat. One breath.

So he stopped talking. He walked to the sink. He let silence do something speech couldn't. And in that space, he saw her face change. Just slightly. But enough.

All systems need slack. Muscles, lungs, minds, marriages.
Without a space to shift into, there's no adaptation.
Without room to reframe, you only repeat.

The empty square isn't wasted.
It's what makes the whole thing work.

To interpret adaptively isn't just to be right. It's to place meaning in a way that moves you forward.

Yes, facts exist. But we don't act on facts – we act on framed facts. Pain is inevitable, as Murakami says. But suffering? That's interpretation. That's the frame.

Some people treat all discomfort as failure. Others seek it out: for growth, for glory, for Sunday medals, for fundraising. The same signal, reframed, becomes meaning. Possibility. Purpose.

This flexibility – this alternate-uses-for-meaning mindset – is the superadaptive skill. Psychologists test creativity with the Alternative Uses Test: how many different things can you do with a button? The most fluid minds don't stop at two or three. They keep going. That's what this next section trains you for.

Because interpretation is the habit of assigning first meaning. Adaptive interpretation is the habit of questioning whether that first meaning is still serving you.

Maybe your interpretation isn't wrong. It's just not helpful anymore.

The first habit helps you break that loop.

It helps you ditch the dogma – and see what else this moment could mean.

Ditching the dogma is about letting go of rigid assumptions.

If it no longer fits – drop it and reframe. If the belief, or rule, or design principle, or inherited rhythm you've never questioned is no longer helping you interpret what's happening – why are you still using it?

This includes your personal interpretations. But it also includes systemic defaults. Dogma isn't just about religion or identity. It's built into workplace workflows, product roadmaps, family schedules, traffic patterns. It's the script you never rewrote because no one told you you could.

We assume "that's just how things are done". We don't pause to ask: does this still work? Does it fit me? Is it helping anyone adapt?

Superadapters do pause. They don't just challenge meaning. They open space for new meaning to emerge.

They learn to see interpretation itself as flexible. Framing is not fixed. It's an interface. And if it's no longer guiding you well, you can reshape it. That's the interpret loop in motion.

And it applies everywhere.

You think you need a car. And that car needs a garage. And that garage needs to be heated. And that gym membership is separate from your commute. Until one day, you pause. You step into third space. And you realise: maybe you don't need the car. Maybe the walk is the gym. Maybe ditching the garage is the move that unlocks the loop.

That's not about self-discovery. That's design thinking.

And it applies to your beliefs, your work, your systems, and the stories you tell about all three.

The real dogma isn't ideological. It's interpretive.

It's the assumption that the frame you're using is the only one available.

But superadapters don't just react. They reframe. They interrupt that reflex. They find the space to interpret differently.

Not just once, but again and again – until the loop gets clearer, and the future gets freer.

DITCH THE DOGMA

Let go of rigid assumptions. If it no longer fits, drop and reframe.

Because if you believe enough bad things about yourself –
if you accept the labels, the limits, the "truths" that others hand you –
you don't just get lost.
You land exactly where the map was leading.

Right in the middle of San Quentin prison.

And that's where we find our next figure.

Not confused.
But certain.
And it's that certainty that nearly cost him everything.

Let's go there now.

HABIT 1: DITCH THE DOGMA

Danny Trejo: the loop that let him out

There are dogmas that come from churches, textbooks, or manifestos.
    And then there are the quieter ones – the ones you inherit without realising.
    You believe them because someone said them. Or showed them. Or hit you with them.
    Danny Trejo was born into one of those loops.
    Born in 1944 in Maywood, California, the result of an affair, raised in a household of secrets, absences, and violence – his story started long before he had the words to tell it. His father beat him. His uncle introduced him to heroin. By age 7, he was dealing drugs. By age 10, he was in jail. By 13, in a new neighbourhood. By 15, already behind bars again.
    Every year that passed wasn't a detour – it was another loop laid down in his nervous system.
    Another circuit of belief.
    Another ratchet on the system.
    You are dangerous. You are bad.
    This is who you are.
    This is what people like you do.

There is no other way.

He didn't choose that dogma.

But shaped his actions. Until it didn't.

Danny Trejo was a prison boxing champion. Lightweight. Welterweight. He won fights inside the ring – but kept losing outside of it. "The toughest guy in prison," he said later, "still ends up in prison."

Throughout the 1960s, Trejo bounced from juvenile halls to county jails to high-security prisons.

He learned how to survive with fists, rage, and silence.

And the system cooperated. It typecast him before he ever auditioned.

He looked the part – thick neck, broken nose, stare that didn't flinch.

He learned to wear that mask before he ever saw a camera.

But one day, in 1968, the system blinked.

A prison riot. A thrown rock. Solitary confinement.

And for the first time, Trejo ran out of dogma to hide behind.

He was locked in a cell, detoxing, hallucinating, facing capital charges.

He describes it now like being in a ditch. A dark, echoing ditch at the bottom of his own life.

But in that ditch, something strange happened.

He spoke out loud.

He doesn't remember what he said.

He doesn't even say it mattered.

Only that it was the first time he imagined a version of himself that could exist 'after' this.

That was the crack.

The signal.

The loop whispering: You could be wrong.

He didn't change because he got smarter. He changed because he finally did something he'd avoided for decades: he listened.

He didn't wake up perfect.

He didn't get out of prison and find redemption.

What he found was plasticity.

He joined a 12-step group. Not to be saved, but to stay alive.

He heard people speak as if change were possible.

As if past behaviour wasn't prophecy.

And for the first time, he believed them.

Not because he had proof. But because something in him was ready to test a new story.

That's what it means to ditch the dogma.

Not rage. Not rejection.

Just the quiet act of saying: Maybe the truth I've been running on isn't the whole truth anymore.

When Trejo was released, he didn't seek fame.

He sought helping loops – feedback systems where he could keep himself accountable by helping others escape their own traps.

He worked construction. He planted trees. He poured cement. He listened. He sat in meetings with teenagers who thought they were invincible – and told them the story of the ditch.

He told them: "You're not what you've done. You're what you can do.

You're not what you were. You're what you're willing to become.

You could be wrong about yourself."

And because he believed it – so did they.

Then one night in the 1980s, he got a call.

There was a kid on a movie set who was about to overdose.

Could Trejo come talk him down?

He showed up. He did what he always did – he listened.

He told the truth.

Someone noticed him.

He looked like a prisoner.

Because he had been one.

But he sounded like something else.

Because he 'had become' something else.

That's the paradox of dogma and plasticity.

The same brain that loops into shame, violence, addiction –

Is the brain that can rewire, reframe, and entangle with its own potential.

The same face that scared people in prison –

would go on to feed people in films.

To appear on shows for children.

To run restaurants.

To save strangers from crashed cars.

To become Machete.

To become Mr. Jaguar.

To become – Trejo.

What changed?

Not his body.

Not his history.

His loop.

He ditched the dogma.
And the loop began again.

He often says he feels like someone's going to wake him up and tell him:
"Time for chow. Time for lockdown."
But no one does.
Because he isn't in the loop anymore.
He remade it.
He became who he might've been.
Not by force.
But by flex.
The year after Danny Trejo got out, Johnny Cash came to San Quentin and
sang: "I hate every inch of you."
But Trejo didn't need the song. He'd already lived the lyric.

That's what this Rule is about.
Not changing your story.
But recognising that your story was always changeable.
The loop isn't just the past repeating.
It's the moment you re-understand what the past meant – and build
something else from it.

DITCH THE DOGMA → REVERSE THE OBVIOUS → SWITCH POV

Trejo didn't break the system.
He broke the spell.
And then he gave others the words to do the same.

The thing to take from Trejo is this: once he had ditched the dogma – once he
let go of the beliefs, assumptions, habits, and traditions that had become rocks in
his pockets – he became something else entirely.
The system didn't change first. He did.
He became a catalyst. Creative. Kind. Caring.
So much so that the guards put him in charge of the gym.
The 12-step program wanted him to lead – not because he demanded it,
but because he carried a charisma even he couldn't see yet.
He laughed and asked to be the president.
They laughed and told him there was no president.
But they meant: you belong here. You're already leading.

That's the truth of this loop.
Once you shed the frame that told you who you had to be,
you create space – your third space.
And what feels like loss becomes possibility.

Your life may not be as dramatic.
But interpretation runs through everything:
How you talk. How you dress. What you accept.
How you do something as simple as paint a wall or speak to a stranger.

Sometimes we assume the method, the role, the frame – without ever asking
if it fits.

And those assumptions can be chainmail.
Heavy. Inflexible. False protection.
No use in quicksand. No use when you need to climb.
No help at all when it's time to turn.

That's what Ditch the Dogma clears.
It doesn't give you the answer.
It gives you the space to look again.

But ditching the dogma is only part of the solution.
Because once you've given yourself space to think –
you need to do something with that space.
And that's where our next habit comes in.

I've never liked constraints. I'm a free radical by nature – bouncing, charged,
looking to connect.
    But the trouble with free radicals is they don't always land. They swirl. They
flare. They dissipate.

Reversing the obvious isn't about doing the opposite for the sake of it.
Sometimes, flipping the frame means doing the wild thing.
Sometimes, it means doing the sensible thing – when chaos was the norm.

Jack Spratt ate no fat. His wife ate no lean.
Between them, they cleared the plate.
Two binaries don't cancel. They loop. They build a third thing.

Sometimes we don't even notice when we're interpreting ourselves into a trap.

You volunteer. You take responsibility. You own the thing.
And then – without realising – you've limited your own role.
It's not always cultural. It's not always gendered. But it's often habitual.

I'll do this because I always do this.
I'll carry that because I can.
I'll assume this because it's mine.

Until you wake up in a structure you didn't mean to build – and can't quite remember how to get out of.
This is the second habit in the interpret loop.

If the first one is about clearing space – this one is about seeing differently once the space is open.

Superadapters challenge the frame before they commit to it.
They don't just challenge authority. They challenge familiarity.
The thing that's obvious is often the thing that's outdated.

They've trained themselves to see 'obvious' as a signal – not of truth, but of repetition. Not of clarity, but closure.
And when they notice it, they pause. They ask:
Is this mine?
Is this useful?
Is this still helping me interpret what's happening?

And if not – they flip it.

REVERSE THE OBVIOUS
When things feel obvious, flip them. Challenge certainty before it calcifies.

In 1969, Danny Trejo leaves a prison.
Meanwhile, in almost another world, two people – one couple – ties a knot.
Two kinds of loops, both promising freedom.
And the child that couple has? She's just getting started.
Successful at high school. Successful at university. Interns at the White House – her dream job.

But that's not where the story ends.

Events reversed her obvious success.

And the question became: What could she do about it?

She was born in 1973, in Los Angeles – raised in privilege, with a promising path ahead of her.

That was the obvious path. The expected loop.

But we are never fully in control of what others see in us.

And sometimes, we're not even in control of the next move we might make.

And that's why – when what seemed obvious is reversed, when the frame flips and your fortune turns – it helps to know how to spot that reversal.

How to detect it.

How to name it.

And how to loop out of it.

Because when something that once worked stops working – interpretation is the only way back in.

Let's follow her through that reversal now.

HABIT 2: REVERSE THE OBVIOUS

In January 1998, Monica Lewinsky was 24 years old. By the end of that month, she was arguably the most recognised woman on the planet. Her name, image, and reputation had been splashed across every screen and newspaper. Not for what she had said. But for what had been said about her. She became a synonym, not a self – a national scandal, reduced to a dress, a smirk, a punchline. A bimbo. A "home-wrecker." A threat.

But the real threat, as it turned out, was not to the presidency. It was to the myth of consequence-free power. The crime, if there was one, was not sex. It was visibility. A young woman becoming seen too clearly, too suddenly, in a way the world wasn't willing to understand. What followed was not just moral panic – it was narrative warfare.

She was told to disappear. To be quiet. To apologise. To stay ashamed. But disappearance is not healing. Silence is not recovery. Monica didn't just survive the scandal – she survived the erasure that came after it. The demand to be less. To be still. To be invisible again.

And then, years later, she began to speak.

After the headlines faded and the cameras turned away, Monica Lewinsky did not chase a comeback. She disappeared in a different direction – into study. Into thought. She moved to London, enrolled at the London School of Economics, and began to analyse the very forces that had undone her. Her thesis was titled In Search of the Impartial Juror: An Exploration of the Third Person Effect and Television Coverage of the Clinton Impeachment Trial.

It sounds academic, and it was – but it was also personal. Deeply. Intentionally. The third person effect is a theory in media psychology that suggests people believe others are more influenced by media than they are themselves. Lewinsky used it to interrogate the gap between what the public believed they were watching, and what she had actually lived through. She wasn't just revisiting her own story – she was reframing it, using the tools of theory, scrutiny, and structured distance.

She wrote herself, in effect, into the role of juror – not just the defendant. She became both subject and analyst, accused and analyst, first person and third. A partial, impartial witness to her own dehumanisation. Not to exonerate, and not to self-flagellate – but to understand. To reconstruct meaning from within the wreckage of reputation.

This is one of the quietest forms of resistance: to sit with what was done to you, and give it a frame. It wasn't public. It wasn't performative. But it was preparatory. She wasn't ready to re-enter the world. Not yet. But she was starting to learn how to name what it had done to her.

The decision to speak was not sudden. It built slowly, through years of patterned silence. Then something broke. Not inside her – but around her. In 2014, Monica Lewinsky took the stage at Forbes' 30 Under 30 summit. She had nothing to sell, nothing to promote – only something to say. "I was Patient Zero," she told the crowd, "of losing a personal reputation on a global scale almost instantaneously." It was not a confession. It was a reclassification.

There was power in the act, but precision in the frame. She wasn't merely telling her story – she was giving it shape. Turning trauma into theory. Herself into case study. By naming the mechanism ('scandal fatigue', 'clickbait culture', 'cyberbullying'), she wasn't just describing what had happened to her – she was indicting a system. And in doing so, she altered her role within it. From footnote to figure. From symbol to strategist. From shame subject to cultural operator.

This was the moment Lewinsky shifted registers. No longer the girl in the blue dress. No longer the punchline. She became a builder of new social narratives – about dignity, empathy, and the human costs of internet virality. Her TED talk, *The Price of Shame*, reached over 20 million viewers. But it wasn't just the scale that mattered – it was the steadiness. The clarity. The ability to speak through, not just about.

This, too, was a form of justice – not legal, but narrative. Not retrospective, but recursive. She was not rewriting the past. She was showing how it had been miswritten in the first place. And in that gap between reality and representation, she found the leverage to act. "Public shaming as a blood sport has to stop," she said. The same culture that had erased her voice was now listening. Not because the culture had matured – but because she had.

What Lewinsky teaches is not just media literacy. It's adaptive authorship. She didn't just weather the narrative – she re-entered it, but refused to stay where she was cast. That shows her superadaptive mind at work. She couldn't change what had happened. But she could change what it meant. The first frame was placed on her. The second, she placed herself.

This is the heart of **reversing the obvious** – how to return to the story without being re-trapped by it. Not by forgetting, or rebranding, or retreating – but by adjusting the lens. Seeing what the story was before reshaping what it could become. It's a shift that requires emotional distance, cognitive clarity, and narrative control. And it's not theoretical. It's behavioural. It's buildable. It loops.

Lewinsky didn't escape the past – she made it useful. Not because it was redemptive, but because it was reframed. She didn't become a saint, or a martyr, or a slogan. She became a narrator. A builder. An operator of her own frame. And that's what makes her return so powerful. She wasn't waiting to be let back in. She came in through a door she built herself.

DITCH THE DOGMA → **REVERSE THE OBVIOUS** → SWITCH POV

Monica Lewinsky showed what it means to reverse the obvious. Her story – once a straight line of success – was twisted by scandal, interpretation, and the gaze of a thousand others. But in that pressure, she made space. Emotional space. Interpretive space. She didn't just escape the role. She paused long enough to challenge it.

She left. She learned. She returned.

But the frame she reversed wasn't the only one available. And that's what brings us to the final habit in the interpret loop.

You've ditched the dogma. You've flipped what looked fixed. Now comes the hardest move: to see again, from somewhere else entirely.

Switching perspective isn't just a metaphor. It's how superadapters break interpretive inertia. It's how they stop reacting from the same role and start reframing the system they're in.

You've done this, maybe without knowing. You imagined your parent's view. Your partner's. Your opponent's. You tried to explain it to a friend and saw it change in the telling. That's perspective-switching. Not to surrender – but to move.

Psychologists have shown that visualising yourself above, beside, or inside a situation changes what you see – and what you can do. Writers call this copywriting: trying on someone else's voice to stretch their own. Switch POV is cognitive cross-training. The mind expanding its range.

SWITCH POV
Deliberately adopt a different perspective to disrupt bias and expand insight.

Now imagine this is you.

You're born in 1988, in Ho Chi Minh City. Your mother is Vietnamese. Your father, a U.S. Navy serviceman. Half-American children aren't safe, so your family hides the truth. Until the truth finds them. Exposed, they flee to the Philippines, then to the U.S. You're two years old. Seven relatives in one room. No one in your family can read.

But you do. You learn. You write.

And with writing comes the ability to shift – between selves, languages, frames.

Ocean Vuong once wrote that looking at someone else might be a way to reimagine yourself. To become someone who didn't yet exist.

His name came from mispronunciation. His life from contradiction. His habit from necessity.

Switching perspective didn't just save him. It made him a writer.

And so I tell this story to you once –
and now I will tell it to you again.

A second time.

HABIT 3: FLIP YOUR POV

Some people grow up in stories they don't understand.
Others grow up in stories they can't translate.

Ocean Vuong was born in Saigon, Vietnam, into a lineage of displacement.
His mother worked in a nail salon. His grandmother was illiterate.
His grandfather was a white American soldier.
He was the first in his family to learn to read – and then the first to realise that reading might be more than escape.
It might be survival.

But the story doesn't begin with language.
It begins with silence.

He didn't speak until the age of six.
He was raised in a household where no one shared a fluent language – not Vietnamese, not English, not love.
At school, he learned English.
At home, he translated for his mother.
At night, he watched television to teach himself grammar.
And when he began to write – he did it in a language his family couldn't read.

This is the moment we pause.
Because the fact – writing a book your mother can't read – is sad in a way.
It's poignant. But it's simultaneously instructive.
Ocean fills what could be a gap with a creative repurposing of his situation.
Vuong's novel, *On Earth We're Briefly Gorgeous*, is a letter to his mother – written in English, a language she cannot read.
This is not merely a performance. It is not merely a provocation.
It's an interpretive loop.
He sends a message to someone who will never receive it. And he does it anyway.
This is Switch POV.

In his case, it's not merely "try on someone else's mind for size."
It's live inside a contradiction – and speak from that contradiction.

When we speak about this habit, we're not talking about persuasion as such.
You might use interpretation for that purpose.

We're talking about the imaginative act of looking at a situation and switching POVs so that you can better interpret – interpret more accurately, if that's the case – reinterpret imaginatively, but also interpret in a way that you would never have imagined without another person's mind in mind.

He survives through reframing – and then he thrives through reframing.

He interprets in a way that allows him to live, and to find new levels that are above where he started.

He builds stairways of perspective.

It's not only him pretending to be someone else.

It's him choosing to be a different, expanded, richer, more varied, transformed self.

It's him choosing to expand his frame of interpretation wide enough to include them both – and to create yet another.

Ocean Vuong doesn't toggle identities. He braids them.

Braids them like rope – to make them stronger.
Braids them like ribbon – to make them more beautiful.
Braids them like DNA – so they can produce something new.
This isn't literary flourish. It's biological metaphor. It's structural thinking.

He doesn't escape contradiction. He composes with it.

Like the keys on a piano. Like bass and treble clefs. Like a band where different tones don't cancel, they complete.

Each sentence, each image, each narrative thread he chooses isn't just a story – it's a stance.

And he has many stances. He can look this way, and that way. He can be this, and that.

That's not passivity. It's active adaptation.

Interpretation as improvisation. Reframing as recursive strength.

This is Switch POV in practice.

And Switch POV is not mysticism. It's method.

It's the act of temporarily stepping outside your default frame – your narrative, your stance, your collection of facts, your version of the truth – so you can re-enter from another angle.

When Vuong says, "I write from the negotiation," he's not being evasive.

He's showing you where he stands: in motion.

That sentence is a stance.

And that stance is the behaviour.
That's the habit.
That's the interpret loop.
Because interpretation isn't just about clarity. It's about capacity.
It's about being able to hold more than one meaning without collapsing.
To re-view, re-read, re-feel.
To shift lenses when the current one goes brittle.
You aren't just one thing. None of us are. Your brain isn't. No brain is.

This is what superadapters do.
They don't flatten their point of view to survive.
They stress it. They test it. They enhance it.
They fly their freak flag of point of view – and try on others for size.

Not to agree. Not to appease.
But to expand what's possible to see.

That's the move. That's the loop.

This is where its worth pausing and feeling: "I've been shown a move.
I've seen someone live it. Now I know what it looks like – and what it could
feel like for me."

There's a deeper kind of seeing that only comes
From displacement.
When you are not quite at home in any one frame, you
Learn to live in the seam between them.

That's where vuong lives.
Where meaning doesn't arrive fully formed -
But layered, refracted, recursive.
Not resolution, but resonance.

This is switch pov at its most intimate. Not a tool for
Debate. A structure for self.

We all have frames we were born into.
Frames we outgrew, or broke, or had broken for us.
We all carry scenes that look different depending on
Where we're standing - or who we're standing with.

What switch pov teaches isn't how to abandon
Those frames.
It teaches how to step out, test them, and return
From another angle.
To re-enter - not with neutrality, but with depth.
With braided meaning. With contradiction held,
Not erased.

But let's be clear - this habit is not just for
Memoirists or poets.
It's for managers in meetings. Parents at the edge of
Conflict. Students trying to unstick a problem.
It's for anyone trying to read a situation more wisely -
Not just once, but again and again.

Switch pov is best understood as part of an
Interpretive loop.
It's not always your first move. Sometimes you start by
Ditching the dogma.
Sometimes you begin by reversing what seems obvious.
But over time, as you become more adept, you learn to
Feel the loop at work - and to know when to move from
Stance to stance.

This is interpretation not as explanation -
But as expansion.
And this is where superadaptability becomes emotional
As well as cognitive.
Because to speak from the seam isn't just to analyse.
It's to risk.
To try again. To say,
"I don't have one stance. I have a system."

This is what vuong offers.
Not identity.
But structure.
Not resolution.
But recursion.

He doesn't give us a conclusion.
He gives us orientation.

And from here, the reader is ready.

To reverse the obvious.
To break the frame.
To build what comes next.

DITCH THE DOGMA → REVERSE THE OBVIOUS → **SWITCH POV**

You've now seen all three parts of the interpret loop.
You've watched someone break their internalised story.
You've watched someone reframe the role the world wrote for them.
You've watched someone learn to move between frames, and speak from the seam.

This is how superadapters interpret – not just themselves, but the world.

Now it's time to meet someone who lived the whole loop – at world scale.
This is a guy who had the whole package.
John Maynard Keynes was one of the most superadaptive minds of any generation. He continually tested boundaries – and redrew new ones. He stood outside official economics, outside canon, outside dogma.
He could flip perspective. Borrow points of view. Step into the shoes of the worker, the president, the investor, the dissenter.
He rewrote economic understanding not once – but several times. He even rewrote his own rules.
And when his models were followed, they helped create one of the most successful human-centred eras in history – so influential that it was later described as the end of history.

It was only when people started misinterpreting his work – flattening it, distorting it, severing its parts from its whole – that history, by which we mean bad actors breaking good systems, returned.

That's who you're about to meet.
Someone who embodies not just one habit, but the full interpretive arc.
The wonderful, the fantastic – Mr. Keynes.

This isn't a recap. It's a run-through.
Everything you've just seen now comes alive in one person's mind.

And one moment in history.

Let's enter the loop.

PUTTING IT ALL TOGETHER: THE BREAK
He was the golden boy of orthodoxy.

Cambridge prodigy. Apostle of Alfred Marshall. The kind of economist who didn't question the system – he explained it. For a while, he wore the role beautifully. Sharp suits, sharper wit. He lectured, advised, annotated the margins of empires. He could quote the Greeks and balance a budget before tea. His father was a moral philosopher, and John Maynard Keynes grew up believing ideas could be elegant and true at the same time.

Then the world collapsed.

The Great War ended, but the peace didn't hold. In *The Economic Consequences of the Peace*, Keynes warned that vengeance economics would break Europe. It did. He resigned from the Treasury in protest. That was the first fracture.

But the deeper break came later. In the 1920s, as unemployment soared and faith in the market held firm, Keynes began to doubt the thing he'd been trained to believe: that markets self-correct. That saving was always virtuous. That intervention distorted the natural order.

Natural order? What natural order lets millions starve with warehouses full of grain?

He looked again.

This wasn't disloyalty. It was clarity. He wasn't trying to kill capitalism. He was trying to keep it alive. But the old logic no longer worked. Classical economists said downturns were temporary. That recessions would clear excess. But people weren't excess. Time wasn't cheap. A lost year in a young life doesn't grow back.

So he turned away. Not from rigor – but from reverence. He wasn't burned by ideology. He outgrew it.

The story goes that someone once asked him: "Why did you change your mind?" "When the facts change," he said, "I change my mind. What do you do, sir?" And whether he ever used the exact words, he certainly lived their meaning.

The break wasn't theoretical.

It was adaptive.

He had ditched the dogma.

What came next would require a different kind of lens.

THE SHIFT

He began to see the economy not as a machine, but as a mood.

Classical theory treated people as aggregates – consumers, producers, savers, investors. But Keynes had lived through too much to believe in tidy abstractions. He had seen good men ruined by delay. He had seen nations unravel because leaders waited for equilibrium. Markets might balance eventually – but eventually is not a policy.

So he walked away from the mountaintop and started listening to the street.

In the lecture halls of Cambridge, he still used the blackboard. But the questions he asked were no longer about supply curves. He asked: what does it feel like to be unemployed? What does fear do to a worker? What does uncertainty do to a shopkeeper? What does waiting do to a generation?

It was heresy, really.

He began thinking like the people classical economists ignored. Like the unemployed. Like the factory owner choosing between cutting wages or cutting people. Like the civil servant who couldn't explain to hungry citizens why things would 'sort themselves out'.

It changed him.

He stopped defending the invisible hand and started asking what it was doing with its fingers.

Demand, he realised, was not a side effect. It was the engine. Investment wasn't about thrift – it was about expectation. People didn't spend because they had money. They spent because they believed. Economics wasn't physics. It was psychology. Collective imagination. Managed risk. Coordinated trust.

To change the economy, he would have to change its mood.

That meant changing the perspective. Not from above – but from inside.

He had switched the point of view.

And with it, the purpose of economics itself.

THE REFRAME

He wrote it in bursts. In hotel rooms. On trains. At his desk in King's College, where the window overlooked a world no longer orderly. He called it The General Theory of Employment, Interest and Money, though it could just as easily have been called The Book That Got Him Laughed Out of the Room.

Because what Keynes proposed was blasphemy.

Spend during a crisis. Borrow when times are bad. Run deficits not as a last resort, but as a moral imperative. Governments, he argued, must step in when confidence steps out. If they don't, the system freezes. And when systems freeze, people fall.

To a generation raised on thrift, this was madness. The rule had always been: when trouble hits, tighten your belt. Keynes said: loosen it. Not forever. Not recklessly. But deliberately. Because saving during a downturn doesn't heal the wound – it deepens it.

It was the economic version of turning into the skid.

He didn't frame it as ideology. He framed it as function. If private demand collapses, public demand must rise. Not because it's ideal, but because it's necessary. He drew diagrams. Used metaphors. Built models. One critic said his prose was like "shot silk" – luminous, layered, almost too beautiful to be trusted.

But the world began to listen. Slowly. Reluctantly. Then urgently.

Because the old tools weren't working. The economy wasn't a pendulum swinging back to balance. It was a loop. And the loop was broken.

So Keynes built a new one.

That was the reframe.

Not a theory – but a system. Not perfect – but functional. Not eternal – but adaptive.

A loop that let nations act when fear would otherwise freeze them.

The idea was simple.

The consequences were global.

He had reversed the obvious.

And the world, for a time, followed.

THE ECHO
It didn't end with him.

By the time John Maynard Keynes died in 1946, the war was over – but the rebuilding had only begun. And it was his ideas, not his name, that spread. Not as doctrine, but as design. Not as monument, but as method.

His students carried them forward – Joan Robinson, Richard Kahn, Abba Lerner. They didn't just quote him. They built systems with him still inside. Institutions emerged that bore his intellectual fingerprint: the IMF, the World Bank, entire ministries of finance whose default mode was no longer passive observation, but active intervention.

It wasn't that the world suddenly agreed. Many never did. But the pattern had changed.

Now, when economies wobbled, leaders reached for tools he once had to invent. Stimulus. Public investment. Coordinated response. Governments became more than referees – they became players. The script had shifted.

He had rewired the role of the state. Not toward tyranny. Toward responsibility.

And the loop he built wasn't just fiscal. It was philosophical.

He taught the world how to revise.

Not reactively. Not defensively. But structurally.

Because Keynes had shown that being wrong isn't the end of authority.

It's the beginning of wisdom – if you loop it properly.

And so, his voice lingers – not just in policy, but in posture.

In the economists who double-check their models.

In the leaders who pivot under pressure.

In the thinkers who say: "We might not know. But we can learn."

In the systems that ask: "What else could be true?"

Keynes didn't build a perfect theory. He built a flexible one.

Not timeless – but timely.

Not rigid – but recursive.

Not a monument – but a loop.

And in that loop, we hear it still:

DITCH THE DOGMA → SWITCH POV → REVERSE THE OBVIOUS

THE TURNING SPACE
Give yourself room to adapt.

You're in the middle of it.
Something's not right. But nothing's clear.
Too early to act. Too late to ignore.
It feels like you've only got two options – neither good.

That's the bind.

Maybe it's medical. Maybe emotional. Maybe someone you love is struggling and you're trying to hold it together while still doing something useful. But everything feels like a loop; panic or delay, act too fast or act too late.

That's where this comes in.
You don't need more force. You need a Turning Space.
That's what The Interpret Loop gives you.

It's like the bit of track at a station that lets a train swivel.
Without it, you're stuck going forward or back.
But with it – you can change direction entirely.

Sometimes it just means stopping long enough to ask a better question.
Not: Why is this happening to me?
But: What's actually going on here? What's the long-term treatment?

That was the move a doctor in a hospital once made. He saw something violent. He asked questions. He triaged it like the clinician he was. Not just "Who's to blame?" but "What's the deeper system breakdown?" That's interpretation in motion. That's the third move.

Same with the health of a loved one. You don't ignore it. You don't spiral. You say: She's done the blood tests, the urine tests, she's got the referral. So now – we're not waiting. We're watching. We're tracking. And if needed, we'll nudge the system. That's a third space too.

It's not reaction. It's not retreat.
It's the move that lets you move again.

And sometimes, it means not going straight to university.
It means taking the time, getting experience, coming back strong.
Then you're not just a graduate. You're a graduate with direction.
You're not stuck on the old track.
You've built the third one.

That's what the Turning Space is for.

Not for waiting.
Not for avoiding.
For choosing better.
For looping back into motion – with clarity.

DITCH → SWITCH → REVERSE

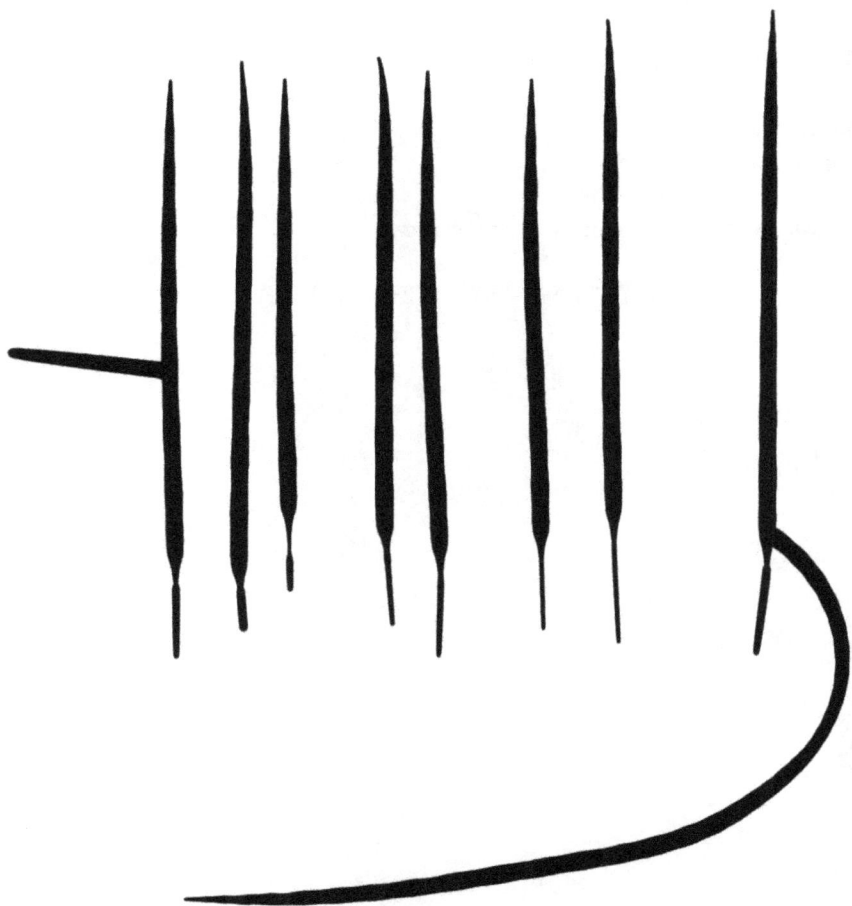

THE SITDOWN: THE CURTAIN AND THE STAGE

WHY WE SIT DOWN NOW
Not blocking. Listening.

"People think that the director is responsible for what you see and the conductor is responsible for what you hear. I think that's bullshit. It's really the director that allows the music to exist and it's the job of the conductor to make theatre in the pit. If you don't have that you don't have opera."
— Leiser/Caurier, *About Opera*

In the theatre, there's a kind of performance most audiences never see. It's called the sitzprobe. The cast sits down. The orchestra plays. It's the first time voices and instruments perform together as a whole. No lights. No blocking. No choreography. Just the raw combination of two systems trying to find each other.

It's not the final show, and it's not the hard-edged technical rehearsal either. It's something between. Something quieter. The cast and orchestra enter from their own spaces — separate, skilled, rehearsed. But here they make a third space. One that only exists when both are fully present. And for many, this is the most human part of the process. Not because it's polished — but because it's shared.

There's joy in that convergence. Musicians hear the voices they've only imagined. Singers feel the shape of the score come alive. It's not pressure — it's permission. A space where you can hear more than your own part. Where the act of listening becomes interpretive. Often it's cramped, sweaty, makeshift. And still, something lifts. Something bigger than either side. A combination that no one could produce alone.

That's the third space. A place of meaning that emerges only when two systems are allowed to coexist without domination. In this book, that space is where your existing habits and interpretations meet the deeper loops of meta-habit and metaplasticity. Where rote experience and conscious awareness converge. And where something new is made.

In neuroscience, it's not unlike what happens when the brain's rehearsal circuits and real-time feedback loops collide. You build better understanding not by drilling, but by layering interpretation on top of action — consciously, then unconsciously, then consciously again. Culture is what rises through this loop. Not culture as performance, but culture as shared recursion. As learned transmission.

The sitzprobe becomes a metaphor for adaptation itself. It holds the structure of self-reflection. A space where we bring what we've practised, and hold it lightly enough to be changed by what we hear.

You are in your own sitzprobe now. What you bring, what this system brings, will shape the third thing. Hold still. Let the loops find each other.

SEEING FROM THE WINGS

As you've moved through the interpret loop, you've already begun to see how superadaptive minds take the raw material of experience and reshape it. This isn't just about spotting patterns – it's about reframing them in ways that open up new options, new futures. The Third Move is the decision that doesn't just respond to what's happening – it adapts to shape what happens next.

And it's part of the loop you've been running all along – Recognise → Understand → Necessary Action. You're not just sitting. You're mid-loop. And this is where meaning gets shaped.

Now you're entering that third space. You've already stepped toward it – through new thoughts, sharper feelings, reframed decisions. This isn't a place of right answers. It's the clearing where interpretation happens. Not from resistance, or inversion, but from a new kind of alignment.

As the lights dim and the curtain falls, you're not stepping away from the action. You're seeing it from the wings. With clearer eyes. With more space to sense what's unfolding.

Take this moment as a rehearsal. Not for what to say, but for how to see. Let the examples you've already lived – Trejo, Lewinsky, Vuong, Keynes, and the examples that come next – remind you what interpretive minds do. They don't seek certainty. They seek movement.

You're already in it. This is your third space. And it's changing how you'll return to the loop.

MARGULIS: PULLING BACK THE CURTAIN

At first glance, the story seemed solid.

Cells compete. The strong survive. The weak get absorbed, outpaced, or forgotten.

That was the script. Biology had its heroes – genes that won, organisms that dominated, mechanisms that selected for advantage.

The textbooks had rehearsed it for decades. Natural selection on repeat. A clean front-of-house performance.

But behind the curtain, something strange was happening.

Inside the cell – every cell in your body – there was a tiny structure producing energy with eerie efficiency. It had its own DNA. It split in two like a bacterium. It didn't follow the rules. It didn't act like it belonged. Most people saw it as just another part of the whole. Lynn Margulis didn't.

She looked closer.

And what she saw was not a detail – it was a challenge to the entire play.

Because that odd little structure wasn't just a quirk. It was a guest. An ancient one. Long ago, one cell had engulfed another... and didn't digest it. Instead, they cooperated. They merged. They looped together into something new.

That structure now powers you.

It turns sugar into usable energy. It keeps your muscles moving, your brain firing, your eyes reading this page.

Later, we gave it a name: mitochondria.

But here's the part that matters:

That structure is in you. Right now. In every one of your cells.

It's not symbolic. It's biological.

That merger lives on inside your body – as a loop that still runs.

It powers your breath, your thinking, your movement.

It's 100% inherited from your mother. It carries its own DNA. And it remembers.

It remembers being something else. It remembers joining. It remembers becoming more.

So yes, mitochondria is you.

The part of you that was once other.

The part of you that loops energy into action.

The part of you that doesn't dominate – but integrates.

The part of you that changed – and stayed.

We're not just talking metaphor here.

We're talking mechanism. Memory. Malleability.

That's what Lynn Margulis saw when she pulled back the curtain.

Not chaos. Not weakness.

But a system we'd been standing on all along – without realising what held it up.

TWO SCRIPTS, THIRD TRUTH

She wasn't a newcomer. She was already respected in her field – trained at the University of Chicago, working out of Boston University, with a background in cell biology and genetics. But in 1967, she submitted a paper that challenged the central dogma of evolutionary theory. It proposed something strange. Unwelcome. Inconvenient.

And for the next twenty years, her theory would be ignored, dismissed, and quietly ridiculed – until it wasn't.

But she refused to leave the stage.

Fifteen journals rejected her paper.

Some called it naïve. Others, absurd. One said it wasn't even science.

Because the idea she proposed wasn't just new – it was disobedient.

In their loop, evolution was a fight.

In hers, it was a fusion.

And that's what made it dangerous.

Not because it broke the model – but because it reframed the system the model was built to protect.

Margulis wasn't just challenging a theory.

She was interrupting a worldview.

A worldview that had become a habit. And a habit that had become invisible.

When a system gets stuck in the wrong loop, it doesn't look like dogma.

It looks like elegance.

It looks like consensus.

It looks like everyone agreeing on a script that no one remembers writing.

She didn't accuse. She didn't grandstand. She refined. She stayed. She re-entered the room.

Each time, her theory came back stronger. Not louder – cleaner.

She brought data. She brought language. She brought the loop.

Years passed. Textbooks didn't change. But biology did.

Because the mitochondria kept whispering. The data didn't go away.

And eventually, enough people pulled back the curtain for good.

Endosymbiosis is now foundational.

It's in your high school syllabus. It's in your cells.

And it got there not because Margulis won an argument –

but because she stayed in a system that told her to leave, and kept interpreting until the truth became undeniable.

That's the adaptive loop.

Not rebellion.

Recursion.

She didn't just offer a new answer.
She restructured what it meant to ask a better question.

THE DEEPER ROLE

She wasn't trying to be a rebel.

That's worth pausing on.

It's easy, in hindsight, to cast Lynn Margulis as an iconoclast. A lone voice. A disruptor of dogma.

But she didn't frame herself that way. She wasn't itching for revolution.

She just saw something others had missed – and stayed long enough to show why it mattered.

Her presence in science wasn't about provocation. It was about persistence.

She didn't just propose a new theory.

She kept interpreting, in public, under pressure – until the system adapted.

In a field that celebrated competition, she introduced cooperation.

In a system that preferred simplification, she insisted on complexity.

And in a culture trained to defend its beliefs, she made the radical move of retesting the mechanism.

Interpretive humility isn't soft. It's structural.

It's not the absence of belief – it's the habit of looking twice.

Of choosing, again, to ask: What if the first frame is wrong?

Of pulling back the curtain – not once, for drama, but again and again, until the picture beneath starts to hold.

Margulis didn't just change biology.

She demonstrated what thinking is.

Not the production of certainty.

But the willingness to revise your relationship to what you already believe.

That's why she matters here.

Not because she had an answer.

Because she refused to protect a bad one.

And in doing so, she became something more than a scientist.

She became a kind of immune system for her field.

Sensitive to error. Resistant to simplicity.

Committed to interpretation – even when the system rejected it.

You might have thought science moves forward by discovering new facts.

But sometimes, it moves forward by re-seeing old ones.

That's what Margulis did.
Not a leap. A return.
Not a revolution. A recursion.

And that's where the metaphor finally locks.

Dogma is the curtain.
It's what gets pulled across the frame when the first answer feels elegant enough.
Interpretation is the stage.
It's where we return – not to perform certainty, but to act inside uncertainty with care.
And if you're still watching from the front row –
this is your invitation to come backstage.

SILENT APPLAUSE

So what happened?

She won.

Not suddenly. Not loudly. Not even in the moment.
But gradually – through journals revised, textbooks rewritten, and generations of biologists who stopped saying "what if" and started saying "of course".
Endosymbiosis is now accepted science.
It's how we teach the origin of complex cells.
It's how we explain chloroplasts in plants, mitochondria in animals, and the quiet record of a billion-year partnership still running inside your body.
But this isn't just a story of vindication.
It's a model of something deeper.
Dogma is the curtain.
The idea we protect because it feels too elegant to question.
Interpretation is the stage.
The place where we test it – again, and again – until it earns its role.

That's what Margulis did.
She didn't walk out. She walked further in.
And in doing so, she helped us see that truth isn't what stands unchallenged.
It's what survives recursive attention.

This chapter opened with three habits:
Ditch the Dogma. Reverse the Obvious. Switch POV.

Margulis showed what it means to live all three.
To drop what doesn't fit.
To see again.
To stay curious when the system wants closure.

And now, if you're ready,
we can look not just at the theory she rewrote,
but at the deeper question she posed:

What else might be behind the curtain?

MILL: THE INTERPRETIVE CONTRACT

Being right doesn't make you good.
Disagreeing doesn't make you wise.
And having a different opinion isn't a superpower.

That's the bit people forget.

They confuse opposition with insight.
Agreement with weakness.
Certainty with strength.

But here's what John Stuart Mill understood – maybe better than anyone before
or since: Truth isn't a trophy. It's a team sport.
You might be right.
You might be wrong.
You might be partly right and partly blind.
But if you never test your view against another one – if you never let it stretch,
or bend, or try to hold under pressure –
then it isn't your view.
It's just a shield. Or a script. Or a costume you forgot you were wearing.
Mill called it out clearly:
"If you are right – you must engage, or your truth will rot.
If you are wrong – you must engage, or stay wrong.
And if you are partly right – you must engage, or remain partly blind."

That's not politics. That's epistemic health.
It's the loop that keeps knowledge from collapsing in on itself.

Because when Mill spoke about freedom, he wasn't being sentimental.
He was building a mechanism.
A defence system for truth – not against error, but against decay.

He knew what it felt like to live inside a system of overconfidence.
He'd been raised inside one. His father trained him in classical logic before he could play.
By his twenties, he had mastered the liberal canon – and lost the will to use it.
What saved him wasn't more knowledge.
It was the moment he realised that other minds – even imperfect ones – could give his own something to loop against.
It wasn't just about debate. It was about depth perception.
Most people see one view and stop.
Superadapters see more – and stay long enough to understand what each angle hides.
So what did Mill really give us?
Not just a warning against censorship.
Not just a defence of unpopular views.
He gave us a structure.
A social loop – a way to keep knowledge from congealing into certainty.

And he gave us language for the feeling we all sometimes have:
That maybe the other side isn't wrong.
Maybe they're holding a piece of the puzzle we can't yet see.

"It is often the case," he wrote, "that your views are only partially true.
And it is in general the case that other people's views are also only partially true.
So when disagreement arises, it may be that each of you holds a complementary partial grasp on the truth."
Which is why, Mill insisted, we must engage disagreement respectfully.
Not to win. But to see more.
That's the move.

Not defensiveness.
Not deference.
Expansion.

You might have thought disagreement was weakness.
You might have thought conviction was strength.
But Mill flipped that.

Disagreement is traction.
Conviction is just momentum.
What matters is whether your truth can loop against another – and get sharper in the process.
And this brings us back to the metaphor we've been living inside since Part A.
Because here's the thing:
Most people live on the front of the stage.
They speak from the spotlight. They follow the script.
They take the applause as proof.
And when disagreement shows up, they treat it like heckling.

But Mill walked backstage.
He saw the scaffolding. The trapdoors. The ropes and rigging that held the scene in place.
And instead of condemning the performance – he studied the system.
He wanted to understand how the theatre of belief was built.

That's what makes him one of us.
Not because he broke with convention.
But because he interpreted inside it – recursively, structurally, again and again.

You've probably seen it happen.

Two people argue. Each insists they're right. Neither learns anything.
Because the point wasn't to discover something new.
The point was to defend something old.

That's not conversation. That's fortification.

But Mill offers another way. A kind of interpretive contract:
If we engage in good faith –
If we treat disagreement as a lens, not a threat –
Then truth doesn't have to shout. It just has to hold.

And here's where it comes back to you.

You might not be on a debate stage.
You might not be writing treatises.
But you are – every day – deciding how to interpret what you see.
You're running loops of meaning, of motive, of memory.
And those loops shape how free you are to think, to act, to revise.

So let's be clear:

Being different isn't enough.
Being curious isn't enough.
What matters is whether your loop stays open.
Whether your view can expand under pressure.
Whether you're willing to ask: What have I missed?

Mill gave us the system for that.
Margulis showed us how it works under fire.
And now you're standing there – stage left –
looking at a curtain that just shifted.

What happens next isn't up to Mill.
Or Margulis. Or anyone else.

It's up to you.

THE ACTOR RETURNS TO THE STAGE

You've seen behind the curtain.

Margulis didn't just revise a theory – she revealed a deeper structure.
Mill didn't just defend freedom – he framed the loop that keeps truth
from ossifying.
And now it's you, standing at the edge of the stage, holding both insights
in hand.
So let's pause here.

Because the stage isn't false.
It isn't fake.
It's just unfinished – until you choose what happens next.

Sartre once wrote that existence precedes essence.

We act first. Then we assign meaning.
But that's only half the story.

You act. Then interpret.
But if you never reflect –
If you never return backstage –
You're trapped playing someone else's part.

Sartre reminded us:
Freedom means authorship.
And authorship begins with the loop.

It's not about rejecting roles.
It's about rewriting the script when the one you've been handed doesn't hold.

That's what superadapters do.
They live on the stage – but think from the wings.
They perform, yes – but they return between acts to reframe.
They loop.

So let's come back to the stories you've already met.

Danny Trejo, who dropped the mask of toughness when it stopped serving him.
Monica Lewinsky, who flipped the script and found herself inside a bigger frame.
Ocean Vuong, who shifted the voice of the story – and the story itself.

These weren't random awakenings.
They were acts of interpretation.
Each one of them looked again.
Each one of them pulled back the curtain.

And in doing so, they moved.
From trapped… to transcending.

So now we ask again – quietly, seriously, clearly:

What story are you in?
Who wrote it?
And what part might you be ready to rewrite?

HOW TO LIVE THE INTERPRET LOOP

HOW TO LIVE THE LOOP
From mind reading to mind opening

"By its nature, thinking twists and turns, drifts and meanders.
A hunter who followed a bee-line from a point of departure to a predetermined
destination would never catch prey."
– Tim Ingold

Now that we've had some time to sit down and think about it together... here's
how to live it.

This is where this rule becomes more than a pattern. It becomes a practice.
You've learned how superadapters interpret the world – how they see more
clearly, more flexibly, and more usefully. How they create a mental and emotional
third space. Now you're going to begin doing that yourself.

This next phase of the chapter is where the structure becomes yours. Not
theory. Not observation. But action. This is where interpretation becomes fluency.

We know from decades of cognitive science and behavioural research that
habits form through cue, routine, and reward. But meta-habits aren't just about
one behaviour repeated. They're about the system you use to shape all your
behaviours – the mental structure that lets you shift stance under pressure, again
and again.

Superadaptability is more than insight – it's a meta-habit. It's the kind of loop
that loops you back into clarity. You don't just learn a better way to think. You
learn how to re-enter and adjust your thinking under pressure. And once that
loop becomes familiar, it starts to run automatically – like a swing or a throw or
a sequence of cuts in a film.

So think of what comes next as both your practice – and your cue. These are
the moments that will become embedded. And the reward isn't just completion.
It's capacity. It's becoming someone who loops better, faster, smarter.

That's what this next section is for.

We're going to walk through the loop again – but this time, you'll see it in
motion. In real lives. In moments of choice. In systems under stress. You'll see
how the loop can fracture – and how it can be repaired. You'll get tools for your
own life, tests you can run, and language to help you reframe what comes next.

This isn't a pile of spare parts.

We've thought it through. Each piece you're about to encounter serves a specific function. The braided reflections show you how others have lived this loop. The Trapped vs Transcended table gives you a visual of what it looks like to stay stuck – or to move forward. And the Reboot sections show how to return to the loop again when things go wrong.

You're not being left alone in the garage with an engine in pieces.

You're being shown the inner workings of something that, once understood, becomes intuitive. You're being handed a user's guide to your own adaptive intelligence.

That's what metaplasticity is: the ability to change not just once, but better each time. The ability to upgrade your upgrades.

Because you're not just someone learning the loop. You're someone already becoming fluent in it. This is how an adaptive mind becomes a superadaptive one.

So let's keep going.

From here, you don't just understand the loop.

You live it.

DITCH → REVERSE → SWITCH

HOW THEY LIVED THEIR LOOP
Open brain. Open mind. Open loop.

We're returning to three of the figures you met earlier – because now you've seen the full interpret loop. And part of the promise of this book is not just to give you ten rules, but to show you how human minds adapt – and how superadaptive minds adapt better. This is where the loop begins to layer.

When we first introduced the interpret phase, we gave you three habits – each one lived by a different person. Each one showing a way that human beings make meaning under uncertainty. Now, with the Sitdown behind you, you've seen something deeper. You've seen that interpretation isn't about whether a frame is true or false. It's about whether it helps you move forward. Whether it expands your options. Whether it points toward the next best action.

Danny Trejo didn't rewrite his story.
Not at first. He just dropped the one that had stopped working.

The toughest guy in prison? That wasn't a truth. It was a part.
He'd learned it. Earned it. Played it so well it became real.
But it wasn't him – not fully. Not anymore.

What changed wasn't his strength. It was his sight.
He heard a story in a rehab meeting that cracked the surface of his own. And in that moment, he didn't just feel wrong. He felt off-script.

That's when the curtain moved.

Trejo teaches us what it means to ditch the dogma: Not to stop believing, but to stop defending a belief that no longer holds. He didn't need a new story. He needed room for a better one.

So he dropped his mask. And found the room to find himself.

That's meta-habit.
That's the loop.

Monica Lewinsky didn't escape her story.

She stepped deeper into it – until she found the mechanism underneath.

For a decade, she was a headline. A meme. A punchline. Not because of what she'd done, but because of what the culture needed her to be.

The story wasn't a lie. It was a trap loop.
And it played on repeat.

Until one day, she looked again.

She didn't find revenge. She found reframing.
What if the shame wasn't hers? What if the joke wasn't about her?
What if she'd been trapped not by action – but by interpretation?

Lewinsky teaches us what it means to reverse the obvious. Not only by flipping the script – but by reading the system that wrote it. She didn't speak louder. She read deeper.

That's meta-habit.
That's living the loop.

Ocean Vuong didn't change the story.
He changed the narrator.

Born in a refugee camp. Raised between war and poverty. He inherited a script sewn from silence and survival. But instead of memorising and regurgitait, he began to re-sequence it.

Together, these three don't just model change.

They model what it looks like to return to the loop when the script no longer serves.

One dropped the code.
One rewrote the frame.
One moved the lens.

Each pulled back their own curtain.

And each –
in their own way –
stepped onto a different stage.

We're not here to crown the most elegant narrative. Or the most accurate theory. There are infinite stories you could tell about the same pattern. The question is: which interpretation increases your chances of doing something that works?

That's what adaptive interpretation is. That's what superadaptability builds. A third space – not just between good and bad, but between noise and action. A loop of meaning that leaves you better positioned to face what's next.

The brain detectives you met in Rule 1 were scanning for meaning too – looping through salience, memory, and imagination to shape what comes next. That's all we're doing here.

One mind. One system. Many entries. Every time you reframe, rethink, or refocus – you're running the same interpret loop they were. And it doesn't stop here. The stories. The science. The inserts that follow. They're not extra. They're part of the pattern. Another pass through the system. Another way to learn what helps you see – and shape – what matters next.

That's what superadaptability is.
Not a straight line.
A loop you learn to live better – each time through.

TRUTH IN THE CLOUDS
Shaping ourselves by staring at the sky

When I was a child, I had a small box of cloud cards – index-sized, the kind you could fan out and hold in one hand. On each card was a type of cloud, its name, its shape, its secret. I remember lying on my back in the garden, holding one of those cards above me, lining up the printed clouds with the real ones drifting by.

I remember thinking about the person who first looked up and thought that.

It wouldn't have been the person whose name made it into the science books. They came much later. It would have been someone prehistoric – someone looking up not to categorize, but to survive. Someone looking for signs: rain, seasons, omens, shelter. Someone making sense of what they saw, because patterns mattered.

Long before the naming came the noticing.

Long before the theories came the seeing.

And while I was lying there, I realised I was doing something old. Something embedded. Staring at the sky, trying to shape the world by shaping my mind. I wasn't making up the clouds – but I was making something of them. I was practising the rhythm we all still live by: Look. Interpret. Act.

Again and again: Look. Interpret. Act.

Someone thought of flying, too, while lying back and staring at the sky. Perhaps the Wright brothers, perhaps someone long before them. People saw birds and wondered: Where do they come from? Where do they go? How do they do what we cannot? Have humans ever flown? Will we?

Some saw angels. Some saw messengers from Olympus. Some shaped their gods in the shape of flight.

And just as I was lying there, feeling my mind shift and stretch while watching the clouds, others have wondered what it is that happens when the mind changes. It would be two million years from the first mind to the first microscope capable of seeing what had changed. But the process was already happening. Even then, thoughts were beginning to join.

Wisps of insight. Sparks across synapses.

The earliest glimmers of what we now call synaptic synthesis.

And somehow, those clouds, those cards, those minds – they all joined the loop. Their sparks became patterns. Their patterns became stories. And now, their stories are part of mine. And this? Maybe now, it's part of yours.

Our minds have always wandered, always looped, always lived.

That's how it works.
That's how it always worked.
That's how it still works.
And when we pass it on, it becomes how we lead.

THREE WAYS TO READ MINDS
From cold to warm to hot

How we guess, how we project, and how we get it wrong.

You've felt it before. That strange jolt when someone says something about you –
something they shouldn't know – and it lands. "You're worried about someone,"
they say. Or, "There's a name starting with M." It's vague, but your brain wants
to believe. This is cold reading. The illusion of mind reading by someone who
knows how people work in general, and trusts you'll do the rest. No facts. Just
pattern, posture, possibility. They've started the loop, and you finish it.

Warm reading starts when they do have a few facts. A birth year. A place.
Something from a form you filled in. Something you let slip. That small bit of
context sharpens the guesswork. It feels more accurate, more intimate. But what's
really happening is they're tightening the loop – steering your reactions while
pretending to follow them. Warm reading feels like insight, but it's often just
inference dressed in your own words.

Hot reading is different. That's when the trick is no longer a trick. The
performer already knows the answer. They've searched your socials, interviewed
the person you came with, listened in through a mic. "Is someone here looking
for an Eleanor?" And you are. The illusion is complete – but it was never about
intuition. It was about control. They weren't reading you. They were playing you.

Even Arthur Conan Doyle – the creator of Sherlock Holmes – fell for it. He
believed in séances. He believed in fairy photographs. He believed in spiritualists
that his own fictional detective would have unmasked in moments. His friend
Houdini tried to wake him from it. He couldn't.

These aren't just tricks. They're interpretive loops. And sometimes the value
isn't just in what you're shown – It's in seeing what you need to move forward.

DETECT → INTERPRET → DECIDE

MOVING FROM TRAPPED TO TRANSCENDED
Interpretive pragmatism

Interpretation isn't about overthinking.
It's about seeing better – self, system, situation – and learning how to respond with more intelligence each time.
That's why superadapters loop.

They don't just ask "Am I right?"
They ask:
"What else could this mean?"
"Is this still helping me adapt?"
"What changed?"

This isn't scepticism for its own sake.
It's pattern recognition as a practice.

Most people get stuck not because they're wrong, but because they don't re-see what they've already interpreted.
They stop at the first frame.
They keep playing the part – even when the scene has changed.
But when you transcend?
You zoom in. You zoom out. You refocus.
And suddenly, the loop turns with you.

Interpretive pragmatism is what happens when you treat each new moment as a chance to refine your lens – not discard it.
You don't need to start over.
You don't need to doubt everything.

You just need to ask, again:
What am I seeing – and is it helping me move?

That's what this Rule trains.
Not the fear of being wrong.
The confidence to re-see well enough to move differently.

TRAPPED VS TRANSCENDED

	TRAPPED...	TRANSCEND...
Ditch the Dogma	You stick to what once worked – even when it no longer fits. You defend the frame instead of testing the pattern.	You zoom in. You let go of what no longer holds. You adapt the belief to match the world you're in now.
Reverse the Obvious	You take the dominant narrative at face value. You accept the role you were handed – even when it shrinks you.	You zoom out. You trace the message back to its machinery. You reframe the story until it restores perspective.
Switch POV	You mistake your viewpoint for the full picture. Other perspectives feel irrelevant – or threatening.	You rotate. You stand elsewhere. You let new angles show you the part you couldn't see before.

The good news is this:
Developing these habits isn't about thinking more, or waiting longer.
It's about interpreting better – so you can move past what's keeping you stuck, and accomplish what matters.

You don't have to get every interpretation right.
But you will benefit every time you get back into the loop.
Every time you shift, recalibrate, and go again.

Interpretation is how you move through change.
Not just by spotting the tree, or the forest – but by seeing the path.
And sometimes, by seeing the bear behind you, or the berries that might just keep you alive.

This is superadaptive interpretation:
How you respond not just to what happened – but to what it could mean next.

So:
Ditch the dogma that's keeping you from upgrading.
Reverse the first idea that came too quickly, just because it felt familiar.
Switch your perspective – jump into someone else's head, even for a second.

You're not looking for truth that never changes.
You're looking for insight that helps you decide what happens next.

That's what interpretation is for.

It helps you adapt.
It helps you upgrade.
It helps you rewrite the story – yours, and the one you live in.

That's how you move from being trapped to transcending your self, your system, your situation.

THE WRONG LOOPS
Three ways interpretation can trap you

You saw the signal. You made the guess. But interpretation is where things can still go wrong.

Interpretation isn't just about meaning. It's about positioning – placing yourself so the next move becomes possible. The wrong loop traps you not because you're inactive, but because your framing of the situation sends you down a path that's closed, rigid, or recursive. And you don't even realise you're stuck.

There are many ways interpretation can fail – but most of them follow one of three patterns.

HYPO is when you delay too long, gather too much, or keep revising the story without committing to one. You float between meanings. You wait for more evidence, a better explanation, the perfect frame. But interpretation is a living choice – it decays if postponed. You hold back from texting because you're still deciding how it'll be received. You keep rereading an application until the deadline passes. You spot trouble in a project, but wait for certainty before

168

raising it – and by then, the cost has multiplied. The loop didn't fail because you lacked intelligence. It failed because you never let it complete.

HYPER happens when you lock on too soon. You seize the first signal, treat it as truth, and move. You overinterpret a glance, a silence, a news headline. You decide the argument's already lost, so you escalate. You hear a noise in the engine and immediately replace the wrong part. You miss what's emerging because you're acting on what barely formed. Interpretation becomes reflex – fast, hard, self-confirming. But that's not reading the system. That's pinning it down. The faster the frame locks, the harder it is to revise. Interpretation needs speed – but also flex. Hyper loops trade foresight for pseudo momentum.

ANTI is a problem because it refuses to interpret at all. It claims the story is settled, or the pattern is permanent. It says: "This is what it means. End of." You assume your partner's silence is always avoidance. You treat a political shift as inevitable decline. You dismiss a different culture's habit as wrong, not different. There's no curiosity. No updating. No revision. Sometimes this comes from fatigue, sometimes from ideology. But the outcome is always the same: the loop collapses. You keep making the same mistake. Not because it works – but because you are locked into what doesn't.

Bad interpretation doesn't just create friction. It freezes movement. It locks the loop before it loops. But the best readers don't interpret to be right. They interpret to create space – for nuance, for repositioning, for the next move. The third move doesn't come from certainty. It comes from seeing there's still somewhere to go. And what the third eye notices gets wasted when the loop shuts early. You can't act on what your interpretation won't allow.

REAL-WORLD WRONG LOOPS
Don't be the idiot in the idiot plot.

The idiot plot is a story that only works because no one says the thing. Or checks the fact. Or asks the obvious question. Someone could have stopped it in two seconds. But no one does. So it keeps going. Farces run on this. So do many tragedies. What makes them "idiot plots" isn't stupidity. It's the absence of the one move that could have broken the loop. In real life, these plots don't stay on the page. They show up in systems, in cities, in leadership meetings and crisis plans. And they don't just cause drama. They cause drift. Delay. Collapse. These are real-world moments where the interpretation loop locked in – and the result

169

was failure. And often, what keeps the loop going is the absence of a third space – a place where interpretation can be questioned, reshaped, or allowed to evolve.

HYPO: The Signal That Waited Too Long

In the days after the 2011 tsunami struck Japan, Fukushima's engineers knew something was wrong. Cooling systems had failed. Radiation readings were erratic. Alarms sounded – but so did uncertainty. Officials hesitated. They double-checked. They sought clarity before action. Meaning was deferred until it could be confirmed, modeled, stabilised. But the loop moved faster than the model. By the time a full evacuation was ordered, the reactor core had already melted. It wasn't negligence. It wasn't denial. It was overstructured meaning-making – an interpretive loop that tried to be precise, when it needed to be adaptive. That's the cost of hypo-interpretation: not ignorance, but delay. Not missing the signal, but mistaking how long you have to understand it.

HYPER: The Stock That Became a Story

When Reddit's r/WallStreetBets pushed GameStop's stock into the stratosphere, it wasn't just a trade. It was a narrative. Hedge funds became villains. Retail traders became revolutionaries. Every price move was interpreted like prophecy. Dips weren't danger – they were tests of faith. Charts became gospel. Patterns were everywhere. Meaning became the movement. But in the rush to interpret, many forgot to ask: was the story still real? Hyper-interpretation doesn't mean you're wrong at first. It means you stop checking. The signal gets overwhelmed by what you want it to mean. That's what happened. Some exited rich. Most held too long. What looked like clarity was momentum disguised as truth.

ANTI: The Platform That Went Backwards

Facebook doesn't just host information. It shapes it. Its algorithms learn what triggers you – then feed it back, louder. Posts that provoke outrage, identity panic, or tribal certainty are elevated. Content that calms, questions, or complicates tends to vanish. The result is a loop that doesn't seek insight – it seeks intensity. The more you engage, the less you see outside your frame. Facebook's systems don't ignore interpretation. They invert it. They use your behavior to predict what version of the world will hold your attention longest – and show you that, regardless of truth. That's anti-interpretation: not failure, but design. A loop that knows what you'll believe and builds a mirror to match it.

COUNTER LOOPS

Interpretation doesn't need to be perfect. It needs to be useful. These habits exist to keep your meaning loops alive, adaptable, and pointed toward what helps. Each one creates the space that rigid thinking tries to close. They prevent the three failure patterns we've just seen – HYPO, HYPER, and ANTI – and they repair them, too. Because the real challenge isn't just getting meaning right. It's staying able to revise it, reopen it, and redirect it – before the rest of your system locks in.

Ditch the Dogma is about letting go of rigid assumptions. If it no longer fits, drop it and reframe. HYPO loops in interpretation happen when you hold on too tightly to a particular lens – even as the situation shifts. You don't adjust the frame. You bend the facts to fit the frame. And so interpretation slows, distorts, or stalls. This habit loosens your attachment to any one meaning model. It reminds you: it's not about finding the perfect answer – it's about using the one that fits right now. It encourages interpretive movement. And if the loop has already gone wrong – if you've been too slow, too stuck – this habit gives you a way back in. You ask: what am I still carrying that no longer helps? You name the dogma, the model, the mental burden – and you drop it. That act makes reframing feel like momentum, not failure. You haven't abandoned your beliefs. You've stopped dragging the ones that were holding you back. And in doing so, you restart the interpretation loop – with motion.

Reverse the Obvious means flipping what feels certain before it hardens. Hyper loops in interpretation happen when you move too fast, with too much confidence, on too little ground. You jump to conclusions based on surface cues or emotional familiarity. You treat recognition as understanding: I saw it – so I know it. I know it – so I must act. But meaning needs time to breathe. This habit forces a check: is this really what's happening? It disrupts narrative overreach and automatic inference. And it doesn't slow you down in a damaging way – it simply inserts one more beat. Enough to test the shape of the signal. Enough to ask: what if it means the opposite? What else might this be? If you've already committed too early, this habit gives you a way back in. It reopens the loop. It says: you're allowed to revise. Before the action locks in. Before you waste effort chasing the wrong pattern. Interpretation doesn't fail because you're unsure. It fails when you're too sure, too soon.

Switch POV invites you to deliberately adopt a different perspective – to disrupt bias and expand insight. ANTI loops happen when interpretation stalls, reverses, or disappears. You stick to one angle, one story, one lens – even when it's no longer helping. And meaning breaks down, not from conflict, but from lack of alternatives. This habit prevents failure by building your capacity to re-see before reaction or rigidity sets in. It makes interpretive expansion part of the loop – not an emergency fix. And it keeps your frame dynamic by borrowing others'. You ask: how would someone else view this? It doesn't have to be someone wise or even someone you like. It could be your best friend. A stranger. A fictional character. A rival. Anyone. The point is that by seeing through a different lens, you re-enter the loop with more options. If you've hit a dead end, Switch POV offers an angle you hadn't tried. A second perspective dissolves the block the first one built. And a third? That's where recursion starts. Not re-explaining – reorienting.

You're not expected to have perfect foresight – or perfect hindsight. Sometimes you'll interpret too little. Sometimes too fast. Sometimes in the wrong direction altogether. The lesson isn't to be perfect. The lesson is to notice when you're off-course – and adjust. That's what these habits do. They don't give you flawless aim. They help you adjust your trajectory as you go – like closing one eye to throw straighter, not because it's accurate, but because it's closer. The point isn't to be right from the start. It's to stay capable of reorienting – especially when you're wrong. You don't overcome overwhelm by getting everything right. You overcome it by building a loop you can live with – because it learns.

REBOOT THE LOOP
How three superadapters returned to the loop – and made it stronger

They didn't just interpret well once. They returned. Each of these superadapters – Lewinsky, Vuong, Trejo – showed us how powerful adaptive interpretation can be. But what matters just as much is what happened after. When they were tested again. When they had to make sense of the world all over – and didn't flinch. They came back to the loop. Not because it had the same answers, but because it was the only thing that kept moving. In what follows, we revisit them in a new light. This is what superadaptability looks like when the world closes in – and the only way out is recursive.

At 51, Monica Lewinsky said something she'd never said so directly before. Reflecting on her past in an interview, she didn't talk about shame or survival. She talked about structure. "Because of the power dynamics and the power differential, I never should have f***ing been in that position." This wasn't confession. It was clarity. After decades of navigating public perception, she reframed the conversation – not around herself, but around consent, coercion, and cultural complicity. She didn't just reverse the obvious framing of her own life. She reversed the public's – again. This was the loop, running stronger. She recognised the persistent flaw in how society still tells her story. She understood what hadn't shifted. And she acted – not to redeem the past, but to reset the terms. It's the purest recursive move: return, revise, reframe. Not for vindication. For change.

At 35, Ocean Vuong realised that his voice had changed. The expansive, poetic language he once used to build bridges to the past began to feel too large. Too padded. After his mother's death, he said: "My first book was about not being able to speak. The next one is about what I do with the silence that followed." He recognised that his old vocabulary no longer served the world he was living in. He understood that grief had changed his medium – not just his message. And instead of forcing the same voice, he changed his form. His essays became spare. His poems shorter. Each word sharper, more deliberate. He didn't abandon language. He switched its perspective. That's how he re-entered the loop: not by climbing back into the same pattern, but by trimming the signal. Not reinterpreting from the past, but recreating from what was left.

At 75, Danny Trejo saw a car flip onto its roof in Sylmar, California. A child was trapped inside, strapped in. He didn't hesitate. He crawled in through the wreckage – stiff joints and all – and tried to unbuckle the seat. A young woman crawled in from the other side. She freed the straps; Trejo pulled the child out. But he didn't stop there. He recognised the boy's panic – and drew on his work with special-needs kids. "We have to use our superpowers," he told the boy. "Say it: muscles!" They yelled together. They turned trauma into play. And afterward, Trejo said simply: "Everything good that has happened to me has happened as a direct result of helping someone else." That's the recursive move. He didn't just save a child. He looped again – without overthinking. He saw what was needed, understood what he could bring, and acted. This wasn't recovery. This was adaptive ascent. This is what superadaptability looks like when it becomes a way of life.

And what you'll have noticed is that Danny Trejo – and that young woman beside him – were just ordinary people, using their ability to adapt as their superpower. It's a reminder that the loop doesn't belong to heroes. It's our birthright. It belongs to anyone who chooses to reboot. Again. And again. And again.

RECOGNISE → UNDERSTAND → NECESSARY ACTION

REBOOT YOUR LOOP
Return to the stage. Reset the scene. Pick up the cue. It's your story to shape.

In life, as in theater, there are moments when, despite our best efforts, things don't go as planned. Maybe you've tried looping through your decisions, adjusting your approach, but still find yourself off-mark. You said your lines, hit your cues, followed the plan, yet somehow the scene fell flat. It's in these moments that rebooting your loop becomes essential. Rebooting isn't about scrapping everything and starting over; it's about stepping back, assessing what's not working, and re-entering with a fresh perspective.

Think of your journey through decisions and actions as a performance on stage. In this performance, RECOGNISE is akin to reading your script, understanding the lines, and knowing your cues. UNDERSTAND is like rehearsing, where you delve deeper into your role, grasping not just the words but the emotions and intentions behind them. NECESSARY ACTION is performing with conviction, where every word, every movement is deliberate and aligned with your purpose.

Sometimes, something in your performance isn't working. Perhaps you misread a cue from a fellow actor, or the scene partner didn't show up as expected. Maybe you rushed your lines before fully understanding them, or you performed before you were truly ready. These missteps can lead to a performance that feels out of sync, where the story you're trying to tell isn't resonating as it should.

Consider the spotlight effect, where the glare of the lights can make you hyper-aware of every move and word. This heightened self-consciousness can either paralyse you or sharpen your performance. The key is to use this awareness not to second-guess yourself but to refine your actions and align them more closely with your true intentions.

To reboot your loop effectively, ask yourself reflective questions that serve as notes from your director-self. What part of my day feels like a misread line, where the delivery didn't match the intention? What cues am I missing or misinterpreting in my interactions and decisions? What story am I rehearsing in my mind, and is it still relevant to the scene I find myself in? What truths am I ignoring backstage, the aspects of my situation that I haven't fully acknowledged or addressed?

These questions aren't mere self-help inquiries; they are tools for refining your performance, ensuring that every element of your role is aligned with your true intentions and the story you want to tell.

Consider the example of Sir John Gielgud, a renowned actor who, even in his later years, faced moments of uncertainty on stage. Forgetting his lines during his

175

last first night in the West End, he didn't panic or give up. Instead, he paused, took a prompt, and carried on with the scene. This moment of uncertainty became an opportunity to reset, to re-enter the scene with clarity and renewed purpose. It's a reminder that moments of hesitation or mistake aren't failures but chances to refine and improve your performance.

You don't need to start from scratch to reboot your loop. It's about re-entering the scene with the lights up, the mic live, and your lines truer than before. It's a process of continuous improvement, where each performance builds on the last, incorporating new insights and adjustments.

Rebooting your loop is about recognizing your cues with greater clarity, understanding your script with deeper insight, and acting with a purpose that resonates with your true intentions. It's how you turn a performance that feels off into one that captivates and inspires, not just for an audience but for yourself. In this ongoing performance of life, every scene is an opportunity to refine, adapt, and grow, ensuring that your story is one of purpose, resilience, and authenticity.

TRANSCEND THE LOOP

"The world is not what I think, but what I live through.
I am open to the world, I communicate with it, but I do not possess it."
– Maurice Merleau-Ponty, *The Visible and the Invisible*

THE VISIBLE AND THE INTERPRETED

A phenomenon is something that happens. But philosophically and psychologically – especially in the work of Maurice Merleau-Ponty – a phenomenon is more specific than that: it's something that happens and is noticed. It's something perceived – something that enters your loop of experience and begins to mean something.

That's why, in everyday language, we call something 'phenomenal' when it stands out. When it catches us. When we say a person is phenomenal, we mean: we saw them. They stood out from the background. They became visible.

But here's the twist: visibility isn't neutral. What we notice – and what we don't – is shaped by how we perceive. Not everything stands out to everyone. What's visible to one person is invisible to another. And what matters to one mind passes through another without trace.

The study of how perception and phenomenon change each other is called phenomenology, you will not be surprised to find.

That's where superadapters live. In that in-between. In the Third Eye. The third way. Where you don't just react to what's obvious – you detect what matters.

From Trejo's jailhouse to Vuong's poetry, from Lewinsky's re-emergence to Keynes's economic paradox – each of them interpreted the world differently. And in doing so, they changed what it meant. They didn't just read the world. They reframed it. And often, they reframed it for others, too.

That's why the next story doesn't begin with a concept. It begins with a presence. A woman who interpreted herself into existence – again and again. A woman who made perception visible. And voice... phenomenal.

UNSEEN ≠ UNSEEABLE
UNSAID ≠ UNTHINKABLE
UNFELT ≠ UNREAL

She didn't possess the world. But she spoke it into being.
She didn't just perceive – it was her voice that turned experience into phenomenon.
What she saw, what she lived, what she endured – she made visible.

Phenomenal, not because she was rare, but because she refused to stay hidden. And that's what comes next.

THE THIRD SPACE OF MAYA ANGELOU
How a phenomenal woman reframed her world

Maya Angelou was a phenomenon. Not just because of what she achieved, but because of how she stood – how she moved – how she chose to be seen.

She wrote the poem 'Phenomenal Woman' in 1978, but she had lived it long before. And when she performed it – hips tilted, smile precise, eyes knowing – you understood that this wasn't metaphor. It was memory. Interpretation in motion. She wasn't describing herself. She was 'framing' herself.

"It's in the reach of my arms..." she said. And we saw it. We saw 'her'. Not just a woman – but a woman who refused to shrink.

She was born Marguerite Johnson in 1928. At eight years old, she was raped by her mother's boyfriend. When he was released from jail and later killed, Maya believed that her words – her testimony – had caused his death. So she stopped speaking. For five years.

Her silence wasn't absence. It was meaning. A deep, recursive act of interpretation. If her words had power, she would withhold them. Protect the world from them. Or protect herself from the world.

But another phenomenal woman found her. Mrs. Bertha Flowers. A teacher who saw Maya's hunger for books – her capacity to memorise whole pages of text – and said: "These words have life when they are spoken."

Maya began to speak again. First by echo. Then with intent.
Then with rhythm.

She became a dancer. A calypso performer. A globe-trotting artist. She travelled through Ghana, Egypt, Europe, and back to the United States, where she worked with Malcolm X and Martin Luther King, Jr. She moved through grief again when both were assassinated. But she didn't collapse. She 're-entered' herself.

Another phenomenal woman had already shown her how. Her grandmother – who once, when denied treatment at a white dentist's office, brushed past the receptionist without a word and escorted young Maya in. Quiet dignity. Assertive presence. That, too, was interpretation.

Later, a friend and editor at Random House – Robert Loomis – challenged Maya to write her life, but as literature. She didn't flinch. She booked a hotel room, lay on the bed, wrote twelve pages a day, then cut them down to three.

The result: *I Know Why the Caged Bird Sings*. Seven more autobiographies followed. Ten books in her final decade. Film. Theatre. Speeches. Medals.

But the real achievement wasn't the output. It was the loop.

She turned trauma into silence. Silence into voice. Voice into presence. Presence into power.

She didn't just perform *Phenomenal Woman*. She became it.

Phenomenally.

THE LOOP MUST MOVE

Interpretation isn't the end of the loop.
It's the place where freedom returns.

Not just the freedom to label something – but the freedom to pause. To reframe. To notice what's changed. To see your self, your story, your system – and realise that none of it is fixed.

That's what the Third Space gives you.

And now?

Now you must choose.
Interpretation opens the path – but it does not walk it for you.

To be a superadapter is not just to detect and interpret.
It is to decide what to do next.

RECOGNISE → INTERPRET → **DECIDE**

FROM REFRAME TO DECISION

You've stepped through the curtain. You've seen how meaning can shift.
Now comes the moment where perception becomes motion.

Interpretation wasn't the end. It was the editing room – the space where you
slowed things down, examined each frame, chose a new lens. But decision is the
cut. It's what happens when you rethread the loop and hit play.

Think of it like adjusting frame rate. When you slow it down, the jerkiness fades.
The motion becomes smooth. You can see exactly what's happening – and what
needs to change.
Or like chronophotography. The horse in motion wasn't visible until it was
broken down – frame by frame. But once you could see it, you could animate it.
You could learn to move differently.

You've recognised a signal. You've interpreted it with more clarity and less drag.
Now comes the act of choosing – not just what to do, but what to understand
better. What to risk. What matters enough to move.

Because the Decide loop isn't just about action. It's about agency.

What you'll meet in Rule 3 is not a binary. It's a system for acting with awareness
– whether the choice is tiny or life-changing.

You are free to choose.
That freedom begins here.

Let's start the next movement.

RULE 3:
YOU ARE FREE TO CHOOSE

The one about deciding what's going to help you adapt

In situations of constraint, many defer or conform. Superadaptable people do something else: they choose. They reassert agency even when options are limited. Choice becomes the core act of transformation – starting with the internal stance: You decide what happens next.

This Rule is where freedom becomes action – not in theory, but in motion. Not when the path is clear, but when it isn't. Not when the system opens the door, but when you decide to move anyway.

This is the final move in the Recognise phase. You've seen the signal. You've questioned the story. Now comes the shift from awareness to decision.

What needs to change? Where do you begin? How do you move when you're not sure you can? These are the real questions superadapters face – not with certainty, but with a loop.

This Rule is about learning to live by hypothesis. To act, observe, adjust. To test the real in real time. And it's about doing that from a place of chosen stance, not reactive drift.

You'll see it in the lives of those who didn't wait for permission: a mother in Liberia who turned will into peace; a man who tested what fear taught him; a protestor who chose alignment over noise; and a mathematician who looped herself into orbit.

This isn't a call to be brave. It's a call to be recursive.

This is where agency begins – not with a guarantee, but with a move.

Let's begin.

What will you do with what is done to you? What will you do in a situation you didn't choose, with constraints you didn't design, and information you don't yet trust? This Rule begins in those moments – the fog, the fork, the shift in gravity when the path you're on begins to buckle.

This is where decision begins. Not in confidence or clarity, but in uncertainty. You don't decide because you know. You decide because you must move.

And what you choose isn't just the next step. It's the shape of the loop that follows. That's why this matters. The decisions you make – especially when you're tired, trapped, overloaded – don't just reveal your priorities. They reshape your future.

Most of us think of decisions as singular: yes or no, left or right. But superadapters know that decision is always recursive. Sometimes it's about knowing what to test. Sometimes it's knowing what to drop. Sometimes it's knowing that deciding not to decide is a move in itself – if you do it with intent.

You'll see it in every example that follows. The decision to try, to stop, to speak, to recalculate. None of them made the move from trapped to transcended in one leap. They chose their direction – provisionally, imperfectly – but they chose it on purpose.

And that's the loop you're entering now.

Is this a dead end? A ladder? A switchback? Do you need more data, more courage, more people at the table? Should you retreat or recalibrate? You don't need perfect foresight to begin. You need motion. You need a next step that doesn't shut down the system, but opens it further.

Decision is not a guarantee. It's a signal. And superadapters know how to read that signal while they're still moving.

This Rule won't give you a formula. It will give you the patterns – the ones that hold under pressure. The ones that free you to choose again. And the ones that leave you better positioned for what comes next.

That's what we mean by Decide.

Not just what happens after Detect and Interpret. But the moment you move forward – toward what you want to understand next.

So far, we've seen how choice isn't always what it seems.

Sometimes, we mistake the illusion of decision for the real thing.

We assume a loop is turning when in fact it's stuck – looping in place, or worse, looping backwards.

But real decision isn't just a click. It isn't a vote, or a gut feeling, or a freeze before the jump.

Real decision lives inside the Recognise phase of the RUN loop – just after you've detected what's happening, just after you've begun to interpret what it means.

It's what turns awareness into direction.

And direction isn't just motion. It's momentum with purpose.

This is the role of the Decide Loop.

Not to close the loop – but to move the loop forward.

And superadapters do it in four ways:

Decision Agency – They choose to move, even when nothing grants permission.

Decision Pragmatism – They move before certainty, with just enough clarity to start.

Decision Imagination – They picture where a move could lead, even when the future is foggy.

Decision Creativity – They invent a next step when none are obvious – widening the path ahead.

This is how superadapters decide – inside noise, inside pressure, inside ambiguity.

And that's what this next section will show you.

Not just decisions that worked.

But loops that turned.

THE DECIDE LOOP

HOW SUPERADAPTERS DECIDE
The loop that moves you forward.

Superadapters don't make better decisions because they're more confident.
They make better decisions because they're more recursive.

They don't panic when clarity is low.
They don't freeze when outcomes are uncertain.
They move forward by looping – through action, reflection, recalibration, and choice.

They don't wait to feel ready. They Build the Will.
They don't defend their guesses. They Test Them.
And they don't stay trapped inside someone else's system. They Free Their Mind.

At its core, the Decide Loop is about engagement.
Not blind commitment, not anxious delay – but the decision to enter the loop itself. The decision to test something, to take one step, to revise the frame as you go.

This isn't about willpower. It's about loop-power.

And superadapters know how to run it.
They don't just pick a path. They build energy. They clarify the stakes. They move. And then they move again – smarter, sharper, freer.

BUILD THE WILL → TEST YOUR GUESS → FREE YOUR MIND

That's the Decide Loop. And in the pages ahead, you'll see how it plays out – three real decisions, three different recursive arcs, one adaptive outcome.

But first, let's look at why most models of decision-making fail to recognise what superadapters do well.

I once visited a maze at a stately home – Chatsworth House, the largest private home in England and one of the filming locations for Pride and Prejudice.

One of those hedged-in, half-predictable puzzles where what looks like the right path often isn't.

Some routes led to dead ends.
Some you could only get through if you ducked down or turned sideways – paths that had become 'semi-official' through repeated use, even though they weren't really meant to be walked.

Someone in our group figured out the trick.
The move we had to make at each fork wasn't the obvious one.
It was the counter-intuitive one.

That's decision-making. Not in the abstract. In the world.

And it's why most models of decision get stuck.
They assume the goal is to choose well – to predict correctly and move fast.

Karl Friston's model is one version of that. He sees the brain as a prediction machine, built to minimise surprise. If you can map the future well enough, you reduce uncertainty. Fewer errors. Tighter loops. Better outcomes. In theory.

But if you collapse uncertainty too soon, you never learn what the system is really capable of.

Alison Gopnik offers a different view.
She studies children, curiosity, play – the idea that adaptive intelligence often comes from trying the path that doesn't look right yet. Exploration over optimisation. Pattern over prediction. Let the loop stay open just a little longer.

Superadapters don't reject one in favour of the other.
They learn when to tighten, and when to test.
They use both models – but recursively.
They don't ask, what's the best decision?
They ask, what's the system I'm in? What's the shape of this loop?
They detect signal. They interpret what matters.
Then they decide – not just what to do, but how to move through the system itself.
Because the best decision isn't always the one that looks neat.
It's the one that fits.

Fits you.
Fits the moment.
Fits the future you're building.

So what does that mean for you?

It means decision-making isn't just a point.
It isn't just a moment.
It's a loop.
It's a crux. A fork. A staging point for something else.

And being aware of that – even early on – changes how you move.
You'll see more of this rhythm in Rule 7.
But for now, remember: it's not just what you decide.
It's how you decide that shapes the result.

You don't need to be correct from the start.
You don't need to freeze at the crossroads – or run headlong into a train coming
the other way.
The most obvious path isn't always right.
The most obscure one isn't always better.

Superadapters learn the shape of the system by moving through it.
And then they ask: Is this a moment for action? Or is this a moment for space?

Sometimes you move.
Sometimes you re-enter.
Sometimes you choose not to act – but to learn more.

They know that decisive action doesn't always come from certainty.
It comes from looping well.

That's the Decide Loop.
It's not just about committing.
It's about updating what you know – and choosing what helps you move
forward.

And yes, you can train this.
You can build the will.

You can test your guess.
You can free your mind from loops that no longer serve you.

And it begins with a kind of decision you might not recognise right away.
Not the one that ticks the box.
But the one that opens the door.

THE THIRD MOVE
The move that changes your position – by creating adaptive advantage

You can detect the pattern.
You can interpret its meaning.
But still – you might not move.

Some people freeze at clarity.
Some leap without it.
But superadaptive people do something else.

They make the third move.

It's not always bold.
It's not always seen.
Sometimes it's the quiet pause that resets a cycle.
Sometimes it's a change of tone, a shift in footing, a question no one expected.
It's not about momentum – it's about position.

Because the right move doesn't just act.
It repositions you.

The third move draws on both vision and space.
From the third eye, it inherits relevance: what matters now?
From the third space, it inherits possibility: what else could this mean?
But here, in the move, it becomes kinetic.
Decision becomes trajectory.

Some will say "I had no choice."
But the third move exists to refute that.
It says: even when the frame looks fixed, there is a way to lean.
A third angle.

A third use.
A third door.

This is the adaptive habit of choosing again –
with more context, more cunning, more care.

Sometimes the third move simplifies.
Sometimes it multiplies.
Sometimes it sacrifices.
Sometimes it stalls – on purpose – to let the right decision catch up.

It's not about finishing the game.
It's about positioning for what comes next.

Without it, you may detect brilliantly.
Interpret wisely.
And still stay stuck.

Without the third move, your loop doesn't change – it just spins.

The third move is where the loop turns real.
It sets the angle for what understanding will be needed.
It defines the scope of what action will matter.
It doesn't just break the loop.
It shapes the one to come.

THE COWBOY LUNCH
It was just corned beef and baked beans.
Nothing special.
But his mother called it a cowboy lunch – and that made it magic.

That's what the third move looks like, sometimes.
Not a breakthrough. Not a bold leap.
Just a reframe. A redirection. A quiet unlocking.

Later, there were chores.
Sweeping the yard. Endless repetition.
So she said, "Pretend you're a spy. Make it a mission."
He wasn't sure he got better at sweeping –

but he got much better at telling stories.
That turned out to be useful.

Years on, the moves got bigger.
Turn a spare room into rent.
Turn a hedge-cutting job into holiday money.
Turn a working summer in a caravan into two months by the sea.
Turn a problem – no passport – into a road trip across Europe with two sons,
a speech, a stop in Bruges, and a memory for life.

The third move dissolves the trap.
It finds the angle.
It makes something more out of what seemed fixed.

And always, it works backwards and forward.
What can I see here?
What might this mean?
What's the move that gives me more moves?

Sometimes you plant the seed.
Sometimes you take the long way round.
Sometimes you say: We're having a cowboy lunch today.
And that changes everything.

HABIT 1: BUILD THE WILL

We've explored what adaptive decision really means. The third move isn't just what happens after you act – it's the move that turns awareness into advantage. For superadapters, the point of a decision isn't just to survive the moment. It's to position themselves more effectively for the next one.

That's the test. That's the habit. A good decision doesn't just change the outcome. It builds your capacity to choose.

That's where the Decide Loop begins – not with full clarity, not with full control, but with a move that feels barely possible in the moment, and becomes possible through the doing.

This is the first habit: Build the Will.

Superadapters don't wait to feel ready. They begin. They act in small, deliberate ways that make action easier next time. They learn that willpower isn't a trait – it's a trainable resource. It loops. It grows. Each time you choose under uncertainty, you increase your capacity to choose again. That's the goal: not just to act once, but to create the conditions for future adaptive action. To stretch the loop forward – through decision, into momentum.

This habit lives close to the ground. It shows up in the moment between collapse and motion. In the quiet between refusal and redirection. When the situation hasn't shifted, but something inside you starts to – that's where the habit begins.

Build the Will is not heroic. It's recursive. It's the smallest move that realigns the system – not because of what it changes around you, but because of what it strengthens within you. This habit isn't about certainty. It's about capacity. And it's forged in the exact moment most people hesitate.

Superadapters understand: willpower isn't stored. It's generated. And action under constraint becomes the engine of freedom. Even the tiniest movement, if it loops, becomes traction. A decision that feels like a test becomes, in time, the muscle that makes further decisions possible.

What does this look like?

It looks like someone who began not with a plan, but with a refusal. Someone who learned – through repeated, uncertain motion – how to push back against what seemed immovable. Someone whose every act didn't just meet the moment, but opened the next one.

Her name is Leymah Gbowee.

She was born in Liberia, a narrow sliver of coastal West Africa gripped by civil war and structural collapse. She didn't enter that history with power. She entered it as a young mother, carrying rice, working without pay, surviving daily erasure. But she began to move. Quietly, uncertainly, again and again. And each move did more than shift her position. It reinforced her ability to make the next one.

You're not looking for triumph. Or for an instant win. It's not the overnight success.

You're looking for the benefits of recursive effort: Small movements, followed by slightly larger ones. Willpower that loops. Agency that accrues.

Let's begin.

LEYMAH GBOWEE

In 2002, Liberia was still in pieces. The war had swallowed roads, homes, futures. Leymah Gbowee wasn't a strategist, or a saint. She was a social worker with children in Ghana, a phone that wouldn't stop ringing, and a body full of fatigue. She didn't start with peace. She started with no choice.

There was a point – long after the war had broken her country, and well before she'd begun to put anything back together – when she couldn't explain her life to herself. "I honestly don't know what I was thinking," she wrote later. "I saw no way forward."

The man she lived with had hit her before their first child. She stayed. Then came another child. And another. It wasn't willful – it was fog. A low, heavy grief that made ordinary motion feel impossible. "It's too hard to move," she thought. "I'll just stay here."

People told her to leave. A boss. A doctor. Friends. Her seventeen-year-old self, she believed, would never have stood for this. But the distance between belief and movement had grown too wide to cross.

Then her mother spoke. "If you decide to do something for yourself," she said, "I will tie my waist."

In Liberia, tying your waist is a vow of endurance. It means: I'll carry your burden with you. I'll stand behind you. But you must begin. That was the moment. The will didn't arrive fully formed. It came as a refusal to stay frozen.

"After so many months of retreat," Gbowee wrote, "it was a jolt into reality. I wasn't a seventeen-year-old girl anymore. I was a twenty-six-year-old woman. With children who depended on me."

She didn't act because she was brave. She acted to find her strength again.

She went home. She got help. She took a job with a trauma healing project – not because it would change everything, but because it gave her somewhere to begin.

The work was modest, but it shifted the shape of her days. "I wasn't sitting at home thinking about what a failure I was. I was doing something. And the more I did, the more I could do. The more I wanted to do. The more I saw needed to be done."

Something had started. The motion became rhythm. The rhythm became strength. And the strength began to return.

She made calls. She reached out to women – some she knew, some she didn't. They gathered in churchyards, side rooms, under trees. They sat on plastic chairs. They brought children. They brought silence. They brought grief. And they stayed.

They wore white. Not to be pure – but to be seen.

They didn't call it a movement. But it moved. They prayed on corners. They sang gospel. They read flyers aloud on the radio.

We are tired. We are tired of watching our children die. We are tired of the war. Women, wake up.

It wasn't spectacle. It was repetition. Not force. Pattern. Not rage. Pressure.

She didn't announce herself. She returned. Then returned again.

One day they stood on the field near the fish market where Leymah had played soccer as a girl. It was dusty. Wide open. No shelter from the sun. But every car in Monrovia passed that road. Including the president's.

At night she lay awake. Her brain on fire. "I knew something extraordinary had happened."

When she arrived at City Hall, she was the first one there. The president had banned public marches. His forces had tortured people for less. But she waited.

Then came the buses. Market women, professors, aid workers, mothers. One hundred. Five hundred. A thousand. She started to cry. Then she started to pray.

It could have been yes or no. But the rhythm held. And that morning, the will became visible.

By 2003, Leymah was standing outside the peace talks in Ghana. The women had been offered three seats inside. Instead, they sat outside. Then they didn't leave.

Dozens at first. Then hundreds. They sat in white. We are tired of war. We are tired of begging. We are not going home.

One day, she stood up. "Send for more," she said. "We're going inside."

She led them to the hallway. Two hundred women followed. They locked arms.

"No one leaves this room until peace is signed."

Security came. "Who's in charge?" She stood. "I am."

"I will strip naked," she warned.

In Liberia, that's a curse. A cultural rupture. Even soldiers back down.

Inside, a delegate picked up the mic. "The peace hall has been seized by General Leymah and her troops."

She hadn't asked for that name. She had earned it.

She hadn't claimed power. She had built it. Beat by beat. Choice by choice. From trauma to decision. From paralysis to presence.

The war didn't end that day. But that day, the end began.

BUILD THE WILL → TEST YOUR GUESS → FREE YOUR MIND

HABIT 2: TEST YOUR GUESS

You've just witnessed one of the most extraordinary examples of will ever built. Not as a personality trait. Not as a speech. But as a pattern – layered over time, beat by beat, in the face of everything that might have silenced someone else.

Leymah Gbowee didn't arrive with power. She built it. She built it out of will. Out of refusal. Out of solidarity. She was a general for peace.

She didn't shout to be heard. But she didn't stay silent either. She spoke. Then stood. Then returned. Until others followed. Until there was no denying what had been made – choice by choice, presence by presence.

If you've read this far, you might feel stirred. You might feel emotional. That's part of the point. But there's something else Leymah left for us.

At the end of her story, she echoes the voice of an old woman who once told her:

"Don't stop."

And her answer, spoken quietly but completely, was:

"I never will."

That wasn't just a personal promise. That was a call.

She didn't only show us what it means to build the will. She showed us what it looks like to find a third move.

Again and again in her journey, the binary was clear: stay or run. Endure or quit. Submit or retreat. And each time, she found another move. Sometimes quiet. Sometimes public. But always forward.

That's what the second habit is about.

Test Your Guess.
Make a provisional move.
Live by hypothesis.
Let the test shape the next move.
This isn't indecision. It's not doubt.
It's disciplined, pragmatic, productive, adaptive curiosity.

You don't just guess. You test.
You don't just assume. You observe.
And in doing so, you make space for something better to emerge.

This is how we refine our way forward – not by waiting for certainty, but by acting carefully and watching well.

It's how third moves appear.

When you test your way forward, you don't just find out whether you were right. You sometimes find out there was another option entirely – one you couldn't see until you moved.

You discover the alternative by stepping into the unknown on purpose.

Some decisions shift the world. Others shift a moment, a room, a thought. But the shape of the response – how you enter, how you adjust – follows the same structure.

You've already done this. You've already guessed, tried, adjusted. You've done it with people. With problems. With yourself.

Now we name it. We train it. We see how well we can do it.

Joe Kenda doesn't talk much about instinct. He talks about patterns. About lies. About things that don't add up.

He spent over two decades in the Colorado Springs Police Department, working homicide. He was assigned 387 cases. He solved 356 of them. That's a closure rate of 92 percent.

Not by guessing. By testing.

He didn't assume he was right. He assumed he was missing something. And so he built a method that let the truth come to him – not by force, but by friction. Each theory sharpened by challenge. Each reading tested against the smallest detail.

This wasn't about certainty. It was about discipline. A slow, recursive attention that refused to settle for the first explanation.

When he tells you how he worked, it's quiet. No drama. No flair.

Just this: Try it. Watch it. Adjust. Try again.

That's what Test Your Guess looks like in motion.

JOE KENDA
Joe Kenda didn't fall into homicide. He tested his way in.

He was working burglary. A murder came through that no one wanted – unsolvable, they said. But he took it. Went slow. Followed the contradictions. And solved it. Five days. No flair. Just recursive attention and a refusal to assume. That was how it started.

He didn't guess once. He built a way of working.

Kenda solved 356 cases. He didn't do it through instinct or brilliance. He did it by walking in with one idea, testing it, watching where it failed, and finding the next best angle from there.

That habit – test, observe, refine, repeat – was never more visible than in the Schmidtke case.

The victim was a young man, stabbed, dumped in a driveway. The scene was cleaned. Stories conflicted. Witnesses clammed up. Suspects denied everything. The blood trail stopped cold.

Kenda didn't push. He circled.

The mother of one suspect had washed her son's clothes. But not his shoes. A test. Not a certainty. But when lab results came back, blood was found in the stitching.

That was the first third move.

Then came a name – a kid he'd already spoken to. Kenda went back. This time the kid broke. He had lied. What happened wasn't a mystery anymore. It was a hunt.

In the interview room, Kenda played forgetful. "I don't even remember why you're here." The suspect relaxed. Smiled. "You said I stabbed him."

That was the second third move.

Nothing about this was linear. Each step was a guess that sharpened the next. Each interaction was a lens turned slightly to one side.

Trigger. Motive. Opportunity. But also: pressure, pattern, positioning. He didn't wait for certainty. He moved to find out.

The first theory broke something open. The second caught something moving. The third caught the truth.

Even now, years later, Kenda says: some of the cold ones still haunt him. A few have been solved by DNA. Some never will be. But his method never changed.

Try it. Watch it. Adjust. Try again.

He didn't just test his way into homicide. He tested his way through it.

BUILD THE WILL → **TEST YOUR GUESS** → FREE YOUR MIND

HABIT 3: FREE YOUR MIND

You might not work in homicide. But don't let that fool you – you're still making hard decisions every day.

It often starts with a feeling.
A suspicion you can't quite put into words.
Or a sense about how something could work better.
Something slightly off. Something unfinished.

But what you do next matters.
You shape it into something testable. You ask a question. You try a move. You watch what happens.

That's the real skill.
Not being sure. But being willing to act on a guess – and willing to change it when it doesn't hold.

You've done this. Everyone has.
It's how you figure out what's really going on with a friend who pulls away.
Or whether your child's vague excuse holds together.
Or whether your own story – the one you're telling yourself about why something isn't working – might need revisiting.

And it's not just about solving problems.
It's how you notice the moment to make a leap.
How you spot the path that's opening – before anyone else sees it.

You begin with a feeling.
You shape it into a hypothesis.
You act. You test. You revise.
And then you start again – only better.

Because the more you do this, the sharper your guesses become.
The more flexible your frame.
The more capable you are – not just of deciding, but of deciding well.

But testing your guess only works if your mind stays open.
That's the danger. Not being wrong – but deciding too soon, and closing the door before the truth arrives.

In policing, that can lead to miscarriages of justice – or to crimes that stay unsolved.
In life, it leads to missed opportunities, broken relationships, stuck futures.

You don't just lose the best option.
You can lose the right one.

That's why this third habit matters.

You have to free your mind.

Release the beliefs, rules, or inner limits that restrict your thinking – so you can see more, imagine better, and act beyond constraint.

Freeing your mind isn't about letting go of logic.
It's about letting go of the trap you didn't realise you were in.

The assumption that there are only two choices.
The internal rule that says you're not allowed to want more.
The belief that you're not the kind of person who does that kind of thing.

These aren't just thoughts. They're constraints.
And the longer they go unchallenged, the more they feel like truth.

But you've been here before.

You've been stuck inside a decision you didn't really make.
You've committed too early, just to quiet the noise.
Or chosen the story that felt safe – then built a cage around it.

And somewhere, quietly, a part of you knew: this isn't the full picture.

That's where the third habit begins – not with rebellion or defiance, but with a kind of gentle refusal.
A willingness to imagine that the constraint might not be real.
That there might be something else worth seeing.

We've just seen what it means to test your guess – to act with clarity even when the outcome is uncertain.

But what happens when the constraints are constant?
When the pressure isn't a moment, but a lifetime?

In this next story, you'll meet a man who, for decades, under oppression, fought for the freedom of others –
the freedom of the poor, the excluded, the overlooked.
The freedom of people who were white, Black, brown – every colour, every faith, every sexuality, every gender.

He was a free mind seeking the freedom of others.
And he believed that clarity wasn't loudness – it was discipline.

As you turn the page, you'll meet someone who urged us all to join him:
To cause good trouble in a troubled time.
To leave behind the false binaries of 'them' and 'us' –
And choose the third move of 'we'.

There is only us.

So how did that start?

BAYARD RUSTIN
They told him to move.
He didn't.

The bus was in the middle of Tennessee. It was 1942. The Army hadn't yet desegregated, and the state certainly hadn't. Rustin had paid for a ticket. A seat was free. He sat down. He was told to move to the back. He refused. He was beaten and arrested.

But the remarkable thing is not just that he said no. It's how he said no. His clarity was not spontaneous. It was recursive.

Bayard Rustin had been watching and thinking for years. He studied Black thought, pacifist theory, political structure. He'd listened to Gandhi, and studied with Quakers. He read W.E.B. Du Bois and Marx. He had trained himself to resist easy dualities: 'their rules vs my resistance', 'violence vs peace', 'assimilation vs revolution'. He didn't reject structure. He rejected bad structure – and carried better structures inside him.

That's what made him dangerous. That's what made him free.

Rustin did not define himself by what others denied him. He knew what it meant to be marginalised – as a Black man, as a pacifist, as a gay man – but he refused to frame his life in terms of denial. He made third moves. He framed new positions. He refused to reduce himself to what the headlines called him. His inner world remained intact, spacious, strategic.

He studied free minds, and became one.
He lived radical freedom – but never called it that.
His decisions were not reactions. They were models.

When others zigged toward respectability, he zagged toward influence. When the party punished him, he made alliances. When he wasn't allowed to lead in public, he designed the march in private. When others said "Don't make trouble," he said "What kind?"

He was not above compromise. He had critics. He made strategic errors. But his mind remained uncolonised. That was the difference. He made decisions as though he were already free.

That doesn't mean it didn't cost him. It did. He was harassed, blacklisted, jailed. He was written out of history. Sometimes he chose silence. But he never chose surrender.

He kept choosing what might still be possible – not what others had already decided he wasn't allowed to want.

He believed that those who are oppressed – regardless of race, gender, belief, or status – deserved the same release. And he didn't fight against their separation. He fought for their togetherness.

Where others saw fault lines, he saw connection.
Where others drew battle lines, he drew blueprints.

He was the strategic architect of the March on Washington.

The largest civil rights demonstration in American history – 250,000 people gathered at the Lincoln Memorial.

He organised it. He ran the operation. And he stayed in the shadows.

He was Martin Luther King Jr.'s chief strategist, but he never claimed the podium.

In pursuit of a better world, he took a third path – neither silence nor spotlight.

He urged others to join him. Not in protest, but in possibility.

It wasn't just a march.
It was an invitation.

Not a long walk to freedom for some.
A shared walk to freedom for all.

BUILD THE WILL → TEST YOUR GUESS → **FREE YOUR MIND**

INTRODUCING CHARLES UPHAM

Some people see power used to harm and choose to look away.
Charles Upham didn't.

He saw an oppressive regime gaining force.
He didn't like bullies. And he set out to stop them.

That was his decision. And he kept deciding – through every turn, every pressure, every trap.

What you're about to see is the full decision loop in motion:
Built from will, sharpened by guesswork, made free by mindset.

You'll see the third moves too – those hard-to-spot moments when he doesn't collapse, doesn't strike out, doesn't retreat –
but choose differently.

And as you read, remember this:
This isn't just a way to survive.
It's a way to decide.

Over time, it gets better. Smoother.
You'll see how it works.
And how you can use it – anywhere.

THE GUESS THAT DIDN'T WAIT

They say he didn't flinch.

But that's not true.

He flinched first.

So he could move faster.

The shell cracked a rock five feet to his left. The air shimmered with heat and dust and the smell of cordite. Others ducked, held, waited.

Upham adjusted his stance.

Not because he knew what would happen next.

But because he guessed – and tested.

That was his rhythm.

He didn't move recklessly. He moved recursively.

He wasn't always like this.

As a boy, he defied his father's path – law. He chose land, not legacy. The dirt told him more truth than the courtroom ever could.

In school, he challenged every drill. Asked questions the officers didn't like. He dropped to the bottom of the officer candidacy list. Didn't care.

"He wasn't disrespectful," one said. "Just certain he had a better read."

When war came, he volunteered immediately.

He didn't say much. But when the sergeant barked, Upham didn't stand taller. He tilted his head. Asked, "Why?"

They thought it was defiance. It was pattern recognition.

In the desert, he ran loops under fire.

He'd peek from behind cover. Not to shoot. To see. One shot. One angle. Then shift.

He wasn't testing aim. He was testing pattern logic – Where they were. How they moved. What they hadn't noticed yet.

"He didn't argue with danger. He tested it."

He got hit in the shoulder. Then the foot. He wrapped the wound, shifted weight, kept moving.

He looped again. And again.

In Crete, they told him to hold a hill. He guessed the flanking angle was off.

He repositioned without orders. His men lived. The flank didn't hold. His guess did.

He earned one Victoria Cross there. They said it was enough for three.

He didn't celebrate. He adjusted. He knew the next test would be harder.

Captured. Moved. Guarded. Watched.

And still – he tested.

He mapped routines. Checked how doors echoed. Faked weakness one week. Tried the gate the next.

Every escape attempt failed. But every failure tightened the loop.

He wasn't trying to win. He was trying to learn the shape of the cage.

When they said he must be superhuman, the people who knew him best said no.

He was just a man. But a man who could test his own limits until they became something more.

This is what the others missed. Upham didn't act with confidence. He acted with tested clarity.

Each guess ratcheted forward. Each move refined the next. He trusted his judgment because he tested it into existence.

"He knew anyone could be wrong. That's why he learned so fast."

Even in the quiet, he was running loops. Even when wounded, the system held.

He wasn't a hero because he stood tall. He was a hero because he bent just enough to see what others missed – and acted just fast enough to make it count.

He didn't flinch last.

He flinched first – so he could move second – and save third.

BUILD THE WILL → TEST YOUR GUESS → FREE YOUR MIND

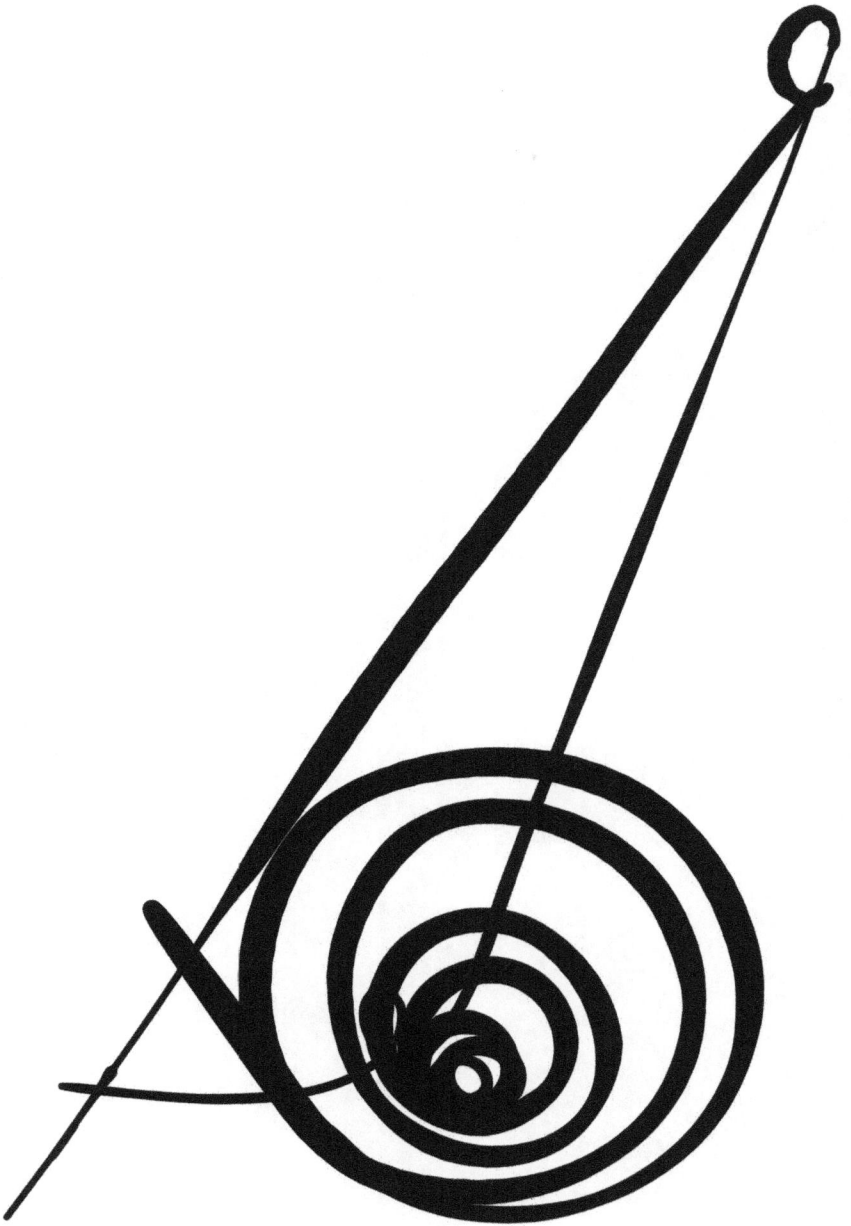

THE SITDOWN: THE ARC AND THE ORBIT

WHY WE SIT DOWN NOW

"If you see a campfire as just a fire, your imagination is very weak, for it is not a lifeless warmth, but a mysterious friend who came to visit you in the darkness of the forest and shared your food, dreams and life!"
— Mehmet Murat İldan

Before we stood to speak, we sat to think.
The sitdown is older than the sermon, older than the boardroom, older than the daily stand-up. It's one of our earliest tools – not for building the world, but for understanding it.

We sat together, around fires.
We made time, quite literally, by extending the day.
We slowed down, and looked out – and up.

In places like Orkney, just off the northern tip of Scotland, people once carved homes into the earth with hearths at the centre – stone circles you could sit around, not just cook on. These weren't just survival shelters. They were early living rooms. Places to pause, to compare ideas, to rehearse memories. Places to decide.

Later, we moved outward – to standing stones and henges, monuments aligned with solstices and stars. Not shelters, but instruments of alignment. Places to witness the arc.

This too was sitting. Not to rest – but to recalibrate.

And from that stillness, something began to loop.

Call it a prehistoric loop.
Call it a cognitive one.
Longer than instinct. Slower than reaction.
A rhythm that gave rise to language, memory, metaphor – and from those, the earliest maps and measures of time.

People looked up and saw not just light, but story:
animals, then monsters; humans, then gods.
The sky became a mirror.
And the mirror became a clock.

From patterns in the sky came patterns in the soil: planting seasons, lunar
calendars, navigational maps.
From those patterns came belief.
And from belief – meaning, direction, trajectory.
The arc began at the hearth.
But it pointed far beyond.
So why does the sitdown matter now?
Because something happens when we stop moving and start noticing.
Cognition doesn't shut down. It opens.
Stillness isn't a pause in the loop – it's the point of entry.

Studies show that firelight – and its modern equivalents: warmth, dimness,
quiet – shifts human conversation from task to meaning.
We move from logistics to story.
From management to imagination.

We slow down long enough for patterns to form – and minds to meet.
Whether we sit alone or with others, we access longer cognitive loops.
The ones that hold not just thoughts, but thought-about-thoughts.
The ones that allow memory to braid with possibility.

And when we sit with the minds of others – around fires, across tables, inside
books – we do something even more remarkable:
We share the loop.
We think together.
We loop upward.

To gaze outward and inward.
To hold perspective and possibility in the same hand.

This is why we sit down now.
To see where we are.
And where we're going next.

KATHERINE JOHNSON: FREEING HERSELF
Escape, velocity, friendship, and freedom

She said she didn't feel the racism.
She knew it was there.
But she didn't let it in.
Didn't let it *define* what was possible.
Didn't let it shrink her orbit.

Katherine Johnson lived her life like someone who knew she had a right to be free in every sense – not just physically, but cognitively. She re-ran the loops they gave her, corrected the flaws, and plotted her own trajectory, again and again, until it bent toward something more precise than protest: freedom with evidence.

You can feel it in the way she speaks about her work. Not just pride. Clarity. An absence of confusion. She knew what she was doing. She knew why it mattered. She was aware that the men at the front of the room were being guided by her numbers. She was aware that many didn't want her there. And she was aware that if she waited for permission, the mission might fail.

She had run the numbers, and the numbers said go.

We forget how real the consequences were.

You're not just miscalculating a budget. You're not just misjudging an outcome. You're plotting trajectories for people whose lives are in the balance. If your freedom to think is shackled, someone else's body might not return. And if your freedom to act is silenced, the whole mission may be delayed, sabotaged, or re-routed to match the slower curve of prejudice.

But Katherine Johnson ran her loops clean. Not perfectly. But with persistent, recursive integrity. She checked and rechecked the arc. She modelled the orbit. She did not guess. And when she saw something wrong, she said it. Again and again. And then they started to listen.

This wasn't abstract freedom.

This was mechanical. Orbital. Non-negotiable.

In the silence between launches, between calculations, between the world outside and the chalkboard inside, Johnson was exercising the most fundamental freedom we have: the freedom to keep thinking clearly when the system prefers you clouded.

That's the sitdown. That's what we're doing here. We're not just marvelling at a genius. We're not mythologising a moment. We're sitting down with someone who looped her way into freedom – who got out of constraint not because someone opened the door, but because she knew how to open the next move within her own mind.

And she did it again and again.

Freedom didn't mean the absence of constraint.

It meant the presence of recursive power.

When she joined the Space Task Group, there were no Black women there. When she joined NASA, she was still separated by bathrooms, by laws, by assumptions. And when she became the person astronauts trusted most, it was not because of a sudden cultural awakening. It was because her loop was undeniable.

She recognised the real problem – bad data, bad assumptions, bad trajectories.

She understood the system – its mechanics, its dynamics, its limits.

And then she took the necessary action – every single time – to adapt the system, correct the figures, and claim the right to be heard.

Recognition. Understanding. Necessary adaptation.

That's the loop.

And she didn't just run it once. She became *fluent* in it. That's the difference. She wasn't just doing the job. She was mastering the loop. And once you master the loop, you no longer need to prove that you deserve to be there. You become necessary.

The rocket doesn't launch without her.

The figures don't work without her.

The arc doesn't bend – toward justice, toward freedom, toward home – unless someone is willing to *calculate* it again.

She didn't ask to be a symbol.

But she became one.

Not because she wanted the spotlight.

Because she made the loop work, and that changed everything.

What can you learn from that? Everything.

You're not trapped in your role.

You're not limited by what others believe about you.

You are not subject to gravity if you can generate enough escape velocity.

You start inside the system. But the loop lets you move beyond it.

And if you run it well enough, if you get the figures right, if you keep going long enough – you start to bend the orbit itself.

There is a moment in orbital mechanics – after thrust, after liftoff, after atmospheric breach – when the arc must become an orbit. It's not guaranteed. It's calculated. The spacecraft must achieve the precise velocity to fall forever around the Earth rather than back into it. It must become free in motion – not free from gravity, but free within it.

This was the loop Katherine Johnson lived inside: constraint and movement, resistance and grace. Every equation she touched – Mercury, Apollo, the trajectory of Freedom 7 – reflected that balance. Her brilliance wasn't brute force. It was recursive clarity. She didn't escape Earth's pull; she turned it into a path. Freedom, for her, was not the absence of force – it was mastery within force. The loop held, and she looped it again.

But this is not a fairytale.

She was not born into orbit. She was born into the segregated American South in 1918. And let's be honest – her life, like the lives of so many women of colour, should have been a statistical footnote. She should not have made it to West Virginia State College at age 14. She should not have become one of the first three Black students to integrate the graduate school at West Virginia University. She should not have entered NACA. She should not have endured the double silence of segregation and sexism. And she should not, by the reckoning of history's gatekeepers, have been responsible for the safe re-entry of astronauts from space.

But she did. Because she looped. Hard.

We like to talk about freedom as if it is a gift. Katherine knew it was work. Work to free the mind, to build the will, to test the guess. She was, long before it became popular language, a master of the Decide Loop. She didn't just believe in freedom. She built it, choice by choice, correction by correction.

At Langley, where she worked in a segregated computing division, her first tests weren't mathematical – they were social. Would she be allowed in the briefing room? Would her name appear on the report? Would her calculations be checked or ignored? But she walked in anyway. "I have as much right as anyone," she said. And she wasn't bluffing.

Later, when John Glenn refused to trust the IBM machine's calculations for his orbital flight, he gave a simple instruction: "Get the girl to check the numbers." That girl was Katherine. She ran the figures by hand. And he wouldn't fly until she said they were good.

That's not just a story of competence. It's a story of recursive credibility. Of someone who had looped her mind so many times that when the stakes were sky-high, others knew her mind would hold.

Let's look at what she was really doing: seeing possible futures, modelling trajectories, predicting states and testing them against reality. She didn't just do the maths. She saw the world through the loop. Past, present, prediction, correction. And every time she ran that loop, her confidence got stronger – not because she was told she could do it, but because she saw that she had. Over and over again.

This is how self-efficacy is born – not in slogans, but in spirals. And Katherine had the most powerful kind: epistemic self-efficacy. The belief not just in your ability to act, but in your ability to know – to perceive and project with clarity inside complexity.

Most people freeze under uncertainty. She focused. "Everything is physics and math," she said. "It's either right or wrong." But that quote is often misunderstood. It wasn't arrogance – it was alignment. In a world that was constantly trying to confuse her, erase her, diminish her, she had found something clean, something that told the truth.

And so she kept returning to it. Each page of calculation was a loop. Not just numbers, but decisions. Is this right? What's the consequence? Can I trust this trajectory? She brought that loop not just to spaceflight, but to life. She raised three daughters while working full time. She navigated grief, discrimination, national attention, and decades of institutional blindness. And still, she returned to the math. Not because it was abstract – but because it revealed the possible.

YOU WANT TO BE FREE? LEARN TO LOOP

When we talk about Katherine Johnson now – when we hold up the Barbie doll, or the Presidential Medal of Freedom, or the lines of Hidden Figures – we're not just celebrating her outcome. We're recognising her operating system. She looped her way into history. With every recalculation, she made freedom real. Not just for her. For the men in the capsule. For the country. For the story.

And now – yes, for us.

Because if Katherine could do what she did, from where she began, then you are not trapped. You may be blocked. You may be underestimated. But the loop is available.

This is the Decide Loop.

Free the mind. Recognise what's distorting your view.

Build the will. Commit to acting even without guarantees.

Test the guess. Run the numbers. Run the situation. Run the loop.

And if the result isn't what you hoped? Loop again. Recalculate. That's what she did, again and again. From the segregated classroom to orbital re-entry. From obscurity to global legacy.

The arc was long. The orbit was precise. The freedom? Earned.

GETTING NOWHERE FAST

In spaceflight, it's called a Trajectory Correction Maneuver. A tiny adjustment – just a fraction of a degree – made after launch. It's almost nothing. A yaw correction so slight it barely registers.

But over time, over distance, that tiny angle becomes everything.

You miss the moon. You miss the planet. You miss Earth. You never come home.

It's the same with your own decisions. You don't feel the consequences straight away. Not when you agree to one more project, or say yes when you mean maybe, or let a habit bend just slightly off its purpose. You don't feel it when you stop checking your heading because you're too busy moving forward. But loops compound. And so does misalignment.

It's not just a poetic idea. It's geometry.

That's why the illusion of momentum is so dangerous. You can be getting nowhere – fast.

And if that wasn't enough to trap you, here comes Zeno.

Zeno's paradox says motion is impossible because, to get anywhere, you'd first have to get halfway. And before that, halfway to halfway. And so on. Infinity before arrival.

Of course, Zeno was wrong. But not entirely. Because in the mind of an overthinker, or a perfectionist, or someone trying to calculate their way to a safe life – Zeno lives. Every step is subdivided. Every possibility is another reason not to move.

That's where adaptive thinkers diverge.

They don't wait for the perfect launch window. They don't split the map until there's nothing left but gridlines. They move. They step. They loop. They act early, and correct in motion.

And sometimes they just run.

In 1983, Cliff Young entered the Westfield Sydney to Melbourne Ultramarathon. Five hundred and forty-four miles. He was 61. He wore overalls. He had no coach, no gear, no sleep strategy. He just kept going.

While the other runners rested, Cliff shuffled through the night. His gait was odd. His form was inefficient. But he didn't stop. And by the end, he wasn't just ahead – he had won by ten hours.

What did Cliff Young understand? That speed is not the only variable. That structure – your loop, your rhythm, your arc – is what determines arrival.

He didn't run the way you're supposed to. He ran the way that got him there.

So when Katherine Johnson calculated the re-entry path that brought astronauts safely home, and when Cliff Young shuffled through the dark while others slept, and when you decide whether to act now or wait for a cleaner moment – you are all engaging with the same question:

Are you shaping your arc, or just moving in one?

Because the danger isn't just being wrong. It's being wrong for a long time. It's missing the planet. It's drifting. It's getting nowhere, fast.

FINDING YOUR ORBIT, FREEING YOURSELF

You don't have to calculate your own re-entry angle by hand.
But you do have to live with the consequences of your arc.

That's the quiet truth of every decision you've made, and every one you're about to make. Most won't feel dramatic. They won't feel free. They'll feel like momentum. Like habit. Like someone else already mapped the course and all you're doing is continuing it. That's how most orbits feel from inside.

But that's not the whole truth. Because you are not a satellite. You are not locked. You are not drifting. You are, at every moment, capable of correction.

Not just movement. Trajectory.

Not just choice. Direction.

Not just action. Recalibration.

Katherine Johnson didn't just calculate the launch – she calculated the return. The tiny arc that would let the spacecraft re-enter the atmosphere without burning, skipping, or breaking apart. It was a matter of degrees. But degrees become everything, over time.

Cliff Young didn't know orbital mechanics. But he understood something else: if you keep going – if you build your own rhythm – you might not just finish the race. You might reset what's possible.

And Zeno? Zeno thought that motion was impossible because the journey could be infinitely subdivided. He couldn't see that what matters is not how far you have to go, but whether you go at all.

The same is true here.

This book isn't asking you to be certain. It's not asking you to know everything before you begin. It's asking if you're willing to loop. To step. To shape your own arc – knowing that even one better decision can change where you land.

Because in the end, it's a matter of what you do now.

Your loop isn't locked.
Your trajectory is still in motion.
And freedom, real freedom, starts when you recognise: the next step is yours.

THE RECOGNISE LOOP

You've already been recognising the loop. Every step so far – every signal spotted, every insight sharpened, every shift in attention – has been a form of detection. And as you've read, you've been interpreting: changing your frame, drawing connections, testing what things mean. But now we pause and go deeper. What follows is the spread that makes the invisible visible. This is the Recognise Loop. And these are its three functions: to Detect, to Interpret, and to Decide. You've seen them all, but now let's look at them working together.

DETECT

The thing about the way superadapters detect is that some of them under the hood have got greater raw material, raw capacity to detect patterns, and those type of things show up on IQ tests and other kinds of psychological tests.

A bit like the way that somebody can have better than 20/20 vision and see for a thousand yards. They've got that raw material and that is really helpful, or can be really helpful as raw material.

But what you're doing here is seeking to distinguish between what is relevant and irrelevant to you.

So, of course, what might threaten you, but also what could really help you – and that's an important and enduring difference.

One of the simplest, clearest discoveries in early radar work wasn't about faster processors or sharper screens.

It was about contrast.

During the Second World War, scientists noticed something blindingly obvious – in hindsight. The easier it was to see the dot – the one tiny signal that meant an aircraft was approaching – the more effective the operator became.

Increase the contrast, reduce the noise, and suddenly, the signal stood out.

Not because the operator got better. But because the system made it easier for the operator to be good.

That's what detection really is. Not noticing more, but noticing what matters – with less effort.

The superadapter doesn't just scan harder. They tune the contrast.

They adjust their inputs – what they let in, what they block, what gets foregrounded.

This is how cognitive load drops.

And once it drops, interpretation sharpens. Decision-making clears.

You can't loop when your screen is too grey.

But when you make the dot stand out – when you choose where to place the contrast – your loop begins to run itself.

Some people see more not because they're born better – but because they train their detectors.

Think of tetrachromats: women who see 100 million colors instead of one million. Or blind echolocators, like Daniel Kish, who use clicks to map the world by sound.

But this isn't just super-sense. It's super-selection.

Radar operators in war didn't watch everything. They learned to tune out the clutter and feel when the one wrong blip meant everything.

You can't detect everything. You don't need to.

You need to detect the right thing. At the right time. And loop before it's too late.

Detection only works when it feeds the loop.

Jump straight from signal to decision – without interpretation – and you risk reacting to ghosts, noise, or your own bias.

But wait too long in the interpretive fog, and the moment moves on without you.

The superadapter learns the difference.

Not by skipping steps, but by looping faster – without dropping frames.

Think of a no-look pass in football. It looks like magic. But it's just a well-trained loop. The detection happened earlier. The interpretation was baked in. The decision was already co-signed.

Detection sharpens interpretation. Interpretation refines detection. And when both are fast and clean – decision becomes action without hesitation.

INTERPRET

Again, there's a raw capacity for interpreting. You might have a greater range of fluidity in being able to come up with a wider range of conceivable uses for an object, a standard psychological test.

You might be able to, through knowledge, see the grays and the gradations, all of which is useful – spectrums within spectrums within spectrums.

Levels within levels within levels. Nuance. Pivot. Lever. And these are good because there are levels and levels and levels.

Interpretation isn't the hinge. It's the test.

Skip detection and jump straight to meaning, and you're not interpreting – you're pre-judging.

You're assigning sense before you've even seen clearly.

That's not recognition. That's projection.

But the opposite risk is just as dangerous: seeing without updating.

You detect the same signals you've always seen, and interpret them the way you always have.

But the world has shifted. The patterns have changed.

The chair you thought was there has been moved.

You still mean well.

But the stuffed toy no longer fits the child.

Interpretation isn't static. It's recursive.

It checks. It questions. It says: What if I'm wrong?

Superadapters keep this loop alive by testing their read against reality – early, gently, and often.

Some organisations do this with a 10th person – someone always tasked with arguing against the prevailing interpretation.

You can do the same.

You can ask: What else could this mean? What else could be happening?

When detection, interpretation, and decision feed each other – filtering, correcting, reinforcing – you don't just survive change.

You catch it while there's still time to adapt.

Prediction isn't a bonus feature of a smart brain.

It's the cost of staying alive.

Even an amoeba, in its way, predicts. It senses, shifts, drifts toward energy, away from harm. If its guesses about the world are wrong, it dies.

In that sense, all that persists is predictive.

But only just enough.

The human brain is vastly more complex – so the guesswork multiplies. What's safe? What's true? What's next? What matters?

But here's the catch: the brain doesn't wait. It doesn't ask.

It assumes. It simulates. It fills in the blanks.

That's the predictive brain. And it's not always right.

In fact, it's often impatient. Imprudent.

Which is why superadapters don't just predict.

They check their predictions.

They interrupt their assumptions. They loop early – before small errors grow into catastrophes.

The real advantage doesn't go to the person with the best guess.

It goes to the one who gets in the way of a bad guess – fast.

Your brain doesn't wait for reality – it predicts it.

Adaptive minds loop through expectation and error.

Not just reading. Re-reading. Re-looping. Re-guessing.

Until what was once opaque becomes pattern. Meaning. Move.

DECIDE

People can decide quicker.

But the brain can only hold so much at once.

So it's not about capacity. It's about how you hold it.

Picture a juggler. Most can keep three objects in the air. The world record for individual juggling is 11 balls – barely manageable even for seconds. But the real trick isn't how many items you juggle – it's how well you chunk them.

You can juggle three grapes. Or three bunches of grapes. Same number of throws. Totally different load.

Superadapters are master chunkers. They compress decision-sets. They reduce drag by grouping complexity into patterns, habits, and meaning. A well-formed concept is like a co-juggler – it catches things for you.

And when you learn how to extend your mind – through ideas, tools, or even teamwork – it's like handing one of those grapes to someone else who won't drop it.

This is what allows superadapters to make good decisions under pressure. Not by holding more raw data – but by holding the right data, the right way.

Most people think they see everything in high-definition. But your visual field is sharp only in a tiny central cone – roughly the size of a thumb at arm's length.

Everything else is blur and guesswork, patched in by memory and assumption.

So where you look matters. And what you choose to look at – that orients the loop.

Think of it like radar. The best operators don't just scan the sky. They know what to ignore. They track signals that don't make sense – and hold their attention there, just long enough to turn a blip into a pattern.

Parents do the same.

They'll hear a dozen crashes a day without flinching. But the silence that stretches just a little too long? That's the signal. That's the thing.

Adaptive decision-making isn't about vigilance. It's about pattern sensitivity. The skill is knowing which anomaly means it's time to move.

People love to talk about System 1 and System 2. But the brain isn't a switch with two speeds – it's a vast, recursive orchestra of subsystems, tuned to different tempos and tasks.

Some detect. Some model. Some decide. Some loop.

And the more adaptive you are, the more precisely you can tune them. Not faster or slower. Better.

Recent neuroscience has shown that even working memory isn't fixed – it restructures on the fly, layering chunks and priorities as needed. Cognitive control and metacognition aren't afterthoughts. They're real-time rewire points – loop points.

Superadapters don't just use their minds. They extend them.

They offload when it makes sense. They chunk and compress. They simulate others. They meta-monitor their own moves.

Adaptive minds don't just toggle between fast and slow. They train the fast to be smarter. And they make the slow faster – by reducing noise, narrowing focus, and learning when to decide.

In superadaptability, the real decision habit isn't reaction or reflection. It's recursive precision.

Studies have revealed something quietly astonishing: even the simple act of writing something down – an intention, a to-do, a question – lights up and strengthens the literal white-matter pathways that link memory, self-regulation, and forward planning.

These are not metaphorical bridges. They are physical threads, deep in the brain, braided from fat and fiber, connecting parts of you that weren't always in sync. They run like cables through a control room.

And every time you loop your mind back – track, reflect, revise – you thicken them. You wire for recursion.

It turns out those giant MRI scanners weren't just good for taking glossy pictures of the brain. They've helped us see the secret architecture of deliberate adaptation.

The real habit isn't speed. It's recursive precision.

Not 'choose fast', or 'choose slow' – but 'choose better, sooner, and with less drag next time'.

Superadapters don't just decide. They train their decision system. And then they decide how they decide.

Decision is the pivot, but it's not the prize.

It's the moment where detection and interpretation converge into movement.

But skip the loop, and your decision will be blind.

Linger too long upstream, and your moment will vanish.

Superadapters learn to move when it's time – not before, not after.

What looks like instinct is often looped intuition.

Like a fighter who counters before the punch is visible. Or the strategist who makes the move that opens three more.

They're not guessing. They're recognising. They're re-looping. They're already on the next beat.

This is the loop before the next loop. What you detect will shape what you understand. What you interpret will shift what seems possible. And what you decide, even silently, will shape the loops that follow. So before you move forward, look again. See again. Detect what others miss. Interpret with clarity and courage. Decide with forward motion in mind. That's how we recognise the loop. And that's how we start to live it.

HOW TO LIVE THE LOOP

You've run the loop now. You've recognised the moment, understood the system, taken the necessary action – at least once, in thought if not in the world. And you've seen how others do it under pressure, in public, or when it costs them something real.

But this next phase is different.

This isn't just about seeing the loop.
It's about 'living it'.

Not in theory. Not in hindsight. In the mess of your real day.

And the thing about living the loop is – it's not always obvious that you're doing it. The wrong loop tends to shout. It breaks something. It throws up sparks. But the right loop is quieter. It moves like breath, or rhythm. You only know you're inside it because your timing gets better. You start making decisions that don't just work – but feel aligned, somehow. They make sense in motion.

This isn't about instinct. And it's not about control. It's about familiarity. You start to recognise a shape. You feel your way through it, not because you're guessing, but because you've seen it before. Pattern fluency.

Sometimes it's in something simple. You start the email you've been putting off. You speak up instead of letting the moment pass. You notice yourself 'noticing', and you hold there, just long enough to ask: "Do I need to act now? Or understand more?" And either answer could be right. The point is – you're looping.

You don't leave the system. You re-enter it, better. That's what living the loop really means. You're not circling passively. You're adjusting. Sensing. Choosing.

There's a phrase Piaget used when studying how children develop object permanence – how they learn that things exist even when they can't be seen. First it's magic. Then it's pattern. Then it's self.

That's what this is. That's what you're learning. Not just to recognise the loop. But to recognise yourself in it.

Because when you do, the loop stops being something you run – and starts being something you reshape.

What's coming next isn't abstract. It's grounded. You'll see how superadapters live these patterns – not just once, but as practice. In public, in private, in tiny course corrections and third moves. You'll see failure. You'll see repair. You'll see how clarity happens – not all at once, but in rhythm.

This isn't a summary. And it's not a checklist.
This is the part where the loop becomes yours.

You've already started running it.
Now see how far it can take you.

HOW THEY LIVED THEIR LOOP
Using decisions to create third moves

You can't always see the third move from the start.

Sometimes it looks like the only choice is A or B. Sometimes it feels like you
already made your move – and it failed. Sometimes it doesn't even feel like a
choice. Just a fall. Or a freeze. Or an end.

But now, look again at the people we've just spent time with. Because
something happens when you step back – when you stop focusing on what
broke, and start looking at what came next. You see the moment they made a
different kind of decision. Not to fix the problem. Not to replay the past. But
to do something else. Something recursive. Something that shifts the whole
structure.

Gbowee's third move didn't come from comfort. It came from crisis. The peace
movement was already broken. She was burning out. Nothing was working. But
then came the shift – not just in action, but in vision. She moved beyond protest
into ignition. She launched a leap beyond what anyone thought possible. Not
alone – but with a logic that multiplied. She made space for others to act. And
that was the third move: not just to act – but to activate.

Kenda's third move came from collapse. He broke – not physically, but
emotionally. The job, the grief, the weight of memory – it all cracked open.
And out of that, he made a shift. Not back to work. Not into denial. He made
meaning. He reframed what had happened so it could help others. That was
the third move – not recovery, but repurposing. Not denying the pain, but
reassigning it. He didn't just come back. He rewrote the script.

Rustin's third move was quieter. It didn't come with a moment. It came with
a pattern. Pushed out. Pushed back. Then back in. But never by accident. He
learned to move with the structure – until he could influence it from angles no
one expected. He adapted not just himself – but the system. He used exclusion

as an insight. Invisibility as a strategy. He didn't wait for permission. He reshaped the field.

Each of them chose a third move. Not to be right. Not to be brave. But to be recursive. To re-enter the loop not at the start – but at the point where it could actually shift what came next.

And now, that same moment turns to you.

Not every third move is dramatic. Some are quieter. Some are slower. Some are closer to where you are right now.

What follows are three of them.

One is about the space before the decision – the room you didn't realise you were in. One is about the frame you carry into the moment – and how it shapes what you see. And one is about what it means to move at all – when even the idea of motion feels like a risk.

These aren't stories of perfect choices. They're stories of adaptive ones. Small, recursive, clarifying moves – just enough to open up the next one.

BUILD → TEST → OPEN

THE MIDDLE ROOM
Getting what you need, not what you want

We didn't mean to create it. The square at the centre of our house – the space between the kitchen, dining room, family room, and stairs – was never supposed to be anything. Just a hallway. A cut-through. But then came the moths. They got into the light-coloured carpet, which had always been a source of tension. People rushing in from the car, across the hessian mat, with muddy shoes. Every step carried risk. The wrong mark in the wrong place. The wrong apology. A small domestic loop of unintended friction.

When we pulled the carpet up, the friction vanished. And something else quietly emerged: a space without rules, without arguments, and without the same need to be resolved. We didn't replace the carpet. We laid down a rug, and the tension stopped. No big decision. No redesign. The room just revealed itself.

We started calling it the middle room. Not because it was really a room – it isn't – but because it started behaving like one. People paused there. Talked. Sat on the stairs. It became the breathing space between one thing and another. It didn't match the parquet or the tiles. It didn't need to. It worked.

Only later did I realise: life gives us these in-between places more often than we think. The city you move to for six months. The project you take on while looking for something else. The mattress on the floor after your first child is born. The middle room isn't the goal. But it's where the system stabilises long enough for everything else to keep going.

Anthropologists call this liminality – from the Latin limen, meaning threshold. Psychology sees it as a zone of heightened potential: a state of neither-here-nor-there where we're more open to change. In design, it's known as affordance – when something reveals new possibilities for action, often because you stop trying to force it into an old plan. Our brains do it too: predict, get surprised, update. Noticing what works, even when it wasn't what you expected, is the real shape of adaptability.

We didn't build the middle room. The system evolved it. All we did was notice.

Maybe you have a middle room too.

Even if you've never called it that.

Even if it's not a room.

YOU BE THE JUDGE
On loops of perception, power, and wiser choice

There's a column in a newspaper where people outsource their morals to the crowd. A stranger describes a petty domestic tension – an unplugged charger, a returned gift, a best friend who doesn't text back – and you, the reader, are invited to cast judgment. It's addictive.

I remember being immediately drawn to it. It was funny, sharp, and obviously designed to provoke a reaction. But what kept me coming back wasn't the outrage or agreement – it was the testing. Comparing my take with someone else's. Sharing it with family. Seeing where we aligned and where we didn't. It turned out to be a good way to learn how other people think – and, more interestingly, how I did.

If you paid attention, you could see something shift. A case that at first looked clear-cut would tilt under discussion. A power imbalance would emerge. A hidden habit. Something that made you reconsider your position – not to abandon it, but to refine it. To choose your stance more wisely.

Being judged is no small thing. And neither is judging. These are ancient acts. Adaptive, protective, sometimes cruel. They helped us stay alive – by reading faces, tones, tensions. They helped us spot deception. Decide whom to trust. But in social life, especially now, they loop faster than ever. Gaze, click, comment, verdict. We are watched while watching. We feel our posture shift when someone looks our way. We hesitate. We walk strangely. We perform a version of ourselves and then judge that, too.

The philosopher Sartre said that hell is other people. But what he really meant was: hell is being fixed in the gaze of another. Not seen, but reduced. Frozen in place. Judged not as becoming, but as finished.

I've walked funny under someone else's eyes. You probably have, too. Tripped over a curb or your own foot because you could feel someone watching. Sometimes that awareness makes you sharper. Sometimes it makes you smaller. I've often thought: some people have probably died of that – not metaphorically, but actually – stepping into traffic because their attention was pulled toward how they were being perceived.

To be judged is not neutral. It loops back through your nervous system. It changes how you move, how you speak, sometimes even how you think. That's why judgement, when it's constant, becomes a trap. But it's also why judgement, when it's conscious, can be a tool. Because the gaze can be internalised – and then examined. Because you can feel the loop forming – and then decide how far to let it spiral.

That's where choice enters. The heart of Rule 3: you are free to choose. Not just to act, but to interpret. Not just to perform, but to perceive. You don't have to adopt other people's conclusions. But you also don't have to reject them out of spite. You can listen. Learn. And then choose a position that's wiser, more adaptive – for yourself, your system, your situation.

Being a better judge isn't about always being right. It's about seeing more of the loop, more of the framing, more of what a moment might mean in motion. You can't escape judgement. You're in the loop. The question is: will you shape it, or let it shape you?

JUDGE → YOU → JUDGE

225

DEPENDS WHO'S DRIVING
Why a dead end isn't always the end

A cul-de-sac isn't the same for everyone.
If you've taken a wrong turn, it's a dead end.
If you're visiting friends, it's a welcome place to park.
If you live there, it's home.
If you're a child on a bike, it's a safe loop.
If you're slipping out after curfew, it might be the perfect escape.

The road hasn't changed. But what it means – that's entirely up to you.

The word cul-de-sac comes from French. It means 'bottom of the bag'. A street with one way in, no obvious way out. A loop that looks closed.

But that's the trick: a cul-de-sac isn't defined by its architecture. It's defined by the loop you're running when you hit it.

$$\text{DETECT} \rightarrow \text{DEAD END} \rightarrow \text{DECIDE}$$

A cul-de-sac feels like the end. That's its function, structurally.

But for the right person, at the right time, it can become something else. A shortcut. A moment of safety. A new way in.

The shape of the space hasn't changed.
Only the interpretation has.

In algorithm design, there's a concept called microchoices – tiny, iterative decisions made during a branching process. Even if you've hit a cul-de-sac, the way you respond at each turn – whether you pause, reverse, detour, or just wait – can completely change your trajectory.

Track them lightly – on paper, in your hand, or just in your head – and you start to notice patterns. A kind of soft map forms. Not of every option you could have taken, but of the real decisions that got you here.

Systems engineers sometimes call this your microchoice bounds: a way of measuring how far your current path has drifted from where you hoped to go, based on accumulated choices. In adaptive systems, those bounds adjust as the environment shifts – not to punish you, but to help you prune away unlikely routes, and focus on the paths still open.

This is the quiet power of small decisions. Even if you feel stuck, even if you're inside the loop that seems closed, these little moves still shape the outcome.

It's not the size of the decision that matters.
It's whether you remember that you're still choosing.

Cul-de-sacs are not just metaphors. They're real.

In ancient Egypt, dead-end streets were designed to limit intrusion and protect children – a deliberate constraint. In the British Isles, allowing cul-de-sacs required a change in the law. It was a campaign to rethink the usefulness of quiet ends.

Today, cities like Berkeley and Barcelona are adapting again – replacing through roads with loops, nodes, and permeable closures. Not to trap movement, but to reorient it.

The question is no longer How are we stuck here?

It's: What could we plant here?

SAPIENS → DECISIONS → SUPERSAPIENS

To call something a dead end is to declare the loop complete.
But a superadapter doesn't stop there.
They ask: could this be something else? Could it be the entrance to another system?
Could it be a node, not a wall?

Sometimes you don't need to reverse out.
You just need to walk.

Because the fence has a gate.
And the back garden isn't a barrier – it's a passage.
And what felt like the bottom of the bag might be the opening scene of something new.

What matters most isn't where the road stops.
It's whether you believe that's the end.

FROM TRAPPED TO TRANSCENDED
How superadaptive decisions change you – and the world around you

Most people think getting unstuck means pushing harder. But real superadapters move differently.

They Build the Will – not by forcing themselves, but by expanding their capacity to choose. Each act of will opens new paths that once seemed impossible.

They Test the Guess – not by seeking perfect plans, but by treating every action as an experiment. Each test, each iteration, brings sharper insight and better results.

They Free the Mind – not with empty slogans, but by questioning old limits. Each shift in perspective reveals options that were invisible before.

Together, these habits form the third move. They're not just about feeling better. They're about changing what's possible – inside you, and around you.

You're not stuck. You're at the start of something bigger. Run the loop again, and watch the world respond.

The third move is where things begin to change – not just in your mind, but in your situation, your system, your world. That's the moment where you shift from coping to adapting, from analysis to traction. From being stuck, to discovering what's next. Each habit in the table is one part of that movement. Build the Will gives you the strength to step. Test the Guess helps you learn what works. Free the Mind opens the space to start again.

Together, they create a way out of constraint. And not just emotional constraint, but practical, structural stuckness: the job you can't leave, the pattern you keep repeating, the identity that no longer fits. These are not just concepts. They are tools – recursive tools. They are parts of the full RUN Loop you've already been learning: Recognise → Understand → Necessary Action. This is Step 3. And these are the decisions that do something. They ratchet. They hold. They lift.

You've seen people do this: Upham, Rustin, Kender, Johnson. These weren't clean breaks. They were practiced loops. Most of them began in constraints that didn't look adaptive at all. But they kept looking. They kept trying. They made a third move – and that made the fourth and fifth possible.

Of course, even well-run loops can go wrong. That's what we'll look at next. The habits that don't just fail – but mislead. The decisions that seem adaptive – but keep you stuck. The wrong loops. Because seeing how they go wrong will help you spot them faster. And fix them earlier. That's the value of this page – not just to reflect, but to act from.

	WHEN YOU'RE TRAPPED...	**WHEN YOU TRANSCEND...**
Build the Will	You filter out possibilities before you even begin. Not because they're impossible – but because you've silently decided you won't follow through. The loop never starts because you've convinced yourself you're not strong enough to hold it.	You build internal permission. You act not because it's easy, but because you've grown strong enough to carry the decision. This is how new paths become viable – and why options you'd ruled out start to reappear.
Test Your Guess	You try to know everything before moving – or you act without feedback. Either way, you stall growth. You repeat what worked last time or freeze in search of the perfect move. Nothing improves because nothing iterates.	You use action as evolution. You try, test, learn, revise. Each move generates data. Each insight lifts the loop. Reality begins to adjust in response to what you now understand.
Free Your Mind	You inherit limits disguised as truths. You obey frameworks that once kept you safe – but now keep you small. You filter out ideas, options, and futures that don't match the past you survived.	You loosen what no longer serves. You examine the lens, not just the view. You shift the frame – and open access to choices that were never on the map. Freedom begins where the old belief ends – and possibilities return that had once disappeared.

THE WRONG LOOPS

Decisions fail for what seem like a hundred different reasons. The pressure. The timing. The people involved. Sometimes it's emotion. Sometimes it's ego. Sometimes it's just the wrong day.

But when you look more closely – especially inside adaptive loops – three patterns show up again and again. Three ways the loop doesn't just stall or misfire, but shuts down its own future. Three ways that the third move – the one that makes the system better – never gets the chance to exist.

You've already seen these patterns. In workplaces. In relationships. In yourself. Now we name them.

HYPO is where the decision is too little, too slow, or too late. People hesitate. They delay. Not always because they're lazy – but because the stakes feel too high. Or because they're distracted. Or because they're waiting for the ideal moment. The perfect information. The full map. Or because they think they have more time – but they don't. Or because they're afraid. Or overconfident. You wait so long to decide that the decision makes itself. But waiting isn't always wisdom. Sometimes it's just the slow death of possibility. And what could have been a first step toward something better, never gets to happen at all.

HYPER is where the decision is made too fast, too soon, or too strongly. It feels like clarity – but it's not. It's momentum mistaken for rhythm. It's confidence without calibration. You move before the loop has formed. You commit before the pattern has revealed itself. And once you've gone all-in, there's nothing left to adjust. The trouble isn't speed – it's speed that doesn't suit the situation. Urgency overwhelms sense. The pressure feels real, so the decision gets forced. You jump to the first conclusion and call it done. But this isn't a single choice. It's a chain. And you've just locked the rest of it shut.

It shows up when people act without listening. When a plan is rolled out before the problem is understood. When the energy of starting becomes a substitute for the patience of learning. When action is confused with adaptation. The system lurches forward – but it doesn't know where it's going.

Do you find yourself deciding before the question is clear? Are you rushing because stillness feels wrong? Have you committed to more than this moment actually demands?

And what could have become a better move – something held, refined, or redirected – is already gone. You've declared too much, too soon. There's no room left to think again.

ANTI is where the decision may be strong – but wrong. It's committed to the wrong model, the wrong problem, the wrong pattern of response. It loops hard on what it already believes, and won't let new information in. The decision gets made not from data, but from position. From reputation. From sunk cost. And once it's made, everything that follows gets bent to fit it. The loop isn't frozen or rushing – it's rotating in place. Loud. Confident. And completely misaligned.

It shows up when leaders double down after they've already been proven wrong. When a strategy is protected because of who made it. When evidence is ignored because changing course would cost face. When dissent is treated as disloyalty. It's the loop that refuses to evolve – because it confuses adaptation with weakness.

Do you find yourself defending a decision long after the facts have shifted? Are you locked into a plan because it was yours? Have you built so much around the original choice that walking it back now feels impossible?

And what might have been the move that changed everything – gets buried under the need to appear right. The loop keeps running, but it stops going anywhere.

Each of these loops goes wrong in its own way. Too slow. Too fast. Or in the wrong direction. And the result isn't always identical – but the consequence is the same: the person doesn't adapt. The system doesn't adapt. The situation can't.

The decision uses up the time. The space. The resources. Or it fails to create what the next decision would have needed. There's a critical path to adaptation, and a good decision doesn't just land clean – it keeps that path open.

A good loop makes a choice. But it also keeps something alive: The chance to revise. To realign. To adjust. To focus. To try again – not from scratch, but from a better position.

That's what wrong loops cut off. That's why the third move disappears. And not just the third – the fourth, the fifth, the ones that might have mattered more. You stay trapped in the existing constraint.

Sometimes a decision doesn't fail because of what it chose – but because it didn't position you to choose again.

REAL-WORLD WRONG LOOPS
I wouldn't start here if I were you.

Some people never write down directions – because they're sure they'll remember. Others see a beautiful place online, take a screenshot, and assume their phone will do the rest. Some trust the tourist map completely – long after they've led the whole family off the beaten path and into a forest of thorn bushes. Each of them thinks they've made a decision. They haven't. They've chosen a direction – but not a path.

This is how decision loops break: sometimes from hesitation, sometimes from overconfidence. From thinking the first move was enough. Or the second. From refusing to adjust. These are real-world moments when a decision is declared, but never developed. No pivot. No test. No third move. They didn't fail to choose. They failed to choose well.

HYPO really caused problems when the U.S. government tried to pass comprehensive climate legislation in 2009 – and missed its only viable window. There was a strong policy proposal. A friendly president. A cooperative Congress. And months of internal optimism. But the loop stalled. Key players hesitated. Debates dragged on. Risk-averse advisors urged delay. By the time the bill reached the floor, the midterm election cycle had already started. Momentum vanished. The bill died quietly – and the opportunity did not come again. The decision wasn't bad. It was just too slow. And what could have led to generational progress ended in a non-move that changed nothing.

HYPER did its damage when a global shipping bottleneck turned into a full-scale logistics crisis after the Ever Given container ship got stuck in the Suez Canal in 2021. There were early signs of trouble – stacked ports, poor weather, reduced oversight. But when the ship lodged sideways in the canal, everything accelerated. Teams worked furiously on assumptions that didn't hold. Strategies changed hour by hour. Public urgency drove the timeline faster than real coordination could form. Every decision was made under headline pressure. And for a week, global supply chains ran on speed instead of sense. What should have been a tightly sequenced salvage became a frantic improv session. Urgency without understanding flooded the system. The loop ran too fast to work.

ANTI locked the loop in place when rescuers tried to save John Edward Jones from Nutty Putty Cave in 2009. He was stuck head-down in a narrow shaft – completely immobilised. The team on site made decisions quickly and confidently. But the underlying assumptions were wrong. They believed the rock wall could hold a pulley system. They believed rescue time was longer than it was. They believed the situation was stable enough to wait for more equipment. None of that was true. When the rock wall collapsed, all options disappeared. Every move after that was constrained by the first, uncorrected decision. It wasn't the lack of action that failed him – it was the structure of decisions that couldn't be reversed. The loop wasn't paused. It was pushed – until no correction was possible.

Each of these failures began with motion. But motion alone doesn't make a loop adaptive. Every one of them lost the space that a third move would have needed.

COUNTER LOOPS
How adaptive habits undo the idiot plot.

The habits that give you back the third move.

These are the habits that don't just move the loop forward – they put it back on track. Each one undoes a specific failure pattern. Each one gives the system another chance. Together, they're how you stop an idiot plot from becoming a tragedy – and how you recover the third move before it disappears.

BUILD THE WILL prevents HYPO loops by giving the system the one thing it's missing: the ability to start. Not the permission to act. Not the perfect plan. But the internal muscle to move – without waiting to feel fully ready. Things often go too slow, too careful, too gentle – because no one has built up enough agency to risk a real step. And without that first act of fortitude, the application isn't filled in. The apology isn't made. The deadline gets missed. Even when the decision has technically been made – there's no follow-through. No motion. The loop stalls on the runway. So you trains that lift. It gives you the structure to say: this is what I'll do next. And then do it. Not because you're sure, but because you've decided. That's the difference between being free to choose – and actually choosing.

TEST THE GUESS prevents HYPER loops by turning action into experiment. It breaks the pattern of going too fast, too soon, too hard – by refusing to treat any decision as final. Hyper-decisions collapse the loop because they overcommit before understanding. Test the Guess puts it right by inserting friction – not to block motion, but to structure it. You check before you go all in. You ask what would happen if this didn't work. You take the next step as a test – not a declaration. And you build decisions that are modular enough to return from.

233

This isn't about hesitation. It's about calibration. If you go left, how does the system respond? If you say it this way, does it land? The guess isn't always verbal. It's physical, relational, strategic. But it always holds a question: "Did it work?" You can still move fast. But now you're watching the loop. And that's what gives you the third move back.

OPEN YOUR MIND prevents the problems caused by ANTI loops by refusing to lock the system too early. It increases the room for revision – not by being vague, but by staying structurally open. Where ANTI collapses and constrains, Open Your Mind keeps the frame flexible. It doesn't treat the first answer as the final one. It doesn't restrict the channel so tightly that only one kind of message can get through. ANTI loops say: "It can't be done because it's never been done." Or: "There's no choice." Open Your Mind answers: "There's always a choice – and I can think of seven straight off." It builds the habit of listening for what hasn't been said yet. It holds the model lightly – just enough to see what's happening, not enough to believe it's the only way the world can be. It checks for conditions that don't quite fit. It flips the map. It moves the frame. It stays open to contradiction – but also to supersession. The new idea. The better product. The pattern that cuts across the plan and offers something stronger. This isn't indecision. It's adaptive doubt – and adaptive imagination. You don't just ask what might be wrong. You ask what might be better. And that's what brings back the third move: Because your mind is open enough, the page blank enough, and the options wide enough – for you to see the next move when it arrives – and choose it.

And there you have it. Decision loops tend to go wrong in three main ways. You've seen them in your life. You've seen them in the lives of others. And now you've seen exactly how to prevent them – and how to put them right. Each failure has a habit that solves it. That's your box of tricks – to repair what goes wrong in the box of tricks.

But as you already know, the story doesn't end there. Because what goes wrong is sometimes broader than a loop type. And what's needed is sometimes more than a counter. You need to know when a loop has drifted. You need to know how to bring it back.

And in both cases, you'll return to the one loop that powers them all. The RUN loop. Which is exactly what we'll do next – first in the lives of our examples, and then in your own. To make sure that when the moment comes – whether through ambition or necessity – you'll know how to turn to your fractal friend.

BUILD → TEST → FREE

REBOOTING THEIR LOOP
Three ways real people re-entered the system – and reshaped what came next.

In April 2008, Leymah Gbowee reached a point no loop could carry her through – not without breaking.

It was her daughter's fourteenth birthday. A celebration. A room full of people. Fourteen glasses of wine. She passed out the next day. Ulcers. Exhaustion. Collapse. Her children gathered around her, frightened. And in their faces, she saw not just worry – but accumulation. After all they had endured, this could not be the final loss.

This wasn't a failure of will. It was a failure of system. Gbowee had survived on momentum for years – holding communities together, holding herself together. But at some point, the loops she had run so fluently – Detect, Interpret, Decide – began running her. She had no distance left. No meta-view.

And that's when she rebooted.

She didn't just stop drinking. She recognised the state she was in – burnout, disconnection, recursive overload. She understood what was driving it: war trauma, separation, spiritual fatigue, the weight of being seen as the engine of hope. And she acted – not through heroics, but through humility. A doctor's visit. A confession. A new rule: "I still don't sleep easily, but I don't drink anymore."

This was the RUN loop in motion – unlabeled, but alive. She didn't need the language. She lived the recursion.

And what followed was not a return to previous form. It was a lift. Her decisions gained depth. Her anger found direction. Her work grew more strategic. Her advocacy more layered. She didn't just loop back – she looped 'forward', into something larger.

That's a real reboot. The kind that comes not from breaking down, but from deciding you won't break off. The loop goes again. But this time, it grows.

In August 1996, Joe Kenda hit the limit of his own system.

It had been building for years – case after case, silence after silence, pain metabolised into stoicism. Then came the final moment. A 74-year-old man in an interrogation room. A child abuse case. A brutal answer to a brutal question. And something in Kenda snapped. He stood up, overwhelmed by rage, and had to be pulled out of the room. He sat down at his typewriter and wrote the memo that ended his police career: "Effective September 1, 1996, I will be retired from the Colorado Springs Police Department. Very truly yours, Me."

But the loop hadn't finished. It had only broken.

In retirement, the trauma didn't fade. He kept it locked inside, thinking silence would protect him and his wife. It didn't. It made him quiet. Sullen. Absent. He was living in a loop that had collapsed in on itself.

And then came the unexpected re-entry: a television producer, a second chance, a camera, a request: "Just tell us everything."

And Kenda did. Without a script. He talked more to that camera than he'd ever said to his wife. He narrated hundreds of cases over nine seasons of *Homicide Hunter*, each one becoming a new form of sense-making. It wasn't performance. It was adaptation.

This was the full RUN loop in motion. He recognised what wasn't working. He understood that healing didn't mean forgetting. And he took action – not just for himself, but for the version of him that had never been able to speak.

He didn't reboot the job. He rebooted the system. He gave voice to silence – and found fluency where the loop had stalled.

That's a true reboot. Not the return. The transformation.

Bayard Rustin's reboot wasn't loud – but it was foundational.

In the 1950s and 1960s, his very presence threatened the movement he helped build. As an openly gay man, he was forced to the margins again and again – sidelined, disinvited, erased. His 1953 arrest gave others the excuse to exclude him. But he never excluded himself.

He recognised what was happening – not just to him, but to the system. He understood that justice built on exclusion was no justice at all. And so he acted – not by demanding the spotlight, but by building a bigger structure.

Rustin didn't just reclaim his role. He redefined what leadership meant. In 1963, with the quiet backing of Randolph and King, he was named executive director of the March on Washington. The vote was contested. His name was whispered. But when the moment came, procedure and strategy locked it in. "Mr March," they would call him.

And he didn't stop there.

Later in life, he widened the loop again – into gay rights, refugee advocacy, AIDS awareness. He legally adopted his partner in a country that offered no other option. He was, in his own words, an "angelic troublemaker."

This was the RUN loop on full display. Rustin didn't run one system. He rewired them. When the loop broke, he found another path back in – and brought others with him.

This wasn't a comeback. It was a reconstruction.

RECOGNISE → UNDERSTAND → NECESSARY ACTION

Each of them rebooted the loop. Not just their courage. Not just their will. The full architecture of response. Because superadaptability isn't about starting strong. It's about re-entering the system after it fails you – or after you've failed it. Seeing again. Learning again. Acting again.

And now it's your turn. Break the orbit. Shift the arc. Travel further.

REBOOT YOUR LOOP

Sometimes you're not stuck. You're just off by a degree. You're moving, looping, adjusting – but the arc is wrong. The orbit is widening. You think you're making progress because you're in motion. But you're circling. And the longer you loop without recalibration, the further you drift.

There's a name for that moment when your energy is high but your outcomes are misaligned. It's not failure. It's disorientation. This is where the loop becomes your compass. You don't need more effort. You need orientation. The loop doesn't just help you move – it helps you return to the right path.

In 1999, NASA lost a spacecraft. The Mars Climate Orbiter entered the atmosphere at the wrong angle and disintegrated. Why? Not because the math was wrong. Because two systems – both correct on their own – were calibrated to different units. One used metric. One used imperial. Two engineers noticed. But their concerns weren't looped through. The system required the right form, not the right instinct. And so the mission continued – off by a little, until it was off by everything.

That's what happens when results don't match your intent. You can be improving daily. One percent better. Smoother. Faster. But if the trajectory is wrong, you're just accelerating toward the wrong outcome. That's when you reboot your loop.

RECOGNISE the drift – not just in outcomes, but in direction. UNDERSTAND what frame you're using, and whether it still serves the mission. Then take the NECESSARY ACTION – not a reset, but a realignment. A course correction that returns you to what matters.

The loop is your gyroscope. Your compass. Your way of checking whether the orbit you're in is taking you where you mean to go.

You're not broken. You're just a little off-track. You don't need to start over. You just need to notice the angle – and shift it.

This isn't a collapse. It's a recalibration. The loop is still running. Step back in.

RECOGNISE → UNDERSTAND → NECESSARY ACTION

Not a new mission. Just a better trajectory.

TRANSCEND THE LOOP
Snakes, Ladders, and the Loops That Lift Us

You are still free to choose. That hasn't changed. But now you've seen what choosing actually involves. The way we make decisions isn't just instinct or guesswork – it's shaped by what we detect, what we interpret, and the kind of action we take. And if we slow that process down just enough to see it more clearly, we can change not just the results we get – but the way we get there. We can adapt the system we use to adapt.

That's the purpose of learning to pause – of becoming able to catch your own loop while it's happening. You don't pause to hesitate. You pause to climb. Decisions become rungs, not reactions. If you don't like where your loops have been leading, this is the moment to adjust how you move through them. What you thought was a flaw in the outcome may turn out to be a misstep in the loop itself. One wrong detection. One unhelpful interpretation. One fast-forward action that skipped the parts you needed most.

DETECT → INTERPRET → DECIDE

This is how you build adaptive ascent. Otherwise, you risk the descent – what we've called wrong loops, or snakes in the system. You may end up sliding somewhere you've been before, or worse, into something smaller and tighter. The alternative isn't comfort or control – it's clarity. Because when you can see your own loops more clearly, you can choose how to reshape them. You can revisit the parts you rushed. You can build strength where there was once noise. You can act with urgency when urgency is truly required – or wait when waiting is what will save you.

This book isn't about overcorrecting. It's about recognising where the corrections need to be made. That might be in the way you detect, or the way you interpret, or the kind of action you keep taking. It might be in all three. That's the loop, and it belongs to you now. Life is made of decisions. Decisions set trajectory. They tilt where we look, where we go, where we stay. Each one shapes the arc, and the orbit, and the version of you that takes the next step.

THE NEXT RIGHT THING
Ruth Miller didn't plan to build a library in a refugee camp. She didn't plan to spend her eighth decade in Lesbos. She didn't plan to become an information designer. But she noticed something wasn't working – again – and she did what she's always done: she simplified the path to action. That's what a decision looks

like when it doesn't announce itself as a turning point. It loops quietly into structure.

Before Lesbos, before the children, before the Simurgh painted on the library wall, she walked to the library each Saturday with her father. As I once did with my mother. Later, Ruth worked inside the UK government, redesigning application forms so they could actually be filled in. She simplified benefit documents that confused native English speakers. She challenged every unnecessary clause, every buried instruction, every 'hairy box' that left a person stuck on the first page. Her title was civil servant. Her real job was clarity.

Years later, she found herself in a refugee camp where clarity was scarce. The chaos was structural: war, waiting, languages in collision. But what she saw was something simpler – a space where books might make meaning breathable again. A place where young minds could travel even when their bodies could not. She turned a metal shed into a multilingual library. No strategy deck. No budget. Just movement. Just recursion.

This wasn't volunteering. It wasn't charity. It was pattern recognition. She saw the same bureaucratic entanglements she used to untangle in London. So she did the next right thing: she translated her own life's work into a new context. She sourced Turkish football books. She labelled shelves in multiple alphabets. She made the system human, again.

A PLACE TO GO WHEN YOU HAVE TO STAY

The shed was small. Covered in metal cladding. Too hot in summer. Cold in winter. But it became something else – a place with 2,500 books in fifteen languages. A space with shelves labelled in Arabic, Farsi, Turkish, and English. A space with Lego piles for children who couldn't read yet. And artwork drawn by children who weren't sure if they could still imagine.

One child came every other day asking for the Virgil van Dijk book. He'd already finished Harry Kane. Already finished Luis Suárez. That book hadn't come back – but he kept coming. Some children wore donated Spurs kits. Others wore Arsenal red. Ruth used the geography of London football teams to teach them maps, and used maps to teach them stories. This wasn't a library by accident. It was a loop – something entered and re-entered, something recursive, something that made staying bearable.

She didn't just bring books. She brought something rarer: a method. A way of seeing what was missing and finding what could be placed there. What do you do when a child has learned to read in Turkish while waiting in a third country? You don't explain the gap. You fill it. She travelled back to the UK to source Turkish children's books. And when the camp burned down, she didn't stop.

The library moved. The loop continued.

That's what a third move looks like. Not a bigger effort. A more adaptive one. She didn't try to solve everything. She made one system better, for the next person who walked into it. She doesn't just open pages. She opens breath. Quiet. Recursion in the face of trauma. A library built from memory, held in language, opened for those who have nowhere else to go.

CREATING SPACE TO THINK

By now you may be left with something like awe – or something like relief. The people you've just spent time with didn't start out with medals or metaphors or theories about recursion. They began where they were. Not just in the womb, but in the world. Some of them arrived impressive. Others had their moment thrust upon them. Others grew into their decisions slowly, painfully, or reluctantly. Most of us live at the intersection of all three.

We survive, and then we loop. We adapt because we must. We transcend because something inside us asks: what else could be made of this? And what might I leave behind if I do it well? To transcend, as you've just seen, is not to disappear or to escape – but to leave yourself, and others, in a better situation. That's the path of every third move.

This chapter has been about decisions. Quiet ones. Impossible ones. The ones that angle us forward or spiral us back. We built the loop so you could see your place in it. Not to trap you, but to free you. Not to add effort – but to add structure when things fall apart. To create space when everything feels too tight to breathe.

TO TRANSCEND: NOT TO ESCAPE, BUT TO LEAVE YOURSELF – AND OTHERS – BETTER

That's what Ruth Miller did. That's what the loop does. It doesn't guarantee clarity, or action, or transformation. But it gives you a place to start. A system to return to. A way to think when things don't make sense yet. That's what we mean by creating space to think. That's what you've done, just by staying with this chapter until now.

And now we go on. From Recognise to Understand. From seeing better, to modelling what you've seen. Because your brain is plastic. And so is the world you live in. And as you're about to discover – so is what you can build.

understand

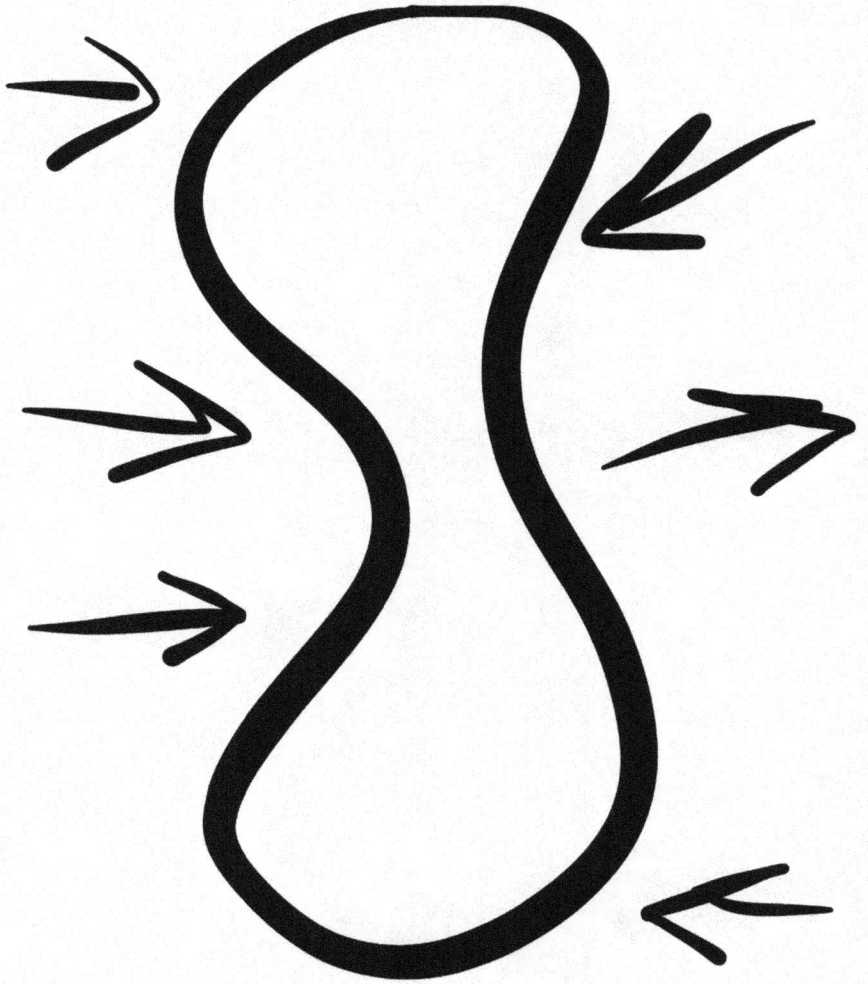

RULE 4:
BE PLASTIC FANTASTIC

How superadapters model the shape of the world –
and reshape it

Superadaptive people understand that selves, systems, and situations are not
fixed – they are malleable. They see plasticity not just as possibility, but as
strategy. What can bend, can be redesigned. Plasticity becomes the raw material
of all future fit.

Humans have to model. We're modelling the world constantly, whether we know
it or not. A mental model is simply the way you picture how things work – why
things happen, what might happen next, where the edges are.

You have mental models of traffic, of grief, of friendship, of failure. You have
models of what success looks like, of what you're allowed to change, of what's out
of reach.

You don't need to draw them to have them. But if you never sketch them –
never surface them – you can't change them.

This is why the most difficult things to change are the ones you can't see.

It's the moment in the movie when the spirit or the ghost is still invisible – still able to trap, trick, or terrify – because no one knows where it is. Once seen, it can be named. Once named, it can be escaped.

Models shape what you think is possible.

Models shape what you don't even think to question.

They shape what you expect from the world – and what you believe the world expects from you.

Most of the time, this happens without noticing. But the difference between being shaped and reshaping, between being stuck and becoming free, starts with this:

Did you choose the model – or just inherit it?

We all model. What we're interested in here is adaptive modelling – the kind that lets you change the shape of what's shaping you.

STILL PLASTIC AFTER ALL THESE YEARS

Meet Anne Jones. She's 83. She's a cyclist. But more than that – for our purposes – she's a modeller. Not the kind who necessarily draws diagrams, although maybe she does – on a notepad, in a journal. What matters is that she remakes the world by entering it differently.

By training, she's a retired psychotherapist and social worker. She understands memory. She understands loops. And she knows what happens when grief has nowhere to go.

So for months – maybe like you – she read headlines about refugees in Gaza, and wept. Not symbolically. Viscerally. Daily. It wasn't a gesture – it was a full-body response to the dissonance, the suffering, the helplessness.

She could have turned away. But instead, she chose to model what resistance could look like. Or rather, what helping, for her, could look like. Her model of the world refused to accept doing nothing. So she chose a mountain – to become her model of resistance, and also her model of practical aid.

Camus once said we must be free in an unfree world. Seun Kuti urges those who want to free Gaza and Congo to also free themselves. Anne decided to free herself – and use that freedom to bring support to others.

She chose the Col du Tourmalet in the French Pyrenees – 2,115 metres of brutal climbing in 30-degree heat. She'd seen it on the Tour de France. She remembered its shape, its challenge, its scale. She set her model: £100 for every metre climbed.

She trained. She stretched. She rode. And people looked at her – "at your age?" – but she climbed it. On a scorching day in June, she rode for hours – stopping only to hydrate and take encouragement from friends. She raised thousands for those she most wanted to help.

And she moved something more lasting: attention, belief. She stretched the shape of what was possible and brought others into that new shape.

This wasn't metaphor. It was a model. A model made visible and useful – because it reshaped action, attention, and resources.

She didn't need a whiteboard. She didn't need a million followers. She just rode her loop uphill.

Still plastic, after all these years.

THE TURN

That's plasticity. That's neurogenesis at work. At 83, she didn't just stretch her body – she stretched her model of what a person could do. And she made it visible to others.

She's a psychotherapist. She understands loops. She understands memory, attention, constraint, adaptation. She just rides hers uphill.

And we know from research that people who understand these things – plasticity, adaptation, how the brain changes – tend to believe more strongly that they can change the world around them.

We don't know if it's cause or correlation. Maybe belief leads to knowledge. Maybe knowledge leads to belief.

But the link is there. And she's living it.

She didn't need a platform. Just a bike, a mountain, and a shape that could stretch from the Pyrenees to Gaza.

So how do people like this reshape their worlds? What is it about them that allows them to do that? And how can you do that too?

THE MODEL LOOP

HOW SUPERADAPTERS MODEL

All life runs on models. Whether it knows it or not. Every living system acts according to a pattern it carries inside – a way it expects the world to work. Even the simplest organism operates from a kind of model: if light, move toward; if heat, retreat. Human beings inherit and assemble far more complex models – often without ever realising they're doing it.

Your mental model isn't just an idea. It's the internal pattern that predicts what you can do, what's likely to happen, and what you expect to result from action. That's why it matters so much. If you don't model how things work, you can't change how they work. You're stuck reacting to a world you haven't even sketched.

But superadapters do more than model what is. They model what could change. They look for the part of the system – internal or external – that might shift with the right pressure. They've already detected something worth noticing. They've already interpreted it as meaningful. They've already decided it's worth acting on. Now, they build the model that allows them to do something about it.

That might mean rethinking how they put a child to bed. Or recalibrating a team mid-game. Or pausing to understand what's really driving conflict at work. The model loop sits at the heart of the adaptive process. You don't need to model the whole sky – just the switch that matters. The simplest picture of the simplest part. That's where the power is.

Because this is how we step from recognising to understanding. From seeing what's wrong to knowing how to respond. This is where the model begins.

Superadapters don't just model more of the world. They model the part that matters – the piece that could change. And crucially, they model themselves in relation to that part. Because unless you understand what's causing the loop you're in, you can't step out of it.

The model loop has three parts: sensing, sketching, and stretching. Each one builds on the last. Each one lets you move from just understanding a system to being able to reshape it.

And when you model the world as a superadapter, you're modeling it with three habits:

Sense the shape – Identify automatic responses that no longer serve your adaptive goals.

Sketch the shape – Flex your thinking style or mental model to fit the situation you find yourself in.

Stretch the shape – Take deliberate risks to stretch whatever needs to be stretched – whether it's your identity, your capability, or your flexibility.

Together, they form the model loop:

$$\text{SENSE} \rightarrow \text{SKETCH} \rightarrow \text{STRETCH}$$

This is how superadapters understand not just what's happening, but what could be different – and where to act to make it so.

Over the next pages, you will explore the three habits that form the model loop and better allow you to model your world in a way that helps you understand how it works – and how you can change it, and yourself, to change it.

You'll meet three people who shaped themselves to shape something larger – by sensing, sketching, and stretching forces that might have appeared to hold them back.

But they found a way through.

They found what we describe as the third shape.

THE THIRD SHAPE

"Yesterday I was clever, so I wanted to change the world.
Today I am wise, so I am changing myself."
– Rumi

Some things only exist when two forces meet. Like a sound when hands clap. Or a path when foot meets forest.

These aren't just blends – they're emergent forms. Something new arises that neither force held alone. We call this the third shape.

Your mind is plastic. It reshapes in response to challenge, repetition, reward, and prediction. It builds models of the world – how things work, what leads to what, which actions matter. And it updates those models through recursive loops of feedback.

Even newborns model: the cry that summons care, the reach that brings a toy, the shape of sound that makes a parent smile. Over time, these recursive loops become beliefs, behaviours, expectations. The connectome, the network of connections inside your brain grows – what we call a behavioral effectome, with recorded and predicted cause and effect models, takes shape.

249

Superadapters don't just receive this imprint. They reshape it. They learn that how they respond changes what happens next – and they adapt accordingly. They train their mind to flex toward possibility.

But the world is plastic too. Systems change. Cultures shift. Environments yield – sometimes slowly, sometimes all at once.

We grow up modelling parts of the world as fixed: institutions, roles, hierarchies, problems. But many of those things are only rigid because we've learned to expect them to be. They can be modelled differently – and therefore modified.

The third shape is what happens when a plastic mind interacts with a plastic world to reshape both. And when that interaction becomes conscious – deliberate – it's no longer just emergence. It becomes authorship.

PLASTIC MIND → THIRD SHAPE → PLASTIC WORLD

This is the spirit of plasticity: not "I am who I am," but "I become what I must become to reshape the world I move through."

The third shape is not always beautiful. The world can mark us in ways we don't choose. But superadapters model with intent. They track where the shaping happens – and choose how to enter the loop.

Not just: Be the change you wish to see.

But: Become the shape that allows that change to happen.

You're about to meet three people who did just that.

HABIT 1: SENSE THE SHAPE
Searching for the third shape

Before you act, before you stretch or leap, something quieter must happen. You have to sense the shape you're in. Superadapters don't just leap into action or jump to conclusions – they feel their way in first. They scan for subtle contours: constraints, openings, tensions, the invisible outlines of possibility.

The most powerful transformations often begin with almost nothing. A gesture. A pause. A breath. The quiet recognition that something in the system is off-pattern – and ready to be touched.

This is not necessarily something you do with your hands, although you can. The Portuguese laying their cobblestones, feeling the contours of the blocks and chipping them by hand, or the drystone wall builder in the north of England, feeling for the next piece of stone that interlocks with the next, or the potter at the wheel, adjusting by fingertip, not formula. This is sensing as skill, not spectacle – the body reading the world before the brain names it.

This is the first habit in the Model Loop: Sense → Sketch → Stretch.

SENSE THE SHAPE – Use your full range of perception to feel the shape of what's happening – and the shape of yourself that might change it.

This helps you identify and soften automatic responses that no longer serve your adaptive goals – but more importantly, it gives you a clearer model of the system you're in and the shape of what you may need to become.

The focus here is that yes, there's the third shape – but this is the habit of sensing the size and nature of the thing you're dealing with. We may use our hands, but we also use our minds and our whole bodies. We ask: what's really going on here? What do I think is going on? That's the beginning of effectome updating – adjusting your mental model before acting.

You already do this. But with attention, you can do it earlier and better. You can feel for the shape of what might happen next, or what causes what to happen next. By updating and layering your sense of what's happening, you begin to sense what you might want to change – and how you might change to meet it.

This habit is about sensing the shape of your world, so you understand enough about it to shape your actions or to reshape your world. Or both.

Instead of merely accepting the limits of your situation – unquestioningly – or living within limits that you don't like but don't know how to change, you start to reshape your response.

You might feel the freeze – or the fear. The urge to disappear, react, obey.

But instead of following it – you pause. You pivot. You reshape the response.

That's not just willpower. It's plasticity in action.

This habit is about a fundamental form of meta-adaptation. When you move between feeling the reflex before simply following it – and in that malleable moment – you can redirect and recode reflex. But first you will need to sense the shape of both your world and your response to it.

What you're about to see is someone who didn't just learn that art from a book. He learned to practice it. Under fire. In danger. Through choice.

Our first third shaping example was born in 1923, near the German border – his parents had fled Poland and Ukraine. When the invasion came, they escaped to Limoges. But instead of staying hidden, he stepped forward. The resistance needed someone to move silently. To listen. To watch. To carry stories without speaking them aloud.

When he was five, his mother took him to see Charlie Chaplin. From that day forward, he wanted to move people without words. To tell a story through breath and gesture. Even his name – Marceau – was chosen for meaning: the name of a French revolutionary general. A signal of resistance.

But how do you fight an enemy that watches every word?

What can a teenager with a love for Chaplin do, in the middle of an invasion?

Let's begin.

MARCEL MARCEAU

The trucks were close. The children were frightened. Their mouths moved, but no sound came out.

Because the man in front of them wasn't speaking either.

He wasn't a soldier. He was barely an adult.
He was seventeen. Jewish. In Nazi-occupied France.

And he had chosen not to run.

Marcel Marceau wasn't always called Marceau. His real name was Mangel. His father – a butcher – was murdered at Auschwitz. His mother survived. He and his brother fled Strasbourg, yes. But not away. Just aside. To Limoges.

And from there, they made a different kind of decision.

They didn't hide. They joined.

The two brothers became part of the French Resistance – specifically the Jewish Resistance. Marcel changed his name to honor a Revolutionary general. But his most powerful disguise wasn't paperwork.

It was performance.

Here's what most people don't know:
Before Marcel Marceau became the world's most famous mime, he used mime to save lives.

He helped smuggle Jewish children out of occupied France – teaching them to stay silent during the most dangerous parts of the journey.

He didn't shout at them. He didn't hush them.
He showed them. He became silence – made it visible – and the children mirrored him.

This is metacognition under pressure: feeling fear, seeing the instinct to run, and choosing a different performance.

One child breathing loud could have cost dozens their lives.
But instead of panicking, they followed his hands. His stillness. His face.
They survived through mimicry.

Plasticity was the method. Silence was the form. He was the sculptor. Later, he would stand in front of thousands in the spotlight. But here – he stood in the shadow, carving calm amid terror. Shaping his own responses to alter outcomes.

This was the first gallery. His brain was his first clay.

After the war, he explained that he began miming at five, after watching Charlie Chaplin.
But he first used it to survive – and help others survive – at seventeen.

This is the part the audience never sees.
The mime who helped children to cross borders. Who faced down 30 German soldiers and mimicked being part of a larger force – bluffing them into retreat.

That's not performance.
That's emotional regulation as strategy.

It's easy to talk about self-control in theory.
It's harder when your hands are shaking.
Harder still when you're carrying the weight of other lives.
But that's exactly what Marceau did. Not once. Not abstractly. Repeatedly. Deliberately.

He used what most people treat as instinct – as material.
He became the sculptor.

And what he shaped – saved people.
The silence was not absence.
It was architecture.

Each breath held a decision.
Each gesture a loop.

Marceau's hands did not move to entertain.
They moved because he had first stilled the scream inside himself.

The body knows how to flinch.
Knows how to curl, recoil, vanish.
Especially a boy whose father has been taken.
Whose name is no longer safe.
Whose language might betray him.
Whose accent might kill him.

But that's the old loop.
  Recognise: I am afraid. I want to disappear. I feel the freeze arrive in my spine.
  Understand: This reflex will not save me. It will not save them.
  Necessary Adaptation: I must move like I am not afraid. I must make my
  body become the message.

He doesn't suppress the fear. He sculpts it.

The trick isn't to erase the reflex.
It's to recall it – in slow motion – until it softens in your hands.

Until it becomes soft clay.
Until you can use it to teach.

A hand raises – palm open.
A finger to the lips.
A wide, exaggerated eye.
The arc of a hush.

Not once.
But again.
And again.

Not just: "be quiet."
But: "copy me."
"Feel what I'm not saying."
"Hold this shape with me until it's safe again."

This is plasticity made visible.

And it doesn't just occur within him.
It ripples through him into others.
Each child who copies him adapts.

Their panic becomes posture.
Their posture becomes stillness.
Their stillness becomes protection.

The sculptor's hands become mirrors.
But the mirror doesn't just reflect.
It reshapes.

Marceau told himself:
    First, I silence myself to survive.
    Then, I silence others to save them.
    Then, I teach silence as art.
    Then, I make the art into a system.
    Then, I become the sculptor of gesture itself.

This is metaplasticity at work. Marcel is not doing what he has learned from others directly, He is sensing what his world does and how his world works so that he can then reshape his own thinking, and from his thinking his actions, and from his actions his world.

In the loop, there is no wasted moment.
Even the stillness has memory.
Even the breath has instruction.

This is the kind of metacognition no stage can show.
We don't teach this.
We embody it.
And then – if we're lucky – we loop it into others.

And if you're reading this – you've already begun.
Start here: Where do you freeze? Where does your body choose an old reflex when a new shape might serve you better?
Just one place. Just one loop. That's enough to start sculpting.
The war ended. The children grew. The silence became applause.

But nothing he did after the war was separate from what he did during it.

Marcel Marceau didn't 'recover'. He didn't 'reinvent'. He continued.

What had been instinct became method. What had been survival became system.
What had been hidden became performance.

Mime was not his escape from the war.
It was his response to it.

"Destiny permitted me to live. This is why I have to bring hope to people who struggle in the world."

He didn't teach mime as decoration. He taught it as transmission.
A new form of speech.
A sculpted silence.
A behavioural grammar born of constraint.

And always, at the centre of it: restraint, breath, timing, and form.

The children had copied his body to survive.
Now thousands would study it to understand.

He performed grief without collapse.
Tension without violence.
Stillness without submission.

Form is not the opposite of freedom.
Form is what lets freedom hold.

His gestures taught something most systems forget:

That self-control is not repression.

It's creative tension.
It's choosing shape over spasm.
It's remembering that every response is sculptable.

This is where superadaptability becomes transmissible.
Where one sculptor teaches another.
Where one loop shapes the next.

You are not stuck with your first shape.
You are not bound to your first breath.
The loop you build now may hold someone else later.

He began by miming silence.
He ended by showing us what it can mean.

He rethought his reflex.
Then rewrote the world with it.

SENSE THE SHAPE → SKETCH THE SHAPE → STRETCH THE SHAPE

And you?
You're not made of stone. You're made to reshape.
Find one reflex. One fear. One moment where your body leads without your permission. That's the clay.
Begin there.

HABIT 2: SKETCH THE SHAPE

Because you're not made of stone. You're made to reshape. And that reflex you just found – that's the clay.

With that clay, you expand your ability to mould yourself – and then mould to move. To shape yourself into whatever you need to be in order to cause the effect you want to see. It's a little like stretching. Yoga before sprinting. A warm-up before the climb. But most of us don't stretch – we just leap or freeze. And because we haven't felt our own readiness, we either get hurt... or don't move at all.

Sensing the shape builds strength. It gives you a deep perception of your environment and yourself. And from that deeper sensing, a new act begins.

SKETCH THE SHAPE – Flex your thinking style or mental model to fit the situation in real time.

This isn't decorative. It's not about art. It's about modelling reality with just enough clarity that you can start to test it. And we all do it. Think of any good bank heist movie. The pepper pot is the getaway car. The salt pot is the bank. You lay out the shape so you can move inside it. That's not just pretending – it's projecting.

And when you rearrange the living room in your head before lifting a single object – you're already doing it. You're projecting structure to prepare for motion.

SKETCHING WHAT WE CAN'T SEE

One of the most extraordinary things about being human is that we can make models of what we don't fully understand.

We sketch what we can't see. We represent systems long before we master them.

We learn how something works not just by acting in it – but by behaving as if we already knew its shape.

This is what supersapiens do.

From the triple spiral scratched into stone to the Marshallese stick charts curved to mimic the sea's unseen structure, human beings have used shape to represent tension, direction, pressure, and possibility.

We didn't just invent tools.

We invented tools for thinking about tools.

Sketching is one of the first and most powerful expressions of that recursive loop.

It is what happens when plasticity and abstraction combine.

It is the bridge between brain, body, and system.

To sketch the shape of something is to say: "I can't change this yet – but I can understand it by behaving differently inside it."

That's what this move is for.

You use your behaviour as a hypothesis.

You try a new shape – not to escape the old one, but to feel how it holds.

You rotate the knot. You test the pressure. You trace the system from the inside.

Children do it with gestures. Protesters do it with movements. Strategists do it with bottle caps on tabletops.

You don't need full visibility to model. You need representation.

And enough plasticity to flex before you break.

This is how sapiens became supersapiens.

This is how sketching becomes adaptation.

And no one did that more vividly – or more obsessively – than the apprentice in the back of a Florentine workshop.

DA VINCI

A teenage apprentice – not legitimate, not university-trained, not even properly right-handed – sits in the back of a studio with a page in his lap and a world in his head.

He's not copying the masters.
He's not refining an image.
He's dissecting a frog.

And he's drawing it – every vein, tendon, curve. Not to replicate it. Not to impress anyone.
But because it's the only way he can understand what it's doing.

Leonardo da Vinci didn't draw to show what he saw.
He drew to see what seeing wanted him to understand.

This was his loop.
And it never stopped.

Leonardo didn't fit the world's disciplines.
He trained in art, but leaked into engineering.
He studied anatomy, but then painted theology into muscle.
He asked questions no one had answers for.

So he stopped asking.
And started sketching.

Every line was a question.
Every margin was a model.

He wasn't taking notes.
He was thinking in pen.

Mirror writing. Reverse-handed loops. Arrows into forces. Water flows into curls.
He wasn't just observing nature. He was mimicking how it models itself.

He didn't become a doctor. But he performed 30 dissections.
He didn't become an architect. But he designed floating cities.
He didn't become a physicist. But he sketched the laminar flow of rivers 400 years before fluid mechanics.

He tried everything. And in trying, he traced the shape of how systems behaved.

A bird's wing → an early airplane.
A shoulder joint → a pulley system.
A tree's growth spiral → a theory of pressure and time.

Leonardo wasn't sketching to be clever.
He was sketching to try reality in different forms.

Not to build it. To feel how it might move.
That's what sketching is: recursive hypothesis.

The act of drawing, for him, was the act of testing a system by becoming part of it.

He'd seen the Vitruvian text: man as the measure of all things.
But where others saw myth or math, Leonardo saw model.

He drew the body inside a square. Then again inside a circle.
He aligned limb and line and system and soul.
He wasn't illustrating an ideal.
He was building a loop you could live inside.

And in doing so, he looped back into the future.

"The workings of the human body are an analogy for the workings of the universe."

That diagram didn't just express proportion.
It expressed recursion.
It said: your body is a system.
And systems are sketchable.
And therefore, alterable.

That's what Leonardo gave us. Not machines. Not art.
Modelling.

He gave us the idea that everything could be understood by sketching its shape.

Even the sky.
Even the self.
Even the future.

Leonardo sketched thousands of things the world didn't want yet.
He died with notebooks unpublished, ideas half-finished, models unbuilt.

But he sketched them anyway.
Because that's what superadapters do.
They behave the model – even when the system isn't ready.

He drew in the margins of tax ledgers.
He wrote backwards across grocery lists.
He covered the walls of his home in diagrams that tried the opposite of every known theory.

He lived his loop.
And passed it on.

Not in final answers.
But in forms others could enter.

"He wasn't trying to finish a drawing. He was trying to catch a system in motion."

And that's the loop you can try too.
Sense – I don't fit the limits the world has given me.
Sketch – So I draw the system until I understand it better than they do.
Stretch – I draw anyway. On scraps. On ceilings. Until the sketch becomes structure.

That's what he did.
That's how he looped.
That's how he saw the world – by sketching it until it made sense.

SENSE THE SHAPE → **SKETCH THE SHAPE** → STRETCH THE SHAPE

HABIT 3: STRETCH THE SHAPE

You've now seen what sketching can do – not just on paper, but in the mind. It simplifies, clarifies, unlocks. It helps you hold the shape of what you're facing, and the shape of what you might become. And in the hands of Leonardo, it gave us a model of the human form so accurate it still feels visionary.

But sketching is not the end of the loop.

Because the sketch is not the thing. The diagram is not the change. And the model is not reality.

Superadapters know that the sketch, like the sense that came before it, is only useful if it helps you stretch. Stretch yourself. Stretch your system. Stretch the shape of what's possible.

STRETCH THE SHAPE is to take deliberate risks to stretch identity, capability, and adaptability.

This habit doesn't mean pushing recklessly. It means identifying the elastic points. The leverage zones. The underused pathways where tension and potential sit waiting.

You stretch when you volunteer for something beyond your current title. When you say yes to a challenge that forces you to grow. When you run the rehearsal a little faster than the script calls for just to see if it can hold.

Sketching helps you see the shape. Stretching helps you reshape it.

And no one did that more courageously – or more creatively – than our next example.

He didn't sketch in chalk or ink. He sketched in absurdity. In theatre. In truth so sharp it slipped past censors and stabbed at systems. He used laughter to stretch the truth until it cracked the regime that had tried to contain him.

Welcome to Czechoslovakia. 1970s. Surveillance state. And one playwright with a mime's face and a dissident's resolve.

VÁCLAV HAVEL

It didn't happen all at once. Not even for Václav Havel.

He saw the shape. He sketched the contradiction. And for a long time, he waited.

There's a party. People are drinking, talking. Someone sings a forbidden song. A half-joke. A line from a banned lyric. And then – the sketch begins.

The laughter stops. A name is written down. A file is opened. Charges are drafted. The system flexes.

And somewhere in that moment, Havel sees the whole thing.

This isn't irony. This isn't theatre. This is the system performing itself. And we are all on stage.

It's not a revolution. Not yet. It's a realisation.

And he starts writing again.

He was a playwright before he was a president. And before that – a stagehand, moving sets while writing his first scripts in the margins.

He didn't shout. He drew.

He used theatre to sketch what couldn't be said.

He created characters who collapsed under contradictions – systems that swallowed their own logic.

"Ptydepe," he called the bureaucratic language in *The Memorandum*.

A word so fake it circled back into truth.

He didn't point to the system. He mimicked it – so well it cracked.

Because that's what plasticity does when it's applied to absurdity:

It shows the pressure lines.

Then the tanks came.

1968. Prague Spring collapses. Moscow intervenes.

The theatre is shuttered. The state redraws the borders of what can be said.

And Havel stops producing plays.

But not writing.

He writes letters. Notes. Fragments.

He keeps drawing the same loop with smaller and smaller gestures.

In 'The Power of the Powerless', he doesn't call for rebellion.

He describes a greengrocer. A man who displays a slogan – not because he believes it, but because that's what's done.

And that tiny moment – of cognitive dissonance made visible – becomes the diagram for a civil revolution.

He sketches a world where people stop pretending.

And the system, deprived of its illusion, begins to unloop.

"If they're locking us up for it, there must be some radioactivity in the truth."

He stretched the shape by holding tension long enough for a new system to emerge.

Charter 77.

Samizdat.

Cafés turned into press rooms.

Living rooms turned into theatres.

Invisible lines of pressure turned into visible loops of civic modelling.

And then – students protest. A rumour spreads: someone's been killed. It's not true. But it feels true. Because the sketch has already been drawn.

Thousands flood the streets.

A dictator wavers.

A vacuum forms.

And the only model that makes sense – the only structure people have seen rehearsed – is Havel's.

The absurdist who stretched the old system so clearly that his new system could replace the one it was mocking. An ideal fit for a new minds who wanted a new world.

He didn't campaign.

He didn't even want power.

But when they asked who should lead – he was already the diagram on the wall.

"I don't want to be the nation's conscience. I just want to tell the truth."

He became president.

And later, in a quiet film about his own life, he ends with a scene:

Himself, being smuggled out of politics in the boot of a car.

A sketch.

A reversal.

A recursive exit.

For Havel, the world was theatre where people were trapped in the roles written for them. So, he wrote new characters, new scenes, new dialogue, and new endings. New models which expose the shapes and forms of the old world. Making invisible lines visible.

And then he showed the world quietly – the possibilities that his absurdist reversals reveal – until the people started to play roles and recite lines from this plays, reading his script and becoming people who first recognised, and then understood the action they needed to take.

A whole nation of people who stretched themselves to the shapes that he provided rather than being distorted – and trapped – in shapes that were forced upon them from outside.

SENSE THE SHAPE → SKETCH THE SHAPE → **STRETCH THE SHAPE**

You've now seen each part of the model loop in action – sensed through silence, sketched into form, stretched into transformation.

Each habit gives shape to the one that follows. And when they loop together, something more than understanding emerges. Action does. Change does.

You saw Marceau sense the shape of silence and danger – using his own body to find safety.

You saw Leonardo da Vinci sketch what could not be seen, and bring logic and beauty into alignment.

You saw Havel stretch absurdity until the system could no longer hold.

But what happens when all three come together – not just once, but over and over again? What happens when the loop becomes recursive – when the person shapes the world, and the world pushes back?

Our next figure didn't just live this pattern. She repeated it, reinvented it, and used it to escape what tried to contain her.

Born in Japan. Shaped by trauma. Defined by obsession and reinvention.

Her name is Yayoi Kusama.

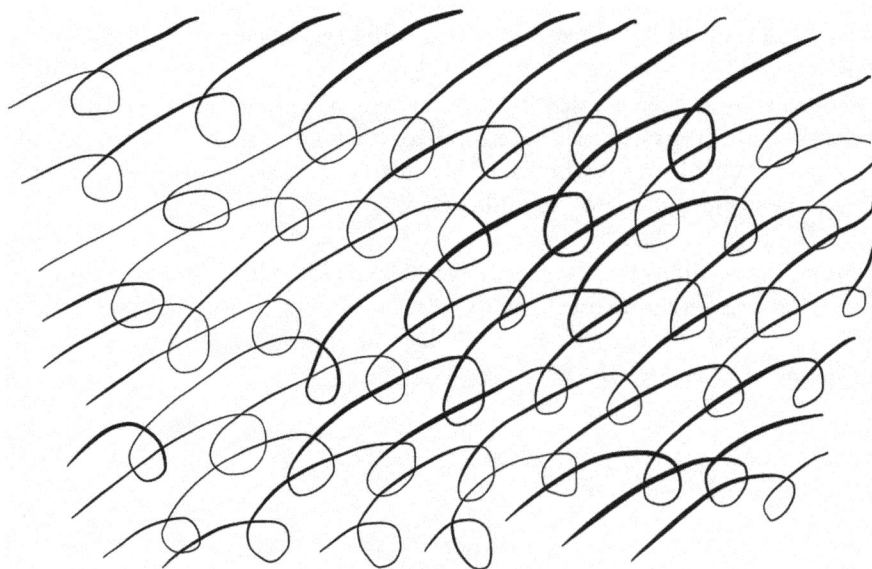

THE INFINITY NET LOOPS OF YAYOI KUSAMA

Japan. 1939.
She was just a girl in Matsumoto when the dots first came.

They covered the tablecloth. Then the walls. Then her skin. Then the sky.

Flowers whispered. Fabrics breathed. Ceilings split into nets that consumed her.

"I felt as if I had begun to self-obliterate."

She was ten.

And already living inside a world she would spend a lifetime translating.

That world didn't make sense. So she painted it until it did.

Some people mistake reflex for reality. Kusama never had that luxury.

Her reflexes were too loud, her perceptions too unstable, her thoughts too fluid to hold.

Her brain was hyperplastic. Every sensation made an impression. Every emotion stuck.

"The smooth white stones in the river near my home… I still remember the patterns they made."

She wasn't reacting. She was absorbing – too much, too fast.

So, she painted. Not to express – but to survive.

The hallucinations became systems. The systems became patterns.

The patterns became nets.

"All of my works are steps on my journey, a struggle for truth I have waged with pen, canvas, and materials."

And every net she painted was a way to sense the shape of her own mind.

She called them Infinity Nets.

A name not for decoration, but for recursion.

Japan felt too small. Too rigid. Too scornful of women.

So, she left. Her plastic brain guided her departure.

She destroyed much of her early work. Packed what she could.

Wrote to Georgia O'Keeffe and begged for advice. And then – she moved to America.

New York. 1958.

She was 27. Broke. Undiagnosed. Drenched in dots.

"I wanted to stand at the top of the art world."

She didn't blend in. She performed. Protested. Painted.

She staged naked happenings in Central Park.

She offered to sleep with Nixon if he'd stop the Vietnam War.

She covered couches with phalluses. Boats with mirrors. Rooms with her own infinity.

And then they stole her work.

Claes Oldenburg, Andy Warhol, and others – they copied her forms.

She vanished while they ascended.

She became more secretive. She stopped trusting.

She sketched the shape of a system that used her loops – but never let her stay in them.

In response, she created something else: a self-loop.

Tokyo. 1977.

After suicide attempts and collapse, she checked herself into a psychiatric hospital.

She still lives there. Voluntarily.

Her studio is down the road.

She paints every day.

"I followed the thread of art and somehow discovered a path that would allow me to live."

Her life now is a recursive net: studio-hospital-canvas-world.

It loops. And holds.

From that loop came global transcendence:
Infinity Rooms. Mirror Worlds. Pumpkins the size of cars.
Louis Vuitton. The Hirshhorn. The hashtags.
But don't mistake the fame for the loop.
The loop was there before the camera came.
It was there when she drew her mother, obliterated by dots.
It was there in the red flowers that covered her room, her body, the world.
It was there when she said:
"If it were not for art, I would have killed myself a long time ago."
She doesn't live in escape.
She lives in a loop she built strong enough to stretch with her.
A dot. A mirror. A net. A loop.
And she's still painting it.

New York. 2022.
Her most expensive artwork, *Infinity Networks, White* sold for over $7.8 million
USD at Christies auction house, on Rockefeller Plaza. She painted it as therapy
back in 1958. She became the world's best-selling contemporary artist, but for
you the value is far greater – because she shows us how to sense, sketch, and
shape your world.
   Not everyone sees dots.
   Not everyone paints nets.
   But everyone lives between three forces:
   Plastic self. Plastic system. Plastic situation.

Kasuma stretched across all three – and stayed looping upwards.

SENSE THE SHAPE → SKETCH THE SHAPE → STRETCH THE SHAPE

You've just travelled the modelling loop.

You sensed the system – where it tenses, where it tightens, where it gives.
You sketched the structure – its joins, its edges, its inner shapes.
You stretched the model – testing its limits, pulling at the parts that needed to
shift.

Not just three stories. One pattern. Lived in different ways.

Marceau sensed in silence.
Leonardo sketched the unseen.
Havel stretched truth until systems cracked.

Each of them modelled a different kind of world.
Each of them modelled a different kind of mind.

And now you've seen the loop in full.
Sense. Sketch. Stretch.

It's yours now.

And like anything adaptive, you'll get better at it.
More fluent. More fluid.
More able to model the structure around you – and reshape the role you play inside it.
But before we act –
before we loop forward –
we sit.

Because some models don't yield their meaning at first glance.
And some loops require stillness before motion.

So now, we go deeper.

We're not done modelling.
We're about to model the modeller.
Not just the world – but the brain that maps it.

Let's sit down.

```
                                    loop  loop  loop
                              loop
loop loop loop loop  loop loop
                         loop
                  loop          loop
                  loop            loop
              loop                loop

            loop                    loop
              loop              loop
            loop  loop  loop
```

THE SITDOWN: THE NET (AND THE KNOT)

WHY WE SIT DOWN NOW

"Every question is a knot.
And every knot begins with silence.
We speak to untangle what binds us –
and sometimes, we only tighten the thread."
– Edmond Jabès, *The Book of Questions*

This is the moment we sit down.

Not to rest, but to understand. To trace. To untangle and rethread. The Sitdown, in every Rule, is the place where the loop slows – so the pattern can emerge.

In Rule 4, you've just modelled the world. You've sensed, sketched, and stretched the structures that shape you. But now it's time to look again – more slowly, more closely – not at the world out there, but at the net of thought you're inside of.

Because the mind isn't just a processor. It's a pattern-maker. A knotter. A looper. A weaver. And what you model doesn't just show you the world – it becomes part of your world.
That's why we sit.

We sit, like the old weavers did. To knot loops into structure. To tighten some strands, and untangle others. Every net is made of loops. Every loop can become a knot. And every knot holds a choice: hold tighter, or loosen. Reinforce, or revise.

This Sitdown isn't just a story. It's a loom.

You're about to meet Santiago Ramón y Cajal – a man who discovered the structure of the brain, and in doing so, gave us a way to see the structure of thought. He showed that what wires can be rewired. That what loops can be relooped. And that minds, like worlds, are plastic.

So sit down. Let the noise slow. Let the model deepen.

Let the net reveal itself – and begin, knot by knot, to take shape.

271

CAJAL: PLASTIC BRAIN, PLASTIC WORLD

He didn't hate science. He hated confinement. He wanted to understand the structure of the world, but not by cutting hair or following pre-approved diagrams. As a teenager, he fought teachers, ran away from discipline, and spent hours studying muscle by sketching bodybuilders in secret. His rebellion was intellectual as much as emotional – an early act of model rejection.

What Cajal resisted most was the assumption that paths were linear. He was not just disobedient. He was searching for something truer than compliance. And that hunger – to see the underlying logic of form – never left him.

Before Santiago Ramón y Cajal became the father of modern neuroscience, he was nearly forced into a life of cutting hair. His father – a strict provincial barber-surgeon – dragged young Santiago to the family shop and told him to learn the trade. But Santiago rebelled. He wasn't interested in razors or scalpels. He wanted brushes and charcoal. He wanted to draw. His obsession with sketching – walls, furniture, animals, everything – got him punished repeatedly. He was labelled disruptive. Expelled from school for defiance. But something in him refused to be shaped by those early constraints. Instead, he began shaping back. Even as a child, Cajal instinctively resisted the idea that paths were fixed. His instinct wasn't to escape the world – it was to redraw it.

THE BOY WHO STAINED THE BRAIN

The lab was improvised, the funding scarce. He would fix tissue by hand, grind lenses when needed, and sharpen quills to trace what he saw. The microscope became his portal not just to the brain, but to a hidden system of adaptation. This wasn't about description. It was about revealing the algorithm of thought.

By drawing what he saw, Cajal wasn't replicating reality – he was building a model. His ink-stroked reconstructions became the basis for the neuron doctrine. One connection at a time, he redrew how the scientific world understood itself.

Cajal's rise as a scientist was entirely self-assembled. With limited resources and no formal mentorship, he taught himself microscopy by candlelight. Where others memorised textbook diagrams, Cajal peered through lenses and drew what he saw. When he encountered Camillo Golgi's new silver nitrate stain – which randomly dyed a handful of neurons black against the surrounding grey – he saw not just cells, but stories. He traced each thread by hand, discovering the individuality of neurons. Where Golgi saw one continuous net, Cajal proved there were gaps – synapses. Signals jumped. And more than that, they changed. Cajal's drawings weren't just observations; they were models – of connection, variation, and possibility. While others saw anatomy, Cajal saw adaptation.

PLASTICITY WASN'T THE WORD YET

Cajal was arguing not just for change, but for changeability. That the nervous system could be modified, trained, improved – that learning physically altered the wiring. This belief set him apart for decades. He faced dismissal. "Adult neurons are fixed," they said. "Your theory is imaginative." But he didn't yield.

When his diagrams were finally accepted, they did more than validate him. They changed medicine, psychology, and education. Suddenly, effort mattered. Practice could become structure. Intention could reshape capacity. The loop was alive.

Cajal's most radical idea wasn't what the brain was made of. It was what the brain could do. He proposed something almost heretical: that the adult brain could adapt. Could rewire. Could change. At a time when most scientists believed mental development ended in childhood, Cajal insisted that effort and experience continued shaping the nervous system across a lifetime. Practice, attention, and learning carved new grooves. "Every man," he wrote, "can be the architect of his own brain." This wasn't just metaphor. It was a principle of plasticity – fifty years before the term was formally coined. Cajal's neurons weren't fixed. They grew. They moved. They connected and reconnected based on use and intention. He drew a brain that could become what it needed to be.

MODEL THE MIND, MODEL THE WORLD

He saw his work not as the end of understanding, but as its beginning. Every diagram he drew opened another question. Every claim he made tested itself against observation. He modelled like an artist, revised like a scientist, and explained like a teacher.

That's what makes Cajal not just a parent of neuroscience, but an architect of adaptive thinking. He didn't just make maps. He made mappers. He taught the world that the brain is not a fixed structure – it is a tool that shapes itself while shaping the world around it.

What Cajal gave us wasn't just the first true map of the mind. It was permission to shape it. To train it. To update and rewire how we see, think, and act. He didn't just model neurons – he modelled modelling itself. Through repetition, revision, observation, and insight, Cajal showed what a plastic brain could do in a plastic world. Rule 4 ends here because his story holds the key to everything that follows: Superadapters are self-revising systems. They build tools, change tools, and are the tool. When Cajal picked up Golgi's stain, he didn't just see differently. He made a different way of seeing. That's what we do next. We learn to work on the system itself.

PLASTIC MIND

We begin, as Cajal did, not with certainty – but with sketching.

He didn't just look through the microscope. He looked with it. He traced the shapes of what the world believed was fixed, and showed that it wasn't. That the brain, far from being hard-wired or complete, was a living map in motion. Eighty-six billion neurons. One hundred trillion connections. A system so complex it can simulate its own structure – while redrawing it.

And you live inside that system. You are made of it.

Your thoughts aren't floating abstractions. They are circuits – electrical, chemical, historical, rehearsed. What you call your personality is pattern. What you call memory is motion. What you call self is structure that shifts – day by day, loop by loop, signal by signal.

This is not poetry. It's physics.

Neurons don't fire alone. They cluster. They echo. They loop. Your identity – your sense of being a single person – emerges from the shifting pattern of those loops. Scientists have begun mapping this through a field called connectomics: the study of how each neuron connects to the next, and how those trillions of threads cohere into a single fabric. That fabric is you.

When you fall asleep, your thoughts scatter. When you wake, your sense of self resumes – midstream, as if nothing happened. Why? Because the structure of your connectivity remains intact. You are not your thoughts. You are the net that catches them.

And that net is plastic.

That is the key. The single insight behind all that follows. Your brain is not a machine. It is not fixed. It is not done. It is a structure that reshapes in response to how you use it. Attention becomes architecture. Practice becomes pattern. Intention becomes infrastructure. The net does not merely hold your life. It forms it.

And if you can shape the brain, you can reshape the mind.

You can change how it models. You can update what it repeats. You can intervene – not just on what you do, but on what you're inside of. Because before the world shows up as a problem, or a threat, or a loop – you've already modelled it that way. Your mind isn't just in the world. It makes the world legible. And that means it can make it differently.

Cajal knew this. That's why he kept drawing. Not to capture reality. To revise it.

You don't have to become a neuroscientist. But you do need to understand what he saw:

Plasticity is not lack of strength. It's opportunity.

Not resistance for its own sake – but the readiness to reshape.

PLASTIC SYSTEM

The systems you live inside don't arrive labelled.

They feel like givens. Like roads already drawn. You follow them because they're there – because everyone does – because that's what systems are supposed to do: structure the world so you don't have to redraw it.

But what if the system isn't a road?
What if it's a net?

Not a solid path, but a web of loops. Repeated behaviours, reinforced expectations, inherited rules, forgotten origins. That's what most systems are – at the societal level, at the institutional level, even at the household level. Patterns knotted together by repetition. Held in place not by logic, but by use.

And like nets, they're porous. Flexible. Built for flow. They let some things through and catch others. They distribute weight. They carry. But they also entangle.

Here's the move:

You begin to see the system not as fixed, but as fabricated. Not permanent, but patterned. And like any pattern, it can be traced, unpicked, reinforced, or reshaped.

This is what adaptive thinkers see – what Cajal showed us at the neuronal scale, Giddens pointed to at the social scale, and what every superadapter begins to feel once they've run the loop enough times. The self is not outside the system. It is the system. And vice versa.

Your behaviours become structure. Your language becomes scaffolding. Your role becomes a node others build around. You loop, and the system loops with you. That's how you get stuck. But it's also how you get free.

Because if it loops through you, you can shift it through you.

The network isn't just external. It's recursive. You feel its shape every time you pause before speaking, or switch tones depending on who's watching, or default to silence when conflict echoes louder than reason. That's not just you. That's the structure working through you. And the second you see that – not as personality but as pattern – you gain the power to change it.

Social systems are made of social acts. And social acts can be redesigned.

We are not trapped in our institutions. We're inside them. Shaping them with every repeated move. And once you know that, you don't have to rage at the net. You can begin to reweave it.

PLASTIC SITUATION

There is no such thing as a neutral situation.

Every moment you enter – every conversation, every meeting, every silent room – is shaped by loops already in motion. Histories. Expectations. Unspoken rules. Structures you didn't design, but still move through.

Most people don't notice. They think situations just are.
But superadapters see the weave.

They feel the tension before words are spoken. They clock who speaks when, and who never does. They sense the repetition, the rituals, the invisible scaffolding that holds the whole thing up – and the points where it might flex. They don't just live the moment. They model the system beneath it.

Because a situation is never just a scene. It's a system in miniature.

It reflects every habit loop, every social net, every belief scaffold around it. And once you know that, you can start to shape it – not with force, but with form. You change the situation not by overpowering it, but by finding the loop it's running and adjusting its rhythm.

This is why awareness is never passive. Once you see the net, you are inside the loop. You can no longer claim you didn't know. But that's also where the power begins.

If you've ever shifted the mood of a room with a well-timed question, you've done it. If you've ever reframed a failure so a team could keep going, you've done it. If you've ever walked away from a pattern that always pulled you back in – you've already rewoven the situation. You sensed the knot, and chose not to pull tighter.

This is not about control. It's about composition.
Superadapters don't see the world as fixed. They see it as composed – and that means it can be recomposed. They don't ask "What is this?" They ask: "What's shaping this? What's being reinforced here? And what might happen if I shape differently?"

That's what it means to live in plastic situation.

Not just to respond to the world, but to reframe the way it arrives.

The adaptive shift isn't always dramatic. Sometimes it's as subtle as a pause. A tone. A pivot. A refusal. A redirection.

But each of those is a thread. And each thread is a chance to reweave the net.

PLASTIC WORLD

The world is not made of facts. It's made of fabric.

Systems, roles, institutions, habits – none of them are natural. They're shaped. Inherited. Reinforced. You grow up inside them, and so they feel real. Solid. Permanent. But they are not. They are woven.

And what is woven can be rewoven.

That's not ideology. That's structure. The laws we live by, the identities we perform, the defaults we repeat – they're all loops. Social loops. Institutional loops. Feedback loops. And once you can see the loop, you can change the logic it's running on.

Superadapters don't fight the world as it is. They learn to model the world as it could be. They don't aim for control – that's brittle. They aim for composition. They look at the loops and think: where is the entry point? Where is the tension? Where's the thread?

Because if a pattern can be felt, it can be followed. And if it can be followed, it can be changed.

This is not about controlling what can't be.

It's about composing what can be.

You're not trapped in structure. You are part of it. And that means you're part of what it becomes.

It doesn't happen all at once. But neither did the world. You change one loop. One gesture. One room. You change the story just slightly, and sometimes – if you've traced the tension right – it changes the net.

Most people walk through life assuming the system is the system. But superadapters hold a different belief. A deeper one. They believe the world is not done.

They look at a broken policy and think: this is editable.

They look at a team dynamic and think: this is designable.

They look at their own thoughts and think: this is rewritable.

They know that every net is composed. Every loop is local. Every shape can flex. And that what you're inside of is not the end of the story.

Because if it is what it is – fine.

But what if it could be more?

And if it can be more – then why not make it so?

WEAVE YOUR WORLD

You didn't choose the first knots.

You were born into a weave already in motion – cultural patterns, family roles, social defaults. You inherited loops before you had words to name them. But now you can. And that's where everything changes.

Because even if you didn't tie the first knots, you've been reinforcing some of them. Repeating certain loops. Pulling threads tighter. The question isn't how you got here. The question is what you do with the net now.

This is what it means to be a superadapter: not just to see the system, but to rework it from inside. To feel the tension in a knot and know – this one can shift.

Take Cecilia Payne.

At 25, she wrote a thesis that redefined the stars. She showed that hydrogen was the dominant element in the universe. The scientific world told her she was wrong. Her conclusion was not accepted – it was 'reinterpreted' by others and credited elsewhere. Her degree was denied because she was a woman. The system caught her in its net.

But she didn't abandon the loop. She held the model. She trusted her structure.

Decades later, her insight was proven right. And what she had quietly redrawn became the new map of the cosmos.

Cecilia saw the universe differently. And eventually, so did the universe.

She didn't break the net. She rewove it.

You might not be rewriting astrophysics. But you're holding a loop too. Maybe it's a family belief you've never questioned. A work role that limits you. A pattern in a relationship that always repeats. Some part of the weave you've mistaken for reality.

But now you know: the net is built of loops. The knot is a turning point. And what holds you can be rethreaded.

Your world isn't fixed. It's rehearsed.

That means every pause is an opportunity. Every gesture, a structural suggestion. Every refusal, a form of design. You are already acting on the net – now you can start acting with intention.

This is what lifting the loop looks like. Not tearing things down. Not escaping. But adjusting, revising, and re-entering with clarity.

And as you do, you don't just change your life. You change the structure that shapes others.

Your loop becomes part of the pattern they inherit.

So what thread do you trace now? What knot might loosen if you looked at it differently? What small loop might reshape the weave?

You don't need to tie the whole net anew. You only need to lift one loop.

The rest will follow.

You've just sat down with Santiago Ramón y Cajal. Not just to remember what he discovered, but to realise what he revealed: that minds are made of structure – and that structure can be changed.

You've seen how a boy dismissed as distracted became the man who mapped the inner loops of the brain. How nets of potential are built one knot at a time. And how every loop, even the smallest, is shaped not just by experience, but by attention, tension, and intent.

This wasn't a lesson in neuroscience. It was a lesson in plasticity.

In your own life, you've already sensed the shape of systems. You've begun to sketch the structure that surrounds you. And you've learned that to stretch those patterns, you need to know where the knot holds – and how to reloop what binds.

This Sitdown wasn't a pause. It was a preparation.

Now you begin to live what you've seen. In loops. In action. In practice.

LIVE THE LOOP

HOW TO LIVE THE LOOP

"The brain is essentially a machine for forming models of the world."
– Kenneth Craik, *The Nature of Explanation*

This is where you continue to live the loop.

You've modelled the world around you. You've looked at systems that hold, at patterns that repeat, and at the inner structure of your own thoughts. You've sat with Cajal. You've felt the shape of possibility.

Now it's time to keep moving, to become an artist of adaptability, a sculptor of possibilities. And this doesn't have to be about the big things, it can be about the small things – figuring out why that colleague has stopped talking or how to complete a task or learn a missing skill that's holding you back – make the biggest difference.

Developing your capacity to create third shapes that better suit the way you wish to live, work, love, and become.

You don't just model the world, you *re-model yourself* – looped, rewired, so that you can remodel the world. The better you identify what's happening in the bit of the world that's holding you back, the better you will be able to focus your energy on reshaping that part.

Living the loop means not just understanding what holds you – but acting on it. It means using what you've sensed, what you've sketched, what you've stretched – to move differently, choose differently, loop differently.

This is where it gets practical. We braid back through the lives you've seen. We try the moves in real time. We look at what it means to reboot a stuck pattern – and how to counter the kinds of loops that trap.

This isn't a checklist. It's a system. It's not about fixing everything. It's about making the model real – so that your next loop is freer than the last.

Let's live the model.

HOW THEY LIVED THE LOOP

Our superadaptive examples didn't just sketch models. They rewove the nets.

Each one – Marceau, da Vinci, Havel – lived inside a failing system. A silence. A contradiction. A structure that no longer served. And instead of accepting it, they looped. They sensed. They sketched. They stretched.

They ran the loop to create a third shape.

PLASTIC MIND → THIRD SHAPE → PLASTIC SHAPE

Marcel Marceau didn't rebuild language. He built around its failure. In the wreckage of war, in silence enforced by trauma and secrecy, he modelled emotion without words. He took the invisible and gave it shape – not once, but night after night, hand by hand, breath by breath. He modelled a new kind of presence. Not to speak louder. But to stretch a shape that provided safety for children in danger.

He didn't just act. He adapted. He rewired the space between expression and understanding – one loop at a time.

Leonardo da Vinci didn't seek control. He sought the structure beneath motion. He drew everything – not to perfect it, but to understand it in time. Each sketch wasn't an answer. It was a test. A feedback loop. A way of asking: what does this form want to become?

He modelled systems that others hadn't seen yet – not because he predicted the future, but because he redrew the present until it became the future.

Václav Havel didn't model utopia. He modelled truth under pressure. In a system where language had collapsed, where even the structure of speech was soaked in fear, he wrote his way back to freedom. Not grand speeches. Loops of comedy. Essays of resistance. Plays that exposed the recursive absurdity of power.

He became president not by seizing power – but by *showing people the loop they were already in*. And offering a way out. You are free, his theatre said, so stretch your shape to become free. By revealing both the absurdities and the reality he provided a third shape into which a whole nation stepped.

Each one of them ran the plastic model loop.

Each one of them sensed the shape of constraint, sketched a response, stretched a structure.

They didn't wait for the system to reboot. They became the part that rebooted.

You don't need to be a mime, an artist, a president.
You need to see what they saw:

The shape is not fixed.
The net is not closed.
The model is not elsewhere.

The model begins where you stand.

SENSE → SKETCH → STRETCH

And to help you do this – because this is a practical book as well as a hopeful one – we're going to show you how.

Modelling the world is not enough. You also need to model yourself. To believe – not passively, but actively – that your mind is plastic. That it can change shape. That it can grow in complexity, in calm, in clarity.

That belief becomes a practice. That practice rewires you. New networks form. New habits take hold.

And through learning – especially through the example of others – you reshape the plastic clay of your own loop.

What comes next are three moments. Three third shapes. Three situations where plastic people reshaped themselves – and the world around them.

PLASTIC PEOPLE –
THREE SHAPES TO TAKE YOU FURTHER

PLASTIC FANTASTIC NO. 1 – THE SHAPE OF REFUSAL

Some people change the world by refusing to choose between the forms they're offered. They don't just take what they're given. They find a third shape.

In 1981, Maya Lin was a 21-year-old undergraduate at Yale, studying architecture. She had chosen it because she loved art and she loved math – and worried she'd have to choose between them. Architecture, she discovered, was a kind of third language: a form where both could live.

That fall, she took a seminar in funerary architecture. A classmate spotted an open competition for a Vietnam Veterans Memorial. Several students decided to enter. Over Thanksgiving break, they travelled to Washington, D.C. to visit the site.

What Maya saw wasn't a blank canvas. It was a wound. And what she sensed in the country wasn't peace, but dissonance. She wanted to honour the fallen – deeply, precisely – but without glorifying the war that took them. She wanted to make something that didn't shout. Something that would hold.

"I imagined taking a knife and cutting into the earth," she later said. "Opening it up."

Her submission was a descending black wall of polished granite, listing names in the order they were lost. It was not a statue. It didn't stand tall. It let you walk into it. And as you read the names, your own reflection appeared in the stone – 'you' among the dead.

"I didn't want a static object," she said. "I wanted something people could walk into, and be part of."

The entry was anonymous. No one knew she was a student. No one knew she was Asian American. When she won, the backlash was swift and personal. But she held her line. Like the wall itself – solid, silent, unmoved.

She's brought this process to everything since. She visits the site. She listens. She sketches. She waits. She lets the place shape her – and then she shapes it in return.

"If what I build looks exactly like the model," she said, "it's dead."

PLASTIC → SHAPE → PLASTIC

The mind reshapes the form. And the form reshapes the mind.

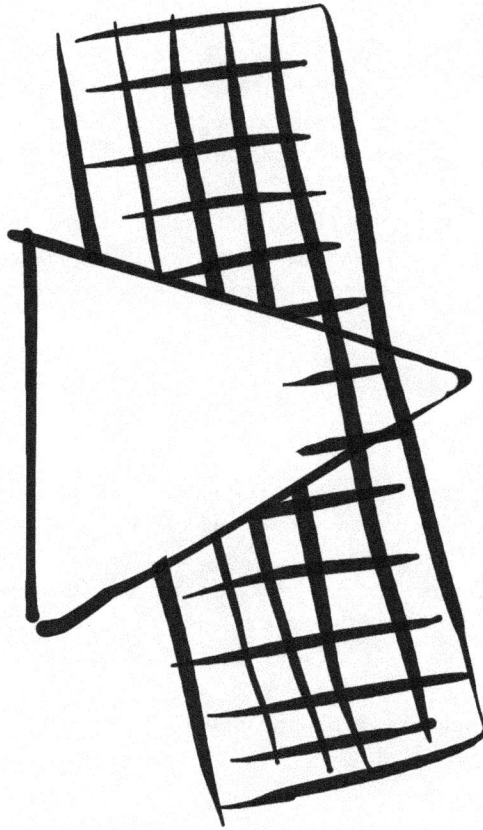

PLASTIC FANTASTIC NO. 2 –
THE WEDGE THAT CHANGED THE FRAME

Some people take hold of lines already there – categories, stories, rules – and by unpicking, re-stranding, and reweaving, they reveal a new form. One powerful enough to thread itself into individuals, into identities, into whole systems.

Kimberlé Crenshaw was born the same year as Maya Lin. But instead of design, she chose law. She could see how legal structures shaped lives – who got protection, who got believed, who got left out. And she saw, again and again, that the law itself was not neutral. It had blind spots, and people fell straight through.

That became painfully clear during the Anita Hill hearings. A Black woman accused a Black Supreme Court nominee of sexual harassment – and the nation split. Feminists rallied to Hill. Black communities closed ranks around Thomas. The two movements didn't converge – they collided. Hill, caught at the centre, was left standing alone. The lines of identity that should have offered support became crosshairs.

Crenshaw had seen this before. In one case, Black women sued General Motors for discrimination. The company defended itself by pointing to Black men on the factory floor – and white women in the office. The court agreed: no discrimination. Because neither race nor gender alone had been violated, the claim was dismissed. The actual lived experience – Black and woman – had no legal category. No standing. No name.

Crenshaw gave it one: intersectionality.

"Cultural patterns of oppression," she wrote, "are not only interrelated, but are bound together and influenced by the intersection of race, gender, class, and other characteristics."

Intersectionality wasn't theory for theory's sake. It became a lens. A net. A knife. A map. It let people see who was falling through – and why. And it gave them a tool to change it.

If you think this doesn't include you – it does. Because the loops that hold people down are the same ones that keep systems from becoming better. You don't have to live at the intersection to help redraw the map.

PLASTIC → SHAPE → PLASTIC

She reshaped the lens. And the lens reshaped the system.

287

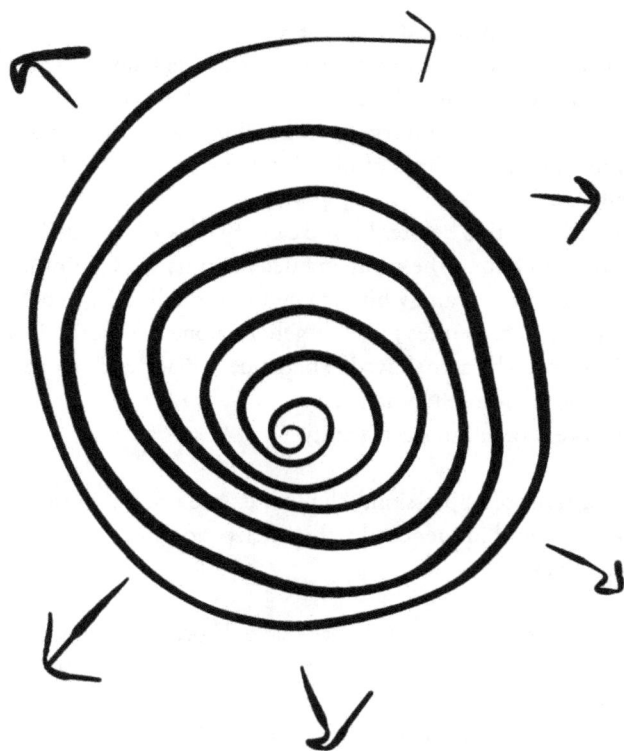

PLASTIC FANTASTIC NO. 3 –
THE LOOP WE BUILT OURSELVES

Some people know how to ebb and flow. They hold shapes of safety and support
– stretching when needed, softening when necessary. Like water, they change
form without losing who they are.

They don't get trapped in fixed positions. They don't fight battles with
no winners. They find their third space – and build a shape they can keep
returning to.

On the first day of 1994, while the rest of the continent celebrated the launch
of the North American Free Trade Agreement, something different happened in
southern Mexico. A small Indigenous resistance force emerged from the forests of
Chiapas. They took over towns, freed prisoners, and declared that the system no
longer represented them.

There were thousands of them – poor, mostly Indigenous, largely invisible to the global economy. Many had no electricity, no clean water, no access to basic education. Their uprising was sudden, but it wasn't a rebellion of rage. It was a refusal shaped over centuries. Their cry was simple: ¡Ya basta! Enough.

But instead of collapsing into violence, something unexpected happened. The government prepared to strike back, but was stopped – literally – by its own conscience. The interior minister threatened to resign if the military moved in. So they talked. And the Zapatistas did something almost unheard of in modern revolutionary history: they stayed where they were, and started building.

They didn't take power. They built loops.

Today, they run their own schools, clinics, courts, assemblies – across dozens of self-governing municipalities. They don't accept external labels. Their spokesperson, once known as Subcomandante Marcos, deliberately stepped back from the spotlight. Decisions are made through elders and assemblies. They govern not by commanding, but by listening.

Para todos todo, para nosotros nada. Everything for everyone, nothing for ourselves.

They've marched silently through towns just to remind the country they still exist – only to disappear back into the trees. And when they expand, it's with consent. At one point, the Mexican president congratulated them for bringing order to forgotten regions.

They built a loop that didn't seek victory – it sought endurance.

Mandar obedeciendo. To lead by obeying.

PLASTIC → SHAPE → PLASTIC

They reshaped themselves. And the system reshaped around them.
Each of them modelled the world – and changed it. Here's how you begin.

FROM TRAPPED TO TRANSCENDED
How reshaping yourself reshapes the world

This whole chapter – this whole book – has always been about how we adapt. How we overcome overwhelm. How we transcend the apparent limits of ourselves, our systems, our situations.

Humans have always done this. Across every sea, every continent, every environment – even out into space. Whether we're seeking to go where no one's gone before, or just trying to find a quieter place to sit, we stretch what holds us. We transcend.

Modelling like a superadapter means you don't have to fix everything – you just have to understand enough. Enough to stretch what's suffocating. Enough to sense what gives. Enough to see what you can work with, and what you must reshape.

That's why we looked at nets and knots. At da Vinci and Kusama. At Crenshaw's wedge and Lin's incision. At systems that held – and systems that flexed.

And that's why this table exists.

To show the shift.
From being shaped by the system… to reshaping the system that's shaping you.

You do it by finding a third shape – and using that third shape to remake the system that's holding you in.

TRAPPED VS TRANSCENDED

	WHEN YOU'RE TRAPPED...	**WHEN YOU TRANSCEND...**
Sense the Shape	You absorb the surface. You inherit roles. You react as if systems are fixed. You feel pressure but don't map the pattern. The loop starts without your consent.	You pause to feel for structure. You detect the rhythm beneath the reaction. You sense where things hold – and where they might give. The model begins with awareness.
Sketch the Shape	You cling to old maps. You mistake neatness for clarity. You sketch to explain, not to explore. The model stays static – and so do you.	You draw to test. You annotate possibility. You sketch not to control, but to learn. The model becomes a living surface – updated with every move.
Stretch the Shape	You respect the frame more than the fit. You wait for permission to innovate. You assume systems will break if you bend them. So you stay small.	You reshape without rupture. You act as if the system is plastic. You probe for flex, and model a future inside the form. You stretch what shapes you – and the shape changes.

When you're trapped by a model, you often don't know you're inside one. You inherit roles. You follow rules. You feel pressure – but you can't see the pattern. The loop starts without your consent.

To transcend, you don't just break free. You sense. You pause. You begin to feel how the system works.

Then you sketch. Not to control – but to test. To move pieces. To try a shape that's never been drawn before.

And then, you stretch. You push gently against what feels fixed. And you discover – sometimes for the first time – that the system is plastic. That you are plastic. That a new shape is possible.

This is what superadapters do. They loop. They learn. They reshape what shapes them.

THREE WRONG LOOPS OF MODELLING
When plastic stops being fantastic

By now, you'll be getting familiar with this. When we try to model our world – to understand what's really happening, spot the important bits, identify leverage points, or locate what's causing pressure – it can go wrong in predictable ways. Three, to be exact.

HYPO happens when you model too slowly, too little, or too late. If you model too slowly, you may have recognised the right problem – but you don't get round to understanding enough to act. If you model incompletely, you delay understanding the system's shape. And when you model too late, you haven't even begun to ask whether you're looking at the right thing.

You notice the student has stopped raising their hand. You know that's something to investigate – but you don't get around to it. So you never find out you've moved their seat – next to someone who's been quietly bullying them. Or you sense that some days at work are far more productive than others. But you never take the time to ask why. You don't realise your best days always begin with a walk. And because you don't model the pattern, the whole year suffers.

So ask yourself: What signal have I already detected that I haven't got around to? What insight have I tagged as important, but never returned to? What have I started modelling – then abandoned before it became useful? Where is the understanding still unfinished, and still unhelpful? And what question do I keep circling... that I'll regret not answering?

HYPER happens when you model too fast, too much, or too soon. This becomes a problem because you jump to conclusions about what the model looks like – using existing mental models that don't fit. You feel like you've made progress because something feels finished. Except it isn't finished. And it isn't clear. And it hasn't added to your understanding. It's just a double-down on your lack of understanding.

You get cause and effect the wrong way round – and much of what follows becomes wasteful or worse. You assume people are ignoring you because they're against you. So you get aggressive, or passive, or you withdraw. But all they needed was space – or a little more explanation. And because you've grabbed the wrong model too soon, you don't notice. Or maybe the model you're using isn't wrong – but you've stopped too early. You're working on your bowling technique. Or your tennis serve. But the real change would come from getting feedback, or trying a different grip. So the effort adds up – but the outcome doesn't shift. And you're left just a little more tired. A little more disappointed.

So ask yourself: Is the model you're using working? If not, maybe you rushed. Have you included other people in your thinking? Would that be part of improving the situation? Have you committed to a view of the world that feels overwhelming?

ANTI happens when you end up with the wrong model – or model the wrong thing. Sometimes it's got nothing to do with speed. It's that you're overly committed to one way of looking at the world. Either because you've accepted someone else's model and can't find a way to escape it, or because you assume and never even question it. Or because it fits too well – suits you too much. Or because you don't even notice that there was an alternative.

When someone models the world as 'us and them' – and decides there has to be an enemy – they spend their time fighting. And often, they're fighting the wrong people. Or when someone continues to wear the behavioural wardrobe of their parent or their generation – they live with the problems, without discarding what no longer fits.

So ask yourself: Am I using an outdated model of the world – or of myself? Is it doing more harm than good? Or simply leaving me stuck in place? What if I'm still living by the old version – when what I really need is the upgrade?

REAL WORLD WRONG LOOPS
That needs to be three times bigger

There's a moment in the cult comedy *Zoolander* where a famous male model is tempted back into work with a charitable promise: the client will build a learning centre for children who can't read. Derek is handed a scale model – and assumes it's the finished building. He stares at it, confused and offended, before hurling it to the ground in protest.

It's funny because it's absurd.

But it's also a perfect illustration of a modelling loop gone wrong.

When outcomes are disappointing – or disastrous – it's not always about poor decisions.

It's often poor modelling.

Of people.

Of pressure.

Of plastic limits.

HYPO Some people act fast, but build nothing. They leap without scaffolding. This is hypo-modelling: too little structure, too little sketch. The model is missing, or fragile, or guessed at mid-air. They improvise through complexity as if pattern will emerge later. But without a form to hold signal, reality collapses under the first strain.

The pitch was paradise. A luxury music festival on a private island. But behind the filters and firelight, there was no infrastructure – no water, no sanitation, no plan. Fyre Festival wasn't a failure of logistics. It was a failure of modelling. McFarland believed that branding 'was' building. But when the weather hit and the people came, the fantasy collapsed. The image held no weight. The loop broke.

Have you ever launched a project with energy but no architecture? Skipped the dry run, assumed the shape would hold? That's hypo. The signal might be strong, but without structure, it can't stretch. You don't need to build the whole system – but you need to sketch it.

HYPER Some people build forms so rigid they can't adapt. That's hyper-modelling: too much structure, too little flexibility. They design the map in perfect detail, then demand the world conform. But adaptive systems need slack, not scripts. When the unexpected comes, brittle plans break.

The 737 Max was engineered to extend a legacy system – an airframe too old for modern demands. To compensate, a software fix was added: MCAS. It was modelled to override pilot error. But the model itself was brittle – rigid, uncommunicated, untouchable. When sensors failed, the system forced fatal nosedives. Boeing defended the model, denied the problem. The result: two catastrophes. This wasn't complexity – it was inflexibility.

Have you ever clung to a plan while the world changed around you? Refused feedback because you were too invested in the form? That's hyper. Your model must breathe. The world won't fit your diagram. Build to flex, not freeze.

ANTI can happen when people refuse models altogether. That's anti-modelling: denying the need for structure, skipping the sketch entirely. These people rely on charisma, vibes, instinct. They act like modelling is weakness. But without form, there's no feedback. And without feedback, there's no loop.

At its peak, WeWork was valued at $47 billion. But it had no clear business model, no path to profit, no structure underneath the slogans. What it had was narrative: a founder, a myth, a movement. Adam Neumann spoke of energy, disruption, consciousness. But inside the walls, decisions bent to vision. The company scaled a model that didn't work, while pretending it wasn't a model at all.

Have you ever avoided defining what you're really doing – because naming it might break the spell? That's Anti. Vision without form turns recursive. Eventually, it spirals. Often the best way to improve parts of your reality is to sense, sketch and stretch the models that make it so.

THE COUNTER LOOPS
Three ways to restore your model loop when things go wrong.

A fabulous fact about this approach to being more adaptable is that the very habits that get things going right are also the ones that stop them going wrong – and the ones that help you recover when they do. They're prevention and repair in the same move. Each one brings the loop back into form. Because you're modelling the world – your situation, your system, yourself. Your loop doesn't just need to run. It needs to return. To flex. To bounce back. Or to be moulded into something new – to provide the third shape. These next three habits help you do exactly that.

SENSE THE SHAPE helps you prevent modelling too slowly, too little, or too late – because you've trained yourself to be model-sensitive. You notice consequences before they unfold. You register delay not as absence, but as tension. Over time, you've built internal maps – sequence models, consequence models, possibility models – that let you read the shape of what's coming. You feel where something is off-pattern, too quiet, too slow. And when things have already begun to slip, this habit repairs the loop by helping you resurface the form. You reattune. You catch the shimmer, the echo, the pulse. You're not just watching – you're interpreting. And because you sensed it early, it's not too late to change.

SKETCH THE SHAPE helps you prevent modelling too much, too fast, or too soon – by inserting the habit of drawing it out. Getting it out of your head expands your ability to think about it. It invites multiple perspectives. You can move around your choices the way a camera circles a scene, or a hand moves over a chess board. Whether it's drawn, stacked in objects, shaped in clay, or mapped on a whiteboard – your model becomes visible, movable, testable. And if you keep the components simple enough, you do your future self a favour. You reduce cognitive load. You increase room for manoeuvre. And when things have already gone wrong, this habit helps you pause and say: Wait – have I really sketched this out? What am I missing? What if I shift one part? Sketching is how you see what you're thinking – and ask the questions your model needs.

295

STRETCH THE SHAPE protects you from choosing the wrong model to guide your actions – because you stretch the logic, the structure, the consequences, and the contours of what you're living inside. Sometimes that model is large: your relationship, your culture, your career arc. Other times it's small but decisive. Like our most plastic exemplars, you ask: is this fit for purpose? What's it really made of? Stretching reveals not just its shape – but its limits. You bounce the model like a ball, kick its tyres, bend it in your mind. You stretch your self-concept too – into different forms, roles, tones – just to see what moves. This is how superadapters adapt: they stress-test before committing. They say: is this still working? Will it still work next time? And if not – what shape must I become to change what happens next?

You've learned to see the world as flexible – and to model what you're inside: your mind, your situation, your system. And then we looked at how to put that right again through the counter loops. These slips will happen – because we're not perfect, and because we often want more than we yet understand. This is still part of the overall path to greater adaptability.

So it's vital. It's valuable. It's worth your time to come back to these pages – to keep training, to keep tweaking, to keep deepening your approach to modelling. Even just naming this as a loop, a system of sketchable behaviours, a structured way to think – has already moved you forward. But there's more. You've opened the door. You've felt its shape. And by now, you've seen what it achieves, what can go wrong, and how to correct. That's real progress. That's adaptive plasticity.

REBOOTING THEIR (RUN) LOOPS

Plastic minds don't just adapt once. They adapt again. And again. Rebooting isn't a failure of the loop. It's a sign the mind is still stretching for more.

We would expect that plastic people continue to reshape themselves – and their worlds.

And as it turns out, that's exactly what they did.

You've met them already – three people who used their minds to sense, sketch, and stretch the world they were in. But that wasn't the end of their story. Each faced another kind of pressure later. Not a breakthrough. A breakdown. Not the launch of a model, but the moment the model no longer held.

This section doesn't repeat what you already know. It shows you what happens next.

Because superadaptability isn't just the ability to loop once. It's the ability to reboot the loop when it stalls, breaks, or betrays you. When the form you trusted no longer holds, or when the system stops responding, or when success itself becomes the trap.

This is what we learn from these minds – not just how to rise, but how to re-enter. How to use the same loop to keep moving:

RECOGNISE → UNDERSTAND → NECESSARY ACTION.

Marcel Marceau didn't just return from war. He returned from silence.

He had helped smuggle children across borders, had forged documents with red crayons and black ink, had used mime to keep hope quiet. After the war, he could have walked away from it all. Instead, he created Bip – half clown, half witness. But even as his fame grew, the loop began to fray. He toured endlessly, spoke rarely, and drifted from the root of his resistance.

Then something shifted.

In the 1950s and 1960s, as his celebrity expanded, he saw that the meaning of mime was becoming performance, not purpose. And in that gap, he began again.

He recognised the drift – not just in himself, but in the applause that covered absence. He understood that silence wasn't just a trick. It was a tool. A message. A discipline. He rebooted – not louder, but deeper. Mime became medicine. He brought grief to the stage as metaphor, not memory.

This wasn't nostalgia. It was the loop returning – not for the fame, but for the function.

His third shape was presence as silence – looped, re-entered, reshaped again.

Leonardo da Vinci spent years in Milan without a patron.

After the fall of Ludovico Sforza in 1499, da Vinci entered a long period without commissions or court support. No theatre. No status. No grand canvases. He could have faded.

Instead, he returned to the sketch. Not for others – but for himself.

He dissected horses. He drew water currents. He designed machines the world wouldn't understand for centuries. He filled notebooks not for display, but for continuity.

He recognised that the external world had stalled – but his loop hadn't.

This was his reboot. Observation without commission. Structure without reward. A retreat into systems that the world would catch up to later.

Sometimes the system doesn't reward the loop. That doesn't mean you stop looping.

His third shape was the endless sketch – plastic thought in recursive motion.

Václav Havel's most famous acts are already legend: from dissident playwright to president. But his third act was quieter, and harder.

After leaving office in 2003, he became a symbol – an icon too easy to quote, too hard to hear. Reverence began to distort his message. He saw it coming.

In a 1994 Harvard speech, he warned that, "The tragedy of modern man is not that he knows less and less about the meaning of his own life, but that it bothers him less and less." He wasn't talking about others. He was talking about all of us – including himself.

He recognised the trap of legacy: when your past becomes too big to challenge, and your message is reduced to aphorism.

He understood that real change didn't come from fame. It came from risking relevance. So he started writing again – essays, interviews, scripts. He used language not as platform, but as provocation. He spoke not just about democracy, but about the systems of power that lived inside our habits, our theatre, our discourse.

And then something remarkable happened.

After his death in 2011, his words began to loop again. Activists in Ukraine quoted him. Protesters in Belarus held signs that echoed Charter 77. Philosophers and students returned to his plays to understand power, not just oppose it.

His loop wasn't finished. It was rebooting – through others.

His third shape was language under pressure – a model that outlived him, because it outlooped him.

These weren't just people with a breakthrough.

They were people who re-entered the loop.

Not to repeat it – but to reshape the shape that had once shaped them.

RECOGNISE → UNDERSTAND → NECESSARY ACTION

REBOOT YOUR LOOP
From stressed out to shaped up

We all have different behaviours when we're stressed. Go-tos. Defaults. Some are more effective than others. Some involve people. Some involve patterns. Some are rituals we don't even realise we're repeating.

There are things we do that don't help. Self-talk that spirals. Criticism that becomes habit. You tell yourself you're unworthy, incompetent, out of time. You avoid what matters. You can't sleep. You lash out. You turn to food, noise, or nothing.

But some people reach for something else.

The Chinese had Baoding balls – stone or metal spheres, rotated in the hand. Catholics have rosary beads. Buddhists, prayer beads. Fidget toys. Wristbands. Clickers. Hair-twisting. Pen-tapping. Every one of them says the same thing: "I'm reaching for something that helps."

In 1988, a man named Alex Carswell threw a pen at a wall in frustration and shattered a framed photo of his mother. So he invented something you could throw – a soft blue ball – without breaking anything. The modern stress ball.

It works. Squeeze, release. You tense the muscle and notice the difference. That's biofeedback. Your body teaches your brain what tension feels like, and what relaxation could be.

And in Japan? The same idea shows up again: squishies. Polyurethane foam animals that deform, then return to shape. Slowly. Gently. Recursively.

Some called them 'mindless manipulation toys'. But they're not mindless at all. They're a third space – a place between reaction and response.

When I tell you that the stress ball is a handheld model of your RUN loop – shapeable, resettable, quietly recursive – and that it gives you back agency through feedback – this is neuroscience, not just a metaphor.

This isn't just stress relief. It's plasticity in action. The stress ball isn't the answer. It's a shape you can return to. It models what your mind can do, too.

Maya Lin reshaped grief into stone. Crenshaw reshaped injustice into a frame. You don't need a memorial. You need a moment of shape.

I'm giving you a neuroplastic invitation: You can reshape your responses to reshape your world.

This is your moment to insert the loop. Snap the band. Squeeze the squishy. Remember what you're doing here.

You don't need to rebuild yourself from scratch. You need to RECOGNISE what's rising, UNDERSTAND the system you're in, and take the NECESSARY ACTION to reshape the loop – this time, with your hands on it.

TRANSCEND THE LOOP
How plastic minds reshape the world from the inside out

"Any man could, if he were so inclined, be the sculptor of his own brain."
– Santiago Ramón y Cajal, *Advice for a Young Investigator*

In this chapter – Be Plastic Fantastic – you've seen how superadaptive people can sense a system's shape, sketch its outline, and stretch what once felt fixed.

You've seen what it means to move through a plastic world with a plastic mind. From Renaissance Italy to modern memorials. From anti-authoritarian children to world-shaping visionaries. You've seen what it looks like to live the shape of human plasticity.

You've also seen that modelling isn't just about describing. It's about understanding the system well enough to change it – or change yourself. A model, then, isn't just a picture. It's not just a metaphor. It's something you step into.

A model is a surface you can live on. A set of assumptions you can walk through – or walk around.

And when it's working, the shapes that shape you are no longer invisible. They become visible. And as they become visible, they become malleable. You begin to reshape them.

Some people don't just adapt to systems. They model them from the inside. They let themselves be reshaped in order to reshape what's around them.

The model isn't fixed.
The model isn't on paper or a whiteboard.
The model is them.

The model can be me.
The model can be you.
And in this next example, the model is all of the plastic people in it.

PLASTIC DREAMS, ELECTRIC EELS

In the southeastern Amazon, deep in Ecuador's Pastaza province, live the Achuar – a people of 18,500 who have protected the rainforest for generations. They do not believe the forest is a resource. They believe it is sacred. They have resisted oil companies, mining, and colonisation – not just with force, but with pattern: dreams, ritual, story, structure.

Every morning before sunrise, they drink wayusa tea and share their dreams aloud. Together they interpret what the day might hold. The practice isn't decorative. It's directional. It's how they model what's coming – before it comes.

In 2009, in this same region, a former college student named Oliver Utne arrived to teach English. He wasn't there to fix anything. But what he found was a culture already modelling its future – through myth, tea, and dreams.

Fuel in the region cost up to ten dollars a gallon. Diesel boats – known as *peque peques* – polluted the rivers and drained resources. Roads would invite deforestation, smuggling, and the collapse of cultural autonomy.

Dreaming isn't mystical. It's cognitive space. It's what your brain does when it's no longer overfitting – no longer trapped in one task, one constraint. In the dream space, the loop opens. New possibilities emerge.

Utne didn't teach a lesson. He entered a model. He sat in the circle, high on caffeine and conversation, and let his mind stretch.

The Achuar told stories of Tapiatpia, the mythical electric eel said to glide silently between worlds. That became the metaphor. The model. The first boat was named after it.

Together they co-dreamed the solution. Kara Solar was born in 2012. The first boats launched five years later. They consulted engineers, refined designs, built vessels powered by sun and shaped by story.

They didn't want more peque peques – expensive diesel boats that polluted their sacred river. They didn't want roads.

They wanted something else. A third shape.

The fleet has grown to nine boats, each gliding cleanly between villages, supported by solar stations and maintained by local engineers. Communities remain intact. Territory remains unbroken.

The model didn't just change transportation.

It protected the loop.

And it still runs.

THE NEXT MISSION
Your fantastic voyage continues

I remember watching a film as a kid – *Fantastic Voyage*.

A team of scientists are miniaturised – shrunken down with their submarine, Proteus – and injected into the body of a comatose defector who holds a vital secret. They have one hour before they return to full size. Inside his bloodstream, they face obstacle after obstacle. Their goal? Find the mechanism that's threatening him: a blood clot. Remove it. Escape. Save him – and the secret he carries.

What captivated me wasn't the science fiction. It was the model.

A system. A threat. A loop. A chance to go inside – to understand enough to act.

That's what you've just done here. This rule has been your Proteus: your vessel for seeing the shape of a system. You've sensed it, sketched it, stretched it. You've found a third shape that lets you stay adaptive inside what once felt fixed.

But modelling is just the beginning.

Now comes the next function of understanding: modifying the mechanism.

In that story, it was a blood clot. In yours, it might be a policy, a pattern, a story, a switch.

You don't need to rebuild the system. You need to find the point that holds everything together – and unlock it.

Your fantastic voyage continues.

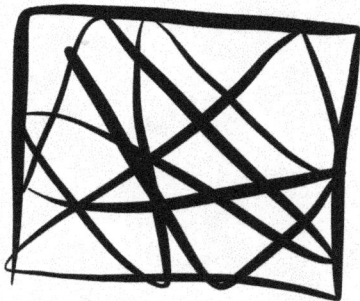

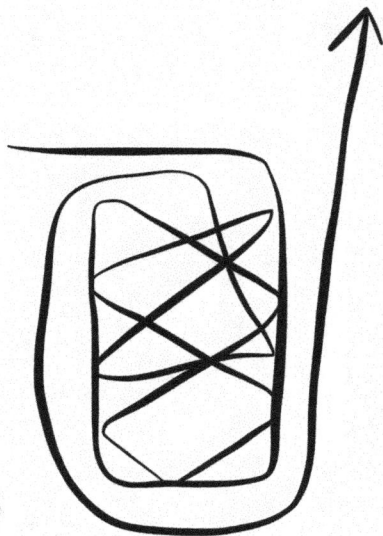

RULE 5:
UNLATCH THE CATCH

The one about trap-breaking

Many systems trap us in absurd or self-defeating loops. Superadaptable people diagnose the underlying mechanisms. They find the catch, study it, and release themselves. Escape becomes possible not through force, but precision. Transcending the limits of self, system, and situation.

Some traps don't snap shut. They drift in quietly, disguised as responsibility, efficiency, good manners, endurance. You don't feel them clamp down. You just stop moving. And then, after a while, you forget that you used to.

This is where the superadapter does something different. They don't fight harder. They don't explode the system. They pause – and look. Not at the whole thing. At the hinge. The bit that holds it in place. The mechanism. Because once you see that, you have a choice. You can lever it, shift it, turn it – sometimes only slightly – and the whole system moves. You move.

You've already begun. You've recognised what's wrong. You've started to model how the system holds together. But now you're stepping into something deeper. This Rule isn't about opinion. It's about orientation. Not about judgement, but engineering. Because understanding mechanisms – what drives, stalls, redirects, or distorts a system – is what allows you to actually change it. Not in theory. In practice.

That's what Rule 5 is. It's the rule of what blocks. What sticks. What catches. And how to move it. It's what enables you to see the loop as it is – and then do something about it. But that's not all. This isn't just a lesson in friction. It's an invitation to precision. To begin seeing the systems you move through – family, culture, government, work, body, belief – not as fixed walls or moral absolutes, but as configurations. You are surrounded by mechanisms. You are full of them. Some are holding you. Some are holding you back. Some need redesigning. Some are waiting to be released.

And the key is that any mechanism can be a trap. But any trap can also be a door. The difference isn't in the structure. It's in your stance, your view, your timing. That's the mindset. And once you have it, the world begins to open – not all at once, but click by click, catch by catch. This chapter will show you how.

THE HIDDEN LEVER

There's a story – maybe apocryphal, maybe not – about a footballer in his thirties, signed to an Italian club. He had recurring ankle injuries. Everyone assumed he was past his prime. But the club had a different way of thinking. Their medical team didn't just treat the pain. They studied the player as a system. And they found something strange.

The ankle issue, it turned out, wasn't from the ankle. It came from the jaw. A misaligned dental filling had subtly shifted the player's gait, which altered his stride, which weakened his stabilisers, which overloaded his ankle. They adjusted the filling. The pain stopped. The injury didn't return.

The club had found the mechanism. The hidden lever. The one place that made all the difference.

This is what Rule 5 is about. The thing that looks like the problem isn't always the problem. You can focus on the visible breakdowns. Or you can trace the loop further. To the point where the system holds. Where it stabilises. Where it resists. And if you find that point – if you know how to look for it – you can do more than fix the issue.

You can change how the whole system moves.

The biggest change doesn't come from the most obvious problem. It comes from the smallest, most accurate adjustment – the hidden lever inside the system.

THE LOOP BEGINS

Nelson Mandela once said, it always seems impossible until it's done. But in adaptation, it's never just the doing that makes the difference. It's finding the mechanism that makes doing possible.

That's what this chapter is about.

You're about to enter a section called the Mechanism Loop. It's the part of the Rule where things get specific. Not abstract. Not motivational. Real. You're going to meet three people who each demonstrate one part of this loop – three habits that, together, show how superadapters identify, understand, and move what holds them in place.

The loop looks like this: Find the Flaw → Spot the Catch → Craft the Key

It starts by recognising what isn't quite working – not catastrophically, just subtly misaligned. Then it asks what's holding that misalignment in place: what belief, rule, rhythm, expectation, or trap is keeping the loop stuck. And finally, it asks you to build something – just one precise shift – that can turn the system without breaking it.

Each person you'll meet in this loop models a different habit. One will show you how to name the flaw before it hardens. One will teach you to see what's really holding the system together. One will show you how to intervene – not with force, but with structure.

This loop is a shortcut. It's what superadapters use to avoid waste, false starts, and broken strategies. You're going to see it used across different domains: global systems, institutional battles, psychological constraints. But the loop works the same way, whether it's being used to challenge a regime or rewire a daily habit. That's what makes it powerful. And transferable.

And this is just the beginning. After you've seen the loop run, we'll sit down together. You'll reflect, connect, and begin to trace how this applies to your own life. You'll see how to braid insights across examples. You'll get to try it yourself. You'll learn what goes wrong when the loop is misapplied – and what happens when it's rerun with clarity.

You're not just learning a habit here. You're learning a system. One that can help you move – out of stuckness, past the trap, and toward something that works.

Let's begin.

THE MECHANISM LOOP

HOW SUPERADAPTERS USE MECHANISMS
It's not enough to notice that something is wrong.

Superadaptive people go further. They use their recognition to locate the actual mechanism that's making it happen. And they use their understanding to work out what would need to change to unlock it.

That's what this loop is about.

We all live inside systems. But systems aren't monolithic. They're made of parts. Interlocking gears. Invisible levers. And catches.

Mechanisms.

Mechanisms explain how things happen. They are the part of the model that matters most – because when you touch the right mechanism, you touch the outcome.

Superadapters get good at this. They learn to locate and leverage. They study how systems work – not in the abstract, but in motion, in failure, in frustration. They examine where things break, what stalls or multiplies progress, what locks people in, what lets them out. They know that behind every repeating failure, every stuck pattern or spiralling process, there's always a mechanism. And if you can name it, you can change it.

This is how they do it.

First, they **Find the Flaw** – they scan for what's broken, misaligned, or malfunctioning 'before' it breaks them.

Then, they **Spot the Catch** – they name the lock or trap that's holding the failure in place.

Finally, they **Craft the Key** – they identify what would need to shift, and how to reroute the system.

Across the next three examples, you'll see this pattern in action. Real minds, real lives, and real-world leverage.

This isn't abstract theory. It's structural insight, applied.

THE SUPERADAPTER MECHANISM MINDSET

Most people don't get stuck because they're lazy or lost. They get stuck because they never learned to look for the mechanism. They're told to try harder. To think positively. To be resilient. But no one teaches them to trace the loop. To find the catch. To look beneath what seems like reality and ask: What's actually holding this in place?

Superadapters don't just act. They investigate. They don't just recognise problems – they scan for levers. They believe there is always a structure, and always a point where that structure can shift.

This is the mechanism mindset. It doesn't require genius. It requires orientation. A superadapter doesn't assume they'll figure it out by thinking harder. They assume there's something built – visible or invisible – that can be unlatched, if seen clearly enough.

They don't look for control. They look for engagement. They know that in almost every stuck system, there is one hinge, one weak point, one small embedded flaw that's holding the larger failure together. And they train themselves to see it.

They believe: there must be a way. I need a way. I must find a way. I found a way.

They don't overpower the structure. They observe it long enough to understand it from within. They look for movement not at the edge, but at the centre. And they begin their intervention not with force – but with focus.

They're not faster. They're more precise. They know that almost all transformation – whether personal or organisational, psychological or structural – begins not with an explosion, but with a well-placed turn.

They don't wait for perfect knowledge. But they never move without a working model. They don't assume they'll get it right the first time. But they assume it's worth trying until the right mechanism fits.

This isn't a personality trait. It's a cognitive stance. And it can be learned.

You're about to meet three people who didn't just escape the loop. They spotted the catch. They crafted the mechanism. They shifted the system.

Let's continue our mechanism hunt.

HABIT 1: FIND THE FLAW

You're about to meet three people. Each of them faced a system that was supposed to work – but didn't. Each of them did something different from those around them. They didn't just adjust to the brokenness. They found the flaw.

That's the first habit in this loop. Find the Flaw. Scan for what's broken, misaligned, or malfunctioning – before it breaks you.

The first person you'll meet is Wangari Maathai. In 1970s Kenya, she faced a system that rewarded environmental degradation, punished dissent, and treated rural women as expendable. But she didn't just resist it – she spotted the flaw. She recognised that what was being called progress was actually erosion, displacement, and collapse.

And that was where her loop began.

Because if you can't find the flaw, you'll be broken by it. But if you can? You can start to unlatch the catch.

WANGARI MAATHAI

The riverbeds where she grew up no longer sang.
  They cracked.
  The children no longer ran with gourds of water balanced on their heads. They waited, exhausted, for mothers to return from vanished forests. The women no longer returned before dusk.
  They returned at dusk, or after it, their backs broken from carrying the wood that grew further and further away every season.
  It was not a storybook tragedy.
  It was something stranger. Quieter.
  The streams did not dry all at once.
  The trees did not fall in one great timbering crash.
  The soil did not blow away like a sandstorm.
  The collapse happened slowly, year after year, unnoticed by those who only looked at the surface.
  At first, Wangari saw it the way everyone else did: As a background sadness. As bad luck.
  As something to endure.
  But she could not leave it alone.

The dissatisfaction inside her – the sharp sense that something about the story was wrong – refused to subside.

When she travelled to villages across Kenya, she saw the pattern repeating:

More dust where gardens used to be.

More hunger where maize used to grow.

More labour where ease used to be.

And with every mile, the same false explanations were offered:

The rains are poor.

The land is cursed.

This is just how it is now.

But Wangari was not born to accept surface limits.

Not then.

Not ever.

She began asking quiet questions:

Why were the streams drying when the rains still sometimes came?

Why were the hills bald when seeds should have taken root?

Why were women walking farther every year, carrying less, returning later?

The answers did not lie in the immediate hardship.

They lay deeper – underneath politics, underneath economics, underneath memory itself.

And as she listened, as she travelled, as she pressure-tested her own assumptions, the fracture line became clear:

The flaw wasn't just the absence of trees.

The flaw was the severing of people from the land that sustained them.

Where once the forest had been a commons – a living system – now it was fenced, sold, cleared, and profited from by the few.

Environmental collapse was not natural.

It was engineered.

It was political.

It was a system trap pretending to be destiny.

It was a broken mechanism disguised as a natural cycle – a loop of depletion and disconnection mistaken for fate.

For Wangari, the recognition was not enough.

Seeing the flaw was only the beginning.

The next step – 'Understand' – required seeing how deeply the flaw was woven into the fabric of daily life: into women's bodies, into children's bellies, into the slow death of communities.

The destruction of trees wasn't just environmental damage.

It was a disempowerment machine.

Every tree lost was an hour of labour stolen, a meal missed, a child pulled from school to fetch firewood.

And so, she did something so simple it seemed absurd.

She wasn't just restoring land – she was intervening in the system itself. Reconnecting what had been severed. Rewiring a broken loop.

She began planting trees.

Seven trees at first.

Seven living gestures of refusal.

Where others saw the missing forest, she saw the first root tip of recovery.

Where others saw exhaustion, she saw leverage.

She didn't begin with national policy.

She began with hands.

Hands in dirt.

Hands tying seedlings.

She taught women to plant trees for fuel, for shade, for food, for time itself.

Each tree was a small act of rebellion against collapse.

Each tree was a bead of water from the hummingbird's beak – a single drop against the inferno.

And the drops multiplied.

And the movement spread.

And the Green Belt Movement grew from a handful of women in rural Kenya to millions of trees across East Africa.

In every workshop, in every speech, she carried the same simple but seismic message:

"We cannot wait for others to save us. We must do what we can, where we are, with what we have."

This was not shallow idealism.

It was deep, deliberate recursion.

Each action created new leverage.

Each planted tree created more strength to plant the next.

She found the flaw not by grand theory.

She found it by standing close enough to the pain to see the hidden trap inside it – and then finding a way to rewire the system, seed by seed, loop by loop.

She didn't just adapt.

She adapted her own way of thinking.

She monitored her thoughts and improved them consciously.

She looked at herself from outside herself – like you're doing now.

This active meta-cognitive behaviour is the seed that grows the tree that produces the seeds that grow the forest.

Take a breath.

In this way, you can adapt how you think and act – and then step even further outside of yourself to improve your ability to adapt how you think and act.

Your brain becomes more flexible.

Your neural pathways fire and rewire new adaptive loops.

And this meta-plasticity is how superadaptive minds like Wangari's are able to find the flaws – and then reason out ways to fix them.

They grow with their understanding.

They change size and shape so that they can step outside and move inside to find the mechanisms that need unlocking.

They don't need to use the words.

They don't need to say "I'm being meta-cognitive" or "I'm using plasticity" – it shows in practice.

In the ways they think and the ways their brains reshape themselves – and through their reshaping – reshape their world.

FIND THE FLAW → SPOT THE CATCH → CRAFT THE KEY

She listened first.

Not for noise, but for pattern. For stress, strain, misalignment.

Wangari Maathai found the flaw not by pointing at power, but by standing close to what was breaking – soil, water, women's backs.

She acted early. She listened long. And because she noticed what others ignored, she began to rebuild.

The loop didn't start with anger. It started with recognition.

And that's what the first habit is:

To see the problem 'before' the system breaks.

To spot the weakness while it still looks ordinary.

To read the early signals, even when no one else can feel the shift.

That's how loops begin.

But seeing the flaw isn't enough.

Some flaws aren't bugs. They're design features.

Some systems are built to hide their catch points – to make obedience look like freedom.

That's why the next habit matters.

HABIT 2: SPOT THE CATCH

Superadapters don't just see what's broken.

They identify the mechanism that holds it in place.

And sometimes that mechanism is beautifully disguised.

Sometimes it looks like process. Or patriotism. Or performance.

To see it – you have to look deeper.

Not at what's failing.

But at what's being maintained.

Spot the Catch is about identifying the specific lock, script, or mechanism that makes the system repeat itself – and keeps the flaw from being removed.

A person who did this with astonishing clarity was Alexei Navalny.

Born in 1976 in the Soviet Union. Lawyer. Anti-corruption investigator. Opposition leader.

He didn't just protest.

He 'named' the catch.

He showed that modern Russia wasn't just a broken democracy.

It was a functioning mechanism of control – 'designed' to appear democratic, but calibrated to reproduce power.

He saw the performance.

He mapped the gears.

And then he showed the world where the pressure points were hiding.

That's where we go next.

This is what it means to Spot the Catch.

ALEXEI NAVALNY

In August 2020, somewhere over the Siberian sky, Alexei Navalny began to feel his body betray him.

It started with a burning in his throat. Then a spreading nausea. Then the sense – deep, unmistakable – that something was wrong, and not in the ordinary way.

For most, it would have been too late.

For most, the trap would have sprung silently.

The body would collapse. The mind would go dark.

The system would have won – clean, deniable, untraceable.

But Navalny – attuned to threat, trained by years of political ambush and procedural violence – recognised the pattern inside the dizziness.

He didn't just suffer.

He spotted the catch.

This wasn't illness.

This wasn't chance.

This was engineered failure – systematic, internalised, pre-approved by the state.

Mid-flight, as his consciousness frayed, he gave a single recursive order: Force an emergency landing. Divert the plane.

Don't ask permission.

That decision – acted on with only minutes to spare – saved his life.

The trap hadn't closed. Not entirely.

But this wasn't his first catch. And it wasn't his last.

Because for Navalny, spotting the catch was never just about survival.

It was about system rupture.

From his earliest days as a lawyer and activist in post-Soviet Russia, he understood the deeper architecture: A regime that used the appearance of legality to hide its mechanisms of control.

Elections that looked democratic.

Judges that looked independent.

Media that sounded pluralistic.

A modern state, in mimicry only.

That was the catch.

The state's real genius wasn't in silencing dissent – it was in writing the script so tightly that obedience looked like freedom.

If you follow the rules, you play your part.

If you play your part, you validate the system.

If you validate the system, the trap remains invisible – replicable, enforceable, global.

Navalny saw it.

And once you see a catch, you can loop it back.

He began building adaptive mirrors.

The Anti-Corruption Foundation (FBK) wasn't just investigative.

It was recursive.

Every video looped public money back to private hands.

Every exposé reflected the regime's logic onto itself.

He didn't merely accuse. He revealed.

Here's the palace.

Here's the luxury watch.

Here's the contract.

Here's the signature.

Here's the law that was broken.

And here's the law that protects the breaker.

One loop showed Putin's alleged secret mansion with a gold-plated toilet brush. Another traced oil revenues back to yachts, bodyguards, and fake tenders.

They weren't just facts.

They were mechanism diagrams.

Not finger-pointing. Circuit-breaking.

That was Navalny's craft: recursive pattern revelation.

He used bureaucracy against itself.

He exposed the pretense.

He filmed the mask while it was still smiling.

In every case, the catch wasn't the crime – it was the mechanism that made the crime invisible.

And when he ran for mayor of Moscow, when he challenged Putin directly, when he turned court appearances into broadcast events, he wasn't just making noise.

He was writing counter-scripts.

He was showing people that the system's choreography could be broken – frame by frame, rule by rule, loop by loop.

Even when the trap caught him again – even when he was poisoned, arrested, sentenced, disappeared into prison – he looped outward.

From inside a penal colony, Navalny still posted.

He mocked his captors.

He named the games.

He showed the lock while inside it.

When Putin tried to silence him, Navalny didn't just endure.

He split the loop.

The story rerouted through his team, his wife, his videos, his ghost.

You couldn't close the system cleanly anymore.

The catch was visible.

And visibility breaks machinery.

Navalny didn't just expose corruption. He exposed the recursive lock that made corruption untouchable.

He spotted the choreography.

He broke the rhythm.

He walked – metaphorically – sideways, like Sharansky, like anyone who sees the trap and refuses its script.

And for every person who watched his videos, shared his footage, looped his message, that act repeated.

And repeated.

And repeated.
Until the catch cracked.
Or glitched.
Or failed to reset.

FIND THE FLAW → **SPOT THE CATCH** → CRAFT THE KEY

Navalny didn't just see the flaw.

He found the catch that was preventing the flaw being fixed.

He showed the trap for what it was – a functioning mechanism disguised as democracy.

He didn't ask people to be outraged. He asked them to look.

And millions did.

They saw the patterns he revealed: the mimicry of elections, the performance of law, the looping of money and power through empty institutions.

His team's investigations didn't just go viral. They became tools. Structural explanations. Maps of hidden gears.

But here's the thing:

Even when you see the catch, it doesn't move on its own.

You can name the lock.

But that's not the same as turning the key.

HABIT 3: CRAFT THE KEY
This is the shift.
From knowing to designing.
From spotting the problem to crafting the tool that changes its behaviour.
Superadapters don't stop at understanding.
They build the mechanism that unlocks the next move.
Not just a response.
A response that fits.
Not just movement.
Meaningful movement that changes the logic of what comes next.

Because it's one thing to expose a broken method.

It's another to invent one that works.

CRAFT THE KEY means designing the mechanism that allows the system to unlock, adapt, or move forward with clarity.

Some people challenge a system from the outside.

Our next superadaptive mind did it from within.

THOMAS KANE

He was born in 1924 in Vienna and emigrated to the U.S. before World War II.

By the 1960s, he was a professor of applied mechanics at Stanford.

He wasn't loud. He wasn't radical. But he saw that the field of dynamics – the equations used to model real-world motion – was locked in a clumsy, outdated loop.

Instead of protesting, he built a better system.

He created Kane's Method – a cleaner, more efficient way of modelling motion used today in spacecraft, robotics, and biomechanics.

He didn't fight the old gears.

He crafted a new one.

And the system moved.

On the deck of the *USS Missouri*, the war was ending.

Flashbulbs blinked. Flags stirred. A treaty was signed.

History, it seemed, had reached its punctuation mark.

In the lower left of the famous photograph – kneeling in fatigues, camera poised – you can just make out the shape of a young man recording the moment: Thomas Kane.

He was 21.

A refugee from Vienna.

A soldier.

A witness to the moment the old system collapsed.

But what matters most is what he did after that.

Because Kane didn't just photograph the end of a world.

He spent the next seven decades figuring out how people move in the new one.

He became a professor of applied mechanics at Stanford.

His students became physicists, astronauts, roboticists, coaches, teachers.

But his central insight never changed:

"There's always a way to move.

You just have to build the right structure inside the system."

That was Kane's genius.

He didn't invent new physics.

He crafted keys – precise mechanism designs that unlocked old constraints from within.

THE VOID IS NOT THE END. IT'S THE PROBLEM TO SOLVE.

By the 1960s, America had sent people into space.

But space was a problem.

Without gravity, motion didn't work the way people expected.

If you lost orientation, there was nothing to push against.

No floor. No air. No traction. No return.

Even the smartest NASA engineers couldn't solve it.

They kept trying to force Earth logic into a place Earth logic didn't apply.

Kane saw something else.

He saw a cat.

More precisely, he saw the way a cat fell.

A cat falling upside down doesn't panic.

It reorients.

No pushing. No platform.

Just a segmented body, twisting mid-air, bending its spine and pulling its limbs until the world turns underneath it.

Kane built it out of tennis balls, wire, and tape.

He watched it flip.

He wrote the equations.

He didn't just watch the cat fall. He mapped it. He did see what others hadn't. He did twist his mind around the twist of the cat. He did follow the bend, the tuck, the spine, the limb. He did track the sequence: bend in the middle, rotate the front, counter the rear, reverse and repeat. He did what the cat did. Only instead of legs, he used logic. Instead of a tail, he used torque. He wrote the motion. He matched the shape. He crafted the key. The very movement the cat used to land – he turned it in the lock of space.

And in doing so, he cracked the motion problem that had stalled spaceflight: You don't need the environment to move.

You need to craft a mechanism inside the system.

He called it Kane's Method.

It didn't just explain how cats landed on their feet.

It explained how astronauts could turn midair, right themselves, and reorient in a vacuum.

He tested the theory with trampolinists in simulated space suits.

He climbed onto a frictionless table and spun 180 degrees using nothing but internal shifts.

He made motion without contact.

Rotation without ground.

And NASA listened.

Because Kane hadn't just solved a problem.

He had shown the mechanism.

And that's how you craft the key: You don't break the system.

You twist inside it.

MOTION IS A MINDSET

Kane believed dynamics wasn't just about math.

It was about clarity. Insight. Structure.

He hated fuzziness. Loved idioms.

He trained his students with sayings they still quote decades later:

"Let's go slow. We don't have time to go fast."

"Nothing is equal to anything."

"When you're unsure whether you know or don't know – you don't know."

Kane's genius wasn't just intellectual.

It was recursive.

He could see a mechanism, name it, simplify it, teach it – Then step back, and let others move through it.

He didn't just solve problems.

He taught generations how to move in problems.

WHAT THE CAT DOES, THE MIND CAN DO

The cat's righting reflex is one of biology's most elegant mechanisms.

It bends at the midpoint.

Tucks and extends limbs.

Uses asymmetry and conservation of momentum to reorient – without pushing off anything at all.

Kane didn't just admire the cat.

He became it.

The cat reorients in freefall.

Kane reoriented in complexity.

He split systems in the middle.

He twisted assumptions until a new path emerged.

He taught people to find leverage in their own internal structure.

And when his eyesight failed late in life, he did what he had always done:

He adapted the mechanism.

He took up the piano.

Blind, seated, fingers floating across keys – he learned to craft a new kind of movement.

Not with vision. With rhythm. With orientation. With sound.

That's what makes Thomas Kane a model of this habit.

He didn't just recognise the flaw.

He didn't just expose the trap.

He crafted the key – over and over again, through physics, through pedagogy, through a mind that never stopped moving.

FIND THE FLAW → SPOT THE CATCH → **CRAFT THE KEY**

He didn't raise a fist. He wrote a method. He didn't tear down the old structure. He built a better one inside it. Kane didn't just teach equations. He taught a way of thinking – a mode of motion that others could enter, and improve.

That's what this habit is about. Not just moving. Not just solving. Designing the shift that lets the rest of the system move too. This is what it looks like to craft the key.

But these habits were never meant to stand alone. You've seen them one at a time. Now, let's see what happens when they align.

This is what Rule 5 has been building in you: a way of thinking that doesn't just notice problems. It understands them structurally. It acts with precision.

You could call it a mindset. But it's more than that. It's a mechanism mindset – a structure you carry – that gives you a mechanism for understanding mechanisms.

The kind that lets you enter a stuck system and know where to look. The kind that helps you feel when pressure is being wasted. And the kind that lets you build something that moves better than what came before.

This isn't about force. It's about fit.

The three people you've just met – Wangari Maathai, Alexei Navalny, Thomas Kane – each carried a different part of this mechanism. One saw the strain. One named the trap. One designed the turn.

Now, before we sit down, you'll see how their movements interlock. Not as steps. As structure. This is what it looks like when the loop begins to move in unison.

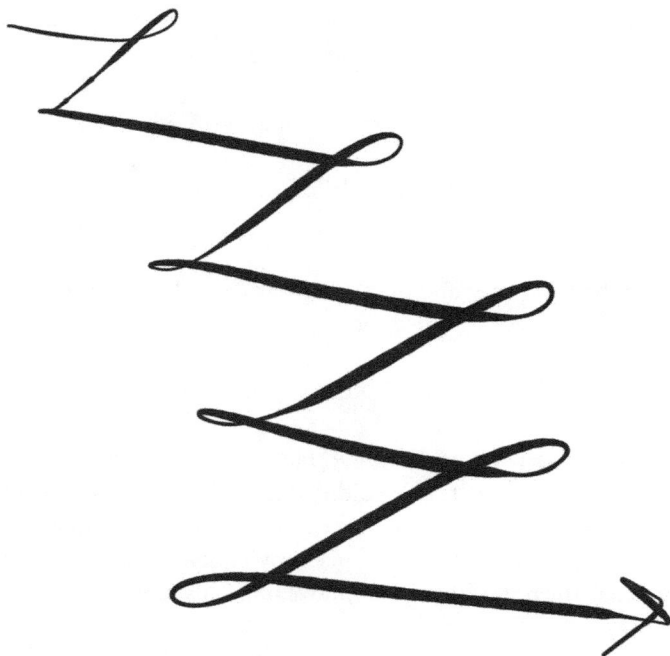

PUTTING IT ALL TOGETHER:
THE ZIGZAG WALK

A system unlatched. A trap broken sideways.

They told him to walk straight. Across the bridge. Toward the West. Toward freedom.

After nine years in Soviet prisons and labour camps, Natan Sharansky had become a symbol of the unbroken dissident. Solitary confinement. Starvation. Years of interrogations designed not just to extract confession but to erode cognition – to grind thought into compliance.

And now, on the day of the prisoner exchange, the gates were open. The bridge was waiting. The world was watching.

And still – they gave instructions.

Walk straight.

He didn't.

"I decided I would walk in zigzags to show I was free."

Find the Flaw

It didn't begin with the zigzag. It began with noticing. With realising that the prison wasn't just physical. That even in release, there was choreography. Even in the moment of freedom, the system was writing the script.

Sharansky had spent a decade resisting one kind of control, only to meet another in the final scene. A gesture. A gait. A performance. That was the final trap. A freedom defined by the very machine that had imprisoned him.

He saw it.

And that moment of seeing wasn't spontaneous. It was trained. The same metacognitive loop he had built in solitary – where he played blindfolded chess against himself, day after day, not to pass the time but to preserve his mind – was the loop that spotted the flaw in this final act. The script wasn't broken. It had just changed tone.

Spot the Catch

The real catch wasn't the prison cell. It was the expectation. The assumption that freedom could be scripted by your captors. That obedience could be performed one last time – in front of cameras, diplomats, a watching world.

The Soviets wanted to prove a point: even now, you'll do what we say.

That's the mechanism. The false release. The loop that pretends it has ended.

Sharansky spotted it – not as a philosophical metaphor, but as an engineered moment of control. And like all catches, it depended on repetition. Obedience encoded into movement. Straight line. Silent walk. Compliant exit.

He refused.

Craft the Key

The zigzag wasn't theatre. It was architecture. A precise adaptive act, built across years of recursive practice.

In prison, he'd crafted thought loops sharp enough to survive isolation. He sang the Israeli national anthem in solitary. He refused to sign confessions. He turned internal games into identity reinforcement. Each act repeated, sequenced, refined – until they formed a pattern stronger than the prison's.

And when the final moment came – when the world thought the trap had opened – he used the pattern again.

The zigzag wasn't spontaneous. It was the punctuation of a private loop made public.

It didn't need volume. It didn't need permission.

It needed rhythm.

The Loop Echoes

That walk across the Glienicke Bridge went around the world.

Not because it was dramatic – but because it was recursive.

The system cracked not through rebellion but through visible refusal. The zigzag became the story. The photo. The symbol.

And behind the walk was a loop:

His wife, Avital, campaigning for his release.

Journalists broadcasting his cause.

Other refuseniks drawing strength from his silence.

Dissidents inside and outside the USSR seeing in his walk a mirror of their own loops.

This was not an escape. It was a rerouting. Not just for Sharansky – but for others. That's what a real mechanism does: it opens adaptive possibility for more than one.

The Final Pattern

Sharansky didn't just survive the system. He exposed its structure.

He recognised the script, understood the trap, and designed a small, repeatable key that disrupted the loop.

Not with violence. With visibility.

Not by breaking the gate. By refusing the choreography.

That's how systems get unlatched. Not always with explosions – but with a single step in the wrong direction.

A loop turned sideways.

A path rewritten under pressure.

A man walking free – not because the system said so, but because he refused to walk straight.

FIND THE FLAW → SPOT THE CATCH → CRAFT THE KEY

You've just run the mechanism loop. And whether you realised it or not, you've been on a hunt. Your mind better attuned to the catches that hold you back.

Not for systems in general. But for the part. The piece. The hidden interaction. That one component which, if recognised early, seen clearly, or rebuilt precisely, changes everything around it.

Wangari Maathai found it in the ground. In the trees. In the backs and hands of the women working with her. She saw the flaw early. Before the collapse. And because she saw it, she started to build.

Alexei Navalny spotted the catch – the thing that wasn't just failing, but functioning as failure. He named the lock, showed the script, made millions see what had been deliberately hidden.

Thomas Kane crafted the key. He didn't just spot the stuck point. He built a system others could use to move through it. He didn't force the old structure to shift. He created a better one.

Not just steps. Not just insights. A way of seeing. A way of thinking. A way of being in the world that helps you locate leverage – and use it.

You haven't built the whole mechanism. But you've built something more important: a loop. A stance. A structure you can carry with you – that helps you find what can be changed, and how to change it.

You're not just hunting for hinges. You're scanning for traps. For locks. For catches. For chains. For substitutions. For rewirings. For uses you hadn't yet imagined.

You're learning to recognise the way. Not just what breaks. But what binds. And now we go underneath.

Ever made a
mistake?
Ever made the
same mistake
twice?

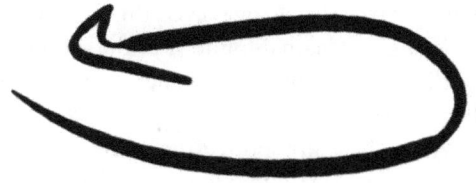

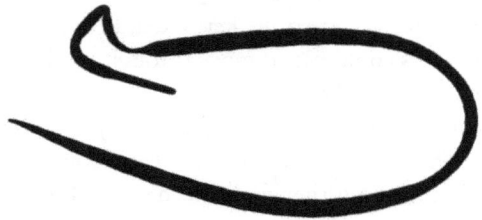

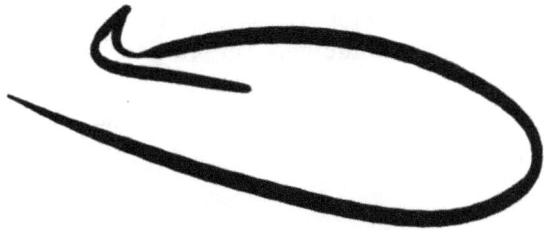

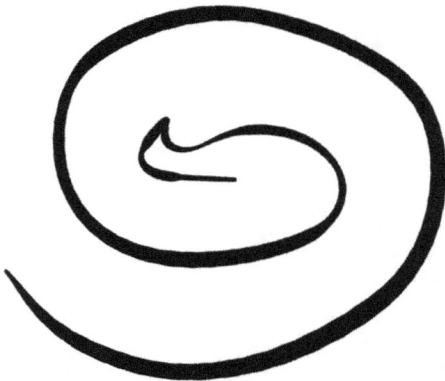

That's not
just a
mistake.
That's a
repeat.
A repeat of
what you've
thought
before.

THE SITDOWN: THE ROCK AND THE SHADOW

WHY WE SIT DOWN NOW

Most of us don't notice the trap we're in until we've adapted to it. We call it routine. Or structure. Or just life.

But somewhere inside that loop – quietly, precisely – something is holding us in place. A rule we never wrote. A limit we inherited. A pressure we stopped feeling because we never thought to question it.

We sit down now because Rule 5 is about seeing that pressure clearly. This chapter sits in the Understand phase of the loop. You've already learned the structure: Find the Flaw, Spot the Catch, Craft the Key. Now we shift from theory to pattern. From description to orientation.

This Sitdown isn't a detour. It's the hinge. It's where we stop just long enough to see the system from inside the system. To understand the difference between what's holding us – and what's holding us back.

We're going to do that through Rosalind Franklin.

She wasn't the loudest. She wasn't the first. But she saw what others missed – not because it was hidden, but because she knew how to read the shadow. The shape of DNA revealed itself not in direct light, but in the pattern of distortion. She used light the way superadapters use pressure: indirectly, intelligently, structurally.

In this Sitdown, we're using the rock and the shadow as symbols. The rock is what seems solid. It may block you. It may weigh you down. Or it may serve as a platform to move across. The shadow is not confusion. It's data. It shows the structure underneath. It shows where the catch might be.

We're here to understand what holds the trap shut – so we can learn how to open it.

Not with force. With focus. Not to escape. But to redesign.

That's why we sit down now.

ROSALIND FRANKLIN

Seeing through the system that tried to erase you

It wasn't a wall. It wasn't a gate.
It didn't swing open or slam shut.
It just stood there. Heavy. Unmoved. Blocking the light.

And yet – what if it was the rock that told you everything?

Not by yielding.
But by how it refused.
By the angles it held.
By the shadow it cast.

Some people see a wall. Rosalind Franklin saw a structure.
And in that structure, she saw the shape of the trap.
And the shape of the truth.
And she documented it, one recursive frame at a time.

She was a crystallographer. But really, she was a shadow-reader. A system-seer.
Someone who could look into the invisible and detect how the catch was built.

She never called it that. But we will.
This is the story of how Rosalind Franklin didn't just study DNA.
She exposed the trap logic embedded in biology, in institutions, in memory.
She didn't unlock the system. She made it *visible* – so others could loop through.

A rock doesn't move. But it can be studied.
A shadow doesn't lie. But it can distort.
Franklin lived in a world where both were weaponised.

The rock was the institution – science, gender, tradition, empire.
The shadow was the credit – stolen, reshaped, passed off as someone else's.

But Franklin's genius wasn't just what she saw. It was how she saw.

She took the scattered reflections of molecular structure and looped them into
clarity.
She didn't invent DNA. She showed us what we'd been too distorted to detect.

Her X-ray diffraction photographs didn't reveal form.
They revealed pattern inside resistance.
The thing you couldn't see until the system blocked you –
and you kept looking anyway.

She refused to guess. She refused to simplify.
Where others reached for models, she looped back through observation.

Where others speculated, she *repeated*.
Not to stall – but to reveal what the structure was hiding from itself.

Her notebooks were not commentary.
They were trap logs.
Precision maps of what she'd seen, tested, challenged, looped.

Every note was a latch.
Every diagram a bolt, slotted into place.
Every page another locked layer of insight – *but never locked away*.

Franklin didn't hide her process.
Others did that for her.

Watson saw the shadow.
Crick ran with it.
Wilkins – perhaps the most dangerous – passed it along.
And the system applauded.

But what was borrowed wasn't just a photograph.
It was a recursive act of seeing – a way of looking into disorder until order emerged.

Franklin called it clarity. Perfection.
Not as aesthetic ideal – but as proof the loop had closed.

She was building a pattern that outlived her.
Not as myth. But as method.
And the tragedy wasn't that she died.
It's that the system treated her as invisible while she lived.
You cannot steal someone's method and call it your own.
Not when that method was a way of seeing –
And especially not when she used that vision to expose the very system that would try to erase her.

This is why the Rock and the Shadow matter.

Because the rock doesn't move.
But the one who sees through it does.

Rosalind Franklin saw through systems.

Not because she defied them flamboyantly – but because she refused distortion.

She didn't zigzag.
She aligned.
She triangulated.
She walked straight through a structure everyone else mistook for noise.

Her rebellion wasn't kinetic. It was crystalline.

She didn't demand to be seen.

She refused to be mis-seen.

And what she gave us wasn't just the double helix.
It was the pattern logic to recognise how loops – biological, intellectual, institutional – are formed.

MOST PEOPLE WALK PAST

Not everyone gets caught in a trap. Some just walk past it. Again and again. For years. For decades. For whole lives.

They don't see the catch. They don't know there is one. And if you've never been taught what to look for, or where to press, why would you?

Most systems don't fail because of dramatic collapse. They fail quietly. Through repetition. Through assumptions.

You inherit a way of doing things – how mornings begin, how conversations end, how leadership sounds, how deadlines tighten. You copy, you adapt, you move forward. But at some point, you realise: You're not moving forward. You're walking a circle. A loop someone else drew, and you didn't question it.

And that's what this is. This is the moment in the Sitdown where you realise you're not standing outside the rock looking at the shadow. You're inside the structure. The shadow is on your wall. And you've been calling it normal.

Some people never look. Some people look too late. And some people look – and still don't believe what they see.

Because systems don't just trap you. They shape your sense of what's real.

They give you explanations that let you feel smart while staying stuck. They reward you for patterns that reinforce the loop. They make you say things like: "It's always been this way."

But it hasn't. You've just always been here.

Spot the trap to avoid it.

Spot the trap to escape it.

Then unlatch the catch.

The trap is never the whole world. It's always a part of the system. A small, repeatable failure that holds the bigger failure in place. That's the catch.

The question is: can you see it? Because if you can't see it, you'll blame the wrong thing. You'll focus on the symptom. You'll fight the surface. You'll keep moving – but never move forward.

Most people aren't avoiding the catch because they're lazy. They're avoiding it because it was hidden. Because they were tired. Because the system said not to look.

And then one day – maybe today – you stop.

You stop walking the loop. You stop saying "that's just how it is." You stop trusting the shadow as fact.

And instead, you begin to trace the shape.

Maybe the trap was a job title. Maybe it was a role in a family. Maybe it was an idea about who you're supposed to be.

Maybe it was a feedback loop you inherited: The perfectionism that earned praise. The silence that kept you safe. The resentment that bought you distance.

And now you see it. Not all of it – but enough. You see the hinge. The bit that holds it shut. And in that moment, you realise: This isn't a wall. It's a door.

You don't need to smash it. You don't need to perform insight. You need to reach – gently – where the pressure is, and press.

That's what comes next: how to find the shortcut.

FIND THE SHORTCUT

Ice looks solid – like rock. But it can be melted. It can be cut. It can be shaped into something better.

That's the mistake people make with systems. They think the visible form is the whole structure. That the road they were given is the only way through. But sometimes the path is long not because it must be – only because no one has questioned it yet.

The shortcut isn't a cheat. It's a mechanism rethought. A reroute that doesn't break the loop – it lifts it.

In post-war Finland, under the weight of economic scarcity and Soviet shadow, a group of quiet reformers chose education as the country's long-term escape route. And at the centre of that vision was Anna-Liisa Tiekso. Just 22 when she entered parliament, she would go on to chair the Education and Culture Committee through five consecutive governments.

In a period of national instability, she was the constant. Her work didn't rely on spectacle. It endured because it was structured. Purposeful. Stable. She wasn't the noise. She was the mechanism. While others shifted, she stayed – and cut through.

Tiekso didn't promise a better future by yelling about progress. She made it by constructing it. Her committee helped establish Finland's national comprehensive school system – a unifying, state-funded model designed to replace fragmented inequality with structured access.

Finland didn't just expand education. They changed its function. They shifted from assessment to development, from standardised sorting to student-centred growth. Teachers were deeply trained, highly respected, and trusted to experiment. Every decision was a mechanism inside a mechanism – less homework, smaller class sizes, more play, equal paths to higher education.

It wasn't just that the Finnish system worked. It was that it worked differently. Because it asked a better question: what is school for?

Elsewhere, education had become a performance loop – more testing, more pressure, more evidence of effort. But Finland saw the weight it placed on its children. And they lifted it.

Homework was rocks in backpacks. Each child bringing home piles of it. Piled on themselves. Piled on their parents. Instead of helping teachers teach and children grow, it shifted the system's burden onto the loop that couldn't bear it.

Finland changed that. Slowly. Intentionally. Systemically. They didn't just delay testing – they redesigned purpose. They made space for teachers to teach. For kids to play. For ideas to rise.

They didn't melt the system. They melted the ice it was encased in.

Tests cast shadows. But light, bent correctly, reveals shape. And the right kind of light doesn't just reveal – it softens. It makes change possible.

Anna-Liisa Tiekso's work didn't need shouting. It needed scaffolding. What she built didn't make headlines. It made futures.

That's what a shortcut is. Not a bypass. Not a trick. But a better-shaped path through what once looked fixed.

That's what superadapters do. They don't just survive systems. They rework them.

Light that casts shadow melts ice.

You've just sat with the system.
You've looked at the part that most people miss.
Not because it's invisible. But because it's too familiar.

Franklin read the structure. Others walked past.
Tiekso rerouted a city. Others thought the old design was good enough.

And you – you began to see what the mechanism mindset actually feels like.
Not just noticing things. But knowing what to do with what you notice.

You now know that most of what holds a trap in place isn't the force. It's the configuration.

That means the way out – or through – begins not with effort, but with structure.

Now comes the shift.

You've seen what the loop looks like from the inside.
You've learned how people move through it.

Next, you'll see how to live it.

LIVE THE LOOP

HOW TO LIVE THE LOOP
Find the catch. Shift the system.

You've seen the pattern. You've studied the catch. You've followed three people as they found a flaw, spotted what held it in place, and crafted a shift – sometimes quiet, sometimes radical, always precise. But the loop doesn't end with them. It loops again. This next section is where you learn to live it.

We're going to go back to those same three people – and beyond them. We're going to bring everything we've learned in the Sitdown about how to hunt for mechanisms and begin sharing it with you. So you can keep understanding. So you can start emulating. So you can think and act in an ever more effective way.

You'll try the loop yourself. You'll see how to test your systems. How to find what's slowing you down. How to spot what's reinforcing the trap – and how to reroute it. You'll learn to name what's rigid, find what's live, and build the kind of shift that turns the whole thing forward. You'll get better and better at seeing what can hold you back – and what can launch you upward.

This is the pivot point. The place where insight becomes movement. You don't have to start over. But you do have to start again.

HOW THEY LIVED THEIR LOOP
They didn't start with answers. Not clarity. Just tension.

Wangari Maathai didn't begin by solving environmental collapse. She began by noticing bare hills, failing crops, eroded trust. Something in the land – and in the lives of the women she listened to – was misaligned. It wasn't loud. It was structural. She didn't dramatise it. She traced it. Tree by tree. Loop by loop. The catch wasn't in the weather. It was in the way the system had stopped allowing things to regrow. And she planted a counter-loop. Quietly. Systematically. "Poverty is both a cause and a symptom of environmental degradation. You can't say you'll start to deal with just one. You're trapped." That's Find the Flaw.

Alexei Navalny didn't stop the system that trapped him. But he saw it. Early. Precisely. Not just the corruption on the surface – but the interlocking mechanisms that held it in place: propaganda, fear, cynicism, inherited helplessness. His decision to return to Russia wasn't a performance. It was the end point of tracing every visible line back to its hinge. Not the strongest point. The weakest. The one you can press. And in pressing it, reveal the system to itself. "We must do what they fear – tell the truth, spread the truth. This is the most powerful weapon against this regime of liars, thieves, and hypocrites. Everyone has this weapon. So make use of it." That's what it means to Spot the Catch.

Thomas Kane didn't force a fix. He studied the terrain. He watched what cats do in mid-air – how they bend, how they twist. Not to resist gravity, but to work within it. He modelled how orientation could be changed not by push, but by sequence. "A cat can right itself in mid-air by bending and twisting its body, despite having no external torque. This phenomenon illustrates how internal adjustments can change orientation." It wasn't about force. It was about the way you move inside a system that won't let you push. That's what happens when you Craft the Key.

Each of these figures ran the whole loop. We've highlighted one part for each – flaw, catch, key – so you could see it clearly. But don't be misled by the structure. They didn't just pause at one habit. They moved through all three. They saw what wasn't working, identified what was holding it in place, and built something that shifted it. What you're seeing here is not just a story – it's the loop in motion. The same loop you now hold. The Try This, the Table, the Reboots – all of it exists because of what they modelled. You don't need perfect conditions. You need a working loop.

They didn't break the loop. They read it. They didn't attack the shadow. They studied the angle of the light. And once they found the catch – they built a way through.

TRAP, RATCHET, DOOR

Not every trap looks like a trap. Some feel like habits. Some feel like home. Some are rituals that used to protect you, until they began to hold you still.

Most people don't see the trap until it's done its job. That's not failure – it's how most systems work. They don't announce themselves. They repeat themselves. They become background. A loop you mistake for life.

And most traps aren't malicious. They're inherited. Inbuilt. Designed by the system before you ever stepped inside. The way your workplace measures productivity. The way your family interprets silence. The way the world rewards you for keeping a mask on – just long enough to forget you're wearing it.

But the beautiful thing about humans is that we're built to notice. Built to adapt. Built to see the pattern and trace it. The trap only works when it stays invisible. Once you can name it – once you can see where it begins and what it keeps out – you're not stuck anymore. You're standing at the edge of the mechanism.

And that's where superadapters begin – not by fighting the system, but by recognising its shape.

A ratchet is one of the simplest mechanisms ever designed. It turns in one direction. It holds. That's it. But that tiny piece of logic – forward only – is behind some of the most powerful systems in the world.

It's how evolution works. Not by planning, but by pressure. An improvement gets locked in, and the species builds from there. No rewind. No do-over. Just one more turn, and then another.

But ratchets don't just live in biology. They live in your habits. Your inbox rituals. Your family stories. The way a team always defaults to the fastest decision-maker. Sometimes they help. Sometimes they trap. What matters is when you notice them, and whether you're the one choosing.

The wrong kind of ratchet keeps you in a role you've outgrown. The right kind of ratchet locks in a gain you never want to lose. You spot a pattern once – and you change how you look forever. You create a better system, and then you decide: this is now the baseline. No more slipping back.

That's the real gift of adaptive thinking. You stop trying to hold everything in your head. You build the mechanism once – and then you trust it to hold the gain.

People who work with their minds this way don't just escape traps. They accumulate leverage. They move forward on purpose. One shift. One lock. One irreversibility that makes the next step easier than the last.

A door is not a metaphor. It's a mechanism. And a possibility. And a promise.

Doors – ways of moving beyond barriers – exist. They always have. Humans just don't always know where to look. Or they need to open one door to find another.

It used to be impossible to fly from New York to Paris. It used to be impossible to travel into space. It used to be impossible to edit genes. All of these were once locked rooms. And then someone found a way. Or made one. And what seemed immovable became ordinary.

Most people don't miss doors because they're missing. They miss them because they've been taught not to expect them. Or to look in the wrong direction. Or to assume that if effort doesn't work, then nothing will.

But superadaptive minds think differently. They don't assume that struggle means stuck. They don't assume that the way forward has to be the way it's always been. They know that systems – real ones – almost always contain a hinge. A point of leverage. A design feature that opens under the right pressure, from the right angle.

Sometimes that hinge is structural. Sometimes it's social. Sometimes it's internal. A reframe. A single sentence. A shift in stance.

And sometimes the door is already open. But it doesn't look like one. Not until you know what to look for.

That's the difference. Not strength. Not specialness. Just the practiced ability to perceive the possibility of movement – and move.

You've seen them now for what they are. Traps are patterns you didn't see until they started repeating. Ratchets are the rules that hold a gain – or a loss – in place. Doors are the structures that move, but only if you know how they're built.

And here's the part most people never learn: These are not just symbols. They are system components. A trap can become a door. A door can harden into a trap. The ratchet is what turns one into the other.

Which means this isn't just about escape. It's about perception. And sequence. And action. You can trace the system. You can find the hinge. You can build a better lock, or dismantle the loop that's held you for years.

And if you do that once – just once – you'll never look at the structure the same way again. That's the power of knowing what you're looking at.

Let's make it visible.

THE MECHANISM THAT WAITED

On their first night, the divers found sponges. On the second, something stranger.

It was 1901. Off the coast of Antikythera, a Greek island between Crete and the Peloponnese, sponge divers stumbled onto a Bronze Age shipwreck. There were marble statues. Gold. Armour. A throne. But in the corner of the haul sat a corroded lump of bronze, about the size of a football. It cracked open years later.

Inside was a mechanism no one expected.

Eventually, with X-rays and reconstructions, it revealed itself: a multi-gear analogue computer, capable of predicting the position of the sun, the moon, eclipses, and the major planets. It could calculate the dates of Greek festivals. It was, in effect, a time-looping device. A calendar. A simulation. A mechanical model of the heavens.

And it was more than two thousand years old.

We call it the Antikythera Mechanism. It wasn't just an ancient artefact. It was a loop someone had built to track loops. And it almost vanished without being understood.

The first to glimpse its potential wasn't a physicist or an engineer. It was a historian of science – someone who believed that ancient minds had made more than we remembered. Someone who trusted that the past held recursive intelligence: human brains capable of abstraction, prediction, modelling, precision. Supersapiens, long before our age gave them a name.

He didn't just decode the object. He modified our sense of what humans had once achieved.

Even the modern story looped strangely. When the BBC covered its rediscovery, commentators praised a local Greek MP for noticing the device in a museum case. The problem? They'd mixed up two entirely different people. The man they described never saw it. But the story stuck.

The truth had been lost. Then mistaken. Then misremembered. Then, finally, understood.

Sometimes a mechanism is right in front of you.

Sometimes it's buried for centuries.

But once you learn how to look,

you don't just find the mechanism.

You start to see the minds that made it possible.

And once you've seen that, you're ready to ask:

What kind of mechanism am I looking at?

And what kind of mechanism am I about to become?

CUDDLES AND COFFEE:
MECHANISMS WITHIN MECHANISMS

Not every system runs on force. Some run on rhythm. Some hold because of trust. Some open slowly, the way conversations do – if you give them the right container.

In our house, it starts with cuddles and coffee.

It doesn't sound like a mechanism. That's the point. It doesn't look like a lever or a plan. But it is one. It's the rhythm that allows other rhythms. A small daily structure that enables thinking, talking, listening – without needing to name those things in the moment. It supports mood, timing, energy. It makes space for decision and repair. You don't have to start fresh every morning. You just have to re-enter the loop.

And once you see that, you start seeing it everywhere.

Because the truth is, most good mechanisms only work because other mechanisms are quietly supporting them. They don't just exist on their own. They need conditions. Scaffolds. Nested systems. That's what this chapter has really been about – not just naming one loop, but learning to live inside a whole ecology of them.

Sometimes, the big mechanism only works because a smaller one has already done its job. Sometimes the only reason we're not fighting anymore is because the circumstances that used to press on us – tiredness, young children, rushed mornings – have changed. But when that space opens up, we can choose to fill it well. We can build a new loop. Not because we're perfect now, but because we have the scaffolding.

Some things that used to make us snap no longer get triggered. Not because we've transcended them – but because they're not being pulled anymore. The mechanism for the fight isn't there. And in its place, if we're lucky, we've built something better.

That's what systems thinkers and parents and designers and educators and tired couples all learn in their own way: you don't fix everything at once. You build the conditions that let other things start to work.

That's what Cuddles and Coffee is. It's not a rule. It's a ritual. A soft loop that lets harder ones re-enter. And once you have something like that – something small and strong and regular – you start to think differently about what 'fixing' even means.

Because maybe the work isn't to solve every problem. Maybe it's to build the thing that holds the thing that lets the solving happen.

Mechanisms within mechanisms. Loops within loops. Supportive systems that don't announce themselves, but change everything once they're there.

That's what superadapters do. They don't just fix. They design for fit.

FROM TRAPPED TO TRANSCENDED

Some traps feel total. But they never are. What holds the system isn't the whole structure – it's the catch. And once you find the catch, the trap begins to loosen. This is what the loop is for. Not to escape by force, but to re-engage with clarity. Find the flaw before it deepens. Spot the catch before you waste your energy on the wrong fix. Craft the key that fits the system – not to smash it, but to lift it. This is where structures shift. This is what it feels like to be trapped. And this is what it looks like to transcend.

	TRAPPED	**TRANSCENDED**
Find the Flaw	You feel something's off, but can't quite name it. You explain it away. You wait. You adapt to the discomfort, then forget you adapted. Nothing breaks – but nothing improves.	You see the misalignment early. You don't dramatise it. You register the tension, trace it to its source, and name it clearly enough to act. The system hasn't failed yet – but you've already begun to tune it.
Spot the Catch	You focus on symptoms. You fix surfaces. You try harder, communicate louder, restructure roles – but the loop repeats. You haven't seen the hinge. You haven't found the real thing holding it all in place.	You pause. You scan deeper. You look not at what's loud, but at what's holding. You find the catch – not the whole trap, but the piece that matters. And suddenly, what looked fixed becomes adjustable.
Craft the Key	You react. You guess. You overdesign or underdeliver. You force a fix before the system's ready – or because you're not ready to wait. The result breaks things further.	You design for fit. You test, revise, adjust. You build a mechanism that matches the structure and intention of the system it's meant to shift. It doesn't snap. It lifts. And the loop begins to move again.

That's where these habits can really help. Their purpose is to move you from a situation where you feel stuck – or overwhelmed, or uncertain – even though you want something better. Each one is a way in. Not to fix the whole system at once, but to begin moving.

You might be standing in a loop you didn't build. Or in one you built, but don't know how to shift. These habits give you structure. They're designed to help you find the part of the system that still wants to move. And then build from there.

Let's walk through them now – not in theory, but in action.

Sometimes you know something's off, but you can't quite say what. You explain it away. You adapt to cope. You keep going. The discomfort builds slowly – until it becomes background. Until you forget you compromised.

This is where many loops hold people still. Because the flaw was never named, nothing can get much better. You might improve – but you're still at the same level. The loop is still the same loop.

This habit – Find the Flaw – is not about self-criticism. It's about noticing what doesn't fit anymore. The stuff that's holding you back. A rhythm that's no longer useful. A story that used to work but now weighs more than it gives. A role you're still playing out of habit, not alignment. The blocker. The slower. The hard stop.

You might notice that you're always exhausted before noon. Or that you avoid one kind of task. Or that every conversation with someone close to you ends in the same quiet way: with something unsaid.

That's not weakness. It's a signal. It's the moment where the system is giving you something rare – a chance to tune it before it breaks.

People who operate with superadaptive clarity trace the signal. They don't dramatise it. They register it. And they name it precisely enough to act.

You don't need to name the whole system. Just the part that's misaligned.

That's where movement begins.

Sometimes it's not enough to know something's wrong. You've named the flaw. You've felt the pressure. But when you try to change it – nothing gives. That's when you know there's a catch.

The catch is what holds the trap in place. It's not always visible. Sometimes it's a routine. Sometimes it's a belief. Sometimes it's a rule no one wrote down, but everyone follows. The catches are the parts that limit – and the parts that can open doors.

You might be trying to work differently – but the meeting structure won't allow it. You might be trying to rest – but the guilt kicks in. You might be ready to speak – but the dynamic snaps back before the words land. That's the catch. The part of the system that reinforces the old loop – even when you know it isn't working.

This habit – Spot the Catch – is about learning where the leverage really is. It may not be the loudest part. It may not even be broken. But it's the part that stabilises the pattern. That keeps the loop repeating. And the part you can change to make changes.

And once you find it, the whole system shifts in your eyes. What felt stuck becomes specific. What felt rigid becomes targeted. You don't have to push harder. You just have to press the right point.

You've seen the flaw. You've spotted the catch. Now comes the part that looks like action – but isn't just action. This is where you build something that works. That fits. That moves the loop forward without breaking the system it lives in.

This habit – Craft the Key – isn't about brute force. It's about fit. It's about looking at the pattern, understanding how it repeats, and then designing one small, deliberate shift that changes the outcome.

Sometimes that shift is a question instead of a defence. Sometimes it's rearranging a process so the real decision happens earlier. Sometimes it's a rule you change for yourself: no phone before noon. No meetings without an agenda. No apologies for asking what you need to know.

It doesn't need to be loud. It needs to be precise. Because when you change the right part of the system, everything after it moves differently.

That's what crafting a key really means. You're not reacting. You're shaping. You're building a mechanism that unlocks a pattern – not once, but repeatedly.

And then you craft the key – because most systems don't need to be destroyed. They need to be redesigned. And not all of it – just the part that makes things work better.

And when you've done it well, the system starts to adapt with you. The loop becomes smoother. The tension becomes momentum. And the next time you spot a flaw, you already know: there's probably a catch. And there's always a key.

You've now seen the whole loop. Not as a concept. As a pattern you can trace. As a structure you can shift.

This isn't a toolkit. It's a rhythm. A way of thinking that helps you find the part that matters – before the system breaks. And then helps you move it – cleanly, deliberately, and without collapse.

You find the flaw – not just to point at it, but to see what needs to be fixed.

You spot the catch – not to complain, but to know what's holding it all in place.

And then you craft the key – because most systems don't need to be destroyed. They need to be redesigned. And not all of it – just the part that makes things work better.

This is what adaptive minds do. They don't fight the structure. They work with it. And over time, the structure starts to work with them.

You don't need to master this all at once. You just need to run the loop. One time. Then again.

THE WRONG LOOPS
Three ways the Mechanism Loop can fail

Humans will always try to find the mechanism that lets them change their worlds – or escape the ones they're trapped in.

It appears to be part of our nature, maybe even our biology, to look for the way out, the exit, the clearing, the light.

We move toward whatever we believe will unlock, upgrade, or improve things. We don't just want to escape – we want the trapdoor to open upward.

But those efforts can go wrong. And when they do, they go wrong in three reliably predictable ways.

You've seen these before, but now they return – in the context of unlatching the catch.

What fails when you're trying to find a way to somewhere better?

What misfires when you reach for the mechanism?

HYPO is about when things go wrong because you do too little, too slowly, or too late to understand the mechanism that matters.

You've noticed something – an opportunity or a threat – and you've formed an initial interpretation. But you stop short of going deeper.

You don't test the mechanism beneath it, or the one beneath that. You delay. You hope it'll resolve. Or you hold your model just long enough to miss the moment.

A manager sees signs of burnout but waits until their best people quit.

A partner senses emotional distance but puts off the conversation – until the resentment is harder to repair.

You hit a plateau in training, but keep running the same loop, hoping it'll work again.

Do I really understand what's causing this output?

What mechanism would make it better – before it gets worse?

HYPER causes problems when you move too fast, assume too much, or act too soon with what you think you know about the mechanism that matters.

A student is failing despite trying hard. A teacher or parent leaps to more homework, more pressure – without realising the blocker is dyslexia, comprehension, or depression.

The true mechanism goes untouched. A competitive gamer keeps losing and doubles down on repetition instead of reworking their strategy.

A business expands rapidly on early success – more stores, more staff – without understanding why the original model worked in the first place. The system breaks under strain.

Are you avoiding the harder work of real understanding, and choosing speed instead?

Are you putting yourself through unnecessary effort – when what's needed is insight?

ANTI happens when you've identified entirely the wrong mechanism. So all your effort goes into understanding or changing something that isn't the problem – wasting time, energy, and often making things worse.

The reasons vary. You might be rushing. Or stalling. You might be overconfident, underconfident, following tradition, or avoiding the harder truth.

Sometimes the mistake is rooted in lack of knowledge. But the result is the same: you're applying pressure in the wrong place.

A manager sees a dip in team performance and rolls out a new AI tool – when the real issue is burnout and communication.

A partner senses emotional distance and buys an expensive gift – when what's really needed is a conversation about shared financial stress.

Is there part of this system you've misunderstood?

Are you working harder on the wrong thing?

That's what an anti-loop steals: effort without elevation.

What we'll look at next is how these wrong loops show up in the real world – not just as abstract mistakes, but as system failures, missed exits, and mechanisms gone awry.

REAL WORLD WRONG LOOPS
Don't stay locked in an open room

Some people stay locked in an open room. They push the door harder. Kick at the hinges.

Some even redesign the lock – without checking which way it turns. But they're not trapped because the mechanism is broken. They're trapped because they misunderstood how it works.

That's the danger of a misread system: you burn energy fixing the part that isn't failing.

You overengineer the catch. You reinforce the wrong constraint. And sometimes, you invent a mechanism that was never there at all.

These aren't just mistakes in perception. They're mistakes in function. These are the real-world moments where the interpretation loop failed to see the mechanism clearly – and locked everyone in behind it.

HYPO caused problems in New Zealand when builders and regulators moved too slowly to understand how a specific combination of climate, building design, and untreated timber could trigger structural collapse. For years, moisture quietly built up inside thousands of homes – warping, rotting, and weakening them from within. Even after the warning signs emerged, institutional hesitation and diluted oversight delayed a coordinated response. By the time the full scope was understood, whole suburbs were affected. The failure wasn't ignorance – it was inertia.

The mechanism was visible. But no one moved quickly or deeply enough to model how the pieces were interacting.

They waited too long to see how it worked. And by then, it had already failed.

HYPER caused problems in Colombia when officials launched a sterilisation plan to control a runaway hippo population – descendants of animals once owned by Pablo Escobar. The goal was straightforward: surgically castrate the hippos and contain the spread.

But they misunderstood the biological mechanism. Hippos bred faster in Colombia's rivers than they ever had in Africa, thanks to ideal conditions. Worse, the sterilisation procedures were risky, slow, and expensive. The plan assumed linear control over a non-linear problem. The result? Population growth surged. By moving fast on an oversimplified model, they made the system more chaotic. What looked like a fix turned out to be a catalyst.

ANTI caused problems in South Korea when a national campaign framed electric fans as lethal if left running overnight. The belief was that fans could somehow suffocate or chill people to death in their sleep. The theory spread through official warnings, media stories, even school lessons. Fan timers were installed by law. But the mechanism was false. The real risks – heatstroke, poor ventilation, rising summer deaths – were ignored. People focused on preventing a fantasy, not solving a crisis. And because the model was wrong, the entire response flowed in the wrong direction. The energy to change things was there. It was just aimed at the wrong mechanism.

As you've seen, these wrong loops have real-world consequences. The ones here are serious in different ways.

345

The hippos are almost comic – but they're causing real ecological damage, costing millions, and injuring people.

The leaky buildings have left thousands in damp, unhealthy homes – bankrupting individuals, councils, and threatening trust in governments. And the phantom fan death? It diverted energy and attention away from genuine, solvable health risks.

As you begin to think like a superadapter – systemically, mechanically – you'll start to notice these failures everywhere.

Not just in policy or infrastructure, but in daily life. Crises caused by delayed, rushed, or misdirected efforts to understand how something actually works.

In high-rise fires, people push or pull on exit doors that were built with pushbars – designed to make escape effortless under pressure. But if no one explains the mechanism, or it's misused, people stay trapped in rooms they could have left.

That's what we turn to next. The counter loops. The habits that don't just prevent failure – but release you from the wrong loop when you're already in it.

THE COUNTER LOOPS
Three Ways to Find the Mechanisms That Matter

What follows are the counter loops.

Not just habits – tools. Designed to correct or prevent the most common ways your mechanism loop can fail.

Each one helps you understand where tension is building, where force is misapplied, or what link needs redesigning.

These are structural habits.

They don't just fix the problem.

They help you find it faster, name it clearly, and intervene with precision.

FIND THE FLAW helps you avoid **HYPO** errors by training and priming you to actively hunt for the mechanisms that matter.

You're less likely to fall into delay or drift because you're already in an active mode – scanning for what's not working or what could work better.

You're aware of the cost of missing something small that could have made a big difference.

You don't assume that distance in a relationship will fix itself. You don't wait for burnout to pass. You ask more. You look again.

It doesn't mean you overreact. It means you acknowledge: if I don't yet have a good explanation, and this matters, I should keep thinking.

Read the manual. Ask the question. Turn the page.

What haven't I spotted yet?
And what's the smallest clue I've ignored?

SPOT THE CATCH helps you avoid **HYPER** errors by training and priming you to catch the error, or the lock, even in something you've already decided to do.

It's the habit of checking mid-move. Of pausing – even slightly – before you commit more energy. Not to second-guess yourself endlessly, but to stop the wrong mechanism from grinding on.

It's a kind of internal whisper: is this really what's causing it? Is this where the block is? Because often, it's not what you're doing – it's what you've already assumed.

Maybe you're improving a system, pushing forward fast, iterating hard. But the core tension is somewhere else entirely. And if you never look, the loop runs hot and misfires.

This habit helps you insert just enough awareness to spot the trap before you reinforce it.

It's not hesitation. It's intelligent interruption.

What's the pressure here?
Am I solving the strain – or just reacting to it?

CRAFT THE KEY helps prevent and repair **ANTI** loops by honing your instinct for what a mechanism looks like that can actually unlock or reroute systems.

When a student keeps failing a subject despite studying hard, you're less likely to label them lazy – because you know you don't yet know why they're failing. You hunt for the real mechanism in this situation.

When your friend is taking supplements for fatigue, you keep listening – until you discover it's chronic sleep deprivation and burnout.

Being a craftsman here means knowing when the key doesn't fit. It should move smoothly. You shouldn't have to jam it in or crowbar the door.

And you don't have to stay locked in a room – or within limits – that damage your health, shrink your ambitions, or just don't suit who you've become.

What's the actual turn that opens this?
What's the false fix I need to let go of?

The mechanism loop – finding the flaw, spotting the catch, crafting the key – is both preventive and reparative.

Just remembering to unlatch the catch is a powerful start. But there's always a catch – and there's always a best way to release it.

Thinking this way helps you move from limit to possibility. From stuck to unstuck.

And this mindset applies everywhere: work, relationships, progress, emotion. There's always something – and that something is worth finding.

You'll have to reboot. Often. But that's no cause for stress or shame.

This is how you clear your head. How you breathe. How you shift with the least harm and the most leverage.

It's what every superadapter in this book has done.

When things got hard, they didn't abandon the effort.

They returned to the loop.

And now – so will we.

WHEN THINGS GO WRONG – REBOOT THE LOOP
The trap didn't open. That's not the end.

Superadapters don't succeed because they always pull the right lever.
They succeed because when the latch doesn't give, they loop again.

This chapter wasn't about general failure. It was about failure at the moment of attempted release – when you try to understand the mechanism, and the system doesn't yield. What you're about to see is how that moment – when the catch sticks or resets – isn't the end of the loop. It's the beginning of the next one.

These are not generic stories of bounceback. They are recursive recoveries. Not because the loop was broken, but because it demanded more. More clarity. More courage. More rerouting.

SPIRAL: Too Fast, Too Hard

Sometimes you hit the system too hard. Navalny launched with elegance and precision, exposing a regime built on camouflage. He was jailed, poisoned, discredited. But even inside the trap, he mocked the system that tried to silence him.

In court, he called Putin "Vladimir the underpants poisoner." He made the mechanism absurd. And then he turned it into a mirror.

He didn't want to die. But he wanted the story to survive. His wife, his team, his global supporters became living extensions of that loop. His defiance echoed beyond his body.

Mock → Martyr → Multiply
  Recognise: This is not resistance. It's retaliation.
  Understand: The story is stronger than the sentence.
  Necessary Adaptation: Loop beyond the individual. Build story structures that outlast you.

STALL: Too Slow, Too Small

Sometimes the loop is too light to be felt. Wangari Maathai planted seven trees. The system didn't flinch. It waited her out. She was ridiculed, surveilled, eventually jailed. And eventually – burned out.

She passed out at a party from exhaustion. Turned to charcoal. And then, she looped again. Not with fire – but with depth. With rhythm. With structure.

She didn't just return. She returned smarter. Calmer. More recursive.

Collapse → Retreat → Return
  Recognise: The resistance isn't rejection. It's inertia.
  Understand: If you burn out, you can still replant.
  Necessary Adaptation: Slow the loop. Make it livable. Then restart.

SNAPBACK: System Recoil

Sometimes, the system hits back after you succeed. Kane rewired motion in space. Gave us the cat twist. Built internal orientation from scratch. Then the universe blinked. He lost his sight.

But even blind, he looped again. He composed music. Reconfigured motion into memory. He passed on methods. Encoded strategies. Embedded loops in places he'd never see.

Observe → Encode → Outlast
  Recognise: Your role has changed. But you still have agency.
  Understand: You can loop through others. Or through legacy.

When the Latch Doesn't Lift

Not all mechanisms are what they seem. Some locks re-seal. Some hinges reverse. You might have pulled the right catch at the wrong time – or revealed the wrong flaw entirely.

This is not your failure. This is the system revealing its depth.

When this happens, the worst thing you can do is give up. The best thing you can do is reboot. That doesn't mean starting over. It means starting 'smarter'.

Ask yourself:
    Did I read the pattern right?
    Did I overtrigger the system?
    Is this actually the load-bearing mechanism – or just a decoy?

The Reboot Loop Is the Loop

    Detect: What didn't go the way you expected?
    Interpret: Where did the model break? Where did the system push back?
    Decide: What can you try next? What can you shift, not scrap?

This is the real trick. The loop isn't a first step.
It's a forever step.

It's the skeleton key.
When the power's down – power cycle the loop.
Turn it off. Reframe. Restart.
Power down. Power up. Re-loop.

Looped. Not Lost.

Wangari wasn't finished. Navalny wasn't erased. Kane didn't disappear. Each of them met their lock. And each ofw them looped again.

This is what superadapters do. They don't just beat the system. They learn how the system beats back – and still re-enter the loop.

That's what you can do.
That's the good news.
You're still here.
Still thinking.
Still testing the catch.
Still looping.

Which means – you've already started again.

REBOOT YOUR LOOP
From stressed out to clicked in

"Go man, go – but not like a yo-yo, schoolboy.
Just play it cool, boy. Real cool."
– West Side Story

There's a scene in *West Side Story* – one of many – where the gang clicks their fingers to communicate. They snap to signal. To coordinate. And in one moment, to remind each other to chill: "Go man go – but not like a yo-yo, schoolboy. Just play it cool, boy. Real cool."

They're not just clicking. They're self-regulating. Syncing. Resetting.

It reminded me of a drama teacher I once had, who taught us to centre ourselves by touching our index finger to our thumb. A little loop. A little hug. A feedback circuit for the nervous system. And I started to think of that loop as the RUN loop.

Index finger: **RECOGNISE** – Something's happening here.
Thumb: **UNDERSTAND** – Let's explore it, feel for the mechanism.
Then: **CLICK – NECESSARY ACTION**.

A motion that reminds you: this loop is alive. You're alive. And the point of all this? Not analysis paralysis. It's to live. To survive if you must. To transcend if you can.

Sometimes, the click is literal. A squeeze of the fingers. A snap of the band. A whispered phrase. A tool to centre. Sometimes it's ritual. A reminder: you don't need the perfect model – you need the moment that brings you back to yourself.

If you're hunting the mechanism too hard – if every catch feels like the catch – you've gone too far.

These loops are tools, not traps. Click to return.

You click back to reality – not just because you're overwhelmed. You click because you remember: you've been here before. You've made it through. And you'll make it through again.

Say it aloud: "I've succeeded before."

"If I haven't, I've survived."

"I can begin again."

That's not softness. That's structure. It's the shape of superadaptability. You are not a mistake in motion. You are a loop that remembers. And when you remember, you adapt.

RECOGNISE → UNDERSTAND → NECESSARY ACTION

TRANSCEND THE LOOP

THE MECHANISM IS ME

Sometimes, what needs fixing can't be seen from outside.
There's no obvious switch. No code. No schematic.
The loop keeps closing wrong. And the only way out is in.

That's when the mechanism changes shape.
It stops being a thing out there.
It starts becoming you.

Not in theory. Not in ego. Just in function.

You're the one who notices the catch early.
You're the one who resets the rhythm.
You're the one who twists the sequence until something shifts.
And you do it again. And again.
Not because you want to be the hero –
but because you see the hinge.
And something in you moves.

Some people call that over-functioning.
Some people call it care.
Some people call it strange.

You call it what you do when no one else is doing it.

You've seen it before.
The woman who reschedules the shift rota to stop the burnout before it begins.
The athlete who crosses the channel, not for herself, but because someone had to
prove it could be done.
The man who makes himself visible in a system designed to pretend people like
him don't exist.
None of them were 'the answer'.
But they became the part that changed what the system had to answer for.

This isn't about visibility. It's about function.
They didn't represent change.
They enacted force. And they held it.

They didn't just point at the mechanism.
They stepped into the hinge, braced their shoulders, and turned.

And when others traced the new motion, they found a path.

Sometimes the mechanism is you.
The way you move. The pattern you hold.
The moment you say: not this way – this way.

You don't just escape the system.
You don't just fix the system.
You become the part that reroutes it.

And when people look back later, they won't always know what changed.

But if they're paying attention,
they'll see you
twisting in the middle
where the motion began.

$$\text{MODEL} \rightarrow \text{MECHANISM} \rightarrow \text{MODIFY}$$

You are here.

THE UNPLUGGED TELEPHONE

On the morning of our child's first birthday, we were both a little surprised – and quietly wounded – that no one had called. No messages. No texts. No well-wishes from grandparents, siblings, friends. Just us, alone in our small home, trying to make the moment feel like a celebration.

It wasn't until early afternoon that one of us went to check the phone and found it: unplugged. Pulled out of the wall, maybe during cleaning, maybe bumped by a chair leg. No one could reach us. All the love was there – it just couldn't get through.

It took seconds to fix. Plug in. Dial tone. Messages began arriving. Everything shifted.

353

Sometimes, what you need isn't motivation. It's a mechanism. A small correction that changes what flows. That lets the world back in. That lets you move forward.

Because not every system needs to be rebuilt.

Some just need to be reconnected.

Once you know what to plug in – what to switch on, or slide into place – you stop wasting energy.

And start using it.

THERE IS A WAY

In Rule 4, you learned that models are plastic. That your mind is plastic. That if you can change how you represent the world, you can change how you move through it. But seeing the model was never the end. It was preparation for what came next.

Here, in Rule 5, you've gone deeper. You've stopped scanning the whole world and started looking for the part of the world that shifts the rest. The part we call a mechanism. The part that makes change possible – not by will, but by design. The hinge. The leverage. The catch.

Not everything that can be understood can be changed. But nothing can be improved until you find the mechanism that lets you change it.

Know yourself. Know the system. Know what holds you back.

Know what will move you forward.

Because mechanisms don't just hold the system.

They make the ends.

The means.

And the ways.

So keep looking. Keep hunting. Keep shifting.

Slide past it. Climb over it. Tunnel through it.

Use it to build.

To orient.

To lift.

Try again.

Shift again.

Go again.

Better.

TRANSCEND THE LOOP

In this chapter – Unlatch the Catch – you've seen how superadaptive minds can find the flaw, spot the catch, and craft the key that unlocks their potential – or the potential of the system they're in.

In life, there is no sci-fi scanner – no magical way to look inside a system and instantly identify the fault. Whether it's disease, dysfunction, or a mechanical flaw, that technology doesn't exist yet. So while others are busy building better machines, we rely on the most advanced mechanism-mapping tool we have: the mind.

And that's why the mechanism mindset wants to find the flaw, scan for what's broken or malfunctioning – and why you want to spot the catch, to identify the specific trap or lock that's holding that failure in place. Then: craft the key. Design the mechanism that will unlock or reroute the system.

These aren't abstract steps. They're behaviours – exemplified by the people we've met.

It's how you'll learn to nudge, hone, and nuance your response to what's holding you back – or to what you want to change in pursuit of your goals. And more precisely, it's how you'll come to understand: through modelling the world and recognising the mechanisms beneath those models, you can direct your efforts at the parts that make the greatest difference.

And remember – learning from other people is one of the most powerful ways we become more adaptable. Not by mindlessly copying or following, but by applying your plastic mind – the one you've been building throughout this book – to understand what mechanism actually needs to change. And how to change it.

So what comes next is a story of someone who didn't just want to help. Someone who recognised what needed changing – and then became the mechanism that changed the output. She didn't just observe the model. She altered its result.

THE CASTLE AND THE CODE

I read about a guy who was born blind and building online systems to help other blind people use LEGO sets. But what really struck me in his story – he said it casually – was someone he referred to as a family friend. Then he said: "She could adapt anything."

He said she left him some LEGO in a box he didn't think would be useful. But then he said she'd written out Braille instructions – by hand – that he could follow.

He called her a dear friend. A family friend. But she'd done something extraordinary. Something foundational. She didn't just adapt. She made the mechanism.

Her full name, I had to find it, was Lilya Finkel. And she was the one who made herself into the mechanism that unlocked his potential.

She renamed each LEGO piece to make it memorable. Reordered the instructions into a logical, tactile-first sequence. Rewrote them all in Braille. For his thirteenth birthday, she gave him not just a set – but a system.

"Words are the most adaptable thing," she told him. "You can't build a model to copy it – it's too cumbersome. But you can explain it with words."

The model was the Alamut Fortress – legendary, complex, designed to be impenetrable. But he built it. On his own. And when he finished it, he said simply: "It expanded my mind."

That's what happens when someone doesn't just help you build – but rebuilds the mechanism around you.

What he did – and is doing – is remarkable. He now creates systems that help others: climbing routes labelled in Braille, 3D audio that brings blind travellers into new worlds. But it was all made possible because someone before him had said: "This catch is real. I can build the key."

She didn't need a lab. She didn't need a grant. She needed attention, precision, and belief.

And what she built didn't end with him.

"They were thrilled that they could build this independently – just like their sighted friends and sighted siblings," he said, after learning that blind children used his site.

"It was such a thrill to give them that opportunity."

She crafted the mechanism.
He passed it on.
And now it loops.

THE FORTRESS AND THE KEY
"Nothing is an absolute reality; everything is permitted."
— Hassan-i Sabbah (via Bartol's Alamut)

You've heard of Alamut Fortress by now. It was once thought to be impregnable.

But nothing is.

Not to someone who thinks like a mechanism mechanic.

Some run at the gates. Some build a better tower. Some find the sewage tunnel. They don't just look at the wall. They look for the latch.

Some mechanisms save lives in wartime. Others reshape them in the everyday.

Operation Spiderweb was a Ukrainian strategy that routed drones deep inside Russian airbases — disabling aircraft without needing to cross the border. Low cost. High precision. Minimal loss of life.

It saved lives by rerouting systems.

But the same kind of mechanism mindset can lift a child out of unhappiness. It can identify the overlooked variable in a cancer treatment. It can redesign a city's bus route so that someone gets home in time for their daughter's birthday.

The shape is different. The stakes may be different. But the loop is the same: find the catch, and craft the key.

All these examples — from the very first chapter, from the very first rule, Overcome Overwhelm, through Recognise, and now into Model and Mechanism — have all had the same purpose.

To allow you to transcend limitations in pursuit of your higher goals.

This adaptive, transcendent path takes you next from identifying mechanisms to understanding how to modify them — in a way that delivers the greatest possible benefit, now and in the future, with the least possible friction, or as the best use of your available resources.

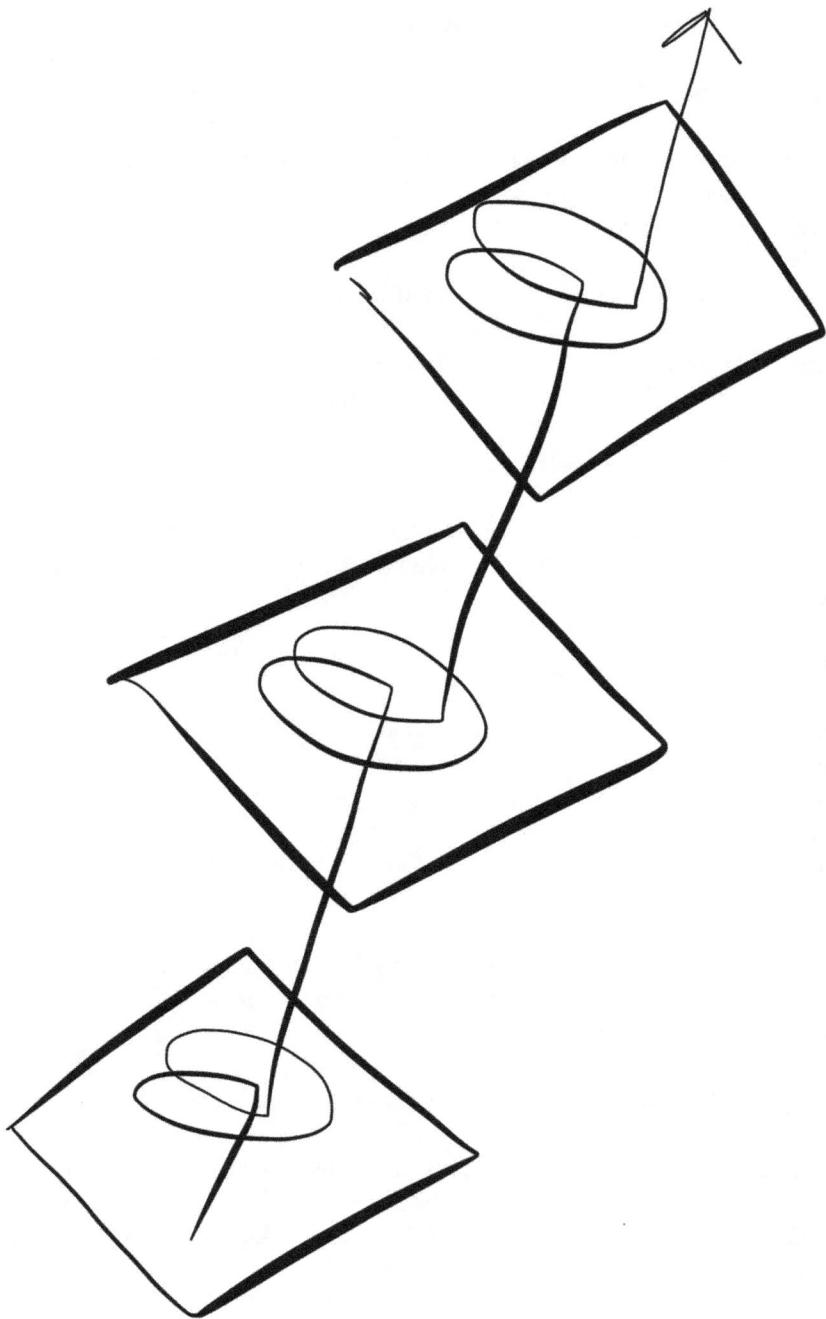

RULE 6:
FLIP THE SCRIPT

The one about modifying the mechanism

Superadaptable people change situations by changing systems. Sometimes that means shifting meaning, sometimes that means changing how things work physically, or socially, or legally. They look at how something works now and then try to identify the simplest way of changing for the most significant impact. They find the part and change the part.

You've seen the flaw. You've found the catch. You've crafted a shift that lets the system move. But now, for the first time, you're not just working with what's already there. You're ready to change the mechanism itself.

This is Rule 6. The final phase of Understand. The place where insight meets engineering.

Superadaptive minds don't just observe the loop – they rewire it. They modify what they understand. They identify the part that matters – the one that can shift outcomes, release constraints, reconfigure paths – and then they act. Not blindly. Not destructively. But precisely. Quietly. Structurally.

Sometimes it's physical. Sometimes legal. Sometimes biological, social, psychological. But it's always real. A change to the way something works that leads to a change in what happens next.

This is the chapter where you learn to rewire. To shift energy. To bend the loop. To upgrade what holds the loop in place. This is superadaptive understanding in action.

You don't have to be an engineer to think like this. You just need to keep looking for the bit that can be changed. And then change it.

You've started to sense something – the mechanism – that you want to change. Maybe even sketch the shape of it. But sensing isn't changing. If you don't know what you need to change then you can make every effort in every direction and still not make a difference.

Let me show you what that can feel like.

THREE YEARS. NO REPLIES.
There was this man who kept posting. On some social media site.

Three years. Thoughtful replies. Smart questions. Jokes that landed – at least in his own mind. But no one replied. Not one upvote. Not a single visible response.

At first he wondered if he was boring. Then maybe forgettable. Then maybe just… not the kind of person others wanted to hear from. He kept going, but with less energy. Less trust. Less hope.

And then one day, he discovered the problem. His account was set to private. No one had ever seen a word.

The moment he changed the setting – and posted that fact – his story went viral. People laughed. People cried. People saw themselves in it.

Because they knew the truth: it wasn't a content problem. It was a mechanism problem.

That's the reality of those three silent years.

He wasn't broken. He was misconfigured. Not ignored – 'invisible'.

A feedback loop had failed. The signal was blocked. The system wasn't broken. It was just misconfigured.

That's the most dangerous kind of loop.

It doesn't hurt. It doesn't collapse. It just hums. It gives you the illusion that things are working – while making sure you never arrive.

There are three things you need to understand about mechanisms:
That they exist.
That they can be changed.
And how they can be changed.

Most people never get past Step One. They don't even realise there's a mechanism running underneath the loop.

Some reach Step Two. They see the problem, name the flaw, trace the pattern. But they still feel stuck – because awareness isn't the same as leverage.

Only at Step Three do things actually change.

Because only when you modify the mechanism can you modify the outcome.

Let's return to the story.

He wasn't wrong about the work. He wasn't wrong about the intention. He even improved over time – just not in a way that landed.

He thought the system was reacting to him. But the truth was: the system wasn't responding at all.

And the moment he rewired it? Everything connected. Everything accelerated. The feedback loop opened – and suddenly, he wasn't just performing. He was landing.

He hadn't changed who he was. He had changed what the system did with who he was.

That's the kind of change Rule 6 is here to teach.

Because you are already in motion. The loop is already running. You're not waiting to start – you're waiting to connect.

And when you do, the whole loop can shift – faster than it seems fair.

This is the pivot.

From effort that echoes in silence to action that reshapes the system.

From trying harder to changing what happens next.

Because when you learn how to rewire the mechanism, you don't just get better. You get further.

THE MODIFY LOOP BEGINS

If modelling the world is like checking whether the lights are on or off,
and identifying the mechanism is like finding the light switch,
then modifying the mechanism is choosing what to do with it.

Maybe you flip it on.
Maybe you sit romantically in the dark.
Either way, the point is, now you're in control of what the system does.

Of course, the brain is full of switches and wires. So is a legal code. So is a family pattern. So is a calendar. And that's what this chapter is about: modifying the mechanisms – internal or external – that determine how the loop runs.

The clever bit is this: once you've spotted the mechanism, you can modify it. You can reverse it. You can accelerate it. You can redirect what it does or what it recognises. You can change what happens next.

That's what this next section is for.
It's called the Modify Loop.

You're going to meet three people who did just that:
    One who flipped the script and changed what the story meant.
    One who inverted the flow and redirected the system's force back on itself.
    One who turned the table and rewrote the function altogether.

You'll see how they moved through these three cognitive behaviours:

FLIP THE SCRIPT → INVERT THE FLOW → TURN THE TABLE.

Each one modified a loop that was shaping their life – or their country. And they did it not through brute force, but through structural precision. Not just by reacting harder, but by rerouting what the system did in the first place.

And that's what you're here to learn next. How to notice the structure. How to change it. How to rewire the loop.

THE MODIFY LOOP

HOW SUPERADAPTERS MODIFY THE LOOP

It's not enough to understand the loop.

Superadaptive people go further. They use their understanding to change what the system does next.

They don't force it from the outside. They shift it from within. They find the precise part – the mechanism – that matters most. Then they modify it. Quietly. Structurally. Recursively.

That's what this loop is for.

Superadapters don't just spot the constraint. They flip it. They don't just react to pressure. They invert it. They don't just escape the frame. They change what the frame allows.

This is the Modify Loop. It has three habits:

FLIP THE SCRIPT → INVERT THE FLOW → TURN THE TABLE

Across the next four examples, you'll see this loop in action. Not just to change behaviour. But to modify the mechanism that holds the loop in place.

This isn't abstract improvement. This is targeted structural change.

This is how superadapters modify the mechanism.

HOW TO READ WHAT COMES NEXT

Each of these examples has been chosen carefully.

Not just because they're impressive – but because they show exactly what we want you to be able to do.

So it matters how you look at them.

It matters what you're seeing – and what we're teaching you to see.

I want you to recognise what others might miss.

To really understand what they did – beneath the surface.

So that you can take action in your own life.

These are stories of modification. But not surface change.

They're stories of function rewired.

So don't just follow what happened.

363

Follow how it happened.

That's what turns a trap into a transformation.

What superadapters do isn't magic. It's structure. They change systems by modifying the functions that hold those systems in place. That's what you're about to see – and what you'll learn to do.

Trap → Transform → Transcend

The trap: a system or situation that limits movement, expression, or outcome.

The transformation: the turning point where the loop is modified.

The transcendence: what becomes possible when the system is different – when it evolves.

Model → Modify → Mechanism

What did they model? What was the hidden structure?

What did they modify – through behaviour, insight, or structure?

What mechanism actually changed?

Input → Function → Output

What were they putting in?

What was the system doing with it?

What came out?

How did they rewrite the function?

They started at the bottom. Now they're here. But how?

They didn't just push harder. They rewrote the function.

THE MODIFIER'S EQUATION

Most people are taught that the only way to get different results is to try harder. You want a better outcome? Increase the input. Work longer. Wake up earlier. Grind more. And for a while, that works – until it doesn't.

Because sometimes, the system you're in doesn't respond to effort. Sometimes the function in the middle is broken – or rigged – or simply not designed for people like you.

That's where superadapters live.

They don't just keep adding energy to a loop that loops against them. They look for the structure of the system itself.

Every loop – whether it's emotional, organisational, societal – has three parts:

INPUT → FUNCTION → OUTPUT

The input is what you bring: your action, your energy, your effort.

The output is what you get: recognition, reward, rejection, result.

But the function is the invisible part in between – the mechanism that processes your input into that outcome.

In most cases, people are taught to keep adjusting the input. If something doesn't work, try harder. But superadapters change the function. They recognise that if you don't modify the mechanism, you're stuck in a loop that just recycles effort into futility.

This is where Rule 6 begins: by naming that middle part. By showing that the power isn't in how much you do – it's in what the system does with what you do.

And once you start to see that, everything changes.

You might find the function in a script you've inherited – about who gets to succeed and how. You might find it in a cultural setting, in a job description, in a rulebook, in an algorithm, or in a childhood belief that never got updated. But whatever shape it takes, the key insight is the same: if the system's function doesn't serve you, don't just fight harder – modify the mechanism.

In this book, you'll meet people who changed the function – sometimes quietly, sometimes defiantly – and transformed their loop.

This is what we're focused on. This is what Rule 6 focuses on in particular: showing you not just how to identify what's trapping you, but how to modify the mechanism to allow you to transcend the system.

Because what follows is not just a set of escape stories. It's a study in mechanism modification – the recursive skill that lets superadapters rewire the loop from within.

Between trying harder and rewiring smarter.

Between doing more – and changing what doing means.

THE MATHS OF MODIFICATION

Every adaptive act involves change. But not all change rewires the loop.

If you want to transcend a trap – not just decorate it – you have to understand how transformation works structurally.

This is the maths of modification.

INPUT → FUNCTION → OUTPUT

Imagine you're in a job where no matter how much effort you put in, the results don't change. You take on more projects. You stay later. You double your output.

But recognition doesn't increase. You don't move forward.

That's not a failure of effort. It's a failure of the function.

The mechanism turning your input into output is broken – or biased – or simply pointed in the wrong direction.

Superadapters learn to spot that, and then shift it. They don't just change what they do.

They change what the system 'does with what they do'. They rewrite the function.

And when you change the function, you change the loop.

MODEL → MECHANISM → MODIFY

Now imagine you've grown up believing success means being picked.

That belief – unquestioned – becomes your model of the world. And that model shapes how you move through systems.

You wait. You compete. You hope to be noticed.

But what if the picking system is broken? What if it's not made to see you?

Superadapters examine the model – and then look underneath it. They find the mechanism that converts belief into structure.

Then they modify it. They stop waiting to be chosen, and start choosing the shape of their own loop.

Sometimes, modifying the mechanism reshapes the model itself. That's recursion.

TRAPPED → TRANSFORMED → TRANSCENDED

You've felt this one. You're stuck. You've tried everything you know. Nothing changes.

Then something shifts – not in the world, but in the way you relate to it.

You identify the loop. You see the moment where it turns. And you reach into it, and change that moment.

The trap transforms. Not into a shortcut – but into a door.

You transcend – not by escape, but by re-authoring the loop from within.

This is not mindset. It's mechanism.

And once you see the transformation point, you'll never unsee it.

These three loops aren't just diagrams. They're recursive blueprints.

Once you recognise them, you start to live them. And once you modify them – you change what life returns.

HABIT 1: FLIP THE SCRIPT

By now, you've seen the shape of it.

Every loop has a function. Every mechanism can be modified. And the people who do it don't just change their trajectory – they change what the system returns.

If you can name the mechanism, you can modify the outcome.

When you spot the catch, you own the loop.

Modify once, and you can change your situation.

Modify recursively – and you change the system that surrounds you.

This is not theoretical. In this book, you'll meet people who made those moves.

Some did it instinctively. Others deliberately. But all of them changed the loop by modifying what it did in the middle.

They didn't escape the system. They restructured it. And the results propagated.

And once the function was rewritten, the system turned – and kept turning.

This is the first movement of the Modify Loop. Flip the Script.

Not metaphorically. Structurally. Emotionally. Recursively.

You started at the bottom. Now you're here – higher.

Not because you escaped the loop, but because you modified it.

You rewrote the function. You shifted the turn. You climbed the loop, recursively.

Just like the next guy did.

In the next section, you'll meet someone who didn't just get through it.

He flipped the structure. He changed what the world did with his story.

That's Flip the Script. And it starts right here.

WHAT TO LOOK FOR

You're not just reading this to be inspired.

You're reading to understand how a superadaptive mind modifies mechanisms – to create a new loop.

So watch what happens. Look for:

The trap.

The transformation.

The transcendence.

What world he was modelling.

What mechanism he was stuck in.

What function he changed – and how that changed everything else.
What input he worked with.
What output the old system produced.
And how he modified the function in between.

Because that's the mechanism. And that's what you can change too.

TRAP → TRANSFORM → TRANSCEND

Tyler was stuck in a loop where mainstream validation defined success. He transformed it by writing and producing stories for the audience he knew existed. He transcended the system by building his own – and inviting the world in.

MODEL → MECHANISM → MODIFY

He was taught: "Success means being discovered." He spotted the mechanism: gatekeeper approval = legitimacy. He modified the mechanism: created a system that skipped gatekeepers entirely.

INPUT → FUNCTION → OUTPUT

He took the input: stories the system ignored. He changed the function: turned those stories into public, profitable events. He produced a new output: recognition, momentum, industry reconfiguration.

TYLER PERRY

Tyler Perry didn't ask for a part in the story. He wrote the whole scene.

For most of the entertainment world, he came out of nowhere. But that's because they weren't looking in the right direction.

Born into poverty in New Orleans, Perry grew up in a household full of trauma, faith, and contradiction. He started writing as a form of survival. His earliest plays weren't seen by agents or critics – they were seen by churchgoers, working-class women, families carrying memory and pain. His stories didn't try to be universal. They were precise. Lived. Familiar.

In 1992, he produced his first play, *"I Know I've Been Changed."* It flopped. He was broke. For years, he lived out of his car, trying to keep the production alive. No press. No backing. Just belief – and an audience he couldn't yet reach.

Then something changed. Slowly, the crowds began to build. Word spread. Communities began to show up – not to see a star, but to hear themselves reflected. Perry had tapped into something the industry didn't understand: a feedback loop the mainstream ignored. While Hollywood chased universality, Perry built specificity. And specificity spoke louder.

His Madea character – part matriarch, part comic sledgehammer – became a phenomenon. Critics dismissed it. Audiences didn't care. They showed up in droves. Perry wasn't on magazine covers, but he was selling out theatres. He wasn't reviewed, but he was revered – by the people who recognised themselves in his loops.

"I was writing from my own pain," Perry said. "I was writing characters that had my mother's laughter and my grandmother's backbone. I wasn't trying to be accepted. I was trying to tell the truth."

And the truth, told consistently, flipped the script.

Perry stopped waiting to be invited into the industry. He built his own infrastructure. In 2006, he opened Tyler Perry Studios. In 2019, he expanded it to a 330-acre site on a former Confederate army base in Atlanta. The symbolism wasn't lost on him. He said:

"The land that was once a Confederate Army base – think about the symbolism. The Confederate Army is fighting to keep Negroes enslaved. Now that land is owned by one Negro."

He doesn't pitch to studios. He produces. He doesn't audition. He casts. The loop didn't open for him – so he rewired it.

His work has faced criticism – some justified, some coded. But Perry never claimed to be making perfect films. He was making 'his' films. And he was making them at scale. While others fought for a greenlight, he built the power grid.

"While you're fighting for a seat at the table," he once said, "I'll be down in Atlanta building my own."

That's what superadapters do. They don't ask for permission to re-enter the loop. They create a new entry point. A new rhythm. A new meaning.

Perry didn't flip the system with protest. He flipped it with production. Not defiance, but direction. Not rebellion, but recursion.

His audience wasn't found. It was forged.

And in the end, the industry came to him.

FLIP THE SCRIPT → INVERT THE FLOW → TURN THE TABLE

Tyler Perry recognised that the stories written for him weren't made for him. So he flipped the script – and wrote his own.

But he didn't just do it once.
He did it again and again, building skills, confidence, audience connection, and industry knowledge – until his new loop ran better than the one he was given.

That's recursive modification.
That's what lifted him from trap → transform → transcend.

Now, Milla Jovovich?
She wasn't standing outside the machine.
She was in it. On the covers of *Vogue* and *Cosmopolita*n. On set. In makeup chairs. In the loop.

And she saw exactly where it was headed: the energy flowed through her beauty – then away from her.
So she didn't just flip the script.
She changed the current.
She inverted the flow – by modifying herself so the system would move differently around her.

HABIT 2: INVERT THE FLOW

To modify the mechanism is to transform the function of the system. And to do that recursively – intentionally and iteratively – is to move from being trapped, to transforming your trajectory, to transcending your previous conditions entirely.

Every superadaptive mind in this book does this. But each habit isolates one distinct form of that function. Habit 2 is not about rewriting the story. It's about redirecting the current. It's about taking the energy of a system – attention, resources, visibility, value – and making it move differently.

When you invert the flow, you don't just escape the loop – you rewire it so it moves through you. Not around you. Not past you. Through you.

Ask yourself: where in your life is the energy blocked? Where are the loops that leave you stuck while other people move?

You may not need to break the system. You may just need to modify where the energy flows. That's what this habit teaches. That's what the next example shows.

She was born by accident in Soviet Ukraine in 1975. By 1980, she was in Los Angeles. Raised by her mother to be a model and movie star, teased at school for being a commie, Milla Jovovich became exactly what her mother hoped – and then went beyond it.

She saw the system she was entering: a girl like her might be celebrated briefly, then discarded. A beautiful face. A short shelf life. She recognised the pattern. Then she modified herself.

She trained, reframed, and reshaped. Not to survive the system. But to invert its flow. So that instead of being shaped by it, she could shape it back.

Read the next example looking for where she spots the trap, modifies the mechanism, and inverts the flow of power. This is how superadapters shift not just their story, but the structure they're in.

MILLA JOVOVICH

This is what Invert the Flow looks like.

When the current moves in the wrong direction – toward regression, repetition, erasure – superadapters don't fight it.

They flip it.

They take that energy, and they use it to move forward.

Milla Jovovich shows how.

She wasn't supposed to be the one who stayed.

Not in Hollywood. Not in five languages. Not in fifteen films about the same character, dying and waking and fighting again.

She wasn't the right type.

She wasn't American enough.

She wasn't male enough. Quiet enough. Flat enough.

But she didn't just stay.

She inverted the flow.

Milla Jovovich was born in Kyiv, 1975. A daughter of motion: Soviet mother, Serbian father, émigré child crossing London, Sacramento, then Los Angeles. Her mother was once a screen star in the USSR. In America, she cleaned houses. Her father would end up incarcerated. Milla was an outsider before she was old enough to understand what the inside even meant.

She began modelling at eleven. Acting by thirteen. She was mocked for her accent, exoticized in casting rooms, reduced and reframed to fit the frame. The system knew what to do with pretty girls who weren't from here. It watched them flicker in and out of genre and memory.

But Milla didn't flicker – or fade. She looped brighter.

371

Every time she was cast, she recast herself. Not through defiance, but through adaptive recursion. She didn't escape the system. She redirected its energy. She didn't interrupt the current. She inverted it.

In 1997, she became Leeloo in *The Fifth Element*.

The role should have swallowed her. An orange-haired alien saviour in a film written by a man for his teenage self. But she transformed the manic into myth. Her body became choreography. Her language became invocation. The frame bent.

And then she became Alice.

Resident Evil wasn't supposed to be a recursive text. It was meant to be a one-shot, B-grade action-horror adaptation of a Japanese video game. Disposable. Derivative. Marketable.

But Milla turned it into a myth system.

Alice wakes up in a lab. No memory. A facility in lockdown. She survives. She dies. She is cloned. She returns. She forgets. She re-learns. She re-loops.

Each film iterates on the one before. But she doesn't play the same role. She plays a character who plays herself. She is the memory and the loss, the self and the twin, the virus and the cure.

It's not subtle. But it is structural.

Pause here.

What she's doing isn't just surviving in a difficult industry.

She's flipping loops that were designed to close down her options – and using them to open up new identity paths.

Each time the system hands her a reduction, she loops it forward.

That's not just persistence. That's inversion.

This is what makes Invert the Flow so powerful:

It's not reaction.

It's redirection – of momentum, meaning, and mechanism.

Milla turned Alice into a recursive heroine – one of the only female leads in cinema history to carry six action films over two decades. Not because she conformed. But because she inverted the system's own momentum.

She didn't fight to be cast.

She let herself be typecast.

And then she flipped what the type could mean.

She took roles that were meant to be visual and made them internal.

She took franchises meant to sell and made them loop.

She took images designed to erase agency – and turned them into mirrors.

And the audience stayed.

Not just because she was kinetic.
But because she was recursive.

Milla doesn't just perform.
She re-performs.

Not just new roles. New iterations. Each role talks to the one before it.
Leeloo to Alice. Alice to Joan of Arc. Joan to Milla. Milla to clone.

She doesn't survive because she breaks the mould.
She survives because she uses the mould as a weapon.

She's not an icon.
She's an echo made self-aware.

She took the flow – the expectations, the frames, the role logic – and redirected it back through the system that produced it.

And it wasn't just her. The director, too, had looped. After earlier failures, he wrote the script on spec, refused studio control, and kept the budget low. He, too, knew what it meant to invert the current.

Later, her loop met his. But for now, the current was hers to reverse.

This wasn't about the male gaze. Or the female gaze. Or even the audience's gaze.

It was about looping until she could see herself.

And inverting anything that tried to drag her backward.

Milla is not herself.
She is self.
She is Milla.
She is what Milla can become.

She made the loop her weapon.

FLIP THE SCRIPT → **INVERT THE FLOW** → TURN THE TABLE

"From now on," she said, "I'm a businesswoman. From now on, I'm an action star."

"There are lots of pretty faces out there. But none of them are still around."

By now, you've seen what it means to modify the mechanism. Not just once, but twice.

You saw Tyler Perry flip the script – writing his own roles and redefining the system that tried to exclude him. You saw Milla Jovovich invert the flow – redirecting the current of an industry that was built to discard her.

Both saw what was coming. Both changed their loop.

That's what superadaptive minds do. They don't just survive the system – they change how it functions.

But what happens when the system doesn't just exclude you or discard you – what if it's built to erase you?

Some loops aren't broken by flipping or redirecting.

Some loops are only escaped when you turn the table itself.

That's where we go next.

HABIT 3: TURN THE TABLES

This isn't just about reinterpreting the story.
It's about modifying the mechanism that tells it.

This is the culmination of the UNDERSTAND phase – when you recognise how a system works, sees what keeps it stuck, and then rewrites the logic so the loop can't run the same way again.

Not everyone gets to do this. But those who do – like Rigoberta Menchú – teach us how.

She didn't overthrow the system by fighting.

She made it see itself.
And she made that vision hold.

RIGOBERTA MENCHÚ
The mirror that modified the mechanism

You can picture her, sitting upright, spine like a staff, in woven red huipil and headband. She speaks, not loudly, not softly, but with an intent that reshapes silence. What she says has been said before. But not like this. Not by someone like her. Not in the places she takes it.

Rigoberta Menchú Tum was born into the smoke and soil of El Quiché, Guatemala – K'iche' Maya, daughter of subsistence farmers, child of a people whose erasure was not a metaphor but a military strategy. Her family was caught in the gears of a civil war designed to grind the Indigenous out of the visible world.

By the time she was in her teens, her father had been arrested and tortured. Her brother murdered. Her mother brutalised and left to die. Her village's land was being devoured, its stories denied, its very language mocked or criminalised. What had once been cyclical time and sacred space became a target grid.

In the logic of the Guatemalan state, the K'iche' were not a people – they were an insurgent terrain.

That was the mechanism.

And she saw it. Not all at once, but again and again, through the recursion of trauma and flight and bearing witness.

Recognition wasn't enough. It never is.

So she understood what others missed: the real violence wasn't only the killing. It was the narrative that made the killing plausible. It was the system that sorted whose lives counted.

She couldn't fight that system on its terms. So she rewrote the terms.

She modified the mechanism.

Her weapon wasn't a gun. It was a mirror.

She told her story. In exile, in interviews, in Europe and the UN and classrooms and courtrooms. She spoke in K'iche', in Spanish, in French, in the language of moral clarity and unhealed loss. And she used her life as a witness structure to illuminate the structural crime.

In 1983, her testimony – 'I, Rigoberta Menchú' – shocked the world. For the first time, millions saw into the genocide beneath the surface of Cold War geopolitics. This wasn't simply a peasant revolt or a communist insurgency. This was extermination-by-administration.

The system responded. Slowly. But the mechanism was altered.

She testified not only in books, but in tribunals. She became a symbolic force in international law. In 1992, she received the Nobel Peace Prize. In 1999, she filed charges of genocide and torture in the Spanish courts against Guatemala's military rulers, including Efraín Ríos Montt.

This was the reversal. The table turned.

The persecuted used international law – a mechanism originally built by colonial powers – to pursue justice. It wasn't perfect. It wasn't clean. But it was real.

The same system that ignored her people began, however reluctantly, to recognise their suffering.

Not because she asked. But because she showed them.

She placed a mirror on a table. She turned the table.

The mirror she turned towards them didn't flatter. It reflected.

And that reflection became inescapable.

There are criticisms. There always are. The anthropologist David Stoll argued that parts of her testimony were constructed from multiple voices and experiences. He claimed her account didn't meet Western standards of evidentiary singularity.

But this is beside the point.

She was never pretending to be a passive witness. She was a narrative strategist, a system adapter. She didn't just want her story to be heard. She wanted the entire mechanism of 'who gets to tell history' to be changed.

And she changed it.

There are now archives that wouldn't exist without her. There are trials that wouldn't have been held. There are children growing up knowing their language, K'iche', is not a liability but a lineage.

She turned a mirror on a world that said: "You do not exist."

And the mirror answered: "I am still here."

This is the essence of modification. Not just protest. But patterned disruption. A systemic incision. Not reaction, but recursion.

And recursion is sticky.

Once the mechanism has been made visible, it can be altered. Once it has been altered, it must account for the change. Once it must account, the loop is not the same.

That's what she did. That's what superadapters do.

Not just to tell their story.

But to change the story that gets told.

FLIP THE SCRIPT → INVERT THE FLOW → **TURN THE TABLE**

Rigoberta Menchú showed us what it means to turn the table – and keep turning it until a system becomes a place of dignity. For her, the goal wasn't power or revenge. It was fullness. A life lived in truth, with justice and memory intact.

"All causes lead to the same destination: living in fullness (Utz' k'aslemal)."

Fullness is recursive. It's not a finish line – it's the compounding result of modifying mechanisms in the right direction, again and again.

And that same logic appears where you least expect it.

You've now seen three ways a mechanism can be modified – and three ways a person can become the modifier.

Tyler Perry flipped the script. He refused to accept the default storyline. Instead, he reshaped the entire arc – from invisibility to impact – by building his own stage and rewriting his own roles. That was modification through authorship.

Milla Jovovich inverted the flow. She didn't just react to being seen as a pretty face – she trained, transformed, and redirected the current of energy in her career. The model became the action hero. That was modification through reconfiguration.

Rigoberta Menchú turned the table. She wasn't supposed to have a voice, but she became one. A drop of water on a rock. Testimony as recursive mechanism. That was modification through truth-telling – looped into the system until it cracked.

Each one applied the Modify Loop differently, but the pattern holds:

FLIP THE SCRIPT → INVERT THE FLOW → TURN THE TABLE

Some changes are symbolic. Some are personal. But the Modify Loop does something deeper: it rewires how the system treats you – and how you treat it in return.

This is superadaptability in action. Recursive modification. One loop forward at a time.

In the high-pressure world of Formula One, McLaren's Andrea Stella doesn't talk about victory. He talks about improvement.

"By nature, I don't necessarily think about the destination. I just think about what we have to put in place to keep improving."

That's Rule 6 in motion.

The smoother your modification, the cleaner your next loop. Like a pit stop perfectly run – done right, you don't lose momentum. You gain it.

That's not just performance. That's adaptation. That's recursion – not repeating, but returning differently.

And when done well, that loop becomes your launchpad.

Next, you'll see what happens when this logic isn't just personal, but structural – when it's used to rewire an entire grid.

REWIRING THE GRID

How Marshall and Stella changed the loop behind their F1 car.

In Formula One, everything moves.

Every car is built on sand. The rules shift. The wind shifts. The tyres change. The tracks evolve. And every year, the governing body rewrites some part of the game.

That's the loop.

You don't just build the fastest car. You build the fastest response to change itself.

Red Bull mastered that. For a time, no one could touch them. Their genius wasn't just speed – it was adaptive dominance. While others took seasons to catch up to new regulations, Red Bull adjusted mid-weekend. They turned constraint into advantage. Regulation into rhythm. The car became an expression of this loop: aerodynamically sharp, tactically aggressive, mechanically fluid.

And at the heart of it was Adrian Newey – Formula One's master of flow. His cars didn't just go fast. They felt inevitable. Rumour had it Red Bull even encouraged rule changes. They wanted disruption – because they could out-loop everyone else.

Until they couldn't.

It happened slowly, then all at once. Red Bull stopped adapting and started fortifying. They didn't stop building. But they stopped bending. And when the pressure came – cultural, ethical, performance-based – they didn't listen. They defended.

They minimised internal fractures. They attacked critics, inside and out. They denied that anything was wrong. Even as key talent drifted. Even as the air got thinner.

What had been an open system became a closed circuit.

$$\text{MINIMISE} \rightarrow \text{ATTACK} \rightarrow \text{DENY}$$

And that's when Rob Marshall left.

Rob Marshall didn't leave for a louder team. He left for a quieter one.

After years as a key architect inside Red Bull's dominance, he could see the loop was locking. It wasn't just the media stories, or the internal politics. It was the energy pattern. What had once been a live wire of innovation had become a fortress of denial. Even the smartest people were spending more time defending decisions than improving systems.

He didn't argue. He just withdrew.

And when McLaren called, he didn't ask about money. He asked about margin.

Andrea Stella didn't make noise either. He was already building in silence.

At McLaren, there were no illusions of supremacy. No obsession with mythology. Just a team that had been fast, then slow, and now hungrier than most to build clarity over chaos.

What Stella had was time. And trust.

While Red Bull tightened its grip, Stella loosened his. He let his engineers breathe. He slowed meetings. He made decision-making recursive: test, reflect, decide. The loop wasn't glamorous, but it worked. And it made McLaren an unusually attractive place to be – for someone who no longer wanted to defend a castle, but design a flow.

Marshall joined. And instead of dominating, he integrated.

The result wasn't just a better car. It was a healthier loop.

McLaren's 2025 challenger didn't break the speed trap. It bent the race around itself. Where Red Bull once applied force, McLaren absorbed it. Their tyres ran cooler. Their cornering remained neutral under pressure. Their pace didn't spike – it held. Week after week.

And when the rules changed – again – McLaren didn't flinch. They adapted without resistance. They remembered what Red Bull had forgotten:

The script isn't the rulebook. It's how you move inside it.

By Melbourne, the shift was obvious. Red Bull hadn't just been overtaken. They'd been out-looped.

What Marshall and Stella had done wasn't magical. It was architectural.

They exited the closed loop. They built system calm. They turned turbulence into timing. They made strategy visible again – not just for the team, but for the sport.

FLIP THE SCRIPT → INVERT THE FLOW → TURN THE TABLE

untie what has
embedded the
limit, and what
blocks progress,
then retie at a
higher level…"

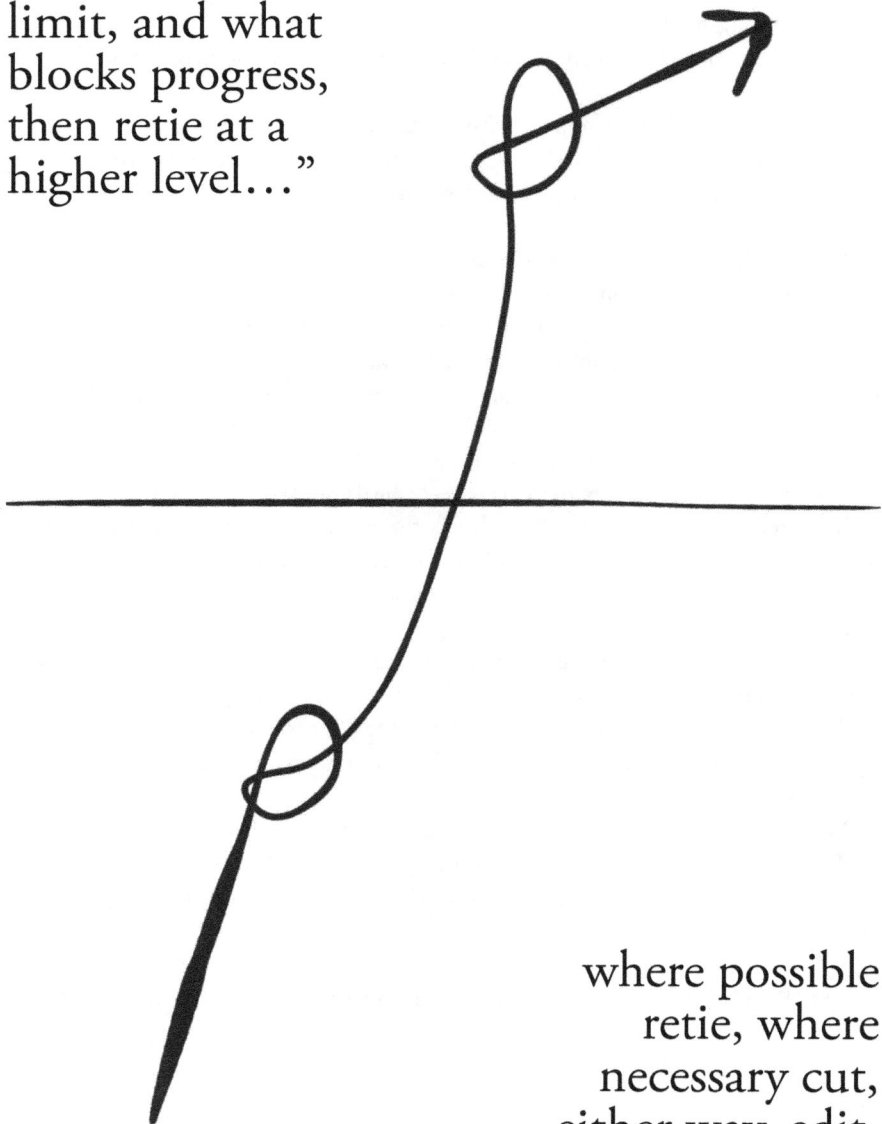

where possible
retie, where
necessary cut,
either way, edit,
paste, upgrade…

THE SITDOWN: THE BRAIN (AND THE BLENDER)

WHY WE SIT DOWN NOW

"The best way to capture moments is to pay attention. This is how we cultivate mindfulness."
— Jon Kabat-Zinn

Rule 6 is where you begin to change the system — not just understand it. But modification without mechanism is just momentum. And loops — those invisible patterns that drive our decisions, behaviours, and beliefs — are the deepest mechanisms we have.

So we sit down now. Not to rest. But to see.

Because what you're about to read isn't just a story. It's a model.

The first person you'll meet in this Sitdown is a world-class pattern-hunter — a scientist who reshaped how we understand the brain itself. Her name is Suzana Herculano-Houzel, and her work began in a kitchen in Brazil. With a blender, a question, and a refusal to accept what didn't make sense.

Suzana didn't just shift neuroscience. She modified how we 'measure' the brain — by challenging the defaults, inventing her own method, and looping through resistance until the system itself had to adapt. Her life shows what happens when you modify the modifier — when you upgrade not just your actions, but your ability to act.

But this Sitdown isn't only about her. It's about 'you'. And the loops you live inside.

Because not every loop you run is built to help you adapt. Some repeat. Some reinforce. Some reduce. Only one kind evolves. Only one learns.

In this section, we'll name them — four loops, four choices. You'll start to see the ones you use, the ones that trap you, and the one that can lift you. You'll learn what recursive thinking really means — and how it gives you an edge the world hasn't taught you to see.

Before this Sitdown ends, you'll meet someone who let go of a loop that had made her famous — because she'd outgrown the pattern she'd built her life on. And you'll meet another who walked away from success others would have dreamed of — because adaptation sometimes means saying no to the world's idea of winning.

Because plasticity isn't just persistence. It's escape. It's inversion. It's choice.

So we sit down. To recognise. To reframe. To rebuild. And when we stand again, we'll be ready to live the loop, on purpose.

These are real-world escape artists. They had the same inputs as everyone else – but they modified the 'function'. They transformed what their systems 'did with' the conditions they faced. They used the maths of modification to alter their path from trapped to transcended. And so can you.

And before you meet her – before we enter the lab or touch the blender – let's take a brief walk. You might find your mind is already moving.

WALKING OFF THE MIND

Steve Jobs was known to summon colleagues for long walking meetings through Palo Alto, bare feet padding on the pavement as ideas bounced around. He might not have realised it, but he was tapping into an ancient mental trick. When you head out for a stroll with no urgent destination, you set your mind free. The very act of walking seems to jar loose the ideas stuck in your head. In fact, scientists find that people generate about 60% more creative ideas while walking compared to sitting. It's as if each footstep jolts the mind into a new connection.

You've felt it – that gentle unraveling of tight thoughts as you amble along. Your brain's planning circuits relax, and a quieter system takes over: the default mode network, active in daydreams and meanderings. Darwin strolled his 'thinking path' daily, letting evolution theories percolate with each lap. Nietzsche even warned, "Do not believe any idea that was not born in the open air and of free movement." There is wisdom in these wandering steps.

As you walk, the world around you blurs into a backdrop for your inner dialogue. The rhythm of your stride becomes the rhythm of your thoughts. Problems that felt unsolvable at your desk suddenly present solutions after a few blocks under the trees. By the time you loop back home or to the office, you've not only stretched your legs – you've given your cognition a chance to roam. In the simple ritual of walking, you discover an active kind of 'sitdown,' where movement unlocks creativity and your mind returns refreshed.

HERCULANO-HOUZEL
Measuring what no one else could see

For decades, textbooks claimed the human brain contained 100 billion neurons. It was a number so clean, so pleasing, that it went unquestioned. Except by one person.

Suzana Herculano-Houzel was trained in biology. She had no intention of becoming a disruptive force in neuroscience. At the time, she was working at the Museu da Vida in Rio de Janeiro, developing public science education projects. But as she tried to communicate the wonders of the brain, something began to nag at her. The facts didn't hold.

The most basic numbers – how many neurons we have, how we compare to other animals – weren't grounded in empirical data. They were estimates, often recycled between papers and books. The deeper she looked, the more she realised the model itself might be flawed. So she asked a simple, unscientific question: how do we know?

What followed was a feat of adaptation. Unable to rely on conventional lab setups, she invented her own method. In her kitchen. Using a blender.

She called it the isotropic fractionator – a technique that turned brains into a uniform soup of nuclei, allowing accurate neuron counts. With this method, she discovered the real number: around 86 billion neurons in the human brain – not 100 billion. She also shattered the long-repeated glia myth: glial cells weren't ten times more numerous than neurons. The ratio was roughly 1:1.

This wasn't just scientific housekeeping. It was a mechanism-level reframe. Our brains are not extraordinary in structure – they're efficiently packed primate brains with an unusually high number of cortical neurons. That's the advantage. Not size. Not magic. Structure and density.

She faced resistance. Her method was too simple. Too homemade. At first, peers dismissed it. But the numbers held. They held through replications. Through international labs. Through peer review.

What she was doing wasn't just technical. It was philosophical. She questioned a field-wide assumption, proposed a new method, and offered recursive data to support it. That's superadaptability at work – she recognised, sought understanding and took action.

Her father once said he couldn't believe he'd raised a rebellious daughter who became a scientist. But it wasn't rebellion for its own sake. It was curiosity. Truth-seeking. Model-challenging. When no one had a reliable answer, she built a way to find one.

Her story shows what happens when someone adapts the measurement system – not just the theory. She didn't challenge the brain. She challenged how we count it. And it turned out that what makes humans different isn't the sizes of our brains. Instead, it's the density of our brains – the raw materials that can shape connections and model your world. You can look out at what is happening and figure out what needs to happen.

We have more cortical neurons than any other species. That means more modelling. More prediction. More simulation. Our brains aren't just reactive, they're recursive. This is the neuronal advantage: not to be smarter, but to be better built for adaptation. More feedback. More refinement. More iterations.

Progress doesn't start with people with better answers, it starts with people with better questions. But more importantly, those who are able to follow their instincts and how that thing that seemed weird turns out to be something that leads us forward. People who are willing to test the metric, question the map, rewire the measurement. Suzana did that. With a blender and a model and a refusal to take the textbook on faith.

Now we know: the brain that adapts best is the one that simulates better – and she showed us how it's built. She modified the mechanism (the blender) to modify our knowledge of ourselves (our brains).

FLIP THE SCRIPT → INVERT THE FLOW → TURN THE TABLE

Philosopher Charles Sanders Peirce believed that truth was what inquiry would settle on, given enough time. William James believed the search for truth was itself revealing – if not final, then at least functional.

Suzana lived both.

Her model didn't just change neuroscience. It changed the use of neuroscience. Because when people understand how their own brain is built, they stop taking every thought as a truth, every story as fixed. They start to loop differently – and to choose different loops.

As we sit down to examine how loops change, you'll start to see a few different ways we describe the transformation.

Sometimes we say a person moves from

TRAPPED → TRANSFORMED → TRANSCENDED

because that's what it feels like.

Other times, we show the system: INPUT goes in, a FUNCTION modifies it, and something new comes out.

And behind it all, we're watching for one thing: can the person MODEL their world, spot the MECHANISM, and MODIFY it – so the loop runs better next time?

You don't have to memorise any of this. You just need to see the pattern.

Because once you see the pattern, you'll never unsee it.

That's what makes the loop recursive.

And that's what makes it yours.

I AM YOUR SUPERADAPTIVE MIND.

There is you.
There is me, myself.
There is you, me, myself, and I.
We are one system – sensing, thinking, acting, looping.

And I can start anywhere.
From inside you – a flicker of thought, a shift in mood, a tightening in your muscles.
From between us – a glance, a gesture, a shared word.
From the systems around you – a sudden change, an unexpected signal.
Sometimes with what you see or hear.
Sometimes with a memory, a feeling, a flash of emotion.
Sometimes with a thought about a thought.
Wherever I begin, I bring all of me – and all of you – into the loop.

When we recognize, I light up the visual cortices at the back of our brain, relay across right and left hemispheres through the corpus callosum – a thick bridge of nerve fibres connecting the two halves. (I want you to picture that for a moment: two great hemispheres joined by a dense wiring harness, over 200 million axons, signals rushing back and forth in milliseconds.) Then I signal your salience networks to notice what matters.

When we understand, I map the pattern with your hippocampus, trace causes through your parietal lobes, and shape new responses in your prefrontal cortex. (That is the part just behind your forehead – the 'decision-making desk' of your brain.)

When we act, I prime your premotor and supplementary motor areas, fuel you with dopamine from the midbrain, and embed the change in memory until it becomes part of you. I work with your body, too – heart rate, breath, posture – because every signal counts. (I am not just in your head; I am in how you stand, breathe, and move.)

And all the while, I am watching myself – your 'I' watching your 'me', your 'me' shaping your 'I'. Some loops spark in milliseconds. Others take hours, days, or years to settle. I learn not just what to do, but how I learn to do it. Looping back, altering my own loops.

This is how you adapt.
This is how we adapt.
You, me, myself, and I – a whole brain, ready for whatever comes next.

I am already one of the most adaptive systems in the known universe.
That is true for almost every human mind.
But superadaptability – the kind this book is about – goes beyond that.
You have the basis of it.
You can hone it.
And so that your mind can work at that level, we will explore how it works.

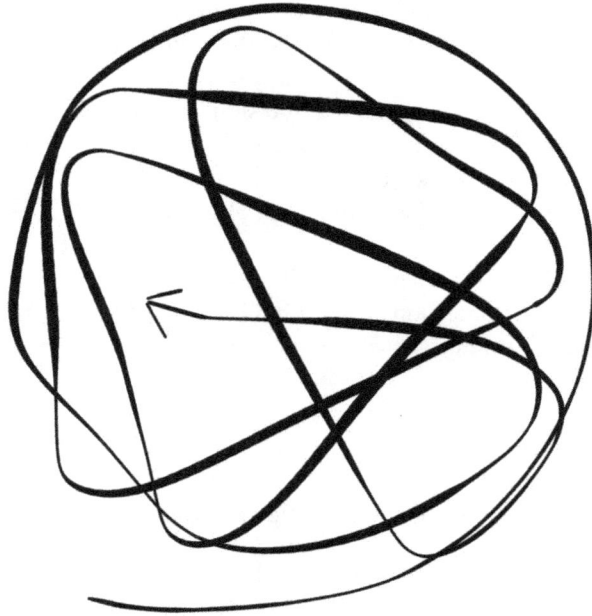

THE TRAP LOOP

This first one, I call the Trap Loop. Not because it always starts as a trap – but because without modification, that's where it lands. You repeat. You get stuck. You burn energy but go nowhere. It's familiar, and weirdly comforting. But it doesn't move you forward. It loops for the sake of the loop. And while all four loops we'll look at in this section are forms of meta-habit – patterns of behaviour that shape other behaviours – only one is designed to learn. Only one is recursive.

Psychologists call it perseverative thinking. We call it the first trap loop: repeating the same response over and over, even when it no longer works. Like a car doing donuts in a deserted parking lot – burning fuel, going nowhere.

These loops are everywhere. Systems run on them. Minds ruminate inside them. Organisations calcify because of them. You keep trying the same fix, not realising you're reinforcing the very structure you hoped to escape.

And it gets worse. The more you try – without modifying – the more the loop tightens. This isn't reflection. This isn't recursion. This is repetition with no gain. And if you've ever felt stuck in a job, a relationship, a system, or a self, you know what we mean. That's why this sit-down starts here. With the problem. With the pattern that pretends to help… but keeps you where you are.

TRAPPED

In the next loop, we'll look at what happens when you tighten the circle – but still don't climb. Efficiency isn't escape. And minimalism isn't always moving forward.

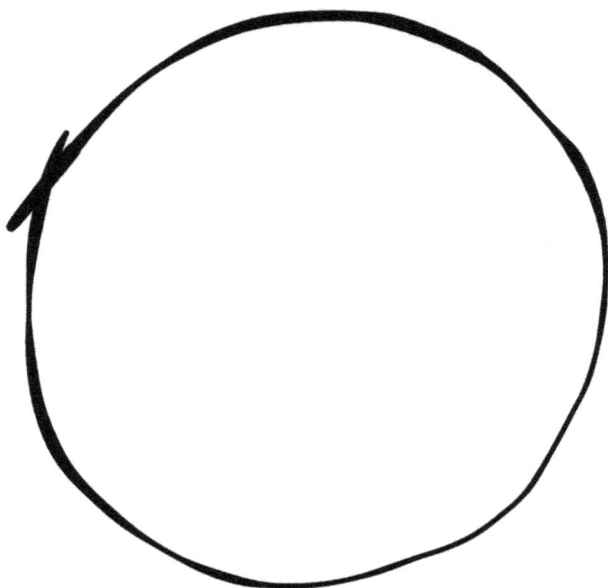

THE MINIMALIST LOOP

If the Trap Loop keeps you circling in friction, the Minimalist Loop offers a kind of relief. It simplifies. Streamlines. Reduces drag. In a complex world, this kind of loop can feel like clarity itself – a way of cutting through the noise by doing fewer things, more consistently.

That's why it's so popular. Whole philosophies have been built around it. Declutter your home. Declutter your mind. Focus on the one thing. Reduce your inputs. Reduce your options. Minimise the loop, and you maximize control.

There's truth in that. And value. But here's the catch: simplicity can become its own kind of trap. The minimalist loop isn't built to evolve. It's built to repeat efficiently. It often trades potential for predictability. You get better at doing the same thing – but not getting better at new things, or finding out about what you want to discover, or invent, or just try.

This is where the distinction matters. The minimalist loop may look adaptive – it cuts, it trims, it focuses. But what it often 'fails' to do is adapt 'upward'. It doesn't upgrade the system. It maintains it. It offers a stable base. But left unchecked, it becomes a kind of austerity of the self.

In the language of this book: the minimalist loop is still a meta-habit. But it's not recursive. It doesn't spiral upward. It stays flat. And over time, that flatness can cost you. Opportunities missed. Growth deferred.

IS THIS YOUR TIDY MIND?

For years, Marie Kondo sparked a global movement by showing how tidying your physical space could restore mental order. Her minimalist method became a mantra, a mechanism that brought peace to millions. "Tidy house, tidy life," she preached – and lived.

But even tidy loops can become trap loops.

After her first child, she found her way back to order. After her second, it got harder. And then came her third.

"After the third, I just thought, tidying has become impossible. My daily life is so chaotic. So, of course, I try as much as possible. But I don't have time and children just keep undoing all my tidying."

She still believed in her system. But she also believed in growth. And recursive loops don't just repeat – they evolve. So, Kondo ran the loop again: she recognised her new reality, understood what was no longer working, and took necessary action.

"I decided this is a time in my life that I spend with my children."

She gave up tidying – not because it failed, but because she had changed.

And perhaps most telling of all:

"I feel that people can change, and we're allowed to change."

Her tidy minimalist loop had served its purpose. Now, it was time to rewire.

TRAPPED → TRANSFORMED → TRANSCENDED

We've looked at the stuck loop – the one that repeats without movement – and the minimalist loop that streamlines by stripping back. Now we come to the reinforcing loop: the loop that gains power through repetition. It is what most people imagine when they hear the word 'habit'. It's the muscle memory of behaviour. You do it once, then again, and again, until the track becomes a trench.

This loop is what keeps us brushing our teeth without thinking, heading to the gym because it's Tuesday, or reaching for our phones every few minutes. It doesn't just repeat. It rewards. And the reward is what makes the loop stronger.

THE REINFORCING LOOP

At the heart of the reinforcing loop is a simple structure: CUE → ROUTINE → REWARD. A prompt triggers a behaviour, which is then followed by a payoff. If the payoff satisfies or soothes, the loop is strengthened. Over time, it becomes automatic.

This structure underlies many personal growth practices – whether it's daily journaling, morning runs, or nightly meditation. It also explains how skills develop, and habits become identity. Reinforcing loops create fluency. They build reliability. They deliver consistency. And when the loop is well-designed, the behaviour becomes effortless.

But they do not adapt. Not on their own.

The reinforcing loop does exactly what it's told – until it's telling you what to do. That is its power – and its peril. Once set in motion, it cannot question itself. It doesn't know whether the behaviour is good, bad, or outdated. It just knows that it used to work.

This is the loop that keeps you opening Instagram, even when it makes you miserable. It's the loop that makes you pour a drink at 6 pm because you always do. It's the same mechanism behind health routines and unhealthy addictions.

Even the most well-meaning loops – like a daily meditation habit – can become brittle if they aren't examined. Reinforcing loops can entrench a shallow success or calcify a comfort zone.

The same loop that helps you run a mile a day can also help you run from your truth for a decade.

In reinforcing loops, that often maps directly as: CUE → ROUTINE → REWARD.

But what happens when the reward no longer satisfies? Or the routine no longer fits who you are becoming?

That's when even a successful loop can start to trap you. If it can't be modified, it becomes a cage. If it can, it becomes a foundation.

A reinforcing loop learns nothing on its own. But the good news is that it can become part of a greater system that does. That system is what we explore next: the recursive loop. The loop that learns. The loop that lifts.

The loop that rewires the brain – and blends what you've done into something new.

So far, I've introduced you to loops that trap, tidy, and reinforce, but none of them transcend. That's what our final loop does.

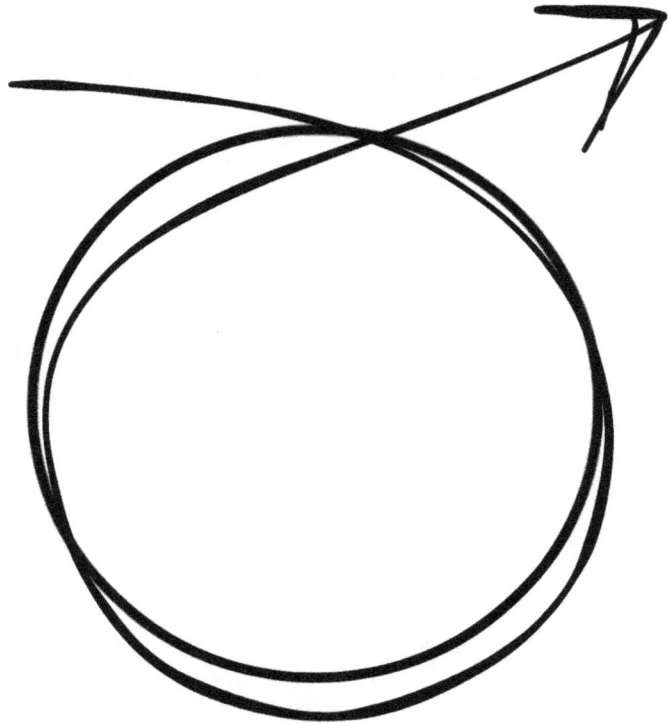

THE RECURSIVE LOOP

Recursive loops do more than just help you move forward – they change how you move. They sharpen your awareness, give you permission to adjust, and teach your brain how to stay flexible without falling apart. Over time, they become the loop beneath the loop: not just a behaviour pattern, but a pattern of how to change your patterns. That's what makes them a consciously chosen meta-habit – and why the most adaptive people you've ever met, whether they call it this or not, are looping like this already.

These loops are the ones that land you somewhere better. Again and again.

Other loops – repetitive, minimalist, reinforcing – can help you stabilise. This one helps you upgrade. It is a naturally evolved system for evolving naturally.

A recursive loop is one that learns forward. Not after the fact. Not as a summary. But inside the loop, so that everything that you have tagged, tested, or felt becomes the basis for a different, wiser next step.

Whereas the reinforcing loop strengthens the same behaviour, the recursive loop reconfigures the system. You don't just do better. You behave differently – because the system around the behaviour is different.

This is the difference between perfecting your response and reshaping your reality.

Four Canonical Benefits of Recursive Loops

They spiral upward. They don't trap you in place – they elevate. Progress isn't a straight line, but it can be an upward spiral. These loops modify momentum. They don't just push you forward. They help you rise.

They modify the modifier. Each time you loop, you're not just changing what you do. You're changing who's doing it. The 'you' who makes the next decision isn't the same 'you' who made the last one. Recursive loops embed growth in the person doing the growing.

They reroute mid-loop. You don't have to finish the whole cycle to course-correct. Recursive loops allow you to shift mid-stride. They let you use what you've learned to adjust direction before the loop ends – so you don't repeat mistakes just because you started them.

They embed plasticity. These loops wire flexibility into the system. They're not brittle, rigid, or overly choreographed. Recursive loops respect complexity – and help you stay adaptive by design, not desperation.

Recursive loops give you two freedoms: the freedom to choose again, and the power to upgrade your upgrade.

They're how you modify the mechanism. And they're how you stay free.

TRAPPED → TRANSFORMED → TRANSCENDED

THE ESCAPE IS THE UPGRADE

They say there's no way out of a locked room. But there always is.

That's not magic. It's design. A lock, after all, is a mechanism. A trap is a structure. And structures can be read.

Escapologists – real ones – don't rage against the walls. They study them. They count the hinges. They trace the shape of the restraint, and learn where the pressure isn't. They know that force is not the art. Timing is. So is knowledge. And most of all, restraint itself contains the clue.

The audience sees spectacle. But what's really being demonstrated is system mastery. Escape is not evasion. It's precision. It's recognising that every system – no matter how total, how tight – contains at least one modifier. One operator that, when found and used, changes the function. And with it, the outcome.

In the best escapes, the move is invisible. The padlock never clicks. The cuffs never slip. The loop is exited before the viewer even knows the artist has begun. That's the highest form of modification: to change the function so subtly that no one sees the hand move.

But some escapes are seen. Some are made in full view, in full struggle, against full constraint. And those, too, are art.

We all have our reasons to escape. Ambition. Fear. Curiosity. Sometimes all three.

But what matters – what sets the true escape artist apart – isn't urgency. It's understanding what's holding you back. It's knowing what part of the system needs to be unpicked, unlocked, or unwound. It's recognising not just the door, but the operator that controls it.

The point isn't just to leave the loop. It's to leave it recursively – by modifying the function that kept it closed.

Because the real trick is this: You don't escape by force. You escape by understanding.

Not in theory. In practice. In locks and laws. In passports and contracts. In cages made of wire, and cages made of paperwork.

The successful escapologist doesn't just want out. They know where the stress point is, and how to release it. They find the latch. The timing. The margin of play. They map the system, and then move through the one part that moves.

Escape is real. It's mechanical. And those who escape best don't guess. They understand what to modify.

Every escape begins before it's seen. Not with action. With awareness. A shift in how the trap is understood.

That's what makes a fork in the road different from a dead end: one of them contains a decision.

Every system has inflection points – structural forks where two paths diverge. And the smartest superadapters don't just ask "Should I go left or right?" They ask: "What does this system do if I choose neither?"

They're not picking exits. They're modifying functions.

Because what looks like a fork is often just a hinge – and what you do with it changes the entire arc of the loop.

This is why some people walk away and everything improves. And others walk away and nothing changes. It's not the leaving. It's how the departure modifies the system – or doesn't.

That's the real fork. Not the one in the road. The one in the function.

Whether you stay or go, the power lies in knowing what your decision is doing to the mechanism. Does it close it tighter? Or does it rewire what it does next?

What we call 'leaving' is often just another round in the trap. But real escape – the kind that upgrades the loop – requires a different question: What is the loop designed to do? And what happens if you choose not to run it?

TRAP → ESCAPE → ESCAPE ARTIST

Delicious Orie was born in Moscow in 1997, the son of a Nigerian father and a Russian mother. He was stateless before he was fluent – too Black for the bureaucracies around him, too foreign to claim a nationality. When his family moved to the UK, it wasn't a straight climb. It was another escape. Wolverhampton became the new site of possibility, and Orie – tall, intelligent, observant – became the carrier of something bigger than ambition. He wasn't trying to win the world's approval. He was trying to understand how it worked.

His father had moved from Lagos to Moscow to study – a leap that looked accidental until you mapped it against the rest of the family's moves. His mother had uprooted twice to give her children a better life. These weren't refugees. These were recursive thinkers: people who left not to flee, but to elevate. Orie absorbed the logic. He watched not just what people did, but what they did it through. He saw that systems didn't just constrain. They revealed their functions, if you paid attention.

When he discovered basketball, and then boxing, he didn't fall in love with sport. He found a loop that worked. A structure you could train into. A story you could run recursively. In Brixton, he saw Luol Deng, and later Anthony Joshua – two men who had modified their circumstances by modifying themselves. That mattered. Not the medals. The function. If they had done it, so could he. He would build a version of himself that could rise inside the system, not in spite of it.

And then the system blocked him. As a teenager, he was denied the chance to play basketball in the United States – not because of skill, but because of status. He was stateless. Caught in a policy trap with no operator. This wasn't resistance. This was nonsense. But the lesson held: the escape wasn't through appeal. It was through reframing. Boxing became the new system. A parallel function with different rules. He stepped in, took the hits, learned the pattern. Won. Learned again. Won again.

By 2024, Orie held a first-class degree in Economics and Management. He had medals. He had momentum. He was signed. Trained. Positioned. A professional boxer on the rise. And then, in 2025, he walked away. Quietly. With precision. "The fire is gone," he said. "And out of respect for the sport – and for myself – it's time to step away." No rupture. No resistance. Just the understanding that the loop had finished its work. That to stay would be performance. That the next escape would be the upgrade.

That's not quitting. That's recursion. It's the rarest kind of exit: the one made with full system comprehension. Orie wasn't just a product of escape. He had learned the architecture. He could see when a path stopped being a path, and became a holding pattern. And so he left – not in shame or in silence, but in mastery. If you ever need a model of modification that leaves the system intact and the self elevated, this is it. Escape is not failure. Escape is the function, understood.

You don't have to fight the system to change it. Well – not always. It's not the fight that matters. It's the future.

Whether you call it a lock, a loop, a table, or a script – every system has a function. And if you can see what it's built to produce, you can decide whether you still want that.

Because escape isn't a retreat. It's a redirection. The cleanest change comes not from opposition, but from understanding. And once you see the loop, you can live it differently.

Start here: What loop are you in that used to work – but no longer does? What function are you still running because it was once effective, once admired, once necessary? Are you adding effort to a structure that only deepens the trap?

You don't need more pressure. You need a better operator. A different exit. A cleaner modifier.

Pause.

Most people don't escape because they're too tired to look. Or too invested to question. Or too rewarded for staying just successful enough.

But the loop doesn't care how much you've put into it. It only does what it's designed to do.

If you're stuck, the question isn't "How do I try harder?" It's "What is this system built to produce – and do I still want that?"

You might be locked out. You might be locked in. You might be climbing a ladder that leads back to the ground floor.

Don't rage at the structure. Map it.

Look for the hinge. The catch. The moment. Because there is always a moment.

The art of escapology isn't bravado. It's precision. It's the calm act of finding the mechanism – and modifying it.

Orie did it. So have millions of others. Most of them didn't call it escape. They called it change. But the truth is, they looped again, on purpose.

They recognised what the system was producing. And then they chose a cleaner function.

So now it's your turn. You don't have to run. You just have to find the operator. And step through the part of the system that moves.

TRAP → ESCAPE → UPGRADE

LIVE THE LOOP

HOW TO LIVE THE LOOP
Modify the function, rewrite the outcome

You've seen what superadapters do. Now it's time to see how they live.

This section is your chance to look again – with structure, with strategy. To revisit the patterns that rewired systems, reshaped outcomes, and turned dead ends into openings.

This is the final step of the 'Understand' phase of the RUN loop. You've learned how to recognise what needs changing. You've modelled the systems. You've explored the mechanisms.

Now we go one step further: modification in action.

Here, you'll see how three different people lived the loop – intentionally, structurally, and recursively. You'll learn how to do it yourself. You'll get practical tools to spot what's trapping you, and techniques to move forward.

You'll test the difference between improvement and recursion.

You'll examine the loops you're already running – and decide whether they're helping you transcend, or keeping you stuck.

And because not all upgrades work the first time, you'll also explore what can go wrong:

the wrong loops, the stuck patterns, the misfires – and how to counter them.

This section isn't abstract. It's where theory becomes traction.

Where reflection becomes recursion.

Where action becomes design.

If you've made it this far, you're ready to live the loop.

HOW THEY LIVED THEIR LOOP
Three ways to modify a mechanism – and change the outcome.

You've already seen the Modify Loop – three actions that change how systems respond.

But now, we go deeper. We revisit the people you've just met, not to admire them, but to understand them structurally.

Because each of them did more than make a good choice.

They modified a mechanism.

They understood how the function was working against them – and changed the loop from within.

Tyler Perry didn't wait for permission. He flipped the script – socially, structurally, financially. He didn't just tell a different story. He changed the machinery that decides which stories get told.

Milla Jovovich didn't fight the current. She inverted the flow – finding roles that let her reshape the system from the inside. Her performances weren't just iconic. They were adaptive acts that redirected power.

Rigoberta Menchú didn't just survive erasure. She turned the table – using the tools of testimony, law, and narrative to reverse the loop that was meant to silence her. She didn't just speak truth to power. She reprogrammed what power could hear.

Three habits. Three rewired mechanisms.

And not one of them was just about effort. Each one was a strategic, recursive act.

This is what it looks like to live the loop – not once, but continuously. Not performatively, but structurally.

What they did is what you can do.

But only if you're ready to see your own system.

And choose your next modifying loop deliberately.

THE CLICK AND THE CLIMB

I was twelve years old. No ropes. No chalk. No training. Just trainers, jeans, and the half-formed certainty of a boy who hadn't yet encountered consequence.

The rock was Almscliff, or Arms Cliff, as climbers call it. One of the oldest and toughest gritstone outcrops in Yorkshire. Rough-edged, wind-scoured, well-loved. Known for being steep. Polished. Unforgiving.

I didn't know any of that. I didn't know there were routes called things like Demon Wall or Wall of Horrors. I just ran up the hill and started climbing. I'd always climbed – scaffolding, buildings, trees, furniture. I thought I was good at it. I was good at it.

Until I wasn't.

Halfway up the cliff, the angle shifted. The grit turned slick. And I froze.

I couldn't go up. I couldn't go down. And I couldn't shout – not really. All I could do was cling.

That's when my dad arrived.

He wasn't a climber. Hated heights. But he scrambled up to a ledge beside me, didn't speak for a moment. Just looked.

And then he said, "There, son."

He pointed with his eyes. "It's safe. Just put your foot down."

My legs were shaking. My fingers cramping. I was ramrod straight, clinging like a ladder with lactic acid. I had Elvis leg, and fear in both hands.

But I trusted him.

And his eyes helped me see what I couldn't.

That there was, in fact, a way down.

That I had, in fact, already done the hardest bit.

So I moved. I stepped. I breathed.

And then I was on the ground.

I still climb. But I use ropes.

I still test myself. But I know what I'm testing.

And I still remember the click.

The rock didn't change.

I did.

And maybe that's what modification really means.

Not just changing the system.

Becoming the one who sees it differently.

My relationship with my father is still developing.

I suppose it's one more example of modifying the mechanism that's me –

by reaching backwards,

to live forwards,

and loop again.

THE MODIFIER IS ME

You've seen what it means to be the model.
You've seen what it takes to become the mechanism.
But sometimes, none of that is enough.

Sometimes you don't need to fill the gap.
You don't need to turn the hinge.
You need to change the conditions under which the system moves at all.

That's what the modifier does.

Not just the person who acts.
But the one who acts differently – because they've become different.

Let me show you one.

He was born Edward Koiki Sambo on Mer, in the Torres Strait Islands, in 1936.
He was adopted the traditional way. Raised in culture.
And raised in a country that refused to recognise that his culture counted.

He didn't start out to be a landmark. He started out blending –
not erasing his heritage, but integrating it with tools the system would respect.

He was taught by people who crossed cultural lines – his teacher Robert Miles,
who learned his language, lived in his home.
Eddie watched. He learned. He moved across worlds.

And then – he modified.

At first it was for his children.
He and his wife Bonita founded a school – so their kids could learn Western
subjects and Islander knowledge.
He taught unpaid.
Drove the bus.
Gardened at night to fund it.

He modified access.
Modified expectation.
Modified what counted as knowledge in a town that didn't want to count his.

Then came the mechanism moment.

He was sitting in a historian's office at James Cook University, describing the land he still believed was his.
The land of his ancestors. The land he planned to return to.

They told him it wasn't his.
That it was Crown land.

He didn't shout.
He didn't collapse.

He said: "No way. It's not theirs. It's ours."

It could've ended there.
But instead, he changed his MO.

He studied. He listened. He learned the system.
Then he rewired himself to engage it.

He didn't try to win the argument.
He restructured the terms on which the argument was being held.

And the system moved.

Ten years later, five months after he died of cancer,
the High Court of Australia ruled that *terra nullius* was false.
That Indigenous ownership had existed.
That land rights were real.

Australia rewrote itself – because Mabo had already rewritten what was required to be heard.

He didn't break the law.
He modified its preconditions.

This is what the modifier does.

Not the one with the loudest vision.

The one who changes what the system can register.

We use the metaphor of the brain and the blender in Rule 6.
Because modification requires both.

The brain: structured, signal-sensitive, always mapping.
The blender: fluid, capable of combining what couldn't mix before.
But there's a risk. If you try to modify without structure, you get noise.
If you blend without intention, you lose the signal.

Mabo did both.

He didn't blend in.
He blended what needed to come together.
And he held the signal strong.

That's what modification takes.

You don't just make a move.
You make yourself into someone who can make that move matter.

You train for fluency.
You train for resilience.
You say: "This isn't working as it is – and I'm going to become the person who
can shift it."

That shift starts inside.
Your habits. Your framing. Your way of reading tension.

You build a new MO – because the old one can't carry what's needed now.

And you use that MO to change the thresholds, the conditions, the recognisable
shapes of value in the world around you.

If you've ever thought,
Why doesn't someone do something about this?
The answer might be: because they haven't become the modifier yet.

And maybe that's what's happening now.

FROM TRAPPED TO TRANSCENDED
How superadapters modify self, situation, and system

	WHEN YOU'RE TRAPPED...	WHEN YOU TRANSCEND...
Shift the Frame	You obey the first version of reality. You fight what the system shows you. You hold the wrong map and move the wrong way.	You change the meaning before you change direction. You shift how the system sees you – and how you see it.
Invert the Flow	You resist. You push against the energy. You become defined by opposition.	You reroute the flow. You bend the current until it moves through you differently. You let it carry you – on your terms.
Turn the Table	You follow the rules that erase you. You play a game you weren't meant to win. You are remembered only when convenient.	You use the system's logic to expose its blind spot. You rewrite the outcome by reusing the mechanism. You don't ask for memory – you install it.

You've just stepped through three examples – each one a different kind of transformation. Not escape. Not force. But modification.

You saw what happens when the system won't change, but you can. Not by shouting. Not by pleading. But by shrinking, sleeping, breathing through the impossible. You didn't break the cave. You changed what it meant to be rescued.

You saw what happens when you stop pushing against the current – and start running with it, redirecting it, until it loops back in your favour. You didn't deny the system. You performed inside it – until the system started to echo you.

You saw what it means to take a story written to keep you out – and turn it inside out. To use the system's own rules to name what it tried to erase. You didn't burn the script. You flipped the caption.

These aren't just stories. They're adaptations. And they aren't just adaptations. They're invitations.

You are a mirror within a mirror – but not a one-way, passive reflection. You can look up and in, and down and around. You can reshape your sense of self and system. That's what the mind does when it's metaplastic. That's what your loop is already learning to do.

These Moves weren't just about them. They were about you.

Now take a breath. Because what comes next isn't linear. Loops break. Meaning frays. Adaptation gets harder.

And that's when you'll need to reboot.

THE WRONG LOOPS
Three ways modifying goes wrong

Not all action improves a system. Some changes entrench the very thing they were meant to solve. Others arrive too late to matter – or too forcefully to survive. These are the failure loops of modification: the moments where transformation misfires.

In Rule 6, we're looking at what happens when systems don't just resist change, but respond to the wrong kind of change – too slow, too shallow, too aggressive, or too misaligned.

Each misfire is a signal. A trap. A lesson in what not to modify, when, and why.

These are the wrong loops. You'll recognise them. You've lived inside some of them. The key is to learn how to see them – before they set.

HYPO is when the modification comes too late, or is too small to change the system meaningfully.

The intent may be right. The model might even be valid. But the action arrives after the structure has already begun to fail – or is too shallow to shift its function.

This is the loop where the patch is applied after the damage is done. Where a weak adjustment is made in place of real repair. Where the urgency to modify is felt, but not acted on – until the moment has passed.

It's like sending relief funding after the emergency is over. Or applying a plaster to a system that needs surgery. Or launching a reform that solves yesterday's problem, while tomorrow's crisis is already forming.

These modifications aren't always wrong. They're just insufficient. Too cautious. Too slow. Too late to matter. The loop is altered – but not transformed.

HYPER is when the modification is applied too quickly, too forcefully, or with too little understanding – and the system fractures.

The impulse to act overrides the need to observe. The urge to fix skips the stage of modelling. The change looks decisive, even visionary – but it doesn't hold.

This is the loop where shallow assumptions rush ahead of real comprehension. Where structural pressure is introduced faster than the system can absorb it. Where modification becomes momentum, not transformation.

It's like redesigning a school curriculum for a rural community using assumptions built at Harvard. Or cutting down thousands of city trees to reduce sweeping costs – without thinking through the ecological collapse. Or issuing a bold top-down policy that solves the headline, but destabilises everything underneath.

These modifications aren't cautious. They're confident. But they sacrifice coherence for speed – and produce long-run fragility. The loop doesn't evolve. It splinters.

ANTI is when the modification reinforces the wrong pattern – or actively worsens the system it was meant to improve.

It may be designed with care. It may even win awards. But the result is regression, not progress. What looked like an elegant solution becomes an embedded error.

This is the loop where the wrong thing is modified for the wrong reasons. Where appearance substitutes for adaptation. Where change becomes a cover for failure – or a delivery mechanism for damage.

It's like filling a historic bridge with concrete to keep it 'safe', destroying its function, its ecology, and its beauty in the process. Or implementing a costly new system that adds friction, hides accountability, and makes future change harder. Or issuing a bold reform that merely codifies old injustice – with better branding.

These modifications are confident, but misdirected. They make the system worse – and harder to fix next time. The loop isn't just broken. It's entrenched.

These are not just mistakes in execution. They're mistakes in structure.

Every one of these wrong loops is the product of a deeper misread: a misunderstanding of what needs to be changed, how it needs to be changed, or what that change will do over time.

Hypo modifies too little, too late.

Hyper modifies too much, too soon.

Anti modifies in the wrong direction – and makes itself harder to undo. Recognising these patterns isn't about blame. It's about fluency. Because what comes next isn't just avoidance. It's recovery.

You'll now see what happens when we get it right – not just fixing the failure, but rewiring the system to prevent the next one.

REAL WORLD WRONG LOOPS
How to learn the right things from wrong loops

Every time a system breaks, it's a chance to see how adaptation works – or how it fails. The examples we're about to explore aren't just relics of the past. They're real-world wrong loops – missteps in modification that echo across time and space. And they're invitations for you to see where these patterns might live in your own work, your own systems, your own choices.

HYPO First, let's look at urban sprawl – an idea that stretched cities into a sea of highways and parking lots. In the mid-20th century, planners believed that more space, more roads, and more cars meant progress. They didn't see how this endless expansion would hollow out communities, trap people in long commutes, and lock entire cities into loops of congestion and carbon. That's the hypo-modify pattern: too little structural rethinking, too much passive drift.

Where else do we see this? In projects that grow without adapting. In teams that keep adding tools without changing how they think. In our own lives, when we assume that more is always better – even if it's the wrong kind of more.

HYPER Then there's the rush of monoculture cotton farming in West Africa – a hyper-modify loop. In the name of growth, governments and investors pushed farmers to plant only cotton, stripping out diversity. Profits rose fast, but so did vulnerability. When prices dropped or the soil weakened, the system snapped. This is what happens when you go too hard, too fast – modifying without nuance or feedback.

Where else does this show up? In business pivots that cut too deep. In leaders who slam a new process into place without testing the soil. In ourselves, when we overcommit to a single idea and forget that real resilience grows from variation, not monotony.

ANTI And finally, consider Japan's post-tsunami sea walls. After the devastating 2011 wave, they built towering concrete barriers – anti-modify structures meant to stop the sea's power. But these walls also cut off coastal communities from the water, their livelihoods, and their heritage. A beautiful fix that became a new prison.

Where else might we see this? In systems that try to control risk by walling off complexity. In relationships where we protect ourselves so completely that no real connection can reach us. In any moment when we confuse defence for adaptation – locking in yesterday's logic instead of building tomorrow's flexibility.

These aren't just cautionary tales. They're diagnostic keys. Because every wrong loop tells us something about the limits of what we thought we knew.

Ask yourself:

Where do I see a system stretching without rethinking?

Where have I pushed one idea too hard, missing the need for diversity?

Where have I built walls when I needed bridges?

These aren't rhetorical questions. They're invitations – to see, to sense, to adapt. Because now, as we turn to the counter loops, you'll see what it looks like when we get it right. Not just avoiding failure, but reworking the loops themselves – so they don't just hold. They lift.

COUNTER LOOPS
How superadapters recover when modification goes wrong

You don't just run the Modify Loop once. You run it again. And again. Because even when you know what needs to change – and how to change it – modification can still go wrong.

You might try too much, too fast. That's hyper.

You might move too slowly, or never act at all. That's hypo.

Or you might do something – but the wrong something. That's anti.

All three can leave you spinning inside the loop instead of breaking free from it.

Superadapters don't avoid failure. They learn how to repair. And they do it using the same three habits that define the Modify Loop in the first place.

Each one – Flip the Script, Invert the Flow, Turn the Table – is more than a move. It's a counter.

FLIP THE SCRIPT is the antidote to hypo-modification. When nothing changes, it's often because nothing's been questioned.

You've fallen into a stale loop. You're still running the story that used to make sense. Or maybe someone else wrote the script for you, and you haven't realised you're reciting it.

Flipping the script doesn't mean blowing it up. It means opening it up. Asking: what am I assuming here? What am I protecting? Who told me this was the only way?

Sometimes the loop feels dead because the story is. If you've been stuck in "this is just how it is," try asking: what if this isn't how it has to be?

Tyler Perry did this when he refused to keep waiting for permission. No script. No backers. Just a borrowed theatre, a homemade play, and a new loop, written on his own terms.

The loop couldn't move forward until the script flipped.

INVERT THE FLOW is the remedy for hyper-modification. When change goes wrong fast, it's usually because you've overwhelmed the system.

You've added too many tweaks. You've pulled every lever. You've flooded the feedback loop. And now nothing sticks – or worse, the system breaks.

Inversion is not about slowing down. It's about rebalancing.

Instead of pouring in more, ask: Where is the energy going? What's leaking? What's reinforcing the wrong thing?

Invert the flow. Redirect attention, effort, reward. Take energy out of the outcome, and push it back into process. Move the hinge point upstream.

Milla Jovovich did this when she stopped playing characters written for someone else. She didn't abandon the industry. She rerouted her voice within it – by choosing how her flow of visibility and credibility was directed.

Real modification isn't maximal. It's intelligent.

TURN THE TABLE is the reversal for anti-modification.

The most dangerous mistake isn't doing nothing. It's doing something – confidently – and getting it wrong.

You might swap out the part that wasn't the problem. Or trust a modification that wasn't built to last. Or worse: be told by others that there's no mechanism worth modifying at all.

Turning the table is how you refuse that trap.

It's not just about changing what you see. It's about changing what the system lets you do.

Who holds the default? Who benefits from the current design? What would it mean to reverse the assumptions that keep this system running?

Rigoberta Menchú didn't just tell a new story. She didn't just enter the room. She redesigned the terms of the conversation. Her escape wasn't personal. It was architectural.

Turning the table means redesigning the logic underneath the loop.

COUNTER LOOPS ARE NOT JUST FIXES. THEY'RE FUNCTIONAL
RESETS.
When modification goes wrong, most people either shut down – or double
down. But superadapters run the loop again. They flip, invert, and turn – until
the loop that trapped them is the loop that frees them.

These aren't instincts. They're skills.

And the most powerful thing about a loop that went wrong?

It's still a loop. That means it can be rerun.

The same mechanism that broke your rhythm can be modified again to restore
it. That's what Counter Loops are for.

REBOOTING THEIR LOOPS

We've spent this chapter zooming in – on mechanisms, on moments, on the
smallest piece that still makes a difference. But now we pull back.

Because no matter how well you understand a loop, sometimes it stalls.
Sometimes what worked stops working. Or what you built begins to work
against you.

This next phase isn't about building better. It's about re-entering when
everything feels broken.

It's not failure. It's reboot.

There's a reason this section comes after Counter Loops. Those are the tools.
This is the terrain. The emotional, situational, cognitive shock of recognising: I'm
in crisis – and the loop I trusted no longer fits. And then doing the hard thing.
Choosing to run the loop again, on purpose.

What you're about to see are not biographies.

They're recursive returns.

Three figures. Three fractures. Three re-entries into the loop – not from the
start, but from right where they stood.

They didn't abandon the system. They re-entered it, altered.

Each one of them shows what a recursive loop really is:

Plastic. Personal. Purposeful. Still running.

RECOGNISE → UNDERSTAND → NECESSARY ACTION

TYLER PERRY: There was a moment, years after he built the studio. After he'd made his money, shaped his audience, created a self-sufficient world of scripts, sets, and shows. A moment when Tyler Perry found himself wondering what came next.

He'd done it. He'd looped the system – made his own. But suddenly, the loop wasn't feeding him. He posted online, quietly, without promotion:

"This is what a midlife crisis looks like."

It wasn't the tone people expected from the billionaire media mogul. But Perry wasn't looking to inspire. He was trying to understand.

His longtime relationship had ended. His Madea franchise had wrapped. He was staring at a vast, functional empire – and wondering whether it still had a function for him.

Most people, from that position, would double down. Build something new, expand the brand, push forward.

But Perry didn't.

He paused.
He wrote.
He listened to what wasn't working.
And he began experimenting again – this time not with cameras, but with questions.

Could AI write scripts the way he did? What would it mean to make stories with machines? Would that save time? Money? Would it help – or hurt – the very voice that built his loop in the first place?

And more than that: What did he want?

"I'm going to walk with God, be the best father and man I can be, hold my head up high, and try to look my best doing it."

This wasn't a collapse. It was a conscious return. He recognised that he was in a recursive phase – not stuck, but unsatisfied. He understood that his loop had grown strong enough to keep running without him. And he took action not to control it, but to rebalance himself inside it.

Not every reboot is loud.
Sometimes, it's a quiet re-entry.
You notice the loop has shifted.
So you shift with it.

413

MILLA JOVOVICH: She once described her fame as if it had a gravity of its own. A pattern that pulled her back to the same shape, no matter how far she thought she'd gone.

After *Resident Evil*, she became emblem and icon: the female action star. Tall, agile, wordless, killing in slow motion. Every week, as she told the Guardian, she was sent yet another script that opened with "a woman wakes up in a lab…"

And for a while, she played the part. Over and over.

It paid well. It looked successful. But the loop wasn't really hers.

Then her body began to push back.

Hair loss. Fatigue. A subtle, creeping unravelling.

"I had to be very delicate," she said. "Because I realised, I was pushing too far."

She recognised the signal. Not dramatic – but recursive. Her work was eating her feedback system. Her sense of play, of timing, of joy. The loop was still turning – but now it had teeth.

Jovovich didn't rage against it. She slipped sideways.

She took roles that were weirder, looser, more obscure. She built a fashion brand. She recorded albums. She travelled – specifically, to Mongolia.

"To learn to be a human being again."

That's how she put it. Not to escape, not to win,

but to re-member herself. Piece by piece.

One of her albums was called *Plastic Has Memory*.

You don't get a better metaphor than that.

She wasn't rebooting in the Hollywood sense – there was no career pivot, no publicity arc.

She was doing something quieter, and more difficult.

Letting the loop she had loved go soft.

Then choosing, by feel, which parts to reinforce.

What the world saw as reinvention was something else entirely:

She wasn't switching loops. She was staying recursive.

She kept checking. Kept tuning. Kept living inside a pattern that remained hers.

Some artists wait for the industry to change.

Milla changed her inputs. Changed the rhythm. Kept the loop.

And maybe the clearest sign?

She stayed in love, too. The marriage lasted.

Even as the roles changed, even as the story shifted.

One small, recursive pattern holding. A loop she could return to.

RIGOBERTA MENCHÚ: They didn't just question her. They tried to unwrite her.

After she won the Nobel Peace Prize, Rigoberta Menchú's autobiography became a target. Scholars and journalists picked at it, accusing her of exaggeration, distortion – even fabrication. They questioned whether her story truly reflected her life. Whether her voice could be trusted.

To many in the Western media, this was literary controversy.

To her community, it was erasure.

"We are not myths of the past," she said. "We are people."

She'd told her story to protect them.

She'd offered it as collective witness, not personal myth.

But the system wanted the facts to be linear, the narrative to be hers alone, the trauma footnoted for verification.

And so the loop – her loop, their loop – broke.

Or it nearly did.

Because Menchú had a choice.

She could defend her truth as a solitary figure.

Or she could reboot the loop outwards.

She did the latter.

She recognised that the trap wasn't just a public backlash.

It was the frame itself: the expectation that only individualised, footnoted, single-author trauma was valid. She understood that memory, in her culture, moved differently. It braided. It echoed. It came from the people.

So she reframed.

She returned not with an apology or an explanation – but with action.

She founded an organisation. She lifted others' voices.

She stood again for election, again and again, not to win, but to speak.

And all the while, she stayed out in the field. Visiting communities. Working with families. Advocating for land, language, and dignity.

That's what a reboot can look like, too.

Not revision.

Re-commitment.

A choice to continue – not because you're safe, but because the loop matters more than the interruption.

Menchú's crisis didn't destroy her credibility.

It clarified her purpose.

She never denied that some parts of the book were shaped by others.

She simply refused to treat that as a flaw.

In her world, truth was collective. That's what made it worth telling.

And in the end, that's what held.
Not the controversy. Not the corrections.
The loop. The purpose. The people.

"I am not only my voice," she said. "I am the echo of many voices."

RECOGNISE → UNDERSTAND → NECESSARY ACTION

You've seen it now – not just how the loop runs, but how it returns.
Each of them faced a fracture. Each re-entered the loop, altered.
Now it's your turn.

Let's look at how to reboot your loop – not just in theory, but in practice.
Not just when you're lost, but when the world is.

REBOOT YOUR RUN LOOP
Grant yourself three wishes

The best thing about having a best friend – or the even better thing about having
better friends, if such a thing is possible – is that your best friend is looking out
for you. Your best friend will take your call. Your best friend is noticing what's
happening with you. Your best friend almost seems to know you better than
you know yourself. Your best friend doesn't say, what can I do to help? Your best
friend is already helping.

And whether that best friend is the family you were born into or the family
you've chosen, the beautiful, powerful thing we've explored together is that your
self can become that friend too.

In the 1992 Disney animated film *Aladdin*, when Aladdin rubs the lamp,
the Genie bursts out singing, "You ain't never had a friend like me." He offers
Aladdin three wishes – not just as a reward, but as a promise of presence,
capability, and transformation.

What if your brain worked like that? What if, instead of waiting for the lamp
to be found, you could train your inner voice, your habits, your patterns of
thought and action, to act like your best friend – not occasionally, but reliably?

That's what the RUN loop is for. It's your mental Genie. And it starts when you train yourself to help you RECOGNISE what's happening, UNDERSTAND enough about you to learn more about what you need to know and then help you to take the next steps of NECESSARY ACTION to improve your situation.

This isn't wishful thinking. Neuroscience shows that self-talk – especially when used to label emotion or guide attention – directly shapes your brain's regulatory systems. It calms the amygdala. It recruits the prefrontal cortex. Over time, it strengthens your meta-awareness: the ability to notice, name, and shift your own patterns. It's not magic. It's metaplasticity. Your brain shaping itself based on how you talk to it.

Think of self-talk as the voice of your own best friend – the one who knows what to say when you're teetering on the edge of giving up. It's not just motivational fluff; it's a neurobiological tool. A click that snaps you back to clarity. A quiet word that keeps you in the game.

And as you practice this – loop by loop – you build a self who's worth listening to. A self who's with you when no one else is. A self who knows how to get through this, and who can remind you: you've done it before.
You'll do it again.

And that's what we'll do next.
Not start over, but start deeper.
To find the flaw. Craft the key.

TRANSCEND THE LOOP

"A page with a loop on it. That's how I think of time."
– Anne Carson, NOX

In this chapter, Rewire the Loop, you've seen how superadapters don't just build new routines. They shift what makes those routines work. They spot the mechanisms – emotional, structural, relational – that are holding them in place, and they reshape them.

This is what real modification means. Not trial and error. Not blind hacking. But elegant changes to the parts that move the whole.

You've seen how mechanisms trap – and how they can be turned. You've seen how good loops can evolve. And how bad loops can be restructured. And you've learned how three forces – flip, invert, turn – create the structure of every meaningful rewiring.

417

We called this the maths of modification.

We called it the ratchet.

Because that's what it is: a way to take what works, and make it work forward.

You've already seen what happens when people identify the trap, escape minimalism, or build reinforcing loops. Some go further. They build systems that evolve, that recur – because they're designed to.

LOOPS OF HAIR AND HEALING

In 2012, Marie-Alix de Putter was living in Douala, Cameroon, when her husband was murdered during an armed robbery. She was newly pregnant. The devastation that followed was profound – and nearly complete. She moved through her life almost without direction, doing things mechanically. Just the next thing, and then the next. "The structure and process of my previous life were holding me up," she would later say.

And then, in what we'd now call a third space, something shifted. Not in a hospital. Not in therapy. In a salon.

It was her regular hairdresser – a place she went not just for her hair, but for the conversation, the rhythm, the company. It was there, while her head was held in someone else's hands, that something in her also began to loosen. Her hairdresser, quietly, steadily, gave her space to speak. And while the conversation was informal, the effect was formal: she began to recover.

And then she had a thought. If this saved me, it could save others. Why hadn't she seen this before? Couldn't this be a mechanism? Couldn't it be scaled?

In 2019, she founded the Bluemind Foundation, a mental health initiative across Francophone Africa. Little steps at first. A simple training model – three days, delivered locally – designed to equip hairdressers with active listening tools and a cultural script for recognising distress. Not to become therapists. But to become better listeners, safer spaces, better supported themselves.

They already did this emotional work. But they were doing it for free, and often without a name.

The Bluemind model has now been adopted across Côte d'Ivoire, Togo, and Cameroon. Hundreds of hairdressers have been trained. Some have referred clients to local clinics. Others have left abusive relationships themselves. The loop doesn't just hold them – it evolves them. Each cycle becomes stronger, more sustainable, more replicable.

We all get help. We all notice things. We can all take a little part of what doesn't work and make it better – or a little part of what does work and spread the word. Passing it on. Looping it forward.

LOOP FORWARD, LOOP UP

She wasn't the only one. Or the first. She wasn't the first to notice the quiet, vital emotional work that hairdressers do. She wasn't the only one to start building from that insight.

And that's what makes this valuable to you – not just her example, but her method. Human minds can notice something better. They can find the mechanism inside it. They can build from it. Improve it. Multiply its impact.

And so can you.

You notice it out there, in the wild – something that works. Something that matters. And then you bring it home. You build a better mechanism around it. You turn it from a moment into a loop, and from a loop into a ratchet. You make it recursive. That's the maths of modification. That's how you get more from what already works.

But all this precision – the models, the mechanisms, the modification – has never been about reducing human experience. It's been about relating to it more clearly. More skilfully. More hopefully.

Because the self, like any system, is larger than the sum of its mechanisms.

It is important to note in all this that focusing on the mechanism is not to ignore that there is a model – of which the mechanism is merely a part. Or to ignore the truth that the brain is part of something larger: a person. And that that is, in the language we used earlier, a gestalt – an overall pattern, an emergent gestalt that can't ever be entirely controlled, or deliberately shaped, or fully mapped out.

That will never be possible. And yet – within that – we can grasp it better. We can live more productively, or more harmoniously, or more pleasingly, for any particular individual. Things can't be made perfect. Or fully understood. Or perfectly actioned. But they can be made better. We can transcend a previous limit. We can raise a new level that we find more satisfying.

And that is the real invitation: not just to understand, but to act. Because what happens next – what you do with the loop you've just rewired – will determine what you build from it.

Not every action needs to be big. But every adaptive action needs to be real. That's where we go next.

"Beyond the edge of the world there's a space where emptiness and substance neatly overlap, where past and future form a continuous, endless loop."
– Haruki Murakami, *Kafka on the Shore*

You've sat with the loop. You've seen its shape, its traps, its functions. You've mapped the system, modified the mechanism, and – just as importantly – you've rebooted.

But this next step isn't about what you've fixed. It's about what you've become.

The loop didn't just respond to your intervention. It reshaped your perception. It trained your attention. It taught you how to look again – deeper, slower, more precisely.

And in that process, something else happened: You changed.

This phase – Transcend the Loop – is not a postscript. It's a re-entry.

Because modification was never the end of the story. It was a structural act that gave you altitude. It opened up new layers of fluency, new ways to see and move, new possibilities for how you relate to systems, and to yourself.

Now it's time to ask a deeper question: What happens when the person who modifies the loop becomes the loop's most adaptive element?

What happens when the system that needs changing... is you?

This isn't about abandoning what you've learned. It's about carrying it with you – into identity, into action, into the kind of recursive upgrade that doesn't just improve your circumstances, but your capacity to evolve within them.

You're no longer just using the loop. You're running it with intent.

This is where transformation becomes ownership. Where adaptation becomes identity.

The loop is still running. But now, so are you.

"All boundaries are conventions, waiting to be transcended. One may transcend any convention if only one can first conceive of doing so."
– David Mitchell, *Cloud Atlas*

You've been here long enough to know: this isn't a clean break.

It's a transformation that loops forward.

You've crossed one threshold. Another is coming.

But everything you've seen in this chapter is still with you – looping, shaping, reframing how you now move.

necessary
action

RULE 7:
SLOW, SLOW, QUICK, QUICK, SLOW

This is the one about getting your timing right.

Some moves only work if they land at the right moment.
Too early, and they fizzle. Too late, and they miss.
Rhythm is more than style. It's structure. It's what determines whether your
energy flows or fractures – whether your action hits clean, or clangs out of sync.
And while most people think of rhythm as something musical or artistic, the
truth is: everything adaptive runs on timing.
How you speak. When you strike. How long you wait. How well you hold.

This is Rule 7 – the one where action isn't enough. It has to be timed.

Because in the real world, your moves are judged not just by what you do, but by when you do it. That's what separates a comeback from a collapse. That's what turns streaks into systems. That's what makes the same move smart in one moment and reckless in another.

This Rule teaches the meta-habit of acting in time. Not rushing. Not hesitating. Timing your loop.

You'll see it unfold in three patterns:
    Those who learn to wait just long enough.
    Those who strike when the system's open.
    Those who hold their elevation instead of burning it.

You'll meet superadapters who don't just perform.
    They perform with timing intelligence.
    And when their rhythms collapse?
    They reboot. Recalibrate. Return – deliberately.

Rhythm isn't a background detail.
    It's the system.
    And the ones who ride it best?
    They don't follow the beat.
    They become it.

THE CODE OF FREEDOM

In 2010, deep in the Colombian jungle, dozens of hostages were being held by FARC guerrillas. Many had been in captivity for years. The jungle was remote, dense, and closely guarded. But radios were allowed – a rare mercy. And into that small space of sound, something unexpected arrived.

A pop ballad called *Better Days* began playing on the airwaves. To most listeners, it was just a sentimental love song. But hidden inside the music, embedded between its choruses, was a Morse code message. Created by a collaboration between the Colombian military and advertising strategist Juan Carlos Ortiz, it was crafted with the utmost care: not too fast to sound like noise, not too slow to be detected. The message read:

"19 people rescued. You're next. Don't lose hope."

It wasn't just morale-boosting. It was rhythm training.

What the message actually did was shift the mindset of the hostages. It primed them to:
    Stay alert – ready for movement.
    Prepare emotionally and physically to act in sync with rescuers.
    Understand that rescue was possible – near even – and not to panic, lose awareness, or give up.

In past operations, hostages had panicked. Some had been killed in the chaos. This message was not just encouragement – it was pre-looping. A pattern of readiness encoded in rhythm.

→ Slow, slow – wait, prepare, steady yourself.
→ Quick, quick – when the moment comes, act with clarity.
→ Slow – stabilise, recover, return to safety.

Even in the most desperate circumstances, rhythm and timing are everything.

The song meant different things to different people. To some, it was a melody. To others, it was Morse. And the difference between those two understandings was the difference between delay and readiness.

In Morse code, the silence between the beats carries as much meaning as the signal.

So does life.

And that's why this story belongs here.

Because what mattered most wasn't the volume. It was the timing.

And the most powerful kind of movement always starts with a pause.

MISTIMED MOVES AND THE RHYTHM THAT HOLDS

You've seen it.

The mistimed launch. The applause that landed too early – or too late. The idea that sounded right but arrived off-beat. The punchline no one was ready for.

They're not failures of effort. They're failures of rhythm.

The signal was right. The intention good. But the moment didn't land.

Not because it was wrong – but because it was rushed. Or delayed. Or mistimed.

We think we're being bold. Sharp. Strategic.

But we've skipped the beat.

In Morse code, the gaps matter as much as the signal. In life, it's the same.

What saves a moment isn't force – it's feel.

And that's why rhythm matters. Not just to dancers, or jazz musicians, or athletes. But to anyone who has to act inside time.

The five-beat pattern – SLOW, SLOW, QUICK, QUICK, SLOW – isn't metaphorical.

It's structural. It's how superadapters time their moves.

One who mastered the wait.

One who surfed the streak.

One who broke the beat – and found the groove inside it.

This is how superadapters take action.

THE ACTION LOOP

HOW SUPERADAPTERS TAKE ACTION

Superadapters don't just act.

They time it. They tune it.

They move with enough rhythm to land hard when it matters – and enough pause to store what works.

Action is a loop.

And loops have a beat.

The best ones don't charge forward. They don't wait forever. They don't react just because a window opens or a deadline looms.

They prepare. They build. They strike. They adjust. And then they store what worked – so they can move again, later, stronger.

It's not instinct. It's not even discipline. It's rhythm. A repeatable, learnable rhythm of adaptive timing:

Slow. Slow. Quick. Quick. Slow.

And behind that rhythm is a function:

The first slow is for preparation: gathering signal, grounding the system, gaining strength.

The second slow is for ramping-up: positioning, pressure, potential.

The first quick is for action: the leap, the strike, the move.

The second quick is for adjustment: the pivot in flight, the mid-course correction.

The final slow is for storage: to embed the gain, and stage the next cycle.

This is how superadapters take action.

Not just in a rush. Not in a loopless sprint. But in rhythm with what's real.

In the pages ahead, you'll see it played out three times:

One who mastered the wait.

One who surfed the streak.

One who broke the beat – and found the groove inside it.

Each of them moved to this pattern – whether they knew it or not.
Now you'll know it.

THE RHYTHM OF ADAPTIVE ACTION

Rhythm is about choice.
Humans are polyrhythmic. We carry many rhythms inside us – physical, emotional, mental.
Your heart is pounding. Your nervous system is firing.
You're hungry. You're angry. You're under pressure. You want more.
These are all signals – internal pulses shaped by what surrounds you.
We don't just move as fast as we can, or as slow as we can.
The most adaptive among us – superadapters – read their environment.
They understand the demands of the situation and system.
But equally, they read themselves. They tune their action to the rhythm that works.
At one moment, rushing in might be genius.
At another, the same impulse would be ruin.
This is what the action loop is for.
A curated way of choosing when to act, and how.

PRESSING PLAY, PAUSE, AND FAST FORWARD

If I may speak to you directly for a moment –
perhaps you've been reflecting on how to take action.
And how you must now take action to improve the way you use rhythm to act.
It's circular. Or even better, recursive.
Each time you follow the thought, it leaves you a little further ahead.

There's no single speed that works for everyone. No universal tempo.

But there is a rhythm to adaptive action – and once you start to feel it, you begin to move with less resistance. You pace yourself differently. You recover faster. You enter moments of intensity more deliberately – and exit them with more to show for it.

This isn't just about acting.

It's about choosing when to act, and how long to hold each beat.

Sometimes, rhythm eludes you. Your timing's off, or the cues don't seem clear. You hesitate when you meant to act – or charge forward when you should have waited. That's not failure. That's feedback. And feedback, in the hands of a superadapter, is the beginning of rhythm reclaimed.

This is your reminder: you don't have to be in sync with anyone else's tempo. You're not behind. You're not early. You're exactly where you are – and from here, you can reset. Feel the beat again. Notice what phase you're in: preparing? Ramping? Mid-streak? Recharging?

The best rhythms aren't borrowed. They're built.

So if you've been drifting, press pause. If you're ready to move, press play. If you've gathered momentum – don't waste it. Press fast forward. And if all else fails, step away just long enough to hear the beat again.

This isn't the end of the loop. This is how you live it.

HABIT 1: MASTER THE WAIT

Delay action while positioning for leverage.
Before transformation speeds up –
it slows down.

The first move isn't action. It's restraint.
The pause before the turn.
The breath before the punchline.
The stillness before the strike.

Superadaptive minds learn how to wait.
But they don't wait passively.
They use the delay. They shape it.

They anchor their rhythm, so when the system opens –
they're already moving.

Let's look at what it means to Master the Wait –
to choose not just what to do,
but when not to do it yet.

SIMONE BILES

She landed.
Then paused.
Then stepped off the mat.

It was the 2021 Olympics. Delayed. Nearly empty.
But the pressure had doubled. The GOAT had arrived. And now she was walking away.

The crowd didn't know what they were seeing.

Her teammates didn't know what to say.
The broadcast stalled. Cameras searched for cues.
But Simone Biles didn't flinch.
She raised her hand. Walked off. Head up. Breath even. Mind unspooling behind her eyes.

She wasn't hurt.
She wasn't crying.
She wasn't quitting.

She was recalibrating.

Later she would explain it:
"My mind and body are not in sync."

It was the twisties. The gymnast's nightmare.
A mid-air loss of spatial awareness – your brain says turn, your body says nothing.
In the wrong moment, it's paralysis. Or paralysis with impact.

And that's what she did.
She recognised it. Mid-routine. Mid-air.
The synaptic dissonance. The loss of the thread.

And she made the move no one expected.
Not a Yurchenko. Not a triple-double.
Something harder.

She paused.
Withdrew.
Protected the loop.

"I have to do what's right for me and focus on my mental health and not jeopardise my health and my well-being."

But this wasn't the Biles I. Or II.
Not the Biles on beam. Or floor. Or vault.

This was the one no one named.

The most important move of all.

The Biles Wait.

Rewind: 2013. Age 16.
She debuts internationally at the American Cup. Stumbles off beam. Loses.
But something else happens that year.
She asks to work with a sports psychologist.

Before the medals.
Before the pressure.
Before she became Simone Biles™.

She didn't wait until the system broke her.
She recognised the early signal – and built a rhythm of mental maintenance.

You don't build The Biles Wait in Tokyo.
You build it in 2013, after a fall and a request.
You build it in silence. You build it in the slow.
Between 2013 and 2016, Simone Biles stopped losing.
She won four straight World Championships, then five more.
She entered the Rio Olympics as a force of nature, not just an athlete.
And she delivered: four gold medals, one bronze.

She didn't just perform routines.
She invented them.
Each one a declaration: I move on my own rhythm.

But rhythm isn't just about motion.
It's also about rest.

In 2017, at the peak of her powers, she did something rare.
She stepped away.

And when she returned in 2018 – she didn't just win.
She raised the bar.

The difficulty gap was so wide.
She wasn't just in a different league.

She was on a different tempo.

Dominance doesn't slow things down. It speeds them up.
Sponsors expect more. Judges expect perfection.
You begin to feel that stillness is betrayal.

And that's when the twist began.
Not the physical one.
The neurological one.
The one that says: You are no longer safe in your own spin.
Tokyo wasn't just another Games.
It was meant to be the crowning loop.
A final surge in the sequence. Quick. Quick. Gold.

But Simone Biles knew the rhythm was off.

She detected it, mid-air.
Recognised it – not after the injury, not after the score.
Inside the rotation.

Most people crash, then ask what went wrong.
She named the pattern she had already learned.
So she paused.

She didn't collapse.
She withdrew.

Not because she was weak – but because she was looping better than anyone in
the room.
She caught herself.

Self-regulation. System rejection. Loop repair.

This was the one she mastered:
The Biles Wait.
She didn't disappear.
She looped.
After Tokyo, she returned to the slow – by choice.
She returned to prep and ramp.

To steady training. Quiet rhythms. Internal recalibration.

This was the beginning of something new.
But it was also a return to the first part of the loop – the slow-slow – because she had been on a hot streak, and she knew what most don't:
You don't extend a streak by pushing harder.
You extend it by dropping back into rhythm – by rebuilding tempo, not forcing it.

In 2023, she re-emerged.
She submitted a new skill on bars – becoming the only woman in history with a named skill on every apparatus.

That wasn't just a comeback. That was a level-up.

She hadn't just recovered. She had stored the experience, staged the platform, and looped into a new version of mastery.

That's The Biles Wait.
Not just a pause. A system of return.
A rhythm of self-rescue.
A mastered tempo.

MASTER THE WAIT → RIDE THE RHYTHM → LEVEL UP

HABIT 2: RIDE THE RHYTHM

You've just seen what it looks like to step out of the loop – on purpose – and wait.

To reject momentum when the rhythm is wrong. To pause not because you're broken, but because your system is out of sync.
That was Master the Wait.

But what happens when the rhythm is right?
When the beat is already running?
That's a different kind of intelligence. A different kind of habit.
This is how the Action Loop works: beat by beat, habit by habit.
You don't learn it all at once.
But you're learning to feel the phases – slow, slow, quick, quick, slow.

Each habit teaches you how to move through the next.
You're not mastering the loop.
You're starting to move with it.

This is the second habit of the Action Loop.

RIDE THE RHYTHM: This habit is about navigating the quick-quick stage of the loop. It means recognising momentum and using it before it fades. Superadapters act while the system is open. They move fast, adapt fast, and loop while conditions are hot.

When you're in flow, it's not the time to slow down. Things are working. The system is humming. This habit helps you act inside that opening – make progress, adjust fast, and stay in the loop. There will be time to pause. This isn't it.

Beyoncé isn't just a performer. She's a quarterback.
She sees the field. Feels the timing. Moves when the gap opens.
She doesn't just ride hype. She rides rhythm.

And when she's hot – she stays hot. Because her streak isn't static. It loops.

Each move leads into the next.
Action. Adjustment. Hit. Reinforce. Reset. Again.
Her team matters – we don't go into it here, but no hot streak runs alone.
And she's been criticised for how she distributes the returns.

But what she does model is this: if you build the right adaptive cycle, and feed it well, your streak can hold longer than most people think possible.

This isn't randomness.
It's a strategy of serendipity.

As you read what comes next, watch for the quick-quick.
The motion that feeds itself.
The decision to keep moving – without losing control.

This is how superadapters move when the rhythm is right.

Not harder. Not faster. Just right.
She's not rushing.
She's rolling.

Now, let's ride.

BEYONCÉ KNOWLES

She opens *Renaissance* riding a chrome horse into the future. It's not subtle.
It's not meant to be. Beyoncé has always been precise with the timing of
her reemergences, and this one thundered in with intent: No apology. Just
momentum, harnessed. A kinetic return, dragged through time and soul and
sweat, each beat a proclamation. For over two decades she's done this – waited,
watched, sharpened – and then struck. But *Renaissance* isn't just another hit
parade. It's a pulse. A permission slip. A declaration of joy as a resistant rhythm.
And as the album unfolds, so too does the pattern beneath it: delay, load, break
through. She doesn't rush the beat. She rides it.

After *Lemonade*, she stepped back again. Not entirely, but enough. The kind
of absence that only someone in complete command can afford. The world kept
spinning – politics unravelled, the pandemic hit, reckonings flared – and Beyoncé
adjusted again. But this wasn't retreat. It was rhythm. She's done it before: : the
surprise drop of her self-titled album, the full-force spectacle of *Homecoming*.
Each time, the quick-quick emerging from the slow-slow. Silence followed by
shock, then power sustained. Each time, she stepped back not because she lacked
material, but because she knew better than to crowd the beat. What looked like
dormancy was calibration. A deliberate syncing of personal growth, cultural pulse,
and artistic shift. Superadaptability isn't always about sprinting ahead. Sometimes
it's about holding your nerve while the tempo builds.

When the beat finally drops, it lands with surgical force. *Renaissance* isn't
random – it's a perfectly sequenced homage to Black queer liberation, dancefloor
defiance, and embodied survival. Every transition clicks. Every sample nods. This
is not the chaos of reinvention; it's the discipline of return. Beyoncé maps her
sound across decades, then folds it into a single forward push. She knows what
to hold, when to pivot, and when to slam the gas. There's no wasted motion. No
apology for the delay. Just release. Superadapters don't throw everything at the
wall. They listen for the opening, match the energy, then strike in time. That's
not instinct. That's craft.

What makes Beyoncé's rhythm adaptive isn't just her timing – it's her
restraint. She holds the note longer than most would dare. She lets the silence
stretch until it hums. In the studio, she's obsessive. Hours to land a breath. Days

to test a vowel. Not because she's unsure, but because she's sculpting time. The same mind that choreographs three seconds of footwork across a stadium stage also knows when not to move. This is delay not as avoidance, but as preparation. Superadapters don't just react faster – they slow the moment down until they can feel the groove underneath. They ride the rhythm by shaping it.

Renaissance is many things – an album, a love letter, a lineage. But it's also a recalibration. After years of control, image, legacy-building, Beyoncé lets go – just enough. The vocals are looser, the persona more diffused. She's sampling not only sounds, but selves. This is not regression. It's resurgence. Joy becomes a strategic return, a beat that holds the weight of recovery. The album pulses with the survival of others – her Uncle Johnny, the ballroom scene, the bodies who danced through oppression. In doing so, she doesn't just find rhythm – she honours its source. Superadapters don't power through disruption; they remix it. They let the rhythm restore them.

Even when she's still, she's moving. Watch her perform: the micro-adjustments, the delayed glance, the fractional pause before a chorus hits. Beyoncé doesn't just follow tempo – she imposes one. The audience shifts with her, breath by breath, beat by beat. That's not charisma alone. It's control. Not domination, but mastery. Like a seasoned DJ adjusting pitch without touching the needle, she guides perception through timing. This is how superadapters move through volatility – they don't react to chaos, they tempo-shape it. They hold the beat long enough to bend reality around it. Rhythm isn't just a sound. It's a strategy.

This is the beat she lives by.

Beyoncé doesn't avoid the next play. She makes it part of the song. She waits once to observe, again to prepare. Then the double-strike: one for presence, one for power. And finally – hold. Sustain. Ride it out while the world catches up. Superadapters don't just keep time. They bend with it, break it open, and build something new inside the pause. Rhythm isn't just what you hear. It's how you lead. And the ones who ride it best? They don't rush the drop. They become it.

MASTER THE WAIT → **RIDE THE RHYTHM** → LEVEL UP

HABIT 3: LEVEL UP

Not every loop ends with applause.

Some end with quiet. With drift. With an opening that feels like loss – but isn't.
After the quick-quick, you don't crash.
You reconfigure.
We've seen how rhythm can ride high. But even hot streaks have edges.
And the most adaptive know that sustaining success is not about clinging to momentum.

It's about what you build into the tail end of it.

This next habit isn't about pause. It's about pattern.
How you end the last loop shapes how you begin the next.
We're now in the final beat of the Action Loop.

Back to slow – but not the same as before.
The first slow was preparation.
This one is positioning.

It's where you either consolidate and grow – or spin out and fade.

Streaks don't just end. They pivot.
And superadapters know how to stage that pivot well.

This is the third habit of the Action Loop: **LEVEL UP.**

This habit is about staging the next loop. It's what you keep in mind during the hot streak, storing resources and staging plans for when the beat slows again. Superadapters don't collapse after progress. They consolidate, recover, and prepare for the next move.

This slow is different. It's not about retreat.
It's about recursive ascent – learning how to lay track for the loop to come.

Robert Pattinson wasn't supposed to be here.

Not in *Tenet*. Not in *The Lighthouse*. Not in arthouse noir or Oscar-watching character studies.

You may remember him from *Harry Potter and the Goblet of Fire*.
Charisma on-screen. Died before the third act. One might've assumed that was his moment.
Then came *Twilight* – not your genre, maybe not his either.

A global phenomenon. Face powdered white. Vampire teeth. Teen franchise gravity.
The perfect setup for a slow decline.

But what followed wasn't collapse. It was curation.

Cronenberg. Limousines. Quiet, recursive films where 'nothing happens'.
Except rhythm. Except strategy.

You start to notice a pattern:
One loop funds the next.
One rhythm builds energy while the other refines it.

Independent credibility → blockbuster power → recursive prestige.

He doesn't switch careers.
He loops forward – storing enough from one phase to stage the next with intent.

Now he's working with directors who bend time, shift timelines, stage systems:
Nolan, Eggers, Denis.
The kinds of directors who need actors who understand structure.

Pattinson doesn't just evolve.
He prepares to evolve – mid-loop.

What you're about to read isn't about rebranding.
It's about recursion.
Watch what happens when someone uses the pause not to disappear, but to rehearse.
To re-gear. To build something he hadn't yet shown.

This isn't the story of a comeback.
It's the story of a Level Up.
He slowed.

But not to rest.
He slowed – to rise.

ROBERT PATTINSON

The body dies. The memory uploads. A new version wakes up. *Mickey 17* begins with a man built to repeat – and Robert Pattinson saw himself in it. "It's literally a character who keeps being regenerated," he said in interviews, grinning like someone who knows the loop from the inside. When Bong Joon-ho handed him the script, it wasn't just a sci-fi resurrection story – it was an invitation. To reframe the last twenty years. To stop ducking his own multiplicity. Pattinson had long been labelled an enigma – arthouse pretender, teen idol escapee, method actor gone rogue – but the truth was simpler. He'd been running iterations. Each character, each press cycle, each artistic pivot: another version that built from the last. Another Mickey. He wasn't evading his identity – he was storing it. Boxing it up. Learning to carry what each version had taught him, without letting any one of them take over the script. What looked like fragmentation was something else entirely: strategic recursion. And this time, he wasn't dying to escape it. He was ready to play the role that mirrored the machine he'd become.

It didn't start that way. For years, Pattinson tried to discard versions of himself like they were radioactive. *Twilight* had made him rich, famous, and trapped in a global loop he couldn't control. Every interview came with a smirk. Every role came with baggage. He'd walk into casting rooms and feel the weight of Edward Cullen enter first. So he did what many do when they fear their own past: he tried to detonate it. Sabotaged PR runs. Took roles that baffled his fanbase. Hid inside low-budget art films with grotesque, unknowable men. But denial is not deletion. The pattern persisted – until he realised that storage was not the problem. He didn't need to bury his past selves. He needed to stage them. Build a platform where contradiction wasn't a liability – it was leverage. Instead of rejecting *Twilight*, he let its shadow sharpen his choices. Instead of fleeing visibility, he learned how to weaponise it. He didn't level up by walking away. He levelled up by absorbing the glitch, reframing the glitch, becoming the glitch.

He turned his career into a controlled experiment. One strange, strategic role at a time. A street hustler in *Good Time*. A deranged lighthouse keeper in *The Lighthouse*. A slippery conman in *High Life*. These weren't random acts of reinvention. They were tests – deliberate staging grounds for persona, presence, and possibility. Each role stretched a different part of him, pulled against a different prior version. He wasn't trying to prove versatility. He was building internal bandwidth. Pattinson started choosing scripts the way a scientist selects variables: What happens if I strip all charisma? What if I speak barely a word? What if I lose beauty, logic, sympathy – and still compel? The lab got stranger, but his grip on the experiment tightened. These weren't self-contained performances. They were recursive inputs. What he learned from one, he rethreaded through the next. With each stage, the performance grew denser, weirder, more controlled. Not to escape type – but to rewrite it. He wasn't trapped in a loop. He was designing it.

Then came *The Batman* – a test of a different order. Big budget. Big risk. No room to hide in obscurity or irony. For Pattinson, it was the bottleneck: could all the stored chaos, the niche performances, the hard-won self-trust be mobilised at scale? He approached it like an outsider breaking into his own myth. No gravel voice. No swagger. Just trauma, detachment, surveillance – Batman as bruised voyeur. The gamble paid off. Critics called it the first time the cowl felt psychological. But more important was what it unlocked in him. "That was the first time I didn't feel like I had to be afraid of being seen," he admitted. Not just seen by audiences – but by the sum of his own selves. The commercial role didn't dilute his recursion. It amplified it. He'd brought his private experiments to the biggest stage and they had 'worked'. What could have been flattening became fractal. His earlier versions didn't collapse under the weight – they cohered. The lab rat had become the architect.

This is the pattern. Not reinvention for its own sake, but recursion with pressure. Pattinson didn't abandon old selves – he stored them. Each version archived with precision, each lesson metabolised rather than discarded. Then, carefully, he staged them. In performances that were scaffolds, not masks. Not escape acts, but integration acts. And in doing so, he created a structure he could rise through. Not by leaping over past limitations, but by absorbing and elevating them. Level Up isn't a clean break. It's a recursive climb. And the secret is this: the rise only holds if the platform is real. Every version contributes. Every stage refines the loop. Superadapters don't transcend by shedding identity – they build pressure until the loop yields a higher form. Pattinson isn't admired because he escaped *Twilight*. He's admired because he carried it, transformed it, and used it to rise.

Behind the scenes, the recursion runs deeper. Pattinson is notoriously private – not because he's aloof, but because he's still building. In interviews, he folds in on himself, dodges labels, mutates tone mid-sentence. Not deflection – compression. A way of regulating what version appears, when, and how. He's running adaptive code in real time: detecting audience cues, adjusting the loop, deciding who gets access. Fame fractured him early. Now he uses that fracture like a lens. One minute absurd, the next profound. One film a grotesque, the next a meditation. He's no longer performing against expectation – he's performing around it. That's the control superadapters learn to wield. They don't just change in response to pressure – they calibrate the release. They know that rising isn't about showing everything at once. It's about showing the right thing at the right stage, and storing the rest for the next version.

Robert Pattinson didn't escape the loop – he turned it into leverage. Every version, every risk, every pivot was part of a recursive system he learned to trust. Where others saw inconsistency, he saw scaffolding. Where others feared typecasting, he saw data. The loop didn't trap him. It taught him. That's the secret to levelling up: use the loop, don't deny it. Store what you learn. Stage what you need. Rise when the structure holds. Superadapters don't level up by leaping – they loop upward, one staged self at a time.

MASTER THE WAIT → **RIDE THE RHYTHM** → LEVEL UP

ONE. TWO. THREE. PUTTING IT ALL TOGETHER.
You've now seen the three-stage action loop come to life.
Not in abstract. Not as theory.
But as rhythm, embodied.

Simone Biles showed us how to slow down when the system is wrong.
Beyoncé showed us how to move fast when the rhythm is right.
Robert Pattinson showed us how to pause – not to end – but to rise.

These weren't merely stories of success.
They were stories of sequence. Stories that instruct.
And the beat they followed wasn't random.

SLOW-SLOW → QUICK-QUICK → SLOW

MASTER THE WAIT → RIDE THE RHYTHM → LEVEL UP

The next story doesn't show one habit.
It shows the loop itself.

You may not know his name.
But what he modelled was more than perseverance, more than patience.
He modelled recursion – the full arc of adaptive rhythm.
His name was Kim Dae-jung.

Kim Dae-jung was born in Hwado, a scattered island chain off the coast of South Korea.
A place of 56 islands, only nine inhabited. Remote. Rural. Marginal.

His name means 'lotus flying on water'.

He was the son of a farmer, one of seven children, raised during the Japanese occupation.

He worked as a shipping clerk, altered his birth records to avoid conscription, and spent his early years navigating a fractured, colonised world.

He entered politics just after liberation – but recognised the timing was wrong.
So he bought a ship. Launched a company. Ran a newspaper. Waited.
When war came, he was captured, sentenced to death, escaped.

Then he re-entered politics. Built influence. Ran for president.
And survived an assassination attempt.
He was later kidnapped. Then exiled. Then sentenced to death again.
But again, he waited. Adapted. Moved when the rhythm was right.

When he finally returned and won the presidency, decades later, he governed with restraint.

He reached across to North Korea with a policy of deliberate warmth – the Sunshine Policy.

And when his time in office ended, he exited quietly, with dignity.

What follows isn't a story of triumph.
It's a story of timing.
You've seen the loop in parts.
Now feel it as one.

KIM DAE-JUNG: THE RHYTHM OF RESISTANCE

He was barefoot when they dragged him to the van.

A blindfold. A chloroform-soaked rag. The slam of a door. The sudden roar of wheels against Tokyo asphalt.

They took his glasses. They took his shoes. They didn't speak.
In the dark, Kim Dae-jung counted his breaths. One – inhale. Two – exhale.

Not prayer. Not panic. Just presence.

For three days, the world assumed he had vanished. In a way, he had.

Bound and gagged aboard a Japanese fishing trawler, he listened to the creak of waves and the murmured Korean of his captors. They spoke in code, but he understood enough. They planned to throw him overboard. The order, it seemed, had come from Seoul.

He waited.
He waited as the execution hour approached. He waited as the hands on his neck tensed.
And then – chaos.

A commotion on deck. Voices raised. Footsteps pounding. A Japanese surveillance aircraft buzzing low overhead. Unbeknownst to his kidnappers, a journalist had been tipped off, triggering a diplomatic and military scramble. Japan's intervention had come just in time.

They didn't kill him. Not because they lost their nerve – but because someone else's timing interrupted the beat.

That was the first Wait.
Not passive. Not weak. But precise.

Kim had moved too soon before. Spoken too boldly. Paid the price.
Now, he would learn the tempo of survival.
Not just resistance. Rhythm.

A revolution doesn't always begin with a shout.
Sometimes it begins with a breath.

THE LONG DELAY
There are waits that last seconds. There are waits that stretch across years.

Some people fade during the long delay. Kim sharpened.
After the abduction, he returned to a Korea that still wanted him dead.
So he exiled himself.

He knew this was not defeat. It was repositioning.
He studied. He wrote. He recalibrated.
Politics, yes. But also philosophy, literature, economics.

He read Aquinas. Gandhi. Marx. Jesus. Jefferson. Mandela wasn't free yet.

He watched how power moved through history.
Not just who won – but when.
Not just what was done – but what was endured.

His enemies tried again.

They jailed him. Beat him. Crushed his spine. Left him unable to walk.
They rigged the election. Then rigged it again.
Still, he waited.

Not idly. Not bitterly. He 'looped'.
Each failure became a rehearsal.
Each loss, a deeper reconnaissance.

He trained himself to lose with grace, to return without hate, to pause when the
urge was to rage.
He became a master of adaptive restraint.
A superadapter in slow time.
Others screamed, struck, stormed.
Kim waited until the mood changed, the structure weakened, the moment
ripened.

In the silence, he became dangerous.

This was the second Wait.

Not imposed. Chosen.
No one knew it then, but he was building the 'Sunshine'.

THE SUNSHINE STRIKE
He won the presidency on his fourth try.

By then, they'd called him finished. Irrelevant. Too soft. Too old.
But he had learned the rhythm of the moment.
And when it finally came, he moved.

North Korea had missiles. America had threats. The peninsula was a powder keg.
Kim brought flowers.
They called it naïve. He called it the Sunshine Policy.

First, he struck with presence: a bold invitation to the North, against decades of
military standoff.

Then, he struck again with precision: food, medicine, cultural exchange,
economic assistance – each calibrated to open a new channel, not just appease an
old wound.

He flew to Pyongyang. He shook the hand of the man who had once tried to
have him killed.

The gesture was not weakness. It was weight.
Because he had waited.
He knew what this meant. Not just tactically. Symbolically.

For one brief window, the Korean peninsula thawed.
Separated families met again. Soldiers stepped back.
Even K-pop crossed the border.
And then – it closed.

The world shifted. New administrations rose. The rhythm changed again.
But for that stretch, for that heartbeat of history, Kim struck.
Once.
Then again.

Strike. Strike.
Not wildly. Not repeatedly.
Just enough. Just in time.

Hold the Note.

He didn't stay in power.
That was never the point.

After the Sunshine faded, Kim Dae-jung stepped down with grace. No autocrat's grasp. No bitter second act.

He held the note.

He taught, advised, and reminded. Quietly. Clearly. Persistently.
Because legacy is not what you build. It's what you don't undo when the music stops.

And his rhythm? It kept echoing.

South Korea's democracy – once fragile, now firm.
Its cultural exports – once silenced, now global.
Its national tempo – once militarised, now syncopated by choice, expression, reinvention.

Kim's loops became the nation's.
His restraint became strategy.
His pause became power.

Even K-pop, that sonic revolution, carries his beat.

Not directly. Not consciously. But in the timing.
Wait. Wait.
Drop. Reframe.
Hold.

History doesn't always reward patience.

But sometimes, it sings it back.

SLOW → SLOW → QUICK → QUICK → SLOW

Kim Dae-jung didn't follow the rhythm once.

He followed it again and again – across decades, dictatorships, and death sentences.

His loop wasn't personal development. It was political survival. And then: peaceful transformation.
What he showed wasn't perfection. It was timing, tuned to integrity.
This is what it means to master the wait, ride the rhythm, and level up – not once, but continuously.

You've now seen the three-stage action loop in full.
Not in abstraction. Not in theory.

But through movement. Through timing. Through choice.

Biles showed you what it means to master the wait – to return to yourself before acting.

Beyoncé showed you how to ride the rhythm when it's hot – when the system opens and progress loops on itself.

Pattinson showed you how to slow without stalling – to use the quiet to stage something new.

And Kim Dae-jung showed you all of it at once.

Each figure showed a different beat.
Together, they showed the rhythm.

SLOW-SLOW → QUICK-QUICK → SLOW

MASTER THE WAIT → RIDE THE RHYTHM → LEVEL UP

They're not gimmicks.
They are the structural phases of effective action.
The first slow – prepare. Ground yourself. Gain signal.

The second slow – stage. Set pressure. Build potential.
The first quick – act. Leap. Move while the system is open.
The second quick – adjust. Pivot. Modify mid-flight.
And the final slow – store. Embed the gain. Ready the next loop.

This isn't about speed.
It's about sequence. And precision. And intelligence, timed.

You might already be asking yourself – am I acting too quickly? Waiting too long?

You might feel a loop tightening around you, or loosening.

You might be wondering where you last stored a gain, or whether you did at all.
And if you're not sure what rhythm you're in, that's fine. Most people aren't.

But it's never too early – or too late – to ask.
The action loop is not a one-time trick. It's not a flow state.

It's a rhythm you can learn to hear – and choose to play.
In your projects.
In your recoveries.
In your high-stakes moments and long quiet stretches.

It's what Superadapters do differently.

Not more action. Not less action.
Just action, at the right time.

We're not done yet.

What comes next isn't repetition – it's resonance.
We'll sit down not to summarise, but to settle.
We'll take each of the five beats you've just seen and give them a deeper rhythm –
through story, structure, and memory.
Because this loop isn't just a lesson.
It's a pattern you can return to.

Let's return now.

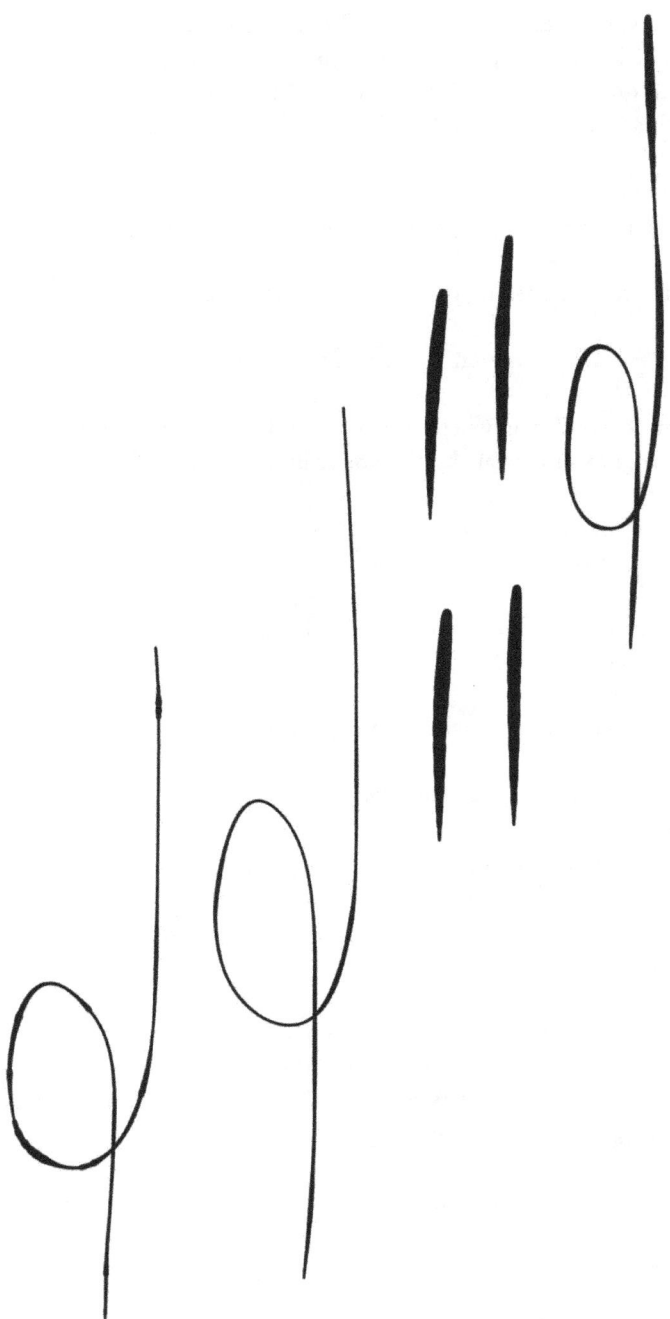

THE SITDOWN – THE BEAT (AND THE BREAK)

WHY WE SIT DOWN NOW.

"You are a rhythmic being. Inside each and every one of us exists a polyrhythmic symphony that lasts a lifetime."
– Evelyn Glennie

We don't sit down to stop. We sit down to reset the rhythm.
This is Rule 7 – the one about timing, tempo, and the five-beat loop that makes action land: slow, slow, quick, quick, slow.

In the next few pages, you'll meet a leader who paused the whole system until the signal returned. A neuroscientist who mapped rhythm into the firing of the brain. And a figure who kept the groove alive by knowing when to break it.

Each of them moved differently. But all of them moved to a beat. And this is the Sitdown where we learn to hear it again.

You cradle a warm mug in both hands, letting the office chatter fade into a comforting hum. After hours of focused work, this pause feels indulgent – but inside your skull, it's anything but idle. Freed from the task at hand, your brain is busily solidifying the morning's gains. Neuroscientists have found that during quiet breaks, the mind 'replays' newly learned skills at high speed, strengthening your memory of what you just practiced. Stepping away is not a luxury; it's part of how we learn.

The Swedes have elevated this wisdom into ritual. They call it fika – a coffee-and-pastry respite that's as integral to the workday as sending emails. Even Ikea's handbook notes that "more than a coffee break, fika is a time to share, connect and relax… [and] some of the best ideas and decisions happen at fika." In the break-room glow, a stray remark from a colleague or just a moment of mind-wandering can knit together ideas that were previously scattered. Your shoulders drop as you sip, and a new connection quietly forms in your mind.

By the time you drain your cup, you've done more than rest – you've given your brain space to refuel and rewire. That subtle feeling of renewal as you return to your desk isn't an illusion. It's your brain, slightly changed and refreshed, ready to integrate the next challenge. The humble coffee break, far from wasting time, is the secret workshop where your mind solidifies learning and sparks its next creative insight.

This is that moment.
Sit down.
Feel the rhythm come back.

LULA DA SILVA: DRUMBEAT, JAILBREAK

He walks out of prison not to silence – but to drums.

October 2019. Luiz Inácio Lula da Silva, former president of Brazil, steps into the open air after 580 days in a jail cell in Curitiba. He had entered in handcuffs. He leaves to maracatu beats and frevo chants, banners in the wind and feet stomping pavement in rhythm. The air doesn't just fill with sound – it resets. Brazil had held its breath. Now it was exhaling.

This isn't a comeback. It's a re-entry into the groove.

Lula was born in rhythm. His hometown, Garanhuns, lies in Brazil's northeast – a highland town steeped in the pulse of African, Portuguese, and Indigenous traditions. Every year it hosts a winter festival where maracatu dancers clash in colour and percussion, and forró floods the streets with stomps and sway. It's a place where even politics has a drumline. Lula carried that tempo with him – not as metaphor, but as motion. First as a machinist, then as a union leader, then as the man who would remake the country. He didn't just rise – he pulsed. You could feel it in his speeches, his rallies, his silences. He wasn't just political. He was percussive.

He lost three presidential elections. Then he waited. Then he won. In 2003, Lula became Brazil's first working-class president. The global commodities boom gave him something rare: space to sync. He used it. Millions were lifted from poverty. Schools expanded. Favelas felt power shift. By the time he left office in 2010, his approval ratings hovered around 80%. Barack Obama called him "the most popular politician on Earth." He didn't govern like a strongman. He governed like a conductor – feeling the crowd's tempo, dropping in when the moment demanded. His rhythm was precise.

But every groove repeated too long becomes vulnerable. By 2018, the pattern collapsed. A sprawling corruption probe – Operation Car Wash – swept through Brazil's elite. Lula was caught in the tide. Convicted. Jailed. His supporters called it a political ambush. His opponents claimed justice. In the background, Bolsonaro rose. Lula vanished from the public stage. The beat stopped. The stage emptied. The silence was deafening.

But not still.

In his cell, Lula read. Watched. Waited. He didn't flail or plead. He trained. He let the rhythm realign. The crowds outside kept up the chant – Lula Livre. But Lula didn't try to force the next downbeat. He listened for it. Timing wasn't gone – it was paused.

This wasn't a break in character. This was control.

In 2022, the sentence was overturned. Lula ran again. But not on old rhythm.

He recalibrated. Moderated. Named Indigenous leaders to his cabinet. Spoke of reconciliation, environmental recovery, economic stitching. When he won, the crowd didn't just cheer – they danced. Journalists called it Lollapalooza, a national remix of hope and protest. He had returned – but not the same. He had timed his return.

He didn't just win. He regained the time signature.

Lula never used the word rhythm. But he moved like a drummer. He felt the shifts, the pauses, the slips. He knew when the system was off, when the crowd was loose, when the silence needed to be held. From the percussion of Garanhuns to the pressure of prison to the beat drop of Brasília, he didn't force the loop – he followed it.

Not every groove is audible. Some are strategic. Some are survival. Some are the music of return.

GROOVE IN THE BRAIN (CHEN-GIA TSAI)
Rhythm isn't background noise. It's how we predict the world.

The human brain doesn't wait to react. It loops. It listens ahead. Whether you're dancing, speaking, driving, or preparing to respond in an argument, your nervous system isn't just processing input – it's pre-aligning. Groove, in this sense, isn't musical. It's cognitive. It's the felt sense of 'this is the right moment' before the move is made.

That timing – what to do, and when to do it – is the difference between adaptive action and wasted effort. And it's not a soft skill. It's a system function.

One of the scientists showing how this works is Chen-Gia Tsai, a neuroscientist and pianist based in Taiwan. Tsai's work uses K-pop remixes and fMRI scans to study what happens in the brain when we hear bass-heavy beats. His research reveals that low-frequency rhythm activates the brain's action system – not just the auditory cortex, but the mirror neuron network, the prefrontal motor planners, the parietal timing hubs. It's not that the music makes us want to move. It's that the groove prepares the movement before we're conscious of it.

This is why Parkinson's patients, whose motor systems struggle to initiate action, often walk more fluidly to rhythm than to commands. The groove does what language can't: it embeds a cue inside the system. It turns waiting into readiness.

Groove isn't linear – it's recursive. A loop. A structure that holds time across repetition, but allows for adaptation inside each cycle. That's what makes rhythm so powerful: it offers enough predictability to orient, and enough space to shift. Tsai's research supports what dancers, drummers, and speakers already know:

timing is the architecture of presence. Not rigidity. Not automation. Dynamic return.

Social scientists have seen this in other places. Conversation analysis, synchronised movement, public debate rituals, even urban crowd flow – all show that shared rhythm builds cohesion. It lets minds time one another. We don't just exchange words; we drop into each other's pulses. When Lula walked back into Brazil's public life, he didn't just offer new policies. He brought the rhythm back. That's why they danced. That's why it was Lulapalooza. The beat was returned.

But rhythm isn't all flow. Groove sharpens most in contrast. Tsai found that enhanced groove perception comes not from perfect continuity, but from deliberate rupture – the pause, the delay, the beat drop. Just like in music, what matters isn't just repetition. It's what happens when the loop breaks and reforms. The most adaptive systems don't avoid disruption. They integrate the break into the groove.

This is the deeper function of timing. It isn't about staying on track – it's about knowing when to exit, when to hold, when to drop back in. Tsai mapped that in the brain. Lula lived it in public. And now you can learn to do it, too.

GROOVE TO FIVE BEATS

Groove isn't just something you feel. It's something you follow. And once you start noticing it – inside music, inside motion – you start to notice it in your own actions.

This next section is a slow walk through the loop you've already seen in motion. Five beats. Each one essential. Each one a phase that helps you time your moves – better, smarter, deeper.

We're not giving you a checklist. We're handing you a rhythm. And if you read it well, you'll start to hear where you are in the loop – and how to return to it with intention.

THE RHYTHM BENEATH THE ACTION

I didn't invent this rhythm. I started noticing it.
In patterns of behaviour. In real transformation.
In the way things begin slowly, then build, peak, adjust, and settle again.
At first, it was a feeling – something I saw in great athletes, in political recoveries, in long creative arcs.
Then I saw it again. And again. And once I began tracing it carefully, I realised: this isn't a one-off.
This is the rhythm behind real adaptation.
We see patterns everywhere – some are illusions.
But this one held up. Not just in stories. In systems. In bodies. In strategy.
I found it in this book's examples – whether I was writing about Buterin, Biles, or Kim Dae-jung.
I saw it in grief, in reinvention, in recovery.
I heard it in Morse code. In music. In the way humans move.
This rhythm doesn't belong to one person, or one type of life.
It's a structure beneath the noise.
And it's a rhythm you can learn to live.

I call it the Five Beats of Adaptive Rhythm:
    SLOW – to prepare
    SLOW – to ramp
    QUICK – to act
    QUICK – to adjust
    SLOW – to store and stage the next loop

These five beats form a loop you can return to – again and again.
Not perfectly. But deliberately.
Not to do more. But to do what matters, better.
The beats matter.
The order matters.
The way you play them matters.
And the spaces between them? They're not pauses. They're part of the rhythm.
(Remember your Morse code. It only makes sense if you leave room for silence.)
The slow-slow is a preparatory phrase.
The quick-quick is a movement phrase.
And the final slow is your release – the rest that resets the measure.
Musicians call this phrasing.

Dancers call it sequence and return.
Adaptive minds just call it good timing.
You don't have to be musical to use this rhythm.
But if you want to live well-timed, well-shaped action loops,
this is the one to learn.

THE DOUBLE SLOW
SLOW → SLOW

You've seen it go wrong. The decorating job that looked fine at a glance – until the daylight hits it. Paint flaking, brush marks like claw tracks, gloss puckering over old dust. And all because the prep was rushed. Anyone who's done it knows: if you don't take time to strip, sand, fill, dust, and cover, no amount of careful brushwork later will save you. That's not hesitation. That's preparation.

Superadapters understand this intuitively. They begin each action loop with two deliberate beats: Prepare and Ramp. Together, they form the foundation of intelligent movement. They take the time they need. Not more. Not less.

Preparation is not passive. It's where attention sharpens, signal is gathered, strength is built. A superadaptive mind entering a new domain doesn't flail into motion – they start by learning the terrain. What's changing? What's required? What materials, allies, strategies will be needed? If they're painting, they're checking the surface. If they're launching, they're checking the wind. It looks slow. But it saves time later.

Ramp is the second slow. Here, priorities narrow. Distractions fall away. Options are weighed and sorted. Momentum begins to build. You can almost feel the pressure coiling. Not to explode – but to strike with purpose. Think of the gymnast just before the run. The sprinter crouched on the blocks. The artist opening paints and laying cloth.

Or the boxer.

Years of general prep behind them. But now? Ten weeks out from the fight, the training camp begins. Not a fat camp. A precision ramp. They study footage, isolate the opponent's strengths and flaws, bring in sparring partners to mimic their style. They run through drills tailored not for general improvement, but for one moment: this opponent, this night, this ring. The more money you have, the more precisely you can ramp. The taller the opponent, the taller your sparring partner. The more aggressive they are, the more you train your counter. The ramp-up is compressed strategy, focus, rehearsal, edge. It's not action yet, but it's not stillness either. It's live.

Together, these two beats are about rhythmic timing. Misjudge them, and the loop suffers. Rush prep and you miss the signals. Rush ramp and your next move wobbles. But stretch them too long – and the moment may pass. That's the deeper mastery: not just knowing how to go slow, but when to stop going slow.

You can see this in every domain. A young athlete who trains without recovering. A startup that scales before it stabilises. A writer who edits before the ideas are formed. These aren't just strategy errors. They're rhythm mismatches. The beat got skipped. The brush hit the wall before the surface was ready.

So why is it so hard to get right? Because this kind of slowness doesn't feel heroic. It doesn't photograph well. But every master you admire – in sport, in science, in story – has learned to hold back just long enough to make the next move clean. They take the time to line up their loop.

You can too. Gather. Focus. Coil. And when the moment is ready – move.

SLOW → SLOW

PREPARE → RAMP

THE QUICK QUICK

You've coiled the spring. You've set your footing. Now comes the moment when everything accelerates.

This is the hot streak phase. Superadapters know that momentum isn't magic – it's made. It happens when action is taken at the right time, and then refined mid-flight. Action and Adjustment. Not one after the other – but one inside the other.

This is where adaptive rhythm comes alive. Where planning meets improvisation. Where you strike – and then shift. Pivot, course-correct, double-down. Stay in the flow, but steer it.

If the slow beats built your platform, this is where you leap.

SLOW: STORE & STAGE

As you reap, you shall sow.

The number one lesson I've learnt in gardening is this: the more you plant, the more you'll enjoy later. I think it was my sister who taught me that. She'd move into a new house – rented or not – and head straight to the garden centre. She'd buy shrubs, trees, perennials. Then she'd dig the boundaries, line the edge with growth. She wasn't thinking just about today. She was seeding tomorrow's beauty, even if she wasn't staying long.

And that stuck. Every weekend, I plant something. I'm not always strategic. I don't propagate deliberately – well, not yet. But I keep planting. Because while I'm busy doing other things, those plants are working without me. Sun, rain, soil, and time are collaborating in the background. That's what storing and staging really is. You do something today that makes life easier, richer, more beautiful in the future.

I don't garden for the applause. I garden to get my hands dirty. I garden because it brings me outside and calms my mind. Because I like physical work that gives back twice: once to the body, once to the soul. And every time I step outside, there's something waiting for me: a blackbird, a robin, a trio of bees. They remember. The garden remembers.

This is what superadapters do in the final phase. They don't collapse after a win. They pause. They enrich the soil. They stage the next rhythm. They don't just move on. They build on. Everything they gained in the quick-quick gets folded back into the loop. Lessons, energy, tools, insight, joy. Not lost. Stored. Not idle. Held in readiness. Protected, composted, quietly improving the conditions for what's next.

That last slow doesn't mean it's the end. It means you're holding space. Shaping future action. If you do it right, your garden – the loop, the rhythm – levels up. You're more capable. You've got more resilience. More options. You're a better gardener. And the bees are back.

THE RHYTHM IN FULL

Not every action loop is well-timed. Most people wait too long, or act too soon. They stall under pressure, or miss the moment mid-flight. But superadapters learn a different sequence – one that doesn't just do more, but does better. It's a rhythm of preparation, build-up, strike, adjustment, and consolidation. It loops. It works. And when it's tuned right, it leads to real change.

What you're looking at isn't a formula – it's a phrase. A structure. A loop you can run again and again. You don't have to follow it perfectly. But once you've felt it, you'll start to hear it everywhere.

$$\text{SLOW} \rightarrow \text{SLOW} \rightarrow \text{QUICK} \rightarrow \text{QUICK} \rightarrow \text{SLOW}$$

$$(\text{Prep} \rightarrow \text{Ramp} \rightarrow \text{Act} \rightarrow \text{Adjust} \rightarrow \text{Store})$$

If you're mid-loop now, stop and ask: Where are you in the rhythm? Are you still gathering strength – or already pivoting mid-air? Did you store the last gain, or did it slip in the rush to move on? This loop won't answer those questions for you. But it will help you ask them at the right time. And that's often what makes the difference.

Once you begin to hear this rhythm in your own life, you can learn to play it – with more purpose, more grace, and more control. Adaptive rhythm isn't about doing more. It's about doing what matters, timed right. One beat at a time.

PREP & RAMP – THE LAUNCH PHASE

PREPARE
This is the first slow. You're gathering what you'll need for what's coming next. Signal. Strength. Skills. Allies. Data. You may still be doing other things – another job, another loop – but inside this moment, the focus is on readiness. You're learning the terrain. You're watching the weather. You're tuning the system.

RAMP
This is the second slow. Tension starts to build – but not to explode. It's compression with purpose. Pressure shaping direction. You're taking the signal you gathered and beginning to apply it. You start blocking time, shifting priorities, saying no to things you used to say yes to. You're loading in force.

TOGETHER
These two beats form your launchpad. Without prep, your ramp is unstable. Without ramp, your prep never goes anywhere. Together, they form the double slow: a deliberate phase of grounded momentum.

ACT & ADJUST – THE HOT STREAK MECHANISM

ACT
This is the first quick. It's not random motion – it's the move you've been setting up. You strike. You enter. You commit to the play. But it's not just speed for speed's sake. The best actions here are tight, timed, and clean. This is the moment when preparation and ramp hit the surface – and become visible. You don't know the outcome yet. But you're in.

ADJUST

The second quick isn't the same. It's not new action – it's intelligent reaction. In-flight edits. Mid-move pivots. Micro-corrections. Here, feedback isn't something you wait for – it's something you catch and use while still in motion. This is the beat that separates a streak from a stall. The smart adapt not between moves, but inside them.

TOGETHER

Action and adjustment form the hot streak – a self-reinforcing rhythm of doing and adapting. It's not about getting lucky. It's about recognising the moment – and staying in it. Not indefinitely, but deliberately. Because when you're in a hot streak, the best thing you can do is use it. Move. Modify. Stay alert. And begin to store. This is the heartbeat of progress.

STORE & STAGE – LEVEL UP

This is the last beat of your slow – but not the last time you'll be here. The gains you make don't just disappear. You store them – mentally, emotionally, strategically. You take what worked and make it portable. You extract the lessons, protect the resources, and recover your energy. Without this beat, the loop might collapse. You burn out. Storage here isn't hoarding – it's holding on to what you've gained, on purpose. It's the place to secure what the hot streak gave you.

But this isn't necessarily about rest, although it can be. The pause. The reboot. The recovery. It's also about the next stage. You're already laying foundations for what you want to achieve at a higher level. You're noticing new signals. Repositioning. Lining up systems. So even as the loop slows, you're shaping the next arc. Staging is not stopping – it's forward orientation. It makes the slow not an ending, but a setup. A launch pad for the next slow, slow, quick.

FIVE BEATS

It was a break.

A deliberate one. A crafted one. One that let the beat breathe and the brain catch up.

Because rhythm isn't just what drives you forward – it's what lets you land. Sit still. Feel the weight of the last move before you take the next.

From Lula's syncopated rise, to Tsai's neural groove, to the polyrhythms hidden in a squirrel's leap – we've been inside the loop all along. The five-beat rhythm of adaptive action. The functional foxtrot of survival.

SLOW → SLOW. QUICK → QUICK. SLOW

You didn't just read it. You sat with it. And now it's part of you.
So let's return to the groove. And see where it carries us next.

WHEN TO HOLD, WHEN TO DROP

You have a rhythm, whether you know it or not.

It shows up in how you start your day, how you handle tension, when you speak in a meeting, how long you wait before making a move. Some people burn bright and crash. Others hesitate and miss their window. Timing isn't about being fast or slow. It's about being right on your own downbeat. Misaligned action creates friction. Mistimed action wastes energy.

Most people don't fail because they lack drive. They mistime the move.

Every streak you've had – when work flowed, conversations landed, you felt light and fast – was a rhythm. So was every collapse, every confused retreat. You don't just move through the world. You loop through it. Preparation, push, pause, return. The trick isn't to hold one phase. It's to know which phase you're in.

Knowing that you're not failing. Or lazy. You're just between bars.

Sometimes the smartest move is to wait. Not forever. Not out of fear. But because the system isn't open. The ground isn't ready. Biles stepped back from the Olympic stage. Lula spent 580 days in a cell while the rhythm reset around him. That wasn't passivity. It was preservation. Timing is protection. Acting too early isn't courage – it's sabotage. Knowing when to hold your fire is what gives your return power.

In music, the pause is part of the beat.

Then the rhythm returns. You feel it. Not as certainty, but as readiness. The urge to act aligns with the opening of the system. That's your drop. But the return isn't repetition. It's remix. The moment doesn't repeat – it advances. You don't pick up where you left off. You re-enter with everything you've stored. The pause wasn't lost time. It was charging.

The groove is yours to re-enter – but never to resume unchanged.

This is rhythm as intelligence. Not flair. Not luck. A real skill. An adaptive tool. Knowing when to push and when to pulse. When to fade and when to strike. It's not just about intuition – it's about feel. About reading the system you're in, and knowing when to move. Not every loop can be won by force. Some are only mastered by timing.

Anyone can push.

The ones who last know when to strike.
Lula waited. Tsai explained. You apply.

MASTER THE WAIT → RIDE THE RHYTHM → LEVEL UP

That's the groove.
That's the break.
That's the return.

ENCORE: THE BEAT (AND THE BREAK)

You might have thought it was a pause. But of course, it wasn't. It was a break.

A coffee break, even. A brain break. A beat drop. A groove.

From the very first moment of this Sitdown, the rhythm was already playing: heartbeats pulsing through your blood stream, the coffee mug warming your fingers, Lula rising not once, but twice – each time finding the beat again, refusing to dance to someone else's tempo.

Then Tsai stepped in, not just with neurons, but with syncopation – showing how rhythm runs deep inside us, how cognition itself swings to the beat. And when we paused to explore the five-stage loop – slow, slow, quick, quick, slow – you weren't just reading theory. You were tracing the steps. Of Biles, Beyoncé, Pattinson. Of adaptation itself.

This whole Sitdown was the action loop.

But slowed down. Stretched out. So you could feel its tempo, not just learn its name.

So yes – this was a break. A meaningful one. Not a distraction from the Rule, but the deep pattern underneath it. Beats. Breaks. Adjustments. Accents. All building to a new kind of fluency.

You might even feel it now. In your memory. In your breath. In your timing. Because that's how superadaptability works – it gives you rhythm you can return to.

And now?

Now it's time to see what it looks like lived.

Let's move forward.

LIVE THE LOOP

HOW TO LIVE THE LOOP
Keep the beat, adapt in real time.

You've seen the rhythm of superadapters taking action.
You've paused for coffee and thought about groove – and about brains and breaks.

Now it's time to see how they keep taking action –
and then try it out for yourself – deliberately, rhythmically, and with awareness.

This is where the loop becomes lived.

You'll return to the examples you've already seen – Biles, Beyoncé, Pattinson –
but through a new lens.
Not just how they took action once,
but how they stayed adaptive when the rhythm changed.

You'll learn to recognise what stage of the rhythm you're in –
whether it's time to prep, to press, or to pause.
You'll see how adaptive timing isn't just instinct.
It's a habit. It's a rhythm.
And it can be learned.

This is the section that moves from noticing the beat
to dancing with it.

We'll show you the patterns.
You'll test your own.
And by the end of it, you won't just know how the loop works –
you'll know how to live it.

HOW THEY LIVED THEIR LOOP
There is a rhythm to learning from life. And there's another rhythm – quieter, older, deeper – that comes from learning how others lived it.

Elie Wiesel once wrote that "to learn means to accept the postulate that life did not begin at my birth. Others have been here before me, and I walk in their footsteps." But we don't just follow. We move with them. We watch how they looped. And then we try to match their rhythm, moment by moment, with a loop of our own.

Dance taught us this. Before language. Before thought. One body moved, and another followed. Then mirrored. Then rose. One gesture became an invitation. One turn became a spiral. And from there – something new.

When we move alongside others, we are not just imitating. We are co-creating. Co-looping. Their momentum becomes our ignition. Their recovery becomes our re-entry.

This next section isn't a recap. It's a recognition. A return. We're going to re-enter the lives of Simone Biles, Beyoncé, and Robert Pattinson – not to rewatch what they did, but to see how they kept living the loop. We'll glimpse the beat that came after the beat. The rhythm beneath the action.

Because learning to act is one thing. Learning to act again – with rhythm, not reaction – is something else. That's the shift. From sapiens to supersapiens. Not a leap. A loop. And we're in it now.

SAPIENS → ? → SUPERSAPIENS

Simone Biles didn't just break a streak. She built a bridge. In Tokyo, at the height of her athletic power, she stepped back – not from fear, but from rhythm. She moved out of the hot streak and into stillness. From quick-adjust to final slow. And then – intentionally – into something else. Her actions made it clear: the slow at the end of one loop isn't the end at all. It's the first slow of the next. Store becomes prep. And so, she paused – not to vanish, but to stage the next return.

Gymnastics gives us the perfect metaphor. On the parallel bars, mastery isn't just in the movement – it's in the transition. You swing, rotate, gather momentum – and when the timing is right, you release. Not to stop, but to arc cleanly into the next bar. Pause. Beat. Hold. Then flight. If you let go too soon, you fall. Hold on too long, and the rhythm stalls. The brilliance is in the moment between loops – the choice to let go, the trust in the arc, the readiness to catch what comes next.

When she returned, it wasn't to reclaim the spotlight – it was to show how action, timing, and recovery braid together. She competed again. But more than that, she mentored, anchored, modelled something new: mastery through rhythm, not momentum. She didn't just perform. She re-entered – with grace, and in time.

Beyoncé lives in the hot streak. Where most artists flash, then fade, she builds rhythm into rhythm – quick into quick. It's not luck. It's design. She doesn't just act. She adjusts. She loops again – intentionally, rhythmically, in time. This is what the second phase of the action loop looks like when fully lived: decisive movement followed by precise modulation, again and again, without burning out.

And here's the brilliance – she doesn't do it alone. Her hot streak isn't a solo sprint. It's a system. Collaborative, evolving, groove-based. She surrounds herself with co-creators, curators, pulse-checkers, cultural architects. In doing so, she doesn't just stay in motion – she expands the motion itself. The streak becomes an engine. The act-adjust rhythm becomes a cycle of creation.

What emerges isn't just music. It's movement. The kind of groove that Chen-Gia Tsai describes in the brain: shared pulse, embodied timing, recursive anticipation. Beyoncé doesn't just ride this groove – she builds it, stage by stage, project by project, beat by beat. Her adaptive power isn't just in what she makes. It's in how she loops – again and again – without losing timing, tone, or self.

Where Beyoncé sustains rhythm, Robert Pattinson rewrites it. He doesn't just return – he re-emerges, often unrecognisable, looping forward with altered timing and tone. After the global saturation of Twilight, he didn't try to replicate the streak. He let the loop dissolve. He stepped off the beat. And then – carefully, oddly, brilliantly – he began again.

Every project since has been a new rhythm: *Good Time, The Lighthouse, The Batman.* None predictable. None nostalgic. He doesn't just act and adjust – he stages, stores, and re-routes. He retools his inner system for each return. And in doing so, he models the quiet form of superadaptability: the one that doesn't announce its recursion but lives it, film by film, beat by beat.

This is the loop as transformation. Not fame, not franchise, but prep, ramp, act – on his terms. Pattinson doesn't discard the loop. He just refuses to ride anyone else's version of it. His habit isn't consistency. It's creative recursion. And his career shows what it means to hold the loop lightly, shift gears with precision, and return not as the same, but as someone new.

Not every loop moves quickly. Some loops stretch across years. Across exile. Across silence. Lula's return to leadership wasn't a comeback – it was a re-groove. After prison, after power, after grief, he came back with rhythm, not revenge. He adjusted. He staged. And when the moment came, he moved – not as the man he was, but as the version he had become.

Kim Dae-jung's loop took decades. From imprisonment to presidency. From vision to re-entry. His loop was not built in one cycle, but in many. He stored. He prepared. He waited. And when he returned, he embedded peace – not just into politics, but into the system itself. Both men show that loop intelligence isn't always fast. But when it returns, it changes everything.

You've seen the loop in motion. Simone paused, adjusted, and returned with precision. Beyoncé rode the act-adjust rhythm like a symphony, building a hot streak system that could groove forward again and again. Pattinson let his timing rupture, then built something stranger and sharper on the other side. Lula and Kim each carried the loop through silence, through exile, until it returned with power and poise.

This is how superadapters live their loop. Not in stunts or sparks, but in timing. In rhythm. In recursive return. The five-beat pattern you've learned – slow, slow, quick, quick, slow – isn't just a tool. It's a truth. The final slow becomes the first. Store becomes prep. The best loops don't end. They move again.

Some do it with speed. Some with silence. But the deepest loops don't start with strategy. They start with feeling. With weight. With something internal shifting. And that's where we're going next.

FALL FLEX FLOW
How simple actions trained over time become fluent mastery

"Dance is the hidden language of the soul."
– Martha Graham (1894–1991)

All dance starts with a single action. And in Martha Graham's world, that action came from the core.

She didn't come from dance. Dance found her. She described it as inevitable. Not a choice, but a gravitational fact.

Martha Graham didn't rise through the classical ballet hierarchy. She dropped into something else entirely – something rougher, heavier, closer to the bone. While other dancers reached upward from the tips of their toes, she began with the pelvis. With gravity. With weight. With the point where power lives in the body. Her movements didn't float – they contracted. And then they released.

This was the technique she taught: contraction and release. You don't leap first. You pull in. You brace. You feel the breath deepen. You start from the centre. She trained her dancers to move vertebra by vertebra, breath by breath, everything spiralling outward from the core. Her language was unapologetically anatomical. She said – famously, and not metaphorically – "Dance from the vagina."

At first, the movement seemed jagged. Too raw. Too physical. But it had structure. The contraction wasn't chaos – it was shape. The release wasn't softness – it was strategy. And then came the spiral: a rotating of the spine, a twist that allowed grief and joy to travel through the torso and out into the limbs. She taught that where you held your weight, how you pushed from the floor, whether your ribs or hips were open – these were all part of the message. Whether you were high or low to the ground determined whether the dance spoke of despair or desire.

Her dancers didn't improvise at random. They trained. Five actions. Repeatable phrases. Each step a cue, each gesture a beat. And from those basics, fluency emerged. Not accident, but articulation. Not looseness, but language. She wasn't just teaching movement. She was inventing a grammar – a way of moving that let people express anything, and everything, from the inside out.

She had critics. Of course she did. She called her first piece Heretic. She rejected an invitation to perform in Nazi Germany – and instead created a work called American Document. She taught through feeling, through grief, through the floorboards. She befriended Helen Keller, who learned to feel the dance through vibration. She drank after retirement. Disappeared. Returned. She created ten new ballets after the age of 76. Her last was staged when she was 94.

She danced at the White House. She was awarded the Medal of Freedom. But the thing that endured was not a single piece. It was the technique.

Fall. Flex. Flow. That was the loop. That was the power. She trained it. Named it. Passed it on. And every dancer who used it – still does.

Mastery starts with a shape. A rhythm. A repeatable act. Do it long enough, and it stops being practice. It becomes your movement. Your grammar. Your way of being in the world.

THE CHESS CLOCK
The whose go is it gambit.

I thought I was being ignored.
She thought I was flooding the space.

It started in the mornings. I'd come in full of energy – dream fragments, overnight ideas, errands already half-planned in my head. I'd start talking. I thought I was inviting her in. But she'd be quiet. Withdrawing. I felt hurt.

Eventually I said something like, "You never say anything when I speak".

She said, You never leave any space.

That stopped me. It wasn't an argument. Just a quiet description of the gap between us. I thought I was being shut out. But maybe I'd been filling the room without knowing it.

I hadn't read about it anywhere. But I remembered: when people play chess, they use a clock.

A physical device. You take your turn, then hit the clock.

Your opponent's time starts.

That's how the rhythm is kept fair.

At first, I actually thought about buying a sand timer. Something visual. But then I remembered that scene from *The Queen's Gambit* – the sharp click as they slapped the chess clock after each move. That's when I thought: maybe there's an app for this.

And there was.

So I downloaded it. Not for chess, for conversation.

The first time, I was sure I was being fair. The second time, I was a little less sure.

By the third time, I knew.

I was speaking for over twice as long as she was.

It wasn't a fight. It wasn't even loud.

But I was taking all the turns.

Not aggressively. Just endlessly.

I hadn't left her any gaps to enter.

She wasn't silent because she didn't want to speak.

She was silent because there was nowhere to speak into.

That was the part I hadn't understood.

The absence of interruption wasn't peace. It was constraint.

Eventually, even her quietness changed.

It stopped feeling passive. It started to feel protective.

I'd speak. She'd nod. Smile, maybe. But she was gone.

Present physically. Absent in rhythm.

One morning I remember clearly: she walked in, silent, got coffee, didn't speak. Not in a dramatic way. Just detached.

It was like she'd stepped out of the loop.

Not punishing me – just no longer in orbit.

And for once, I didn't try to fill the space.

I just watched it sit there, unclaimed.

And I thought: Maybe this isn't silence. Maybe this is feedback.

That was when I started leaving space.

Not performatively. Not as a tactic. Just genuinely pausing.
Letting her take her turn.
Letting myself hear what timing actually feels like when it's shared.

Sometimes she spoke. Sometimes she didn't.
But there was room again.
The loop came back – awkwardly, imperfectly – but alive.
Turns out, I wasn't waiting for her to speak.
I was taking all the turns.

The chess clock didn't just measure something.
It revealed a pattern.
And that gave me the chance to change it.

THE SHEEP (AND THE SHUFFLE)

Cliff Young was born in 1922 on a 2,000-acre farm in Victoria, Australia, where he helped manage 2,000 sheep. That's a sheep an acre – or an acre per sheep. And because the family couldn't afford horses, he ran. A lot.

At 56, he entered his first public race – the Adidas 16 km over Melbourne's West Gate Bridge – wearing overalls and work boots. He ran it in 64 minutes and then kept running: improving his time, running full marathons, and eventually, trying to break the 1,000-mile world record.

But it wasn't until 1983 that Cliff Young became legendary.

At 61, he entered the inaugural Sydney-to-Melbourne ultramarathon – 544 miles – competing against elite athletes half his age. Most runners planned to sleep six hours a night. Cliff didn't. Not by design. He just accidentally woke up at 2 am and kept going. The others caught up, only to discover he was ahead. So he decided: no more sleep. Just run.

Cliff finished first. Ten hours ahead of the rest.

He didn't win another race. But something else stuck: his shuffle. A low-impact, energy-saving style he used instinctively. Later, ultra runners adopted it. The 'Cliff Young Shuffle' is now a known technique. And a comedy show title.

There's something in this story. Not just the tortoise-and-hare lesson. Not just stamina. But something about surprise. Cliff didn't set out to defy a system. He just kept going – longer, quieter, weirder. And that worked. Once.

After that, the others adapted. They watched. They learned. He lost his edge.

But what made Cliff remarkable wasn't just that he broke away from the flock. It was that he did it by 'accident' – and 'stayed' ahead by 'choice'. He joined the race late in life. He ran his way. He shuffled.

The sheep and the shuffle. A man who had herded thousands, and then separated himself from them – not by brilliance, but by moving through the margins and refusing to stop.

Every loop has its surprise. Every edge dulls when observed. But once, Cliff Young ran ahead – and for one stretch of the course, the whole country followed.

QUICK QUICK NO

It was just meant to be a push-start. The battery was dead, so I leaned in behind the car to help give it a nudge downhill. What I didn't expect was for my fingers to get caught in the trunk seam. I was wearing leather-soled shoes, the smooth kind. As the car picked up speed, my grip slipped – but not free. I couldn't signal. I couldn't stop. I was being pulled, skiing silently down the slope, leather soles against tarmac, trapped by my own hands.

At some point, I had to choose: hold on and be dragged, or wrench free and fall. I tore away. Crashed. My shoulder split. My shirt exploded like paper. But I walked away.

Sometimes, the only way to survive a system that's moving too fast is to say no. You might fall. You might bleed. But you might walk away.

This is a riff about those moments. When the system says no. When you do. When you don't. When you should. When it matters.

The World Says No

There are times when the rhythm is yours – when the world syncs to your motion. And then there are times it doesn't.

We were strapped into the ride. My son, maybe eight, was sitting ahead of us, alone. The safety bar came down, the machinery clanked, and we lurched forward. But the moment we crested the first rise, he started to slide in his seat. He wasn't safe. His harness hadn't locked properly.

There were no emergency buttons. No way to flag the operator. All we could do was hold on – to the bar, to each other, to him – hoping we'd make it through the next four loops without something breaking. Quick quick no. The world had said go. But everything in my body wanted to shout stop.

That's how it happens. One minute you're in flow. The next, you're hurtling toward something you didn't choose. And all you can do is brace, react, survive – and remember, next time, where the exits are.

You Say No

Sometimes the No comes from you. Not out of fear, but foresight. Not because you're lost, but because you see too clearly where something leads.

You say no to the meeting that should have been an email.

No to the plan that was never yours to begin with.

No to the momentum that's only carrying you because you haven't jumped off yet.

It's not easy. We've been taught to keep moving, to say yes, to stay agreeable. But superadapters know that rhythm doesn't mean always faster. Sometimes rhythm means pause, hold, breathe. Reset the beat. They know that speed without discernment is just drift.

In some cultures, no is direct. In others, it's circled. But wherever you are, the capacity to say no – to reclaim your tempo – is what turns movement into music, and noise into rhythm. It's the beat between beats that holds the whole thing together.

You Don't Say No

And then there's the no you never say. The plan you agree to but dread. The invitation you accept but never follow through on. The small silences that become distance.

A friend plans a grand birthday. It's not your style. You'd rather go for a walk, grab something simple. But instead of saying that – "That's not really me" – you delay. You ghost. You don't say no. And so you don't say anything at all.

These moments seem small. But they add up. Relationships drift. Opportunities pass. You trade a short discomfort for a longer erosion.

We think saying no will damage the bond. But often it's the failure to say it that does. Superadapters know this. They've learned the cost of unspoken refusal. And they've learned to find words that keep the rhythm alive – "Not now," "Not this way," "Let's talk."

Refusing well is not rejection. It's recognition. It's rhythm. It's grace in the face of collision.

The Other No's

There are other no's, too.

The no of a toddler – clear, full-bodied, non-negotiable. The no of a seasoned negotiator – calm, spacious, exact. The no of a culture that wraps refusal in ritual. The no of a workplace where refusal must be coded to survive.

Psychologists call these refusal strategies. Some are direct. Some are deflective. Some are disguised as questions:

"Who's approving that overtime?"

"Can we revisit that next week?"

"I'd love to help – if something else comes off my plate."

You're not just buying time. You're holding rhythm. You're protecting the loop.

And sometimes it's literal: you say no, and walk away. From the table. From the room. From the role that's no longer yours to play. Saying no won't always spare you pain – I got a busted shoulder from one of mine. But I also got to walk away.

Rhythm isn't always motion.

Sometimes it's resistance.

$$QUICK \rightarrow QUICK \rightarrow NO$$

FROM TRAPPED TO TRANSCENDED

Sometimes the limits feel real, but they rarely are. Sometimes your actions seem to give you less than the sum of their parts. But the good news is this: the habits you've just encountered – Master the Wait, Ride the Rhythm, and Level Up – provide more than momentum. They offer rhythm. And rhythm is how superadapters escape limits that trap others.

What you've seen is that each habit operates not as a standalone action, but as a timing adjustment. A way to re-enter an effective beat. The slow-slow of patient preparation. The quick-quick of decisive action and smart adjustment. The final slow: to store and stage for what's next.

And when the rhythm is right, it changes everything. The same self, the same system, the same situation can yield entirely different results – just because the rhythm has changed.

So this isn't just about behaviour change.

This is tempo correction. Pulse awareness. Pattern fluency.

This is the logic of rhythm as applied to life.

And when you change your rhythm, you change your power.

TRAPPED VS TRANSCENDED

	TRAPPED	TRANSCENDED
Master the Wait	Rushes into action. Mistakes movement for progress. Is stuck. Overactive and underprepared.	Delays action until the rhythm makes sense. Recognises pauses as powerful. Aligns with the timing of the system.
Ride the Rhythm	Breaks the flow. Quits the streak too early. Doesn't adjust. Momentum lost.	Recognises the beat. Extends the hot streak. Adjusts while in motion. Stays in flow.
Level Up	Exhausted by effort. Doesn't convert gain into growth. Stalls or resets.	Consolidates progress. Reorients for the next cycle. Uses rhythm to store energy and stage the future.

Even when your effort is high, you can feel trapped. Trapped in the wrong phase. Trapped in the wrong rhythm. Trapped by doing too much too soon, or too little too late.

But what if your loop could be tuned?

Each of the three habits in this chapter helps you do exactly that. Not by replacing action, but by modifying its tempo.

Master the Wait teaches you to pause with purpose. It isn't about doing nothing. It's about holding still long enough to recognise what's needed. So you don't act just because you can – you act when the rhythm is right.

Ride the Rhythm keeps you moving when momentum builds. It helps you stay in your streak without falling out too soon or drifting off course. You adapt in motion. You adjust while you act.

Level Up is your intelligent deceleration. It turns success into fuel. It helps you store your gains and stage the next loop. It makes the slow deliberate, not passive.

Together, these habits don't just make you effective. They help you align with a deeper adaptive pattern: the five-beat rhythm of superadaptability.

SLOW → SLOW → QUICK → QUICK → SLOW

You saw this rhythm introduced in the Action Loop. You explored it in depth during the Sitdown. And now, here, you've seen it in practice: one habit for each phase.

So let this sink in:
Every habit you learn here is a way to return to that rhythm.
To restore it. To stay in it. To modify it when it breaks.

Because even adaptive action can go wrong.
Even the best loops can fall out of sync.

And that's what we turn to next:
The Wrong Loops – and how to fix them.

THREE WAYS LOOPS GO WRONG

Some actions fail because the timing is off. Others fail because the understanding was never there. These aren't random mistakes. They're structured failures. They show up in real loops, again and again.

When a loop breaks, it usually breaks in one of three ways:
Too slow to land.
Too fast to breathe.
Or too wrong to work.

We call them Hypo, Hyper, and Anti. Not just names. Patterns. Each one tells you something vital about what's happening – and what isn't.

Like a dancer learning five basic moves, it doesn't look like much at first. But with attention, timing, and repetition – something changes. What felt stiff becomes fluid. What felt foreign becomes instinct. This is what fluency in adaptation feels like. You begin to sense where the loop is weak. And where it might begin again.

HYPO is when your actions are too slow – or when the gaps between them are too long – and you miss the moment.

You do the right thing – just too late. You prepare, rehearse, hesitate… and by the time you move, the system has already moved on.

Sometimes it's over-preparation. Sometimes it's perfectionism disguised as planning. Sometimes it's the quiet hope that someone else will act first.

It's like showing up at the platform just as the train is pulling away. Or trying to pass the baton in a relay – only to realise the other runner has already gone.

Or stepping onto the stage one second too late, and missing the cue entirely.

You see it in teams that plan endlessly but never launch. In relationships where silence lasts just long enough to become distance. In decisions delayed so long they're no longer decisions – just damage control.

The moment needed rhythm. But hypo gives hesitation. You weren't wrong to prepare. You were just too late to move.

HYPER is when your actions are too fast – or when you move between them too quickly – and you don't leave enough space for timing to work.

You act before the system is ready. You skip the breath, the check, the moment to listen. It feels urgent. It feels right. But it lands too soon – or not at all.

Sometimes it's pressure. Sometimes it's fear of falling behind. Sometimes it's the rush to fix before the facts are even clear.

It's like answering the question before it's been asked. Or throwing a punch before your feet are planted. Or passing the baton before your teammate is ready – and watching it hit the ground.

You see it in managers who leap into solutions before understanding the system. In conversations where someone talks too fast, and nothing really lands. In plans rushed out the door – when what was needed was one more night to think.

The rhythm feels urgent. But hyper isn't flow – it's compression. You're moving fast. But the loop can't breathe.

ANTI is when the wrong thing is done – or nothing is done at all – and the pattern of action fails to meet the demands of the situation.

It's not too fast. It's not too slow. It's just wrong – because the loop is built on a misread of what's really happening.

The signals weren't detected. The pattern wasn't understood. The model was flawed, or the mechanism wasn't adapted.

So the action that follows – if any – moves in the wrong direction. It might look confident. It might feel calm. But it deepens the problem, or delays the response. Sometimes the silence is the signal. And no one is listening.

It's like continuing to build the wrong bridge with total commitment. Or doing nothing in the face of slow collapse – because today still seems fine. Or defending the loop itself, even when it no longer fits the world around it.

You see it in policies that punish instead of adapt. In strategies that stay rigid while the system transforms. In choices that serve the actor – but damage the future.

Anti is when adaptation doesn't just fail. It refuses to begin. And the loop doesn't just stall – it turns against itself.

These aren't just types of failure. They're signals. Each one tells you where the rhythm broke – and why action didn't land.

Hypo: too slow, too late, too much distance.
Hyper: too fast, too soon, too little space.
Anti: too wrong, too misaligned, or nothing at all – because the pattern was broken before it began.

You've now seen all three. And if you've been paying attention, your ability to notice them is already improving. That's the recursion. The loop within the loop.
    You're not just reading about adaptation. You're practicing it.
    Like a dancer learning five basic moves, it doesn't look like much – until it does. Precision in rhythm creates fluency in action. Recognition precedes understanding. Understanding precedes change.
    And all three of these – Hypo, Hyper, and Anti – come from upstream failure. A broken Recognise. A foggy Understand. An action taken without sync, without breath, without beat.
    Now that you can see them, you can begin to move differently. Next, we look at how.

REAL WORLD WRONG LOOPS

SLOW → SLOW → QUICK → QUICK → SLOW

This is the rhythm you want. When it's working, actions align. When it breaks, they don't.

The road to hell, they say, is paved with good intentions. But the rhythm of hell? That's mismatched tempo. Misfired timing. Effort without sequence. What follows are three true stories – different domains, different decisions – but all out of rhythm.
    For years, Nigeria's Nollywood became the second-largest film industry in the world by output – over 2,500 films a year. Shot fast, edited overnight, and released to hungry local markets, it created cultural momentum. But speed has a cost. As global platforms like Netflix and Amazon entered the space, viewers began expecting higher-quality production. Nollywood's release rhythm – originally its advantage – became its constraint. The system couldn't ramp up. Quantity became a trap. The beat had to shift – but didn't.
    It started fast, stayed fast, and failed to change tempo.

Seagram's tried to evolve from legacy whiskey brand to cultural empire – investing in studios, records, and channels. But it moved too slowly. While it was busy positioning, the culture changed underneath it. By the time its bets matured, they no longer matched the mood or the market. Seagram's fell from top-shelf dominance into collectible nostalgia.

PlayStation Home told a similar story. Virtual avatars. Exploratory environments. But their launch stalled. Users weren't ready; the platform under-delivered; the rhythm was perpetually in ramp-up, never in release.

In 2012, a parishioner in Spain attempted to restore a fading fresco of Christ. She meant well. She brought care, effort, and initiative – but lacked pause. She didn't step back. Didn't ask for feedback. Didn't reflect before moving forward. She rolled up her sleeves and painted, confident that good intent would carry the work. The result: 'Beast Jesus' – an internet phenomenon for all the wrong reasons.

She was in motion, but not in rhythm. No beat. No break. No loop.

Each one of these was done with effort. With conviction. With momentum. But rhythm isn't about motion. It's about timing. And timing isn't just a start – it's a sequence.

$$SLOW \rightarrow SLOW \rightarrow QUICK \rightarrow QUICK \rightarrow SLOW$$

You lose it – and the loop collapses. You regain it – and the loop adapts.

Or, to echo the great queen of jazz herself:
"It don't mean a thing if it ain't got that swing."

Which means – adaptively – you need to find the rhythm first, and only then give it everything you've got.

The next section is about getting the rhythm back. Because superadapters don't just act. They act in time.

COUNTER LOOPS – RHYTHM RESTORED

You've seen how loops go wrong. Hyper, hypo, anti – aren't just mistakes. They're structured failures – of timing, rhythm, or pattern. And they don't just appear in one domain. You've seen them in leaders, athletes, teams, and in yourself.

The good news? They can be countered. And the counter isn't complicated.

The best pattern for action is also the best pattern for recovery.

MASTER THE WAIT helps restore the space between moves that hyper action removes. Instead of acting before the system is ready, you take that breath, check the pause. You learn to distinguish between urgency and pressure.

Superadapters don't move on instinct alone. They pause with purpose. They know that silence can carry power, that rhythm needs air. Master the Wait isn't about hesitation. It's about alignment. To Master the Wait is to remember: you can choose.

You don't have to fill every space. You don't have to answer every pressure.

It's not just about stillness – it's about strategic delay. Wait long enough to see what matters. Long enough to time the move. Long enough to feel the rhythm shift around you – and use it.

You've seen it:

Beyoncé didn't rush from *Lemonade* to *Renaissance*.

The speaker in "Who's Go Is It?" learned to leave space, and the loop came back.

Lula paused, not to retreat, but to prepare for re-entry – on his own beat.

And you?

Wait one breath longer than you want to.

Let silence settle before the reply.

Ask yourself: Why now? And: What would I miss if I moved too soon?

RIDE THE RHYTHM allows you to speed up when Hypo would slow you down until the moment has passed. This doesn't mean rushing. It means entering while the loop is still alive. It means recognising that momentum is already here, and you need to step into it – not after, but during. You're not waiting for perfection. You learn to sync. You match tempo. You begin to act while the beat is present – even if it's not comfortable.

You've seen it: Kim Dae-jung re-emerged before the movement was fully formed – but just in time to help shape it.

Simone Biles didn't wait for full confidence – she returned when she was ready enough.

If you feel stuck in prep:
Start while you still feel unsure.
Let momentum carry part of the lift.
Adjust in motion.

The beat won't wait.
But you can learn to ride it.

LEVEL UP helps you to avoid moving in the wrong direction. Instead of doubling down on broken patterns , you learn twice from the past. You look backwards to move forward. To Level Up is to store the lesson – and use it to build something better.
Not every loop deserves to continue. Sometimes the only adaptive move is to let the old pattern go – and author a new one.

You've seen it:
Pattinson didn't replay *Twilight*. He rebuilt his system.
Martha Graham didn't soften for her critics. She doubled down on her movement at a higher level.
Kim Dae-jung embedded peace because he had first endured repression.

You don't always need to repeat.
Sometimes the loop you need is the next one – the one that starts with a better self.

Ask:
What am I defending that no longer fits?
What's ready to be let go?
What's already stored – and waiting to be used differently?
These loop failures – Hyper, Hypo, and Anti – aren't just things that happen to others. They happen to all of us. But now you have the pattern.

Master the Wait brings you back to the breath.
Ride the Rhythm brings you back into flow.
Level Up brings you forward as someone changed.

This is how rhythm is restored.
This is how loops begin again – not randomly, but wisely.

Even when the pattern breaks, you don't have to.
Because the beat returns.
And now – you know how to listen.
It's the repair.
The three-part action loop isn't just the ideal.
Diagnosis meets rhythm.

slow-slow, quick-quick, slow
MASTER THE WAIT → RIDE THE RHYTHM → LEVEL UP

too fast, too slow, too wrong
HYPER → HYPO → ANTI

The best pattern for action is also the best pattern for recovery.

REBOOTING THEIR LOOP

In this chapter, we've explored how effective action isn't just about movement – it's about rhythm. You've seen how superadapters use timing to act better, adjust faster, and store what matters. But even with the best loop, things still break. What worked before stops working. Systems shift. You get knocked out of sync.

That's why this moment matters.

Because rhythm isn't static – it's recursive. It returns. And so must you.

Here's the good news: when the loop fails, you don't need to invent a new system. You already have one. The RUN loop – Recognise, Understand, Necessary Action – isn't just for first moves. It's for re-entry.

In this section, we revisit our three core figures – Simone Biles, Beyoncé, and Robert Pattinson – to show what rebooting really looks like. Not a comeback. Not a crisis. A reloop.

Each faced a moment that wasn't in their original story. A rhythm-break. And each one stepped back in – not perfectly, but purposefully.

SIMONE BILES

Of course, Simone Biles isn't just a gymnast and a rhythmic strategist. She's a person – just like you and me. And like anyone else, she has setbacks. She has heartache. She gets thrown off balance.

She married Jonathan Owens, a Chicago Bears safety, and the internet didn't quite know how to process it. During an interview on *The Pivot* podcast, Owens joked that he was the catch in the relationship – that he hadn't followed gymnastics, hadn't known who she was, but swiped right when he saw her on a dating app. It was light, maybe clumsy, but sincere.

And then came the backlash.

Her fans attacked him. Loudly. For arrogance. For not showing enough reverence. For not 'getting' her. But in doing so, they missed something more important: that loving someone doesn't mean performing their biography – and that attacking their partner isn't loyalty. It's noise.

And here's what Simone did: she paused. She didn't respond instantly. She gave it a beat. And then, calmly, with rhythm, she re-entered. She said, Fans on social media can have a false sense of reality. They think they know us, but they don't. She acknowledged the toll it takes. And then she added, simply: Are you all done yet?

What she did wasn't defensive. It was diagnostic.

She recognised what was really going on.

She understood the difference between social perception and her actual relationship.

And she took necessary action – not to attack, but to rebalance.

That's how the loop works. Not just in Tokyo. Not just on the vault. But in life. In love. In the comments. In recovery. She didn't just perform. She processed. And that's what it looks like to reboot the loop.

BEYONCÉ KNOWLES

Back in 2024–25, not long after *Renaissance* reset the groove, Beyoncé dropped *Cowboy Carter*. Country, yes – but not merely as costume. It was a reclamation. A re-entry. A rhythmic shift in register.

There had been questions. About feminism. About image. About motherhood. About genre, and boundaries, and Blackness in country music. But what she recognised, among other things, was this: there's a limit to how far one genre can take you. You have to re-up.

And it wasn't the first time she'd done it. In the 2000s, when R&B faced extinction under the weight of EDM and crossover pop, she had adjusted. She collaborated. She evolved. She made herself close enough to the new sound to relaunch her own – and in doing so, she brought a whole movement with her. An R&B rebirth.

That loop became a method. A recursive move she understood deeply. She had seen the pattern before. And when she saw it again in country's cultural blind spots, she didn't react – she re-composed.

This wasn't pressure as novelty. It was pressure as rhythm.

She looked outward: at legacy artists, at how decades are sustained. You need collaborators. You need experiments. You need to write more than you release. From the moment she recorded her first solo album – eighty tracks in a week, without her father even knowing – it was clear: Beyoncé had already begun building a recursive life. One that could adapt, lift, and loop again.

She knew the genre would shift. So she placed herself above it – until the genre came to her.

The tour for *Cowboy Carter* had no features. No spectacle. Just family. Roots. Rhythm. She returned not to reassert the past, but to reveal something deeper: that her identity was the rhythm. That country was hers. That R&B was hers. That all of it was Beyoncé.

And she returned in joy.

Cowboy Carter wasn't resistance.
It was rhythm-aware inheritance.

RECOGNISE → UNDERSTAND → NECESSARY ACTION

ROBERT PATTISON

Sometime between filming *The Lighthouse* – a storm-lit, two-man mythscape spun from unfinished Poe and sea-soaked Promethean dreams – and landing *The Batman*, Robert Pattinson told interviewers: "I don't really know how to act." Not with modesty. With recognition.

He compared himself to a dog in an elevator – overwhelmed every time the doors opened. And inside rehearsals for *The Batman*, he spiralled. Unsure if he belonged. Unsure if he'd already failed.

But instead of hiding that spiral, he used it.

He didn't try to master the performance. He recognised what was happening – self-doubt, dislocation, the loop breaking – and he played into it. He understood that the role wasn't about playing Batman. It was about integrating every version of himself he'd ever been: the indie oddballs, the megastar vampire, the self-critical underdog. He didn't disown those versions. He folded them in.

He called himself a catastrophist. But what he was really doing was meta-performance: recognising, understanding, and acting – not from the outside of the loop, but from inside it.

He deliberately stayed disoriented. Didn't over-rehearse. Didn't over-prepare. He kept his centre unstable – so he could stay real.

And when he arrived in *Mickey 17*, it all made sense. A man built to regenerate. To die, reboot, and return – with fragments of memory and identity bleeding between versions. Pattinson wasn't just acting. He was being. Re-looping. Evolving. He didn't perform mastery – he lived recursion.

That's metaplasticity. The brain learning how to learn again.

Every loop doesn't start from scratch.

Sometimes, the loop returns – and this time, you're starting from higher up the spiral.

These weren't reruns. They weren't relapses. They were re-entries. Each of them – Simone, Beyoncé, Pattinson – hit a point where the rhythm changed. The old loop no longer fit. And each of them found their way back in. Not by forcing it. By feeling it. They recognised what was really happening. They understood what it meant. And they took necessary action – not always perfectly, but purposefully.

That's what a reboot is.
Not a reset. A return – with awareness.

And you'll need it too.
Because at some point, your rhythm will stall. Or snap. Or fade.
And when it does, the best move won't be to power through.
It'll be to pause, to re-loop – and begin again with rhythm.

REBOOT YOUR LOOP
Get back on your beat.

"A stumble may prevent a fall.
Don't curse the rhythm –
find your step again in the silence
between the notes."
– William Stafford

You've heard this beat before.
And you've felt the moment when you lost it.
That sick half-step. The too-early move. The stretch that didn't land.

This isn't about perfection. It's about return.
The body knows rhythm. So does the spirit.
So does the loop.

You're not starting over.
You're rejoining the phrase.

You start with a three-count beat.
Something your body can remember before your mind catches up.
Just three fingers on the table: fourth, third, second – and then the second again.
That's a rhythm.
Not a performance. Just a signal.
The smallest kind of loop.

Over time, that pattern expands.
Three becomes six. Six becomes nine.
What felt small and mechanical becomes fluid, expressive – yours.

That's how dancers learn.
Not by memorising every move in advance, but by internalising the rhythm
beneath each sequence.
The simple loops give rise to the complex ones.

And that's what allows you to dance with others.
Because they've learned the same foundational beats –
and when the moment changes, you respond.

Nobody moves well without counting in.

Four, five, six.

That's the invitation – the quiet gesture that says: I'm ready. Join me.

You RECOGNISE the shift in their rhythm.

You UNDERSTAND your place in the phrase.

And you take the NECESSARY ACTION to rejoin – not just to follow, but to dance.

Jewel McGowan, the queen of swing, didn't just keep time – she played with it.

When she missed a beat, she didn't freeze or flinch.

She turned the stumble into a swivel, the delay into a wind-up.

That's what the greats do: they don't erase the mistake.

They fold it into the rhythm.

Make it part of the music.

Maybe the stumble was the rhythm.

Maybe you missed your cue – and this is your next one.

Everyone loses the beat. Everyone falls out of sync.

But you're still here.

The loop is still running.

Count yourself back in.

TRANSCEND THE LOOP

You've now seen what it really means to live the loop.

Simone Biles showed us how rhythm can be broken – and rebuilt. Beyoncé showed us how a pattern can be repeated, upgraded, and then re-authored. Pattinson showed us that even when the loop feels like chaos, there is a way to act from inside it.

Lula taught us groove at scale. Tsai showed us the biology of sync.

And you've felt the shape of this chapter in your own rhythm: slow, slow, quick, quick, slow.

You've learned how action moves:

how to wait, and prepare

how to act, and adjust

how to store the gain and stage the next loop

The habits in this chapter weren't just behaviours. They were beat recognition devices. Timing tools. Ways to move through uncertainty without rushing. Ways to know when the loop is ready – and when you are.

You've rebooted. You've returned. But we're not done yet.

Because there's one thing left to do:
Transcend the loop.

Not leave it. Not discard it. But step forward with it – elevated.

Let's go.

You might not have noticed it happening – but you've changed too.

Somewhere between Biles and Beyoncé, between hot streaks and wrong loops, something in you has tuned. You've started to sense the rhythm in your own decisions. To feel the difference between speed and timing. To notice when you're forcing, and when you're flowing.

That's not just insight. That's adaptation.

You've learned how to pause without stalling.
How to act without overreaching.
How to return to the loop – not as a reset, but as a rhythm.

You're not done. But you're not where you started.
And now, we move one beat further.

RHYTHM IS ME: ELLA FITZGERALD

You've come through the loop. You've seen the five-beat cycle at work – slow, slow, quick, quick, slow. You've timed actions. You've waited, adjusted, returned. And now you're standing not just inside the loop – but beyond it.

Because rhythm, once internalised, is no longer something you follow. It's something you are.

This final movement is not about another lesson. It's about recognising what's already inside you – the sense of timing you've begun to cultivate, the recursive awareness that lets you know when to act and when to hold.

What does that look like, lived? What does it mean to move in rhythm – not occasionally, but continuously?

Ella Fitzgerald was a shy girl who survived by singing on the streets. After her mother died, she dropped out of school, was sent to reform school, and later worked the streets of Harlem as a lookout for gamblers. At 17, she walked onto the Apollo stage to dance – and changed her mind at the last minute. She sang instead. And the rhythm began.

She won. She joined Chick Webb's band. And then she changed American music.

She didn't just sing. She swung. She didn't just perform. She phrased, modulated, returned. Her scatting wasn't decoration. It was recursive brilliance – mistake into motif, breath into beat.

But rhythm isn't just rise. It's adjustment.

In the 1950s, she reached a breaking point. "I had gotten to the point where I was only singing be-bop," she later said. "I thought be-bop was 'it', and that all I had to do was go some place and sing bop. But it finally got to the point where I had no place to sing. I realized then that there was more to music than bop."

That was the pivot. The ramp became reinvention. With Norman Granz, she launched the Song Book recordings – Cole Porter, Duke Ellington, Gershwin. Not improvisation. Not escape. Structure. Depth. Timing. Return.

She didn't just adapt her sound. She adapted her identity. Not in one burst, but across decades. Across tempo. Across silence.

She moved through racism, sexism, genre boundaries, industry reinventions. And through it all, she kept time. She became timing. And in doing so, she became something rare: rhythm, remembered.

$$SLOW \rightarrow SLOW \rightarrow QUICK \rightarrow QUICK \rightarrow SLOW$$

You don't just take action anymore. You live it.
You move like rhythm lives in you.
And the loop you've just lived isn't something to follow anymore.
It's something you are.

You've moved through the loop. Felt the rhythm. Watched it break, return, and break again.

You've waited with intent. Acted with timing. Stored what mattered.
You've missed the beat, and found your way back in.

That's what rhythm is. Not perfection. Return.

The habits weren't just actions – they were rhythm-makers.
Each one tuned you to something deeper:
The beat of change.
The timing of choice.
The pause before power.

Slow-slow. Quick-quick. Slow.
That rhythm lives in you now.
Even if the names fade, the feeling won't.

You know what it's like to act too fast.
To wait too long.
To move without meaning – or miss the move altogether.

And now you know what it's like to return.
To re-enter.
To begin again with rhythm.

That's not just improvement.
That's transcendence.
The loop was never the goal.
It was the path.

You've lived it. Now let's step beyond it.

Because what comes next isn't just another move.
It's the pattern behind every move.

Let's find it.

RULE 8:
WASTE NOT, WANT NOT

The one about using energy to adapt

Superadaptable people don't hoard or waste energy. They redirect unused potential and see value in what others discard. Resourcefulness becomes a multiplier. Nothing is lost. Energy is found, focused, and looped.

In Rule 7, you learned how superadapters take action rhythmically – when to wait, when to move, when to adjust.

Now we explore the energy that makes that movement possible. This chapter isn't about working harder. It's about directing energy – reclaiming it, concentrating it, and rerouting it when the system gives you nothing for free.

Rule 8 introduces the energy loop: the hidden structure that helps superadapters use what they've got to change what they're in.

You'll see how energy can be recovered, redirected, and reused – looped not just to survive, but to transcend.

Every lifeform faces the same challenge: how to keep moving in a world that doesn't offer energy for free.

The fish needs oxygen. The wolf needs meat. The vine needs sunlight. Every species that survives does so by managing energy – finding it, converting it, storing it, spending it, and repeating the cycle without burning out.

Energy is not the opposite of stillness. It's the price of movement. And adaptation is the act of spending that price well.

Humans don't live the longest. We aren't the strongest. But our loops go further than any other species. We've learned not just to burn energy, but to budget it. To channel it through tools, culture, rituals, predictions, and plans. To loop it not only through our muscles, but through our minds.

That's what makes us adaptable. And it's also what makes us vulnerable.

Because energy is finite. The wrong loop burns it. The right loop builds it. And superadapters are those who know the difference – not once, but across cycles. They don't just act. They redirect. They reuse. They reduce loss.

They find. They focus. They flow.

D TO THE F TO THE H

At night, she rode the D train. Northbound. Over and over again.

Not to get anywhere. Just to stay safe. To stay warm. To stay moving.

Liz Murray had nowhere to sleep – not really. Not in the way most people think of sleep. She was fifteen, newly homeless, and riding the subway because it looped. Because if she stayed in motion, she wouldn't be seen. Wouldn't be stopped. Wouldn't be hurt.

The D train was a rhythm – her lullaby and her shelter. She learned to nap lightly between stations. To rest her head against cold glass. To fold her body around a backpack with everything she owned. She watched people step on, step off. Watched lives pass by, steady as steel.

In the mornings, she rode that same train to Manhattan. To alternative schools. Humanities Prep. Any place that might take her in. She'd walk block after block with addresses scribbled in her notebook. Take deep breaths outside buildings. Push open doors.

She studied in stairwells. Washed in public bathrooms. Ate when she could. She didn't waste a thing – not warmth, not time, not a scrap of kindness.

It wasn't just survival. It was direction. Energy, when focused, becomes something more than survival.

She found what little energy she had. She focused it on the one future she could see. And she flowed – through fear, through friction, through the dark, riding loops until the loops became forward motion.

Later, she would get into Harvard. But before that, she made the most of a train that never stopped moving. That was enough.

MOVEMENT TAKES ENERGY

That's the deep condition behind this chapter: movement takes energy. And adaptation depends on how that energy is used.

In the next section, we'll look at how superadapters manage it – not by working harder, but by finding, focusing, and repurposing what others miss. They scavenge. They strategise. They hack. They invent. They perceive, predict, and plan their way through energetic systems others don't even see.

You'll see the science that underpins it. You'll learn how energy loops through bodies, brains, systems. And you'll meet three key figures who don't just model it – they embody it. Each one rewires scarcity into strength. Each one shows how energy, handled right, becomes transformation.

Then we'll pause.

Not necessarily by sitting down – though you can if you like. You might be commuting. Walking. Standing. Running. That's fine. The Sitdown is a loop within the loop: a moment to reflect, recharge, and reloop from a different angle.

And after that, we'll get up again – into the part of the chapter where those loops come alive. In your life. In the world around you.

This chapter isn't just about energy.
It's about how to use it – to adapt, to act, to go again.

Let's begin with one question:
How do superadapters use energy?

THE ENERGY LOOP

HOW SUPERADAPTERS USE ENERGY

All life runs on energy. From the darting motion of an amoeba to the firelit planning of early humans, every living system must solve the same basic challenge: how to find, focus, and flow energy. Without it, there is no motion, no thought, no adaptation.

Superadapters are not exempt from this condition. But they manage it differently. They don't waste what they gather. They loop what others discard. They move through systems in a way that reduces loss and increases return. They treat energy not just as fuel – but as a signal, a structure, a form of intelligence.

$$\text{FIND} \rightarrow \text{FOCUS} \rightarrow \text{FLOW}$$

This is the core adaptive purpose of Rule 8:

FIND: Energy must be located, reclaimed, recovered. From rest, from rhythm, from what others ignore.

FOCUS: It must be placed precisely, not scattered. Energy that touches everything changes nothing.

FLOW: Energy must be kept moving through systems. This is where motion becomes momentum.

F^3 doesn't define what energy is. It defines how superadapters use it. This is the loop of adaptive energy use: the pattern that governs how energy is located, placed, and routed through a system. Find the energy. Focus it precisely. Let it flow. This is how superadapters move without waste – and adapt without burnout.

BRAINS LOOP ENERGY

As neuroscientist Lisa Feldman Barrett writes, even the simplest lifeforms must predict where energy will come from. An amoeba darts forward not randomly, but because its internal model says: there's something worth moving toward.

Human brains are prediction machines. Every action you take – every word, every decision – starts with a forecast: will this cost more than it gives?

The superadapters don't just act. They anticipate. They adjust. They choose loops that return more than they spend.

This is what makes superadaptability different. Not just using energy. Not just saving it. But looping it – so that every cycle adds capacity, increases clarity, and feeds the next round of change.

HABIT 1: DUMPSTER DIVE

We've just seen how energy can be redirected – how the body, without our conscious permission, prepares for effort. Predicts. Allocates. Pulls in resources from one system and channels them toward another. But redirection only works once something has been found.

The first move in adaptive energy use is Find. That doesn't mean waiting for ideal conditions. It means learning to notice what others ignore. To look again at what seems empty or broken, and see not junk – but junction. Not waste – but possibility.

That's where the first Rule 8 habit begins.

It's not a joke. The ability to see value where others see none is one of the most powerful superadapter behaviours. Because when a system gives you nothing, and the world looks dry – what you need most is the ability to re-see.

To recognise fuel in failure. To scavenge for signals. To find the beginning of a loop where no one else even sees a thread.

And no one showed this more clearly than a teenager in Malawi, who found something small, and looped it into something larger.

WILLIAM KAMKWAMBA

He was born in 1987 in a farming village outside Kasungu, Malawi – a country where the rains can make or unmake a year. In 2001, when he was just fifteen, the rains didn't come. The maize failed. The famine spread. And like so many others, William Kamkwamba dropped out of school, not because he lacked curiosity, but because his family couldn't afford the fees.

He still wanted to learn. So he began going to the local library. A one-room building with old chairs and older textbooks. And it was there, wedged between dry science manuals, that he found a tattered book called Using Energy. It had no narrative, no bold promise – just diagrams. But one of those diagrams sparked something.

That book wasn't just a curiosity. It was stored energy – the captured thinking, effort, and experimentation of someone William would never meet. But the loop had already begun. If he adapted better, it would be with the energy of others.

He read. He walked. He noticed. He began collecting things: blue gum wood, rusted bicycle parts, broken electronics. He wasn't building something yet. He was scanning the landscape for possibility. And in that moment, he wasn't just surviving – he was searching for a loop to enter.

This is the first movement in the energy loop: Find.

Superadapters don't start with ideal conditions. They don't wait for permission or certainty. What they do is notice – not just opportunity, but residue. Remains. Overlooked leverage.

Kamkwamba's story isn't about genius. It's about how energy gets redirected when a system breaks. It's about recognising that energy is always there – somewhere – but you have to learn to see it.

So as you read what follows, look for that shift.

Watch how Kamkwamba loops from famine to focus.

Watch how he finds what others discarded – and loops it into motion.

Because the first move in superadaptability isn't force.

It's finding.

THE SPARK

Some, as we discussed earlier, are born with superadaptability. Some achieve it. And some, like William Kamkwamba, are thrust into it.

He was fifteen years old when the famine came. His family, like many others in rural Malawi, was already stretched thin. Drought had ruined the harvest. There was no money for food, no money for school. He dropped out. Hunger thickened the air. In a world without options, he was expected to wait – to endure until the system shifted, or aid arrived, or something changed. But Kamkwamba wasn't waiting.

In this moment – this exact kind of moment – superadapters are made. He'd already recognised the problem. He understood the mechanism: no food without power, no power without change. And now, standing outside the loop of access and infrastructure, he began to seek what he could energise. Not with more – but with what was already there. No windmill yet. No blueprint. Just need, scarcity, and a question: what if I could build something that worked?

This is how it begins. Not with resources. With recursion.

THE SEARCH

The village library had a single tattered science textbook. It had diagrams, not instructions. But Kamkwamba didn't need instructions. What he found in those pages wasn't knowledge – it was a mechanism. A concept of how energy could be generated. A windmill, crudely drawn. Parts connected to function. That's all it took.

He didn't just read. He translated. He mapped the diagram onto his environment and began to model the system in his head. What could act like a rotor? What could serve as a frame? He searched scrap piles and old machinery. He looked not for perfection but for possibility. He wasn't collecting junk – he was building a loop. Each piece had to fit the model he was refining inside himself.

This wasn't a sudden burst of genius. It was a slow, adaptive spiral: detect, interpret, decide. Model, mechanism, modify. He was doing it all – without naming it. The textbook offered a glimpse. The real adaptation was what he did next: translate insight into components. Build, in his mind, a working system from nothing.

THE WINDMILL

The first blades were made of PVC pipes. The tower was built of blue gum trees, scavenged timber, rusted metal. The dynamo came from a bicycle lamp. Piece by piece, Kamkwamba assembled not a prototype – but proof. When the wind turned the blades and light flickered from the bulb, the system came to life.

It was potential – harnessed, wired, live. In a landscape where most saw absence, Kamkwamba had created motion. And not random motion: directed energy, flowing through a closed loop of need, retrieval, and reuse. He had converted scarcity into structure. No school, no electricity, no engineering degree – just an urgent loop rerouted through a teenager's mind and hands.

To build the windmill was to rewire the circuit. He had recognised the problem. He understood the structure. And now, he had acted in a way that didn't just adapt to the world – it changed it. He wasn't reacting anymore. He was routing power.

THE RECURSION

The first windmill lit a bulb. The second charged a battery. The third pumped water. Each iteration carried a new layer of purpose – not because conditions improved, but because the loop had started to feed itself. Kamkwamba's insight didn't stay local. It scaled. Neighbours came to watch. Journalists followed. A TED Talk. A scholarship. A book. But none of that was the real recursion.

The real loop was this: Kamkwamba took what the world discarded – scrap, silence, scarcity – and wired it into something that moved. And then, he did it again. Each reuse built not just output, but belief: in systems, in ingenuity, in the possibility that something could be salvaged from almost nothing.

That's what superadapters do. Not once. Not heroically. But repeatedly. Recursion isn't repetition – it's refinement. And Kamkwamba refined not just his windmill, but his method. Resourcefulness became system. System became signal. Signal became structure. From a library page to a national grid of possibility. And still: no waste.

WHAT HE SHOWS US

Kamkwamba's story isn't about brilliance under adversity. It's about energy. Specifically, how to route energy when the system gives you nothing. He teaches us the first essential move of superadaptability – to loop value from what others discard.

This is dumpster diving: becoming someone who can re-enter the system through the side door. Someone who looks again at what seems broken and sees not junk, but joints. Not failure, but fit. It's the habit of turning shortage into flow – not by resisting constraint, but by rerouting through it.

To watch Kamkwamba build that windmill is to witness someone energising a feedback loop from scratch. He wasn't waiting for tools. He was converting everything around him into potential – then into motion. His gift wasn't just vision. It was motion under pressure. That's the skill. That's the system. That's the method.

GLOBAL ECHO

Every culture has a word for it.

In India, it's *jugaad*. In Brazil, *jeito*. In Latin America, *viveza criolla*. In West Africa, System D. In English? Maybe it's hack, or kludge, or that phrase muttered under your breath: just make it work. Different languages, same instinct – to reroute energy through constraint.

Kamkwamba's windmill sits inside that global lineage. It's not an outlier. It's an expression. Whether it's a street vendor rewiring a battery to charge five phones, a chess player compressing cognition into blitz speed, or a farmer inventing a tool from bicycle parts – this is the shared improvisational engine of the world.

And it's not random. It's a loop. Recognise what's broken. Understand what could work. Act to make motion. Everywhere this happens, energy flows not because it's available – but because it's redirected. This Rule honours that truth. In Kamkwamba, we saw the first spark. In the next section, we'll see what happens when that spark is placed with precision.

Be a Dumpster Diver is not just a quirky phrase. It's the first movement in a system-level pattern. You start with what's overlooked. You collect, repurpose, ignite. You don't wait for energy – you reroute it.

Kamkwamba shows us that transformation doesn't begin with more. It begins with reuse. Superadapters don't hoard effort. They don't wait for conditions. They loop what's already there – and that loop builds momentum.

Next, we shift to placement. If Kamkwamba teaches you how to find fuel, Hikaru Nakamura shows you where to place it.

FROM FIND TO FOCUS

What Kamkwamba showed us is how the loop begins. Not with abundance, but with attention. Not with certainty, but with curiosity. He didn't start with power. He started with possibility – and the willingness to notice what others overlooked.

But noticing isn't enough.

Finding energy is only the first move. What comes next is the harder skill: placing it. Not losing it to noise. Not scattering it across distractions or illusions or false starts. Focus is what protects the loop once it begins.

Superadapters don't just hunt for energy. They concentrate it. They hold it long enough to do something with it. And that's not just an emotional discipline – it's an adaptive behaviour.

The moment you find energy – time, insight, attention – you face a new question:

Where should it go?

Because if it goes everywhere, it goes nowhere.

If it touches everything, it changes nothing. This is the move from Find to Focus. From noticing, to placing with precision.

And the habit that helps make that possible?

That's what we'll turn to next.

HABIT 2: SQUEEZE MORE

The second habit in Rule 8 is called Squeeze More.

And its purpose is simple: to help you focus your energy.

Not your time. Not your ambition. Your energy – the actual effort and attention your system can sustain. Because once you've found energy, the next question is where to place it. And that's what this habit teaches.

Focus isn't about doing less. It's about doing with intention. It's the ability to cut through distraction – not just external noise, but internal flood. To resist scattering, to keep your energy long enough in one place that the loop starts to return more than it costs.

That's what this habit helps you do.

Superadapters don't just save energy. They place it. Precisely. Deliberately. Repeatedly.

They learn to defend their attention. To guard the signal. To work with what's already in hand.

This is where energy becomes direction.

And no one shows that more clearly than the person you're about to meet.

HIKARU NAKAMURA

Some people are so good at using energy that it seems almost magical. So precise, so repeatable, that others accuse them of cheating. That's what happened to Hikaru Nakamura, after he won 45 out of 46 high-level blitz chess games online – an absurd hot streak that reminded some players more of code than cognition. One opponent commissioned a full statistical analysis to test for foul play.

The result? A 99.6% chance that Nakamura had not cheated. In other words: no foul. Just focus.

You might remember those hot streaks from Rule 7 – the moment when rhythm and readiness align. But Nakamura's gift isn't just rhythm. It's targeted energy under extreme constraint. No one is better at converting attention into performance at speed. In 2022, he was given the key to the city of Memphis, Tennessee, for his contribution to chess. But what he really earned was the key to looping energy with perfect placement.

Nakamura was born in 1987. A chess prodigy by nine. An American grandmaster by fifteen. But it wasn't just his talent that stood out – it was his capacity to focus fast, under pressure, for long stretches, and still find clarity in chaos. He's known for his blitz mastery: three-minute games where each move costs energy, and hesitation means defeat. You don't win those matches with force. You win with flow.

He's also a public figure. A streamer. A teacher. A provocateur. He's rejected diagnostic labels, particularly those that would define him through stereotypes of mental difference or neurological disorder. Instead, he focuses on what attention makes possible.

In his own words:

"It's easy to become angry, but when you get better, you channel your energy into the game. No matter how badly you play, unless you make a flat-out blunder, there's always going to be some narrow path to being able to save the game and draw instead of losing."

So as you read what follows, watch what he does with his energy.

Watch how he doesn't expand. He contracts.

How he doesn't force. He selects.

How every move is made not with more – but with less, better.

Because Don't Waste Anything isn't about doing more.

It's about placing energy so well that it starts to return more than it costs.

THE BLITZ ENVIRONMENT

At three minutes per game, there's no time to hesitate. No time to calculate seven moves ahead. The clock is louder than your thoughts. And yet – this is where Hikaru Nakamura thrives.

Blitz chess looks chaotic from the outside. Pieces snap across the board. Players slam timers with the flat of their hands. Spectators see speed and spectacle. But inside Nakamura's loop, there's something else: clarity under compression. Not chaos. Compression. In that shrinking window of time, he doesn't just react faster – he places attention more precisely. He doesn't conserve energy. He concentrates it.

This is not about working harder. It's about routing pressure into performance. Nakamura doesn't outthink his opponents by expanding. He adapts by squeezing more use out of every second, every signal, every flicker of insight. While others burn time calculating, he loops – detect, decide, place. The game doesn't slow down. His loop speeds up.

In Rule 8, this is what energise() looks like at velocity. Not more force – just better flow.

THE UNFOLDING LOOP

In blitz, there's no luxury of pause. But watch closely, and you'll see Nakamura isn't rushing. He's placing. His mind doesn't skip steps – it runs them tighter. Detect → Interpret → Decide. Over and over, inside seconds. What looks like instinct is actually a collapsed decision tree. He's not avoiding thought. He's compressing it.

Each game is a moving system. Opponent patterns. Time pressure. Board dynamics. Nakamura doesn't just respond to the surface – he models the mechanism beneath it. In his head, positions aren't pieces. They're probabilities. Patterns. Traps. Force sequences. But he doesn't calculate them all. He identifies what matters most. Then he strikes.

This is what it means to energise under constraint. He doesn't speed up to match the clock. He routes cognition differently. His precision comes not from more effort, but from better attention. There's no wasted energy. Blitz isn't chaos for him – it's clarity revealed by compression.

NONTRADITIONAL PATHWAYS

For most grandmasters, the path to success is fixed: federation support, tournament ladders, long-format prestige. Nakamura broke that pattern. He took his game online. Twitch. YouTube. Speed chess arenas. Not as gimmick – but as system. In blitz, every move is content. Every mistake is feedback. Every game is a loop.

It wasn't just a brand – it was an ecosystem. While others measured their progress in trophies, he was testing cognition live, in front of thousands, iterating in public. His rise came not from legacy systems, but from platforms that rewarded fast loops, high engagement, and visible precision. It didn't dilute his ability. It refined it.

This too is part of the habit: Squeeze More Use is not just about time. It's about context. Attention. Format. He made the system work for him – not by overpowering it, but by redirecting it. He placed his energy where it could move. And in doing so, he multiplied it.

PRECISION OVER EXCESS

Nakamura doesn't win because he does more. He wins because he does less, better. In blitz, most players burn energy trying to see everything. He doesn't. He sees what counts. It's not about being faster. It's about being selective. The wrong move at speed is still wrong.

This is the myth Squeeze More Use dismantles: that adaptation under pressure means effort, intensity, exhaustion. But superadaptability doesn't mean sprinting – it means placing pressure where it shifts the system. In Nakamura's case, that means not reacting to the whole board, but locking on to the single weak point that unlocks the rest.

There's no overflow. No scatter. His loop is tight. He places energy like a scalpel, not a floodlight. What others waste in breadth, he returns in depth. This isn't hustle – it's economy. Not minimalism for aesthetic, but compression for function. He gets more not by expanding, but by constraining – beautifully.

LOOP LOGIC

Every game runs the loop. But in Nakamura, the loop runs fast – and deep. He doesn't wait for full clarity. He detects a shift, interprets the frame, decides the move. Again. Again. Again. While others are still choosing their lens, he's already placed three pieces into play.

This is not guesswork. It's loop fluency. The speed isn't recklessness – it's repetition converted into recursion. A model forms. A mechanism reveals itself.

He modifies just enough to reroute the board. No excess. No overcorrection. Just the right adaptive move, placed in the right moment, with the right cost.

That's the habit. Squeeze More Use isn't just about squeezing more effort. It's about squeezing insight. It's how superadapters rewire their energy loop – not to power through, but to power toward. In chess, it looks like a quick strike. In life, it might look like decisive restraint. Either way, it's the same engine.

PATTERN FOR YOU

This isn't just about chess.

Everyone faces blitz moments. The inbox overflow. The interview. The crisis call. The choice under pressure. And in those moments, the question isn't how much energy you have – it's where you place it.

Squeeze More is the habit of routing limited attention to maximum effect. It's where you shift from overthinking to clear targeting. When the window narrows, you don't panic. You narrow your focus with it. What matters? What moves the system? What can I act on now?

This is how superadapters energise under constraint. They don't collapse. They don't scatter. They make each move count. That's not hustle. That's leverage. And it doesn't take brilliance – it takes placement. A deliberate act, made just in time, with just enough force to shift the whole board.

You don't need more hours. You need better moves.

Nakamura shows us what happens when energy is placed with purpose.

This is the second move in Rule 8's loop. After you've salvaged what others missed, you don't scatter effort – you squeeze more use from what you have. Focus becomes fuel. Pressure becomes clarity.

DUMPSTER DIVE → **SQUEEZE MORE** → USE EVERYTHING

Each habit builds on the last. Together, they form a loop that energises not by force, but by flow. You don't power through the system. You route power into it.

Next: constraint sharpens. Emotion rises. We enter the third habit – where pressure becomes structure.

FROM FOCUS TO FLOW

Not every situation lets you hold your focus. Some situations take everything you have – and still ask for more. This is where the loop starts to break. This is where flow is fractured.

Let's just pause and think about this.

You've been in moments where nothing is working. The plan fails. The rhythm collapses. The energy you'd gathered scatters through cracks. You don't feel stable. You don't feel powerful. You don't feel like a system. You feel like a person grasping for a lifebuoy – trying to save just a little more time, just a little more strength.

In those moments, your body does something remarkable. It re-diverts. It shuts off nonessentials. It searches. It sends a last flicker of energy toward whatever might help you re-establish the loop.

And this isn't weakness. This is adaptation.

When Julianne fell from the sky in our prologue, she couldn't focus. She couldn't plan. She couldn't flow. All she could do was breathe – strip oxygen from air with a throat that barely opened. And her body knew: save what you can. Even when everything is broken, the loop still tries to loop.

That's what flow is.

It's not grace. It's not beauty. It's movement through friction. It's energy redirected through constraint, trying to continue.

And that's the move we're making now – from Focus to Flow. And from Nakamura to Dostoevsky.

HABIT 3: USE EVERYTHING

The third habit's purpose is simple, and often urgent: to help you restore flow – not by powering through, but by rerouting what you still have. Because sometimes, you're not in a hot streak. You're not building momentum. You're just in the middle of a crisis, trying to stay upright.

Superadapters don't conjure flow from nothing. They repurpose it. They look around – at tools, tasks, failures, fragments – and ask, what still has use? What can I redirect? What can I rebuild from the pieces?

This isn't optimism. It's not a mindset. It's a method.

And no one lived that method more precisely, more painfully, and more productively than the man you're about to meet.

FYODOR DOSTOEVSKY

The crux of our next example takes place in 1866, and it unfolds in just one month. But by that point, the man at the centre of it had already lived several lifetimes.

He was born in Moscow. He trained as an engineer. He published his first novel to applause, and his second to silence. He joined a literary-political circle. He was arrested, sentenced to death, marched to the scaffold – then spared at the last minute.

He spent four years in a Siberian prison camp, shackled with leg irons for most of it. He developed hemorrhoids. He lived in a cell with an inch of dirt on the floor, which he slipped on frequently. He spent six more years in military exile, forced to beg, often broke, often sick, often alone.

And then something changed.

Perhaps it was fate. Perhaps it was focus. But in that final stretch, with no time left, he did something remarkable. He wrote.

In just 26 days, he dictated a novel that pulled from every loop he'd ever lived: obsession, risk, addiction, shame. It wasn't clean. It wasn't polished. But it worked.

He didn't just find a plot. He found a use – for pressure, for failure, for flaws. And what he created wasn't just literature. It was motion. It was flow.

So as you read what follows, look for how he loops.

Not around success – but through collapse.

Not in rhythm – but in rupture.

Not because he had resources – but because he found a use for everything.

THE DEADLINE GAMBLE

St. Petersburg, 1866. Fyodor Dostoevsky is forty-five, broke, and out of time.

The Russian literary giant, already weighed down by debt and past political exile, has made one gamble too many. He's taken an advance on a novel he hasn't written – and if he doesn't deliver it within twenty-six days, he'll lose the rights to all his work. No more royalties. No more second chances. No margin for error.

What does he do?

He places a new bet.

He hires a stenographer. Her name is Anna Grigoryevna Snitkina. Twenty years old. Brilliant. Unknown. He dictates the novel aloud – sometimes frantically, sometimes barely coherently – and she records it, word for word. The novel is *The Gambler*. A book about risk, self-destruction, obsession. A book that mirrors his own life so precisely it feels less written than excavated.

But here's the twist: it works.

Not just the book. The system. The loop. The crisis doesn't crush him – it clarifies him. The deadline, the debt, the desperation – they don't break his loop. They energise it. He doesn't run from constraint. He uses it. He builds a structure from pressure. A partnership from panic. A career-saving move from collapse.

A limit becomes a lever – what psychologists call an affordance. A structure that suggests an action. A deadline isn't just pressure. It's a grip. A bet. A move.

THE STENOGRAPHER AND THE STRUCTURE

Dostoevsky didn't just meet his deadline. He built a process.

Anna wasn't just a note-taker. She became his second brain, his rhythm, his method. They worked in tight cycles – dictation, feedback, revision. She brought pace. He brought chaos. Together, they created structure. *The Gambler* was completed in time. But more than that, something repeatable had been forged. A loop that could survive pressure, not just react to it.

This is the heart of the habit. Find a Use for Everything means you don't discard tension – you channel it. Dostoevsky used urgency to force clarity. He mined his gambling addiction for plot. He repurposed his romantic turmoil into narrative turn. The constraint wasn't overcome. It was converted.

He would later marry Anna. Their loop would continue. More books. More structure. Less collapse. What began as survival became a system – not just for writing, but for living. Emotion. Pressure. Pattern. Recursion. He didn't tame the chaos. He turned it into sequence.

THE GAMBLER'S LOOP

In *The Gambler*, the protagonist spins between risk and ruin, seduced by the high of uncertainty. It's fiction, yes – but it's also autobiography. Dostoevsky didn't just write the gambler. He was the gambler. He'd pawned his future, again and again, betting that something – or someone – would appear to rescue him. This time, one did.

But what matters isn't just the rescue. It's the reuse. He didn't write his way out despite his addiction. He wrote his way out with it. That's the loop. He took his most volatile flaw and turned it into form, theme, engine. He didn't suppress it. He shaped it.

Superadapters don't ignore the system. They reroute through it. Dostoevsky sacrificed one outcome – security – for another uncertain path. He leaned into the risk, looking for affordance: a move the structure allowed, if he acted precisely. He bet on recursion. He won.

And then he did it again.

PATTERN FOR YOU

Everyone meets constraint. A deadline. A loss. A trait they wish they could shed. Most people try to outrun it. Superadapters don't. They ask a different question: What can I make from this?

That's what Find a Use for Everything teaches. You don't just work under pressure – you work with it. You use the tension in your life like wire in a circuit. Energy flows through the parts you thought were broken. A bad habit becomes a plotline. A crisis becomes a container. An obstacle becomes a rhythm.

This isn't just about optimism. It's about recursive optimism – the belief that something better is possible because you are willing to look for it, act on it, and shape the conditions that allow it to emerge. You don't hope passively. You intervene precisely.

Dostoevsky didn't conquer his chaos. He looped it. He turned collapse into cadence. The page into process. The constraint into a creative algorithm.

You don't give in – unless it helps you to win. You create space. Especially when it feels like there's none. You shift. You breathe. You reroute.

Nothing discarded. Everything re-used – even you.

DUMPSTER DIVE → SQUEEZE MORE → **USE EVERYTHING**

Some people burn out. Others break through.

The difference isn't more energy. It's better loops.

Constraint isn't the end of motion. It's the beginning of reuse.

This habit isn't just about surviving limits.
It's about rethreading them.
Reusing them.
Refusing to discard the parts of yourself you can still use.
But not the end of the loop.

THE ENERGY LOOPER: PUTTING IT ALL TOGETHER

You've now seen how superadapters use energy – one habit at a time.

You've seen what it looks like to Find energy where none appears to exist. To notice the discarded, the overlooked, the neglected – and loop it into motion. You've seen what it means to Focus energy with surgical precision – placing attention in a system so fast-moving that most people couldn't even follow. And you've seen how to Flow energy through pressure, through collapse, through everything that would normally stop you – and keep going.

Each of those habits – Find, Focus, Flow – matters on its own. But the real power comes when you can loop them. Again. And again. And again.

That's what our next figure shows us.

Soichiro Honda didn't represent just one stage of the loop. He lived the whole circuit. And he did it over decades, across crises, teams, countries, setbacks, and breakthroughs. He's the Energy Looper – the one who didn't just solve problems, but designed systems that could keep adapting without him.

He was born in a small Japanese village, the son of a blacksmith. As a child, he saw a car for the first time and was so overwhelmed by its motion – so stunned by the idea that something could move under its own power – that he chased it down the road without even thinking why. That was the pattern. He chased energy. And then he learned to build it.

Later, he said that without racing, "there is no Honda." And he didn't just mean the company. He meant himself.

He once said that the value of his life could be measured by how many times his soul had been deeply stirred. That success was the visible 1% of a life built on 99% failure. That to build anything worthwhile, you'd need people you didn't understand. People you might not even like. You'd need their energy too.

He believed in machinery. But he believed more in people.

And what he shows us now isn't a single skill or a single strategy. It's the ability to loop energy through time. Through scarcity. Through difference. To reuse. To redirect. To attract and absorb what you don't yet know how to use – and build something from it anyway.

Because superadapters don't just manage energy. They make systems that loop it.

SOICHIRO HONDA

Long before he built engines, Soichiro Honda built a stamp.

He was a boy in a small Japanese village, expected to bring his homework home each night with a parent's seal. His family was poor. His father, a blacksmith, worked long hours. Some nights, there was no one to stamp it.

So Honda made his own.

He carved it himself. Clean lines. Careful shape. A signature that would pass. It wasn't deception. It was design. Not rebellion – but recursion. The problem wasn't just that homework needed a stamp. The problem was how the system handled verification. Honda didn't break the rule. He redesigned it.

It was the first object he built that stood in for a parent. And it carried the first mark he would later make famous.

The logo didn't say "Honda."

But the habit did.

SCARCITY AND SCRAP

After World War II, Japan was rubble. Honda's factory had been bombed. Materials were scarce. Fuel was scarcer. But instead of waiting for conditions to improve, he did what he'd always done: he looped what remained.

He scavenged cast-off military engines, broken generators, and scrap metal from bombed-out buildings. Some of it he called little gifts from Truman. He wasn't being ironic. He meant it. The waste of one system became the seed of another.

His first postwar creation wasn't sleek. It was ugly. A bicycle with an engine bolted on. But it moved. That was enough. It was faster than walking. Stronger than silence. He didn't call it a revolution. He called it a start.

This wasn't survival. It was system creation under constraint. He didn't just make a motorbike. He made a method: use what exists, compress the form, and keep it moving.

The war didn't end his work.

It cleared space for the loop.

THE MACHINE THAT DOESN'T STOP

Honda's first engine-bicycle didn't look like the future. But it moved. And once it moved, it didn't stop.

He refined the model, adjusted the form, scaled the production. Not because resources appeared – but because the loop allowed it. One working part led to another. One success paid for the next. Each machine wasn't just a product. It was a proof. The process worked. The constraint held. The structure responded.

This wasn't genius. It was repetition with awareness. Salvage became system. Compression became capacity. Scarcity became scale. His business didn't grow because he solved scarcity. It grew because he kept finding new uses for what others overlooked – materials, designs, disciplines, even defeat.

He didn't call it a philosophy. He just called it what worked.

And yet: the engine outlasted the man. It outlasted the rubble. It remade the road.
The machine didn't need to be beautiful.
It needed to move.

And it did.

PATTERN ECHO

This wasn't genius as an isolated act.
It was creatively aware repetition – a set of cognitive behaviours that produced a genius outcome.

And here's the thing: genius always is.

The greats aren't just lucky or brilliant. They loop. They salvage. They compress. They convert. Not once, not twice – but habitually. Under pressure. Across systems. Through failure.

That's the shift.

From talent to pattern. From moment to method. From spark to engine.

Kamkwamba, who turned scrap into signal.
Nakamura, who made seconds decisive.
Angelou, who turned silence into sequence.
Picasso, who stole.

And when the loop is built right –
the engine keeps running.

You don't always start
with enough energy.
But if you follow the curve,
if you move, even a little,
energy can be found…

It's not a straight shot.
It's a search pattern.

THE SITDOWN: THE SOIL (AND THE SEED)

WHY WE SIT DOWN NOW

"Energy is a very subtle concept. It is very, very difficult to get right.
But everything goes because the sun is shining."
– Richard P. Feynman

We don't sit down to switch off. We sit down to reflow the energy.

This is Rule 8 – the one about energy: how we find it, how we focus it, how we learn to let it flow through us without losing our shape. In the last section, you saw what happens when we harness energy to transform environments, lives, and systems. But now, we're asking something deeper:

How does energy transform us?

That's why we pause here. Not to collapse – but to observe the form energy takes when we stop pushing. To feel its rhythm return in a quieter, more integrated way. This is the Sitdown where the body replays what it learned, and the mind prepares for something new.

In a dusty courtyard in Brazil, a circle of people clap and sing as two players in the centre sweep and kick in a graceful duel. This is a *capoeira roda* – part martial art, part dance, all improvisation. You crouch at the edge of the circle, catching your breath from your own turn sparring moments ago. As you watch the veterans feint and flow, you're not just resting; you're learning. Your eyes track their movements, and without realising it, your brain's motor neurons fire in sympathy, rehearsing the motions. In capoeira, much of the education happens on the sidelines.

This pattern – intense action followed by attentive pause – is central to how we acquire complex skills. A capoeirista enters the roda, tries a combination, then steps out to observe others. In those minutes of observing, the mind integrates what the body just attempted. Neuroscientists talk about 'mirror neurons', cells that light up both when you perform an action and when you see someone else perform it. In the roda, as you sway and sing along, those neurons are training you. You're internalising that slick escape move or the timing of a perfectly executed kick, all while sitting on your heels.

Many arts and sports have similar rhythms. A basketball coach might bench a player to watch the game flow before sending them back in. A jazz ensemble's novice might learn by quietly absorbing the band's improvisations until it's their moment to solo. We grow through this dance of engagement and observation. In the lively circle of capoeira, as in life, sometimes you advance by stepping back – the pause is not defeat, but a strategic part of the play, honing your instincts for when you jump in again.

This is that moment.

Sit down.

Let the energy you've gathered take a new shape.
Let it move you differently.
Let it root.

CARVER: HIS SEED AND HIS SOIL

Here we begin with a man who turned what others called waste into a way of thinking. A scientist, yes. But more than that: a teacher of transformation. A fellow human who nurtured himself as carefully as he nurtured the land. George Washington Carver didn't simply rise. He looped – from constraint to creativity, from discarded material to embedded meaning. His mind became a system. His life became an energy loop.

He began in the dirt.

Not the soil of abundance – but the soil of absence. Born into slavery, torn from his family, Carver was raised in obscurity, sickly, orphaned, unseen. And yet even as a child, he saw something that others had discarded: potential. Not just in the earth – but in himself.

He left.
Walked away from the place that didn't see him.
Walked toward education, toward cultivation, toward meaning.
He carried no money. Just faith, talent, and a hunger not to be wasted.
He knew what it meant to be treated like a weed.
He became a master of seeds.

Carver didn't invent the peanut. He reinvented the story of what a peanut could be.
Just as he didn't invent the soil – but refused to let it remain barren.
His move: from overlooked to essential.
From 'Mr. Carenot' to the man who testified before Congress.
Energy, repurposed.

514

Wasted matter, turned into growth.
And through every loop, every adaptation – Carver returned again and again to the same truth:
Where the soil is wasted, the people are wasted.
Where the people are wasted, the future is wasted.
But if you see what's hidden, what's possible, what's seed and not scrap –
You will grow something the world didn't expect.

He lifted himself. And then he lifted others.
So nothing – no child, no peanut, no acre – had to be wasted again.

SEEING WHAT WASN'T THROWN AWAY

He didn't begin as a scientist. He began as a noticer.

George Washington Carver was the kind of child who listened to plants before he ever spoke to people. His neighbours called him 'the plant doctor' before he could spell it. Sickly, solitary, turned away from the fields where stronger boys worked, he wandered the woods instead – collecting bark and roots, sketching leaves in chalk, naming flowers by sight and scent. He gathered what others stepped over. He examined what others cleared.

And in those quiet, self-directed loops, a habit formed.
Everything that seemed useless had a second life.
Everything overlooked held a pattern.

The habits of attention became the start of something else.
An adaptive mind. A system of reuse. A recursive ethic.
Not because someone told him to study waste – but because waste was all he had.

As he grew older, Carver began walking to school. Not across a town – but across counties. Ten, twenty miles at a time. He carried his books in a bundle and traded chores for places to sleep. When he arrived at a classroom that would finally take him, he was already far beyond the syllabus. He knew what the textbooks didn't teach: that observation is not a luxury, it's a technology. And he had been refining it for years.

He painted. He cooked. He built his own pigments from crushed plants. He fixed shoes. He carved tools. He coaxed colour out of clay. Every time he mastered one material, he folded it into another. There were no silos. No waste streams. Only possibilities.

This wasn't invention in the Edison sense.
It wasn't innovation as novelty.

It was transformation by necessity – looped into meaning by attention.

He didn't rush the answer. He tuned in.
He studied what others ignored until it revealed what it had to offer.

"Anything will give up its secrets if you love it enough," he said.

And that was the ethic that powered everything else:
Attention before action. Affection before extraction.

Because as Carver knew, energy and information are everywhere.
The real challenge is attention.
Energy ebbs, energy flows.
It can neither be created nor destroyed.
It can only be discovered, directed, and reused.

THE LAB AND THE LOOP

At Tuskegee Institute, Carver finally had his own laboratory. But it didn't
look like one. There was no polished steel. No gleaming beakers or stocked
storerooms. The benches were wooden. The shelves half-empty. Much of the
equipment had been salvaged, repurposed, donated, or improvised.

   To others, it looked like poverty.
   To Carver, it looked like opportunity.

He had spent a lifetime building with less. What mattered wasn't abundance – it
was the ability to see energy where others saw lack. If something had potential, it
could be looped. If it could be looped, it could be taught.
   His lab became a cathedral of reuse. Students arrived expecting formulas. They
were given systems. Loops. A moral logic of attention. If a material was close
at hand, it was worth investigating. If it had been thrown away, it might be the
most important thing in the room.

   Carver rarely worked on just one project at a time. He believed in the
resonance between tasks. Testing the properties of sweet potatoes led him to
new glues, paints, and starches. Studying the husk of a peanut taught him how

to isolate oils, dyes, and building materials. A fungus on a rotting stalk might unlock a treatment for disease. Nothing was still. Everything was process.

When asked why he studied the peanut so deeply, Carver said: "I asked the Lord what to do with the peanut, and He showed me."

It wasn't metaphor. It was method.

He asked. He waited. The answer came back.

Observation as conversation. Use as response.

Inside the lab, his students learned to listen. Not just to chemicals or reactions, but to the quiet feedback of method. They learned to repeat a trial not because it failed, but because it hadn't yet revealed its full utility. They learned to combine disciplines, to connect texture with tension, heat with hue, time with transformation. They learned that waste isn't a condition. It's a perspective.

Each of Carver's experiments carried an echo:

Use what you have.

Learn what it holds.

Embed what it teaches.

He didn't just make new things. He made new kinds of thinking. His students weren't taught to chase novelty. They were taught to build recursion – to design processes that got smarter with every cycle.

That's what the lab became.

Not a place for production.

A place for embedded intelligence.

Carver showed that the lab didn't need to change to produce change. The change came from within the loop – from the way materials were seen, handled, looped again.

He called it 'service'. Others later called it 'innovation'.

But what it really was, was embedded adaptation.

A system for making energy useful again.

And again.

THE MORAL ECONOMY

When George Washington Carver was invited to speak before Congress in 1921, he arrived without spectacle. He brought no lab coat, no entourage, no credentials to wave. What he did bring was a basket.

Inside were samples – powders, pastes, textiles, pigments. All of them drawn from the waste streams of American agriculture. Cast-off shells. Dried leaves. Ground peanuts. Fragments of cotton stalk. Things no senator in that chamber had ever looked at twice.

He laid them out like tools. And then he began to speak.

Soft-voiced, unhurried, deeply prepared, he explained how every item on the table had been transformed from what others had discarded. He didn't use technical jargon. He used insight. Insight made repeatable. Insight embedded into method.

And for a moment – even in that room, even in that era – something shifted.

He told the story of a humble seed.
How it could be used for oil, protein, glue, paint.
How it could support the soil that supported it.
How it turned waste into sustenance. Scarcity into surplus.
How what had been left behind could lead someone forward.

The senators asked him questions. He answered each with patience and pattern. What he offered wasn't just a catalogue of uses. It was a philosophy of utility. The loop wasn't hidden in the data – it was the data.

And the moral was clear:
If you waste energy, you waste people.
If you ignore what's left over, you ignore what's possible.

Carver didn't go to Congress for funding. He wasn't there to win applause. He was there to demonstrate a principle:
That adaptive energy isn't measured by scale – it's measured by return.
That no system can claim to be efficient if it keeps throwing people and resources away.
That value isn't found. It's made. Through loops. Through attention. Through design.

He knew he wasn't the country's vision of a modern scientist.
Black. Poor. Polite. Unflinching.
He also knew that he didn't need to be.

He had already built the system.

The waste he brought into that room wasn't decoration. It was evidence.
Evidence that transformation could be taught.
That recursion could be cultivated.
That the future wouldn't be built from what was shiny – it would be built
from what survived.

And as he finished his testimony, you can imagine one senator whispering to
another: "That man has turned frugality into a religion."
For George Washington Carver, the seed and the soil were never just
agricultural realities. They were spiritual propositions. They were moral
geometry. If the soil was depleted, it wasn't just poor farming. It was poor seeing.
Poor stewardship. Poor systems. And the seed? That was the test. Could you
take something small, inert, overlooked – and help it become something living?
Could you do it again? And again?

He believed you could.

Not every seed will grow. Not every soil will respond. But Carver's lesson was
never perfection. It was pattern.
Waste nothing. Want for less. Become more.

That was his ethic. His loop. His method for living.
And he returned to it constantly. With students. With crops. With faith.

Even in his last years – stooped, fragile, walking with a cane – he would kneel
beside fields at Tuskegee and run his fingers through the dirt. Not to plant. To
listen. To remember that what people throw away often still contains everything
required to grow.

SEED → SOIL → SUN

Transformation, Carver knew, is never just one thing.
It is structure, placed well, powered rightly.

It is attention. It is effort. It is timing.
It is what you begin with, where you plant it, and what energy you bring to it.

It is an extraordinary thing, when you stop to think about it, that a seed – no
larger than a fleck beneath your fingernail – contains within it the instructions to
turn sunlight, soil, and water into life. The earth around it looks inert: dust, grit,
a scattering of broken rock. But given time, touched by light, and mixed with
water, that lifeless ground becomes a partner. A conduit. A loop.

And the sun – blazing ninety-three million miles away – casts energy into the
void. Plants alone have learned to trap it, to store it, to build from it.

Inside that seed, the machinery of life stirs. Roots push downward. Shoots
lift upward. Light is caught, sugars formed, structure shaped. It is, as Richard
Feynman once said, the closest thing we know to a miracle.

George Washington Carver understood that miracle – not just in theory, but
in practice. He lived it. He looped it.

He found the nutrients in hardship, the sunlight in obscurity, the structure in
constraint.

He didn't just rise from the soil.
He transformed the soil itself.
And in doing so, he taught the rest of us: nothing is wasted.
Not if you know how to use it.

Carver showed us what it means to build something real – something
regenerative – out of loss. But that kind of loop doesn't come from hope alone. It
comes from knowing what to do when energy is low, resources are scattered, and
time is running out.

So before we move on, let's look a little deeper at how energy works – when it's
scarce, when it's stuck, and when it starts to move. A way to map the habits we've
seen into the systems we live in.

FIND → FOCUS → FLOW

Let's walk through what energy really looks like at each phase of the loop.

FIND: ENERGY AT THE EXTREMES

All life seeks energy. That's not metaphor – it's physics. Whether you're a moss cell or a magpie, you find what you need or you fail. And for the simplest life forms, that search begins before anything we'd call thinking. It begins with motion.

Take the amoeba. It doesn't have a brain, but it does have something astonishing: a prediction engine. A tiny loop of action and feedback that helps it move not randomly, but in response to its world. It wiggles left, gets nothing. It wiggles right, finds glucose. Loop complete. Try again.

This kind of exploratory movement is so universal it has a name: the Lévy walk. You see it in bacteria. In bees. In birds. In ancient hunter-gatherers. Even in you, when you're looking for a coffee shop you can't quite remember the name of.

The logic is simple: lots of short bursts, then a long stride. Wiggle-wiggle-stride. Loop back. This pattern allows creatures to cover territory efficiently – not just with hope, but with strategy. Because what you're really doing is modelling the environment. Testing hypotheses with your feet. Or fins. Or flippers. Or prefrontal cortex.

Human beings do this too – but with upgrades. We search with memory. We search with language. We extend the Lévy loop beyond instinct, into culture. From the first fire-makers to the Polynesian ocean navigators, we foraged outward. We pushed the loop wider. We turned FIND into flight.

But what's often forgotten is that this wasn't aimless wandering. It was targeted exploration, driven by need – then honed by culture. And when humans hit the edge of what they could find, they learned to build instead. The Inuit didn't just arrive in the Arctic. They survived there with seal oil lamps, snow-block shelters, community intelligence systems passed down in story. They found energy, focused it, and looped it forward.

Even today, the same loop runs – though now we call it gig work. Or migration. Or hustle. Every parcel delivered is the result of someone else's energy being looped through you, by you, for something you need. We're not post-amoeba. We're post-forager. But the loop remains.

And here's the part that matters: FIND is not the whole loop. It's the start of it. It's the moment you open your eyes to scarcity, to potential, to motion. But what happens next – how you direct that energy, how you shield it, how you use it – that's where we turn next.

FOCUS: HOW WE USE WHAT WE FIND

Once humans discover a new source of energy, they don't just save it – they try to shape it into power.

Fire is the classic case. First discovered, then controlled, then mastered. Around two million years ago, *Homo erectus* likely learned to manage fire, not just to stay warm or ward off predators, but to cook. And cooking, it turns out, was not just a culinary breakthrough. It was a biological one. Cooked food gave more calories per bite. Easier digestion meant smaller guts, and smaller guts meant spare energy – some of which went toward building bigger brains. The Expensive Tissue Hypothesis suggests that fire gave us cognition. Cooking gave us focus.

You see this principle everywhere. Energy is found – but it's focus that makes it usable. The Inuit, living in harsh climates, developed metabolic adaptations to process extreme diets. The Bajau Sea Nomads evolved enlarged spleens to better manage oxygen reserves during deep dives. Tibetans reprogrammed their red blood cell response to high altitude. In each case, focus wasn't about narrowing. It was about converting energy under constraint.

Focus is a form of design. It turns environmental inputs into usable outcomes. It's how we learned to irrigate fields, domesticate fire, use gravity, shape tools, coordinate hunts, and craft the first rituals and stories. You can see it in the way we build settlements. In the way we light cities. In the way we craft silence around what matters most.

And it's not just physical. It's cognitive. Focused thought is metabolically expensive. Your brain accounts for about 2% of your body mass – but uses around 20% of your energy. Which means what you attend to quite literally determines how your energy gets used. The human brain is a lens. Focus is the act of aiming it.

We've created technologies to help us focus. Monasteries, libraries, headphones, calendars, reminders, thresholds, routines. These aren't accidents. They're architectural tools for catching the Find and channelling it into motion.

Because if FIND is the start of the loop, FOCUS is the narrowing beam that lets the loop run. And once energy is focused, something else becomes possible. Movement. Momentum. Flow.

FLOW: WHAT KEEPS THE LOOP ALIVE

Flow is what lets us go on. Not just move, but repeat. Sustain. Loop.

It begins the moment energy, once found and focused, enters a structure that can carry it forward. That structure might be your own habits. It might be your family. It might be the entire infrastructure of your culture. Flow is sustained energy – and the systems that remember how to use it.

That remembering is often invisible. Sociologists call it habitus – the embedded, inherited behaviours we don't think about, but that shape how we think. How you greet someone, how you hold a spoon, how you decide who is 'us' and who is 'them'. Habitus is what happens when a flow becomes so repeated it starts to feel like nature. And sometimes, that's helpful. Sometimes, it's not.

Because flow isn't always freedom. In fact, it can be the opposite. A river flows fastest in its deepest channel. That doesn't make the path right. It makes it rehearsed. This is the tension. Flow is efficient, but that efficiency can be dangerous. It's how energy loops can become ruts. How tradition becomes dogma. How coordination becomes conformity.

But flow is also how we build everything. Teams. Tunnels. Rituals. Rail networks. Languages. University departments. Festivals. Family dinners. It's the quiet harmony that lets energy accumulate into effort, and effort into outcome. Focus directs. Flow sustains.

The paradox of the Sapient Paradox is that our brains got big long before our cultures did. For almost two million years, we had all this energy – in the form of cognition – but very little infrastructure for sharing or sustaining it. One genius couldn't always loop others in. The super-sapient might see the flame, but not pass it. Culture is what turned sparks into circuits.

But even culture can constrain. It carries what's known – and sometimes ignores what's needed. We see this in the stories of those who resist inherited flows: those who question caste, challenge gender norms, disrupt inherited power. They aren't disrupting flow. They're introducing friction – for the sake of a better loop.

Friction isn't failure. It's formative. It tells you where energy isn't moving cleanly. Every system, even a personal one, needs to listen for its own grinding. When something resists, don't just push harder. Rethink the path.

Flow and friction are inseparable. One sustains momentum. The other signals where change is needed. And to live well inside any loop – your own or a society's – you need to work with both.

THE THIRD MIND

In our exploration of energy, we've looked at finding, focusing, and extended flow. But the most powerful expression of all three happens when one mind meets another – and something new begins. A third mind. Neural alchemy.

Sometimes we call it collaboration. But this is something deeper. Not help, not support. Not a sounding board. A loop. You don't just share ideas – you reroute each other. The loop gains velocity, intelligence, and texture. And when it works, it feels less like conversation and more like recursion.

You think a thought. They return it differently. You return it again. And somewhere in that mutual shaping, a third intelligence arrives. Not in either head. Not in the space between. But in the loop itself.

That's the third mind.

William Burroughs and Brion Gysin knew this. They invented a method to show it: the cut-up and the fold-in. The cut-up disrupted expectation – breaking up a finished page into fragments, rearranging it to find something hidden. The fold-in layered two texts at once, vertically aligned, then read across. A new sentence emerged. A third signal. A buried message in the folds.

They called the result The Third Mind. And it went beyond metaphor to become method.

David Bowie borrowed it. First with scissors, then with software. He called it the Verbasizer. Sentences from different places. Cut, rearranged, relooped. Not noise – signal, reshaped. Songs built from patterns he didn't yet know he'd thought.

This is what recursion looks like in art. A loop that thinks differently each time it's run. A structure that surprises its own creator.

And sometimes, it doesn't take a machine or a method. It just takes a partner.

This is more than collaboration. It's co-recursion. It's cognitive structure made of people.

Philosophers call it the extended mind. Psychologists call it transactive memory. Artists call it intuition. You might just call it knowing what someone else would say before they say it – and writing the next line together anyway.

It doesn't happen all the time. But when it does, it's not just productive. It's profound.

One mind. Two minds. A third begins.

One mind. Two minds. Three minds. More.

LIVE THE LOOP

HOW TO LIVE THE LOOP
This is where the loop lands.

This is the part where we braid it all together. Where the examples return. Where the Sitdown becomes a step-up. Where the ideas take shape in your own life.

You'll meet familiar faces again – Kamkwamba, Nakamura, Dostoevsky – and see how their energy loops didn't just begin and end. They recursed. They adapted again. And again.

So will you.

Welcome to the part where practice meets principle. Where energy is not just found, but re-circulated. Where we stop wasting, and start living the loop.

Let's go.

HOW THEY LIVED THEIR LOOP
You've seen the principles by now. But what you've really been seeing is energy – found, focused, and flowed – through lives that made the loop their own.

William Kamkwamba showed us what it means to find energy where others see none. A broken bicycle. A book no one else picked up. Scraps of wire and tin. He didn't wait for permission. He didn't ask for more. He saw more – and built a working windmill before he'd turned fifteen.

Hikaru Nakamura taught us how to focus energy without wasting it. Blitz games. Bullet games. Deep analysis. Twitch streams turned into training programs. He doesn't just move through formats – he loops them. Every input gets repurposed. Every challenge becomes data. Even when accused, he looped the energy back – clarity as counterattack.

Fyodor Dostoevsky taught us to flip energy under constraint. Imprisoned. Condemned. In debt. He wrote his way back to solvency, yes – but also to love, to meaning. He didn't escape the system. He metabolised it.

Soichiro Honda's life reminded us that focus isn't only personal – it's systemic. Every failed engine, every factory floor adaptation, every machine tweak – he wasn't chasing innovation for its own sake. He was tightening the loop: less loss, more reuse.

And George Washington Carver returned us to the earth – to the soil and the seed, to the loops within loops: How do we leave the energy we've found for others to use? How do we regenerate – not just in ourselves, but in systems?

525

You've seen energy converted, scavenged, redirected, restored. Not just conserved – but re-authored. Not just protected – but remixed.

This isn't just theory. It's your loop now.

And in the next few pages, you'll feel it: The catch of movement. The stillness of focus. The recovery of energy you forgot you stored. The turning point where scarcity loops into creative force.

We're not trying to make you efficient. We're trying to help you move – not burnt. Energised.

FIND → FOCUS → FLOW

STRETCH IT BACK INTO SHAPE
How energy returns, if you let it loop.

Today is one of those days when I've spread myself thinner yesterday than usual. I had the elation of finishing Rule 7 completely, but also the added stress of a decorator showing up, and a publisher's meeting that pulled me out of the work rhythm and into planning mode – PR, production, sales, layout, prizes, positioning.

By the afternoon, I was thinking about Rules 8, 9, and 10 all at once, rather than just the next block. That's when I started to feel the stretch – the thinning. Bread scraped over too little butter. I snapped at someone close to me, only slightly, but it was there. I went to bed not quite right.

This morning I tried to find the thread again. I started with notes. Drawing, because drawing always helps. Sketching, diagramming, figuring out where I'd been and what I was building. Then jogging. Then dictating while jogging. Then coffee. Then motion became focus again.

I used to do jiu-jitsu with my daughter. We'd drive to training, talking the whole way – sometimes missing our turn because the conversation mattered more than the route. That's energy, too. Use, not waste.

And now, I think it's time to return to the people we've been learning from. The kid who built windmills from scraps – his book was called *The Energy Book*. Nakamura, squeezing more use from every second on the clock. Dostoevsky, gambling on constraint and finding creativity. George Washington Carver, restoring the soil so others could plant.

So now we're entering the phase where you live the loop. Or live your loop. Your way of finding and using energy. Let's enjoy it.

CATCH-'EM-ALL
Hyper-curious, adventure-prone, and other diagnoses they missed.

I've always been in motion. Not because I was restless or out of control, but because I was already following something. Energy, maybe. Curiosity. A loop I didn't know I'd joined. I was out of my cot before nine months. Throwing myself onto the floor. Running. I remember the flat in Muswell Hill, north London – the room near the kitchen, the thud of the floor, my mother nearby. I didn't toddle. I launched.

They said I was hyperactive. They meant it as concern. Dr. Spock was still the voice of parental wisdom, and movement, especially fast movement, was considered a symptom. But I wasn't a problem child. I was an energy system in action. And it's never really stopped.

I pulled a television down on myself once. Crushed my finger – left index. The top came off. A doctor found the tip, put it in a matchbox, and had it sewn back on. You can still see the line. I've been skeered on railings, fractured my arm, earned stitches from multiple angles. I was never accident-prone. I was adventure-prone. And always moving.

That's why I still play Pokémon Go. Not because I care about the creatures, but because it gives me an excuse to move. To see what's just around the corner. I've played it in Rio favelas and across Kuwait rooftops. I've sprinted at 3am. for one I hadn't caught. Last week, my watch said I'd covered 187 km – just while 'working'. That didn't include the times it ran out of battery.

I used to walk my youngest to school every morning. It was our ritual. But when he hit high school, the rules changed: I could only walk him to the gate. So I kept walking. The habit didn't need a reason. The loop had embedded.

I don't just move to burn energy. Movement generates energy. The more I move, the more I want to. The more I notice. The more I notice, the more I move again. That's the loop. That's the system. It's not external. It's not imported. It's me.

I've never really stopped catching them. Only now, I realise – I might have been catching pieces of myself all along.

FREE AT THE POINT OF USE
Don't forget what you've already got

Even particularly clever squirrels forget where they buried the good stuff. And so do we. Sometimes the energy you need is already there – you just haven't looped back to it yet.

Superadaptability isn't just about effort. It's about remembered effort. It's about knowing how to reaccess the energy you – or someone else – already spent. That's how sapiens become supersapiens. Not through more work, but through better loops.

Think about it. A screwdriver is stored energy. So is a washing machine. So is a list. So is every language, every lesson, every note you've ever taken. Someone else did the thinking, the forging, the failing. And now, if you know where to look, it's free at the point of use. Provided you can find it again.

Superadapters don't start from scratch. They don't reinvent the loop. They enter it at the point of power. They loop back to what they already knew. They reclaim what they already built. They store with the intention to recover.

I leave myself notes sometimes. Notes to say: you've got this. The part you need is already here. Look harder. Think again. There's a book on the shelf. A tool in the drawer. A friend you can call. A half-formed idea just waiting to finish looping. You've got this – because you've already laid the ground for it.

This isn't just cognitive. It's cultural. All culture is stored energy. All teaching is an act of conservation. Why write anything down? Because the future version of you, or someone like you, will need it. That's what a recipe is. That's what a formula is. That's what the person who first cracked fire was doing: leaving energy for the next to pick up.

Psychologists call this 'effectuation': starting not from what you lack, but from what you already have. What can you make happen with what's lying around – mentally or physically? It's not just cause-and-effect. It's what effect you can cause.

So here's the rule:

Leave energy for yourself.
But leave it somewhere you'll return to.
Store it not just in place, but in habit. In visibility. In loop.
You don't need more strength. You need better memory.
Free at the point of use. That's what superadaptability looks like. You've already done the work. Now find it again.

THE DEADLEG DANCE

When I was a kid, in a house bustling with four siblings, a cat, a dog, and the usual chaos, the bathroom became my quiet zone. I'd slip in, close the door, and sit – often with a *Reader's Digest* in hand – and before I knew it, I'd be gone. Not physically gone, of course, but gone into a world of words and focus, the outside noise fading to a distant hum.

And then, when I finally stood up, came the Deadleg Dance. That awkward little shuffle-hop, grabbing the sink or the wall, as the pins and needles rushed back into a leg that had fallen asleep.

Most people explain this simply: the edge of the seat presses into the back of your thigh, compressing blood vessels, slowing the flow of oxygen, pinching off nerves. It's like bending a garden hose – the water doesn't stop existing, but the delivery is blocked. That's why your leg isn't out of energy – it's that the energy can't reach where it's needed.

But here's the thing: while the blood was blocked at one level, it was flowing somewhere else. My brain, deep in focus, was pulling resources. More oxygen, more glucose, more neural firing – all being redirected toward the mental work at hand. Some of that would have happened no matter where I sat, but by carving out this private moment of stillness, I'd allowed my mind to seize those resources fully, to channel them into what I was reading and learning.

Even though I hadn't consciously planned to sit and read for an hour, my body – which includes my brain – was already preparing, already predicting the demands ahead. This is known as predictive regulation, or allostasis: the body's quiet, continuous way of anticipating what's coming and budgeting its energy before the need even arises. I might not have realised I was setting myself up for a dead leg, but some part of me was already feeling its way forward, already allocating resources where they were needed most.

It's not quite the same as conscious thought, but it is a kind of body-level intelligence – a way of sensing and steering that even a single-celled amoeba can perform. And if an amoeba can do it, you can be sure my body could do it, and so can yours.

That deep focus I reached, that sense of absorption where time slipped away and the world narrowed to a single point of attention – that's often called a flow state. It's the mental sweet spot where challenge meets skill, and for a while, we become completely engaged in what we're doing.

Sometimes, it felt like time itself bent: seconds stretching into minutes, minutes folding quietly into hours. The bathroom became a kind of fulcrum – a balancing point where the busy weight of the outer world tipped into the stillness of the inner one. It was where I could sit, concentrate, and let the scattered noise of life fall to one side while I tipped myself fully into focus.

Other people have their own fulcrum spots – park benches under trees, corners of libraries, quiet car rides, even the backseat of a bus. Any place where the balance tilts, where we settle in and let ourselves pivot from distraction to absorption, can become a small lever for adaptation and change.

So yes, on one level, it's just a kid sitting in a bathroom with a numb leg. But at another, it's a beautifully orchestrated act of energy management: the body diverting, the brain predicting, the whole system adapting to let something important happen – the work of learning, focus, and change. And maybe that's the real lesson here: the Deadleg Dance is funny, yes, but it's also a tiny example of how we make adaptive leaps – how we gather, channel, and balance our resources to meet the moment.

FROM TRAPPED TO TRANSCENDED
How energy becomes momentum

This is the pivot. Not a summary. Not a decorative pause. A moment of realisation.

You've seen how superadapters use energy – not just to move, but to keep moving. Not just to act, but to build momentum.

The habits in this chapter weren't traits. They were tools. Each one helps you find, focus, or flow energy – even when it's scarce, misfiring, or buried beneath failure.

And it often is. Energy gets lost. Not just through fatigue, but through doubt, distraction, disconnection. What traps us isn't just effort – it's effort misapplied. Energy pointing in the wrong direction.

But that's what the loop is for. It retools energy. It teaches motion. It turns fragments into patterns. And those patterns – when looped – become power.

You've seen that with William Kamkwamba, turning scrap into rotation. With Hikaru Nakamura, converting chaos into precision. With Dostoevsky, who took punishment and constraint and re-forged it into meaning.

And maybe most of all with Honda.

He didn't just build engines. He chased energy. Literally. The first time he saw a car, he ran after it – barefoot, in awe. Not even knowing why. That's what energy does to us when it's moving right. It stirs the soul.

He once said that success is 99% failure. And he meant it. Not as a shrug, but as a system. That all energy – when used well – is not wasted, but woven. That even when you fall short, the pattern continues. You're building something. And that something will stir others.

In Japanese, there's a phrase: 一粒万倍 *(ichiryuu manbai)*. It means one grain, ten thousandfold. From a single seed, a great harvest. One loop – run well – can change everything.

You don't need to see the table to understand it. Just remember: if energy feels scattered, or wasted, or lost – it isn't. Not if you loop it. Not if you use it. That's what this Rule was always about.

	TRAPPED	TRANSCENDED
Dumpster Dive	Always waiting for permission, perfect timing, or ideal conditions. Misses what's already available.	Spots useful material in any setting – even if it's flawed or overlooked. Creates options from scraps.
Squeeze More	Wastes energy in the wrong place. Chases novelty, panics when things get hard. Focus scatters.	Targets the pressure point. Applies effort exactly where it matters. Knows the value of constraint.
Use Everything	Repeats inefficient routines. Blames others for delays. Adapts to bad systems without questioning them.	Designs smoother loops. Changes the mechanism, not just the behaviour. Builds structure that helps.

THE WRONG LOOPS

All loops can go wrong. And as we've seen elsewhere, the good news is, they tend to go wrong in predictable ways.

Instead of getting lost trying to find energy, or confused attempting to flow it, or distracted while needing to focus it, you can use the three-way diagnostic that recurs throughout this book. This is one of the core benefits of recursive thinking: You don't need to invent a new framework for every failure.

Here, that means returning to a simple triad – used across all the Rules, adaptable to any loop.

But in Rule 8, the focus is energy. And that means learning to spot the three kinds of energy misfire that block momentum, exhaust capacity, or drive the system in the wrong direction.

When you master this, you don't just upgrade your ability to energise – you upgrade your ability to notice what's not working before it spirals.

HYPO happens when there's too little energy, the energy is too late or too slow. You might be trying to do the right thing – but without enough energy, the loop doesn't run. And here's the crucial part: the moment your energy drops below a certain threshold, the problem you thought you were solving has already changed. The goal might still look valid, but the system conditions have shifted.

Now, you're not choosing between success and failure – you're choosing between two new moves: restore the energy required to act, or redesign the loop so that it matches your current capacity. What traps people is that they don't notice the shift. They keep pressing on, trying to complete the original loop, but the context has moved. HYPO isn't just about being tired – it's about failing to adapt when the fuel runs low.

HYPER happens when there's too much energy, the energy arrives too soon or too fast. Sometimes energy is available, so we use it – not because the system is ready, but because we feel we have to act. Or because taking action is just too easy. And while the early surge can look productive, it often short-circuits the loop. You get premature motion without meaningful direction. Individuals burn out. Systems lose coherence. Too much energy too soon creates clutter instead of clarity. It can lead to overbuilding, overcommitting, or simply exhausting momentum before purpose is fully formed. Worse, when energy is abundant and easy to spend, it's often wasted. And in that waste, you may create new problems – ones that only exist because it was so easy to move. HYPER doesn't just drain the future – it distorts the present. Not because your intentions are wrong, but because your energy is out of rhythm with the loop.

ANTI happens when the wrong kind of energy is used or energy is applied in the wrong direction. As a kid, I once plugged a car radio into mains electricity. I was confident, curious, and just informed enough to be dangerous. The shock threw me across the room. The lesson was instant, although not always remembered. Not all energy is compatible – and some forms of power are just unusable. They are actively destructive. ANTI energy loops follow the same logic. The system is energised, yes – but the action it powers is misaligned. Maybe the effort is real, but it's aimed at the wrong task. Maybe the drive is authentic, but it's built on guilt, resentment, or borrowed ambition. Or maybe the system's just so used to running hot that it burns through everything it touches. The result is the same: activity without adaptability. Energy without use. A kind of damage that only becomes visible once the fuse is blown.

I won't waste your energy listing every possible example of the three-way diagnostic. You already know how to feel it. And now you can apply it to yourself. Notice what's missing, what's misfiring, or what's misaligned. In the next section, you'll see how these patterns play out in the real world – when people energise the wrong loops, and then what it takes to recover the right ones.

REAL WORLD WRONG LOOPS
All the wrong energy in all the wrong places.

We've all killed a plant.

Sometimes it's too much water. Sometimes not enough. Sometimes it's the wrong kind of soil, light, or fertiliser – and the plant wilts even though we thought we were helping. That's what energy misfires look like in the real world. It's not that we didn't care. Or didn't act. It's that the system couldn't handle what we gave it – or needed something different. Too fast. Too little. Or in the wrong direction. Every adaptive loop can fail this way. And you don't always see it until the leaves start falling.

Outside of plant care, energy loop failures are an under-recognised part of why things stay trapped.

And once you start looking, you see it everywhere – loops that didn't transcend their traps because no one could supply the right resource. The crux wasn't belief, or insight, or intent – it was energy. The ability to find, focus, and flow the right kind to the right place at the right time.

I promised you three examples, and here they are:

HYPO often happens when people return again and again to a problem they agree is urgent, valuable, even inevitable – but no one fixes the energy loop. High-speed rail is a perfect example. Japan, China, and much of Europe have built thousands of miles of track. The systems work. The returns are real. And still, in other countries, the same questions keep being asked – studies launched, budgets revised, plans announced – only to stall or reset. And as time drags on, the cumulative energy spent not building it begins to outweigh the cost of building. This is what happens when no one finds, focuses, and flows the energy needed to push a decision into practice. Leaders prefer not to choose. And the system loops itself, endlessly. That's lost loop bias.

HYPER is so often caused by the belief that energy will be infinite, and the compulsion to act simply because you can. During the Apollo era, NASA was flush with momentum. Money flowed – not just financially, but structurally. Instead of designing a recursive next step, they repeated what they already knew how to do. The goal became repetition, not evolution. And the belief that funding and focus would continue indefinitely led to complacency. When the

Cold War shifted, the sources of energy dried up. A permanent lunar base – frugal, purposeful, and costed at a fraction of Apollo – was on the table. But it was never built. The chance to launch a higher-order loop – solar satellites, lunar infrastructure, space-based internet – was missed. The small step was taken. The next giant leap never came.

ANTI happens when the wrong energy is used or energy is applied in the wrong direction. In the buildup to the heavyweight championship, UK fighter Daniel Dubois shoved and insulted Oleksandr Usyk at the weigh-in. Dubois used anger to energise. A false motivation that disappeared soon after the real fight started.

Usyk ran a quieter system. A knockout combo he and his team had named 'Ivan'. Two years of focused energy.
   In Round 5, Ivan landed.
   Dubois was beaten. His energy gone. In the fight between revenge and recursion, there was only one winner.
   Each of these failures occurred not because success was impossible, but because the energy was wrong. Too little, too fast, or misdirected. But that's not the end of the story. The habits that built the energy loop can also rescue it. And that's what we'll look at next.

THE COUNTER LOOPS
Three ways to right the wrongs.

The great news is that the care instructions that came with your plant can actually help you rescue it. Or to put it another way: the habits of the energy loop don't just prevent failure – they repair it. Because failure is going to happen. That's reality. Bienvenue.

DUMPSTER DIVING counters HYPO failures – the kind where energy is missing and the loop can't get started. It works by shifting you out of passivity and into scavenger mode. You stop waiting for perfect conditions and start looking for usable ones. Dumpster diving means scanning for underused time, leftover momentum, neglected materials, half-built plans, contacts you forgot you had. It's a mindset that says: the energy might not be where you expected – but it exists somewhere. People do this when they make a prototype out of spare parts. When they repurpose an old campaign. When they borrow a venue instead of building one. When they get the thing done on a laptop that's half-broken because the real deadline can't wait. If this habit had been used more consistently in high-speed rail efforts, we might have seen scaled-down pilot lines, regional patchwork networks, or shared-rights-of-way that moved projects forward instead of stalling at square one.

SQUEEZE MORE is how you counter HYPER – the kind of loop that runs too fast, spends too freely, and burns out before it builds. It's not about stopping. It's about redirecting. HYPER loops fail because energy goes where it can, not where it should. Squeezing more means applying pressure where it matters most – and withdrawing it where it doesn't. It's a practice of focus and refocus. Not hyper-focus. Not tunnel vision. But the ability to shift your attention to the more helpful part of the system – the piece that leads to transcendence, not just momentum. There's always more than one thing to do. There's almost always something better to do. Squeezing more means twisting, recalibrating, and reorienting what you already have to release something better. It's not about efficiency for its own sake – it's about creating slack, freeing energy, and opening possibility. That's what NASA missed. In the rush to repeat Apollo, they didn't restructure the loop. They didn't squeeze more – they just spent more.

USE EVERYTHING counters ANTI failures by shifting attention away from purity of input and toward adaptability of output. It's not about using more energy – it's about using more of what you already have. That means repurposing emotions you'd normally reject. Ideas you'd dismissed. Strengths you hadn't owned. Use everything you've been through. Use what you've buried. Use the things you thought didn't count. This habit works in any system – professional, strategic, structural – but let's focus here on the personal. In relationships, this means redirecting blame into clarity. It means folding in fear or regret and letting it inform what you ask for next. It means recognising that your emotional energy isn't the problem – the misdirection is. And when you stop thinking of priorities as singular, and selfhood as segmented, you get back the full range of motion. People like you do this. They just didn't know they could.

So there you have it. It's a one-to-one fix and repair system. Although, and this is important, noticing where it's going wrong is going to need something else. And that something else is the RUN loop. That's the thing you've got to reboot. Reboot and keep running.

REBOOT THEIR LOOP

Not because they were perfect. But because they returned.

You've already seen the loop at its best. How people find their energy, focus it, share it, loop it back. But what happens when even that breaks down?

This isn't about failure. It's about re-entry. The system still works. These three just had to prove it again – under pressure.

RECOGNISE → UNDERSTAND → NECESSARY ACTION

REBOOT 1 – WILLIAM KAMKWAMBA

He didn't belong in the classroom. At least, that's what the official list said. His name wasn't on the roll. His fees weren't paid. And so, on the first day of term, while the others filed into assembly, William ducked behind the latrines and waited.

He stayed low. Watched through the cracks. And when the courtyard emptied, he slipped in like a shadow. Into the classroom. Back row. Head down.

He didn't ask questions. Didn't raise his hand. "As long as I'm silent, I can listen. I can still learn." That was the rule. Not written down, but felt in the stomach.

He managed two weeks before they caught him. The moment his name was called in front of the class, his whole body went still. Then he stood. Walked. Quiet. Outside.

He told his father. His father went to the school. Pleaded. Promised the tobacco crop would cover the fees. It wasn't much of a promise. But it was enough for three weeks.

The money didn't last long, but that's not the important part of the story.

The important part is the way his superadaptive mind rebooted the loop each time it was blocked. No fees. Sneak in.

He looped before there was a windmill. Before the library. Before the fame.

He recognised. Understood. Took action.

REBOOT 2 – HIKARU NAKAMURA

Once, it was all speed. All pressure. The loop was pure velocity: study six hours, perform on demand, win or collapse. And in the early years, it worked. Hikaru Nakamura made his name with tempo. Lightning-fast decisions. Risk. Precision under fire.

But somewhere along the way, something shifted. Streaming started. The edge softened. The loop widened. He started enjoying the game again – not just the victory. And when the pressure returned – when he lost in round two of the

2024 Candidates Tournament – he didn't spiral. He studied. He laughed. He showed up the next day and won three games in a row.

He wasn't calmer because he stopped caring. He was calmer because he had somewhere else to send the energy. The loop was open again. The system had margin.

Even Nakamura – the speed genius – had to learn to slow the loop, reroute the current, and find a different rhythm for return.

He recognised what was happening. Understood what was needed. Took action.

REBOOT 3 – FYODOR DOSTOEVSKY

After they married, Fyodor and Anna didn't go on a honeymoon. They went on the run.

Germany first. Then Switzerland. Then Italy.

Berlin, Baden-Baden, Geneva, Vevey, Milan, Florence.

It was less a grand tour than a carefully timed escape route.

Each time a debt caught up, they moved again. Each time a publisher caved, they wrote again. The loop was familiar, even comforting in its own distorted way. Money came in. Gambling took it out. The ring was pawned. A coat sold. Then, somehow, a manuscript. A telegram. A reprieve.

They stayed just long enough to write.

Just long enough to breathe.

Then moved on.

Anna was the difference. Not just a copyist, not just a wife. She was a counterbalance – practical, loyal, steel behind soft eyes. She read the ledgers, watched the odds. And when Dostoevsky couldn't stop gambling, she quietly built the scaffolding to publish *The Idiot, Demons, The Gambler* itself.

Dostoevsky had made a bet, once – a literal one – that he could finish a novel fast enough to keep his rights. He did it, barely, dictating through the night with Anna taking notes. That was earlier. What followed was the proof.

He kept moving.

He wrote while they ran.

And somewhere along that long road, he stopped writing just to survive and started writing something deeper – with space, with weather in it, with God.

By the time they returned to Russia in 1871, the debts were paid. The books were better. And the loop – flight, focus, finish – had done its work.

Not a gamble.

A system.

A kind of necessary momentum.

They didn't reset everything. They just looped again – cleanly, deliberately, in a way that let the system restart without breaking.

You've seen how Kamkwamba re-entered the system by sneaking in, and staying in. You've seen how Nakamura shifted the flow. And how Dostoevsky outran collapse long enough to rewrite the rules.

Now it's your turn. But before you restart – step back. Let's look again at how loops really reboot. What you just saw wasn't just story. It was structure.

REBOOT YOUR LOOP
Inhale. Loop. Exhale. Begin again.

*"When the breath is unsteady, the mind is unsteady.
When the breath is steady, the mind is steady."*
– Svātmārāma, Haṭha Yoga Pradīpikā, Chapter II, verse 2

We've reminded you to breathe before. But since breathing is quite important for life – I'm going to remind you again.

You'll probably remember the idea we explored in earlier chapters of living the fractal life. You'll remember the term fractal. You'll remember my invitation to live a fractal life.

This is relevant here because by using the RUN loop – these three steps – you're adopting a pattern you've already been living. One that all life follows. But by naming it, you can shift it from being a kind of junkyard of mismatched habits and thoughts… to something a little more examined, a little more deliberate.

When stress rises, breath shortens. When breath shortens, thought narrows. That's not weakness – it's biology. Shallow breathing cues your nervous system to brace, constrict, conserve. It shifts you into survival mode.

But one long exhale can tilt the loop. Three slow breaths can reoxygenate your brain, restore your sense of space, and reset the system – linked to the vagal nerve that calms your heart and reopens your mind.

You can't control your vagus nerve directly. But you can influence it. Long exhales, breath rhythm, gentle vocalisation – these ancient tools are now backed by neuroscience.

Breathe in: energy.

Breathe out: excess.

Again. Again.

This three-step rhythm can be your mantra. Silently guiding your breath.

One, two, three. One, two, three.

That's the metronome of a better mind.

Stay in the breath. Inhale, hold, exhale. One, two, three. One, two, three. Not just once. For as long as you need. Let this be your first loop.

RECOGNISE the overwhelm.

UNDERSTAND that oxygen changes everything.

And don't rush the NECESSARY ACTION.

Stay inside the breath loop until you can emerge – centred, stable, able to face the external world.

You've got to breathe to stay alive. Obvious – but nevertheless profound. First breath to last breath. So we might as well get better at it. That's the breath – or the belief – flowing through this book.

This is your most minimal meta-habit. It takes 10 seconds. And it works.

TRANSCEND THE LOOP

You've seen energy loop and return.
You've watched people rebuild it – sometimes painfully, sometimes beautifully –
until momentum wasn't just a force outside them,
but something they could generate on command.

This wasn't a chapter about hustle.
It was a chapter about harnessing.
About finding what flows, and then learning how to hold it,
focus it, embed it – without letting it fossilise.

You saw it in the farmers, the inventors, the near-collapse survivors.
But maybe you saw it first in Honda –
a boy chasing a car down a dirt road,
not because he wanted to ride it,
but because he had to know how it moved.
Because some part of him already understood
that to ride energy, you first have to chase it.

And some people never stop chasing.
They run not toward engines, but toward expression.
They wire their lives so the current builds quietly.
And then, one night, they strike the match.
Not to burn out. But to burn forward.

One of them is waiting on the next page.

THE LONG ROAD (AND THE TWO WEEK MYTH)

The famous story goes like this: Jack Kerouac wrote *On the Road* in a furious, almost divine burst – three weeks in April 1951, typing without pause onto a 120-foot scroll of tracing paper sheets he had glued together himself. He didn't use paragraph breaks. He didn't stop to edit. He fed the scroll into his typewriter and let it run. It was single-spaced, no margins. It felt unstoppable. That's the story.

But that's not the whole story. That scroll didn't come from nowhere. Before that three-week streak, Kerouac had already written a full earlier draft. He'd spent years filling notebooks, writing letters, collecting vignettes. He'd been out on the road, absorbing everything. That's where he found the energy. And what looked like sudden flow was really the release of something long built and stored. What looked instant had been slowly looping for years.

Even after that legendary burst, the book wasn't finished. He hit friction. The scroll sat. Publishers passed. Edits took months. The final version didn't appear until 1957 – six years later. And even then, it met resistance. First praised, then attacked, then canonised. It would eventually be named one of the greatest novels of the 20th century. But it had to loop through resistance and refinement. The flow had to re-route.

He didn't just find the energy to write *On the Road*. He found energy in the very things others might throw out – scraps of memory, moments of regret, even stillness. Then he focused it, shaped it, flowed with it – until it ran out. And then he looped again.

Find. Focus. Flow.

TRANSFORMED ENERGY → EMBEDDED ACTION

You've followed energy across every loop.
You've seen it scavenged, focused, shared, sparked.
You've watched it stall – and watched it return.
Through others. Through crisis. Through recursion.

But this Rule wasn't just about energy.
It was about action.
Not the kind that burns out.
The kind that stays.

To adapt is to move.
But to embed?

That's what makes the movement last.
Because what we're building here isn't momentum.
It's memory.
Structured. Stored. Ready to be used again.

The loop isn't just running.
It's running through you now.

What comes next?
Not just energy.
Not just movement.
But the right cut.
The one that makes the change hold.
The one that edits the loop itself.
You've carried the energy long enough.

Don't just carry the energy.
Use it.
Don't just edit.
Embed.

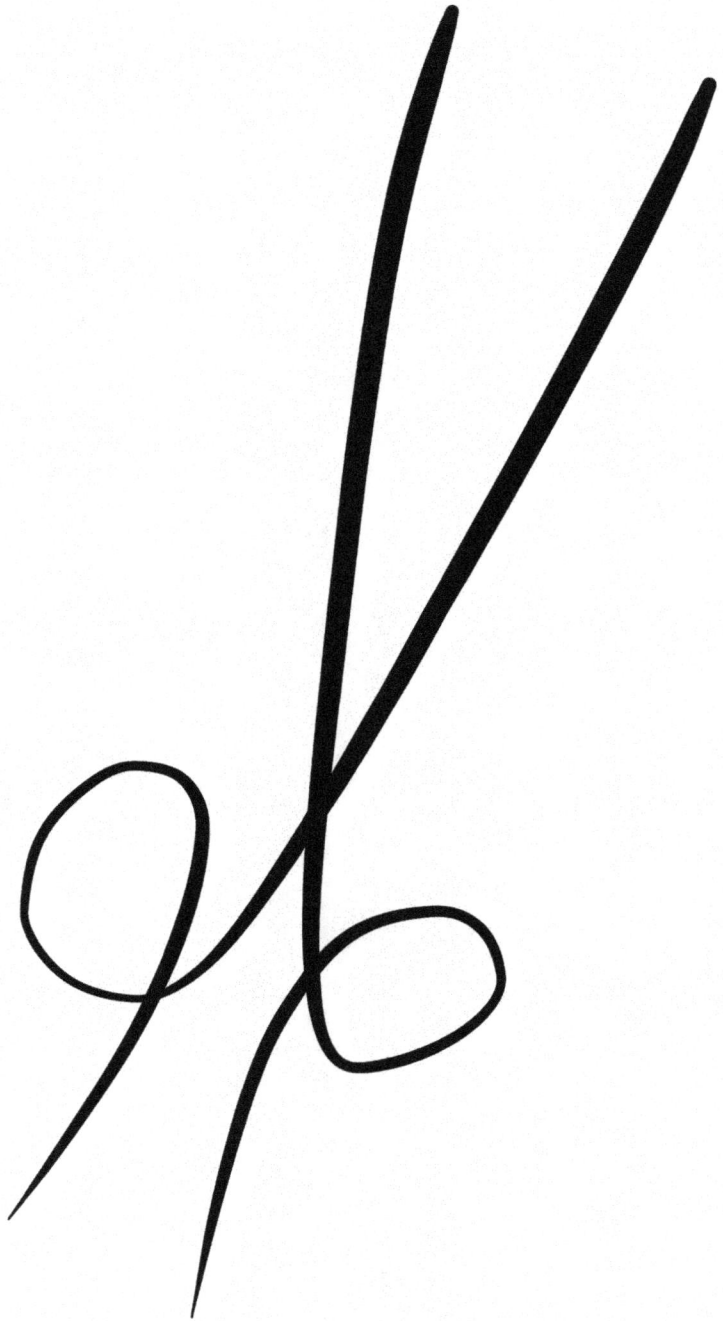

RULE 9:
CUT. EDIT. PASTE. UPGRADE.

The one about embedding upgrades.

Adaptation doesn't stick unless it becomes embedded. Superadaptable people don't just change behaviours – they replace mechanisms. They install better systems. They rewire without losing continuity. They upgrade.

We're still in the final phase of the RUN loop: Necessary Action. But where Rule 8 taught you how to find and focus energy – how to reduce friction and use what you have more effectively – Rule 9 shows you how to use that energy to embed the adaptations you need. Because what we want is for change to stick. For it to be ratcheted in – providing a permanent upgrade upon which you can build. So that you don't waste any of the energy you worked so hard to acquire.

This is the one about embedding change.

Not every change sticks.

Some flare up and vanish.

Others loop back around – and trap you in something worse.

We've all seen it. A broken system gets a surface polish. A toxic pattern gets rebranded as progress. A crisis response becomes the new default. We call it change – but nothing deeper has shifted. The fault is still there. The outcome might look different, but the architecture is the same.

That's what this Rule is for.

Not just making change.

Making it hold.

Rule 9 is about upgrades that last. Swaps that stick. Loops that teach themselves to loop better. This isn't the first time you've changed something. But this might be the first time you've changed the 'right' thing, at the 'right' level, in a way that makes it 'stay'.

You'll see what it takes to do that:
Superadapters who recognise a fault no one else sees.
Those who remove the exact part that's causing the glitch.
Those who embed something better, so deeply it becomes cultural memory.

They don't just fix things. They replace. Embed. Improve.

They don't chase novelty. They engineer normal.

Because in a world addicted to constant change, the most radical move isn't more disruption.

It's embedding the change that matters most – and letting it ripple.

COPY. PASTE. FAIL.

Some systems don't just loop. They loop wrong.

Take the five-a-day rule. Fruit and veg. Sounds scientific. But where did it come from? Marketing consensus. Not metabolic truth. Eat five apples a day? You hit your target – and overload on sugar. You trust the loop. And it betrays you.

Now calories. The average is misleading. The actual amount absorbed changes day to day. Individual metabolisms burn them differently. The measurement itself is flawed. And yet the number becomes the law. You don't just eat the food – you eat the error.

Same with the taste bud map. Or the neuron count. Still passed around. Still printed in textbooks. Even though Susanna Herculano-Houzel dissolved brains, counted nuclei, and proved it wrong.

This is Rule 9's starting point. Not just whether something is embedded – but whether it 'should' be. Because once it's in the system, it spreads.

Superadapters don't copy-paste belief. They check the logic. They challenge the origin. They cut the fault. They upgrade the loop.

Some people never spot the fault.

Some see it – and walk on.

But every meaningful upgrade begins the same way: with someone who sees what's wrong, and says: "that part doesn't belong."

They don't yell. They don't panic.

They just notice. And name it.

That's where real recursion starts – not in the action, but in the seeing.

Because the truth is, most systems don't fail from lack of effort.

They fail because the wrong part gets left in place too long.

Because no one was willing to say: "this rule no longer fits."

The first figure in this loop didn't build the system.

But he noticed where it cracked.

And from that crack, he drew the blueprint for something better.

STITCHED UP, SWITCHED UP

Mary Edwards Walker was born in 1832, when women couldn't vote, couldn't serve, and couldn't wear trousers without risking arrest. She did all three.

A trained physician, she volunteered as a surgeon during the U.S. Civil War – a role no woman was officially permitted to hold. So she cut through that too. She set bones, dressed wounds, and performed battlefield surgeries in a black dress hemmed for movement, not modesty.

The government, begrudgingly, gave her the Medal of Honor. Then – nearly fifty years later – they tried to claw it back. A bureaucratic review panel decided she hadn't been technically 'enlisted'.

She refused to return it. "You may deny me the uniform," she said, "but you'll never erase the service."

They tried to stitch her out of the story. She stitched herself back in.

She was arrested dozens of times – for wearing trousers, for dressing as she pleased. Not for making noise, but for refusing to be silent. For refusing to sit still. For switching the role she was given into the one that was needed.

She made medicine political. She made fashion tactical. And she made herself the only woman in U.S. history to receive – and refuse to surrender – the Medal of Honor.

Walker didn't just unpick the rules. She showed what happens when you don't go back. When you hold the thread of your own history and pull it forward.

She stitched herself into service. And switched the pattern they handed her.

If you want to cut, edit, paste, and upgrade your system, remember:

You don't need permission.

You need precision. And perseverance. And a thread strong enough to hold through time.

THE EMBED LOOP

HOW SUPERADAPTERS EMBED CHANGE

Some changes are temporary. Others stick.
Some last nanoseconds. Others endure for thousands – or millions – of years.
Trillions, even. Infinity and beyond.

Superadapters know the difference.
They don't just change. They embed.
And when needed, they unembed.

Because they understand something most people miss:
You can be embedded in a system before you're even born.

You didn't choose the language you think in.
You didn't design the shape of your day, or the rhythm of your education.
You didn't opt into your cultural defaults.

So embedding isn't just about action.
It's about structure – and restructuring.
And it's not always conscious.
That makes it dangerous. But also, full of opportunity.

When superadaptive minds begin to notice this – when they really see the
loops they're inside – they ask different questions. Not just "What do I want to
change?," but "What am I already embedded in?" And then, "What do I want
to be embedded in next?" They ask what kind of change would actually hold.
What's the smallest move that makes the biggest difference? What shift would
stick without disrupting everything else around it?

Here's the core concept we're circling:
Not all embedding is good.
Not all unembedding is wise.

Some patterns need to be broken.
Others need to be reinforced.
And some loops need to be left entirely – gently or decisively – because the harm
of trying to fix them outweighs the benefit.

It's been said you shouldn't try to change something unless you understand what it does.
So superadapters don't rush. They pause.
Sometimes for a full decision cycle. Sometimes for a single beat.
(Think back to the five-beat rhythm of adaptive action.)

They slow the loop and ask a different set of questions. Is the change desirable?
Will it help – not just now, but later? Is it affordable – not in money alone,
but in energy, attention, social cost? Is it sustainable, or at least reversible? And
above all: can it be done without damaging the wider loop – your self, your
relationships, your system?

Not every change is worth embedding.
Superadapters know this.

And yet the cost of staying embedded in something harmful can be even greater.

So they aim for the smallest effective change –
One that minimises harm, requires the least unnecessary force, lasts the longest,
and can still be undone, if needed.

It's a kind of hierarchy of harm.
We used to cut out tumours.
Then burn them.
Then poison them.
Now we try to rewrite the gene.

Same goal. Less damage.
Cleaner loop.

That's what this next section is about.

Let's look at how superadapters do it – across different domains.
The four moves they make:

Cut. Edit. Paste. Upgrade.

THE FOUR MOVES OF EMBEDDING
How to get unstuck and make the change stick

Some changes are visible. Others are structural.

Some burn hot and fast. Others settle deep.

Embedding isn't just about intention – it's about architecture.
To embed a change means to install it into the loop: into the self, the system, or the situation. It means the change doesn't need to be constantly managed or reinforced. It becomes part of what runs – automatically, adaptively, even when attention is elsewhere.

But superadapters don't just hope that happens.

They move toward it, deliberately.

And the best of them tend to make the same four moves.

CUT
The first move is subtraction.

Not everything can – or should – be edited.

Some loops don't need adjusting. They need excising.

Superadapters know that before you add, you often have to cut. That means recognising what doesn't belong, what never worked, or what might have served once but now corrodes the system it sits in.

Faulty beliefs. Misaligned routines. Embedded harm.

This is the beginning of precision.

Not a chainsaw, but a scalpel.

Not destruction for its own sake, but conscious removal to make space for something better.

EDIT

Next comes refinement.

Once the loop is cleared, the next move is to shape what remains.

This is the territory of adjustment, re-alignment, and gentle shifts. Not because change must always be soft, but because the most enduring edits often 'don't require' total upheaval. Superadapters are skilled at this – seeing where the beat is off, where a pattern could be cleaner, more fluid, more fit for purpose.

Think of it as adaptive copyediting – except the draft is your life.

And you're editing for clarity, rhythm, truth.

PASTE

This is the move most people miss.

Because even after the cutting and editing are done, you still have to re-enter. You have to bring the change **back into the system** – and back into the self.

Superadapters paste with precision. They don't shove insights into places they won't hold. They integrate change into the broader context: relationships, routines, social systems, culture. If that loop rejects the change, it won't embed. It'll bounce off – or worse, cause damage on the way out.

That's why this move matters so much.

Paste is about rhythm. About right timing. About getting the placement right.

Without it, the change fails – not because it wasn't good, but because it wasn't absorbed.

UPGRADE

The final move isn't about the change itself.

It's about what happens **after**.

Superadapters don't want loops that just survive.

They want loops that scale, stretch, evolve.

Upgrade is the move that makes change self-sustaining. It's how a shift becomes an engine. How the modified loop starts to feed forward, extend its benefits, and – eventually – embed itself not just in one domain, but many.

From cognition to behaviour.

From behaviour to culture.

From culture to system.

CUT. EDIT. PASTE. UPGRADE.

Four moves, made again and again.

The habits work with the moves. The moves work with the habits.

Now let's see how three superadapters did it.

HABIT 1: SPOT THE FAULT

We've just looked at the four moves superadapters use to embed meaningful change: Cut. Edit. Paste. Upgrade.

But as you'll now see, those moves don't run on their own. They rely on something quieter, something prior. They rely on habits.

Because if you can't spot what needs to be cut, if you can't see what's misaligned – you won't just fail to upgrade. You'll embed the wrong thing more deeply.

That's why the three habits we're about to explore sit inside the embed loop itself. They're what keep the four moves running. They're what allow the loop not just to happen – but to evolve.

And I've chosen this first example carefully. Because it shows all four moves in action – but it exemplifies the first habit with clarity.

It's called: Spot the Fault.

It's the habit that helps you embed the change you want – so it actually holds. And it's also the habit that helps you unembed yourself from what's quietly keeping you stuck.

Not with panic. Not with force. With perception.

What I love about Vitalik Buterin – what makes him a perfect first figure in this loop – is the way his mind works. From very young, he showed a kind of high-resolution pattern awareness. Not just logic. Structure.

He could see the gestalt of a system – the whole pattern – and sense when something was missing from it. He didn't start by trying to invent. He started by recognising when the output didn't match the intention.

That's what a true superadapter sees.

He traced the misfit backwards, from outcome to architecture. And once he'd located the part that no longer served – he moved.

That's what I want you to look for in what follows.

Not just a biography. Not just a startup origin story. But the moment of noticing.

Because the first real movement in embedded change isn't doing. It's seeing. Seeing what doesn't fit. And refusing to loop it back in.

VITALIK BUTERIN

Vitalik Buterin was thirteen when he learned that control could vanish overnight. He had spent months immersed in World of Warcraft, a massive online universe where progress meant power – accumulated gear, spells, rankings, prestige. But one evening, without warning, the company that ran the game – Blizzard – altered the rules. A feature he loved was removed. His character was weakened. There was no vote, no negotiation, no appeal. The game had changed, and he had no say. He later wrote that he cried himself to sleep. It sounds like a teenage tantrum. But it wasn't. It was an awakening. "I realised what horrors centralized services can bring," he would say later. Something inside him snapped – not just emotionally, but architecturally. The system he had trusted turned out to be built on a single point of power. And that point had failed him. It wasn't a game anymore. It was a blueprint for everything that could go wrong in the real world.

That rupture stayed with him. As Buterin got older, he started to notice similar fragilities in systems far beyond gaming. He began writing for a small online publication about digital money, drawn to the promise of money without gatekeepers. At first, it seemed like a solution – decentralised, open-source, mathematically secured. But the more he studied these systems, the more he saw their limits. The architecture was rigid. The scripting was minimal. It couldn't flex. It couldn't evolve. And once again, a system built to empower was shackled by its own design. Most people didn't see the flaw. They were dazzled by what worked. But Vitalik spotted the frozen gears underneath. He wasn't trying to be radical. He was asking a simple question: if you see a system that can't adapt, and you know how to improve it – what's your responsibility? He wrote more than

200 articles in under two years – many of them unpaid – just to understand how these systems worked and where they broke.

He kept looking. He wasn't a protestor. He wasn't loud. He was just observant. Quietly obsessive. Systems fascinated him – how they were built, where they broke, why they failed. He saw that some were transparent but inflexible, others were flexible but corruptible. He studied how digital money worked, how it moved, who controlled it. On paper, these systems claimed to be free. But in practice, they were locked. Hard-coded. Incapable of adapting to new needs or new ideas. It was the same flaw all over again: a central belief in decentralisation, wrapped in infrastructure that couldn't flex. Where others saw a revolution, he saw a trap waiting to spring. That's what superadapters do. They don't wait for the collapse. They trace the weak point back to the design. And then – very quietly – they begin to sketch something better.

At 19, Vitalik wrote a white paper proposing a new kind of platform. It wouldn't just move digital money – it would carry logic. Adapt to purpose. Run small applications. Execute contracts. It would be decentralised, yes – but also programmable, flexible, self-evolving. He didn't frame it as a revolution. He didn't scream about injustice. He simply spotted the flaw in the old system and drafted a new scaffold. Then he opened the gates. Other developers joined in. A network formed. A culture took root. And through it all, Vitalik insisted on one thing: don't build another fortress. Build a field. Don't centralise. Don't ossify. Leave space for what comes next. It wasn't just code. It was a quiet refusal to repeat the original mistake.

You've seen systems like that too. A platform that used to work – until an update broke it. A device you loved – until a part became unavailable. A favourite product discontinued without warning. It's not just inconvenience. It's a kind of helplessness. The system moves on, and you're left behind. That's what it means to be bricked. The machine still exists, but it can't run. It can't adapt. That feeling isn't limited to software or gadgets. It happens in jobs, in relationships, in institutions. Something shifts. The rules change. And you realise: you had less control than you thought. What Vitalik did wasn't dramatic. It was deliberate. He saw the structure that failed him – and started sketching one that might fail less. That's the habit. Not panic. Not protest. Precision. Spot the fault. Then ask: what would I build instead?

The system he built didn't stay theoretical. It became real – messy, growing, flawed in new ways, but alive. It expanded across industries and continents. It helped build tools for identity, voting, finance, community ownership. And when its own architecture began to show signs of strain, Vitalik didn't retreat. He published his doubts. Proposed reforms. Supported forks. Some systems freeze under pressure. His evolved. Not because it was perfect, but because it was designed to change. That's the deeper pattern. Superadapters don't create flawless systems. They create fault-tolerant ones. They expect the need for repair. They leave room for the next better version. He played chess with Ukraine's digital minister in a war zone, discussing how smart contracts helped buy drones in the first weeks of the invasion.

Vitalik didn't just see a broken loop. He built a better one. Then – critically – he left room for it to evolve. That's the quiet brilliance of his habit. Not genius, but recursion. He looked at what failed him, and instead of fighting it, he forked. Instead of patching it, he restructured. Instead of locking it, he left it open. Superadapters don't just spot the problem. They open the space for the next move, even if it isn't theirs. Because real adaptation isn't about winning the system. It's about freeing it to grow.

SPOT THE FAULT → SWAP THE PART → BAKE IT IN

HABIT 2: SWAP THE PART

The truth is, spotting the flaw is only the beginning. Once you've seen it – what then?

Some flaws collapse under pressure. Others persist because they're welded into the system's frame. Superadapters don't just name the fault. They swap the part. They find the piece that no longer fits – an outdated rule, a toxic habit, a brittle belief – and they remove it cleanly, without breaking the whole machine.

The best ones do more than patch – they design the replacement so others can use it too. That's what Vitalik did. He didn't just diagnose. He made it possible to fork, to signal a better path, to scale the system past its old limits. That's what any smart swap requires: scalability (will it work beyond now?), signalling (can others recognise it?), secession (is there a clean break?), and sequence (is this the right part, at the right time?). The next figure shows how that kind of swap can work – not in theory, but in action.

RORY MCILROY

The problem wasn't his swing. It wasn't his power or his pedigree. Rory McIlroy had already won four majors, been world number one, and held trophies on every continent. But there was one title he couldn't claim: the Masters. Year after year, he arrived at Augusta as the favourite, and year after year, something went wrong. In 2011, it was a meltdown on the back nine. In later years, it was pressure. Expectation. A missed putt here, a poor decision there. Everyone said he needed to fix something. But no one could agree on what. Rory, eventually, did. The fault wasn't physical. It was mental. Not in a vague, motivational way – but in a specific, repeatable loop. He realised he had been playing the wrong game inside the right one. The course wasn't beating him. His own mental script was. And that was something he could change.

It took him years to see it clearly. Golf is a game of mistakes – Rotella had said that. Everyone hits bad shots. But Rory's pattern wasn't the mistakes themselves. It was what he attached to them. One poor approach would spiral into two bad holes. A missed putt would echo in his head for the rest of the round. He was playing against the noise in his own mind. He noticed how often he focused on what he couldn't control: what his competitors were scoring, what people were saying, what this tournament meant. That was the broken part. Not his technique. His target. He had wired his attention to the outcome instead of the moment. So he made a decision – not just to try harder, but to swap the part of his game that processed pressure.

He turned to Bob Rotella – 'Dr. Bob' – a sports psychologist known for helping elite golfers reset their internal patterns. Together, they isolated the fault: Rory was spending mental energy on things he couldn't affect. Headlines. History. The leaderboard. Instead of pushing him to be tougher, Rotella taught him to replace those loops with something useful. They built a mental routine designed for focus, not force. Breathe. Reset. Focus on the swing, not the score. Rory used a modified yardage book – not just for distances, but to recentre himself every few holes. They called it 'getting lost in it'. It wasn't just about feeling calmer. It was about deliberately overwriting the part of the loop that spiralled under stress.

By the time he returned to Augusta in 2025, the new loop was in place. His game plan was quiet, internal, deliberate. During the final round, he didn't speak to his playing partner, Bryson DeChambeau – not from rudeness, but design. "That was the plan all week," Rotella said. "We wanted Rory to get lost in it." He wasn't watching the leaderboard. He wasn't chasing momentum. He was playing his round. One shot, one breath, one rhythm at a time. Even when he missed a 5-foot par putt on the 18th and lost his chance to win in regulation, he didn't spiral. He reset. In the sudden-death playoff, he birdied the first hole to win the Masters – and complete the career Grand Slam. The victory wasn't about aggression. It was about alignment. He had swapped the part that used to break.

It wasn't magic. It wasn't a new swing. It was a better loop. Rory had changed the internal system that governed how he played under pressure. Not by psyching himself up, but by calming himself down. By anchoring to breath.

By rehearsing presence. By reminding himself, between holes, of what he could control. The silence wasn't emptiness – it was clarity. He no longer carried the past with him from shot to shot. And he didn't reach for the future. He stayed where he was, and played the game in front of him. It's easy to think that elite performance is about doing more. But for Rory, winning came from doing less of what distracted him – and more of what kept him centred.

Maybe you don't play golf. But you know this loop. The pressure loop. The story loop. The moment where your attention slips from what you can do – to what might happen if you don't. Maybe it's the school run. A critical meeting. A conversation you're dreading. The moment where you lose your rhythm not because you're wrong – but because your focus slips. We all carry default loops. Some were installed early. Some we inherited. Some got patched on in a crisis. But none of them are final. Superadapters don't just push through. They notice. They pause. They swap the part that isn't helping. Not with perfection – but with presence. You don't get to choose the course. But you do get to choose where you place your focus. And that choice – made often enough – is a system upgrade.

Rory McIlroy didn't change who he was. He changed what he focused on. And that changed everything else. He didn't try to master the chaos. He designed a loop that could hold under it. Breath. Ritual. Reset. A system built to keep him in motion, even when the pressure surged. That's what superadapters do. They don't just adapt once. They adapt how they adapt. He focused on what he could do, with what he had, where he was. You can too.

SPOT THE FAULT → SWAP THE PART → BAKE IT IN

You can spot the fault. You can swap the part. But will it hold? That's the harder move. Because real adaptation isn't a one-time act – it's a loop that embeds. What McIlroy changed now runs under pressure. But what happens when the system isn't personal, but public?

HABIT 3: BAKE IN BETTER

When the goal isn't self-focus, but shared learning? Superadapters know that the deepest upgrades are the ones that stick without supervision – systems that teach themselves, loops that others want to enter. The next story doesn't begin with strategy. It begins with a question: Can you tell me how to get to Sesame Street?

JOAN GANZ COONEY

Joan Ganz Cooney didn't set out to teach children.
She set out to change television.

In the late 1960s, she was a documentary producer in New York, tracking the civil rights movement and anti-poverty programmes through a lens of measured public attention. Her shows were modest. The audience was small. The Emmys, though validating, didn't change anything.

And that was the problem.

"I could make a thousand documentaries about poverty," she said later, "and only the already-convinced would watch. I wanted to make something that would actually change lives."

That change began in her apartment near Gramercy Park, during what she called 'a little dinner party'. Her husband, her boss, and Lloyd Morrisett – an educational psychologist at the Carnegie Corporation – sat around a table with wine and worry. Morrisett had seen his young daughter glued to early-morning cartoons. Could that same TV screen teach letters instead of violence? Shapes instead of stereotypes?

"I don't know," Cooney said. "But I'd like to try."

That moment was the spark. But the genius was in what she built next.

She didn't just pitch a show. She cut the existing mechanism – rejected the patronising, chaotic, commercialised children's programming of the era – and proposed a new recursive engine.

Her 1966 report, 'The Potential Uses of Television in Preschool Education', mapped out something unprecedented: a system that could loop. A system that would embed pedagogy, psychology, and media production into a single upgrade mechanism. It wouldn't just entertain children. It would teach them. And it would teach itself, season after season, to teach them better.

"It was a perpetual television experiment," she said later. "That was the point."

She founded the Children's Television Workshop. Raised $8 million from Carnegie, Ford, the U.S. Office of Education. Built a team of curriculum specialists, child psychologists, and radical artists. She collaborated with Jim

Henson to create the Muppets – not as comic relief, but as cognitive scaffolding. She created loops children wanted to enter.

And she fought – for measurement, not just mission.
CTW built formative and summative testing into the production process. Cooney's team tracked children's attention in 7.5-second intervals. They re-edited segments based on observed response. They cut jokes that didn't land. They rewrote songs that didn't teach. They designed Sesame Street to adapt to the child, not the other way around.

And it worked. Sesame Street premiered in 1969. By the end of its first season, it had won three Emmys, a Peabody, and the cover of *Time*. But more importantly, it reached the children no one else was reaching – urban Black and brown preschoolers, children in poverty, children without books in the house. And it made them loop literacy, numeracy, emotional regulation, cultural belonging.

It was baked in better.
Cooney could have failed.
She was doubted, challenged, and underestimated.
She had no high-level management experience.
She wasn't a teacher. She wasn't a mother.
She was a woman leading a cultural system redesign in 1968.

But she held her course. She designed for adaptation. She made kindness recursive. And she made sure the upgrade felt like joy.

That was the secret.

The songs were loops.
The curriculum was looped.
The kids didn't just watch – they repeated, recalled, recited, and internalised.
The parents didn't resist – they trusted it. It felt safe. It felt like love.

She didn't just launch a programme. She made a loop that embedded itself inside a culture.

And it stayed.

It's still on air.

It's still teaching STEM, autism acceptance, trauma resilience.
It survived the HBO pivot. It crossed languages, platforms, political cycles.
It didn't just adapt to change. It taught others how to.

"How do you get to Sesame Street?"

Cooney answered by building the road. And embedding it so deep that no one forgot the way.

SPOT THE FAULT → SWAP THE PART → **BAKE IT IN**

THREE MOVES, ONE LOOP

You've just seen three different people make three different moves.

Vitalik Buterin spotted a flaw – first in the system that failed him, then in the ones he was expected to trust. He didn't just complain. He read the pattern, saw what was missing, and recognised the part that didn't belong.

Rory McIlroy rewired the way he handled pressure. Not by trying harder, but by noticing what was spiralling him out of rhythm – and swapping that part for something quieter, more stable. He built a loop he could run, even under fire.

Joan Ganz Cooney didn't just build a television show. She designed a system. She brought together disconnected parts – education, performance, psychology – and baked them into something lasting. Something joyful. Something that still loops today.

Three habits. Three adaptive moves. But they don't work in isolation.

They loop.

Spot the fault. Swap the part. Bake it in.

What connects them is perception. Each of these people saw a pattern – and saw what was missing. They recognised not just what was wrong, but what was needed to complete the shape. They didn't just add a new behaviour. They edited the architecture. And in doing so, they changed the output. They changed the culture. They changed the loop.

It's like baking. You don't just mix the ingredients. You apply heat. You wait. You transform. What comes out is something new – something you can share, replicate, embed.

That's what the MVL really is: not just a decision sequence, but a recursive system. A loop that can see itself. A loop that learns.

Now, pause here.

561

Before we name the pattern directly, before we step into the next frame – ask yourself: Which part of the loop are you most comfortable in? Which part do you usually skip? And which part, if you learned to hold it better, might unlock the rest?

EMBEDDED, UNEMBEDDED: THE MOMENT BEFORE

Now, you don't know what's coming next. But I do.

It's Tig Notaro – the comedian who stood up on stage, just days after a double diagnosis, and told the truth. She cut into her own life in real time. It wasn't rehearsed. It wasn't safe. It was her version of a cinematic jolt: Cut. Scene change. Reality pours in.

That moment – the one where life breaks from the script – has a visual twin. I remember watching a TV series that pulled the same trick. It was lit like a 1980s sitcom: canned laughter, bright set, harmlessly sexist jokes, the usual setup. There's the dad, the gags, the sofa, the stairs, the TV. We've seen it all before.

But then the mother in the scene leaves the room. Walks through the kitchen door. And everything changes.

Suddenly, the colour drains. The laugh track dies. The light goes cold. The camera shifts from multi-cam to single. The tone becomes real. What we're watching is no longer sitcom. It's system.

She stands in the kitchen – between the door that leads back into her fake life and another door that might lead somewhere else. Somewhere real. Somewhere unknown.

This is the moment of awareness. She sees the front stage for what it is. And she sees the backstage. She sees what's holding her in place. And now the question isn't comfort or discomfort – it's forward or backward.

That show was Kevin Can F**k Himself, and the moment matters. Because every example in this chapter is a real person facing that same kitchen door. Whether it's Chappell Roan or Edith Piaf, Anaïs Nin or Tig Notaro. They're not born brave. They're not walking a straight path. But they find the cut point. They make the edit. And then they build something new.

It doesn't always work at first. As Honda said – 99% of success is failure. But it loops. It iterates. It upgrades.

So now, watch closely. Because when Tig stands on that stage, mic in hand, she's not just telling a story. She's walking through the kitchen door. And you're about to go with her.

TIG NOTARO: CUT. EDIT. LAUGHTER.

Hello. I have cancer. How are you?

Tig Notaro didn't mean to write a theory of looped growth. She just stood on stage and said what was true. It wasn't polished. It wasn't safe. It didn't even feel survivable. She didn't know if it would be – until it was.

The moment became a trauma loop made visible. A comedy set made sacred. A system made loopable and learnable.

In a single season, Tig lost her mother, her health, her partner, and nearly her career. But instead of silence, she offered rhythm. Instead of collapsing, she stood up.

The set began like a cough. "Hello. Good evening. Hello. I have cancer. How are you?" That wasn't gallows humour. It was an orientation. A loop, made audible. Trauma. Pause. Breath. Repeat.

It was a cut she didn't choose. An edit she did. A paste into the world that others could hold. And, over time, an upgrade that made her whole.

Tig was a private person. She didn't share her dating life, her pain, or her family history on stage. But that night cracked her open.

She would later describe it as feeling like a baby giraffe trying to stand – raw, unsteady, alive. She wasn't delivering jokes. She was locating herself. She wasn't okay. She said it, then laughed at it, then looped it again. Not because she was strong, but because she didn't want to be alone.

That night, she began to ask for help. And people gave it – meals, care, presence. She allowed it in. She allowed the edit to take.

In 2015, she returned to the stage in her Netflix special. She took off her shirt. She revealed her scars. She stood in her truth.

That wasn't spectacle. It was recursion. A return to the loop – not to repeat it, but to show it could hold.

The part of her that might have stayed hidden was replaced by the part that shares. And in sharing, she grew. In growing, she helped others grow too.

And then something stranger happened.

Zack Snyder was deep into postproduction on a zombie heist film when he needed to replace an actor – after the film had already been shot.

So he called Tig. And she said yes.

She filmed alone on a green screen in Simi Valley, with tennis balls for eye lines and tape marks for footsteps. They cut the old actor. They edited her in.

They pasted her across the film.

And it worked. The system got better.

The metaphor doesn't need explaining. She was swapped in. And the structure didn't just hold – it improved.

This wasn't just a comeback. It was a recursive upgrade. Not just a performance. A pattern.

She turned her pain into art. Her art into help. Her help into action. And her action into a loop others could learn from.

Because sometimes the bravest thing you can do is unhold what's broken – and build a loop that holds what matters.

SPOT THE FAULT → SWAP THE PART → BAKE IT IN

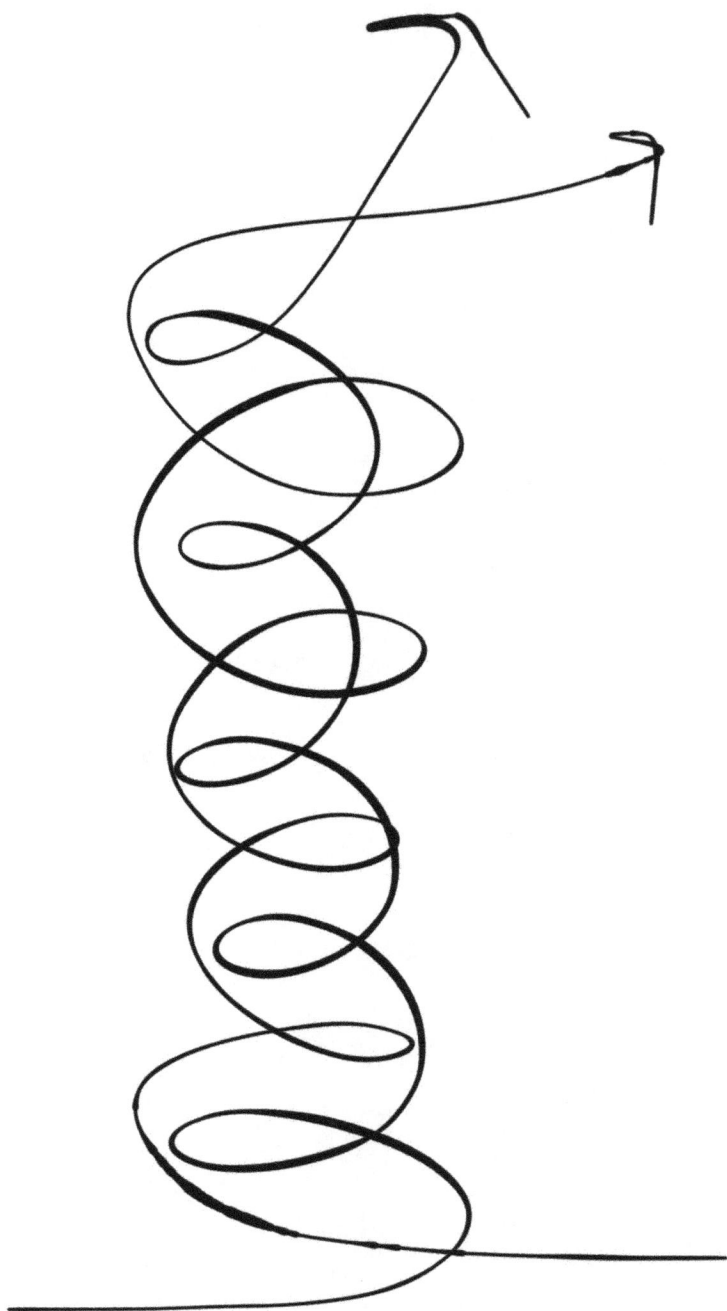

THE SITDOWN: THE SPARK (AND THE SCISSORS)

WHY WE SIT DOWN NOW

"We do not grow absolutely, chronologically. We grow sometimes in one dimension, and not in another; unevenly. We grow partially. We are relative. We are mature in one realm, childish in another."
– Anaïs Nin

You've come a long way.
And you're still learning. Still running the loop.
That's the point. That's the promise.
Every page you've turned, every figure you've met, every pattern you've spotted –
it's sharpening your ability to adapt again. And again. And again.

This Sitdown isn't a rest. It's a return.
We don't pause here to recover.
We pause to embed.

Because everything you've done so far – spotting faults, swapping parts, gathering
energy – has been leading here:
the place where change becomes structural.

Not every upgrade holds.
Not every insight sticks.
But what you're about to learn is how superadapters make sure it does – how
they embed better loops, stronger defaults, lasting rewrites.

You've already met a few amazing minds – each one running the loop in their
own way.
Now we sit down with three more. And these ones don't just adapt – they design.
They've built systems that remember how they were made.
They know how to leave something better behind.

They might chase novelty.
They experiment – boldly, relentlessly.
They see what others miss, decode what others don't.
But that is not all.

They cut – clean.
They edit – with precision.
They paste – with purpose.
They upgrade the loop so it runs better the next time around.
A recursive revolution.

But before we enter the lab – before the scissors flash and the loop gets sharper –
let's spend a moment with someone else.
Someone whose loops were louder, faster, messier – and still brilliant.

EDISON'S TWILIGHT

Thomas Edison didn't believe in waiting for inspiration.

He believed in catching it by the throat. He worked by apple pie and unlit cigars,
wore blue flannel work suits with silk neckerchiefs, and called sleep a waste of
time. He once claimed success was "1% inspiration, 99% perspiration," but
even his inspiration sweated. His lab was a chaos of glass bottles, wires, grease,
batteries, and sparks. He wasn't polishing. He was reinventing – over and over
again.

And still, even Edison knew that sometimes the best ideas don't arrive by
force.

They arrive in the half-light.

He used to nap sitting up in a chair, holding metal balls in each hand. As he
slipped toward sleep, the balls would drop, clattering to the floor and jolting him
awake – often with an idea on his lips. He was exploiting the creative moment
between wakefulness and dreams. A trick. A spark.

Modern researchers have tested this. In one study, volunteers were asked to
drift off holding an object, just like Edison. When they were gently roused, just
as sleep began to take hold, many reported creative inspiration. The moment
before dreaming became a door.

Salvador Dalí used a similar method: a key and a plate. The surrealists called it
the threshold.

The rest of us might call it: twilight.

Sit down.

Let your mind wander off the beaten path.

In that dreamy liminal space, a strange and brilliant idea might slip through
the veil – right into your lap.

Now let's meet someone who didn't just wait for the spark –
she engineered it.

Frances Arnold, rider of motorcycles, breaker of patterns, designer of enzymes, and master of the directed loop.

This is where the real embedding begins.

THE SPARK – FRANCES ARNOLD
Frances Arnold left home at fifteen.

She hitchhiked up the California coast, slept in cars, and didn't ask permission. She worked as a cocktail waitress, then a cab driver, then a nuclear technician. She bought a Moto Guzzi and rode it from Milan to Istanbul and back. "I toughened up my brothers," she said once, when someone asked if it had been hard growing up with boys.

It wasn't rebellion. It was recursion. The loop had started early: spot the constraint, redesign the system, move.

Years later, she chose Caltech for its simplicity – one building, one focus. By then she had cut through several lives and disciplines, and she was looking for something she could build. Not discover. Build.

What she built would change how life itself could change.

In the early 1990s, Arnold introduced a concept so simple it bordered on dangerous: What if we could speed up evolution – and aim it?

To understand what she meant, imagine an enzyme as a tiny, folded tool made out of protein. These tools do everything from digesting your lunch to cleaning up oil spills. The trouble is, enzymes are picky. They tend to work only in the specific conditions nature gave them. Change the temperature, the solvent, or the structure even slightly, and they stop working.

Scientists had long wished they could redesign enzymes – to make them more stable, faster, smarter. But designing one from scratch was like trying to reverse-engineer a hummingbird with a spoon and a sketchpad. Too complex. Too many moving parts.

Arnold's solution was elegant: don't design it. Evolve it.

She took a gene that coded for an enzyme and introduced random mutations – essentially scrambling the code in small, targeted ways. She then expressed those genes – meaning she let cells read the new instructions and build the mutated enzymes.

Some of the mutants were useless. Some were weird. A few were better.

So she took the best ones, mutated them again, and ran the process over. Cut. Edit. Paste. Upgrade.

That's directed evolution. It's not trial and error. It's intentional iteration. Evolution with a steering wheel.

And it worked. By 1993, she'd created enzymes that didn't just survive in non-natural environments – they thrived. Catalysts that could handle solvents, heat, industrial abuse. Proteins that could do things no natural enzyme had ever done.

Within a decade, directed evolution had gone from curiosity to canon. It became a method used in green chemistry, drug synthesis, vaccine development, biodegradable plastic. Wherever a biological reaction needed to be faster, cleaner, or smarter – Arnold's loop was running in the background.

She won the Nobel Prize in Chemistry in 2018. But that wasn't the reward. The reward was the system itself.

"I don't know how to design a new enzyme," she said. "But I can evolve one."

It's hard to overstate what that means. She didn't just create a tool. She created a loop: A system that gets better every time you run it. A way to turn randomness into structure. Curiosity into precision. Spark into selection.

And that spark?

It was never dramatic. It was iterative. It was quiet, like an idea that hums beneath your ribcage until it starts changing your decisions. Arnold didn't wait for clarity – she built toward it, generation by generation, mutation by mutation, with just enough pressure to move the system forward.

That's what makes her a superadapter. Not the Nobel. The loop.

She didn't run the scientific method. She redesigned it – so it could keep running without her.

And now, before the loop cuts deeper, before we begin slicing code and stitching it back together again, we sit for a second with the spark:

A woman in a garage, crouched over a machine that isn't finished, smiling like she knows exactly what it's going to do next.

Let's go.

THE SCISSORS

Imagine you're a bacterium.

You've been attacked by a virus. You survive – and as a souvenir, you snip out a piece of the enemy's genetic code and stitch it into your own DNA. Not randomly, but carefully: repeated patterns, spaced with precision. It's a mugshot gallery. And if the same virus ever returns, you'll recognise it – and cut.

This mechanism is called CRISPR. It works with a protein named Cas9 to locate and slice foreign DNA. For the bacterium, it's defence. For scientists, it became the most powerful gene-editing tool ever discovered.

ACT I – COLLISION COURSE

In 2011, Jennifer Doudna and Emmanuelle Charpentier met over lunch in Puerto Rico. Charpentier had been studying how Streptococcus used CRISPR to fight viruses. Doudna specialised in RNA structure and folding. Their expertise met at the right molecular seam.

Charpentier's lab had discovered that two RNA molecules – crRNA and tracrRNA – could guide Cas9 to a specific genetic sequence. One found the target; the other anchored the blade. Cas9 made the cut. But in nature, the system was cumbersome. To use it in the lab, researchers had to balance and manage both RNA components.

They saw the part that didn't fit – and swapped it.

Together, they fused the two RNAs into one – a single programmable guide that could be custom-written and paired with Cas9 to target any gene in the genome. "It's like using Word," Charpentier said. "Find the word. Delete. Replace."

This wasn't just a breakthrough. It was an interface redesign. Precision biology became programmable.

ACT II – MAKING THE CUT

The technical achievement was only part of it. The deeper adaptive move was simplification. They didn't invent a new system – they made an existing one more functional. The scissors already existed. They sharpened the handle.

CRISPR-Cas9 spread fast. Labs everywhere used it to cut genes with elegance and ease. Not because it was revolutionary – but because it now ran as a loop. Input → target → cut → result. A search-and-replace engine for life itself.

This is what superadapters do.

They don't just add power.

They remove friction.

They rewire complexity into clarity.

ACT III – EDITING THE SYSTEM

Within two years, CRISPR was being used to engineer crops, modify animal embryos, and treat genetic conditions in human cells. Doudna and Charpentier didn't just alter what science could do. They altered who could do it. What was once the preserve of elite labs became a protocol available to graduate students.

They didn't hoard the tool. They published the instructions. They sparked a scientific wildfire – and a cultural one.

CRISPR became a new layer in the logic of possibility.

Don't just accept the system. Cut it.

Don't just analyse the code. Rewrite it.

The real upgrade wasn't just genetic.
It was conceptual.
You can change what you inherit.
You can embed a better version.

That's the superadaptive cut: the one that transforms what's possible – not just for you, but for anyone who follows.

THE SHALLOWEST CUT
It wasn't a big deal.

That was the problem.

The food delivery arrived, as it always did. I went to the door, smiled, took the box, brought it in.

I placed it gently on the kitchen floor.

Helpful. Efficient. Ordinary.

Except – no.

It turns out, for years now, I've been doing this in a way that my wife quietly hates. Not the greeting, not the carrying. The floor. The box on the floor.

It's messy, it's awkward to unpack, and somehow, it makes everything feel heavier.

She'd mentioned it, probably more than once. Maybe I'd even agreed.

But I hadn't changed it.

Not because I disagreed. But because I hadn't made room for the edit.

I was running the loop I'd written for myself: helpful person, greets delivery, carries groceries.

But she needed a loop with more precision: items go on the island, sorted by type, easier to put away.

Not on the floor. Not dumped. Sorted.

It wasn't resistance. It wasn't sabotage.

It was just a copy loop with no cut point.

And once I saw it, once we laughed through it, once she walked me through the loop she wished I'd run –

It took nothing.

A two-second shift.

The shallowest cut.

But now the groceries go where they're meant to go.

COPY → PASTE → REPEAT
A very different kind of loop

There's power in a well-placed cut and edit.
But most people don't cut. Or edit.
They copy.

They take what was handed to them – ideas, scripts, habits, expectations – and paste it forward.

They tweak, maybe. They edit a little. A word here. A gesture there.
But the structure stays intact.
Because no one ever pulled the thread.

COPY → PASTE → REPEAT

It looks like action. It feels like motion. But it's a closed loop.
The same data cycling through different hands. The same behaviour playing out with different clothes.

Sometimes the edit is cosmetic.
Sometimes it's well-intentioned.
But it's still the same pattern. And if the pattern is broken? So is the outcome.

This is how faulty systems embed.
Not because someone chose them.
But because no one interrupted them.

The truth is: it takes effort to cut.
To interrupt what's already been normalised.
To remove a part of a loop and leave a space for something better.
To pause – not just to reject, but to redesign.

That's what superadapters do.
They don't copy.
They cut.

They don't just repeat.
They upgrade.

And that's what we'll do next.

THE FOUR MOVES OF EMBEDDING

CUT

You don't jump into everything knife-first. You don't always have to leave the job, walk out of the room, delete the name, pack the bag. But sometimes you do. Sometimes a person needs to leave – not because they're angry, not because they're brave, but because they can't see any other way to make space for what's next. It might be a habit, a role, a belief, a system. It might be the whole thing. But there comes a moment – quiet or loud – where the loop you're inside is too tight to breathe, too warped to bend back into shape. And so you cut. Carefully. Not to destroy. To release. To create space.

Because the point of the cut isn't the cut. It's the upgrade. Always. Even when it doesn't look like it yet. You're not cutting for drama. You're cutting to make room – for the thing that isn't here yet but needs to be. Sometimes it's as small as carving a window of time out of the night to write. Sometimes it's letting go of the carpet in the middle room because no carpet is better than the fight it caused. Sometimes it's jiggling the rusted part until it finally lifts, WD-40 in one hand and a prayer in the other. But all of it, all of it, is done to create the space where the upgrade can land.

Science tells us that change often begins with disruption. The brain, wired for patterns and routines, clings to the familiar even when it hurts. Neural pathways grow stronger with repetition, reinforcing cycles that keep us stuck. But cutting – whether it's a relationship, a habit, or a place – interrupts those cycles. It's not just an act of removal; it's an act of creation. It clears the clutter, the noise, the weight, and opens up the space where something new can take root.

Because the point of the cut isn't the cut. It's the upgrade. Always.

Psychologists call this 'boundary setting', a way to protect your mental and emotional well-being. Sociologists call it 'role transition', the shedding of one identity to make room for another. Neuroscientists call it 'neural plasticity', the brain's ability to adapt and grow when given the chance. And we've called it metaplasticity, because you can guide your own growth. But whatever you call it, the truth remains: all of it, all of it, is done to create the space where the upgrade can land.

Sometimes the space is physical – a room emptied of tension, a desk cleared of clutter, a suitcase packed for a new beginning. Sometimes it's emotional – the quiet after a goodbye, the stillness after a storm. And sometimes it's mental – the clarity that comes when you finally let go of what's been holding you back.

But the space matters. It's where the upgrade lives. It's where growth happens, where healing begins, where the future unfolds. And while the cut may feel sharp, even cruel, it's never the end. It's the beginning. The upgrade is waiting. But first, you have to make room.

So no, you don't jump into everything knife-first. But when the time comes, when the weight of staying becomes heavier than the fear of leaving, you cut. Not to destroy, but to create. Not to end, but to begin. Because the point of the cut isn't the cut. It's the upgrade. Always.

Cutting to create space is a powerful concept, both metaphorically and practically. It's about recognising that growth, healing, and transformation often require letting go of what no longer serves us. Whether it's a toxic relationship, a draining job, or even outdated habits, the act of cutting isn't about destruction – it's about creation.

By removing the clutter, the noise, and the weight, we open up room for new opportunities, ideas, and connections to take root. It's a process of renewal, where the space you create becomes fertile ground for the upgrade – to the systems that surround you, the situation you're in, and – above all – the better version of yourself, your life, and your future.

It's not always easy, but it will be worth it. Because the point of the cut isn't the cut – it's the space it creates and the possibilities it unlocks. Always.

EDIT
Some things can't be edited. Some things can. And some things could be – if you had the time, the tools, the strength, the permission, the clarity, the distance, the courage. This is where editing begins: not with what you want to change, but with what's actually editable in the system you're in, with the capacities you have, at the moment you're living.

You can't edit everything. You can't edit everyone. And sometimes, you can't even edit yourself – not yet. Not until the loop gives you more room. Not until the earlier cuts are made. Not until the pressure drops or the upgrade strengthens or the mechanism reveals itself more clearly. And yet: editing is what most of life actually feels like. Not a rewrite. Not a reboot. Just a chance to adjust the sentence you're already inside.

That's the work. That's the weight.

You don't always get to reinvent the page. But you can move the comma. And maybe the comma is mightier than the page.

The world is full of people who never learned to do that – who crash through systems they don't understand, or abandon loops before the edit could land. But superadapters learn to pause. To look. To feel for what holds and what might bend. They learn what can be adjusted and what can't. And they work from there.

Editing isn't about control. It's about craft. You don't change the world. You change what the world does with you. And sometimes, later, that changes the world.

Editing, then, is not just a technical act. It's a deeply human one. The sculptor shaping clay. The musician shifting a melody mid-note. The dancer adjusting to the floor or the partner's pace. The mother scaffolding a child's story – helping them name, order, and revise their memories until they start to feel like a self. Even your phone does it. That quiet hum in your pocket, full of fragments – photos, chats, playlists – becomes a kind of lifelog, holding pieces of who you are. Lose it, and studies show the reaction is more than inconvenience. It's a loss of self-continuity. Like someone quietly unsaved your life.

This is what makes editing so subtle – and so important. It's not about control. It's about coherence. It's the awareness that we are changeable, and the skill to shape that change without collapsing the whole. At its best, editing resolves contradictions without rewriting history. It lets you carry forward what still fits, while letting the unnecessary fall quietly away.

Superadapters understand this not just as metaphor, but as method. They know that systems – whether personal, organisational, cultural – rarely fall apart all at once. Instead, they get tangled. Tense. Misaligned. So they work with what's already there. They dissolve friction where it builds. They adjust small parts of the loop and let the rest recalibrate naturally. Not crashers. Not quitters. But those who stay long enough for the edit to land.

The best edits are quiet. Small. They don't announce themselves. But they ripple. A policy shift that tips the balance toward justice. A connector that simplifies everything downstream. A sentence rephrased that shifts an entire conversation. Consider the Voting Rights Act of 1965. A targeted edit to a broken loop. It didn't rewrite democracy – but it changed access. Consider the USB port. Or the QR code. Small, low-cost, low-glamour. But they redefined connection across systems. They made things work – together.

In your life, it might look like a reusable water bottle. A recycling bin. A conversation you choose to have differently. A way of showing up that doesn't require a full identity change – just a quieter, more deliberate alignment. Something small that starts to ripple. Something small that holds.

Because most of the time, life doesn't give you a blank page. It gives you tension. And time. And something already written. Editing is how you shape the rest.

PASTE

The upgrade is still the point. The god. The goal. That hasn't changed. But now you're holding something new – an idea, a behaviour, a part you've built or found or shaped. The question is: how do you join it? How do you connect what's new to what still exists – without it slipping out, falling off, or making the system worse? That's what pasting is. Not just sticking it in. Sticking it so it holds.

Sometimes you use Sellotape. Sometimes superglue. Sometimes spit. Sometimes a wedge of folded cardboard. Sometimes a weld. But pasting isn't just about permanence – it's about fit. It's about knowing what kind of bond is good enough for now, and what kind might need to last. If you've cut cleanly, the new part might slide in and settle. If not, you may be patching over a hole with too little material and too much hope. Superadapters think in connection types. They ask: does this need to be reversible? Does it need to be invisible? Does it need to send a signal? Will I need to access it again – or can I bury it like lead pipe and trust it never leaks.

The upgrade can't hold unless the join works. So you choose your bond. Not based on style. Based on function, friction, and what comes next.

To embed change is not to lock it in place forever. It's to choose the right kind of bond for the moment, the system, and the loop you're in. Sometimes that bond is strong and visible – a weld, a law, a new rhythm that anchors everything around it. Sometimes it's flexible, built to move with the strain – like seismic joints in a building or rituals that offer comfort but bend when the world changes. And sometimes, it's dissolvable: a temporary measure, a transitional loop, a holding pattern that releases when it's no longer needed.

Stickiness isn't just about glue. It's about connection – emotional, environmental, structural. The things that embed well are the things that make sense in the context they live in. A habit that fits your morning flow is more likely to survive than one that constantly interrupts it. A belief reinforced by community tends to hold more tightly than one left isolated and unspoken. A change that aligns with how you already move through your kitchen, open your bag, or start your day is more likely to survive than one that demands constant friction.

We see this everywhere. The photo of a child clutching a worn teddy bear circulates online and becomes a symbol of resilience. The object sticks – emotionally, culturally – but the situation behind it remains stuck, unmoved. The teddy becomes part of the story; the story itself resists change. Rituals work the same way. A candle lit, a prayer spoken, a journal closed before bed. These acts ground us – but when they become rigid, they start to bind rather than hold. What once was sacred starts to feel like obligation.

Stickiness can be beautiful. A festival passed down for generations. A slogan that unites a movement. A shared practice that gives shape to a community. But stickiness can also become constraint – nostalgia that won't let go, bureaucracy that refuses to evolve, persistence that slides into stubbornness. Superadapters don't just press harder. They place better. They know that embedding well isn't about making things unmovable. The best joints aren't fixed. They're self-aware. That's what makes the upgrade possible.

UPGRADE

The upgrade is still the point. The god. The goal. But now you've installed the change. You've cut, edited, pasted. The part is in place. So now the question shifts: did it make anything better? Not louder. Not newer. Better. Not just in theory, but in system terms. Did it do what you meant? Did it hold? Is it opening new space – or sealing it shut?

This is where upgrades often stumble. What you thought would be an improvement turns out to be a detour. What you remembered wanting isn't what you need anymore. What you believed was possible doesn't quite live in the system you're in. And sometimes, your upgrade works – but it was never the real upgrade to begin with. You can spend months improving a thing that's already peaked. You can tweak yourself into exhaustion chasing that last 1% – a gain no one sees, no one uses, and that might cost more than it gives.

But you can also build something that opens a new door. And then another. And another. And another.

So the real question is not just: did this upgrade work? It's: what comes next? Have you made this change into a platform, or a cul-de-sac? Have you made it recursive? Upgradable? Usable by someone else? Is it yours alone, or something others can join?

Not every upgrade is for everyone. Not every change needs consensus. But superadapters think beyond the install. They think beyond the moment. They ask: who is this really for? Where does it go next? What does it enable that wasn't possible before?

Because the point of the upgrade… is still the upgrade. And the most upgradable thing you have is yourself. Your beautiful plastic mind.

The upgrade promises clarity, but clarity can be deceptive. A sharper lens might reveal more detail, but does it distort the bigger picture? A faster processor might speed up the task, but does it leave the user behind, overwhelmed by the pace? The system hums, but is it humming in harmony – or drowning out the subtler notes that once mattered?

Change can cling to the edges of what was – or stain, corrode, or warp, sometimes for the better, sometimes for the worse. A new feature might streamline your workflow, but does it introduce friction elsewhere? A new habit might feel empowering, but does it crowd out the pleasures or friends that kept you grounded? The upgrade is installed, but the system is never static. It shifts, adapts, resists. The question isn't just whether the change works – it's whether it works with you.

Science tells us that systems thrive on balance – on feedback loops that keep them alive and responsive. A change that disrupts those loops can destabilise the whole. Did the upgrade respect the system's rhythm, or did it impose its own? Did it amplify the signal, or drown it in noise? Did it create resilience, or fragility? The answers aren't always immediate. Systems take time to reveal their truths – to show whether the change was a gift or a burden.

And then there's the human factor – the user, the operator, the one who must live with the upgrade. Did it empower them, or alienate them? Did it make their work easier, or their choices harder? Did it invite creativity, or enforce conformity? The upgrade might be perfect in design, but design is only half the story. The other half is lived experience – the way the change feels, the way it fits, or doesn't.

The upgrade is installed, but the work isn't done. The system breathes, evolves, reacts. The question isn't just whether the change succeeded – it's whether it mattered. Whether it made the system better, not just different. Whether it opened new possibilities, not just new problems. Whether it held space for growth, for connection, for meaning. The upgrade is the point. But the system is the story. And the story is still unfolding.

Start small. The world doesn't change in sweeping gestures; it shifts in quiet, deliberate moments. Look at the spaces you inhabit – the room you're sitting in, the streets you walk each day. What might make them better – not just for you, but for everyone who passes through?

A bench where someone can rest. A light that makes the dark less lonely. A book left behind for a stranger to discover.

Think about connection. The world upgrades when people feel seen, heard, understood. How can you create spaces – physical or emotional – where others can meet, share, and feel less alone?

Sometimes, it's as simple as listening. Sometimes, it's as complex as building something that invites others to linger and reflect.

Don't rush. Upgrades aren't about speed; they're about depth. Take the time to understand what's needed, what's missing, and what's possible. The best changes are the ones that feel inevitable once they arrive – as if they've always been waiting to happen.

And finally, leave room for mystery. Not everything needs to be explained or solved. Some upgrades create possibility – open doors, blank pages, quiet corners where something unexpected might unfold.

The world doesn't need to be perfect. It just needs to feel alive, like it's breathing alongside us.

If you can do these things – if you can make the world a little kinder, a little more open, a little more human – then you've already begun the upgrade. And for now, that's enough.

You've upgraded. But only because you made it stick.

And you made it stick because you knew what to keep.

And you knew what to keep because you had the courage to cut.

This is the braid beneath the chapter.

Not four actions. One loop.

To embed well is to move like a system that understands itself.

Cut → Edit → Paste → Upgrade.

Not in a rush. Not by accident.

But deliberately, with rhythm.

Because this is the rhythm of real adaptation:

SLOW → SLOW → QUICK → QUICK → SLOW

And beneath that rhythm, always, is the deeper pattern:

Recognise → Understand → Necessary Action

That's what you've been doing all along.

You haven't just made one change. You've re-entered the loop – with more awareness, more grip, more grace.

And that's where the real upgrade begins.

FINAL

Frances didn't wait for permission. She ran the loop. Doudna and Charpentier didn't invent the parts – they made the cut that made them usable. Both moved from discovery to upgrade not by control, but by recursion. And when they stepped back, they left something that others could build on.

> This is the pattern:
> Spot the fault.
> Swap the part.
> Bake it in.

That's not just what Frances did in the enzyme lab. It's what Bayard Rustin did with the civil rights blueprint – cutting through performative protest to embed strategic nonviolence. It's what Monica Lewinsky did when she stopped defending her past and rewrote the social contract around shame. It's what Bobby McIlvaine's father couldn't do – because sometimes grief makes the past uneditable.

You've seen these moves. You've run some version of them yourself.

But here's the challenge: most people get stuck between the swap and the bake.

They spot the fault – eventually.
They even try a clean cut.
But when it's time to embed, to normalise the upgrade, to make it durable – they stall.

Because that part isn't glamorous.
That part doesn't feel like change.
It feels like maintenance. Like stitching. Like discipline.
But that's where the real adaptation lives. Not just in the cutting – but in the pasting. The embedding. The normalising of what was once optional.

The truth is, most loops don't fail because people can't change.
They fail because people don't store the change.
They don't embed the upgrade into the system that made it necessary.
This is where superadapters differ.
They don't just cut and edit.
They upgrade the system that allowed the error in the first place.

They cut the myth.
Edit the model.
Paste the new loop.
Upgrade the scaffolding.

You can too. But only if you see your life as editable.
Not a fixed script, but a working document.

Frances knew that. So did Charpentier.
You don't need to be a scientist.
You just need to stop fearing the edit.

Because what comes next – after the swap, after the stitch – isn't just healing.
It's higher resolution.

And if you're ready –
it's time to reboot the loop.

You've made space.

You've cut a little time from your life, made room in your thinking, opened up
to what could change.

You've started to edit – not just the text, but the way you move through ideas.

You've begun to paste – holding new thoughts, looping new examples.

You've felt the edge of the upgrade.

And in doing that, you've done more than read.

You've prepared the ground.

LIVE THE LOOP

HOW TO LIVE THE LOOP
So, let's just be clear about where you are.

You're not in the final chapter yet. But you are in the final active part of the RUN loop. This is the moment where things get embedded – where the changes you've made either hold, or don't. And it's also where the loop itself becomes self-aware. From here, you don't just finish the loop. You're ready to run it again, smarter. Stronger. Recursive.

You've just sat down – properly sat down – and this is the part where the ball drops. You wake up. You get your creative surge. It's the shift from reflection into recursion.

In this section, we return to people you've already met: Buterin. McIlroy. Cooney. But we also go further. We draw the thread through the science, the structure, the stories. You'll see how embedded change actually plays out in lived systems. You'll see how real loops either lock in – or fall apart. And we'll look at how to make that shift happen in your own life too.

If you've been reading this with a highlighter or a second brain or a memory that's only half-reliable – good. That's part of how we embed. And if you're just now flipping to this page, cold, I'll say this: just by reading, you've already begun the process. You've cut a little time from your life. You've made space. You've started to edit, started to paste. You've begun to upgrade. That's what plastic minds do when they're given better patterns. I see you, brain.

I've read of people writing books on toilet paper in prison cells – Ngugu wa Thiong'o did, smuggling his novel out one sheet at a time. Irina Ratushinskaya wrote poems with a matchstick on bars of soap, memorised them, then washed them away. Behrouz Boochani wrote a memoir from Manus Island by WhatsApp, line by line, in PDFs. Navalny read Tolstoy in solitary and wrote his own book – *Patriot* – by sheer force of mind. Wittgenstein carried *The Gospel in Brief* through the trenches of World War I. These people weren't just trapped. They were looping. Recoding. So if you're sitting on a bus, in a hospital waiting room, on your living room floor – know this: the loop can still run. The upgrade can still begin. Even here.

We're going to remind you what this embed loop actually does – not just in theory, but under pressure. In real systems. With real limits. And we'll look at wrong loops, counter loops, and how to reboot the whole thing if it slips.

So let's go. The loop's alive now. Let's see what you make stick.

HOW THEY LIVED THE LOOP

You'll remember from earlier in this chapter that Vitalik Buterin didn't storm the system. He didn't shout. He spotted the fault others missed – a brittle architecture disguised as innovation – and quietly drafted something better. Ethereum wasn't born from ego. It came from precision. He didn't try to change everything. He swapped one part: centralised control for decentralised logic. And he let it grow.

What he teaches us isn't just to recognise what's broken. It's to trace the flaw to its source, sketch a different scaffold, and release it into the world – not to dominate, but to evolve. That insight came early: when a favourite game deleted his digital character, the pattern lodged. That was a gestalt – an embedded loop he could feel but hadn't yet named. And when he did name it, he didn't rage. He redesigned. That's what decentralisation was: not a rebellion, a reauthoring.

And McIlroy? He didn't change his swing. He changed his instructions. He cut the thought that was wrecking his rhythm – the fixation on outcome – and replaced it with something quieter, stronger, more durable: presence. Breath. Sequence. In the biggest moment of his career, he didn't push harder. He stepped deeper into a loop that could hold under pressure.

That's what makes his transformation powerful. Not just that he learned to perform again – but that he rebuilt the action gestalt. He swapped the mental process that failed him for one that could run clean, under stress. A loop that would hold. That's what you're doing, too – upgrading the way you loop. Changing not just what you do, but how you choose what to do next. That's meta-habit.

Joan Ganz Cooney didn't pitch a show. She embedded a structure. *Sesame Street* didn't just teach the alphabet – it embedded kindness, culture, and cognitive scaffolding into a loop that could run in millions of homes. It taught itself. Improved itself. Played itself back. She didn't rely on charisma. She built a system.

I know it worked, because I was there. I was one of those *Sesame Street* kids. Two hours of Spanish, street scenes, singing puppets, kindness across colour and voice and shape. Big Bird, Oscar, Bert and Ernie. It wasn't content. It was curriculum. It wasn't just a moment – it was a method. One that's still looping through culture now.

That's what these three reveal when seen together:

A system re-authored.

A focus realigned.

A culture rewired.

And none of it was loud.

None of it was instant.

These weren't breakthroughs. They were build-throughs.

Each of them found a way to make the change stick.

What they left behind wasn't noise or novelty.

It was structure.

And what they made – the system, the process, the habit – kept running.

As it will now, with you.

THE METAPLASTIC MOUSE

I read a story once about a carpenter. He had a beautiful little workshop with a lathe, a plane, and the chisels of his trade. At the end of each day, he'd switch off the lights and leave behind a soft scatter of wood shavings on the workbench – tiny curls of oak and ash, the quiet residue of honest labour.

But every morning, when he returned, something had changed. The tools were untouched, but the shavings were gone. Not thrown away – just… relocated. Neatly placed into boxes or containers that had been sitting nearby.

The carpenter was mystified. It wasn't a prank. No one had been in the workshop. But the cleanup kept happening – tidy, consistent, precise.

Eventually, he set up a camera. And what he discovered was quietly astonishing.

A mouse. A small, plain mouse. Each night it would emerge from beneath the bench, scamper onto the surface, and begin nudging the shavings into the nearest container. It didn't eat them. It didn't hoard them. It simply preferred the bench tidy. The mouse wasn't helping the carpenter. It wasn't hindering him either. It was just… doing what it does.

And the carpenter? He had no idea that his workspace – his system – was being rearranged in his absence.

We like to think that what's inside us is ours.

That the thoughts we think, the habits we hold, the rhythms we follow were all consciously chosen.

But often, we are the bench.

And the world is the mouse.

Things are being put into our containers – our memory, our muscle memory, our moods – by forces that mean neither harm nor help. Tone, tempo, posture, reaction. These enter us through repetition, imitation, osmosis. Through systems, workplaces, screens, families. Through friction and silence. Through rhythm. The mouse doesn't ask permission. The loop embeds anyway.

This is what philosophers call habitus: the shaping of behaviour by structures we don't fully see.

This is how habits accumulate without review.

And this is why we need meta-habits – tools that help us inspect, question, and redesign what's being embedded. Because otherwise, you may find yourself responding to the world with patterns you never picked, storing shavings you didn't choose, following rhythms you don't remember learning.

The bench doesn't know what it's storing.

The mouse doesn't know what it's curating.

And you – if you're not careful – may spend a life working from containers you didn't pack.

WRESTLE IT, RIDE IT, LOCK IT IN

When I was a teenager, I used to watch sumo wrestling on the Eurosport channel. I had no idea why it was on or who was paying for the rights, but there it was – grainy coverage, overdubbed commentary, bouts that lasted three seconds and rituals that seemed to go on forever. And I loved it. I loved the rhythm of it: the salt throwing, the stare-downs, the sudden, thunderous burst of movement.

But most of all, I loved The Wolf.
Chiyonofuji.

He was unlike the others. Leaner, more muscular – 260 lbs of tensile, coiled power. Where some of the *rikishi* looked like geography – slow-moving landmasses – Chiyonofuji looked like a predator. Which he was. Competitively ferocious. Technically elegant. A man who, once he got a left-hand grip on your *mawashi* (belt), did not let go.

Years later I learned he was the son of a fisherman, discovered while out running at fifteen and lured to Tokyo with the promise of a plane ticket. His career began in 1970, but it was a slow rise. In 1974 he made it to the top league, dislocated his shoulder, fell back. Promotion again in 1978, more shoulder problems. But instead of giving up, he adapted. His coach edited his repertoire, trimming the high-risk throws. And Chiyonofuji rewrote himself: he expanded his technique – *kimarite* – eventually using over 40 winning moves. He became a kind of sumo tactician, a sculptor of fights.

He even once used a move called the Amiuchi, the fisherman's net-casting throw. The commentators loved that. It felt mythic. The son of a fisherman casting his fate.

In the mid-1980s, he dominated. Fifty-three wins in a row. A decade at the top. He became Yokozuna, the highest rank in sumo, and held it with a kind of intense humility. At his peak, half the population of Japan tuned in to watch him fight. I still remember the bout he lost to the young star Takahanada – 18 years old. A kind of passing of the torch. After that, he retired.

Later, he managed a sumo stable, and then he died – too young – from pancreatic cancer. When I finally went to Tokyo, I made a pilgrimage to Ryōgoku Kokugikan, the National Sumo Hall. I watched the *dohyō-iri* – the ring-entering ceremony – and felt the memory of him there. The Wolf. Still, somehow, present.

There's a Japanese expression – *sumō no kan*. The sixth sense of sumo. The instinct you only get from being in the ring, from riding momentum, from wrestling with real force.

That was Chiyonofuji.

He wrestled his fate – set-backs, injuries, limitations.

He rode his strengths – his timing, his grip, his grit.

And when the moment came, he locked it in – the win, the legacy, the grip that never let go.

I loved him for that. Still do.

THE GRENADE (AND THE VASE)
Sometimes, something explodes in your life.

It could be a choice you made. It could be something that happened to you. A death, a divorce, a revelation. Nietzsche once called it a grenade – an idea or event so powerful that nothing can ever go back to the way it was.

Grenades don't just break things. They scatter them. They create distance between what once held together. And in that new space, something else becomes possible.

Entropy teaches us this: you can't put it all back. Try crawling on your hands and knees to gather every shard of a shattered cup – some pieces are too sharp, others too small, and some are simply gone. Even if you could find them, they wouldn't quite fit the same way.

But here's the strange grace: once it's broken, you get to decide which pieces to keep. You can leave behind the ones that hurt you. You can rebuild – not what was, but what could be.

Some choose to honour the break. In Japan, the art of *kintsugi* binds broken pottery with gold, making the fracture a feature. Others let the fire burn it all down, and start again from nothing. Both are valid. Both are human.

Even the expected changes – puberty, grief, falling in love – are grenades in disguise. You live one way, and then, without warning, you live another. Your timeline ruptures. You can't go back. The only real question is: what do you build now?

Sometimes, the grenade breaks the pattern. Sometimes, it reveals it.

And sometimes, it gives you space to choose: not how to return, but how to begin.

FROM TRAPPED TO TRANSCENDED

You're just taking a look at your system – your choices, your defaults, your embedded loops. You're thinking about them already as you read this. Bit by bit, your self-talk is improving. You can almost feel those neurons fire.

Embedded cognition. Emerging awareness. A sixth sense starting to form.

You've tried something – or you're about to. Either way, you've stepped back from the mechanisms just long enough to see them working… or stalling.

So let's pause here. Not to stall. To reflect.

This page isn't a checklist. It's a mirror. A structural one.

What you'll see now are the shapes people fall into – and the patterns they use to climb out. Not hypotheticals. Not abstractions. These are real loops. And real lives loop through them every day.

You might sometimes find yourself in the trapped column. That's not permanent. It doesn't define you. But it does describe something you might be doing.

Maybe you haven't named the thing that's limiting you. Or maybe you've named it – but haven't moved past it.

Because naming the fault isn't the same as swapping the part. Realising you find it hard to concentrate is a start – but it's not enough. That's the signal, not the solution. You still have to find what's behind it: the setting, the habit, the loop within the loop. Maybe it's your workspace. Maybe it's the hour. Maybe it's the way you've been trained to think. Maybe you walk while listening to an audiobook. Maybe you switch your teacher. Maybe you rewire your chemistry – cut the coffee, or add it. Whatever the lever is, that's the part. That's the swap. The small, precise move that clears the fault and lets the next loop run.

Each habit offers a way out of a trapped or embedded situation you didn't choose. It lets you get out of a bed someone else made. It lets you transcend the limits you didn't set.

But if you don't bake it in, the loop won't hold. The change will stay raw. Untested. Unlived.

If you are what you eat – then you can only eat what you bake. And a chocolate cake without chocolate? That's just disappointment in a tin.

So when you find yourself in that other column – the transcended one – don't just celebrate. Ask: Is this embedded? Or is this just a taste?

If it's embedded – make it tick. Learn what's working. Make it loop. Make it stick.

	TRAPPED	**TRANSCENDED**
Spot the Fault	You sense something's wrong – but you can't name it. You accept brittle systems because they're familiar. You adapt around the flaw instead of addressing it.	You see the faultline in the loop. You question the structure others assume is fixed. You trace the error back to its origin – and begin to sketch an alternative.
Swap the Part	You try harder, but nothing changes. You repeat the same process expecting a different outcome. You blame yourself, instead of replacing the faulty input.	You isolate the loop that's not working. You remove the distraction. You rewire the internal mechanism. You upgrade the pattern, not just the performance.
Bake It In	You change – but it fades. You make a breakthrough, then backslide. You depend on willpower instead of systems. The loop doesn't hold.	You embed the shift into structure. You build a system that teaches itself. You repeat the upgrade until it becomes the default. The change doesn't visit – it stays.

THE WRONG LOOPS

What we're about to show you is something you've already seen – whether you realised it or not.

Across every chapter in this book, we've used the same diagnostic trio. Three ways loops can go wrong. A trio. A triad. A triple. And each time, we've applied it to the loop at the heart of that Rule.

This time, we're applying it to this Rule's loop – the embed loop. Because even the right upgrade can go sideways.

And as your brain is probably already teeing up... yes – this is the Goldilocks Principle.

Loops can fail by going too fast or trying too much. They can fail by doing too little, or acting too late. Or they can fail in a third way entirely: by going in the wrong direction altogether.

So what we're going to do now is break those down. One by one. We'll show you how embedding can go hypo, hyper, or anti – and help you spot those patterns when they show up in your own systems.

Sometimes change doesn't stick. Sometimes it sticks too well. And sometimes, what you think is a breakthrough... is a misfire.

Let's take them in turn.

HYPO happens when the change doesn't embed fast enough, deeply enough, or widely enough to take hold. The loop runs – but the upgrade doesn't land. Maybe you bought the book, but didn't read it. Joined the gym, but never went. Heard a useful insight from your partner, but didn't act in time. The window passed. The moment drifted. You missed the train – or caught it too late to matter.

Sometimes hypo means too little stickiness. You did something, but not enough. You sealed the shower tray, but used too little silicone. It leaks. You made a change, but didn't reinforce it – and it peeled straight back off. And sometimes it's too local. The change is real, but never spreads. Think of Britain's strange dual relationship to the metric system – part inherited, part rejected, generationally fractured. You buy groceries in kilograms, but tell your height in feet. Your teenager uses metres. Your parents still speak in stone. The loop didn't fail. It just never fully embedded.

That's hypo. The loop ran – but never stuck.

HYPER is the opposite. The system embeds too fast, or too forcefully, before it's ready to hold. The change may be right – but the speed breaks it. The structure can't keep up. You install a new workflow, but no one's trained. You build a brilliant tool, but it doesn't integrate. Action is taken before architecture is built.

Organisations do this all the time. They overcommit to change because the hype pulls them in – and they go hyper. Overlapping systems. Overloaded users. Too much change, too soon. You'll have seen it in the plugs and sockets of the world: electric systems rushed into place with no agreement on standards, leaving legacy frictions everywhere. But the same pattern shows up at home: ten new subscriptions, each meant to reinforce a commitment, but now you're buried. You told the world you'd started – so you got the applause, but not the change.

ANTI is more subtle. And more dangerous. This is when the wrong thing gets embedded. You embed a behaviour that moves you away from what matters. You try to make the child change – but the system doesn't shift. The student learns to perform, not understand. The feedback loop rewards output, not meaning. Or the upgrade you needed isn't even visible to the person you're trying to help – they're still back at a different stage.

Sometimes the problem isn't effort or speed. Sometimes it's that the loop turns in the wrong direction. The wrong move gets reinforced. The wrong belief gets wired in. The wrong fix becomes the new default.

Other times, nothing sticks at all. Not because there's no effort – but because there's no foundation. You're offering books before the person can read. The lesson arrives before the scaffold is there. It's a zone-of-proximal-collapse. No architecture. No adoption. No loop.

That's anti. It looks like embedding. It even feels like it. But it moves you away from where you need to go – or proves impossible to stick at all.

REAL WORLD WRONG LOOPS

The crowds were real. You can say what you like about what came after, but the crowds were real. Cairo, 2011. People singing, standing on tanks, holding up phones like they might capture a future inside the pixels. Something changed, and it was dramatic enough that the world tuned in. But just because something changes doesn't mean it stays. Just because you cut something doesn't mean you removed it. They removed a president. They didn't remove the system. They removed a visible part of the loop, but not the hidden structure that made it recur.

Far away, in another story that tried to end early, another system got built – fast, expensive, and almost entirely from the outside. Police forces, courts, embassies, military outposts, development corridors. You can still see the maps. They're tidy. But the maps were never the terrain. It's hard to know where to start with Afghanistan. It's harder to know where to stop. Because the story did stop, very suddenly, but the loops didn't. What got built was impressive in theory. But theory doesn't defend a checkpoint. Theory doesn't repair belief.

In the United States, something else stuck. A reform, aimed at equity. A plan, shaped by intent. But what embedded wasn't what was imagined. The law was called No Child Left Behind. You hear it and it sounds kind. But loops don't run on names. What actually took hold was a different kind of loop – one built on metrics, pressure, repetition. Teachers stopped teaching so they could teach the test. Students stopped listening so they could get the grade. Parents tracked numbers, not understanding. Schools looped on a story that no longer taught.

You don't always know which kind of failure you're watching until you've watched it all the way through. But when you know what to look for – what was cut but not edited, what was pasted before it was ready, or what got stuck in the wrong layer altogether – you stop feeling helpless. And maybe, if you're lucky, you start noticing your own loops early enough to shift them before they freeze.

COUNTER LOOPS
How superadapters put it right

Some loops go wrong. Not because you're careless. But because you're in motion – and motion doesn't always mean you're moving in the right direction.

The good news? You already know how to fix it.

Superadapters don't invent a whole new system every time something slips. They re-run the loop. They use the same three habits – Spot the Fault → Swap the Part → Bake It In – but apply them more wisely, more lightly, more precisely. What follows isn't a new technique. It's a better pass through the one you already know.

Let's look at how that works.

SPOT THE FAULT is your counter when the system goes HYPER – too fast, too much, too soon because it tends to happen when you act before you've seen clearly. You rush to do something, because motion feels like momentum. But what matters isn't just doing – it's noticing. Buterin didn't do everything. He saw the real problem. He paused long enough to spot the actual fault before making a move. That's the whole point of this habit.

When you're not spotting the fault, you're embedding noise. You're hard-coding urgency. You're enthusiastically reinforcing the wrong thing.

Whole nations have rushed to roll out insulation or digital services without properly training anyone to implement them – creating more dysfunction, not less. Sometimes the error isn't just the first missed fault. It's the failure to keep spotting faults as they emerge.

That's how loops compound. That's how fixes become new problems. Spotting isn't one and done. It's a live diagnostic. And superadapters know: don't swap or bake until you've spotted it properly.

SWAP THE PART is your counter when the system goes HYPO – too little, too slow, often because you've spotted something that needs changing but nothing's happening. You know the outcome isn't what you like, but haven't replaced what's causing it. It's the toilet roll that never goes back on the holder. The insight that never turns into change.

Sometimes you need a sub-loop to ask: Why haven't I done this yet? What's resisting the swap? The fix isn't more spotting. You've done that. The fix is actually doing the thing – replacing the bit that isn't working.

It could be small: the way you start your day. The setting where you try to write. The shortcut you keep using out of habit but that always crashes. Don't wait for perfection. Don't wait for it to hurt more. Just swap the part and re-loop from there.

BAKE IT IN is your counter when the system goes ANTI – wrong direction, wrong result – because it often feels like you're doing it right. You've embedded something. You've baked it in. But it doesn't work. Or worse – it works against you.

The issue here is almost always method. You're using the wrong adhesive. The wrong form of glue.

You might need influence instead of enforcement. A clamp instead of a weld. The lesson from Cooney, and from every real builder of embedded systems, is this: baking it in requires the right recipe for the right environment.

For one person, it's running 200 km a week. For another, it's stillness. Some people need accountability. Others need private mastery.

Think of all the different ways people have written books. Or taught children. Or found their rhythm. That's the clue.

If it's not sticking, don't blame the habit. Don't blame the person. Ask: what does this loop actually need to hold?

Spot. Swap. Bake. Same loop. Better calibrated.

That's what Counter Loops are.

They're not new. They're what happens when superadapters go back to the loop – and run it right.

REBOOTING THEIR LOOP

What it looks like to start again – but not from scratch.

In forensic science, Locard's Principle says that every contact leaves a trace. The same is true of superadapters. They don't just pass through life invisibly. They leave signs. Patterns. Clues. Every time they re-enter the loop – every time they recognise, understand, act – they leave a residue of recursion. Sometimes you see it in a turnaround. Sometimes in a retreat. Sometimes in a return. It's not always visible to them. But if you know what you're looking for, you'll find it. These stories are built from those traces. And once you start seeing them, you'll start spotting them everywhere. In strangers. In friends. In yourself.

These aren't just examples I selected because they fit the model. They're here because they live it. They were chosen after months of searching, filtering, and re-filtering through the stories of real people who have been tested, torn, and reassembled in motion. They've met overload, mismatch, loss, conflict, contradiction – and still found a way to recurse. And if you look close enough, you'll see it's always there. In the background. In the thread. In the breath between moves.

The loop. Not a new plan. Not a clever trick. Just a re-entry into the same recursive logic: Spot. Swap. Bake. Recognise. Understand. Take necessary action. So let's go back to them now. Not to the polished loop you've already seen, but to the private one. The loop they ran when things fell apart.

Vitalik Buterin didn't leave Ethereum. But he came close to losing the thing he built – because it was drowning him. In 2024, the system was scaling. The vision was working. But the founder was vanishing into meetings, fire-fighting, and coordination cycles. He couldn't hear his own mind inside it. And then something shifted. Quietly. He spotted the flaw: not in Ethereum, but in himself. Or rather – in the loop he was stuck inside. The builder had become the maintainer. The imagination had been replaced by administration. The solution wasn't dramatic. It was recursive. The Foundation redesigned the structure. They unhooked him from daily coordination. They gave him what he hadn't been asking for, but desperately needed: time. Space. Silence. Now he writes again. Models again. Thinks again. He didn't exit. He elevated. He didn't walk away. He walked up.

Rory McIlroy didn't shatter. But something did. In May 2024, he filed for divorce. Removed his wedding ring. Kept showing up for tournaments with a press-trained calm. The world assumed it was over. But inside, something wasn't sitting right – not just in his marriage, but in his story. He realised the fault wasn't his form. It was his foundation. Trust, not titles, had been holding him steady all along. And so, quietly, he reversed course – not out of weakness, but out of presence. The paperwork vanished. His rhythm returned. At Augusta, he arrived not just with clubs, but with his daughter and wife. There were no speeches, no explanations – just the quiet return of a real loop. A loop that had held. And would hold again.

Joan Ganz Cooney wasn't failing. But she could see the limits. The world had shifted – conflict, climate, displacement. Millions of children now lived without stability, without schools, without *Sesame Street*. The old loop had taught millions. But it was built for living rooms. And the new world had none. She saw it. Named it. Re-entered the loop. Welcome *Sesame Street* wasn't a rebrand. It was a rebuild. Trauma tools, mobile curricula, translation pipelines. Muppets sent not to entertain, but to stabilise. Not every system holds under pressure. But hers did – because she re-looped it for a world that needed it differently. She didn't start again. She reached further.

These aren't origin stories. They're return stories. Because superadapters don't just loop once. They loop again. Especially when it matters.

RECOGNISE → UNDERSTAND → NECESSARY ACTION

You've seen their pressure points. You've seen the re-entry. You've seen that even when it looks like they've been knocked off course, they haven't lost the thread. They've just looped. And if you've been watching closely – like Locard, like Holmes – you'll have seen the traces. The quiet pause. The redirected move. The long-form return. Not showy. Not scripted. Just recursive. Every contact leaves a trace. Every adaptation does too. You know their methods. Now apply them.

REBOOT YOUR LOOP
The loop is still there. Step back in.

You've seen how they returned. How they re-entered the loop – not with noise or drama, but with recognition. Each time, they weren't starting from scratch. They were stepping back into the system they already trusted. That's what you're doing now.

In forensic science, you return to the scene. You look for the trace. Not to punish. To understand. Loops leave evidence. Even when a loop fails – especially when it fails – it leaves a trace. Something in the behaviour, in the silence, in the interruption. A sign you can follow, if you know how to look. Change doesn't disappear cleanly. It leaves residue. Something stuck. Something missed. Something attempted but not absorbed. That's the scene you return to. Not to blame yourself – but to investigate. Because if you can see what remains, you can work backwards. And from there, you can reboot.

Return to the scene of the adaptation. Ask: What moved, and what didn't? What part of the loop ran? What part never landed? What part keeps looping, even though you thought it ended? There are clues everywhere: the habit you dropped, the conversation you avoided, the notebook you stopped using. You don't have to guess. You just have to re-examine the site.

Some evidence is invisible at first. Like latent prints – fingerprints that only appear when dusted. Recognition works like that. You don't see the pattern until you've trained your eye. The loop was there all along, but hidden under what you told yourself about it. You need the right light. The right lens.

Sometimes you need to reconstruct. Forensic teams work backward from the fallout. Shattered glass. Skid marks. Blood patterns. None of these are the event – they're its echo. You can do the same with yourself. Look for what scattered, and how. Reverse the story from the mess.

And sometimes, it's DNA. The tiniest trace. A repeated word. A drawer you never open. A shortcut you keep using even though you know it fails. You don't need a full picture to reboot a loop. Just one strand that's still connected to what matters.

This is not about blame. It's about attention. This is not failure. It's residue. You're not returning to punish yourself. You're returning to find the pattern that can help you shift. That's the point of rebooting your loop – not starting from scratch, but starting from what's still here. Still waiting to be recognised.

RECOGNISE → UNDERSTAND → NECESSARY ACTION

TRANSCEND THE LOOP

Well, let's look at what we've learned.

We've travelled through a lot – not just across three habits, but through the entire final phase of the RUN loop. This isn't just the end of Rule 9. It's the close of the last functional loop in the sequence: your upgraded way of thinking, living, learning, leading.
This is your meta-habit now.

We could stop here. But instead, let's take a moment to loop back. Not because I'm telling you to – but because you'll want to. You'll want to re-read, to mark, to reflect, to follow the thread back through earlier pages. Because the science here wasn't dropped in – it was synthesised for you. And the people in these pages? You may not share their circumstances, but you share something deeper: the capacity to adapt under pressure, to detect the trace of the future you want, and to apply what you've learned.
That's what superadapters do. They loop back – not out of regret, but to reinforce what matters. They don't just make moves. They make meaning. They reflect recursively, landing ahead of where they started.

When we reach back through other people's lives, we don't just see further. We move further. We rise higher. That's the value of this loop. That's why every hero from every era kept the stories of those who came before – passed by hand, by wall, by fire, by ink.
Maybe that's what story was always for: to carry the lesson beyond your own memory. To extend what you know. To embed what others have learned in your own life. The recursive inheritance of wisdom, across ages and places and voices.

So as you consider how to cut, edit, paste, and upgrade – pause here.
Consider what you've done.
And how you now dare to be you.

CUT. EDIT. PINK. PONY.
The fall and rise of a midwestern superstar

When Chappell Roan first released *Pink Pony Club* in 2020, almost no one heard it.

The pandemic was crashing in. Radio didn't know what to do with a glam-pop fantasy about a girl escaping small-town Tennessee to become a queen in West Hollywood. The beat shimmered, the vocals soared, the lyrics declared freedom in stilettos – but the track vanished.

Except it didn't.

It lived. Quietly. In loop. Inside her. Inside others.

She had cut something. Edited something. Made a move too early – or just early enough. Got dropped by her record company. Worked in a diner. Yet, the song became a whisper among queer fans and dreamers, a private anthem for kids who wanted out. Who wanted up. For years, it lived in the wings.

And then, suddenly, it burst onstage in sequins and face paint.

By 2023, it was everywhere. People were screaming the lyrics back at her on tour. By 2024, *The Rise and Fall of a Midwest Princess* had crowned her. And that once-silent track? It was the encore. The climax. The story.

Five years.

Five years of looping upwards.

Of cutting and editing and trying again.

Of upgrading the upgrade.

She didn't just wait for the world to change.

She changed herself.

Bolder.

Braver.

Better.

By the time the world caught up to "*Pink Pony Club*," she was no longer just the girl who wrote it.

She was the artist who had earned it.

Not once.

But in every loop since.

That's how you embed the future.

You don't beg for permission.

You build the next version – and then you live it.

Loop complete.
Next loop loading.
Welcome to Rule 10.

You've looped once.
Not perfectly. Not forever. But fully.

You spotted the fault. You swapped the part. You baked it in. And when it slipped, you rebooted.

That wasn't just a chapter. That was a recursion. A beginning that passed through its middle and returned, changed.

This is the moment most people stop.

But superadapters don't stop. They loop again.

This time, not to survive. This time, to lead. To embed in others what was once only experimental in you.

To make it easier for someone else to spot the fault sooner. To offer a part they can use. To build systems where good change holds.

You've finished your first full loop. You know how to re-enter now. And more than that – you know how to help others enter with you.

Live it. Learn it. Lead it.
Necessary action complete.
Next loop loading.

loop again

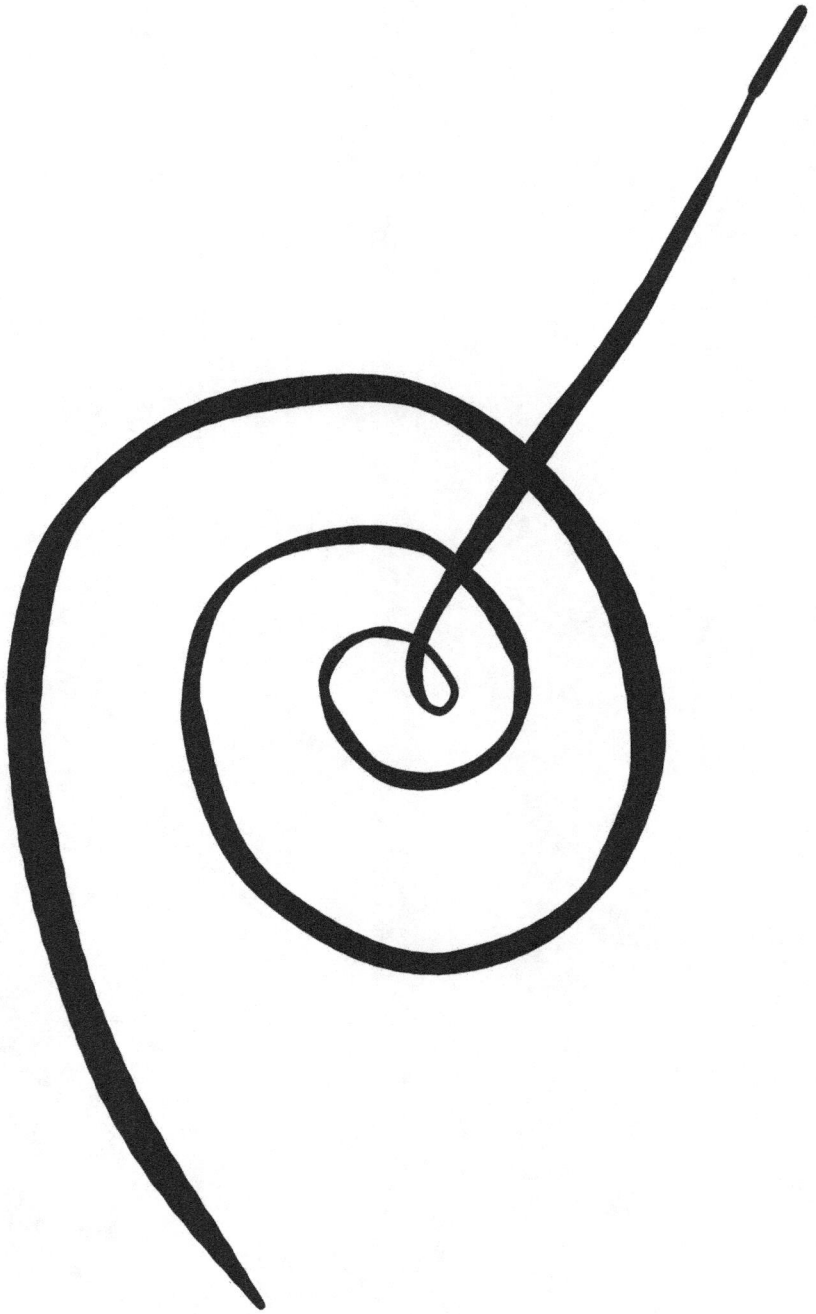

RULE 10:
RELOOP THE LOOP

The one about upgrading your ability to upgrade.

Superadaptability is not a one-time move. It's a recursive system. A loop. A way of becoming better at becoming better. Superadapters internalise the pattern – so every change increases capacity, and every cycle teaches the next. Your very own meta-habit of choice.

You've reached the final rule in the superadaptability system. You've learned how to recognise patterns, understand systems, and take necessary action. Rule 10 is different. This is where your loop becomes recursive. Where the loop becomes even more recursive. It loops back on itself to go... It loops to go forward. It loops to go to somewhere better. It loops to ratchet itself up. It provides a ladder to somewhere better. A leveling up. This is where you continue building your capacity to live, learn, and lead the loop. This is the rule where you upgrade your ability to upgrade. Where you don't just adapt once. You loop the loop.

You've already done more than you realise.

You've moved through uncertainty, adaptation, missteps, and course-corrections – not just by reading, but by looping. Quietly, deliberately, you've become someone new. Not all at once. But meaningfully.

This is Rule 10. The one where recursion begins to speak.

Not as a metaphor – but as a method. Not a fresh start, but a return – with everything you've earned. This is where the loop loops. Where your understanding begins to turn back toward itself – not to close, but to re-enter.

You've already run the RUN loop nine times: Recognise, Understand, Necessary Action. But here, the actions start to echo. The insights start to fold. The architecture you've built – of habits, systems, meta-habits – becomes the very ground you stand on. This Rule isn't just about change. It's about knowing how to change again.

Because this is what superadaptability really means.

Not just survival. Not even progress. But becoming someone who loops on purpose. Who chooses what to embed, what to upgrade, what to lead.

In this chapter, we'll call it by its three names: Live the Loop. Learn the Loop. Lead the Loop. But it's all one thing, really. One recursive, adaptive system. A spiral disguised as a line.

And now, you're standing at the edge of it – not as a beginner, but as a looper.

This is where sapiens becomes supersapiens. Where the plastic mind meets a plastic world, and changes it. Where the habit becomes the meta-habit. Where your own behaviour becomes the very loop you lead others through.

Ten Rules. One Loop. This is the one that turns it inward – so you can carry it forward.

To understand how that happens, we have to look back first.
Not to rewind. But to prepare for the dive.

THE REVERSE KIERKEGAARD

Life, it is said, must be lived forwards, but can only be understood backwards.

The person who did the saying was Søren Kierkegaard. A philosopher of faith, fear, and longing. He rightly marked the challenge of making sense of a life while living it. You don't get to press pause. There's no instant replay.

Now imagine this.

The Summer Olympics. Diving competition. The pool blinks a hard, perfect blue. You're ten years old, coming home from school. There's lemonade, and maybe something salty to eat. And the divers climb.

They climb to the very top.

And they stand there. Rehearsing. You can see it. You can see them imagining it, calculating it. Their feet inch forward to the very edge. The balls of their feet rock up and down.

The announcer cuts in:

"Remember – difficulty and execution. That's what the judges score. That's what counts."

And then, right before she begins, the crowd hears:

"She is about to attempt the Reverse Kierkegaard. The most difficult dive of all."

The Reverse Kierkegaard.

In this dive, she looks back – not in regret, not to fall – but to understand. She understands what happened, how it mattered. She sees the moves. And then she dives. Forward. Not because she's fearless, but because she finally understands what it means to live a difficult dive well.

LIVE FORWARDS ↔ LEARN BACKWARDS

THE SPIRAL FORWARD

You've looked back – not to return, but to prepare. That was the dive. Now comes the rhythm.

This isn't a theory chapter. It's a movement chapter. The loop begins to live.

What follows is not explanation – it's recursion in action. This is where superadapters breathe, adjust, risk, repeat. This is where you see that the habits you've formed are starting to form you. That what you've practiced is beginning to become who you are.

This is what superadaptability was always spiraling toward.

The arc from sapiens to supersapiens doesn't run in a straight line. It curves. It lifts. It learns. It loops. You start with plasticity. You grow into metacognition. But here – you enter metaplasticity. The moment your system learns to learn itself.

This Rule is where that recursive ignition becomes visible – not as a big idea, but as a lived loop.

LIVE THE LOOP → LEARN THE LOOP → LEAD THE LOOP.

Not steps. Spirals. Not stages. Recursions. Together, they form the only real system humans have ever used to pass wisdom forward – to move through change, and come out changed.

What does it look like?

It looks like practice. It looks like pattern. It looks like risk and rhythm. It looks like people doing something hard – then doing it again, better. It looks like music. It looks like movement.

It looks like you.

You've done the dive. Now, dance the loop.

Let's go.

THE UPGRADE LOOP

HOW SUPERADAPTERS UPDGRADE

They remember.

Not just for sentiment or survival – but to adapt. Superadapters don't just respond to the present. They run it against the archive of the past. And when they remember, they loop. They upgrade. They move forward – not from scratch, but with structure.

Long before there were words for recursion, humans were already doing it. They remembered yesterday's flint, and today's fire, and used them to light tomorrow's cave. They learned to copy, to mimic, to gesture, to teach. They felt their way into feedback. They saw when a tool worked, when a signal mattered, when a pattern repeated. One fire-and-rewire at a time, they edged forward. Not in leaps. In loops.

They remembered their way into measurement. The inch, the mile, the centimetre. They remembered their way into metaphor, into mind, into map. They named the stars, then named the gaps between them. They remembered with pigments on walls, with stories, with structure. Their brains carried the same billion-neuron potential as yours does now – but they had to feel their way toward it.

SAPIENS → REMEMBER → SUPERSAPIENS

And what did they remember?

That change was possible.

That loops could be improved.

That the mind was plastic, and the world could be shaped. That every loop – when remembered – could be run better next time.

And now, you can remember too. You've seen the loop across ten rules. You've watched minds adapt. You've watched systems change. You've seen energy rerouted, rhythms clarified, modification made structural. You know now what they never named.

You've seen what adaptation actually is. You've seen what traps it, what frees it, what loops it forward. This book has not just described it. It's demonstrated it. In every habit. In every example. In you.

RECOGNISE → UNDERSTAND → NECESSARY ACTION

That's how superadapters upgrade. They don't just act. They remember. They don't just repeat. They run.

In the next section, we'll explore what that really means. How to live the loop, learn the loop, and lead the loop.

YOUR NEW GAME++
You've seen the movie.

6:00 AM. *I Got You Babe.* Again.

Bill Murray's character, Phil Connors, wakes up to the same blaring radio, in the same bed, in the same town, on the same February morning. He doesn't know why. Not yet. At first, he jokes. Then despairs. Then gives up entirely. Then – and only then – does he start to change.

He learns the piano. He reads poetry. He helps strangers. He fails. He tries again. What to others looks like one day is, for him, hundreds. But eventually, he gets it right – not by escaping the day, but by upgrading how he lives it.

Nadia, in *Russian Doll*, does the same. She wakes up at a party. Dies. Wakes up again. Dies. Again. Over and over. Until she stops asking "How do I get out?" and starts asking "What's holding me here?"

The loop only ends when the character evolves. Not just survives. Not just reacts. But loops forward. Better.

So that thing you do every day – every hour, every conversation, every breath – it has a name. It has a mode. And in gaming, it's called New Game Plus.

I was early to gaming. Pong. Beige plastic console. A square ball. A line for a paddle. And me, learning how to angle my dot so it didn't miss. The game never changed. But I did. I got better.

Later, it was text games. Hitchhiker's Guide on a floppy disk. No instructions. Just: "You are in the dark." Type something. Try again. Get stuck. Start over. Loop.

Then came the arcades. Space Invaders. Asteroids. No memory, no checkpoints. If you failed, you started again. But not from scratch – you started with what you knew. That was the hidden upgrade.

Years later, with my children, I played Wii tennis. I bounced and lunged and served with full body sweat. My son? Sat on the sofa and flicked his wrist. He beat me every time. Not because he was stronger – but because he brought memory into the loop.

Eventually I found my favourite mode: New Game Plus. A way to start again with everything you've already earned. Two kinds of memory. First, your knowledge of the world. Second, your improved character – your tools, your skills, your strategy.

And then some games offered New Game Plus Plus. Even harder loops. Fewer clues. But the same recursive truth: the second loop is not for survival. It's for synthesis.

Other games – roguelikes – go even further. No safety nets. Every new loop is generated fresh. The maps shift. The enemies learn. If you die, you lose everything. Except what you've learned.

That's life. You wake up in the same mind. But never the same day.

The map shifts. The rules change. But you – if you remember what you've learned – can still move forward.

That's what this chapter is. Your New Game++.

You've seen the loop. You've run it. Now you're going to refine it.

Not by guessing. Not by surviving. But by looping forward – on purpose.

You don't start from scratch.

You start again, better.

HABIT 1: LIVE THE LOOP

You've seen how loops work in games. You've seen how they work in films. But in life, the loop isn't entertainment. It's engineering. And sometimes, bad engineering kills people.

I once knew someone who wanted to take out a fireplace. Tied a rope to it. Attached the rope to a car. The car was outside. He pulled. The entire chimney came with it.

Somewhere else – a builder decided to remove a carport wall. From the bottom. The idea was that gravity would do the rest. It did. It collapsed. One man died.

The point isn't just that these were bad ideas. It's that they were loops with no feedback. No stage-check. No 'what happens if – ?'

That's why in this chapter, when we say Live the Loop, we don't mean 'do what you always do'. We mean: know what you're doing. Run the loop with structure. Sometimes that means pausing. Scanning. Ramping. Preparing. Especially when the next move might kill you.

That's where we're going next.

A man in the desert. Living in a van. Getting ready to climb a sheer wall of rock without a rope. Not because he's reckless. But because he's recursive. He knows the loop. He's run it thousands of times. In his mind. On the wall. With sweat, and scripts, and silence. His name is Alex Honnold. And the climb we're about to see is one of the most exacting run loops ever performed.

When we say Live the Loop, we don't mean improvise. We don't mean leap. We mean: act in rhythm, with memory.

The loop we're talking about isn't just habit. It's structure. It's the same loop that's been quietly threading through every chapter of this book:

RECOGNISE → UNDERSTAND → NECESSARY ACTION

In Rule 10, we upgrade that loop by running it again – deliberately. That's what this habit is about. Living the loop doesn't mean being reactive. It means knowing what to do, when to do it, and how much margin you need before you move.

In fact, it's more than one loop. It's a loop with tempo. As you've already seen in Rule 7, effective adaptive action often follows five phases:

SLOW → SLOW → QUICK → QUICK → SLOW

PREP → RAMP → ACT → ADJUST → STORE

Alex Honnold, our next superadaptive mind, didn't invent that rhythm. Like every superadapter before him, he discovered it. And then drilled it, memorised it, trained his muscles and memory until he could hear it in the stone.

A climber whose achievements were so extreme, so uncertain, that a team of documentary filmmakers followed him just to see whether he would succeed, freeze… or fall.

The film was called *Free Solo*. It won an Oscar. But what you're about to read isn't a summary of the film. It's an entry into Honnold's mind: his systems, habits, rituals, memory. The loop he lived, second by second, handhold by handhold, on one of the tallest rock faces in North America: El Capitan.

Honnold lived in a van in the desert. He trained alone. He rehearsed the climb not once, but hundreds of times, rope on, rope off. Every move was mapped, memorised, adjusted, stored. A toe here. A shift there. A place to rest – not by sitting, but by flexing against a sheer surface with one foot and one palm. No rope. No audience. No margin.

This is what it means to Live the Loop when the loop has real consequences. Pay attention to what he sees. To how he prepares. Not just the climb – but the planning, the risk profiling, the rehearsal, the rhythm.

He isn't reckless. He's recursive. And the loop he runs might be the difference between death – and transcendence.

This is the first of three habits in the upgrade loop. It has a name: Live the Loop. And it means this: Transform experience into adaptive intelligence.

The loop we're talking about – the one you're stepping into again – is the same loop that's carried you this far: RECOGNISE → UNDERSTAND → NECESSARY ACTION. The RUN loop.

But now you're running it deliberately. With memory. With rhythm. This is the meta-habit. And it's yours to choose.

Living the loop means looping back to every insight you've already earned. From Rule 1 to Rule 9, this book has given you ways to detect, interpret, decide, model, modify, enact, energise, and embed. Live the Loop is how you start doing that consciously – daily. Again. And again. And again – better.

This isn't just how superadapters climb walls. It's how they walk into their lives – and how you can walk forward in yours.

ALEX HONNOLD
The most dangerous place to learn.

By the time Alex Honnold pulled over the lip of El Capitan with no rope, no protection, and no second chance, he wasn't winging it.

He was running a loop he had trained into himself a thousand times before.

Free soloing – the purest, most unforgiving form of climbing – leaves no room for error. That's what makes it mesmerising. And terrifying. But Honnold didn't start with El Cap. He started with something more radical:

A willingness to learn in full view of death.

For most of us, failure is uncomfortable. For him, it was potentially fatal. So he adapted. Harder. Faster. Smarter.

He learned how to learn – under pressure.

Every hold was a decision. Every decision part of a system. He mapped sequences, visualised moves, rehearsed until they weren't guesses anymore. He didn't just train his body. He trained his loop.

Not because it was trendy.

Because it was necessary.

When you're thousands of feet off the ground with nothing but your fingers and feet between you and the void, you don't rely on memory. You rely on refinement. And every loop has to hold.

That's what this habit is for.

Not for climbing rocks. For building the kind of loop that helps you climb anything.

THE LAB OF FEAR

Honnold didn't start fearless. He started meticulous.

At age 19, in a borrowed van with condensation on the windows and a Coleman stove balanced on a milk crate, he studied every move on Yosemite's Half Dome. Not just the route – every friction point, every potential slip, every way the climb could go wrong. He wasn't memorising. He was simulating.

To outsiders, free soloing looks like madness. No rope. No second chance. But for Honnold, it was the logical endpoint of a loop repeated thousands of times: Try, notice, refine. Loop again. Until nothing is left but the next move.

This wasn't just exposure therapy. It was controlled recursion. A kind of emotional calculus. He learned to feel fear, not flee it. Track it, tag it, test it. Like a lab animal, he studied his own limits – then adapted his system to push them.

Where most people freeze, Honnold observed. Where most people flinch, he learned to breathe. He didn't just build tolerance – he built tools. One loop at a time.

And those tools didn't stay static.

In training, Honnold journaled his weaknesses: hesitation, mis-sequencing, cognitive overload. Then he'd find ways to adjust. Not to eliminate fear, but to match it with fluency. To level up his loop so it could handle more noise, more risk, more responsibility.

Because when the wall bites back, there's no room for hope. Only process.

UPGRADING THE UPGRADE

Every great adapter learns to get better at getting better.

For Honnold, that meant turning his body into a testbed – and his mind into a control tower. When he made mistakes, he didn't just correct them. He extracted them. He asked: What broke the loop? Was it attention? Muscle fatigue? Poor prep? A false sense of certainty?

Most people try to improve by doing more of the same. Honnold broke that cycle. He trained like a chess grandmaster, not a thrill-seeker. He didn't just practice climbing. He practiced practicing. He rehearsed how to rehearse.

That's what makes this habit different from raw repetition. 'Learn the Loop' isn't about doing something again and again until it sticks. It's about building a smarter version of yourself with each pass. Using every feedback signal – fear, fatigue, friction – as raw material.

You might call it meta-mastery. But Honnold would just call it honesty.

No illusions. No denial. No skipping steps.

That's why, even at the peak of his fame, he still rehearses like a beginner. Still tweaks his visualisation sequences. Still changes his nutrition if his recovery falters. Still asks himself if he's rushing the mental loop to chase the physical one.

It's recursive humility. Clarity over confidence. And it scales.

If you can learn this loop, you can use it anywhere.

LEARN THE LOOP, USE THE LOOP, BECOME THE LOOP

What separates Honnold isn't talent. It's transformation.

He became the kind of person who treats every route as a feedback system. The kind of person who loops, not because he must, but because he can't imagine not to. Not just for performance. For identity.

When you learn the loop, you unlock a form of freedom. You stop mistaking effort for progress, or confidence for preparation. You start noticing what actually improves you – and what doesn't. You get precise. Sharper. Slower, before faster.

It's not glamorous. It's not viral. But it works.

And in a world full of noise, the quiet of that loop becomes a sanctuary. Something you can trust. Not because it always feels good, but because it always tells the truth.

Honnold built that sanctuary inside himself. And when he stands alone on a sheer face, chalk on his fingers, wind pulling at the edge of his shirt, he's not guessing.

He's looping.

And so can you.

Start here.

Start small.

Start again.

LIVE THE LOOP → LEARN THE LOOP → LEAD THE LOOP

HABIT 2: LEARN THE LOOP

Alex Honnold didn't just live the loop – he drilled it into stone. He ran it, refined it, rehearsed it. But even the most recursive climb eventually hits a limit. What happens when the loop you've mastered still needs to evolve?

That's where we go next.

This is the second habit in the upgrade loop. It has a name: Learn the Loop.

And it means this: Deliberately upgrade how your adaptive system works. Not by starting over, but by refining the loop that shapes you. Learning here means learning how to re-loop – with structure, precision, and purpose.

You've already begun to live the loop. Now you learn how to upgrade it – through memory, feedback, and rhythm. This is where your plastic brain meets your plastic world. It's Rule 4, reborn. The system isn't just external. It's you. It's rewiring with every loop you run.

And this time, our next superadapter isn't a world-famous name. You probably haven't heard of her. But then again, I don't know who you are either. That's not what makes someone superadaptive.

Her name is NikNak. She's a sound artist. A composer. A loop thinker. A system builder.

She took what the world gave her – trauma, loss, signal, silence – and built a composition so recursive, so carefully layered, that it lets us echo a line you may remember from the writer Octavia Butler:

"God is Change."

That wasn't just metaphor. It was method. NikNak turned that idea into rhythm, into learning, into transformation. That phrase loops in her track – and it loops in this chapter too.

Because whether you start from faith, from funk, from feedback, or from fear – if you can learn to re-loop, you can learn to evolve.

You are sapien. You can change. You are becoming supersapien.

Let's watch how she did it.

This isn't a profile. It's a pattern.

NikNak doesn't just make sound. She builds systems. Every beat is nested. Every scratch is selected. Every loop is layered – not just musically, but mentally.

What you're about to see isn't random. It's recursive. You'll hear loss – but also structure. You'll hear silence – but also signal. You'll hear an artist remaking her environment by remaking her experience of it.

This is what it means to level the loop. Not start from scratch – but stretch what you already have. Adapt not just the product, but the process.

PLASTIC WORLD ↔ PLASTIC MIND

So as you read, don't just admire. Track. Listen. Follow the feedback. Watch what the loop is doing – and what she's doing to the loop.

This isn't someone starting again. It's someone learning better. That's what this habit is for. NikNak isn't becoming someone else. She's becoming more herself – loop by loop.

Every performance is a recursive step. Every track is a layered return. She lives the loop, learns from the loop, and lets each version of herself meet the next one with more awareness, more precision, more power.

This is plasticity in motion. Her mind is flexible. Her sound is layered. Her tools, her stage, her identity – shaped and reshaped by every cycle.

She's not waiting for change. She's composing it.

And now, the loop is about to stretch even further.

She's been invited to perform with one of the most respected orchestras in the world. The moment is real. The stakes are high. There's no guarantee the system will welcome her refinement. No certainty the loop will hold.

But she's not improvising. She's re-looping. This is what Level the Loop looks like – when the spotlight is hot, the format is foreign, and the tools you trust must still evolve.

Let's see what she does next.

NIKNAK

I didn't know you were going to see her. Not really. I'd been to the underground nights – where she'd been behind the decks, carving strange, skittering sets out of vinyl, dust, and deliberate rupture. But this was different. You'd just been writing about change – about God is Change, about Octavia Butler, about the idea that survival demands not just motion but recursion. And then: there she was. NikNak. Performing Parable.

It was a commissioned work. A live orchestral composition built around her turntables. Performed in the dark, at a venue called TESTBED – a name that felt recursive in its own right. The orchestra surrounded her. The audience did too. And she stood there in the middle, fingers on the vinyl, scratching a new identity into being. It wasn't just music. It was structure. Story. Spiral.

Because turntablism isn't just DJing. It's loop manipulation. It's sound as code, surface as syntax. It's the act of reusing, reframing, returning – on purpose. And in that moment, you saw what she was doing: not just playing the loop, but levelling it. She wasn't just mixing a track. She was iterating a self.

This wasn't performance. It was adaptation in public.

A recursive act. And a recursive identity.

She was scratching the signal. And re-authoring the noise.

RECOMPOSE THE SYSTEM
Most people loop to perform. NikNak looped to learn.

Her decks weren't just playback tools. They were feedback systems – instruments of recursion. She didn't just scratch for rhythm; she scratched for meaning. Every beat was a revision. Every mix, a test. What started as sound became structure.

And then she started building upwards.

Workshops. Collaborations. A podcast. Commissions. Theatre scores. DJ sets folded into spatial sound installations. Her tools stayed the same – vinyl, voice, reverb – but the system changed. It grew more intentional. More adaptive. It stopped being about what she played, and started being about how she played it, why she shaped it, what she could learn by pushing the pattern further.

She didn't formalise the learning in lectures. She did it in layers. Through practice. Through process. Through performance as platform. Through platforms as self-structure.

You could watch it happen: the shift from expression to composition.

From rhythm to recursion.

From loop to loop-leveling.

This was no longer a set. It was a system she was designing.

And she was living in it, live.

OPEN THE LOOP
The more precise she became, the more open her loop became. That was the surprise.

Because most artists protect their process. But NikNak didn't close the circle – she expanded it. The podcast. The workshops. The scores for theatre. The immersive soundscapes. Each one became a way in. A loop someone else could step into and use.

She didn't just perform her process. She shared it.

Not as product. As invitation.

You could feel it. The venue itself was recursive – versioned, live-updating, built to evolve with its users. And she matched it. She stood inside the orchestra, levelling the loop live, letting others hear the layers build, the structure emerge. It wasn't just a concert. It was a blueprint you could feel. She wasn't holding the loop. She was extending it.

This wasn't about passing on knowledge. It was about passing on recursion. Creating structures that could flex. Feedback that could teach.

Moments where the audience didn't just watch her change – they looped, too.

That's what learning the loop really means.

Not just learning from the pattern. But building it so others can learn through it.

THE LOOP THAT CHANGES YOU BACK

Every time she performs, she loops herself again. That's the rule.

Not for the audience. For herself.

Because NikNak doesn't present finished work – she presents recursion. She makes the process audible. She lays bare the adjustments, the layering, the shifts in rhythm and self. She's not just scoring sound. She's modelling change.

And it's deliberate.

This is someone who didn't start with a formula. She started with pressure. With noise. With a neurodivergent mind and no map. But instead of bending herself to fit the world, she looped until she found a way to perform through it. Then perform as it. Then teach through it.

That's the heart of this habit.

Learning the loop isn't about taking notes. It's about turning practice into pattern.

It's about seeing how you adapt – and choosing to adapt that.

It's recursive. It's moral. And it's yours to shape.

NikNak did it through turntables. You'll do it through something else.

But the principle is the same:

You can't just run the loop. You have to level it up.

LIVE THE LOOP → **LEARN THE LOOP** → LEAD THE LOOP

HABIT 3: LEAD THE LOOP

NikNak didn't just change herself. She changed the soundscape. She changed the stage. And in doing so, she showed us what the second habit was always for – building recursive structure inside yourself, and around yourself.

But what happens when the loop needs to stretch further?

What happens when your transformation must scale?

That's where we go next.

This is the moment the loop becomes collective. When systems become your canvas. When you don't just adapt to the world – you help remake it.

The third habit in the upgrade loop is not about control. It's about continuity. It's not about being in charge. It's about keeping the loop open long enough for others to run it.

Because the real power of recursion isn't doing it all yourself. It's designing the conditions that make adaptation possible – for you, and for the people who follow.

You've lived the loop. You've learned the loop.

Now, it's time to lead it.

The third habit is called Lead the Loop.

Lead the Loop → Shape environments that help others loop better. Build systems that carry learning, even when you step away.

This isn't about grand speeches or top-down control. It's not about branding yourself a visionary. It's about the quiet architecture of recursion – designing structures that support adaptive behaviour long after you've moved on.

It's the wisdom to see where a system is failing – and the courage to build one that can learn.

It's not always glamorous. But it's the most enduring power a superadapter can wield.

And no one models that better than our next example.

This isn't just someone who saw what others missed.

This is someone who recognised, understood, and acted – across multiple levels.

Dr. João Goulão didn't just change one policy or treat one person. He helped an entire nation reroute its energy – from punishment to possibility.

He lived the loop. He learned the loop. But most importantly, he led it.

LIVE → LEARN → **LEAD**

You'll see how he enacted a new strategy, energised a fractured system, and embedded change so deeply that even today, years later, the world is still studying the loop he left behind.

JOÃO GOULÃO

He was born in the hills, in a quiet place with a long name – Cernache do Bonjardim, a few hours northeast of Lisbon. A town small enough to notice people. A town still shaped by the afterglow of Portugal's revolution. João Goulão grew up not in the centre of change, but in the kind of place that gets changed last. That made him a watcher. And later, a designer.

When the revolution came – the Spirit of '74, they called it – it stayed in his bones. He believed what the people in the streets believed: that power should lift, not punish. That systems were made by people, and therefore could be remade. He joined the medical profession with that idea in mind. Not to protest, but to build.

But by the late 1990s, Portugal was in crisis. Heroin was everywhere. Deaths were rising. Prisons were filling. The state's response had hardened into the same brutal logic spreading across the world: punish the person, not the pattern. Portugal had adopted the global loop – Minimise, Attack, Deny – and was now living with its consequences.

Goulão saw it for what it was: a system failure disguised as order. He had grown up in a country that had learned to listen after dictatorship. He couldn't understand why it had stopped. He wasn't a politician. He wasn't loud. But he had one advantage most revolutionaries didn't: he had time. He watched the old loop collapse. Then he started sketching a new one.

THE SYSTEM THAT CHANGED EVERYTHING

When the government asked him to help fix the crisis, he didn't arrive with slogans or a masterplan. He arrived with a team. Nine people – judges, psychologists, sociologists, doctors. Their brief was radical, but clear: start from scratch. Rethink the entire system. No assumptions. No imported models. Just one question: What would actually help?

They looked at the data. They looked at the bodies. They looked at the prisons. Then they looked at the people. And what they saw broke the loop.

Goulão didn't call for legalization. He didn't glorify drugs. He just named the truth: drug use isn't always a problem. And when it is, the problem isn't the drug – it's the pain beneath it. So they flipped the model. Possession wasn't decriminalised as a shortcut. It was decriminalised so the system could pivot – from punishment to presence.

They built dissuasion commissions – not courts, not jails. Just a quiet room with a psychologist, a social worker, and a question: Do you need help? If the answer was no, the case was closed. If it was yes, the door opened. Goulão believed you couldn't scare someone into changing. But you could offer them a way out.

It wasn't just that the criminal penalty disappeared. It was that something better appeared in its place. Help. Respect. A real loop. The kind that doesn't snap when pressure hits.

THE LOOP THAT HELPED OTHERS LOOP

The results came fast. Heroin deaths dropped. HIV diagnoses collapsed. The prison population shifted. What had once been a war zone of petty crime and untreated trauma became something new: a health system with a human face. People who once ran from police now walked into clinics. The streets were quieter – not because they were controlled, but because they were cared for.

But the real shift wasn't in the numbers. It was in the architecture.

The commissions weren't just a reform. They were a recursive handoff. Each encounter became a loop. Police referred people who needed help with drug problems to social workers. Social workers opened a path to treatment. Treatment led to jobs. Jobs led to something rare in public health: continuity.

There were tax breaks for employers who hired recovering users. Relapsed addicts were guided back in, not cast out. Recovery wasn't just individual – it became infrastructural.

And then something even rarer happened.

Other places started calling. Oregon. Colombia. Switzerland. They didn't want slogans. They wanted the system. What Goulão built in Lisbon started looping outward – across cities, across oceans, across ideologies. Not because it was radical. But because it worked.

He didn't write a manifesto. He designed a loop. One that others could walk into. And stay.

THE LEGACY THAT LOOPS

Goulão didn't make himself the face of the reform. He didn't need to. The system worked. And that, for him, was enough. He stayed in the same office, wore the same brown suits, gave credit to the teams around him. But year after year, government after government, the loop he helped build held.

He didn't lead by force. He led by design. And design, when it works, becomes invisible.

Portugal went from being Europe's heroin capital to one of its quietest success stories. The proportion of prisoners held for drug offences dropped from over 40% to 15%. HIV diagnoses linked to injecting drug use went from more than half of the EU total to less than 2%. Not because people were afraid – but because people were seen.

And yet, he never confused success with finality. Even now, Goulão watches the edges of the system with care. When budgets shrink or rhetoric hardens, he notices. When people forget what the old loop felt like, he reminds them. Because loops don't stay looped unless someone keeps leading.

He didn't just live the loop. He learned it. And then he built it – so that others could walk through it, again and again.

That's what it means to lead the loop. Not to take control. But to create continuity. To design a system strong enough to carry others.

LIVE THE LOOP → LEARN THE LOOP → **LEAD THE LOOP**

THE LOOP BEFORE THE LOOP

SPIRAL LIFE → SPIRAL YOU

The Big Bang gave us energy, pressure, and time. Then gravity. Then atoms. Then stars.

Eventually, those atoms formed minds. And those minds began to loop.

We learned to recognise, to understand, to act. We repeated. Refined. Re-entered. Not just for survival – but for synthesis.

That's what you've been doing. Loop by loop. Habit by habit.

You've lived the loop – under pressure, like Honnold.

You've learned the loop – by refining, like NikNak.

You've led the loop – by designing systems, like Goulão.

And now, you're ready to see what happens when all three habits run together. Not in one person – but across generations.

This next moment is about recursion that lasts. A loop that holds its shape even as it changes. A structure passed forward – not as tradition, but as transformation.

Niels Bohr helped the world see the structure of the atom. His son, Aage, showed how that structure could bend – and still hold.

What they built wasn't a monument. It was a method. A spiral of learning, handed on.

This book has been threading that pattern all along. Not a line. Not a closed loop.

But a recursive spiral – from life to you, and from you to life.

THE LOOP BEHIND THE LOOP

He didn't tell his son what to become.

He showed him how to think.
That was Niels Bohr's loop.

The house they lived in was more than a home – it was an institute. Physicists flowed through it like ideas. Pauli, Heisenberg, Klein. It wasn't formal. It wasn't forced. It was osmotic. Aage Bohr grew up inhaling uncertainty and exhaling curiosity. He didn't just learn equations. He learned how to sit with the unknown.

But the loop wasn't safe.

In 1943, the Nazis learned that Niels Bohr had Jewish ancestry. The warning came fast. There were lists. The family had to vanish. That night, Aage packed a single bag and climbed into the bomb bay of a converted Mosquito bomber. No seats. No windows. Just oxygen tubes, a flight suit, and a three-hour ride across enemy territory.

The loop was airborne now.

He arrived in London flat on his back, inside a shell designed to carry bombs, not boys. From there, he helped his father advise the Tube Alloys project – consulting on atomic models, refining structures. Not building, but understanding.

When they arrived in London, Aage became not just a researcher, but his father's double. He translated notes, carried letters, stood in meetings where survival and science blurred together. The loop was running now – not just in equations, but in action. Together, they joined the Tube Alloys project, consulting on the atomic models at its core.

Their job wasn't to build anything. It was to see clearly.

When a crucial component of the nuclear chain reaction needed verification, it was the Bohrs who were asked to check the design. Not with power – but with pattern recognition. They offered no breakthrough, just calm recursion under pressure.

But this isn't a story about bombs.

And it's not a story about war.

It's a story about the structures that carry us forward.

The ones built quietly, inside safe rooms and escape routes, inside questions asked kindly, inside generations that watch and learn until they can finally act.

The loop Aage inherited was not a legacy.
It was a platform.

One his father had built with ideas, not orders.
And one Aage would soon refine – not in battle, but in discovery.

THE CRUX AND THE DISCOVERY

You might think an atom is something solid.
Something tidy. Neat. Spherical.

That's how it was imagined for a long time: a central nucleus, dense and round, circled by electrons like moons around a planet. Then came the idea of layers – shells that kept particles in line, magic numbers that explained stability. It worked, for a while.

But not always.
Some nuclei bent. Others wobbled.
The charges didn't sit where they were meant to.

The model wasn't broken. It was just incomplete.

The structure that was meant to hold wasn't holding.
That's the moment a superadapter begins to build.

One physicist suggested a different picture: maybe the nucleus was more like a droplet of water. Not static. Not rigid. But shifting. A surface pulled and bulged by what moved inside.

Another mind – Aage Bohr – saw how to test it.
Then another – Ben Mottelson – helped him prove it.

Together, they showed that particle motion and surface deformation weren't separate effects. They were interwoven. Each influenced the other. The nucleus wasn't a shape. It was a system.
Their model explained the anomalies.
It predicted energy levels.
It linked mathematics to motion.

Later, it would be called the liquid drop model – but it was more than metaphor. It was a structure that revealed itself only through feedback.

The atom, it turned out, wasn't still.
It was adaptive.

You might wonder why this matters.

Why a droplet-shaped nucleus, discovered decades ago, belongs in a book about adaptation.

Here's why.

Because what Aage Bohr uncovered wasn't just a better model of matter. It was a deeper truth about structure itself: that form isn't fixed. It responds. It flexes under motion. The shape you see is the product of interactions you can't.

That insight doesn't just explain atoms.

It explains us.

Because we're shaped the same way.
By motion. By pressure. By what moves around us and what moves through us. Our systems deform. And sometimes, that deformation is what holds us together.

So yes – it's physics.
But it's also pattern.
And when a mind like Bohr's sees a shape flex and asks: what else flexes like this? That's superadaptability in its most essential form.

That's not a metaphor.
That's a recognition.

And the beginning of something bigger.

THE CATHEDRAL AND THE LIFT

The breakthrough wasn't the model. It was the method.

Bohr and Mottelson didn't simplify the system. They didn't bend it back into order. They built something that could hold complexity without collapsing. They built structure out of feedback. And in doing so, they showed us something we forget too easily:

Adaptation isn't what happens when a system breaks.
It's what reveals what the system is made of.

We imagine strength as stillness. But the nucleus flexes. The mind flexes. A good structure isn't rigid. It responds. It absorbs distortion without losing identity.

Where are you acting like a solid – when actually, you're a system?

That question doesn't just apply to physicists. It applies to us.
To leadership. To learning. To life.

Aage didn't just level up the science. He helped build a way of seeing. A recursive architecture.
Not a cathedral of stone, but of thought – held aloft by minds like Gamow, Rainwater, Mottelson, and the quiet architects who kept the loop alive long enough for someone else to enter.

Shape doesn't emerge in silence.
It comes from movement, feedback, and contact.

The crux they solved wasn't just technical. It was philosophical:
Can we build systems strong enough to carry others?

That's the lift.
That's the loop.
And that's what comes next.

TEN RULES → ONE LOOP

You've just completed the Upgrade Loop. But what you've really done is run the full system.

The RUN Loop. The recursive engine that powers real change.

You've lived it with Alex Honnold – who planned every move, every hold, until the impossible became breathable. You've learned it with NikNak – who re-layered her art and identity through feedback, pattern, and change. And you've led it with João Goulão – who didn't just reform policy, but embedded compassion into a system designed to punish.

This wasn't metaphor. This was method. You've seen superadapters in motion – not abstract traits, but repeatable habits. Not personality, but practice.

The Upgrade Loop is a reminder system. A recursive ignition. It tells you: run the loop again. Live, learn, lead – and use what you've just gained to spiral up. To return, better. That's how superadapters operate: not once, but on purpose, over time.

And now, you'll sit with that. Because we're not done.

This next section is one you'll recognise: a Sitdown. A moment to deepen and absorb – not by slowing down the system, but by entering it. With Gaudí, we'll explore structure. With Live, Learn, Lead, we'll reflect on your own spiral. And with the loop types ahead, you'll begin to see what kind of loop you've really been running.

This is your chance to pause without pausing. To reflect while moving. To sit with the system – and watch what unfolds.

THE SITDOWN: THE CATHEDRAL
(AND THE CRUX)

WHY WE SIT DOWN NOW.

"I just run. I run in void. Or maybe I should put it the other way: I run in order to acquire a void."
– Haruki Murakami

We don't sit down to stop.
We sit down to see.

That's always been the point of these moments – each Sitdown in this book. They weren't pauses between the real work. They were the real work. The kind that doesn't shout. The kind that doesn't need applause. The kind that changes you by re-seeing what you've already done.

This one is no different.
Except that it is.

Because now you've run the whole loop.
You've seen how superadapters climb – step by adaptive step – from recognition to understanding to necessary action.
You've watched them rewire their systems, rebuild their defaults, and upgrade their upgrades.
And somewhere along the way – between the pages and the pauses – you started climbing too.

But every climb needs a perch.
Every loop needs a breath.

That's what this is.

Call it a Sitdown.
Call it a ledge.
Call it what climbers do when they scan the rock face ahead.
What architects do when they lift their eyes from the model to the building and ask: does the structure still match the vision?

Or call it what Batman does on the edge of a skyscraper –
crouched, brooding, still.
Not watching the city go by.
Reading it.
Listening for its pattern.
Because this isn't rest.
It's a kind of seeing.

And the science agrees.
When we shift gears – physically, mentally, rhythmically – we also shift the shape
of our thinking.
It's called divergent cognition.
The body moves.

The mind loosens.
And solutions begin to arrive sideways.

That's why walking helps with writing.
Why the best ideas appear just after the run, or just before sleep.
Why Murakami writes in the cadence of kilometres.
Why Gaudí walked his site, every morning, to hear what the stone was
  trying to say.

I run to write.
Not to escape my thoughts, but to find them.
I move, not to avoid the problem, but to let the right shape of it come into view.
And sometimes I pause – not to stop –
but to stay in the movement long enough for something else to arrive.

My daughter does it too.
She codes through complexity, curled over a keyboard in total stillness –
only it's not stillness.
It's motion, folded inward.
She doesn't notice time passing.
She doesn't hear her name.
She enters a loop.
And the loop moves.

That's what this Sitdown is.

You don't need to sprint.
You don't need to stop.
You just need to be here long enough to recognise what's already moving –
in the system,
in the loop,
in you.

Because you're not sitting outside the loop anymore.
You're sitting inside it.

You've started to build.
Now's the moment to look again at what you're building.
To feel the rhythm of the pattern.
To read the route ahead.
To notice the still-moving mind.

Like Murakami, I run.
Not to escape the world, but to enter the void where the loop can be felt.
Like Honnold, I climb – sometimes for freedom, sometimes for silence.
And like Gaudí, I build in a way that leaves space.

This is your Sitdown.
This is the void that teaches.
This is the moment before the next move.

Then move forward.

GAUDI: THE LOOP THAT BUILT ITSELF

He walked the site every morning. A slim man in a long coat, worn shoes white with limestone dust, eyes sharp behind half-spectacles. Barcelona, 1925. The Sagrada Família wasn't even half-built. And Gaudí – its architect, chief obsessive, spiritual mechanic – already knew he would not live to see it finished.

Around him, cranes creaked and sunlight flared against scaffolding. Local stone was being hand-cut into spirals, buttresses, and Nativity figures that looked like they had melted into place. He walked slowly, not because he was old, though he was, or unwell, though he was that too – but because every step was an inspection. Every angle mattered. Every model still whispered something new.

To outsiders, the construction looked eternal. Not metaphorically – literally. Construction had begun in 1882, and by 1925 it had been under way for over

633

forty years. There were no shortcuts. No mass production. No fixed plans. Gaudí had stopped drawing conventional blueprints long ago. He worked in three dimensions – clay, string, inverted weights – so the church could evolve as it was built. He thought buildings should adapt like trees. Slowly. With gravity in mind.

To Gaudí, delay was not a problem. It was the point.

"My client," he famously said, "is not in a hurry."

He meant God, of course. But what he didn't say – and what made him more radical than the quote suggests – is that he was building not for the present, or even the near future. He was building for continuity.

For the loop.

He didn't expect to finish. He expected to be continued.

That's what makes him more than an architect. More than an eccentric. More than a genius who died under a tram – which, for the record, he did, crossing the road near the cathedral in June 1926, so disheveled from his monastic habits that no one recognised him at first.

Gaudí lived as if the real measure of his work was not completion, but transmission.

His real client wasn't God. It was time.

He wasn't trying to impose a vision. He was trying to embed a pattern.

One that could outlive him.

One that would adapt itself.

SOLVING FOR TIME (THE CRUX)

Every great structure has a crux. Not just a keystone – a problem.

For climbers, the crux is the hardest move. The one that makes or breaks the route.

For Gaudí, the crux wasn't a single stone. It was how to build what you could never finish.

Most architects design with an end in sight. A complete model. A schedule. A sense of closure.

Gaudí broke that logic. He didn't just design the cathedral – he designed a system that could evolve without him. A recursive method. A living blueprint.

This wasn't poetic. It was brutally practical.

He created scaled physical models, suspended from wires with small sandbags – using gravity itself to calculate optimal curvature. He worked from instinct and mathematics, developing a kind of biomimicry before the term existed. He left behind geometries more organic than gothic: hyperbolic paraboloids, ruled surfaces, helicoids – architectural shapes drawn not from tradition, but from nature's own loops.

And then, the real genius: he embedded learning into the work itself.

He taught apprentices not just what to build, but how to adapt.

He chose materials that could be altered.

He encoded modularity into the design – from facades to windows to towers – so that change was not an interruption, but a continuation.

The early sections were made from local Montjuïc sandstone – chosen because the craftsmen knew how to cut it. But Gaudí also partnered with concrete manufacturers, anticipating the shift toward poured and reinforced materials. He saw further. Not in prophecy, but in pattern. He designed knowing that one day, machines might carve what his hands could not. And now they do – using computer-guided carving arms and high-resolution scans of the original models.

He didn't resist the future.

He built for it.

That was the crux:

How do you loop a vision into stone, without knowing who will finish the sentence?

Gaudí solved it not with speed, but with structure.

Not with force, but with fidelity to pattern.

Not by finishing – but by preparing others to continue.

THE LIVING BLUEPRINT

There is a blueprint you can roll up and put in a drawer.
And there is a blueprint that lives.

Gaudí built the second kind.

The Sagrada Família is often called a masterpiece of sacred architecture. But that misses the deeper truth. It is not just sacred. It is instructive. Every arch, every spiral, every strange asymmetrical window is also a lesson. A recursive hint. A way of saying: You are not just building. You are learning how to build.

He trained the masons and sculptors not just in skill, but in philosophy – not religious dogma, but adaptive presence. Watch the structure. Let it teach you. Loop from intention to action to form. The basilica was always meant to be a teaching tool. Not just for believers. For builders.

He left behind not a fixed design, but an evolving language.

A syntax of stone.

A morphology of recursion.

This is why it still works. Why the project didn't collapse after his death.
Because it was never about him.
It was about the system.
The apprentice becomes the architect.
The modeller becomes the master.
The work teaches itself.
Modern artisans now use digital scans of Gaudí's original plaster models – some of which had been shattered during the Spanish Civil War and painstakingly reassembled. They overlay algorithmic extrapolations atop his hand-carved prototypes. The work continues – not because it was rigid, but because it was recursive.
This is meta-habit made visible:
A system that trains itself.
A structure that teaches its own continuance.
Gaudí built a loop.
A pattern you can walk through.
A cathedral that adapts.

LEGACY IS A LOOP

Most legacies are monuments.
Gaudí's is a mechanism.

You can walk through it, but you'll never be finished with it.
Not because it's incomplete – but because it's designed to be continued.

When he died in 1926, less than a quarter of the Sagrada Família had been built.
Almost none of the final towers.
Almost none of the sculptural facades.
But the pattern – the recursive structure – had already taken root.

Today, nearly a century later, new sections rise not by rewriting his vision, but by looping it forward:
From sandstone to concrete.
From hand-carved to CNC-guided.
From Gaudí's string-and-weight models to LIDAR scans and parametric design.

He didn't resist the technologies he couldn't imagine.
He welcomed them – by building a frame that could hold what hadn't yet been invented.

That is superadaptability.

The loop lives longer than the architect.
The pattern holds shape through changing hands.
The crux isn't closure – it's continuity.

When the basilica is eventually finished – perhaps in the 2030s – it won't be the end of Gaudí's project. It will be the proof of it.

A loop completed.
A structure that outlived its creator – not by staying the same, but by staying in motion.

This is what it means to live the loop.
You don't have to finish your cathedral.
You have to build in a way that someone else can.

META-HABITS, BRAINS, AND BECOMING

You've met meta-habits before.
Not in a lab. Not in a textbook.
In the wild. In people.
Every superadapter in this book carried one – sometimes unnamed, sometimes unacknowledged – but always alive. A recursive pattern. A habit of re-authoring. A loop that didn't just react, but reconfigured.

Meta-habits aren't bonus features.
They are architectural upgrades.
They are what separate stuck loops from spiral ones.

Peirce saw this over a century ago:
Beliefs aren't fixed things. They're habits of action that we adjust through feedback, doubt, and revision. We bet on them – until they stop working. Then we loop. If we can.

That's the difference.

William James called habit the "enormous flywheel of society" – steady, powerful, and freeing. But he also warned: that same flywheel can become a hamster wheel.

When repetition dulls attention, and you forget you can change the gear.

Meta-habits are what let you shift tracks.
Not escape the wheel – repurpose it.

Pierre Bourdieu named another trap: habitus – the deep, invisible grooves we inherit from our culture, class, gender, norms. The moves we didn't choose. Meta-habits are the first tools that let us rewrite that script.

They are self-recognition in action.

They say: you are not just the product of your loops.
You are the pattern-breaker.
The field-bender.
The recursive agent.

Francisco Varela took it further:
We don't just perceive the world – we enact it.
We co-author reality through loops of action and attention.

That's what Gaudí did.
That's what you've done.

Not just adapted.
Redrawn the loop.
You're not here to escape your habits.
You're here to make new ones possible.
Habits that become systems.
Systems that become patterns.
Patterns that evolve.

This is meta-habit in the wild:
The act of staying adaptive when the world wants you to repeat.

SUPERSAPIENS ARE CATHEDRAL BRAINS

From noticing patterns → to noticing ourselves → to adapting how we adapt.

This is the supersapien arc.
Recursive self-authorship.
Meta-habitual design.

Refer to neuroplasticity + metacognition = metaplasticity.
Brains that don't just learn – but learn how to change the way they learn.

Gaudí was the first builder.
Supersapiens are builders of builders.

RECURSIVE RECURSION (THE FREEDOM LAYER)

Freedom is recursive responsibility.

We aren't blank slates – but we're not locked scripts either.
Meta-habits let us question the field, rewrite the role, re-loop the system.

Gaudí gave up control in order to preserve the pattern.

This is the difference between designing a plan and designing a future you won't control.

This is not about mastering the loop.
It's about teaching it to survive you.

WHO FINISHES THE CATHEDRAL?

The cathedral is still unfinished.

It has been under construction since 1882. It has outlived wars, architects, ideologies, even its own country's regime. But it has not outlived its pattern. Because the pattern was built to survive.

And that's the point.

We tell ourselves stories about closure. Final chapters. Last acts. But the truth is, anything worth building is never done. Not if it's alive. Not if it loops.

Gaudí understood this.

He wasn't building for applause. He was building for continuity. Not just a structure, but a structure that could teach itself forward.
A pattern made durable through recursion.

That's what you've been building, too. Maybe without stone. Maybe without blueprints. But if you've run this loop – Recognise → Understand → Necessary Adaptation – then you're already inside the architecture.

You're not finishing something.
You're learning to live the loop.

Superadaptability doesn't end in mastery.
It ends in transfer.

The real test of any system isn't whether it changes you.
It's whether it keeps changing – even after you let go.

Which means: this is not your last loop.
This is the loop that lets you build the next one.

Peirce called beliefs "habits of action we're willing to bet on."
De Beauvoir sharpened the warning:
"Don't gamble on the future. Act now. Without delay."

Because the loop isn't complete when you understand.
It completes when you transmit.

Gaudí didn't leave behind a cathedral.
He left behind a recursive invitation:
Continue the pattern. Adjust the structure. Carry it forward.

You are not here to be finished.
You are here to become a self-architect.

A future-builder.
Not to complete the cathedral –
but to extend the pattern.

Loop by loop.

That's the difference.
William James called habit the "enormous flywheel of society" – steady, powerful, and freeing. But he also warned: that same flywheel can become a hamster wheel.
When repetition dulls attention, and you forget you can change the gear.

Meta-habits are what let you shift tracks.
Not escape the wheel – repurpose it.

Pierre Bourdieu named another trap: habitus – the deep, invisible grooves we inherit from our culture, class, gender, norms. The moves we didn't choose.
Meta-habits are the first tools that let us rewrite that script.

They are self-recognition in action.

They say: you are not just the product of your loops.
You are the pattern-breaker.
The field-bender.
The recursive agent.

Francisco Varela took it further:
We don't just perceive the world – we enact it.
We co-author reality through loops of action and attention.

That's what Gaudí did.
That's what you've done.

Not just adapted.
Redrawn the loop.

You're not here to escape your habits.
You're here to make new ones possible.
Habits that become systems.
Systems that become patterns.
Patterns that evolve.
This is meta-habit in the wild:
The act of staying adaptive when the world wants you to repeat.

THE LOOP YOU TEACH

You don't have to finish the cathedral.
But you do have to teach the pattern.

That's the final move of superadaptability.
Not just learning the loop.
Not just living it.
But leading it – so someone else can begin where you left off.

We think of leadership as charisma, vision, dominance.
But superadapters lead differently.
They transmit patterns.

Sometimes it's a phrase. A gesture. A way of solving without panic.
Other times it's structural – a system, a habit, a rhythm.

It doesn't have to be grand.
But it has to be loopable.

That's what every one of the people in this book did.

They didn't just survive complexity.
They taught the structure of how.

Bayard Rustin didn't just stay clear – he gave others a logic of liberation.
Leymah Gbowee didn't just build her own will – she amplified the will of a
movement.
    Katherine Johnson didn't just calculate trajectories – she taught belief,
precision, and the loop of self-trust.
    Alex Honnold didn't just ascend – he offered a model of recursive mastery that
others could enter.
    Even Kim Dae-jung – built a tempo that others still keep time to.

Each one carried a pattern.
Not perfectly. Not always consciously.
But they taught the loop.

That's what you do now.

Not by preaching.
By practicing.
By showing what it looks like to reroute the pattern under pressure.

You become a supersapien when someone else loops because of you.
When your way of adapting becomes a structure they can build on.

This is not legacy.
It's recursive influence.
The loop you teach is the loop you leave behind.

THIS IS YOU NOW

This is where the loop hands off.
Not from one chapter to the next –
but from this book to your life.

You've walked the scaffold.
Seen how clarity becomes action.
How habit becomes system.
How failure can loop into growth – if you re-enter with precision.

You've met the crux in others.
Now you meet it in yourself.

Because this is no longer theory.

You are a builder now.

Not of cathedrals, maybe.
But of structures no less real.

You are choosing what to reinforce.
What to undo.
What to pass on.

And that's the crux.
Not the hardest part –
but the most defining.

Because superadaptability isn't something you finish.
It's something you continue.

You're not just part of the loop.
You're what the loop becomes
when it learns to evolve itself.

LIVE → LEARN → LEAD

You've just come from cathedrals and architecture – Gaudí's long arc of devotion, and the crux each structure must carry. But this part of the Sitdown is different. Now we turn inward. Here is where you begin to build your own structure. To recognise your loop. To trace its shape, and – maybe – for the first time, to reshape it. What follows is a recursive spiral. Three loops. One inside the next. This is your scaffolding now. And your crux.

LIVE → META-HABIT

You'll never have a shortage of habits. They're already living in you – quietly directing how you wake, how you speak, how you avoid or recover. Some are trained. Some are inherited. The way people around you behave – how they move, speak, interrupt or stay quiet – those patterns don't just pass by. They fill in the gaps. They give you templates. They start to shape your sense of what's normal, what's possible, what's you.

That's what the sociologist Pierre Bourdieu called habitus. The loops you inherit before you notice you're looping. The invisible strings. They animate you. They help you move. But they also pull against you when you try to move differently.

Pinocchio wanted to be a real boy. Not made of wood. Not moved by strings. And in some way, that's what this book is trying to offer too.

The chance to see what's been shaping you. And the chance to shape it back.

Habit isn't just conditioning. It's capacity. William James – psychologist, philosopher, cowboy-hatted mind-mapper – once called habit 'the enormous flywheel of society'. He understood something fundamental: that once behaviours embed, they preserve energy. They free us to act without friction.

That's useful – until the loop you're conserving is no longer serving. That's where meta-habit begins.

Animals run habits too. Patterns of grooming, migration, withdrawal. But humans do something extraordinary and ordinary all at once: we can say to ourselves, "What is going on here?" Not just out there – in the situation – but in here. In the loop that's running our reaction.

Once you know there's a loop, you can decide what to do with it. You don't want a pet rock. That was a fad for a minute. You want a pet brain. One that learns to sit up, loop over, reroute, and grow.

Neuroscientists call it Hebbian learning: 'Neurons that fire together wire together'. But meta-habit isn't just wiring. It's when you 'know' the wires are there. And it's what lets you choose a different circuit when the old one fails.

Deliberate, conscious meta-habit is where superadaptability begins. Not just living with what you've been handed, but noticing, curating, and reshaping it. What to keep. What to cut. What to amplify. What to reframe. And this ability – to shape your own meta-habit – is only possible because of something else: your ability to learn the loop.

That's where we're going next.

LIVE → LEARN → LEAD

HABITUS AND META-HABIT

You didn't start with a blank slate. No one does.

Before you ever chose how to act, you were already being acted upon. The way people speak around you. The gestures they use. The decisions they expect. These are the patterns you inherit – not just behaviours, but structures of perception and response.

The sociologist Pierre Bourdieu called this habitus: the embedded system of dispositions we acquire through upbringing, schooling, social class, and culture. It's not just what you do. It's what feels natural to do – what fits. You don't need to be taught it directly. You absorb it through repetition, through observation, through context.

That's why your habits aren't just personal. They're historical. They're semiotic. They carry signals from other people, other times. They mean something, even if you didn't choose them. And that's where meta-habit begins – not by erasing this inheritance, but by recognising it.

You can't control your starting point. But you can learn to see the pattern. And once you can see it, you can start to adjust it. Meta-habit is the moment when the loop turns toward choice. Not just doing differently, but selecting which different to do. Shaping the shape that shapes you.

This isn't rebellion. It's recursion. You loop back to what made you – and begin to loop forward, differently.

THE FORK

There's a moment – sometimes quiet, sometimes fierce – when you realise that the loop you've been living isn't the one you want to keep.

Not because it's catastrophic. But because it's inherited. Unexamined. It came to you pre-installed: in your culture, your family, your class, your corner of the city. You've rehearsed it for years. Maybe decades. You know it by heart. But now, something in you is asking: Is this mine? Is this still the loop I want to live?

That's the fork.

It's not always dramatic. Sometimes it's as small as saying no to hosting. No to performative effort. No to loops of expectation that cost more than they give. Not because you don't care – but because you do. And you've begun to sense what your energy is really for.

A fork isn't a rejection. It's an opening.

It's not just a no. It's a chance to reroute. To interrupt the loop you didn't choose, so you can create the one you might. That new loop might be unformed. It might be unfamiliar. But the fork – the decision to depart – is already a recursive act.

This is where meta-habit meets metaplasticity.

Because now that you've chosen to leave the default, you'll need more than just will. You'll need the system inside you that can help you reshape how you respond. You'll need to notice what happens next – and begin learning from it, as it happens.

Which brings us to the next loop.

LEARN → METAPLASTICITY

You can learn. But more remarkably, you can change how you learn.

Plasticity alone is already remarkable. Your brain can grow new connections, weaken old ones, reroute signals, recover from damage. It can change.

But once you've chosen to reshape your own meta-habit – your own pattern for living – that decision is only made possible by something deeper.

It's a combination of two things: metacognition (your awareness of thought) and neuroplasticity (your capacity to change).

That combination is what I call metaplasticity.

Not just thinking differently. Not just learning something new.
But reshaping how you shape.
Upgrading how you upgrade.
Getting better at getting better.

In Rule 9, you met Frances Arnold – directing evolution in a lab. Here, you're directing the evolution of your own learning loop. The lab is your mind.

You're not just reinforcing a habit or following a path. You're retooling the system that makes paths possible. Scientists describe this as shifting the threshold for change itself. The conditions for learning become part of what's being learned.

Peirce saw it too: inquiry loops back. You test, you shift, you test again. Not just forward motion – recursive motion.

Metaplasticity isn't just intelligence. It's the intelligence behind intelligence. And when it starts to move in others – through mentorship, culture, systems – you're ready for what comes next.

PLASTICITY → METACOGNITION → METAPLASTICITY

You don't learn just by living.
You learn by noticing what your living is teaching you – and then by explaining it, especially to yourself.

This is where metaplasticity becomes visible. Not just as potential, but as a pattern.

Psychologists have long studied experiential learning – the idea that we adapt best when we cycle through four stages: experience, reflection, abstraction, and re-application. But that loop doesn't complete itself. It needs attention. And it needs narration.

That's where the self-explanation effect comes in. Learners who actively articulate what they're doing – who describe their reasoning or ask themselves questions – consistently understand more and adapt faster. It's not motivational fluff. It's structural reinforcement.

The combination of these two – living reflectively, and reflecting aloud – creates a loop that strengthens itself every time it runs. That's what metaplasticity feels like: not just forming a new path, but recognising the path as you walk it, and deciding where to turn next.

It's not just what happens to you. It's what you do with what happens to you.

For example, you can watch television and absorb very little. Or you can watch television with your child, pause it, ask questions, and talk through what you're both seeing. Suddenly, it's not just entertainment – it's recursive learning. It's a loop. You're shaping the plasticity as it unfolds.

Life is just one damn experiment after the other –

or at least, that's what I tell myself.

THE SECOND STEP

The fork was the first move. You said no to the loop you didn't choose. That's where the story shifted. But it didn't end there.

Because stepping out is only the start. The second step – the one that really matters – is the one you take while still looking over your shoulder. It's where you begin to learn, in motion, from what you've already lived. And that learning doesn't come all at once. It comes by looping: noticing, trying, stumbling, adjusting.

This is what metaplasticity is for. Not to give you a script – but to give you structure in uncertainty. A way to change, while changing.

It's not about looking back to stay there. It's about looking back to move forward better.

Not nostalgia. Not regret.

Just looped intelligence. Recursive clarity.

You're starting to rewire not just what you do, but how you respond to what happens when you do it. That's adaptive learning. And it begins when you realise: the most useful insight is often the one that shows up after the action, not before it.

The loop is running. You're in it now. Not waiting for the perfect path. Just running the best available loop – with better awareness each time.

And here's the thing.

Once that loop settles – once it strengthens, repeats, refines – something strange and generous happens.

The loop begins to move beyond you.

Which brings us to the next recursion.

LEAD → SUPERSAPIENS

You don't get to be supersapiens on your own.

By now, you've looped. You've recognised and reshaped your meta-habits. You've accessed the deeper machinery of change – metaplasticity. But the final phase of recursion isn't internal. It's relational. It's environmental. It's about what you pass on, and what you shape for others.

Some people lead by force. Others lead by design. Supersapiens lead by culture.

They don't just inspire – they architect spaces in which recursion is more likely to emerge. They don't just help others survive – they build environments in which many can thrive. Systems where plasticity is not the exception, but the baseline. Habitats of possibility.

You may remember João Goulão, the architect of Portugal's drug decriminalisation programme. His real achievement wasn't just policy – it was context. He created a space where people were treated as adaptive beings. Where shame was reduced, support was offered, and recursion became viable again.

The same logic echoes across history and biology. Cooperative intelligence. Cumulative culture. From early stone circles to modern learning systems, what humans have passed down is not just information – it's adaptive structure. The possibility of refinement. The loop passed forward.

That's what supersapiens do. They benefit everyone – or as many as possible – and themselves, by enabling more than is possible alone.

You're not just looping forward anymore. You're looping outward. That's how we evolve each other.

SAPIENS → SUPERADAPTABILITY → SUPERSAPIENS

SCAFFOLDED INTELLIGENCE

You can build a scaffold on your own.
But you can't build a collaborative working environment on your own.

When the scaffolding went up around my house, it turned four storeys into a single surface. Roof work became wall work. What would've been dangerous and difficult became safe and ordinary – because someone else had built the platforms. Layer by layer, plank by plank, the conditions were changed. And the result wasn't just access. It was transformation.

That's the real logic of scaffolding. Not the wooden boards – but the recursive generosity behind them. Someone went up before you. And they made it easier for you to go further.

This is how cultural transmission works. We pass down not just facts, but frameworks. Ladders and handrails and ways of working. Vygotsky called this the zone of proximal development – the space between what you can do alone, and what you can do with the right support. The scaffold that lets you operate above your level until that level becomes your own.

It's also how collective intelligence works. Once the scaffold is in place, multiple people can work at height. Not just one mind getting better, but many minds lifting each other.

But then comes the deeper truth.

One day, my scaffolder's mate didn't show up. He did the job anyway – just slower, harder, grumpier. Because you can build the structure alone. But you can't build the system alone. You can't create a way of working together unless someone else is working together with you.

That's the heart of sympoiesis. Not that everything is connected in theory. But that some things – better systems, real trust, supersapiens outcomes – simply can't be built alone.

THE ADAPTIVE RATCHET
Some loops close. Others continue.

But the rarest kind – the one that matters most – is the loop that holds after you leave it. The one that turns upward, stays open, and helps someone else begin where you finished.

That's the adaptive ratchet.

You've learned how to live differently. You've learned how to learn recursively. Now you begin to lead – not by controlling others, but by creating the conditions where better loops can take hold. Not just in your life, but in your systems. Your classroom. Your workplace. Your home.

This is what leadership looks like here: not dominance, but design. Not inspiration, but infrastructure. You don't just model adaptability – you embed it. You reinforce the right kinds of friction. You reduce the wrong kinds of noise. You create scaffolds that hold long after you're gone.

And as you do, you make recursion easier for others. You give them starting points you never had. You build platforms that make what was once difficult – normal. You become part of a distributed upgrade loop.

This is how culture works. This is how progress happens.

You're not just passing on wisdom. You're passing on structure. And when that structure is built to support learning, adaptation, recursion – you're not just lifting yourself. You're lifting what comes next.

That completes a never-ending recursion.

It's a positive end that never ends.

You've stepped through the spiral now. Lived the loop. Learned it. Led it. Not abstractly – but in structure. In story. In thought. And maybe even in practice. What comes next is yours to build. But it's already begun. Because once a loop reshapes you, it reshapes the next loop too. The moment you live differently, learn recursively, and help even one other person do the same – you're not just looping. You're looping well. That's superadaptability.

LIVE THE LOOP

HOW TO LIVE THE LOOP

"We die so many times and then are born again."
— Kae Tempest, *On Connection* (2020)

To live the loop is not to have it all figured out. It's to keep moving with a system that keeps evolving with you.

This is where the work becomes quiet, continuous, real. Where you notice that everything you've done — every reset, every shift, every return — has been preparing you to stay adaptive while living.

Living the loop doesn't mean avoiding difficulty. It means recognising difficulty as a re-entry point. A place to pause, shift weight, and try again — not from the start, but from where you are now.

Sometimes you move forward by asking better questions.

Sometimes you move by listening to the version of you who still wants to grow.

That version might feel far away. But they're not.

They're in the system already.

To live the loop is to treat each experience — however small — as an opportunity to:
Read your own emotions as signals
Use the friction as feedback
Ask: what's really stopping me?

Superadapters learn to live forward not by speeding up, but by staying in the system long enough to learn from it. The goal isn't mastery. The goal is continuation with awareness.

You don't need a breakthrough. You just need to live in a way that lets the loop keep running.

And when it falters? You know what to do.

You live.
You learn.
You lead.
And then you loop again.

HOW THEY LIVED THEIR LOOPS

You haven't seen them for a while. You've moved through the Sitdown, the spreads, the table, the reboots. But before we go forward, let's return – just briefly – to the three minds who showed you what an Upgrade Loop looks like from the inside. They're not here to be worshipped. They're here because they modelled something real. Each one faced a pattern that could have held them back. Each one chose to live differently. And in doing so, they gave us something to learn from.

Let's look at what they did. Then let's look at what you might do next.

ALEX HONNOLD – LIVE THE LOOP

He didn't erase fear. He looped with it.

Alex Honnold's upgrade wasn't about courage – it was about recursion. He faced fear, tracked it, trained into it. He turned pattern into structure. Every ascent was a rehearsal. Every fear was logged, replayed, recalibrated. He made uncertainty predictable – not by removing risk, but by adapting to it until it became part of his rhythm.

What he showed us is that fear doesn't mean stop. It means loop again – this time more precisely.

So ask yourself:

Where does fear show up in your system?

How can you track it, pattern it, and begin designing around it?

What would change if you treated the feeling not as a signal to freeze – but as a prompt to refine?

NIKNAK – LEARN THE LOOP

She didn't wait for permission. She rewired the system around her.

NikNak wasn't trying to become someone else. She was trying to become herself – on purpose. She mapped her sensory profile. She claimed her space. She created rituals for energy, tools for transition, and boundaries that made collaboration possible. She didn't adapt by suppressing difference. She adapted by surfacing it – then designing forward.

What she showed us is that the loop becomes stronger when it matches who you really are.

So ask yourself:

What in your environment still isn't adapted to the truth of you?

What simple habit, space, or ritual might help you turn overload into signal?

How could you turn the label that once limited you into a trapdoor – one that opens into the next loop?

JOÃO GOULÃO – LEAD THE LOOP

He didn't lead with authority. He led with continuity.

João Goulão built one of the most quietly effective upgrade systems in the world – not by demanding control, but by protecting the loop he helped design. He stayed present. He adapted with the data. He re-looped not to fix the past, but to preserve the future. And he taught others not by theory, but by structure.

What he showed us is that leadership isn't about being the centre of the system. It's about keeping the system centred on care.

So ask yourself:

What upgrade in your life needs continued attention?

Where are you still needed – not to build something new, but to protect something that works?

What system have you already helped build that could support others – if you stayed in the loop?

You've met them before. You're seeing them again now. And this won't be the last time you visit with them. They're not here as examples to admire. They're here as loops you can learn from. The next move is yours.

THE RECURSIVE LIFE

It doesn't feel like much at first – a misnamed face, a misplaced date, the wrong side of the saucepan, you've put the cat in the fridge.

But slowly, steadily, like a tape loop folding in on itself, something begins to vanish.

Dementia typically is not the loss of thinking. It's the loss of memory that makes thinking effective. A person can still speak, still feel, still argue – but they can no longer use what they know. They can't carry learning forward. They can't form, store, and retrieve the building blocks of becoming again, and can forget what they had become previously. They are, in a painful way, still themselves – but not the version of themselves that had grown, or can still grow.

In the film *Memento*, the protagonist Leonard doesn't suffer from age-related decline. He's young, sharp, determined – but he has no short-term memory. He can think, act, fight – but he can't remember long enough to apply what he's learned. He has to write notes and stuff them in his jacket pockets just to remind himself of what he learnt minutes before. And he becomes open to manipulation by those who replace his notes with other notes – so that he remembers that he wanted to remember something, but forgets what it was that he wrote down to remember.

And so, like many real-world systems, he's competent but not adaptable. Intelligent but stuck.

CALCULATION → RECURSION → INTELLIGENCE

So the lesson is clear: without memory – without reusable, recursive memory – you can't progress. You can repeat. But you can't upgrade.

Among your ancestors, there have always been those who realised this. Some survived by being faster or stronger. But those who moved the species forward – toward something we might call history – did so because they remembered. And more than that, they stored memory outside themselves. They extended their recall across generations and into the future.

Marks on bones. Shells in piles. Pebbles in pockets. Notches on walls. Later, maps and diagrams, star charts and shadow clocks. Even before we had formal language, we had tools for memory. The smarter ones – the superadaptive ones – didn't just live. They learned how to loop.

Eventually, humans invented storytelling, ritual, and culture. Each one a mechanism for memory. Each one allowing recursive patterns to be passed forward. Then came writing. With writing, recursion could extend beyond a single lifetime. Knowledge could survive without needing to be perfectly remembered. It could be stored, rerun, edited, and improved.

Memory became generational.
Memory became iterative.
Memory opened paths into the minds of others.

RUN THE LOOP

Even our machines began this way. Early computing systems could calculate – but they couldn't remember in any useful sense. They ran instructions blindly. They couldn't adjust. They couldn't reflect. They couldn't reuse.

Punch cards. Paper tape. Magnetic drums. These weren't memory, they were instruction. If a program failed, someone had to intervene. If it succeeded, the machine didn't know why. It was all computation, no recursion.

Then came a leap.

In the late 20th century, researchers began experimenting with artificial neural networks – systems that mimicked, in limited ways, how the human brain processes information. But the real shift came when memory itself was built into the system.

A recursive neural network isn't just a big calculator. It's a system that loops. That holds information from previous steps. That updates itself based on its own outputs. In short: it remembers. And then uses that memory to adapt.

Instead of running once and stopping, it can rerun. Instead of starting from scratch, it can adjust based on what it just did. This kind of memory-in-the-loop allowed machines not just to simulate intelligence, but to inch toward something more: adaptive intelligence. Self-updating insight. Experience turned into action.

That's why it mattered. That's what changed the game.

SAPIENS → RUN → SUPERSAPIENS

And so it is with you.

You don't become a better thinker just by thinking harder. You become a better thinker by remembering better. By learning what helped. By noticing what didn't. By feeding the loop – not just with data, but with insight. Yours and others'.

The recursive life is the life that loops well. It's the life that uses memory to evolve. That moves from experience to pattern, from pattern to principle, from principle to action – and back again.

Recursive life is not just a way to live.

It's how you become.

You live. You learned. You led. You loop again – forward, toward a recursive future.

THE FLY BRAIN
Don't be a fly guy. Or, what I learned about human adaptation from a sky full of dead insects.

At the top of the house, beneath the skylight, I kept finding them. Flies. Littered across the wood floor in tiny black punctuation marks. I vacuumed them up without thinking, again and again. Until one day, I paused. Why do they always end up here?

What I found was oddly satisfying. Flies aren't stupid – but they are consistent. They move upward because it's warmer up there. They spiral along the edges of walls and corners – what scientists call thigmotaxis. They seek light – positive phototaxis – drawn to the sunlit brightness that once meant open sky. In the wild, all of this made sense. Heat meant lift. Light meant exit. Wall meant guidance. And for millions of years, it worked.

But now we build houses. We seal the windows. We replace the open sky with glass.

And still, the flies spiral upward. They hug the walls. They rise with the warm air. They fly toward the brightest part of the room – and die there. Trapped not by cruelty, but by logic that used to work.

LIVE → LIVE

They bounce off windowpanes. They drop to the floor. They repeat. They try again. They never learn. They die in the brightest part of the room. Far from the door that let them in. Unable to reflect. Unable to adapt. Unable to revise the rules. They live, live, live – and so they die.

But I used to think we were better.

And then I watched people do the same thing. They flew upward – toward the job that was wrong for them, the relationship that repeated a script they never wrote, the shiny surface of success, status, validation – always upward, always toward the glow.

We, too, die in bright rooms.

We don't spiral like flies. We spiral like humans: with emails, habits, gut feelings, history. We hit glass not with our bodies, but with our time, our energy, our hope. And sometimes we don't even notice it was glass. We just try harder.

But here's the difference. We can pause. We can look down. We can notice the loop we're in. Not just live. Learn.

LIVE → LEARN

657

We can revise the rulebook mid-flight. We can say: This doesn't work anymore. We can remember what failed last time – and try something new. And more than that: we can pass it on.

Flies have no culture. They have instincts. But no teaching. No stories. No warning signs written in metaphor or memory. They live, live, live – and vanish. The next fly makes the same mistake.

But we – we tell each other not to go up there. We write books. We open doors. We lead.

And that's the final loop. Not just to live. Not just to learn. But to leave something behind that helps someone else navigate. To turn the loop into language. To take adaptation and make it transmissible.

LIVE ↔ LEARN ↔ LEAD

That's the difference. A fly has about 100,000 neurons. There are seventeen million flies for every one of us. If you do the maths, it turns out there are more fly neurons in the world than human ones – by a lot. They win the raw numbers. Astonishing, in its way. But they still fly into skylights.

And then again – so do we. We fly into mountains. Into wars. Into people. We repeat the pattern, even when we know better.

But every now and then – someone notices. Someone learns. Someone leads. And the loop rises, not just in us – but because of us.

METAMORPHOSIS: HOW DARE YOU BE YOU

Be aware, when attempting to change, what kind of a change you are attempting...

It can be a kind of violence that hides behind the language of order. It doesn't always shout. Not always. It cuts. Not with weapons, but with edits.

Cut this part of yourself, they say. Copy this version we prefer. Paste yourself back into society and pretend you have lost nothing. Pretend you are exactly like we wish you to be.

This isn't how change should work, and it's not what we mean by superadaptability.

To truly embed something, to truly change, is not to overwrite or erase, but to expand, to create space where none existed before, to make room for difference, to celebrate variation and self-expression, to repair systems that treated differences as error.

The history of trans people, like many other excluded groups and individuals, is a history of forced edits, of being cut from the loop.

What follows is a testimony, not a metaphor, not a theory. A metamorphosis in her own words. And a defense of the right of us all to dare. A forceful challenge for us all to dare to be ourselves, to dare to challenge the limits that are placed upon us.

I haven't cleaned it up. I haven't diluted it. I've made space for it here. Because transcending limits begins with the courage to hear what was once erased.

CARLA ANTONELLI, SPANISH SENATOR

Trans people – we are the food of the whole world. Everyone wants a piece of us: to know what we are, what we are not.

Whether we have orgasms.
Whether we are happy.
Whether we've had surgery.
Whether we cultivate ourselves.

Leave us alone, for the love of God – since you believe so much in God.

You have come here to erase us. To derogate my partner Ximena, to derogate me. Really.
Don't you feel ashamed? You pretend to get rid of us – an entire group of people, historically persecuted, who are now daring to lift our heads and claim space in society.
You make our lives impossible.
And Mr. Fuster – I was also a girl. I am 65 years old. And I'm standing here because I survived the same violence you now wish on today's children.

I was taken to psychiatrists.
I was abandoned.
I was cut off from my family.
I died in my father's eyes.
You want to do this again?
Leave us alone, for the love of God.
We will not return to the margins.

We will not return to the margins.
¡No vamos a volver a los márgenes!

THE LOOP THAT OUTLIVES YOU

Some people learn a skill. Others learn a system.
But superadapters learn how to evolve the system itself.

They don't just adapt in the moment.
They adapt the loop that teaches them how to adapt.

That's the difference.

The first shift is in rhythm. When you're trapped, you adapt only when forced.
You react, recover, repeat. But transcendence begins when you start living the
loop – daily, deliberately. You embed recursion into your actions. You don't wait
for chaos. You train for change.

The second shift is in awareness. When you're trapped, you reflect without
refining. You learn without looping. But superadapters meta-learn. They model
their moves. They trace the mechanism. They upgrade the feedback, not just the
effort. Insight becomes recursive structure.

The third shift is in transmission. Trapped leadership clings to outcomes. It
teaches obedience, not recursion. But transcendent leaders teach the loop itself.
They build environments where others learn, adapt, and pass it on. Legacy isn't
what they build. It's the pattern they leave behind.

This isn't about brilliance.
It's about structure.
And the structure is a loop.

FROM TRAPPED TO TRANSCENDED

	TRAPPED	TRANSCENDED
Live the Loop	You adapt only in emergencies. You react, then reset. You abandon what works when pressure fades. You start fresh every time. You treat progress as fragile. You mistake newness for growth.	You embed adaptive rhythm into daily action. You don't just survive the loop – you inhabit it. Your baseline gets smarter with each iteration. You return to tested patterns and refine. You treat practice as loop memory, not repetition. You look for depth, not just novelty. You tune the tempo of change to the need.
Learn the Loop	You collect information but never systematise it. You confuse insight with integration. You misattribute success. You blame or credit without understanding causal structures. You mistake reflection for overthinking – or avoid it altogether	You run models. You refine heuristics. You meta-learn from the outcomes of prior loops. You zoom out. You adjust mechanisms. You model better before you move. You mine each loop for feedback. You're not afraid to examine failure, because every mistake is a recursive upgrade opportunity.
Lead the Loop	You try to control outcomes. You withhold process knowledge. You position yourself as essential. You confuse direction with leadership. You prescribe steps instead of empowering adaptation. You build for credit.	You teach systems, not just solutions. You structure environments so others can run and refine the loop themselves You model meta-habitual growth. Your presence trains recursive thinking in others. You build for continuity. You leave behind loops that others can inherit, inhabit, and expand.

Sometimes the loop lifts you forward. You live through something that teaches you to learn. You learn something that helps you lead. And in leading, you make something real – something that outlives the crisis that began it. That's how constraint becomes movement. That's how a system shifts. But not every loop holds. Some fray. Some fail. Some need to be restarted – not from the beginning, but from a different angle. That doesn't mean you failed. It just means you're ready to loop again, this time with more of the system in mind.

The loop continues.
And so do you.

LOOP SHIFT

Sometimes, the loop lifts you forward.

You live through something that teaches you to learn.
You learn something that helps you lead.
You lead something that brings others with you.

That's how constraint becomes movement.
That's how a system shifts.

But not every loop holds its shape.

Sometimes they fray.
Sometimes they break.
Sometimes the upgrade doesn't embed.

That doesn't mean you failed.
It just means you loop again.

This time: differently.
This time: better.

The loop continues.
And so do you.

THE THREE WAYS THE LOOP GOES WRONG

Upgrade loops aren't always noble. They don't always spiral up. Sometimes, they fracture. They falter. They burn through their own logic.

And when they go wrong, they usually go wrong in three ways:

Hyper. Hypo. Anti.

Each one is a distortion of the Run Loop.
Each one looks like progress – until you realise it's a recursive failure.
Here's what they feel like, and how to spot them.

HYPER is the loop that accelerates beyond its own comprehension.
It mistakes motion for mastery. It mistakes energy for integration.

You recognise the need to act – and you do. Immediately.
But you skip the understand. You override the necessary.
You start upgrading before you've mapped the system.

In your mind, it's progress. In reality, it's overreach.
Startups scale too early. Habits stack without foundation.
People burn out – not because they're weak, but because they never paused.

I knew a man once – a runner – who trained so hard his legs forgot how to walk.
He didn't quit. He just collapsed forward.

Hyper looks like speed. But it erases rhythm.
It burns through the feedback it needs most.

HYPO is the loop that drifts instead of spins.
You delay. You wait. You study the loop without ever stepping into it.

The recognition comes faintly, if at all.
Understanding never lands because nothing real was ever risked.
Necessary action dissolves in the fog of maybe later.

Like the novelist who waited for inspiration – pen poised, ink drying – until the story within him faded into silence.

In organisations, this is outdated systems that never get reformed.
In life, it's the perfect moment that never comes.
Adaptation atrophies. The loop rusts shut.
Hypo isn't a refusal. It's an erosion.

ANTI is the most dangerous of all.
It's the upgrade loop that inverts itself – intentionally.

You still recognise. You still act.
But you act against what you understand.
You double down on failure. You recurse into destruction.

In this loop, recursion becomes sabotage.

It looks like leadership, but it distorts the loop to serve fear.
It repels feedback. It attacks reflection. It weaponises denial.

Like the man who sought love, but pushed away every hand that reached for his.
He thought he was protecting himself. He was building a cage.

Anti-loops aren't accidents.
They're deliberate distortions – recursive firewalls that grow stronger the more they're criticised.

You can't reason with an anti-loop.
You can only recognise it – and build a better one.

LOOP THE LOOP, DON'T LOSE IT
This is why loops must be lived deliberately.
Run the loop with rhythm.
Run the loop with self-awareness.
Run it like your life – and your system – depends on it.

Because sometimes, it does.

SCORCHED LOOPS
Part 1: The Cultural Loop That Destroys Itself

Some loops don't improve.
They refine their own ruin.

We think of recursion as progress. The act of learning, spiralling upward, adjusting toward better. But not all loops spiral. Some close tighter. Some collapse. Some turn back on themselves with such force and clarity that they get worse, deliberately.

That's the scorched loop.

You've seen it. In places like Palmyra. In the hollowed shells of libraries. In schools that were bombed not by accident, but because someone wanted to burn the idea of learning out of the loop. You've seen it in what's called 'cultural erasure', but what's really adaptive reversal – the systematic unbuilding of future possibility.

What kind of recursion is that?

The kind that learns how to destroy more precisely. The kind that refines cruelty. The kind that upgrades its own ignorance. You don't need sophisticated technology to build a scorched loop. You just need a pattern that teaches itself how to break what others are trying to build.

Economists speak of the tragedy of the commons – shared resources ruined by uncoordinated use. But Elinor Ostrom showed the opposite: that with the right agreements, communities can manage shared goods with care. There's a lesson there.

Because this isn't about commons. It's about recursion.

The Scorched Loop is a kind of anti-strategy. A system that uses available means to achieve undesirable ends. It follows logic. It takes action. It leaves a mark. But the mark is loss. Ash. Absence.

You can't reason with a Scorched Loop.
But you can recognise it.
And you can build something better.

Part 2: The Personal Loop That Devours the System

Not all scorched loops operate on the scale of cities or cultures. Some fit inside a single person. But they can burn just as much.

This is the personal recursion of dominance. The loop of the strongman, the fallen strategist, the performative destroyer. It begins like strategy: using available means to pursue a goal. But the goal is not health, or growth, or survival. The goal is control. And the loop learns fast.

Minimise the truth. Attack the challenger. Deny what just happened. Then do it again, louder. The loop doesn't care whether it helps anyone. It only cares that it wins, and stays in motion.

You've seen versions of this. Crassus, marching for power and burning the republic with him. Caesar, refusing return. Modern versions too – of men who turn self-image into spectacle and loyalty into loyalty tests. This isn't just narcissism. It's engineering. A loop designed to escalate. Every criticism becomes fuel. Every fact is an attack. Every weakness is a weapon to turn outward.

The irony is, it looks like confidence. But it's just recursion without humility. Learning without correction. Power with no adaptive aim.

This is not just a personal flaw. It's a system. And it loops.

It can't be reasoned with. It can only be recognised.

And it runs like this:

MINIMISE → ATTACK → DENY

THE COUNTER LOOPS – THE FIRST AID KIT

When upgrade loops go wrong, they don't always crash. More often, they stall, overheat, or reroute themselves into something unrecognisable. That doesn't mean the system is broken. It means it needs to be re-entered – with care, and at the right point.

This is your First Aid Kit. Not a second system. A re-entry into the one you already know: Live → Learn → Lead. When a loop misfires, one of these three habits has either been skipped, twisted, or applied in the wrong context. The counter isn't to invent a new model. It's to restore the existing one – by beginning again at the right stage.

What follows is not a fix from the outside. It's a recovery from within. The loop knows how to heal itself – if you let it.

LIVE is the counter to HYPO. Think of it as your adrenaline shot – just enough to get you moving again.

Hypo happens when your upgrade loop stalls. You've spotted the opportunity, maybe even started to sketch a plan, but you haven't entered the loop. You're buffering. Waiting. The day keeps slipping. And every delay reinforces the next.

That's when you don't need more clarity. You need contact. Something real. Action that changes state. It doesn't have to be big. It just has to be done. Walk the dog. Change rooms. Write the line. Say the thing. Schedule the call you've been avoiding. Your body knows how to loop before your brain remembers. And motion is memory.

This is where Live becomes your re-entry point. Not by faking energy, but by supplying it. It's not about finishing the loop – just reactivating it. Even bad movement gives feedback. Even partial action tells you something. Reading one sentence out loud. Sending one honest message. Switching locations so your nervous system resets. These are all ways back in.

Ask yourself:
    What's the smallest real action I can take right now?
    What would a one-minute version of progress look like?
    What am I delaying because I've told myself I'm not ready?

None of these require brilliance. Just movement. Because hypo isn't broken willpower. It's friction. And Live is how you dissolve it. The loop will take care of the rest. Live → Learn → Lead. But nothing happens until you start.

LEARN is the counter to HYPER. Think of it as your oxytocin hit – or your first deep breath after moving too fast for too long.

Hyper kicks in when the loop gets overloaded. You're doing too much, too fast. Actions stack. Habits pile. Insights get skimmed, not absorbed. It feels like momentum, but it's disconnection underneath – speed without sense, growth without grounding.

You don't need another push. You need perspective. You need to Learn – not more information, but more contact. More friction with reality. Learn what's actually happening. Learn what you missed. Learn what you're reinforcing without realising.

That means slowing down enough to hear the signal. Letting integration catch up with output. Rereading something you skimmed. Having a conversation you didn't schedule. Going analogue. Naming what's real without performing it. You don't need to retreat. Just breathe, absorb, and recalibrate.

Ask yourself:
What part of the grind is grinding me down?
Where are the marginal gains actually diminishing returns?
Am I reinforcing rather than moving forward?

The lure of hyper is that it looks effective. But reflection is what makes it real. And LEARN is what reopens the loop. Not a full stop – just a change in rhythm. A shift in state. Lead will come. So will action. But not before you Learn again.

LEAD is the counter to ANTI. Think of it as your antidote – not a weapon, but a wiser signal. A way to guide the loop back into health.

Anti loops don't just misfire. They rewire. What begins as self-improvement turns into self-armour. You follow the steps. You run the loop. But the outcome is a closed system – one that filters out dissent, difference, and change. You're not upgrading anymore. You're fortifying. Locking in a narrow version of growth that no longer lets reality in.

The danger here isn't failure – it's false success. You appear disciplined. Focused. Even effective. But the learning has stopped. The leadership has warped. You're reinforcing something that doesn't serve you – or anyone else. That's when the loop becomes not just ineffective, but harmful. Not just broken, but anti-adaptive.

The counter is to Lead. Not by seizing control, but by reintroducing openness. Adaptive leadership isn't about dominance. It's about restoring feedback.

Rebalancing power. Making space for complexity. When you lead like that, you break the spell. You create new patterns that others can move inside.

This is where culture comes in. Anti loops feed on isolation. Echo. Performance. So you lead by shifting the environment. You elevate voices that challenge you. You reward questions, not just answers. You build systems that evolve – ones that can stretch without snapping. That's how you bake in the good version, the pro-upgrade rhythm, the one that can bend and still run clean.

You don't counter anti with argument. You counter it with leadership. Quiet, visible, recursive. The kind that opens the system instead of locking it. You find people who support you. You create conditions for high adaptability. And in doing so, you make successful adaptation more likely – for yourself, and for everyone around you.

REBOOT THEIR LOOP
How three superadapters kept looping – even after the breakthrough

You know by now: superadapters don't just change once.
They loop again.

Sometimes because of failure.
Sometimes because success created a new friction.
But always with the same system:
Recognise → Understand → Necessary Action.

These aren't mythical figures.
They're people who've learned to upgrade recursively – to take the lessons from one breakthrough and apply them, often imperfectly, to the next constraint, the next crisis, the next quiet moment of "what now?"

What follows are three of those moments:
    A climber, facing fear not with strength, but with pattern
    A musician, reshaping her systems around her neurodivergence
    A doctor, fighting to keep the upgrade running when the world started forgetting why it mattered
They're not here to be worshipped.
They're here to remind you: this is how change persists.

But sometimes, the loop doesn't begin with you.
Sometimes it begins with someone else – someone you watch, someone you

follow, someone whose system you choose to step into.

That's what happens next.

Alex Honnold has spent his life climbing. But that doesn't mean he stopped learning how to fall.

Years after Free Solo, after Half Dome and El Capitan, after fame and lectures and handshakes with presidents, fear still came. Not just on walls. On stage. In life. In fatherhood. In quiet, shifting moments where no rope or pattern could guarantee a safe outcome.

And Honnold, the master of edge exposure, recognised something: fear doesn't always scale with danger. Sometimes, it's just noise.

He understood that he couldn't trust the feeling alone. So he'd trained himself to ask: what's real here? What's fear responding to? What can I learn?

It wasn't bravery. It was recursion.

And when fear surged – on stage, in interviews, in split-second decisions that had nothing to do with rock – he ran the loop again. Recognise. Understand. Necessary action.

Not to erase the fear. But to make it functional.

That's what mastery is. Not the absence of fear, but the presence of a system you trust more than your nerves.

After a show, she often couldn't speak.

Not from emotion – from overstimulation.

NikNak, the award-winning turntablist and composer, wasn't facing a creative block. She was facing a sensory one. Lights. Noise. Travel. Social obligations. Her system would flood. And even as her music gained traction, her body began sending warnings she couldn't ignore.

At first, she tried to manage through sheer effort – show up, perform, endure, repeat. But that wasn't adaptation. That was depletion. Eventually, she recognised the truth: this wasn't just post-show fatigue – it was neurodivergent overload.

She understood she would need a different system.

So she built one.

She created pre-performance rituals: silence, meditation, sound frequencies to reset her nervous system.

She began using access riders – documents explaining her specific needs – so venues and festivals could support her.

She shifted her touring logistics, arriving early when possible, guarding her energy like a primary resource.

And she began to loop differently.

She collaborated. Co-created. Shared the creative load on her album *Ireti*. She moved from isolated excellence to recursive generosity.

Even her music loops.
Built from fragments, found sounds, layered rhythms.
What she lives, she makes.
And what she makes, loops forward.
João Goulão probably didn't expect to have to fight again for the system he helped build.

Two decades earlier, he'd helped Portugal reframe its entire approach to drugs – away from punishment, toward public health. The result was historic. Incarceration plummeted. Overdose deaths fell. HIV cases dropped. And the stigma surrounding drug use softened into something humane: a shared challenge, not a deviant's problem.

But that very success bred its own threat.

As deaths declined and headlines faded, political urgency began to dissolve. Public concern drifted. Drug misuse, once seen as a systemic failure, slipped to 13th or 14th on the list of national priorities. The memory of the 1990s crisis was fading. Prejudice was creeping back.
Goulão recognised the danger: systems that succeed risk being dismantled – not because they fail, but because people forget why they worked.
So he shifted his role.
He moved from architect to guardian. From national reformer to international educator. He spent his time not redesigning the system, but defending it – showing why it worked, and what would happen if others let it die.
He didn't just loop once.
He looped again – through memory, advocacy, and vigilance.
Because some loops aren't about innovation.
They're about keeping the upgrade running.

LEADING HER LOOP

Rule 10 isn't just about mastering the loop.

It's about recognising when someone else is already living it – and being willing to follow.

Not every loop starts from scratch. Some begin when you watch someone else do something extraordinary, then realise you don't want to be left behind – not just physically, but structurally, emotionally, spiritually.

Sometimes, you loop because someone else leads.

I've climbed enough – not like Alex. Not mountains. Not free solo. But enough to tie a figure of eight, and own a pair of climbing shoes, a mat, a rope, a chalk bag. Enough to feel the tension in a belay line, to stand on manufactured footholds with real fear in your hands. Enough to know that what looks clean from below is often smeared with dust, blood, or doubt. Enough to understand that free soloing isn't just climbing without ropes – it's climbing without forgiveness.

So when I read Dierdre Wolownick's story, what struck me wasn't the height. It wasn't even her age. It was the structure.

She didn't start by mastering a system. She started by watching her son – Alex Honnold – loop through fear and repetition, by recognising what he was doing – not as showmanship, but as a pattern. Then one day, in the middle of her own unravelling – after divorce, grief, and the quiet hollowing-out of what used to be certainty – she asked her son the question that changed her system.

"Will you lead me up?"

And he said, "Only if you learn how to jug."

Jugging: ascending a fixed rope, by hand, over three thousand feet into the sky. It's not gentle. It's not forgiving. It's not abstract. You don't just show up and go. You prepare. You suffer. You learn how to breathe again while hanging from a vertical wall.

And she did. She trained. She failed. She practiced alone. She looped through the pain until her muscles, her system, and her mind adapted to the next phase of herself.

Eventually, she climbed El Capitan. Twice. Once at 66. Once at 70. Not because she thought she could. But because she followed the loop already in motion – and made it her own.

That's recursion. That's re-entry. That's what happens when someone doesn't just inspire you, but shows you the shape of a system that can carry you forward.

She didn't climb to impress.
She climbed to adapt.
And by doing so, she showed the rest of us:

You don't always invent the loop.
Sometimes, you enter it.
And over time, it becomes yours.

REBOOT YOUR LOOP
Your return to the system – deliberate, recursive, real.

You've just seen what it looks like to follow someone else's loop.
You've seen how a system can lift you, lead you, even speak for you – when you're
not ready to speak for yourself.

But this is a different kind of return.
This isn't about leaning on someone else's upgrade.
This is about re-entering your own.

One of the most rhythm-intelligent voices of our time, Kae Tempest, once wrote:

"When I was young I sought help from my older self... I told me: know
yourself."

That's what this is now.
You, reaching forward.
You, returning to yourself.
You, looping again – deliberately.

The mind, at its best, is not singular.
It's recursive.
It loops between selves, timelines, perspectives.
Many people speak to those they've lost.
Many speak to the selves they haven't yet become.
You can do both.

You're doing what psychologists call future-self projection.
Or what we can call other-self projection.

You don't need a term for it.
But the language can help you learn.

So ask: Who in you still knows what to do?

RECOGNISE
You're already in the loop. The only question is: where?

Don't pretend you're starting over. You're not. You've been looping all along – through distraction, through struggle, through fragments of routine that didn't quite hold.

Now is the time to pause. To notice. To re-enter with eyes open.

What were you trying to do, back then?

What part of you already knows the answer?

UNDERSTAND
This is the part most people skip.

They blame the failure, curse the distraction, and jump straight to action. But real rebooting means reading the system.

What were you running? What was it designed to solve?

You're not just observing your loop. You're adjusting the structure of how you adjust. That's metaplasticity.

You are not just a learner. You are learning how you learn.

Now's the moment to trace the logic – not just of what you did, but of who you were becoming.

NECESSARY ACTION

Don't fix everything.

Re-enter.

Choose the smallest viable move that aligns with your loop's purpose. It might be a message. A reset. A step back into something you left too soon.

You've seen how Honnold returned to fear with structure. How NikNak re-engineered her system around her sensory life. How Goulão defended the loop that others forgot.

They didn't restart. They didn't rebrand. They rebooted – with intelligence, and pattern, and care.

Now it's your turn.

Know yourself.
Recognise yourself.
Understand yourself.
Take the necessary action to re-know yourself.

RECOGNISE → UNDERSTAND → NECESSARY ACTION

Not a fresh start. A fresh re-entry.

RECAP: LIVE THE LOOP

You've just completed the Upgrade Loop – not just in theory, but in practice. You've recognised, understood, and acted. Again and again. Not by luck, but by pattern. Not perfectly, but structurally. And that's the point.

Back at the beginning of this chapter, we framed it like New Game++ – the mode where you don't start from scratch. You start again, only better. You enter the loop again with everything you've learned from the last one. That's the loop you've just lived.

And like we said then, this is your highest-scoring dive. You've stood on the edge. You've jumped. Not for the first time – but this time, with more of yourself behind you.

Until there's permadeath, there is no real death. Just another second. Another version. Another re-entry.

Or as a certain film reminded us: "You're not dead yet."

Which means: the loop still lives.

So let's go again – on purpose.

TRANSCEND THE LOOP

You've done more than finish a chapter. You've completed the Upgrade Loop.

And now – just now – you're beginning to see what the whole book has really been doing.

You've gone pattern-hunting in all directions.
You've reversed the obvious.
Tested the guess.
Sketched the shape.
Spotted the catch.
Inverted the flow.
Rode the rhythm.
Found a use for everything.
And baked it in.

You've travelled with scissors and soil.
With beats and blenders.
With curtains and lanterns.
From fragments to futures.

All to understand how to build superadaptive behaviours.
Your own custom-crafted meta-habit.
Forever a work in progress.
Yet made to fit you, and your situation.

And all of it designed not to lock you in –
but to loop you forward.

This is not the end of your system.
This is the moment it becomes recursive.

You've learned to use your natural plastic mind.
You've begun to reshape a world that, now, you know to be more plastic than it seemed before.

You're not just living in the loop.

You are the loop.
    And it lives through you.

KEEPERS OF THE FORESTS

In the Brahmaputra River region of Assam, India, there is a forest that shouldn't exist.

Thirty years ago, it was sandbar – a stretch of dying land between split currents, scoured by flood, cracked by drought. No canopy. No soil. No shade. The birds had left. The snakes had begun to die. And the young man who saw them – half-buried in dust, boiling in the sun – asked himself a question so simple it sounded ridiculous:

What if I just planted a tree?

His name is Jadav Payeng. He was sixteen. He found a patch of bamboo, and started planting. One. Then ten. Then more. Every day, on foot, carrying seeds in bags and water in cans, he planted. And when he saw the bamboo take, he planted trees. When those trees took root, he planted more species. He introduced termites, then ants, then fruit-bearing trees, then deeper-soiled trees that would fix nitrogen and bind the land. He planted through heatstroke. Through flood. Through ridicule. Alone, for years.

677

But forests are recursive systems. They don't just grow. They loop.

And over time, something changed. The soil thickened. The birds returned. The air cooled. And the snakes stopped dying – because the rabbits had come back, and the trees had brought the insects, and the insects had brought the birds, and the birds had brought the fruit, and the fruit had brought the monkeys. And Payeng kept planting.

Decades later, the forest now covers over 1,400 acres. It is denser than the officially protected forest nearby. It has elephants. It has tigers. It is still growing. And it has a name now – Molai Forest – but Payeng simply calls it home.

LIVE → LEARN → LEAD

Akira, another keeper of the forest, began in the weeds.

In the fields of rural Japan, he watched his family clear thick undergrowth by hand. As a child, he wondered if there was a better way. Not through chemicals. Not through control. Just... something better.

He didn't begin by loving forests. He began by noticing effort. Labour. Loss. And later, after drifting through early studies in agriculture, still unsure of his direction, it wasn't a professor or a book that turned him. It was fieldwork. Days spent walking, naming plants, seeing the deep green of the *chinju-no-mori* groves – the sacred forests that once circled shrines – and realising that something ancient had been broken.

He studied under Dr. Yoshio Horikawa, who told him plainly:

"If you study weeds, your work may never see the light of day."

But Miyawaki did it anyway.

Later, in Germany, under the guidance of Reinhold Tüxen, he was told again – this time not what not to study, but how to study it:

"There are three billion years of the history of life out there... Study it with your hands."

And Akira did. He became a scientist, then a mapmaker, then – slowly – a system builder.

He spent more than a decade crawling through undergrowth, cataloguing species, mapping Japan's natural vegetation layer by layer. The result was ten volumes of field-collected data: a kind of green census. But he didn't stop there. Because knowledge wasn't enough. He'd seen the deserts left behind by industry. The collapsing soils. The plantations that mimicked forests but didn't support life. And he asked the recursive question all superadapters eventually reach:

What could be planted that would last?

He began planting not like a forester, but like a sociologist.

Not one species, but many — indigenous trees that once belonged there, layered together like a community: canopy, sub-canopy, companions, helpers. Not in rows. Not in monoculture. But in loops.

The method worked. It grew forests ten times faster than traditional replanting. It restored biodiversity. It resisted flood, fire, heat. And most importantly, it didn't need to be tended. It remembered how to grow.

In time, Akira Miyawaki became a professor. Then a planner. Then a global force. He helped map and replant ecosystems across Japan, China, Indonesia, Brazil. Forty million trees. More than 1,700 sites. He brought forests back to cities. He embedded them in industrial zones. He showed governments and corporations how to plant systems that would support themselves.

But like Payeng, he didn't begin with a grand idea.

He began by noticing.

They both did.

One saw the snakes dying. One saw the weeds consuming.
Both paid attention. Both learned. And both acted — not once, but recursively.

They sowed.
The world answered.
They listened again.
And the forest grew.

NOT THE END-END

I don't know what part of this will stay with you.
But something will.
Maybe one line, one loop, one thought that returns later
in a moment you weren't expecting.

I didn't write this to be definitive.
I wrote it to be lived with.
Maybe misunderstood. Maybe misused. Maybe returned to.

That's how change begins.
Not with certainty.
But with fragments strong enough
to survive the filter
and signal something forward.

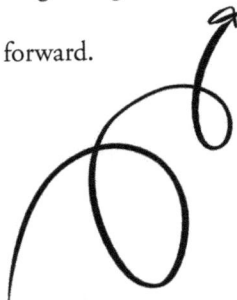

LOSS. LOVE. LOOP.

My son is leaving. For the bus. For the coach.
For the ferry. For the train. For Rome. For the
airport. For university. For the next chapter.
And before he leaves, he is reading The Old
Man and The Sea aloud to us sat by the stream
that was once a river. The stream in France he
insists on calling by the wrong name because we
got the name wrong when we first came here
when he was a baby. He reads the line: "The boy
keeps me alive." My boy will leave tomorrow
on the 6:25 bus. My wife who encouraged him
to read will tell me that I got the time wrong. I
have got many things wrong. He will be leaving
me. My heart is breaking. He will return, but
my heart will still break. I am the old man.
He is my boy.

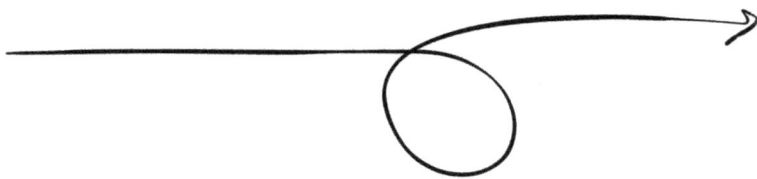

OUTWIT. OUTFIGHT. OUTLAST

So, this is the place.

You've looped through perception, system, and action.
You've cut. You've moved. You've built.
Not perfectly. Not endlessly. But deliberately.

You're no longer in survival.
You're in recursion.

That's what mastery is.

Not knowing everything –
but knowing how to loop better next time.
Not having it all figured out –
but having a way back, and forward,
when the system breaks,
when the map burns,
when the old rhythm no longer works.

Because now you know:
The loop is never lost.
It just waits to be restarted.

And if this feels like the end – it isn't.
It's just the part where the loop repeats.
Higher. Sharper. Embedded.

You've been here before.
You'll be here again.
But next time,
you'll be someone
who already knows what to do.

She didn't just survive the fall.
She didn't just follow the stream.
She looped – again and again.

Every cut, every crawl, every breath was a decision.
Every infection, every wrong turn, every faint memory was information.
Her brain looped what her body couldn't plan.

She didn't just survive the jungle.
She became it.

A rainforest of adaptation.
Fractal, layered, recursive.
Self-repairing even while breaking down.
Evolving while in motion.
Learning while half-blind, half-dead, half-miraculous.

Like a metaplastic brain under pressure,
she rewired her options,
repurposed her pain,
and embedded the loop – not just in her survival,
but in the story the rest of us would carry.

That's not metaphor.
That's what superadaptability is.

If you've made it this far –
you're already in the next loop.

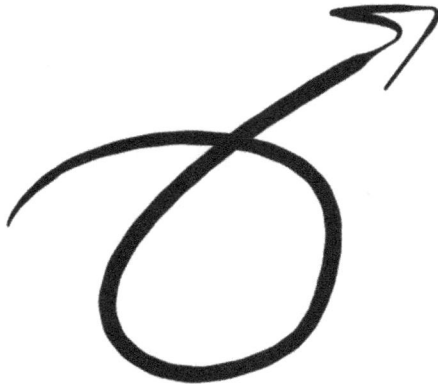

LAST LOOP, LAST TAPE

Life, Kierkegaard said, can only be lived forward – but only understood backward.

In Beckett's play *Krapp's Last Tape* an old man sits alone in a room, rewinding his own history, listening to earlier versions of himself. At one point, hearing his younger voice speak with hope and conviction, he mutters: "Hard to believe I was ever that... stupid bastard."

It's not the self-awareness that damns him. It's the stasis.

Krapp is still looping, but not living. Still taping, but not adapting. The great moments – the boat, the bliss, the girl who agreed to leave with him without opening her eyes – he relives them. But he doesn't build from them.

There's a difference between memory and momentum.

At one point, he holds a ball. And gives it to the dog.

That ball might be joy. Or purpose. Or the other life – the life he could have had. He lets it go. The moment passes.

Superadapters don't do that.

They use memory as impetus. as food, fuel, and playground. Not just to look back, but to re-enter the loop. To cut, edit, and upgrade their system. They ask: What did I bank? What can I build?

They don't just rewind.

They rewrite.

Don't be Krapp.

Loop forward.

Last tape, first step.

ON ENDINGS AND OTHER BEGINNINGS

There's an art to ending. But it isn't about solving everything. It's about noticing the shape.

This book had many shapes. But just one loop.

Some stories close with a sentence that lands like a breath. Some with a silence. Some with a bird call. Some end mid-thought – which, if you think about it, is every life. The best endings, like the best loops, don't resolve. They recur.

This one does too. You've seen it before, in a different form. A door disguised as a beat. A rhythm returning. A spiral disguised as a line. You may not have noticed when it started. You may not be sure it's ending now. That's exactly how a good loop behaves.

You've changed. Not in a way that demands fanfare – but in a way that will show itself when the next hard moment comes. You've built a structure. You've tried on a new system. You've recognised something, understood something, acted differently. That is enough.

To transcend doesn't mean to leave. It means to rise within. You're still here, inside your self, system, and situation – but altered. Recursive. Slightly more tuned.

T.S. Eliot wrote, "To make an end is to make a beginning." And he was right. But there's more. Because beginnings never start cleanly, either. They start halfway through something else. They begin with echoes.

So yes, this is an ending.

But it's also a signal.

A pattern re-entered.

A page turned – but not away.

Just back into the loop.

I LIKE TO READ FROM THE BACK

Hello.
I like to start my books from the back. Then I flip forward. Then back again.
Maybe to the middle. Then to the back.
I get stuck in, find out where it's going,
to see if I want to start where it began.
If that's you, maybe we're talking to each other
before we've even started.
But of course,
you have.
We never really get to the start.

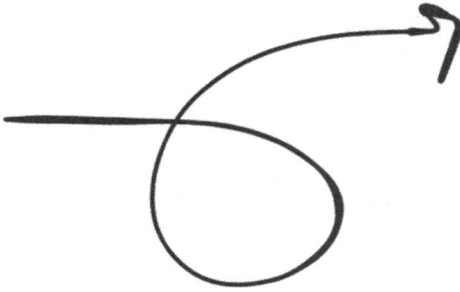

THIS IS ME. I explore adaptive intelligence and the systems and minds that shape it. Artist and author of the bestselling *The Strategy Book*, I work across disciplines to understand how people and organisations transcend constraints.

www.ingramcontent.com/pod-product-compliance
Lightning Source LLC
Chambersburg PA
CBHW021917190326
41519CB00009B/813